◉ Goes beyond the printed textbook

Media Essentials is now integrated with *VideoCentral: Mass Communication*, providing an ongoing insider's look at the media industries. Throughout the book, look for this symbol ◉ directing you to the VideoCentral site to watch related videos. The videos feature experts in their fields like Noam Chomsky, Amy Goodman, Junot Diaz, Anne Rice, and *Media Essentials* author Richard Campbell, along with discussion questions that help you think critically about the media. **See the inside back cover for information on how to access VideoCentral.**

VideoCentral ◉
bedfordstmartins.com
/mediaessentials

Based On: Making Books into Movies
Writers and producers discuss the process that brings a book to the big screen.
Discussion: How is the creative process of writing a novel different from making a movie? Which would you rather do, and why?

Includes valuable study tools

Each chapter concludes with Chapter Essentials, a powerful study guide that outlines key concepts and terms from the chapter. The book's companion site at **bedfordstmartins.com/mediaessentials** includes more free study aids such as pre- and post-chapter quizzes to help gauge your understanding of the material, streaming headlines from a variety of news sources, a Media Portal that helps you find the best media-related sites on the Web, and access to *VideoCentral: Mass Communication*.

Offers a lot for little money

With its concise format, clean design, and accessible coverage, *Media Essentials* is an easy book to use, for a reasonable price — **up to 40 percent less than other mass communication books.**

For more information about *Media Essentials*, please visit **bedfordstmartins.com /mediaessentials/catalog**.

MEDIA ESSENTIALS

MEDIA ESSENTIALS

A Brief Introduction

Second Edition

Richard Campbell
MIAMI UNIVERSITY

Christopher R. Martin
UNIVERSITY OF NORTHERN IOWA

Bettina Fabos
UNIVERSITY OF NORTHERN IOWA

with

Jimmie L. Reeves
TEXAS TECH UNIVERSITY

BEDFORD/ST. MARTIN'S
Boston • New York

For Bedford/St. Martin's

Publisher for Communication: Erika Gutierrez
Developmental Editor: Jesse Hassenger
Production Editor: Kellan Cummings
Senior Production Supervisor: Dennis J. Conroy
Marketing Manager: Stacey Propps
Copy Editor: Denise Quirk
Indexer: Kirsten Kite
Photo Researcher: Sue Barlow at Magellan Visual, Inc.
Permissions Manager: Kalina K. Ingham
Art Director: Lucy Krikorian
Text Design: TODA (The Office of Design and Architecture)
Cover Design: Donna Dennison
Cover Art/Cover Photo: Frank Herholdt / Alamy
Composition: Cenveo Publisher Services
Printing and Binding: RR Donnelley and Sons

President, Bedford/St. Martin's: Denise B. Wydra
Presidents, Macmillan Higher Education: Joan E. Feinberg and Tom Scotty
Director of Development: Erica T. Appel
Director of Marketing: Karen R. Soeltz
Production Director: Susan W. Brown
Associate Production Director: Elise S. Kaiser
Managing Editor: Shuli Traub

Manufactured in the United States of America.

7 6 5 4
f e d

For information, write: Bedford/St. Martin's, 75 Arlington Street, Boston, MA 02116
  (617-399-4000)

ISBN 978-1-4576-0108-8

Acknowledgments

About the Authors

Richard Campbell, director of the journalism program at Miami University, is the author of *"60 Minutes" and the News: A Mythology for Middle America* (1991) and coauthor of *Cracked Coverage: Television News, the Anti-Cocaine Crusade, and the Reagan Legacy* (1994). Campbell has written for numerous publications, including *Columbia Journalism Review*, *Journal of Communication*, and *Media Studies Journal*, and he has served on the editorial boards of *Critical Studies in Mass Communication* and *Television Quarterly*. He holds a PhD from Northwestern University.

Christopher R. Martin is a professor of journalism at the University of Northern Iowa and author of *Framed! Labor and the Corporate Media* (2003). He has written articles and reviews on journalism, televised sports, the Internet, and labor for several publications, including *Communication Research*, *Journal of Communication*, *Journal of Communication Inquiry*, *Labor Studies Journal*, and *Culture, Sport, and Society*. He is also on the editorial board of the *Journal of Communication Inquiry*. Martin holds a PhD from the University of Michigan and has also taught at Miami University.

Bettina Fabos, an award-winning video maker and former print reporter, is an associate professor of visual communication and interactive media studies at the University of Northern Iowa. She is the author of *Wrong Turn on the Information Superhighway: Education and the Commercialized Internet* (2003). Her areas of expertise include critical media literacy, Internet commercialization and education, and media representations of popular culture. Her work has been published in *Library Trends*, *Review of Educational Research*, and *Harvard Educational Review*. Fabos has a PhD from the University of Iowa.

Jimmie L. Reeves is an associate professor of electronic media communication at Texas Tech University. Reeves is co-author of *Cracked Coverage: Television News, the Anti-Cocaine Crusade, and the Reagan Legacy* (1994), and has written for numerous publications including the *Village Voice*, *Columbia Journalism Review*, and *Television Quarterly*. Though his doctoral studies at the University of Texas focused on television criticism, his current scholarly interests have shifted to electronic gaming.

Brief Contents

Preface

THE MEDIA WORLD IS COMPLEX, dynamic, and constantly changing—
so much so that it's difficult to keep track of it all. Since the mid-2000s, the
evolution of the Internet, the emergence of powerful computing platforms and
mobile devices, and the growth of massive corporations that dominate our
media landscape, the ways that most of us use and consume media and the ways
that media messages saturate our lives have fundamentally changed. When we
published the first edition of *Media Essentials*, our goal was to help students
and instructors keep up with the changing media landscape by focusing on the
fundamentals of media studies, and this continues to be our goal in the second
edition — so that no matter how the media continue to evolve, students will
have the critical tools they need to understand what's *really* going on.

Media Essentials distills media industries and major concepts (such as digital
convergence and legal controls) down to their essence. Each chapter offers inci-
sive historical context, frames key concepts up front, and uses pivotal examples to
tell the broader story of how different forms of media have developed, how they
work, and how they connect to us today. For example, a brand-new Chapter 10,
"Electronic Gaming and the Media Playground," starts out by exploring the roots of
electronic gaming in early twentieth-century penny arcades, then goes on to explain how new technologies facilitated the medium's evolution into computer and
console games played in arcades and at home and its eventual development into a
socially driven mass medium. It then "follows the money" through an in-depth section on the economics of the video game industry, moves into discussions of regulation and its implications for democracy, and, in a new Converging Media Case
Study box, discusses the ways converged gaming devices affect other parts of the
media landscape. In addition to this wealth of content offered in every chapter,
Media Essentials is still thirty percent briefer than competing books; the coverage
is succinct, accessible, and peppered with memorable examples; and the book's
unique approach — distilling media information to its core — allows instructors to
add in personal research or social perspectives that are important to them.

Since its initial publication, we have been excited by the success of the book,
and by positive instructor feedback. But as media continue to grow and change, so
too must *Media Essentials*. In preparing the second edition, we talked to instructors and students alike to find out what additions we could make to the book, and
let that feedback shape the revision process. We found out that instructors wanted
to see more on media topics like video games, country music, trade magazines,
and streaming music. They also wanted more coverage of concepts like media
convergence and media literacy, and a greater multimedia component. The second

edition of *Media Essentials* now includes coverage of these topics and many more so that it is more current, flexible, and informative than ever.

Media Essentials emphasizes convergence — and practices it, too, by combining print and digital media into a single accessible package. For the second edition, we have expanded the book beyond the printed page, with videos offering vivid insider perspectives on the mass media industries. These selections from *VideoCentral: Mass Communication*, fully integrated into the text and accompanied by discussion questions, offer additional material for the classroom or home. In addition, there are many more options for supporting the digital aspect of teaching with *Media Essentials* and guiding the learning experience, from e-books to *MassCommClass*, a comprehensive and integrated online course space.

Features of *Media Essentials,* Second Edition

Clear, streamlined, and accessible. Thirty percent briefer than competing texts, *Media Essentials* still addresses all the topics typically covered in introductory books. From the media industries (e.g., books, radio, TV) to legal controls, it offers just the right amount of detail to ensure that students pull the information together, make connections, and develop media literacy.

A great structure for learning. *Media Essentials* offers a chronological table of contents and consistent organization in each chapter: a brief history, the evolution of the medium, a look at economics, and sections covering the medium's relationship to democracy, media literacy, and convergence. This consistent focus and organization helps students make their way through the material and grasp themes both big and small. Under each major heading, a highlighted preview paragraph signals key ideas and contextualizes them in order to guide students through the material.

The best coverage of industry economics. Unique Money In/Money Out headings in every industry chapter help students understand the dollars and cents that go into and come out of that medium. These headings shows students the bottom line, explaining the complex relationship between the production, distribution, and consumption of each medium as well as the specific players involved.

Learning tools that help students "get it." In each chapter opener, a bulleted list of objectives highlights what students should expect to learn, while timelines preview important historical events necessary for understanding the chapter's theme. Media Literacy Case Study boxes address particularly relevant topics in greater detail and help students think critically about them. Finally, each chapter concludes with Chapter Essentials, a powerful study guide that helps students review material and succeed in the course.

A compelling design and an affordable price. A clean yet eye-catching design makes *Media Essentials* a book students will want to pick up and read. The text's attractively small size makes it easy to carry and more student-friendly. And if that's not enough, *Media Essentials* costs about forty percent less than competing introductory texts.

New to This Edition

Fully integrated VideoCentral clips. The new VideoCentral feature merges and converges *Media Essentials* with resources on the Web. Video clips, added to every chapter, get students to think critically about the text and the media by giving them an insider's look at the media industries through the eyes of leading thinkers—including Noam Chomsky, Amy Goodman, and Junot Díaz—who address topics like net neutrality, the future of print media, media ownership, and more. These clips are showcased in the margins throughout the book, prompting students to visit the VideoCentral site, where more than forty videos are accompanied by thoughtful questions that invite students to offer their own analysis and reactions—perfect for media response papers and class discussions. For ideas on how to integrate VideoCentral into your course, see the Instructor's Resource Manual. For a complete list of available clips and access information, see the inside back cover or **bedfordstmartins.com/mediaessentials**.

A new video game chapter. Chapter 10, "Electronic Gaming and the Media Playground," explores the electronic gaming industry from its origins to its emergence as a mass medium. It addresses a high-interest topic for students—one with increasing importance in the broadening world of mass media.

Increased coverage of mass-media convergence. A brand-new Converging Media Case Study box in each chapter reflects on the ever-changing media landscape. These boxes address topics like print-Web publishing synergy, 360-degree music licensing, multifunction video game consoles, advertisements in naming rights, and more.

A stronger emphasis on media literacy. The Media in a Democratic Society sections at the end of each chapter have been updated to cover issues like niche cable channels, music-label conglomerates, and the messages of mass-audience movies. In addition, Media Literacy Case Studies in each chapter consider new developments in music downloading, economic news coverage, the future of television programming, and more.

Updated industry coverage. Throughout the book, examples, statistics, and visuals have been updated to reflect the current media environment, with student-friendly references to social media, Netflix, video games, cyberbullying, *The Hunger Games*, *Modern Family*, and more.

Student Resources

For more information on student resources or to learn about package options, please visit the online catalog at **bedfordstmartins.com/mediaessentials/catalog**.

Student Site for Media Essentials at bedfordstmartins.com/mediaessentials

Free study aids on the book's Web site—such as pre- and post-chapter quizzes—help students gauge their understanding of the text, assess their strengths and weaknesses, and focus their studying. Students can also keep current on media news with streaming headlines from a variety of news sources and can use the Media Portal to find the best media-related sites on the Web. In addition, students can access other online resources such as *VideoCentral: Mass Communication.*

MassCommClass for Media Essentials at yourmasscommclass.com

MassCommClass is designed to support students in all aspects of the introduction to mass communication course. It's fully loaded with the *e-Book for Media Essentials*, videos from *VideoCentral: Mass Communication*, the *Media Career Guide*, and multiple study aids. New functionality also makes it easy to upload and annotate videos, embed YouTube clips, and create video assignments for individual students, groups, or the whole class. Adopt *MassCommClass* and get all the premium content and tools in one fully customizable course space; then assign, rearrange, and mix our resources with yours. *MassCommClass* requires an activation code.

Media Essentials e-books and digital options

The *Bedford e-Book for Media Essentials* includes the same content as the print book and allows students to add their own notes and highlight important information. Instructors can customize the e-book by adding their own content and deleting or rearranging the chapters. Another option is the Bedford e-Book to Go, a PDF-style e-book downloadable to your laptop or tablet. Digital versions of *Media Essentials* are also available through our publishing partners' sites: CourseSmart, Sellwood, Barnes & Noble NookStudy, Kno, CafeScribe, or Chegg. For more information, see **bedfordstmartins.com/ebooks**.

Media Career Guide: Preparing for Jobs in the 21st Century, Seventh Edition

James Seguin and Sherri Hope Culver; ISBN 978-0-312-56082-9

Practical, student-friendly, and revised with recent statistics on the job market, this print guide includes a comprehensive directory of media jobs, practical tips, and career guidance for students considering a major in the media industries. The *Media Career Guide* can also be packaged for free with the print text.

Instructor Resources

For more information or to order or download the instructor resources, please visit the online catalog at **bedfordstmartins.com/mediaessentials/catalog**.

Instructor's Resource Manual

James E. Mueller, Christopher R. Martin, Bettina Fabos, and Richard Campbell; ISBN 978-1-4576-1288-6

This downloadable manual provides instructors with a comprehensive teaching tool for the introduction to mass communication course. Every chapter offers teaching tips and activities culled from dozens of instructors to teach thousands of students. In addition, this extensive resource provides a range of teaching approaches, tips for facilitating in-class discussions, suggestions for using VideoCentral in and out of class, sample answers for the VideoCentral discussion questions, writing assignments, outlines, lecture topics, lecture spin-offs, critical process exercises, classroom media resources, and an annotated list of more than 200 video resources.

PowerPoint Slides

PowerPoint presentations to help guide each chapter's lecture are available for download at **bedfordstmartins.com/mediaessentials** on the instructor side.

Test Bank

James E. Mueller, Christopher R. Martin, Bettina Fabos, and Richard Campbell; ISBN 978-1-4576-1289-3

Available in print and as software formatted for Windows and Mac, the Test Bank includes multiple choice, true/false, fill-in-the-blank, and short and long essay questions for every chapter in *Media Essentials*.

About the Media: Video Clips DVD

This free instructor's resource includes more than fifty media clips, keyed to every chapter in *Media Essentials*. Designed to be used as a discussion starter in the classroom or to illustrate examples from the textbook, this DVD provides the widest array of clips available for the introduction to mass communication course in a single package. Selections include historical footage of the radio, television, and advertising industries; film from the Media Education Foundation; and other private and public domain materials. The DVD is available upon adoption of *Media Essentials*. Please contact your local sales representative for more information.

Questions for Classroom Response Systems

Questions for every chapter in *Media Essentials* help integrate the latest classroom response systems (such as i>clicker) into your lecture to get instant feedback on students' understanding of core concepts as well as their opinions and perspectives.

Content for Course Management Systems

Instructors can access content specifically designed for *Media Essentials* for course management systems such as WebCT and Blackboard. Visit **bedfordstmartins.com/coursepacks** for more information.

The Bedford/St. Martin's Video Resource Library

Qualified instructors are eligible to receive videos from the resource library upon adoption of the text. The resource library includes full-length films; documentaries from Michael Moore, Bill Moyers, and Ken Burns; and news show episodes from *Frontline* and *Now*. Please contact your local sales representative for more information.

Acknowledgments

We wish every textbook author could have the kind of experience we've had while working on *Media Essentials* and would like to thank everyone at Bedford/St. Martin's who supported this project through its many stages, including Macmillan Higher Education Presidents Joan Feinberg and Tom Scotty, Bedford/St. Martin's President Denise Wydra, Director of Development Erica Appel, and Marketing Manager Stacey Propps. We are especially grateful to Publisher Erika Gutierrez for her leadership and passion; to Executive Editor Simon Glick for his creative guidance; to Development Editors Stephanie Ventura and Jesse Hassenger; and to Editorial Assistant Alexis Smith for her contributions to our art program additions. We also appreciate the tireless work of Managing Editor Shuli Traub, who oversaw the book's extremely tight schedule; Project Editor Kellan Cummings, who made sure we got the details right with help from copy editor Denise Quirk and proofreaders Virginia Rubens and Marcell Rosenblatt; and Senior Production Supervisor Dennis J. Conroy, who oversaw production and kept the book on schedule. We are also grateful to our research assistant, Susan Coffin.

We extend particular and heartfelt thanks to our collaborator and contributor Jimmie Reeves, for all of his ideas and expertise. His knowledge of the media industries, especially the world of electronic gaming, has been invaluable; the second edition of *Media Essentials* would not have been the same without him.

We also want to thank the many fine and thoughtful reviewers who contributed ideas to *Media Essentials*: Ajje-Ori Agbese, *University of Texas Pan American*; Julie Andsager, *University of Iowa*; Jerome D. DeNuccio, *Graceland University*; Jennifer Fleming, *California State University – Long Beach*; Peter Galarneau Jr., *West Virginia Wesleyan College*; Mary-Lou Galician, *Arizona State*

University; Neil Goldstein, *Montgomery Country Community College*; August Grant, *University of South Carolina*; Jennifer Greer, *University of Alabama*; Jodie Hallsten, *Illinois State University*; Allison Hartcock, *Butler University*; Kirk Hazlett, *Curry College*; Amani E. Ismail, *California State University, Northridge*; Sharon Mazzarella, *James Madison University*; Daniel G. McDonald, *Ohio State University*; Gary Metzker, *California State University–Long Beach*; James E. Mueller, *University of North Texas*; Robert M. Ogles, *Purdue University*; Daniel A. Panici, *University of Southern Maine*; Kenneth Payne, *Western Kentucky University*; Zengjun Peng, *St. Cloud State University*; Samantha Phillips, *University of Miami*; Selene Phillips, *University of Louisville*; David Pierson, *University of Southern Maine*; Jennifer Proffitt, *Florida State University*; Arthur A. Raney, *Florida State University*; Steve H. Sohn, *University of Louisville*; Mark Steensland, *Pennsylvania State – Erie*; Carl Sessions Stepp, *University of Maryland*; Melvin Sunin, *Pennsylvania State–Erie*; Mike Trice, *Florida Southern College*; Richard West, *University of Texas at San Antonio*; Mark J.P. Wolf, *Concordia University Wisconsin*; and Yanjun Zhao, *Morrisville State College*.

Special thanks from Richard Campbell: I am grateful to all my former students at the *University of Wisconsin–Milwaukee, Mount Mary College*, the *University of Michigan*, and *Middle Tennessee State University*, as well as to my current students at *Miami University*. Some of my students have contributed directly to this text, and thousands have endured my courses over the years—and made them better. My all-time favorite former students, Chris Martin and Bettina Fabos, are coauthors, as well as the creators of our book's Instructor's Manual, Test Bank, and *About the Media* DVD. I am grateful for all their work, ideas, and energy.

Special thanks from Christopher Martin and Bettina Fabos: We would also like to thank Richard Campbell, with whom it is a delight working on this project. We also appreciate the great devotion, creativity, and talent that everyone at Bedford/St. Martin's brings to the book. We would like to thank reviewers and our own journalism and media students for their input and for creating a community of sorts around the theme of critical perspectives on the media. Most of all, we'd like to thank our daughters, Olivia and Sabine, who bring us joy and laughter every day, and a sense of mission to better understand the world of media in which they live.

Please feel free to e-mail us at **mediaessentials@bedfordstmartins.com** with any comments, concerns, or suggestions!

Contents

7   Movies and the Impact of Images   193

**8 Television, Cable, and Specialization in Visual
Culture** 225

10 Electronic Gaming and the Media Playground   291

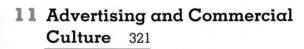

MEDIA FRAMING INDUSTRIES

11 Advertising and Commercial Culture 321

12 Public Relations and Framing the Message   355

MEDIA EXPRESSIONS

14 Legal Controls and Freedom of Expression 415

15 Media Economics and the Global Marketplace 447

16 Social Scientific and Cultural Approaches to Media Research   477

MEDIA ESSENTIALS

As this image from Times Square, New York, demonstrates, the media—in all their varied forms, from television news to online advertising—function as an essential part of our lives.

1

Mass Communication: A Critical Approach

As new technologies become both greater in number and more widespread in use, our relationships to the media continue to change and deepen. Mass media are more adaptive and less contained than ever, and disconnecting from them is no longer as easy—or desirable—as it once was. In a recent study at the University of Maryland, two hundred college students agreed to go without media for a twenty-four-hour period and then write about their experiences. While some students did complain about the lack of access to MP3 players and the difficulty of avoiding television screens, for many of them the experiment felt more personal. Without text messaging, phone calls, e-mail, or Facebook, students felt cut off. "Going without media," noted the project's director, "meant going without their friends and family."[1] Engaging with media isn't just a leisure activity; it's a major component of how many of us live our lives.

Similarly, the nonprofit organization TV-Free America used to sponsor an annual "TV Turnoff Week" during which thousands of participants swore off television for seven days. The event was meant to prompt people to think about the place of television in their daily lives. The last "TV Turnoff Week" was held in 2008; TV-Free America has since changed its name to the Center for SCREEN-TIME Awareness (CSTA) and worked with the anticonsumerist group Adbusters to reinvent its media-abstinence campaign. The result of this collaboration is the reformulated "Digital Detox Week," encompassing more than just television when it encourages consumers to turn off their screens (though underneath the description of Digital Detox Week on the Adbusters Web site is another, potentially contradictory message: "Get updates on Twitter"). This transition verifies that we have crossed a threshold into a media environment where screens affixed to smartphones, laptops, and tablets bring the powers of television, the Internet, books, and movie screens to almost any imaginable location.

THINKING ABOUT OUR RELATIONSHIP with all the small, medium, and large screens in our world generates many compelling questions. For example, what does research tell us about how media both reflect and shape our world? What roles and responsibilities do mass media have? What is our role in media processes such as the development and distribution of content? And how (if at all) should these processes be changed? In this book, we take up such questions by examining the history and business of mass media as well as scholarly research into how media and people interact. We take stock of the media's positive and negative aspects, seeking ideas for ways to use media to improve the quality of our lives.

At their best, in all their forms, the media try to help us understand the events and trends affecting us. At their worst, they can erode the quality of our lives in numerous ways. For one thing, media's appetite for telling and selling stories can lead them to misrepresent those events or exploit them (and the people they most affect) for profit. Many critics disapprove of how media—particularly TV, cable, and tabloid magazines—seem to hurtle from one event to another, often dwelling on trivial, celebrity-driven content rather than meaningful analysis of more important events. Critics also fault media for failing to fulfill their responsibility as a watchdog for democracy—which sometimes calls for challenging our leaders and questioning their actions. Finally, the formation and growth of media industries, commercial culture, and new converging technologies—smartphones, laptop computers, digital television—have some critics worrying that we are now spending more time consuming media than interacting with one another.

Like anything else, mass media have their good sides and bad, their useful effects and destructive ones. And that's why it is so important for us to acquire media literacy—an understanding of the media that are powerfully shaping our world (and being shaped by it). Only by being media literate can we have a say in the roles that media play around us.

In this chapter, we take steps to strengthen that literacy by:

- tracing the evolution of mass communication—from oral and written forms to print and electronic incarnations

- examining mass media and the process of communication, including the steps a new medium travels on its journey to mass medium status, and the role that mass media play in our everyday lives

- considering two main models of media literacy—cultural and social scientific—which reflect different approaches to understanding how mass communication works and how media affect us

- taking a closer look at cultural approaches to media literacy

- taking a closer look at social scientific approaches

- exploring ways of critiquing the mass media and reflecting on the importance of doing so

The Evolution of Mass Communication

The mass media surrounding us have their roots in mass communication. **Mass media** are the industries that create and distribute songs, novels, newspapers, movies, Internet services, TV shows, magazines, and other products to large numbers of people. The word *media* is a Latin plural form of the singular noun *medium*, meaning an intervening material or substance through which something else is conveyed or distributed.

We can trace the historical development of media through several eras, all of which still operate to varying degrees. These eras are oral, written, print, electronic, and digital. In the first two eras (oral and written), media existed only in tribal or feudal communities and agricultural economies. In the last three eras (print, electronic, and digital), media became vehicles for **mass communication:** the creation and use of symbols (for example, languages, Morse code, motion pictures, and binary computer codes) that convey information and meaning to large and diverse audiences through all manner of channels. And in the era we're experiencing today, these channels have also converged, changing the dynamics of media production, distribution, and consumption that held for much of the twentieth century. For example, you can now read magazines in their print edition as well as their online version. And you can watch movies at theaters as well as on your iPhone.

The Oral and Written Eras

In most early societies, information and knowledge first circulated slowly through oral (spoken) traditions passed on by poets, teachers, and tribal storytellers.

These army cadets from the 1940s train in sending and receiving Morse code, one of the earliest mass communication technologies.

However, as alphabets and the written word emerged, a manuscript, or written, culture developed and eventually overshadowed oral communication. Painstakingly documented and transcribed by philosophers, monks, and stenographers, manuscripts were commissioned by members of the ruling classes, who used them to record religious works and prayers, literature, and personal chronicles. Working people, most of whom were illiterate, rarely saw manuscripts. The shift from oral to written communication created a wide gap between rulers and the ruled, in terms of the two groups' education levels and their economic welfare.

These trends in oral and written communication unfolded slowly, over many centuries. Although exact time frames are disputed, historians generally date the oral and written eras as 1000 B.C.E. to the mid-fifteenth century. Moreover, the transition from oral to written communication wasn't necessarily smooth. For example, some philosophers saw oral traditions (including exploration of questions and answers through dialogue between teachers and students) as superior. They feared that the written word would hamper conversation between people.

The Print Era

What we recognize as modern printing—the wide dissemination of many copies of particular manuscripts—became practical in Europe around the middle of the fifteenth century. At this time, Johannes Gutenberg's invention of movable metallic type and the printing press in Germany ushered in the modern print era. Printing presses—and the publications they enabled—spread rapidly across Europe in the late 1400s and early 1500s. But early on, many books were large, elaborate, and expensive. It took months to illustrate and publish these volumes, and they were usually purchased by wealthy aristocrats, royal families, church leaders, prominent merchants, and powerful politicians.

In the following centuries, printers reduced the size and cost of books, making them available and affordable to more people. Books could then be mass-produced—and they became the first mass-marketed products in history. This development spurred significant changes: specifically, an increasing resistance to authority figures, the rise of new socioeconomic classes, the spread of literacy, and a focus on individualism.

Resistance to Authority

Since mass-produced printed materials could spread information and ideas faster and farther than ever before, writers could use print to disseminate views that challenged traditional civic doctrine and religious authority. This paved the way for major social and cultural changes, such as the Protestant Reformation and the rise of modern nationalism. People who read contradictory views began resisting traditional clerical authority. With easier access to information about events in nearby places, people also started seeing themselves not merely as members of families, isolated communities, or tribes, but as participants in larger social units—nation-states—whose interests were broader than local or regional concerns.

New Socioeconomic Classes

Eventually, mass production of books inspired mass production of other goods. This development led to the Industrial Revolution and modern capitalism in the mid-nineteenth century. The nineteenth and twentieth centuries saw the rise of a consumer culture, which encouraged mass consumption to match the output of mass production. The revolution in industry also sparked the emergence of a middle class. This class was comprised of people who were neither poor laborers nor wealthy political or religious leaders, but who made modest livings as merchants, artisans, and service professionals such as lawyers and doctors.

In addition to a middle class, the Industrial Revolution also gave rise to an elite class of business owners and managers who acquired the kind of influence once held only by the nobility or the clergy. These groups soon discovered that they could use print media to distribute information and maintain social order.

Spreading Literacy

Although print media secured authority figures' power, the mass publication of pamphlets, magazines, and books also began democratizing knowledge—making it available to more and more people. Literacy rates rose among the working and

Before the invention of the printing press, books were copied by hand in a labor-intensive process. This beautifully illuminated page is from an Italian Bible from the early 1300s.

middle classes, and some rulers fought back. In England, for instance, the monarchy controlled printing press licenses until the early nineteenth century to constrain literacy and therefore sustain the Crown's power over the populace. Even today, governments in many countries worldwide control presses, access to paper, and advertising and distribution channels—for the same reason. In most industrialized countries, such efforts at control met with only limited success. After all, building an industrialized economy required a more educated workforce, and printed literature and textbooks supported that education.

Focus on Individualism

The print revolution also nourished the idea of individualism. People came to rely less on their local community and their commercial, religious, and political leaders for guidance on how to live their lives. Instead, they read various ideas and arguments, and came up with their own answers to life's great questions. By the mid-nineteenth century, individualism had spread into the realm of commerce. There, it took the form of increased resistance to government interference in the affairs of self-reliant entrepreneurs. Over the next century, individualism became a fundamental value in American society.

The Electronic and Digital Eras

In Europe and America, the rise of industry completely transformed everyday life: Factories replaced farms as the main centers of work and production. During the 1880s, roughly 80 percent of Americans lived on farms and in small towns; by the 1920s and 1930s, most had moved to urban areas, where new industries and economic opportunities beckoned. This shift set the stage for the final two eras in mass communication: the electronic era (whose key innovations included the telegraph and television) and the digital era (whose flagship invention is the Internet).

The Electronic Era

In America, the gradual transformation from an industrial, print-based society to one fueled by electronic innovation began with the development of the telegraph in the 1840s. Featuring dot-dash electronic signals, the telegraph made media messages instantaneous—unencumbered by stagecoaches, ships, or the pony express.[2] It also enabled military, business, and political leaders to coordinate commercial and military operations more easily than ever. And it laid the groundwork for future technological developments, such as wireless telegraphy, the fax machine, and the cell phone (all of which ultimately led to the telegraph's demise).

The development of film at the start of the twentieth century and radio in the 1920s were important milestones. But the electronic era really took off

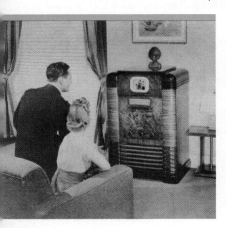

In the 1930s and 1940s, television or radio sets—encased in decorative wood and sold as stylish furniture—occupied a central place in some American homes.

in the 1950s and 1960s, with the arrival of television—a medium that powerfully reshaped American life.

The Digital Era

With the arrival of cutting-edge communication gadgetry—ever smaller personal computers, cable TV, e-mail, DVDs, DVRs, direct broadcast satellites, cell phones, PDAs—the electronic era gave way to the digital era. In **digital communication**, images, texts, and sounds are converted (encoded) into electronic signals (represented as combinations of ones and zeros) that are then reassembled (decoded) as a precise reproduction of, say, a TV picture, a magazine article, a song, or a voice on the telephone. On the Internet, various images, text, and sounds are all digitally reproduced and transmitted globally.

New technologies, particularly cable television and the Internet, have developed so quickly that those who had long controlled the dispersal of information—for example, newspaper editors and network television news producers—have lost some of that power. Moreover, e-mail and text messages—digital versions of both oral and written culture—now perform some of the functions of the postal service and are outpacing some governments' attempts to control communications beyond national borders.

Media Convergence

The electronic and digital eras have ushered in the phenomenon of **media convergence**, a term that has two very different meanings. According to one meaning, media convergence is the technological merging of content in different mass media. For example, magazine articles and radio programs are also accessible on the Internet. And songs, TV shows, and movies are now available on computers, iPods, and cell phones.

Such technological convergence is not entirely new. For instance, in the late 1920s, the Radio Corporation of America (RCA) purchased the Victor Talking Machine Company and introduced machines that could play both radio and recorded music. However, contemporary media convergence is much broader because it involves digital content across a wider array of media.

The term *media convergence* can also be used to describe a particular business model by which a company consolidates various media holdings—such as cable connections, phone services, television transmissions, and Internet access—under one corporate umbrella. The goal of such consolidation is not necessarily to offer consumers more choices in their media

Today, using our computers, we can listen to a radio talk show, watch an adventure movie, or download a favorite song, as old media forms now converge online.

CONVERGING MEDIA
Case Study

Disney and Steve Jobs

Convergence—both as cross-platform media integration and as ownership consolidation—is an essential aspect of communication industries in the twenty-first century. Though the cultural, economic, and technological forces driving this megatrend are larger than any single individual, people have shaped this process. Steve Jobs, who died in 2011, clearly ranks as one of the most influential.

Jobs was just twenty-one and a college dropout when he cofounded Apple Computers with Steve Wozniak in 1976, leaving in 1985. In 1986, he bought what would later become Pixar Animation Studios, signing a deal with Disney to cofinance and distribute feature films, including *Toy Story*.

Thanks to his successes in the movie business, Jobs enjoyed a triumphant return to Apple in 1996, where he would eventually become CEO. With Jobs at the helm, Apple became the world's leading maker of mobile devices, a key innovation in the evolution of media convergence. His support of the iPod, the iPhone, and the iPad were pivotal in the convergence revolution in which one device can be used to listen to music, surf the Internet, stream a movie, play an electronic game, make phone calls, and send text messages. But his legacy also includes the other type of media convergence—consolidation of the media industries into a new oligopoly composed of a few powerful conglomerates.

During the first decade of the new century, Steve Jobs served as a member of Disney's board of directors, a result of the company's purchase of Pixar in 2006.[1] By 2009, shortly after Apple became the country's biggest music retailer, Disney became the world's largest media company.[2] The company's subsidiaries and affiliates are organized into four business segments: Media Networks (ABC, ESPN, the Disney Channel, and Radio Disney);

Studio Entertainment (Walt Disney Studios, Pixar, Marvel); Parks and Resorts; and Consumer Products. Disney has also launched a segment called Disney Interactive Media Group, which creates "interactive entertainment and informational content across multiple platforms including online, mobile, and video game consoles around the globe."[3]

Though Apple is not part of the Disney family of companies, the Jobs connection resulted in several joint ventures. Most notably, Jobs launched the video iPod in 2005 by publicizing a deal with Disney to sell ABC shows like *Desperate Housewives* and *Lost* on iTunes, fusing the content creation of one conglomerate with the hardware and distribution of another. This link between the technological convergence Jobs and his company championed and the business convergence embraced by Disney and their competitors typifies the changes experienced in recent media history—changes that will doubtless continue with new technology and shifting conglomerates.

In the following chapters, we will consider how media convergence has changed the way we read; the way we listen to music and watch television; even the way we connect with others. Ultimately, grasping the significance of media convergence is a key to understanding how the media world now works.

but to better manage resources, lower costs, and maximize profits. For example, a company that owns TV stations, radio outlets, and newspapers in multiple markets—as well as in the same cities—can deploy one reporter or producer to create three or four versions of the same story for various media outlets. The company therefore can employ fewer people than if it owned only one media outlet.

The convergence business model offers more profits to those companies that downsize—or converge—their workforce while increasing their media holdings in many markets. But while it's easy to see the benefits for media owners, this model presents serious disadvantages for society. It limits the range of perspectives from which messages are delivered, as media content becomes concentrated in fewer and fewer hands. For instance, as conglomerates buy up more and more newspapers and employ fewer reporters, citizens are exposed to a narrower range of interpretations of news events. Simultaneously, media owners' personal biases and interests—for example, in culture, politics, and economics—gain more influence. That's because the content they control gets disseminated more widely than content controlled by smaller companies or media outlets.

Both forms of convergence are changing the ways media are distributed and consumed. While much media content is still produced by traditional media industries (the music industry, the film industry, the publishing industry, and so forth), distribution channels have expanded to include a great variety of services and devices. This in turn has caused an ongoing economic shift, where cable and Internet providers, cell phone companies, and digital retailers like Amazon or iTunes receive a greater share of the money spent on media consumption, while traditional outlets like movie theaters, book stores, and record labels may struggle. Media consumption still absorbs a massive amount of time and money, but convergence ensures that this time and money will be flowing in new, different directions.

Mass Media and the Process of Communication

To understand how mass media shape the communication process, let's look at the stages a medium goes through on its journey to becoming a mass medium. Then let's examine the ways in which the media have affected everyday life.

The Evolution of a New Mass Medium

A new medium emerges not just from the work of inventors, such as Thomas Edison, but also from social, cultural, political, and economic changes. For instance, the Internet arose to meet people's desire to transport messages and share information more rapidly in an increasingly mobile and interconnected global population.

Typically, each media industry goes through three stages in their evolution. First is the novelty or *development stage*. During this stage, inventors and technicians try to solve a particular problem, such as making pictures move, transmitting messages between ships and shore, or sending mail electronically.

Second is the *entrepreneurial stage*, in which inventors and investors determine a practical and marketable use for the new device. For example, the Internet has some roots in scientists' desire for a communication system that could enable their colleagues across the country to share time on a few rare supercomputers.

Third is the *mass medium stage*. At this point, businesses figure out how to market the new device as a *consumer product*. To illustrate, Pentagon and government researchers developed the prototype for the Internet, but commercial interests extended the medium's usefulness to individuals and businesses.

Debating Media's Role in Everyday Life

Even as far back as ancient times, human beings have always discussed and debated the media's merits and dangers. The earliest recorded debates in Western society about the impact of the written word on daily life date back to the ancient Greeks—in particular, to Socrates, Euripides, and Plato. These men argued over whether theatrical plays would corrupt young people by exposing them to messages that conflicted with those promulgated by their teachers.

Today, we still debate these sorts of questions. At the turn of the twentieth century, for example, newly arrived immigrants to the United States who spoke little English gravitated toward vaudeville shows and silent films, which they could enjoy without having to understand English. These popular events occasionally became a flash point for some groups. For example, the Daughters of the American Revolution, local politicians, religious leaders, and police vice squads feared that these "low" cultural forms would undermine what they saw as traditional American values.

Since then, print, electronic, and digital communications have extended their reach, and people have begun spending more time consuming them (see Table 1.1). Mass media now play an even more controversial role in society. For instance, some people are frustrated by the overwhelming amount of information available. Others decry what they view as mass media's overly commercial and sensationalistic quality. In their view, too many talk shows exploit personal problems for commercial gain, and too many TV shows and video games feature graphic violence.

People also keep grappling with the question, "To what extent do mass media shape our values and behaviors, and to what extent do our values and behaviors shape the media?" Researchers have continued searching for answers to this question. For example, some have designed studies to determine whether

TABLE 1.1 // HOURS PER PERSON PER YEAR USING CONSUMER MEDIA

Year	Total TV	Broadcast & Satellite Radio	Newspaper	Consumer Internet	Video Games	Total*
1999	1,427	939	205	65	58	3,280
2002	1,519	991	194	147	70	3,430
2006	1,555	975	179	190	82	3,499
2009	1,562	984	165	203	96	3,555
2012	1,597	729	150	197	142	3,515
Seven- and Eight-Year Changes						
1999–2006	+128	+36	–26	+125	+24	+219
2006–2012	+42	–246	–29	+7	+60	+16

*Total hours includes time spent with recorded music, consumer magazines, consumer books, home video/DVD, box office, interactive, TV and wireless content, and time spent media multitasking—using media simultaneously.

Source: Veronis Suhler Stevenson Communications Industry Forecast.

Mass media play a significant role in capturing important historical and controversial events. This Pulitzer-winning photo by Stanley Forman, "The Soiling of Old Glory," shows a white teenager attacking an African American lawyer with a flagpole bearing the American flag at a protest over court-ordered busing to desegregate schools in Boston on April 5, 1976.

watching violent TV shows makes viewers more likely to commit violent acts. Other scholars argue that violent TV shows don't cause violent behavior in viewers. Rather, people who already have violent tendencies are drawn to violent TV shows. Still others suggest that different variables—such as age, upbringing, or genetic predisposition—might be the root causes of violence. Research into such questions of media and violence hasn't yielded conclusive answers. But it does encourage us to keep asking questions and to examine the approaches we use to analyze the media's role in our lives.

Finally, people have expressed concern about the financial power of mass media industries. In the United States, these industries earn more than $200 billion annually, and reinvest those revenues to research how we choose our media content, what we do with that content, and how media companies can better serve our needs and influence our behaviors (from shopping to voting) so they can make more money.

Like the air we breathe, mass media surround us, and we often take its impact, like that of the air, for granted. If we don't take it for granted, we frequently can't agree on its quality. To monitor the media's "air quality" more proactively and productively, we must become media literate. We can start by examining several models for understanding media's nature and impact.

Media Literacy: Ways of Understanding

Experts have used a variety of approaches to understand how the media work and what influence they have on our lives—in other words, to strengthen our media literacy. These approaches include the linear model of mass communication (which focuses on the communication process), the cultural model (which views mass communication as a cultural characteristic and uses anecdotal evidence to interpret media), and the social scientific model (which uses data gathering and analysis).

The Linear Model

The linear model represents a traditional approach to interpreting media content. The model attempts to explain how a mass medium actually communicates messages and how we understand those messages. According to this model mass communication is a *linear process* by which media producers deliver messages to large audiences. **Senders** (authors, producers, organizations) transmit **messages** (programs, texts, images, sounds, ads) through a **mass media channel** (newspapers, books, magazines, radio, television, the Internet) to large groups of **receivers** (readers, viewers, consumers). In the process, **gatekeepers** (news editors, executive producers of TV shows and movies) filter those messages by making decisions about which messages get produced for which audiences. This linear process allows **feedback**, in which citizens and consumers, if they choose, return messages to senders or gatekeepers through letters, phone calls, e-mail, Web postings, or talk shows.

The problem with the linear model is that it doesn't capture certain complexities of the mass communication process. In reality, media messages do not always get to their intended receivers, nor do receivers always interpret these messages in the way media producers want. For example, people might ignore an advertisement or a new movie, or draw an entirely different message from a magazine article or TV show than what the content creator intended to communicate. The cultural and social scientific models have since developed more sophisticated approaches to media study that improve on the limitations of the linear model.

Often, popular stories and characters evolve in our culture over time, acquiring new meaning. Consider the classic 1931 film *Frankenstein* (top) and the 1974 parody *Young Frankenstein* (bottom). How does each story reflect changes in cultural attitudes?

The Cultural Model

The cultural model of media literacy views media content as a part of culture. Culture consists of the ways in which people live and represent themselves at particular historical times—as manifested in things like fashion, sports, architecture, education, religion, science, and media.

As cultural forms, the media help us to make sense of daily life and to articulate our values. When we listen to music, read a book, watch television, or scan the Internet, we assign meaning to that song, book, TV program, or Web site. And different people often assign different meanings to the same media content. Take the Harry Potter book series. Some readers see the series as an innocent coming-of-age children's story. Others interpret it as more adult literature containing pointed metaphors about good and evil that parallel current political events. Still others construe the series as a tool for luring children into a life of witchcraft. And others use the books merely for entertainment, inventing Harry Potter parodies in almost every imaginable media form.

We describe this model for understanding media content as cultural because it recognizes that individuals assign diverse meanings to messages, depending on personal characteristics such as their gender, age, educational level, ethnicity, occupation, and religious beliefs. According to this model, audiences actively affirm, interpret, refashion, select, or reject the messages flowing through various media channels. One manifestation of this active audience in the digital age is the Internet *meme*. Coined by British evolutionary biologist Richard Dawkins, the term has come to mean a digital experience—a video, a sound recording, even just a catchphrase—that is passed electronically from one consumer to another—sometimes with new variations (remakes, remixes, mash-ups, and so forth)—often very quickly. This widespread, rapid transmission is often referred to as *viral*, and includes brief cultural touchstones like Rebecca Black's "Friday" video, Charlie Sheen's use of "winning," or Three Wolf Moon T-shirts. Unlike network celebrities and corporate brands, the meme is a product of an interactive culture in dialogue with itself.

But even as we shape media content, it shapes us, too. For instance, during the recent wars in Afghanistan and Iraq, journalists' work increased people's awareness of the wars and in some cases altered attitudes toward them. Graphic depictions of the wars' human toll prompted many people to vocally oppose the wars. This opposition in turn influenced political leaders to reconsider their military strategies.

Thus, the cultural approach to studying the media critically analyzes media content, the ways in which audiences interpret the content, and the circumstances of how the media produce such content.

By analyzing the news media's coverage of the recent wars in Afghanistan and Iraq, the cultural model shows how media content shapes attitudes and beliefs. Graphic portrayals of the human casualties caused many people to oppose the wars.

The Social Scientific Model

The social scientific model also asks important questions about the media, but is informed by an approach that tests hypotheses with measurable data. The model has its roots in the natural sciences' pursuit of objective research. But as social scientific researchers know, applying rigorous social scientific methods to the study of human behavior is much less reliable than applying such methods to a highly controlled chemistry or physics laboratory environment.

Nevertheless, social scientific research has provided valuable insight into questions about how the media affect us and has become more sophisticated with the rise of electronic and digital media in the twentieth century. Early research looked at the effects of media like movies, and used electric mechanisms attached to viewers' skin to detect heightened responses to frightening or romantic scenes. More recent research has continued to test hypotheses about media effects, using controlled laboratory experiments. For example, researchers might set out to chart the relationship among stereotypical magazine representations of women of color and readers' occupational expectations for women of color in general.

Politics and public opinion also have long attracted the interest of media researchers, beginning with the rise of **survey research** in the twentieth century. Today, media researchers—working for universities, news organizations, the government, and political parties—conduct regular national and regional surveys to take snapshots of the public's opinions on all manner of issues. They also use that information as a basis for action. For example, public opinion researchers (usually working as consultants for political parties or campaigns) test words, ideas, and images on small focus groups, to see how different ways of framing a topic such as "global warming" or "climate change" affect voters' decisions.

Just as media research can help political candidates formulate their campaign strategies, it can also help businesses develop and market their products. For instance, consumer product companies use quantitative methods to track the effectiveness of their advertisements. Hollywood studios regularly screen-test movies to figure out which ending works best for viewers. Ratings services track audience numbers for radio, television, and Web sites—compiling immense stores of data that companies use to gauge the effectiveness of their ad spending.

The goal of social scientific media research, then, is to develop testable hypotheses (or predictions) about the media, gather relevant data, and then determine whether the data verifies the hypotheses.

A Closer Look at the Cultural Model: Surveying the Cultural Landscape

In the pages that follow, we examine the cultural model of media literacy, which provides many ways to study media content through the lens of culture. We discuss two metaphors researchers use to describe the way people judge different media content, and present ways to trace changes in our cultural values as media adapt and change.

The "Culture as Skyscraper" Metaphor

Throughout the twentieth century, many Americans envisioned our nation's culture as consisting of ascending levels of superiority—like floors in a skyscraper. They identified **high culture** (the top floors of the building) with "good taste," higher education, and fine art supported by wealthy patrons and corporate donors. And they associated **low** or **popular culture** (the bottom floors) with the "questionable" tastes of the "masses," who "lapped up" the commercial "junk" circulated by the mass media, such as reality TV shows, celebrity gossip Web sites, and action films.

Some cultural researchers have pointed out that this high-low hierarchy has become so entrenched that it

Animated comedy series like *South Park* reflect a mix of high and low culture with their often raunchy parodies and attacks on what the creators perceive as hypocrisies within society.

powerfully influences how we view and discuss culture today.[3] For example, people who subscribe to the hierarchy metaphor believe that "low" culture prevents people (students in particular) from appreciating fine art, exploits high culture by transforming classic works into simplistic forms, and promotes a throw-away ethic. These same critics also accuse low culture of driving out higher forms of culture. And they argue that it inhibits political discourse and social change by making people so addicted to mass-produced media that they lose their ability to see and challenge social inequities (also referred to as the "Big Mac" theory).[4]

The "Culture as Map" Metaphor

Other researchers think of culture as a map. In this metaphor, culture is an ongoing process—rather than a vertically organized structure—that accommodates diverse tastes. Cultural phenomena, including media—printed materials we read, movies and TV programs we watch, songs and radio shows we listen to—can take us to places that are conventional, recognizable, stable, and comforting. They can also take us to places that are innovative, unfamiliar, unstable, and challenging.

Human beings are attracted to both consistency and change, and cultural media researchers have pointed out that most media can satisfy both of those desires. For example, a movie can contain elements that are familiar to us (such as particular plots) as well as elements that are completely new and strange (such as a cinematic technique we've never seen before).

Tracing Changes in Values

In addition to examining metaphors of culture that we use to understand media's role in our lives, cultural researchers examine the ways in which our values have changed along with changes in mass media. Researchers have been particularly interested in how values have shifted during the modern era and postmodern period.

The Modern Era

From the Industrial Revolution to the mid-twentieth century—which historians call the **modern era**—four values came into sharp focus across the American cultural landscape. These values were influenced by developments that unfolded in the modern era and the media's responses to those developments:

- **Working efficiently.** As businesses used new technology to create efficient manufacturing centers and produce inexpensive products more cheaply and profitably, advertisers (who operate in all mass media) spread the word about new gadgets that could save Americans time and labor—reinforcing the benefits of efficiency.
- **Celebrating the individual.** Media described and interpreted new scientific discoveries, enabling ordinary readers to gain access to new ideas beyond what their religious leaders and local politicians communicated to them. With access

to novel ideas, people began celebrating the individual's power to pick and choose from ideas instead of merely following what leaders told them.

- **Believing in a rational order.** Being modern also meant valuing logic and reason and viewing the world as a rational place. In this orderly place, the printed mass media, particularly newspapers, served to educate the citizenry, helping to build and maintain an organized society.[5]
- **Rejecting tradition and embracing progress.** Within the modern era was a shorter phenomenon: the **Progressive Era**. This period of political and social reform lasted roughly from the 1890s to the 1920s and inspired many Americans—and mass media—to break with tradition and embrace change. For example, journalists began focusing their reporting on immediate events. They ignored the foundational developments that led up to those events, further reinforcing the notion that the past matters far less than the present and the future.

The Postmodern Period

In the **postmodern period**—from roughly the mid-twentieth century to today—cultural values changed shape once more, influenced again by developments in our society and the media's responses to those developments. Cultural researchers have identified the following dominant values in today's postmodern period:

- **Celebrating populism.** As a political idea, **populism** tries to appeal to ordinary people by setting up a conflict between "the people" and "the elite." For example, populist politicians often run ads criticizing big corporations and political favoritism. And many famous film actors champion oppressed groups, even though their work makes them wealthy global icons of consumerist culture.

- **Reviving older cultural styles.** Mass media now borrow and then transform cultural styles from the modern era. For example, in music, hip-hop deejays and performers sample old R&B, soul, and rock classics to reinvent songs. And in the *noir* genre of moviemaking, directors use moody photography and retro costuming to create the same look and feel of movies crafted in the earlier era.
- **Embracing technology.** Even as we and our media can't seem to get enough of retro cultural styles, we passionately embrace new technologies. The huge popularity of movies that feature technology at their core—like *Transformers: Dark of the Moon* and *Avatar*—testifies to this paradox.
- **Embracing the supernatural.** Some people have begun challenging the argument that scientific reasoning is the only way to interpret the world, and have gravitated

Directed by the Wachowski brothers and released in 1999, *The Matrix* is both a reflection and a critique of the postmodern period's value of embracing technology. The film's innovative special effects would come to define the look of many action films in the early 2000s.

toward traditional religion or the supernatural. Mass media reflect this shift. For example, since the late 1980s, a host of popular TV programs emerged that featured mystical themes—including *Twin Peaks, Northern Exposure, The X-Files, Buffy the Vampire Slayer, Charmed, Lost,* and *The Vampire Diaries.*

A Closer Look at the Social Scientific Model: Gathering Data

The social scientific model of media literacy differs in key ways from the cultural model. In this section, we examine those differences in more detail. We compare analyses of two studies to show the contrast between the two models. And we look more closely at how social scientific researchers gather data to analyze the content of media messages and consumers' responses to those messages.

Comparing Analyses of Cancer News Coverage

Cultural and social scientific media researchers often study the same topics—but they ask different types of questions about those topics. For example, two studies recently analyzed news coverage of cancer. The study informed by the cultural approach, titled "Constructing Breast Cancer in the News: Betty Ford and the Evolution of the Breast Cancer Patient," explored a historical turning point in how the media and consumers interpret breast cancer. The study centered on how the news media covered First Lady Betty Ford's mastectomy operation in 1974. The author of the study concluded that coverage of Ford's mastectomy still influences contemporary news coverage of breast cancer today. Specifically, many stories about breast cancer patients emphasize "the need for breast cancer patients to maintain their femininity."[6]

Research by social scientists asked a question about cancer news coverage that was perhaps less expansive, but more measurable. In an article titled "A Comprehensive Analysis of Breast Cancer News Coverage in Leading Media Outlets Focusing on Environmental Risks and Prevention," researchers analyzed the contents of newspaper, television, and magazine accounts of the topic over a two-year span. The researchers didn't interpret the meanings of the news stories (as cultural researchers might have). Instead, they focused on the data they gathered, describing it in more objective terms. For example, the authors noted that "about one-third of the stories included prevention content, primarily focusing narrowly on use of pharmaceutical products. Little information described risk reduction via other individual preventive behaviors (e.g., diet, exercise, and smoking), parental protective measures, or collective actions to combat contamination sites."[7]

Gathering and Analyzing Data

The social scientists analyzing cancer news coverage used a technique called **content analysis** to gather data. Through content analysis, researchers code and count the content of various types of media. For instance, they total up the number of news stories that contain specific types of information regarding the topic in question (such as how to prevent cancer), count song lyrics containing references to a topic (e.g., sex), or total up the number of occurrences of certain behaviors (e.g., violent acts) shown in a set of movies.

But content analysis is only one way to gather data using the social science approach. Researchers also conduct **experiments** using randomly assigned subjects (college students are a popular test subject) to test people's self-reported recall of or reactions to media content. To illustrate, experimenters might use devices such as eye-trackers to record what part of a page or screen each viewer is watching.[8] Researchers can also gather data through surveys they've designed or use data from the many surveys the federal government funds and makes available.

Critiquing Media

To acquire media literacy, we can read the findings of cultural and social science researchers who have studied various aspects of the media. However, both models have their limits; thus, it's important to view their conclusions with a critical eye. We can also learn to critique media content ourselves in a methodical, disciplined way. Whatever approach we use to develop media literacy, it's helpful to always keep in mind the benefits of a critical perspective.

Evaluating Cultural and Social Scientific Research

Examining the findings of both cultural or social scientific research on media can help us follow a **critical process** that consists of describing, analyzing, interpreting, evaluating, and engaging with mass media. But the two models have strengths and weaknesses that are important to keep in mind. The cultural model is best at recognizing the complexity of media culture and providing analyses that draw on descriptive, critical, historical, ethnographic, political, and economic traditions. Yet this model has a downside: While cultural studies can help us see media from

MEDIA LITERACY
Case Study

Bedouins, Camels, Transistors, and Coke

Upon receiving the Philadelphia Liberty Medal in 1994, President Václav Havel of the Czech Republic described postmodernism as the fundamental condition of global culture, "when it seems that something is on the way out and something else is painfully being born." He described this "new world order" as a "multicultural era" or state in which consistent value systems break into mixed and blended cultures:

> For me, a symbol of that state is a Bedouin mounted on a camel and clad in traditional robes under which he is wearing jeans, with a transistor radio in his hands and an ad for Coca-Cola on the camel's back. . . . New meaning is gradually born from the . . . intersection of many different elements.[1]

Many critics, including Havel (who died in 2011), think that there is a crucial tie between global politics and postmodern culture. They contend that the people who overthrew governments in the former Yugoslavia and the Soviet Union were the same people who valued American popular culture—especially movies, rock music, and television—for its free expression and democratic possibilities.

The same familiar tools of American popular culture—Facebook, Twitter, blogs, and mobile phones—have also aided a democratic uprising (dubbed the "Arab Spring") across North Africa and the Middle East. Using cell phones and 3G wireless routers (allowing for Internet connections on-the-go),

citizens have documented the atrocities perpetrated by totalitarian regimes.

One such regime, headed by Syrian dictator Bashar al-Assad, has been methodically gunning down thousands of antigovernment protesters since 2011. Syrian activists like Rami Jarrah began using Twitter and Facebook as platforms for communicating events in Syria to a global audience and for describing "the massacre of innocent people right in front of [his] eyes." Even after he was forced to escape from Syria to Cairo, Egypt, Jarrah has helped establish the Activists News Association, which gathers every video Syrian citizens take and sends it to global news agencies. "You have over 1,000 videos filmed every day, maybe more. What we see on TV is really just a small percentage of what is filmed." The developing global market and the resulting global connectivity have thus made it increasingly difficult for political leaders to hide repressive acts from the rest of the world.

At the same time, we need to examine the impact on other nations of the continual influx of popular culture—the second biggest American export (after military and airplane equipment). Has access to an American consumer lifestyle fundamentally altered Havel's Bedouin on the camel? What happens when CNN or Facebook is transported to communities in remote African villages?

What happens when Westernized popular culture encroaches on the rituals of Islamic countries, where the spread of American music, movies, and television is viewed as a danger to tradition? These questions still need answers. A global village, which through technology shares culture and communication, can also alter traditional rituals forever.

To try to grasp this phenomenon, we might imagine how we would feel if the culture from a country far away gradually eroded our own established habits. This, in fact, is happening all over the world as U.S. culture has become the world's global currency. Although newer forms of communication such as phone texting, Facebook, and Twitter have in some ways increased citizen participation in global life, in what ways have they muted the values of older cultures?

Our current postmodern period is double-coded: It is an agent both for the renewed possibilities of democracy and for the worldwide spread of consumerism and American popular culture.

Source: Kristen McTighe, "Syria's Faceless Voices Risk Their Lives by Speaking Out," March 14, 2012, www.nytimes.com/2012/03/15 /world/middleeast/15ihtm15-syria-blog.html

APPLYING THE CRITICAL PROCESS

Investigate the influence of American popular culture on other parts of the world. Look at stories on the home page of at least four international news sources from four different countries. If you are fluent in other languages, good; if you read only English, try the *Guardian*, the *Independent*, the *Telegraph* (all UK), the *Mail & Guardian* (South Africa), *Sydney Morning Herald* (Australia), the *Globe and Mail* (Canada), *NHK* (Japan), *The Straits Times* (Singapore), AlJazeera.net (Qatar), and *The Times of India.*

DESCRIPTION Describe the content of the four newspapers, with particular regard to any U.S.-related content.

ANALYSIS What patterns emerge in the U.S.-related content? Does the content have to do with international politics, sports, entertainment, or some other topic? What percentage of the stories on the home page of each

newspaper is about the United States or American culture? Are there any other countries that dominate the news in each newspaper?

INTERPRETATION Does your analysis support the idea that U.S. culture is influential throughout the world? Does the United States have any rivals to the global strength of its culture?

EVALUATION Discuss the advantages and disadvantages of American culture becoming so popular worldwide. Is there evidence that other cultures are influencing American culture? Is that a good or bad trend?

ENGAGEMENT Continue to read international newspapers, and consider the influence of culture from other countries on the United States. Contact an editor at your local newspaper and ask why an important story you saw in an international paper isn't news here.

new perspectives, the conclusions laid out in a particular study may just be the author's interpretation. They may not necessarily explain cause-and-effect connections in situations other than what the author examined.

The social scientific model seeks to develop and test theories about how the media affect individuals and society in measurable ways. This approach produces conclusions based on "hard" numbers, which policy makers often find comforting. It may suggest a clear chain of cause and effect, or at least a statistical relationship between the media and an effect.

One way to critique the media is to analyze the highly stylized advertisements and information that appear before us. In the poster for the 2011 film *Mission: Impossible—Ghost Protocol,* what is being sold, and what does it reveal about American audiences?

But like the cultural model, the social scientific model has limits too. For example, the options provided in a multiple-choice survey question might not cover all the possible responses that participants could give. As a result, the researchers obtain an incomplete picture of how people respond to particular media. Also, definitions of what is being measured may confuse things. To illustrate, researchers might count a bonk on the head shown in a movie as "an act of violence," even though the event could be purposeful, accidental, deserved, or part of a character's fantasy. Researchers can thus neglect to ask more nuanced questions, such as whether accidental incidents of violence have a different effect on movie viewers than purposeful acts of violence. Finally, many social scientific studies are limited to questions that their funding sources—the government, media industry associations, or granting agencies—ask them to study. This situation further constrains the scope of their research.

Ultimately, though, the quality of any media research—cultural or social scientific—depends on the nature of the questions asked and the rigor of the method used. Oftentimes, "triangulating" with three or more approaches to test a question makes for much stronger conclusions. For those of us seeking to strengthen our media literacy by consulting research, the best approach may be to balance findings on a particular question from both the cultural and social scientific models.

Conducting Our Own Critiques

If we want to conduct our own critiques of specific media, we'll need a working knowledge of that medium—whether it's a book, TV show, song, movie, video game,

THE CRITICAL PROCESS BEHIND MEDIA LITERACY

Becoming literate about the communication media involves striking a balance between taking a critical stand (developing knowledgeable interpretations and judgments) and being tolerant of diverse forms of expression (appreciating the distinctive variety of cultural products and processes). Finding this balance in a media-literate critical perspective involves completing five overlapping stages that build on one another.

Stage One: Description

Develop descriptive skills associated with breaking down a story into character types and plot structure. Focus on how music, dialogue, camerawork, and editing come together in a way that encourages audience engagement. Master the terms and understand the techniques of telling stories in a particular medium.

Examples
- Describe how the conventions of the documentary are used in sitcoms like *Modern Family* or *The Office*.
- Describe the use of retro-sounding music in *It's Always Sunny in Philadelphia*.

Stage Two: Analysis

Focus on and discuss the significant patterns that emerge during the Description stage. Make connections. How does this song or story connect with other items of popular culture?

Examples
- How does the satirical approach of *The Colbert Report* compare to that of *The Daily Show with Jon Stewart*?
- What are the similarities and differences between *Fox & Friends* and NBC's *Today*?

Stage Three: Interpretation

Interpret findings. Ask "What does it mean?" If there is a distinct pattern, what is the cause or reason? Consider whether comedy, irony, and satire complicate this stage of the critical process.

Examples
- What does the presence of criminal protagonists mean for shows like *Dexter*, *Weeds*, and *Breaking Bad*?
- What does it mean when Jeff Dunham fashions a comedy act around "Achmed, the Dead Terrorist"? Why do Dunham's fans find the "I keel you" line so funny?

Stage Four: Evaluation

Arrive at a critical judgment that goes beyond your personal tastes. Does the media product under analysis cause harm? Does it inspire thought? Does it perpetuate a dehumanizing view of a group? Does it promote active citizenship or passive consumerism?

Examples
- The movie adaptation of *The Girl with the Dragon Tattoo* depicts scenes of rape and torture. Should the movie be condemned for promoting violence against women?
- The villain in *The Muppets* (2011) is a greedy oil tycoon. Is this film anticapitalist propaganda?

Stage Five: Engagement

Make your voice heard. Take action that connects your critical perspective to your role as a citizen. Become involved in doing your part to challenge media institutions and make them accountable.

Examples
- Write letters to media editors about blind spots in news coverage.
- Contact companies that perpetuate harmful images of women in their advertising and recommend more socially responsible ways of selling their products.

magazine, radio show, or some other form. For example, suppose our goal is to develop a meaningful critique of the TV show *Dexter* (in which the main character is a serial killer), Rush Limbaugh's conservative radio program, or weekly magazines' obsession with Kate Middleton. In each case, we will have to thoroughly familiarize ourselves with the show, program, or magazines in question and start thinking about what messages they seem to be conveying. As we begin this process, we will also need to transcend our own preferences and biases. For instance, we may like or dislike hip-hop, R&B, pop music, or country, but if we want to criticize the messages in one or more of these musical genres intelligently, we need to understand what they have to say and consider why their messages appeal to particular audiences.

Familiarization and a certain amount of self-conscious detachment, then, are the preliminaries of a rigorous process that moves beyond matters of taste or, worse, a cynical, wholesale dismissal of culturally significant experiences. Becoming truly media literate requires mastering this critical process and applying it to our everyday encounters with the communication media. The process encompasses five steps: Description, Analysis, Interpretation, Evaluation, and Engagement (see "The Critical Process behind Media Literacy" on page 25).

Benefits of a Critical Perspective

Developing an informed critical perspective on the media enables us to participate in a debate about media's impacts on our democracy and culture. For instance, on the one hand, the media can be a force for strengthening our democracy and making the world a better place. Consider the role of television in documenting racism and injustice in the 1960s—coverage that encouraged the Civil Rights movement. Or consider researched media reports that have stimulated interest in and tolerance of diverse cultures around the world (see "Media Literacy Case Study: Bedouins, Camels, Transistors, and Coke" on pages 22–23).

On the other hand, the media have also helped to create a powerful commercial culture in our nation—a culture in which fewer and fewer multinational corporations dominate our economy and generate more and more of the media messages we consume. A society in which only a few voices are

Powerful celebrities like Oprah have a profound influence on popular opinion and belief. Developing an informed critical perspective on the media allows individuals to engage in discussions about their impact on the world.

telling us stories about what's important, what our values should be, and how we should behave is hardly a healthy democracy.

Because media constitute forces for both good and ill, it's that much more important for each of us to think carefully about which media we consume, what messages we draw from those media, and how those messages are affecting our actions, the quality of our lives, and the health of our democracy. We need to ask additional questions, such as the following:

- Why might some people continue clinging to either/or thinking about media (such as "high-brow" versus "low-brow" books or movies) when so many boundaries in our society have blurred? Does this either/or thinking reflect a desire to keep people in their "proper" socioeconomic class?
- What does it mean that public debate and news about everyday life now seem just as likely to come from Oprah, Jon Stewart, or bloggers as from the *New York Times*, *NBC Nightly News*, or *Newsweek*?[9] Can we no longer distinguish real news from entertainment? If so, does this affect how well informed we are?
- How can we hone our awareness of the economic interests fueling the messages delivered through the media we consume? For example, do you listen to a talk show on a radio station that survives on advertising revenue? If so, ask yourself how the host might distort information (for instance, deliberately inciting conflict between guests) to attract more listeners and therefore bring in more advertising revenue. (Advertisers only want to spend money on ads that will reach as many people as possible.) If such distortion is taking place, how reliable is the information you're consuming by listening to the show?

Unfortunately, we can't rely only on professional media critics or watchdog organizations to do all the work of critiquing the media for us and analyzing their effects on our lives. Each of us is also responsible for doing some of that work ourselves. As you read the different chapters in this book, you'll learn more about each type of media—and you'll hone your ability to examine them with a critical eye.

CHAPTER ESSENTIALS

Now that you have finished reading this chapter, you can use the following tools:

REVIEW

Understand the Evolution of Mass Communication

- **Mass media** are industries that create and distribute songs, novels, newspapers, movies, Internet services, TV shows, magazines, and other products to large numbers of people. **Mass communication** is the creation and use of symbols (such as languages, motion pictures, and computer codes) that convey information and meaning to large and diverse audiences through all manner of channels (pp. 5–6).

- In the oral and written eras (1000 b.c.e. to the mid-fifteenth century), information and knowledge circulated through spoken traditions (oral) and then through manuscripts (written) commissioned by elites (p. 6).

- In the print era (starting in the mid-fifteenth century), wide dissemination of manuscripts became possible, thanks to the emergence of movable type and the printing press. Mass production of books spurred four significant changes: resistance to authority, the rise of new socioeconomic classes, the spread of literacy, and a focus on individualism (pp. 6–8).

- In the electronic and digital eras (the late nineteenth century to today), the telegraph, radio, and television (electronic media) made messages instantaneous and reshaped American life. **Digital communication**, whereby images, texts, and sounds are converted into electronic signals and reassembled as a precise reproduction of an image, a piece of text, or a sound, has changed the rules about who controls the dispersal of information (pp. 8–9).

- The electronic and digital eras also ushered in **media convergence**, which can refer to the technological merging of media content (such as the availability of a magazine article in print and online form) or to a business model used by media companies that consolidate media holdings to reduce costs and maximize profits (pp. 9–11).

Explain How Mass Media Relate to the Process of Communication

- A new medium goes through three stages on its journey toward mass medium status: the novelty (or development) stage (inventors or technicians try to solve a particular problem), the entrepreneurial stage (inventors and investors find a marketable use for the new device), and the mass medium stage (businesses figure out how to market the new device as a consumer product) (p. 12).

- Human beings have long debated media's merits and dangers. Some people today are worried that mass me[...] cial and sensationalis[...] lence, and that they ha[...] power (pp. 12–13).

The **post**[...]
genc[...]

Describe How Media Literacy Represents Ways of Unde[...]

- One approach to **media literacy**—or the attempt to understand how the media work and what impact they have on our lives—is the linear model. According to this model, **senders** (authors, producers, organizations) transmit **messages** (programs, texts, images, sounds, ads) through a **mass media channel** (newspapers, books, magazines, radio, television, the Internet) to large groups of **receivers** (readers, viewers, consumers). **Gatekeepers** (news editors, TV and movie producers) filter those messages. Citizens and consumers return **feedback**, or messages, to senders or gatekeepers through letters, phone calls, e-mail, "tweets", or talk shows. The linear model doesn't capture certain complexities of the mass communication process (p. 14).

- The cultural model of media literacy views media as characteristics of a culture and recognizes that different people assign different meanings to media content. Adherents believe that even as we shape media, they shape us (p. 15).

- The social scientific model seeks to test hypotheses about media's effects by gathering and analyzing measurable data. Politicians and businesses often use such research to formulate strategies (pp. 16–17).

Describe the Cultural Model of Media Literacy in Greater Detail

- Cultural researchers of media have offered several metaphors to describe how people judge different media content. The "culture as skyscraper" metaphor holds that some people associate **high culture** with characteristics such as "good taste," higher education, and fine art, and **low or popular culture** with characteristics such as the "masses" and commercial "junk" (p. 17).

- The "culture as map" metaphor holds that culture is an ongoing process that accommodates diverse tastes and that various media can satisfy human desires for both familiarity and newness (p. 18).

- Cultural researchers trace changes in values that accompany changes in media. The **modern era** saw the rise of values including efficient work, celebration of the individual, belief in a rational order, and rejection of tradition and embracing of progress (in particular, during the **Progressive Era**).

...tmodern period witnessed the emergence of values including celebration of **popu- lism**, a revival of older cultural styles, an embracing of technology, and an interest in the supernatural (pp. 19–20).

Describe the Social Scientific Model of Media Literacy in Greater Detail

- Social scientific media researchers ask different types of questions about media than cultural researchers ask. In a comparison of studies analyzing news coverage of cancer, a study informed by the cultural model explored how coverage of Betty Ford's mastectomy informs news coverage of cancer today, including an emphasis on women's need to maintain their femininity. A study informed by the social scientific model reported data-based findings, such as the percentage of news stories that included content about how to prevent cancer (p. 20).

- Social scientists use **content analysis** to gather data—they code and count the content of various types of media. They also conduct **experiments** to generate data, and gather data through **surveys** (p. 21).

Explain Why Critiquing Media Is Important and How to Approach This Activity

- Citizens can examine the findings of cultural and social scientific research on media to follow a **critical process** consisting of describing, analyzing, interpreting, evaluating, and engaging with mass media. Both models have strengths and limitations (p. 21).

- To conduct our own critiques of specific media, we must acquire a working knowledge of each medium we want to study, as well as transcend our own preferences or biases regarding the media we're studying (pp. 24, 26).

- A critical perspective on the mass media is valuable because it enables us to take part in debates about the media's impact on our democracy and culture (pp. 26–27).

STUDY QUESTIONS

1. Explain the interrelationship between *mass communication* and *mass media*.
2. What are the stages a medium goes through before becoming a mass medium?

3. Describe the skyscraper model of culture and the map model of culture. What are their strengths and limitations?
4. What are the major differences in how the linear, cultural, and social scientific models approach the study of media?
5. Why is the critical process important?

MEDIA LITERACY PRACTICE

We began this chapter by considering the consequences of media deprivation. For this exercise, we ask you to try it for one day.

DESCRIBE the experience of giving up all media for one day—including television, radio, movies, books, magazines, newspapers, and the Internet (even connections on a mobile phone).

ANALYZE the patterns you discover. Which media were the most difficult to avoid using? Which were the easiest?

INTERPRET what these patterns mean. For example, what missing elements (e.g., news, social contact, entertainment) affected your daily life the most? Did the deprivation experience open up new possibilities for you?

EVALUATE the role of the media in your life and in your social circle. What is good and bad about it? Is it too easy to demonize all media as "bad"? Is it too easy to overindulge in media content?

ENGAGE with the community by telling your story to local news outlets, on a social-networking page, or on a relevant Web site. Or, ask your instructor to collect your entire class's media deprivation outcomes for public presentation.

⊙ ONLINE RESOURCES

Go to **bedfordstmartins.com/mediaessentials** for review quizzes, links, and more.

Visit the site's **VIDEOCENTRAL: MASS COMMUNICATION** section for videos like the one on page 12. There, you can find additional exclusive videos related to Chapter 1, including:

THE MEDIA AND DEMOCRACY

This video traces the history of media's role in democracy from newspapers and television to the Internet.

2

Books and the Power of Print

The most successful books of this generation include J. K. Rowling's Harry Potter series. The series, which follows the exciting life of orphan Harry Potter as he attends Hogwarts School of Witchcraft and Wizardry, has broken all commercial-success records: More than 450 million copies of the books in sixty-seven languages had been sold by 2011. The final book, *Harry Potter and the Deathly Hallows*, was released in July 2007 and sold 13.1 million copies that year, becoming the fastest-selling book in history. Rowling's books have received several honors, including a commendation from the Carnegie Awards and the Whitbread Children's Book of the Year award in 1999.[1] The series has also expanded across media platforms, most famously in blockbuster movies.

The series' successes are measured not only in book sales and a new interest in reading among children and adults, but also in profitable movie franchises. And while the books inspired people to see the movies, the movies also inspired people to read books from other fantasy authors. Rowling's successes revived interest in the older *Lord of the Rings* trilogy by J. R. R. Tolkien (also made into movies) and C. S. Lewis's *Chronicles of Narnia* series (spawning yet more movies). Other, more recent book series to make the leap into multimedia franchises include the *Twilight* saga and the *Hunger Games* trilogy.

The latest evidence that books still matter in a world where digital media dominate our mediascape is the Wizarding World of Harry Potter. Opened in 2010, this theme park establishes the world of Rowling's stories as a vacation destination and serves as a reminder that books—the oldest mass medium—survive because they originate some of the biggest ideas and stories that resonate even outside the mediated experience.

FOR HUNDREDS OF YEARS—before newspapers, radio, and film, before television and the Internet—books were the only mass medium. Books have fueled major developments throughout human history, from revolutions and the rise of democracies to new forms of art (including poetry and fiction) and the spread of religions. When cheaper printing technologies laid the groundwork for books to become more widely available and quickly disseminated, people gained access to knowledge and ideas that previously were reserved only for the privileged few.

With the emergence of new types of mass media, some critics claimed that books would cease to exist. But so far at least, that's not happening. In 1950, U.S. publishers introduced more than 11,000 new book titles; in 2010, that number reached more than 315,000 (see Table 2.1 on page 36). Though books have adapted to technology and cultural change (witness the advent of e-books), our oldest mass medium still plays a large role in our lives. Books remain the primary repository of history and everyday experience, passing along stories, knowledge, and wisdom from generation to generation.

In this chapter, we trace the history of this enduring medium and examine its impact on our lives today by:

- assessing books' early roots—including the invention of papyrus (the first writing surface) and the printing press, as well as the birth of the publishing industry in colonial America

- exploring the unique characteristics of modern publishing, such as how publishing houses are structured

- taking stock of the many types of books that now exist, from a variety of print books to the electronic and digital books available today

- examining the economics of the book industry, including how players in this industry make money and what they spend money on to fulfill their mission

- considering the role of books in our democracy today as this mass medium confronts several challenges

The Early History of Books: From Papyrus to Paperbacks

Books have traveled a unique path in their journey to mass medium status. They developed out of early innovations including papyrus (scrolls made from plant reeds), parchment (treated animal skin), and codex (sheets of parchment sewn together along the edge and then bound and covered). They then entered an entrepreneurial stage, during which people explored new ways of clarifying or illustrating text and experimented with printing techniques such as block printing, movable type, and the printing press. The invention of the printing press set the stage for books to become a mass medium, complete with the rise of a new industry: publishing.

Papyrus, Parchment, and Codex: The Development Stage of Books

The ancient Egyptians, Greeks, Chinese, and Romans all produced innovations that led up to the creation of something that looked roughly like what we think of as a book. It all began some five thousand years ago, in ancient Sumeria (Mesopotamia) and Egypt, where people first experimented with alphabets. Initially, they drew pictorial symbols, or *hieroglyphics*, on wood strips or pressed these symbols into clay tablets, then tied or stacked these objects together to form the first "books."

Then, in 2400 b.c.e., the Egyptians began gathering reeds from plants found along the Nile River and rolling the plants into scrolls they could write on—called **papyrus** (from which our word *paper* is derived). Between 650 and 300 b.c.e. the Greeks and Romans adopted papyrus as well. Gradually, **parchment**—treated animal skin—replaced papyrus in Europe. Parchment was stronger, smoother, more durable, and less expensive than papyrus. Around 105 c.e., the Chinese began making paper from cotton and linen, though paper did not replace parchment in Europe until the thirteenth century because of questionable durability.

The first protomodern book was probably produced in the fourth century by the Romans, who created the **codex**, sheets of parchment sewn together along one edge, then bound with thin pieces of wood and covered with leather. Whereas scrolls had to be rolled and unrolled for use, a codex could be opened to any page, and people could write on both sides of a page.

TABLE 2.1 // ANNUAL NUMBERS OF NEW BOOK TITLES PUBLISHED, SELECTED YEARS

Year	Number of Titles	Year	Number of Titles
1778	461	1945	6,548 (World War II)
1798	1,808	1950	11,022
1880	2,076	1960	15,012
1890	4,559	1970	36,071
1900	6,356	1980	42,377
1910	13,470 (peak until after World War II)	1990	46,473
1915	8,202	1996	68,175*
1919	5,714 (low point as a result of World War I)	2001	114,487
1925	8,173	2004	160,919
1930	10,027	2006	274,415*
1935	8,766 (Great Depression)	2010	316,480
1940	11,328		

Changes in the Bowker Annual's methodology in 1997 and 2006 resulted in additional publications assigned ISBNs being included in their count.

Sources: Figures through 1945 from John Tebbel, A History of Book Publishing in the United States, 4 vols. (New York: R. R. Bowker, 1972–81); figures after 1945 from various editions of The Bowker Annual Library and Book Trade Almanac (Information Today, Inc.) and Bowker press releases.

Writing and Printing Innovations: Books Enter the Entrepreneurial Stage

Books entered an entrepreneurial stage with the emergence of **manuscript culture**. In this stage, new rules about written language and book design were codified—books were elaborately lettered, decorated, and bound by hand. Inventors also began experimenting with printing as an alternative to hand lettering and a way to speed up the production and binding of manuscript copies.

CHAPTER 2 // TIMELINE

2400 B.C.E.
Papyrus
Made from plant reeds, papyrus is first used as paper and rolled into scrolls.

1000 B.C.E. The Earliest Books
The Chinese make book-like objects from strips of wood and bamboo.

Fourth Century C.E. Codex
The first protomodern book is produced by the Romans.

600 Illuminated Manuscripts
These books are created by priests and monks throughout Europe.

1000 Movable Type
The Chinese invent movable type, significantly speeding up printing time.

Manuscript Culture

During Europe's Middle Ages (400 to 1500 c.e.), Christian priests and monks transcribed the philosophical tracts and religious texts of the period, especially versions of the Bible. Their transcriptions took the form of **illuminated manuscripts**, books that featured decorative, colorful illustrations on each page and that were often made for churches or wealthy clients. These early publishers developed rules of punctuation—for example, making distinctions between small and capital letters, and leaving space between words to make reading easier. Some elements of this manuscript culture remain alive today, in the form of design flourishes such as the drop capitals occasionally used for the first letter in a book chapter.

Block Printing

If manuscript culture involved advances in written language and book design, it also involved hard work: Every manuscript was painstakingly copied one book at a time. To make mechanically produced copies of pages, printers in the third century in China came up with an innovation that made mass production possible.

These Chinese innovators developed **block printing**. Using this technique, printers applied sheets of paper to large blocks of inked wood in which they had hand-carved a page's worth of characters and illustrations in relief. They derived these carvings from authors' and illustrators' works, which could range from plays and scriptures to instructional materials (such as advice about how to plant crops). The oldest dated block-printed book still in existence is China's *Diamond Sutra*, a collection of Buddhist scriptures printed by Wang Chieh in 868 c.e. to honor his ill mother.

Illuminated manuscripts were handwritten by scribes and illustrated with colorful and decorative images and designs.

1453 Printing Press
Gutenberg invents the printing press, forming the prototype for mass production.

1640 The First Colonial Book
Stephen Daye prints a collection of biblical psalms.

1751 Encyclopedias
French scholars begin compiling articles in alphabetical order.

1800s Publishing Houses
The book industry forms prestigious companies that produce and market works of good writers.

1836 Textbooks
William H. McGuffey publishes the *Eclectic Reader*, helping American students learn how to read.

Movable Type

The next significant step in printing came with the invention of movable type in China around the year 1000. This was a major improvement (in terms of speed) over block printing because, rather than carving each new page on one block, printers carved commonly used combinations of characters from the Chinese language into smaller, reusable wood (and later ceramic) blocks. They then put together the pieces needed to represent a desired page of text, inked the small blocks, and applied the sheets of paper. This method enabled them to create pages of text much more quickly than before.

The Printing Press and the Publishing Industry: Books Become a Mass Medium

Books moved from the entrepreneurial stage to mass medium status with the invention of the printing press (which made books widely available for the first time) and the rise of the publishing industry (which arose to satisfy people's growing hunger for books).

The Printing Press

The **printing press** was invented by Johannes Gutenberg in Germany between 1453 and 1456. Drawing on the principles of movable type, and adapting a device from the design of a wine press, Gutenberg's staff of printers produced the first so-called modern books, including two hundred copies of a Latin Bible—twenty-one of which still exist. The Gutenberg Bible (as it's now known) was printed on a fine calfskin-based parchment called **vellum**.

Printing presses spread rapidly across Europe in the late 1400s and early 1500s. Chaucer's *Canterbury Tales* was the first English work to be printed in book form. Many of these early books were large, elaborate, and expensive. But printers gradually reduced books' sizes and developed less-expensive grades of paper. These changes made books cheaper to produce, so printers could sell them for less, making the books affordable to many more people.

CHAPTER 2 // TIMELINE continued

1870s Mass Market Paperbacks
"Pulp fiction" paperbacks become popular among middle- and working-class readers.

Mid-1880s Linotype and Offset Lithography
New printing techniques lower the cost of books in the United States.

1926 Book Clubs
Book-of-the-Month Club and Literary Guild are formed.

1960s Professional Books
The book industry targets various occupational groups.

The spread of printing presses and books sparked a major change in the way people learned. Previously, people followed the traditions and ideas framed by local authorities—the ruling class, clergy, and community leaders. But as books became more broadly available, people gained access to knowledge and viewpoints far beyond their immediate surroundings and familiar authorities. Some of them began challenging the traditional wisdom and customs of their tribes and leaders.[2] This interest in debating ideas would ultimately encourage the rise of democratic societies in which all citizens had a voice.

The Publishing Industry

In the two centuries after the invention of the printing press, publishing—the establishment of printing shops to serve the public's growing demand for books—took off in Europe, eventually spreading to England and finally to the American colonies. In colonial America, English locksmith Stephen Daye set up a print shop in the late 1630s in Cambridge, Massachusetts. There, he and his son printed *The Whole Booke of Psalms* (known today as *The Bay Psalm Book*), marking the beginning of book publishing in the colonies. By the mid-1760s, all thirteen colonies had printing shops. Some publishers (such as Benjamin Franklin, who published several popular novels by British author Samuel Richardson) grew quite wealthy in this profession.

However, in the early 1800s, U.S. publishers had to find ways to lower the cost of producing books to meet exploding demand. By the 1830s,

The weekly paperback series *Tip Top Weekly*, which was published between 1896 and 1912, featured the most popular dime novel hero of the day, Yale football star and heroic adventurer Frank Merriwell.

1971 Borders Is Established
The chain formation of superstores begins.

1995 Amazon.com
The first online book distributor is established.

2007 Harry Potter
Harry Potter and the Deathly Hallows has record-breaking sales of 13.1 million copies.

2007 Kindle
Amazon.com introduces the Kindle, the most successful e-book reader to date.

2011 Borders Closes
The chain closes all of its stores as brick-and-mortar stores lose business to digital sales.

machine-made paper replaced the more expensive handmade varieties, cloth covers supplanted costlier leather ones, and **paperback books** with cheaper paper covers (introduced from Europe) all helped to make books even more accessible to the masses. Further reducing the cost of books, publishers Erastus and Irwin Beadle introduced paperback **dime novels** (so called because they sold for five or ten cents) in 1860. By 1885, one-third of all books published in the United States consisted of popular paperbacks and dime novels, sometimes identified as **pulp fiction** (a reference to the cheap, machine-made pulp paper they were printed on).

Meanwhile, the printing process itself also advanced. In the 1880s, the introduction of **linotype** machines enabled printers to save time by setting type mechanically using a typewriter-style keyboard. The introduction of steam-powered and high-speed rotary presses also permitted the production of even more books at lower costs. In the early 1900s, with the development of **offset lithography**, publishers could print books from photographic plates rather than from metal casts. This greatly reduced the cost of color ink and illustrations and accelerated the production process—enabling publishers to satisfy Americans' steadily increasing demand for books.

The Evolution of Modern Publishing

As demand for books skyrocketed, the publishing industry morphed to satisfy it. Companies that participated in this industry, often called publishing "houses," were initially small and focused on offering the works of quality authors. Over time, these companies were snapped up by major corporations with ties to international media conglomerates. However, regardless of what subject matter they focus on or who owns them, publishing houses are structured in similar ways to carry out the process of attracting authors, developing manuscripts, and marketing published books.

Early Publishing Houses

The modern book industry in the United States developed gradually in the 1800s with the formation of "prestigious" publishing houses: companies that identified and produced the works of respected writers.[3] The oldest American houses included J. B. Lippincott (1792); Harper & Bros. (1817), which became Harper & Row in 1962 and HarperCollins in 1990; Houghton Mifflin (1832); Little, Brown (1837); G. P. Putnam (1838); Scribner's (1842); E. P. Dutton (1852); Rand McNally (1856); and Macmillan (1869).

Between 1880 and 1920, as more people moved from rural areas to cities and learned to read, Americans became interested in reading all kinds of books—novels, historical accounts, reference materials, instructional resources. This caught the attention of entrepreneurs eager to profit by satisfying this demand. A savvy breed of publishing house—focused on marketing—was born. These firms included Doubleday & McClure Company (1897), the McGraw-Hill Book Company (1909), Prentice-Hall (1913), Alfred A. Knopf (1915), Simon & Schuster (1924), and Random House (1925).

The Conglomerates

Book publishing sputtered from the 1910s into the 1940s, as the two world wars and the Great Depression turned Americans' attention away from books. But as the U.S. economy recovered during the 1950s and 1960s, the industry bounced back. Major corporations and international media conglomerates began acquiring the smaller houses to expand their markets and take advantage of the **synergy** (the promotion and sale of different versions of a media product across the various subsidiaries of a conglomerate) between books and other media types.

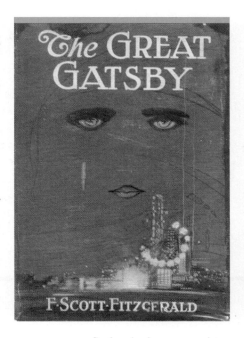

Scribner's—known more for its magazine in the late 1800s than for its books—became the most prestigious literary house of the 1920s and 1930s, publishing F. Scott Fitzgerald (*The Great Gatsby,* 1925) and Ernest Hemingway (*The Sun Also Rises,* 1926).

Nowadays book publishing is dominated by a handful of these giants. For example, the CBS Corporation owns Simon & Schuster and its imprints, including Pocket Books; and News Corp. owns HarperCollins and all of its imprints, including Avon (see Figure 2.1 on page 42). The largest of the publishing conglomerates is Germany's Bertelsmann. This company controls about one-third of the U.S. trade book market. (Trade books are sold in bookstores and constitute about 10 percent of the total U.S. book market.) Through its focused acquisition strategy, Bertelsmann has become the world's largest publisher of English-language books.[4]

The consolidation of the book industry has raised concerns among observers who mourn the loss of the older houses' distinctive styles and their associations with renowned literary figures like Mark Twain and Nathaniel Hawthorne. Moreover, the large corporations that now define the industry's direction can buy needed resources (such as paper, printing, and binding services) at a discount and thus charge less for their product. They also have huge marketing budgets. Few independent publishers have been able to compete against them, which ultimately has reduced the range of books now available to consumers.

FIGURE 2.1 // FIVE LARGEST
TRADE BOOK PUBLISHERS
(NORTH AMERICAN REVENUE
IN MILLIONS OF DOLLARS)

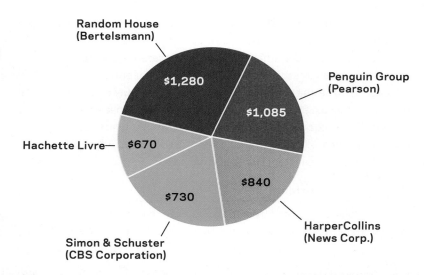

Random House (Bertelsmann): $1,280
Penguin Group (Pearson): $1,085
HarperCollins (News Corp.): $840
Simon & Schuster (CBS Corporation): $730
Hachette Livre: $670

Source: Jim Milliot, "Penguin, Hachette Gained in Tough 2008," Publisher's Weekly, May 4, 2009, www.publishersweekly.com/article/CA6655851 .html?q=revenue.

The Structure of Publishing Houses

Regardless of their size or the types of books they publish, publishing houses are structured similarly. For example, they have teams or divisions responsible for acquisitions and manuscript development; copyediting, design, and production; marketing and sales; and administration. And unlike daily newspapers but similar to magazines, most publishing houses pay independent printers to produce their books.

The majority of publishers employ **acquisitions editors** to seek out authors and offer them contracts to publish specific titles. For fiction, this might mean discovering talented writers through book agents or reading unsolicited manuscripts. In nonfiction, editors might examine unsolicited manuscripts and letters of inquiry or match a known writer to a project (such as a celebrity biography). Acquisitions editors also handle **subsidiary rights** for an author—that is, selling the rights to a book for use in other media, such as a mass-market paperback or as the basis for a screenplay.

After a contract is signed, the acquisitions editor may turn the book over to a **developmental editor** who helps the author draft and revise the manuscript by providing his or her own feedback and soliciting advice from reviewers. If a book is to contain illustrations, editors work with photo researchers to select photographs or find artists to produce the needed drawings or other graphics. Then the production staff enters the picture. While **copy editors** fix any spelling, punctuation, grammar, or style problems in the manuscript, **design managers** determine the "look and feel" of the book, making decisions about type styles, paper, cover design, and layout of page spreads.

Simultaneously, the publishing house determines a marketing strategy for each book—including identifying which readers will be most interested in the forthcoming title, deciding how many copies to print and what price to charge, and selecting advertising channels for reaching the target customers. Marketing budgets usually make up a large part of a publishing company's expenses, and marketing managers are often fairly high up in the organization.

Types of Books: Tradition Meets Technology

Until fairly recently, books of all kinds took printed form: pages bound together through various devices (such as glue or spiral wire) and enclosed by a cover (cardboard, leather, paper). But with the rise of electronic and digital publishing, book formats have expanded beyond print to include audio ("books on tape," now available as CDs or MP3 downloads) and e-books (which are accessed on the Internet and read on a computer or a handheld device). Regardless of the format, however, books are still highly diverse in terms of their subject matter.

Print Books

Today, the publishing industry produces titles that fall into a wide variety of categories—everything from trade books and textbooks to mass market paperbacks and reference books. These categories have been formally defined by trade organizations such as the Association of American Publishers (AAP), the Book Industry Study Group (BISG), and the American Booksellers Association (ABA).

Trade

One of the most lucrative markets in the industry, **trade books** include hardbound and paperback books aimed at general readers and sold at commercial retail outlets. The industry distinguishes between adult trade, juvenile trade, and comics and graphic novels (which contain pictures rather than type). Adult trade books include hardbound and paperback fiction; current nonfiction and biographies; literary classics; books on hobbies, art, and travel; popular science, technology, and computer publications; self-help books; and cookbooks. Juvenile book categories range from preschool picture books to young-adult or young-reader books, such as the Dr. Seuss books, the Lemony Snicket series, and the Harry Potter series.

Professional

Professional books target various occupational groups, not the general consumer market. This area of publishing capitalizes on the growth of professional specialization that has characterized the U.S. job market, particularly since the 1960s. Traditionally, the industry has subdivided professional books into the areas of law, business, medicine, and technology-science. These books are sold mostly through mail order, the Internet, or sales representatives knowledgeable about the various subject areas.

Textbooks

Textbooks such as *The Eclectic Reader* have served a nation intent on improving literacy rates and public education and are divided into elementary through high school (el-hi) texts, college texts, and vocational texts. In about half of the states in America, local school districts determine which el-hi textbooks are appropriate for their students. The remaining states, including Texas and California, have statewide adoption policies governing which texts can be used. Unlike el-hi texts, which are subsidized by various states and school districts, college texts are paid for by students (or their parents) and are sold primarily through college bookstores. The increasing cost of textbooks has led some students to trade, resell, or rent textbooks or to download them more cheaply from sites like Amazon.com or BarnesandNoble.com. For the 2007–08 school year, the average college student spent between $921 and $988 on textbooks and other required course materials.[5] (See Figure 2.2 on page 45.)

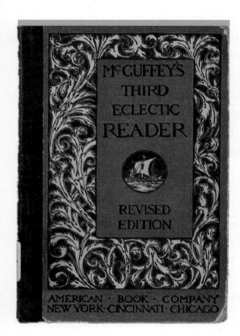

First published in 1836, McGuffey Readers helped enable the nineteenth-century U.S. literacy movement and the wave of western expansion. After the Civil War, they were the standard textbooks in thirty-seven states. With 130 million copies published since the first edition, the readers are still in print and in use, with the latest revised version published in the late 1990s.

Mass Market Paperbacks

Unlike the larger-sized trade paperbacks, which are sold mostly in bookstores, **mass market paperbacks** are sold on racks in drugstores, supermarkets, and airports as well as in bookstores. Contemporary mass market paperbacks—often the work of blockbuster authors such as Stephen King, Danielle Steel, and John Grisham—represent the largest segment of the industry in terms of units sold. But because the books are low priced (under $10), they generate less revenue than trade books. Paperbacks first became popular back in the 1870s, when middle- and working-class readers popularized dime novels. In 1939, when publisher Pocket Books lowered the price of these books from fifty or seventy-five cents to just twenty-five cents by slashing costs such as author royalties, readers devoured even more of them.

A major innovation in mass market paperback publishing came with the **instant book**, a marketing strategy that involves publishing a topical book quickly after a major event occurs. Pocket Books produced the first instant

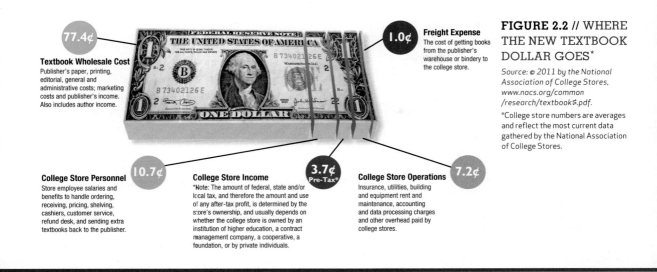

FIGURE 2.2 // WHERE THE NEW TEXTBOOK DOLLAR GOES*

Source: © 2011 by the National Association of College Stores, www.nacs.org/common /research/textbooks.pdf.

*College store numbers are averages and reflect the most current data gathered by the National Association of College Stores.

77.4¢

Textbook Wholesale Cost
Publisher's paper, printing, editorial, general and administrative costs; marketing costs and publisher's income. Also includes author income.

1.0¢

Freight Expense
The cost of getting books from the publisher's warehouse or bindery to the college store.

College Store Personnel **10.7¢**
Store employee salaries and benefits to handle ordering, receiving, pricing, shelving, cashiers, customer service, refund desk, and sending extra textbooks back to the publisher.

College Store Income
*Note: The amount of federal, state and/or local tax, and therefore the amount and use of any after-tax profit, is determined by the store's ownership, and usually depends on whether the college store is owned by an institution of higher education, a contract management company, a cooperative, a foundation, or by private individuals.

3.7¢
Pre-Tax

College Store Operations **7.2¢**
Insurance, utilities, building and equipment rent and maintenance, accounting and data processing charges and other overhead paid by college stores.

book, *Franklin Delano Roosevelt: A Memorial*, six days after FDR's death in 1945. However, these books suffer from the same problems that their TV counterparts do: Because these accounts are cranked out so quickly, critics have accused them of containing shoddy writing, exploiting tragedies, and lacking in-depth analysis and historical perspective.

Religious

The best-selling book of all time is the Bible, in all its diverse versions. Over the years, the success of Bible sales has created a large industry for religious books, and many religious-book publishers have extended their offerings to include serious secular titles on such topics as war and peace, race, poverty, gender, and civic responsibility. After a record year in 2004 (twenty-one thousand new titles), this category has seen a slight decline. Yet it continues to play an important role in the book industry, especially during turbulent social times.

Reference

Reference books include dictionaries, encyclopedias, atlases, almanacs, and volumes related to particular professions or trades, such as legal casebooks and medical manuals. Encyclopedias and dictionaries traditionally have accounted for the largest portion of reference sales. But these reference works have moved mostly to online formats since the 1990s in response to competition from companies offering different formats. These rival formats include free online or built-in word processing software dictionaries, search engines such as Google, and online resources like *Wikipedia*.

WIKIPEDIA

English
The Free Encyclopedia
2 431 000+ articles

Deutsch
Die freie Enzyklopädie
767 000+ Artikel

Français
L'encyclopédie libre
676 000+ articles

Polski
Wolna encyklopedia
514 000+ haseł

日本語
フリー百科事典
500 000+ 記事

Italiano
L'enciclopedia libera
458 000+ voci

Nederlands
De vrije encyclopedie
449 000+ artikelen

Português
A enciclopédia livre
408 000+ artigos

Español
La enciclopedia libre
374 000+ artículos

Русский
Свободная энциклопедия
204 000+ статей

search · suche · recherche · szukaj · 検索 · ricerca · zoeken · busca · buscar
поиск · sök · 搜索 · søk · haku · cerca · sök · пошук · căutare · ara · hledání · sanību

[English ▾] [→]

100 000+
Català · Česky · Deutsch · English · Español · Esperanto · Français · Italiano · Nederlands · 日本語 · Norsk (bokmål) · Polski · Português · Русский ·
Română · Suomi · Svenska · Türkçe · Українська · Volapük · 中文

Since its launch in 2001, *Wikipedia* has grown to include more than nineteen million entries in 270 languages. Despite the controversies about bias, inconsistency, and incorrect information, the site is one of the most popular on the Web for general information.

University Press

The smallest market in the printed-book industry is the nonprofit **university press**, which publishes scholarly works for small groups of readers interested in specialized areas such as literary theory and criticism, art movements, and contemporary philosophy. While large commercial trade houses are often criticized for publishing only high-selling, mainstream books, university presses often suffer the opposite criticism—that they produce mostly obscure books that only a handful of scholars read.

Electronic and Digital Publishing

Within the formal categories discussed above, publishers are continually experimenting with alternatives to the printed-book format to remain competitive and to leverage the advantages of new technologies now available in the digital age. Examples of these alternatives include audio books and e-books.

Audio Books

Audio books (once known as "books on tape," though they now are available primarily on CD or as MP3 downloads) became popular in the 1990s and early 2000s and generally feature actors or authors reading versions of popular fiction and nonfiction trade books. Indispensable to many sightless readers and older readers with diminishing vision, audio books are also popular among readers who have long commutes by car or train, or who want to listen to a book while doing something else, like exercising. By the early 2000s, audio books were readily available on the Internet for downloading to iPods and other portable devices.

E-books

For about two decades, publishers have been exploring the idea of **e-books** to attract readers who have strayed to other media forms. In their most basic form, e-books are accessed on a Web site and read on a computer. The more heralded consumer version involves electronic books that can be downloaded to portable reading devices.

Despite years of predictions that such e-books would become a significant force in publishing sales, the e-book market never materialized. Then, in 2007, Amazon introduced a new e-book reader—the Kindle—that it hoped would make e-books so easy to download, store, and read that the market would finally take off. Unlike earlier e-book readers, Amazon's Kindle uses a wireless connection that enables consumers to directly buy and download offerings from a selection

VideoCentral⊚
**bedfordstmartins.com
/mediaessentials**

Anne Rice
Novelist

Books in the New Millennium
Authors, editors, and bookstore owners discuss the future of book publishing. **Discussion:** Are you optimistic or pessimistic about the future of books in an age of computers and e-readers?

of books, newspapers, and blogs from its online store (a version of Amazon's bookstore). Book downloads take less than a minute. Now, Amazon delivers 105 e-book downloads for every 100 paper-based books sold.[6] In 2011, in recognition of the boom in sales, the *New York Times* started publishing e-book best-seller lists in fiction and nonfiction. That same year, Amazon began selling its basic Kindle for $79, breaking the $100 mark, and also introduced the more expensive color touchscreen Kindle Fire. E-book apps are now available for iPods, iPads, Androids, and mobile phones, as are Nook apps for Barnes & Noble's own popular e-book device (see Figure 2.3 on page 48). The giant Borders bookstore chain, in contrast, missed the e-book boom, which many believe contributed to its bankruptcy in 2011.

The Economics of the Book Industry

To serve customers profitably, the book business (like other mass media industries) must bring in money while also investing in needed resources. Publishers make money by selling books through specific channels (such as brick-and-mortar stores and online stores) and by selling television and movie rights. And they spend money on essential activities such as book production, distribution, and marketing.

Money In

Compared with other mass media industries, book publishing has seen only a relatively modest increase in revenues over the decades. From the mid-1980s to 2010, total revenues went from $9 billion to about $27.9 billion. But the industry continues to seek new and bigger sources of growth. Publishers bring in money through a variety of channels.

Book Sales

The most obvious source of revenue for publishers are sales of the books themselves—whether they're in print, audio, or e-book form. There are several main outlets for selling books:

1. **Brick-and-mortar stores.** These include traditional bookstores, department stores, drugstores, used-book stores, and toy stores. After the 2011 bankruptcy of Borders-Waldenbooks, book sales are now dominated by the single largest chain, Barnes & Noble. Barnes & Noble operates more than 705

Amazon.com CEO Jeff Bezos presents the Kindle Fire, a color touchscreen version of its popular Kindle electronic reader. E-readers like the Kindle Fire attempt to transform books from paperbound purchases at brick-and-mortar stores to a completely online experience.

The Strand is an independent bookstore in New York City. Open since 1927, it is famous for its "18 miles of books," which include more than 2.5 million new, used, and rare books.

superstores, though it closed its remaining smaller B. Dalton bookstores in 2010. The rise of book superstores—along with competition from online stores—severely cut into independent bookstores' business, dropping their number from 5,100 in 1991 to only about 2,200 today. Many independents have formed regional or statewide groups to develop survival tactics.

2. **Online stores.** Since the late 1990s, online booksellers have created an entirely new book-distribution system on the Internet. The trailblazer is Amazon.com, established in 1995 by then-thirty-year-old Jeff Bezos. In 1997, Barnes & Noble, the leading retail store bookseller, launched its own heavily invested and carefully researched bn.com site. In 1999, the American Booksellers Association also launched BookSense.com to help more than a thousand independent bookstores establish an online presence. The strength of online sellers lies in their convenience and low prices, especially their ability to offer backlist titles and the works of less famous authors that even superstores don't carry on their shelves. Many online customers also appreciate the ability to post their own book reviews at online stores, read those of fellow customers, and receive book recommendations based on their searches and past purchases. As book readers turn to e-books, online stores are better situated for this transition. By 2011, customers were buying more e-books than print books from Amazon.

FIGURE 2.3 // E-BOOKSTORE PURCHASES BY IPAD OWNERS

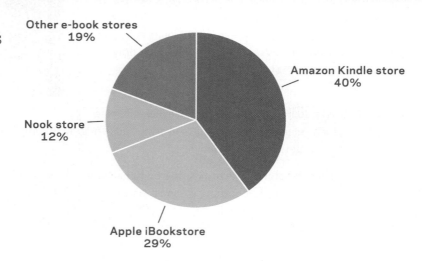

Other e-book stores 19%

Amazon Kindle store 40%

Nook store 12%

Apple iBookstore 29%

Source: Jim Milliot, "Amazon Ups Its Edge," Publishers Weekly, January 24, 2011, http://www.publishersweekly.com/pw/by-topic/industry-news/bookselling/article/45861-amazon-ups-its-edge.thml.

CONVERGING MEDIA
Case Study

Self-Publishing Gets Redefined

Between 2008 and 2010, e-book sales rose over 1,000 percent.[1] Media convergence—in the form of e-book readers and e-ink apps for tablets and laptops—is clearly changing the way people read books. But there is another dimension to the e-book revolution that is even more threatening to the traditional print publishing powers: Media convergence is also transforming the way people publish books. Amazon's Kindle Direct Publishing has made self-publishing so cheap and easy that, as one Amazon executive put it, "The only really necessary people in the publishing process now are the writer and reader." [2] Amazon is also taking on more of the roles of a traditional publisher, having set up its own dedicated publishing arm.

Of course, self-publishing has been long stigmatized as a vain enterprise (hence the term "vanity press"). To be self-published has been equated with amateurism and work that is not worthy of the considerable expenses and promotional resources associated with one of the big publishing houses. In the new media landscape, however, those notions are becoming increasingly inaccurate. John Locke, the first self-published author to join the Kindle Million Club, sells his crime novels for 99 cents a copy and has mastered the strategic use of blogging, Twitter, and e-mail to build a devoted fan base.

A number of established authors have also started testing the waters of self-publishing e-books. But the publishing industry response to these flirtations can be harsh. For instance, when Kiana Davenport e-published a compilation of award-winning short stories, her publishing house, declaring she was "sleeping with the enemy," canceled the publication of a forthcoming novel and has threatened litigation if she does not return the $20,000 advance.

The established publishers have reason to guard their turf: Self-published authors need not pay 10 percent to a literary agency, and they receive a significantly larger piece of the overall pie. Whereas the authors of paper-based books claim royalties of between 5 and 15 percent, authors with Amazon receive between 35 and 70 percent of the purchase price.[3]

But Amazon's entry into the publishing world is not limited to simply giving self-published authors a platform. They are also signing authors to their own publishing arm, which produces books in physical and electronic forms through a more traditional (albeit more secretive) process.[4] Publishers may soon face the kind of competition that booksellers have seen from Amazon over the past decade—and self-publishing authors may still struggle against authors with greater promotional muscle behind them. Media convergence is creating some new avenues; it's also generating more potential traffic.

3. **Book clubs.** Book clubs, similar to music clubs, entice new members with offers such as five books for a dollar, then require regular purchases from their list of recommended titles. The Book-of-the-Month Club and the Literary Guild are two examples, both launched in 1926. Originally, this business model helped generate revenues when bookstores were not as numerous as they are today. But since the 1980s, book clubs' sales have declined.

4. **Mail order.** Mail-order bookselling was another tactic introduced before bookstores became a major channel for selling, now used primarily by trade, professional, and university press publishers. A mail-order company, like a book club, immediately notifies readers about new book titles. This channel appeals to customers who want to avoid the hassle of shopping in stores or who want their purchases (for example, of sexually explicit materials) to remain private.

Regardless of what channel a publisher sells its books through, trade publishers are constantly on the hunt for the next *best-seller*—inspired by the huge success of Harriet Beecher Stowe's abolitionist novel *Uncle Tom's Cabin*, which sold a then-whopping 15,000 copies in just fifteen days back in 1852. (A total of 3 million copies flew off the shelves before the Civil War.) A best-seller can come from anywhere—a celebrity who pens his or her autobiography, a respected scientist who offers a provocative new perspective on artificial intelligence, a first-time novelist whose work is chosen for Oprah's Book Club.

Indeed, publishers have learned that TV can help sell books. Through TV exposure, books by or about talk-show hosts, actors, and politicians sell millions of copies—enormous sales in a business where 100,000 units sold constitutes remarkable success. In national polls conducted from the 1980s through today, nearly 30 percent of respondents said they had read a book after seeing the story or a promotion on television. A major force in promoting books on TV was Oprah's Book Club. Each selection by the club—before it made its transition online to Book Club 2.0 in 2012—became an immediate best-seller.

Over the years many movies have been based on books. *The Hunger Games* is a recent example. Movie rights bring in substantial revenue for the book industry.

TV and Movie Rights

Many TV shows and films get their story ideas from books, a process that generates enormous movie-rights revenues for the book industry and its authors. The most profitable movie-rights deals for the book industry in recent years have included the Harry Potter films as well as Peter Jackson's movie adaptations of J. R. R. Tolkien's Lord of the Rings series (first published in the 1950s). Books and their adaptations create desirable cross-promotion. HBO's adaptation of *A Game of Thrones*, the first book in George R. R. Martin's A Song of Ice and Fire series, pushed Martin's work to the top of best-seller lists and promoted the publication of the fifth book in the series, *A Dance with Dragons*. TV or movie promotion can also boost sales in new media: In September 2011, Martin joined Amazon's "Kindle Million Club," meaning that e-book sales of his work have exceeded one million downloads. Even classic and *public domain* books (no longer subject to copyright law) can create profits for the book industry. For example, in 2011, a screen version of Charlotte Brontë's 1847 novel *Jane Eyre* boosted sales of the reissued novel.

Money Out

To generate sales, publishers must spend money on producing books, distributing their products, and promoting or marketing newly launched titles.

Production

To produce books, publishing houses have expenditures such as overhead (including salaries for the employees who edit and design books) and paper, printing, and binding. Also, as part of their contracts, authors sometimes require that publishers pay them *advance money*, an up-front payment that's subtracted from royalties later earned from book sales (see Table 2.2). Typically, an author's royalty is 5 to 15 percent of the net price of the book. New authors may receive little or no advance from a publisher, but commercially successful authors can receive millions. For example, *Interview with a Vampire* author Anne Rice hauled in a $17 million advance from Knopf in a contract for writing three more vampire novels.

Distribution

Distribution costs include maintaining inventory of books to be sold and fulfilling orders (shipping books to commercial outlets or college bookstores). Publishers

TABLE 2.2 // HOW A PAPERBACK'S REVENUE IS DIVIDED

Despite their low profit margins, mass market paperbacks remain an important segment of the book industry. For example, two-thirds of Random House's income comes from paperbacks. A Random House paperback, retail priced at $10, breaks down this way:

Author royalty	$1.50
Publisher's costs	$2.00
Paper, printing, and binding	$1.00
Retailer	$5.00
Publisher profit	$.50

Source: Arianne Cohen, "A Publishing Company: Random House," New York, http://nymag.com/news/features/2007/profit /32906/.

monitor their warehouse inventories to ensure that enough copies of a book will be available to meet demand. Anticipating demand, though, is a tricky business. No publisher wants to be caught short if a book proves more popular than originally predicted. Nor does it want to get stuck with books it can't sell, as the company must then absorb the cost of returned books. As one way to avoid both of these costly scenarios, distributors, publishers, and bookstores have begun taking advantage of digital technology to print books on demand rather than stockpiling them in warehouses. Through this technology, they can revive books that would otherwise have gone out of print because of limited demand—and avoid the expense of carrying unsold books (see "Converging Media Case Study: Self-Publishing Gets Redefined" on page 49).

Marketing

Publishers spend a significant amount of money on marketing, which includes advertising and generating favorable reviews. For trade books and some scholarly books, publishing houses may send advance copies of a book to appropriate magazines and newspapers with the hope of receiving positive reviews that can be used in promotional materials such as brochures. A house may also send well-known authors on book-signing tours and arrange radio and TV talk-show interviews to promote their books. College textbook firms "seed adoptions" by paying instructors an honorarium to review a book that's in development, by sending free examination copies to potential adopters, and by promoting new titles through direct-mail brochures.

To help create a best-seller, trade publishing houses often give large illustrated cardboard bins, called *dumps*, to bookstores to display a particular book in bulk quantities. Large trade houses buy shelf space from major chains to ensure prominent locations in bookstores. Publishers also buy ad space in newspapers and magazines and on buses, billboards, television, radio, and the Web—all to pump up interest in a new book.

Books in a Democratic Society

Books have played a vital role in our democracy—not only by spreading the notion of democracy itself but also by disseminating ideas that inspire people to drive change. For example, Harriet Beecher Stowe's *Uncle Tom's Cabin* sparked outrage over slavery, helping to end the institution in the 1860s. Rachel Carson's *Silent Spring* exposed the perils of the pesticide industry in the 1960s, prompting the American public to demand reform. And Michael Pollan's *The Omnivore's Dilemma* has people thinking about the ethical and nutritional issues connected with factory farming and buying more locally raised meats and vegetables. Books have enabled people to freely share ideas, discuss those ideas' merits and flaws, and make informed choices—all key elements in

MEDIA LITERACY
Case Study

Banned Books and "Family Values"

Ulysses by James Joyce, *The Scarlet Letter* by Nathaniel Hawthorne, *Leaves of Grass* by Walt Whitman, *The Diary of a Young Girl* by Anne Frank, *Lolita* by Vladimir Nabokov, and *To Kill a Mockingbird* by Harper Lee have all been banned by some U.S. community, school, or library at one time or another. In fact, the most censored book in U.S. history is Mark Twain's *The Adventures of Huckleberry Finn,* the 1884 classic that still sells tens of thousands of copies each year. Often, the impulse behind calling for a book's banishment is to protect children in the name of a community's "family values."

APPLYING THE CRITICAL PROCESS

DESCRIPTION Identify two contemporary books that have been challenged or banned in two separate communities. (Check the American Library Association Web site—www.ala.org—for information on the most frequently challenged and banned books, or use the LexisNexis database.) Describe the two communities involved and what sparked the challenges or bans.

ANALYSIS Look at the patterns that emerge: the main arguments for censoring a book, for defending these particular books, or for holding any middle-ground positions or unusual viewpoints raised in your book controversies.

INTERPRETATION Why did these issues arise, and what do you think are the actual reasons why people would challenge or ban a book? For example, can you tell if people seem genuinely concerned about protecting young readers, or are they really just personally offended by particular books?

EVALUATION Who do you think is right and wrong in these controversies? How are First Amendment protections of printed materials significant here?

ENGAGEMENT Contact your local library and ask what policies they have in place to respond to book challenges, and whether they observe the ALA's annual Banned Books Week each September.

any democracy. Indeed, the ability to write whatever one wants has its very roots in our founding documents: Amendment I of the U.S. Constitution's Bill of Rights guarantees freedom of the press.

Though books have long played this crucial role and will continue to do so, they face several challenges that threaten to dilute their impact. These challenges include the persistence of censorship, a decline in reading, and the loss of old books to physical deterioration.

Censorship

Throughout human history, rulers intent on maintaining their power have censored or banned books to prevent people from learning about alternative ideas and ways

The Lorax, by Dr. Seuss
was challenged for "criminalizing
the foresting industry."

BANNED BOOKS WEEK
Celebrate Your Freedom to Read
www.ala.org/bbbooks

Banned Books Week is an event sponsored by the American Library Association to raise awareness of challenges to reader freedoms and attempts to ban books.

of living. For example, in various parts of the world, some versions of the Bible, Karl Marx's *Das Kapital* (1867), *The Autobiography of Malcolm X* (1965), and Salman Rushdie's *The Satanic Verses* (1989) have all been banned at one time or another. (For more on banned books, see "Media Literacy Case Study: Banned Books and 'Family Values'" on page 53.)

In the United States, censorship and banning of books are illegal. But citizens can sometimes force the removal of books from public or school libraries if enough people file a formal complaint—a **book challenge**—about subject matter they find objectionable in particular books. The American Library Association (ALA) compiles a list of the most challenged books in the United States. Common reasons for challenges include sexually explicit passages, offensive language, occult themes, violence, homosexual themes, promotion of a religious viewpoint, nudity, and racism. The ALA defends the right of libraries to offer material with a wide range of views, and does not support removing books on the basis of partisan or doctrinal disapproval.

This tension between citizens' desire to suppress printed materials they find objectionable and the desire to uphold freedoms guaranteed by our Constitution has long characterized our democracy—and will likely continue to do so.

Books and Community

As we enter the digital age, many bookstores are closing, from the small, independent stores to even the megachains that once threatened smaller stores. Bookstores of all shapes and sizes can offer more than sales: book clubs, author readings, and other live events, as well as a general sense of community. Though their aim is more commercial, many bookstores have taken on roles once assigned to public libraries, as social gathering spaces for readers. But just as libraries now face slashed budgets, many bookstores find it difficult to compete with the discounts of online retailers, or the convenience of e-books. In many cases, a customer choosing a local bookstore over online options will essentially mean agreeing to pay a higher price to support the face-to-face social interaction of brick-and-mortar bookstores.

Physical Deterioration

Many older books, especially those from the nineteenth century printed on acid-based paper, gradually deteriorate. To prevent loss of the knowledge in these books, research libraries have built climate-controlled depositories for older books that have permanent research value. Also, recent projects by Xerox and Cornell University have produced electronic copies of old books through computer scanning.

The Google Books Library Project represents a similar effort. Begun in 2004, the project features partnerships with the New York Public Library and several major university research libraries to scan millions of books and make them available online and searchable through Google. The Authors Guild and the Association of American Publishers initially resisted having Google digitize books without permission. Google responded that displaying only a limited portion of the books was legal under "fair use" rules. Both sides worked to finalize an agreement in 2009, which would make millions of current and out-of-print books available for sale, with Google and authors and publishers sharing the revenue.

An alternative group, the Open Content Alliance, was dissatisfied with the Google Books Library Project's intent to restrict scanned book content to Google's search service. The alliance started a competing nonprofit service in 2007 that partners with the Boston Public Library, several New England university libraries, and Yahoo! to digitize millions of books with expired copyrights and make them freely available through the Internet Archive.

Censorship, the decline of bookstores and libraries, and physical deterioration of books all present daunting challenges to books as a mass medium essential to our democracy. But like other mass media, books—and the people who love them—have adapted as needed to keep this medium alive and vital. Witness the proliferation of book-discussion groups, the greater array of formats through which books are now available, and the power of a writer like J. K. Rowling to resurrect a passion for reading in children and adults alike. The ultimate value of books is their ability to encourage the exchange and exploration of ideas. Clearly, they are still serving this purpose—despite the challenges and changes that have re-shaped this oldest of media.

CHAPTER ESSENTIALS

Now that you have finished reading this chapter, you can use the following tools:

REVIEW

Evaluate the Early History of Books

- Books first developed due to innovations made by the Egyptians, Greeks, Chinese, and Romans. Egyptians created **papyrus** (scrolls made from plant reeds) in 2400 B.C.E. Gradually, people began writing on **parchment** (treated animal skin) because of its durability and cheaper cost; by the fourth century C.E., Romans created the first protomodern book with the **codex** (sheets of parchment sewn together along the edge and then bound and covered) (p. 35).

- Books entered the entrepreneurial stage in the Middle Ages, at which time people explored new ways of writing. This led to the emergence of **manuscript culture** whereby priests and monks advanced the art of bookmaking with **illuminated manuscripts** that featured decorative, colorful illustrations on each page. At the same time, inventors experimented with printing techniques that sped up the hand-lettering process, such as **block printing**, in which printers applied sheets of paper to large blocks of inked wood onto which they had hand-carved a page's worth of characters and illustrations, and movable type (pp. 36–38).

- The invention of the **printing press** by Gutenberg between 1453 and 1456 allowed for the mass production of books such as the Bible. (The first Gutenberg Bible was printed on a fine calfskin-based parchment called **vellum**.) This advancement marked books' move to the mass medium stage, complete with the rise of the publishing industry two centuries later. By the 1830s, **paperback books** were introduced in the United States, and by the 1870s **dime novels** (coined as **pulp fiction**—a reference to the cheap, machine-made pulp paper they were printed on) were made accessible to the masses. Meanwhile, in the 1880s, the introduction of **linotype** machines enabled printers to save time by setting type mechanically using a typewriter-style keyboard, and the introduction of **offset lithography** in the 1900s allowed publishers to print books from photographic plates rather than from metal casts—cutting costs and saving more time (pp. 38–40).

Outline the Evolution of Modern Publishing

- Initially, publishing houses were small and focused on offering the works of prestigious authors, but over time—by the 1950s and 1960s—they were snapped up by major corporations with ties to international media conglomerates that took advantage of **synergy**, or the promotion and sale of different versions of a media product across the various subsidiaries of the conglomerate (pp. 40–41).

- Regardless of the size or type of books published, all publishing houses are structured similarly: **Acquisitions editors** seek out authors, offer them contracts, and handle **subsidiary rights** (the selling of the rights to a book for use in other media); **developmental editors** help the author draft and revise a manuscript by providing feedback and soliciting reviewer advice; **copy editors** fix spelling and other grammar issues; **design managers** determine the "look and feel" of a book; and marketing managers identify consumer patterns and help determine business plans accordingly (pp. 42–43).

Explain the Types of Books That Exist

- Until recently, books of all kinds only took printed form. Some of the categories include **trade books** (hardbound books and paperbacks aimed at general readers and sold at commercial retail outlets); **professional books** (targeted at various occupational groups, not the general consumer market); **textbooks** (educational books divided into elementary through high school, college, and vocational categories); **mass market paperbacks** (sold on racks in drugstores, supermarkets, and airports) and **instant books** (an innovation in mass market paperback publishing that involves putting out a topical book quickly after a major event occurs); religious books; **reference books** (including dictionaries, encyclopedias, atlases, almanacs, and volumes related to particular professions or trades); and **university press books** (nonprofit scholarly works for small groups of readers) (pp. 43–46).

- With the rise of electronic and digital publishing, book formats have expanded beyond print to include audio books—known originally as "books on tape" (later avilable on CDs and as MP3 downloads), which became popular in the 1990s and early 2000s—and **e-books**—digital books read on a computer or electronic reading device. Publishers in the e-book market are continually trying to find ways to make improvements on printed books (pp. 46–47).

Understand the Economics of the Book Industry

- The book business makes money by selling books through brick-and-mortar stores, on-line stores, book clubs, and mail order, and also by selling TV and movie rights (pp. 47–51).

- The book business spends money on essential activities such as book production, distribution, and marketing (pp. 51–52).

Consider the Role of Books in Our Democratic Society

- Books have played a vital role in democracy by spreading its very notion and disseminating ideas that have inspired people to drive change (pp. 52–54).

- Despite the crucial role of books, they face many challenges. For example, censorship prevents people from learning about alternative ideas or ways of living. Although censorship is illegal in the United States, citizens can sometimes force the removal of books from public or school libraries—a **book challenge**—about a subject matter they find objectionable. In addition, the physical deterioration of books poses problems (pp. 54–55).

STUDY QUESTIONS

1. Why was the printing press such an important and revolutionary invention?
2. Why did publishing houses develop?
3. What are the main ways in which digital technologies have changed the publishing industry?
4. What are the main sources of revenue in book publishing?
5. How do books play a vital role in our society?

MEDIA LITERACY PRACTICE

Although there are more than a quarter million new books published every year, it's sometimes too easy to forget about the oldest mass medium when we talk about "the media." To reconsider the impact of books, investigate the influence of books on another medium: the movies.

DESCRIBE the current state of movies by developing a list of the top twenty movies from the past year.

ANALYZE your list by noting patterns: Which movies were based on books, and which movies later inspired books?

INTERPRET what these patterns mean. For example, are only popular books made into movies? Do movies increase the sales of related books, or launch new books?

EVALUATE the synergy of books with movies. Do movies bring attention to books that might otherwise go unnoticed, or do movies completely overshadow books?

ENGAGE with the community by contacting your local library or a bookstore. Since reading for pleasure strongly correlates with academic achievement, you could work with the library or bookstore to develop a promotion or reading series built around the influence of books on movies.

▶ ONLINE RESOURCES

Go to **bedfordstmartins.com/mediaessentials** for review quizzes, links, and more.

Visit the site's **VIDEOCENTRAL: MASS COMMUNICATION** section for videos like the one on page 46. There, you can find additional exclusive videos related to Chapter 2, including:

TURNING THE PAGE: BOOKS GO DIGITAL
Authors discuss how e-books are changing both how books are consumed and how they are written.

TABLETS, TECHNOLOGY, AND THE CLASSROOM
Students and teachers discuss the use of tablet computers as classroom textbooks.

3

Newspapers: The Rise and Decline of Modern Journalism

In 1887, a young reporter left her job at the *Pittsburgh Dispatch* to seek her fortune in New York City. Only twenty-three years old, Elizabeth "Pink" Cochrane had grown tired of writing for the society pages and answering letters to the editor. She wanted to be on the front page. But at that time, it was considered "unladylike" for women journalists to use their real names, so the *Dispatch* editors, borrowing from a Stephen Foster song, had dubbed her "Nellie Bly."

After four months of persistent job hunting and freelance writing, Nellie Bly earned a tryout at Joseph Pulitzer's *New York World*, the nation's biggest paper. Her assignment: to investigate conditions at the Women's Lunatic Asylum on Blackwell's Island. Her method: to get herself committed to the asylum. After practicing the look of a disheveled lunatic in front of mirrors, she wandered city streets unwashed and seemingly dazed, and acted crazy around her fellow boarders in a New York rooming house.[1] Her tactics worked: Doctors declared her mentally deranged and had her committed.

Ten days later, an attorney from the *World* went in to get her out. Her two-part story appeared in October 1887 and caused a sensation. Nellie Bly's dramatic first-person accounts documented harsh cold baths; attendants who abused and taunted patients; and newly arrived immigrant women, completely sane, who were dragged to the asylum simply because no one could understand them. Bly became famous. Pulitzer gave her a permanent job, and New York City committed $1 million toward improving its asylums. Through her courageous work, Bly had pioneered what was then called *detective* or *stunt* journalism. Her work inspired the twentieth-century practice of investigative journalism.

ALONG WITH THEIR INVESTIGATIVE ROLE, newspapers have played many roles in Americans' lives. As chroniclers of daily life, newspapers both inform and entertain—providing articles on everything from science, technology, and medicine to books, music, and movies and stimulating public debate through their news analyses, opinion pages, and letters to the editor. Moreover, newspapers form the bedrock for other mass media. TV, radio, and online outlets like Google all rely extensively on newspaper journalists' work for their content. While print journalism may not be as eye-catching as TV news footage or as up-to-the-minute as online news reports, it offers a much more in-depth, long-term examination of events than these other media.

Still, newspapers struggle mightily to stay in business in today's digital age. Most are losing money as ad revenues have been dropping steadily for some time; to make matters worse, ad revenues fell 30 percent in 2009 alone in the wake of the global financial meltdown, and the erosion continued with a drop of 7 percent in the first quarter of 2011.[2] Some newspapers, such as the *Ann Arbor News* and *Detroit Free Press*, began publishing a print version only two or three days per week; others like the *Seattle Post-Intelligencer* now publish only online; and many—like the *Chicago Tribune* and *Philadelphia Inquirer*—have declared bankruptcy. U.S. newspapers have lost readers as well as their near monopoly on classified advertising, much of which has shifted to popular Web sites like craigslist.com. Industry observers now regularly ask, "Can this mass medium survive much longer?"

In this chapter, we examine newspapers' unique history, their role in our lives, and the challenges now facing them by:

- exploring newspapers' early history, including the rise of the political-commercial press, penny papers, and yellow journalism

- assessing the modern era of print journalism, including the tensions between objective and interpretive journalism

- considering the diverse array of newspaper types in existence today, such as local and ethnic papers as well as the underground press

- examining the economics behind print journalism

- taking stock of the challenges facing newspapers today, such as industry consolidation and the digitization of content

- considering how newspapers' current struggles may affect the strength of our democracy

The Early History of American Newspapers

Human beings have always valued **news**—the process by which people gather information and create narrative reports to help one another make sense of events happening around them. The earliest news was passed along *orally* from family to family, and from tribe to tribe, by community leaders and oral historians. The first known *written* news account was developed by Julius Caesar and posted in Rome in 59 B.C.E. In the fifteenth century, the development of the printing press accelerated people's ability to disseminate news through the printed word, and now, with the Internet, people can get the latest news—in real time—about events happening practically anywhere in the world.

Yet after the news moved from oral to written form, it soon shifted from an information source accessible only to elites or local readers to a mass medium that satisfied a growing audience's hunger for information. In the earliest days of American newspapers (the late 1600s through the 1800s), written news took on a number of different formats—political analyses printed on expensive, handmade paper; cheaper accounts printed on machine-made paper; sensationalist and investigative reporting. Each of these formats fulfilled Americans' "need to know"—whether they wanted coverage of the political scene, exposés of corruption in business, or even a humorous or entertaining perspective on current events.

Colonial Newspapers and the Partisan Press

Inspired by the introduction of the printing press in Europe, American colonists began producing their first newspapers in the late seventeenth century. One function of these publications, collectively known as the **partisan press**, was to critique government and disseminate the views of the different political parties that had begun to emerge and sponsor newspapers. Another function of these early papers was a commercial role, serving business leaders by offering the latest updates on markets and reporting on ship cargoes arriving from Europe. The partisan piece of the early press evolved into the editorial pages we see in today's newspapers, while the commercial function of these early papers foreshadowed today's business sections.

The first newspaper, *Publick Occurrences, Both Forreign and Domestick*, was published on September 25, 1690, by Boston printer Benjamin Harris, but it was banned after just one issue for its negative view of British rule. In the early 1700s, other papers cropped up, including Benjamin Franklin's *Pennsylvania Gazette*—which many historians regard as the best of the colonial papers. The *Gazette* was also one of the first papers to make money by printing advertisements alongside news.

One significant colonial paper, the *New-York Weekly Journal*, was founded in 1733 by the Popular Party, a political group that opposed British rule. *Journal* articles included attacks on the royal governor of New York. The party had installed John Peter Zenger as printer of the *Journal*, and in 1734 he was arrested for *seditious*

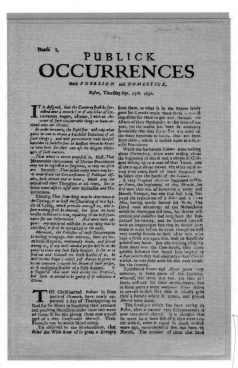

The first colonial newspaper, *Publick Occurrences, Both Forreign and Domestick,* was published in 1690 and banned after one issue for its negative portrayal of British rule.

CHAPTER 3 // TIMELINE

1690 First Colonial Newspaper
Boston printer Benjamin Harris publishes *Publick Occurrences, Both Forreign and Domestick.*

1734 Press Freedom
John Peter Zenger is arrested for seditious libel; jury rules in his favor in 1735—establishing freedom of press and newpapers' right to criticize government.

1827 First African American Newspaper
Freedom's Journal is founded.

1828 First Native American Newspaper
The *Cherokee Phoenix* is founded.

libel when one of his writers defamed a public official's character in print. Championed by famed Philadelphia lawyer Andrew Hamilton, Zenger won his case the following year. The Zenger decision helped lay a foundation—the right of a democratic press to criticize public officials—for the First Amendment to the Constitution, adopted as part of the Bill of Rights in 1791.

By 1765, the American colonies boasted about thirty newspapers, all of them published weekly or monthly. In 1784, the first daily paper began operations. But even the largest of these papers rarely reached a circulation of fifteen hundred. Readership was largely confined to educated or wealthy men who controlled local politics and commerce (and who could afford newspaper subscriptions).

The Penny Press: Becoming a Mass Medium

During the 1830s, a number of forces transformed newspapers into an information source available to, valued by, and affordable for all—a true mass medium. For example, thanks to the Industrial Revolution, factories could make cheap, machine-made paper to replace the expensive handmade kind previously in use. At the same time, the rise of the middle class, enabled by the growth of literacy, set the stage for a more popular and inclusive press. And with steam-powered presses replacing mechanical presses, publishers could crank out as many as four thousand copies of their

Andrew Hamilton defends John Peter Zenger, a New York printer arrested for libel in 1734. Zenger eventually won his case, which established the precedent that today allows U.S. journalists and citizens to criticize public officials.

1833 Penny Press
Printer Benjamin Day founds the *New York Sun* and helps usher in the penny press era.

1848 Associated Press
Six New York newspapers form the Associated Press (AP), relaying news stories around the country via telegraph.

1883 Yellow Journalism
Pulitzer buys the *New York World*; the battle with Hearst's *New York Journal* heats up in 1895 during the heyday of yellow journalism.

1887 Nellie Bly
Nellie Bly's first article on the conditions in women's insane asylums is printed in the *New York World*, an early effort in investigative journalism.

Founded by Benjamin Day in 1833, the *New York Sun* helped usher in the penny press era, bringing news to the working and emerging middle class.

newspapers every hour, which dramatically lowered their cost. Popular **penny papers** soon began outselling the six-cent elite publications previously available.

The First Penny Papers

In 1833, printer Benjamin Day founded the *New York Sun*, lowered the price of his newspaper to one penny, and eliminated subscriptions. The *Sun* (whose slogan was "It shines for all") highlighted local events, scandals, and police reports. It also ran fabricated and serialized stories, making legends of frontiersmen Davy Crockett and Daniel Boone and blazing the trail for Americans' enthusiasm for celebrity news. Within six months, the *Sun* had a circulation of eight thousand—twice that of its nearest competitor. The *Sun*'s success unleashed a barrage of penny papers that favored **human-interest stories**: news accounts that focused on the daily trials and triumphs of the human condition, often featuring ordinary individuals who had faced down extraordinary challenges.

In 1835, James Gordon Bennett founded another daily penny paper, the *New York Morning Herald*. Considered the first U.S. press baron, Bennett—and not any political party—completely controlled his paper's content. He established an independent publication that served middle- and working-class readers. The

---

CHAPTER 3 // TIMELINE continued

1896 Modern Journalism
Adolph Ochs buys *The New York Times*, jump-starting modern "objective journalism."

1913 First U.S.-Based Spanish Paper
El Diario-La Prensa is founded.

1955 First Underground Paper
Village Voice begins operation.

1980 First Online Paper
Ohio's *Columbus Dispatch* becomes the first newspaper to go online.

Herald carried political essays and reports of scandals, business stories, a letters section, fashion notes, moral reflections, religious news, society gossip, colloquial tales and jokes, sports stories, and, later, reports from the Civil War fronts. By 1860, the *Herald* had nearly eighty thousand readers, making it the world's largest daily paper.

Changing Business Models

As they proliferated and gained new readers, penny papers shifted their business models. Previously, they had been funded primarily by the political parties that sponsored them, and their content emphasized overt political views. But as they expanded, they realized they could derive even more revenues from the market—by selling space for advertisements and by hawking newspapers on the streets and through newsstands. As their business model shifted, editors began putting their daily reporting on the front page, moving overt political viewpoints to the editorial page.

As ad revenues and circulation skyrocketed, the newspaper industry expanded overall. In 1830, about 650 weekly and 65 daily papers operated in the United States, reaching a circulation of 80,000. Just ten years later, the nation had a total of 1,140 weeklies and 140 dailies attracting more than 300,000 readers.

The First News Wire Service

In 1848, the enormous expansion of the newspaper industry led six New York newspapers to form a cooperative arrangement and found the Associated Press (AP), the first major news wire service. **Wire services** began as commercial and cooperative organizations that relayed news stories and information around the country and the world using telegraph lines (and, later, radio waves and digital transmissions). In the case of the AP, which functioned as a kind of news co-op, the founding New York papers provided access to their own stories and those from other newspapers.

1982 Postmodern News
Gannett chain launches *USA Today,* ushering in the postmodern era in which news is modeled after television.

2001 Dominance of Chains
Top 10 newspaper chains control more than one-half of the nation's total daily newspaper circulation.

2007 Online Growth
Most newspapers offer some kind of online news service.

2007 Joint Operating Agreements
Joint operating agreements (JOAs) remain in place in ten U.S. cities.

Such companies enabled news to travel rapidly from coast to coast, setting the stage for modern journalism in the United States. And because the papers still cost only a penny to buy, more people than ever now had access to a widening array of news. Clearly, newspapers had moved from the entrepreneurial stage to the status of mass media.

Yellow Journalism

Following the tradition established by the *New York Sun* and *New York Morning Herald*, a new brand of papers arose in the late 1800s. These publications ushered in an era of **yellow journalism**, which emphasized exciting human-interest stories, crime news, large headlines, and easier-to-digest copy. Generally regarded as the direct forerunner of today's tabloid papers, reality TV, and newsmagazine shows, yellow journalism featured two major characteristics:

1. Overly dramatic—or sensational—stories about crimes, celebrities, disasters, scandals, and intrigue
2. News reports exposing corruption, particularly in business and government—the foundation for *investigative journalism*

The term *yellow journalism* has its roots in the press war that pitted Joseph Pulitzer's *New York World* against William Randolph Hearst's *New York Journal*. During their furious fight to win readers, the two papers ultimately took turns hosting the first popular cartoon strip, *The Yellow Kid*, created in 1895 by artist R. F. Outcault. Pulitzer, a Jewish-Hungarian immigrant, had bought the *New York World* in 1883 for $346,000. Aimed at immigrant and working-class readers, the *World* crusaded for improved urban housing, better treatment of women, and equitable labor laws, while railing against big business. It also manufactured news events and printed sensationalized stories on crime and sex. By 1887, its Sunday circulation had soared to more than 250,000—the largest anywhere.

The *World* faced its fiercest competition when William Randolph Hearst in 1895 bought the *New York Journal* (a penny paper founded by Pulitzer's brother Albert) and then raided Joseph Pulitzer's paper for editors, writers, and cartoonists. Hearst focused on lurid, sensational stories and appealed to immigrant readers by using large headlines and bold layout designs. To boost circulation, the *Journal* invented interviews, faked pictures, and provoked conflicts that might result in eye-catching stories. In 1896, its daily circulation reached 450,000. A year later, the paper's Sunday edition's circulation rivaled the *World's* 600,000.

Yellow journalism has been vilified for its sensationalism and aggressive tactics to snatch readers from competitors by appealing to their low-brow

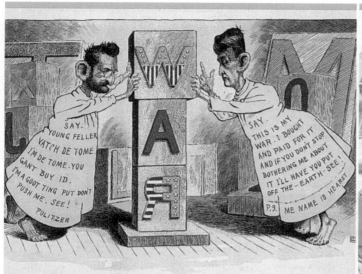

Generally considered America's first comic-strip character, the Yellow Kid was created in the mid-1890s by cartoonist R. F. Outcault. The cartoon was so popular that newspaper barons Joseph Pulitzer and William Randolph Hearst fought over Outcault's services, giving yellow journalism its name.

interests, but this unique era gave birth to several newspaper elements still valued by many readers today—such as advice columns and feature stories. It even laid the foundation for the prestigious Pulitzer Prizes, which today recognize quality writing, reporting, and research in such categories as poetry, history, international reporting, editorial cartooning, public service, and explanatory reporting.

The Evolution of Newspapers: Competing Models of Modern Print Journalism

In the late 1800s, as newspapers pushed to expand circulation even further, two distinct types of journalism emerged: the story-driven model, which dramatized important events and characterized the penny papers and the yellow press; and "the facts" model, an approach that seemed more impartial and was favored by the six-cent papers.[3] Provocative questions arose: Could news accounts be entirely objective? Should reporters actively interpret the meaning of particular events for readers?

As observers wrestled with these questions, newspapers also began changing shape in response to technological advances. These advances included the introduction of color printing and the digitization of text and images—innovations that would ultimately transform the world of print journalism.

"Objectivity" in Modern Journalism

Throughout the mid-1800s, the more a newspaper appeared not to take sides on its front pages, the more readers it could attract. Also at this time, wire service organizations were serving a variety of newspaper clients in different regions of the country. To satisfy all their clients, newspapers strived for impartiality—presenting "the facts" and leaving it up to readers to interpret the facts' implications for their own lives.

Adolph Ochs and the *New York Times*

The ideal of an impartial, or purely informational, news model was reinvented by Adolph Ochs, who bought the *New York Times* in 1896. Through wise hiring, Ochs and his editors rebuilt the paper around substantial news coverage and provocative editorial pages. To distance the *Times* from the yellow press, the editors also downplayed sensational stories, favoring the documentation of major events or issues and developing a powerful marketing message touting the *Times* as the higher-brow choice.

With the Hearst and Pulitzer papers capturing the bulk of working- and middle-class readers, managers at the *Times* initially tried to use their straightforward, "no frills" reporting to appeal to more affluent and educated readers. In 1898, Ochs also lowered the paper's price to a penny. Soon middle-class readers gravitated to the paper as a status marker for the educated and well-informed. Between 1898 and 1899, circulation soared from 25,000 to 75,000. By 1921, the *Times* had a daily circulation of 330,000 and a Sunday circulation of 500,000.

"Just the Facts, Please"

Early in the twentieth century, with reporters adopting a more "scientific" attitude to news- and fact-gathering, the ideal of objectivity took firmer hold in journalism. In **objective journalism**, which distinguishes factual reports from opinion columns, modern reporters strive to maintain a neutral attitude toward the issue or event they cover. They also search out competing points of view among the sources for a story, in an effort to provide balanced coverage.

The story form for packaging and presenting this kind of reporting has been traditionally labeled the **inverted-pyramid style**. Developed by Civil War correspondents,[4] inverted pyramid reports were often stripped of adverbs and adjectives, and began—as they do today—with the most dramatic or newsworthy information. They answered the questions who, what, where, when (and, less frequently, why and how) at the top of the story and then narrowed the account down to its less significant details. This approach offered an important advantage: If wars or natural disasters disrupted the telegraph transmissions of these dispatches, at least readers would get the crucial information.

Known for getting information and presenting news in a straightforward way—without the opinion of the reporter—the *New York Times* was the first truly modern newspaper. It established itself as the official paper of record by the 1920s and maintains a venerable reputation today.

Interpretive Journalism

By the 1920s, people began wondering whether the impartial approach to news reporting was sufficient for helping readers understand complex national and global developments. As one news scholar contended, it was partly as a result of "drab, factual, objective reporting" that "the American people were utterly amazed when [World War I] broke out in August 1914, as they had no understanding of the foreign scene to prepare them for it."[5] Such concerns triggered the rise of **interpretive journalism**, which aims to explain the ramifications of key issues or events and place them in a broader historical or social context.

Editor and columnist Walter Lippmann insisted that while objectivity should serve as journalism's foundation, the press should do more. He ranked three press responsibilities: (1) "to make a current record"; (2) "to make a running analysis of it"; and (3) "on the basis of both, to suggest plans."[6]

In the 1930s, the Great Depression and the Nazi threat further spurred newsmagazines and radio commentary to provide more rigorous analysis of global events. First developed in the partisan era, editorial pages also made a strong comeback. More significant, political opinion columns proliferated. Between 1930 and 1934 alone, more than 150 syndicated columns sprang up. Yet newspapers began carefully separating news and opinion pages, so readers could more easily distinguish between them.

The rise of radio in the 1930s intensified tensions between the objective and interpretive models of print journalism. As radio gained in popularity, broadcasters increasingly took their news directly from papers and wire services. Seeking to maintain their dominion over "the facts," some newspaper editors and lobbyists argued that radio should provide only interpretive

MEDIA LITERACY
Case Study

Covering Business News

The recent financial crisis and subsequent recession spotlighted newspapers' coverage of issues like corporate corruption. For example, since the beginning of the crisis in 2008, articles have detailed the collapse of major investment firms like Lehman Brothers, the GM and Chrysler bankruptcies, the fraud charges against Goldman Sachs, and of course all the scandals surrounding the subprime mortgage/home foreclosure crisis.

But this coverage has not always been so prevalent. Over the years, critics have claimed that business news pages tend to favor issues related to management and downplay the role of everyday employees. Critics have also charged that business coverage favors positive business stories—such as managers' successes and promotions—while minimizing negative business news (unlike regional newspaper front pages, which often emphasize crime stories). Like other business managers, many news executives prefer not to offend investors or potential advertisers by running too many investigative reports. Even in the recession years, some papers focus more on unemployment numbers, the stock market, and corporate earnings than investigating possible wrongdoing in the business world. Magazines like *Rolling Stone* have run more in-depth articles about economic issues.

But in an era of bankruptcies, bailouts, and Occupy Wall Street, newspapers must share some of the investigative responsibilities. One of the great scandals of 2011 demonstrates how news literacy often requires sampling multiple sources when delving into stories about corporate corruption. Media mogul Rupert Murdoch was forced to withdraw his $12 billion takeover bid for British

Sky Broadcasting after a phone-hacking scandal involving key figures in his publishing empire brought down one of the Britain's oldest newspapers, the *News of the World*. In the continuing fallout of the phone hacking scandal, Murdoch's News Corp. announced in 2012 that it would divide its publishing companies (newspapers and books) from its entertainment holdings (television and movie studios).

A rival paper, the *Guardian*, played a prominent role in publicizing the lurid details of the case. Reporter Nick Davies continued to investigate the *News of the World* after the police, the government, and the rest of the press accepted the News Corp. story that the hacking of British royal family members, including Prince Charles, was an isolated event. When Davies discovered that James Murdoch paid more than $1 million in hush money to cover up another instance of phone hacking, the scandal took on new life, reaching a tipping point when Davies reported that the *News of the World* had hacked into the phone calls of Milly Dowler, a missing teenager. Davies revealed that the hackers had deleted

Dowler's voice messages so they could listen to new ones—a transgression that gave her parents false hope that she was still alive. This revelation damaged News Corp. from top to bottom; intrepid reporting from Nick Davies and the *Guardian* curtailed Murdoch's stranglehold on British politics and media.[1]

Davies, then, demonstrates that courageous reporting can make a real difference on a grand scale, even or especially if it involves standing up to a media conglomerate in the news business. Imagine what might have been avoided if such investigative journalism had addressed the abuses of Wall Street and the too-big-to-fail banks in the lead-up to the financial collapse of 2008. The story of journalism taking on a corrupt conglomerate should inspire business reporters to do more than function as cheerleaders for corporate interests.

APPLYING THE CRITICAL PROCESS

DESCRIPTION Choose two major newspapers and investigate how they covered the phone-hacking scandal and other media business stories. How does the coverage differ in terms of the number of articles devoted to the scandal in May, June, and July of 2011? How many editorial and opinion pieces are devoted to the scandal during this three-month period?

ANALYSIS How do the two newspapers characterize the scandal? Are there differences in the editorial treatment of Rupert Murdoch and his son James?

INTERPRETATION Write a two-to-three paragraph critical interpretation of the "meanings" of the scandal proposed by the two newspapers. Are there differences

in the coverage of Murdoch being forced to withdraw his bid for British Sky Broadcasting?

EVALUATION Determine which papers and stories you would judge as good and which ones you would judge as weaker models for how business and media stories should be covered. Are some elements that should be included missing from the coverage? If so, make suggestions.

ENGAGEMENT Contact a business editor from a newspaper and ask how he or she makes content decisions. What kind of business and economic reporting catches the editorial department's eye? What considerations are made when business editors decide what to cover?

commentary. Other print journalists argued that it was interpretive stories, not objective reports, that could best help newspapers compete against radio. However, most U.S. dailies continued relegating interpretive content to a few editorial and opinion pages.

It wasn't until the 1950s—with the outbreak of the Korean War, the development of atomic power, the deepening of the Cold War, and the U.S. anticommunist movement—that newspapers began providing more interpretive journalism. They did so in part to compete with the latest news medium: television. And their interpretive material often took the form of an "op-ed" page—which appeared opposite the traditional editorial page. The op-ed page offered a wider variety of columns, news analyses, and letters to the editor.

Literary Journalism

By the late 1960s, national turmoil—stirred up by assassinations, Civil Rights protests, the Vietnam War, the drug culture, and the women's movement—had many middle- and working-class Americans questioning traditional authority. Key institutions, including journalism, lost some credibility. As a result, journalists began exploring new models of reporting as a way to regain readers' favor.

Jon Krakauer is a current practitioner of literary journalism. He is known for his books about the outdoors, including *Into the Wild*, about the travels of the late Christopher McCandless.

Literary journalism (sometimes dubbed "the new journalism") adapted fictional techniques, such as detailed setting descriptions and extensive character dialogue, to nonfiction material and in-depth reporting. This form of journalism had first surfaced in the late 1930s and 1940s, but it gained popularity in the 1960s, especially in magazines like *Rolling Stone*. In daily newspapers, literary journalism took the form of longer feature stories on cultural trends and social issues, augmented with detailed description or dialogue. While writers such as Tom Wolfe, Norman Mailer, and Hunter S. Thompson were the big names in literary journalism initially, today writers such as Jon Krakauer (*Into Thin Air*, *Under the Banner of Heaven*) and Adrian Nicole LeBlanc (*Random Family*) keep this tradition alive. (See Chapter 13 for more information on the culture of journalism.)

Journalism in the Technology Age

In the early 1980s, two technology advances—an emphasis on color printing and digitization of news content—ushered in a new brand of journalism that looked and operated quite differently from earlier forms. *USA Today*, launched in 1982 and influenced by television, led the way in the use of color and brevity of content. And in 1980, the *Columbus Dispatch* became the first paper to go online.

USA Today Colors the Print Landscape

USA Today made its mark by emphasizing visual style over substantive news or analysis and using brief news items to appeal to busy readers with shortened attention spans. Now the most widely circulated paper in the nation, *USA Today* represents the only successful launch of a new major American daily newspaper in the last several decades. Demonstrating keen marketing savvy, *USA Today* uses TV-inspired color and design. The paper also employs a writing style that mimics TV news—casting many reports in the present tense rather than the past tense to create a sense of immediacy.

Online Journalism Redefines the News Process

Today, rather than subscribing to printed news-papers, many people start their day by logging on to the Internet and scanning a wide variety of free news sources, including print papers' and cable news channels' sites, newsmagazines' sites, blogs, and news headlines aggregated by search engines such as Google. This development has reshaped the way the news process works.

USA Today was the first daily newspaper to intentionally copy television, both in the TV-like look of its street vendor boxes and in its brief, compact stories.

Specifically, the advent of online journalism has radically speeded up the news cycle: In mere moments, stories about anything ranging from a politician's scandalous affair to a rampaging chimp to the discovery of a possible cause of autism can be posted in every possible place on the Internet—complete with audio and video. And these accounts can be updated practically in real time. Printed newspapers, not wanting to be left behind, have felt compelled to cover the stories attracting the most interest online. This reactive behavior can sometimes create an avalanche effect, whereby a small story that appears first on the Internet cascades through cable, network news, and then newspapers. Such stories stay in the public eye perhaps far longer than they would have in pre-Internet days, and they can take on a magnitude that may be out of proportion with their real significance.

Categorizing News and U.S. Newspapers

Just as approaches to journalism have varied over the years, a variety of newspaper types have arisen to fulfill different readers' needs. These types (some of them published daily; others, weekly or monthly) include local, regional, and national papers as well as papers catering to specific ethnic groups or alternative perspectives on politics and values. With this diversification, newspapers have succeeded in reaching a wider array of communities.

Small Local Papers: Focus on Consensus

Local newspapers, especially small weekly papers with circulations under five thousand, tend to promote social and economic harmony in the regions, counties, or municipalities they serve. These papers practice **consensus-oriented journalism**. Often published once a week, small local papers provide community calendars and meeting notices and carry articles on local schools, social events, town government, property crimes, and zoning issues. Their publications primarily seek to foster a sense of community, though they may also explore discord and problems plaguing the localities in which they're based.

Regional and National Newspapers: Focus on Conflict

In contrast, regional papers, which are sometimes called "metro dailies" when their circulations are over a hundred thousand, and national papers, like *USA Today* or the *New York Times*, often promote **conflict-oriented journalism**, in which front-page articles focus on events or issues (such as government corruption or spikes in crime rates) deviating from social norms. Journalists for these publications see their role as going beyond neutral fact-gathering to offer competing perspectives and conflicting sources on such issues as education, government, poverty, crime, politics, and the economy.

Ethnic and Minority Newspapers

Historically, small-town weeklies and dailies have served predominantly white, mainstream readers. However, since Benjamin Franklin launched the short-lived German-language *Philadelphische Zeitung* in 1732, newspapers aimed at ethnic groups have played a major role in assimilating immigrants into American society as well as helping them retain and solidify their cultural identity. Today, the United States has many thriving foreign-language daily and weekly newspapers.

VideoCentral ◎
bedfordstmartins.com
/mediaessentials

Community Voices:
Weekly Newspapers
Journalists discuss the role of local newspapers in their communities.
Discussion: In a democratic society, why might having many community voices in the news media be a good thing?

These newspapers serve some of the same functions for their constituencies—immigrants, disabled veterans, retired workers, gay and lesbian communities, the homeless—that mainstream papers serve, covering similar events, issues, trends, and developments. However, they interpret these from the perspective of their constituents' priorities and interests. For example, a paper catering to gay men and lesbians may publish articles on new rulings regarding gay marriage—a topic often covered in mainstream papers. Yet the minority paper's articles will focus on legal developments threatening gay men's and lesbians' rights and present ideas for taking defensive action.

African American

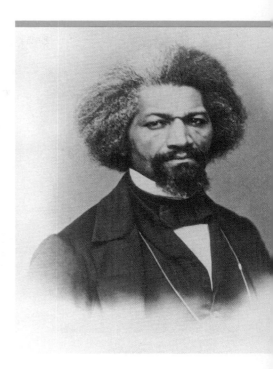

The first newspaper published in the United States aimed at black readers, *Freedom's Journal*, operated from 1827 to 1829. It opposed the racism apparent in many New York newspapers and offered a voice for the antislavery, or abolitionist, movement. Since 1827, more than 3,000 newspapers have been edited and owned by African Americans, including Frederick Douglass's *North Star*. With an average life span of nine years, early publications took stands against race baiting, lynching, and the Ku Klux Klan. They also promoted racial pride long before the Civil Rights movement began. More than 180 mostly weekly African American papers survive today, including Baltimore's *Afro-American*, New York's *Amsterdam News*, and the *Chicago Defender*, which celebrated its one hundredth anniversary in 2005. But this number is down from 300 in 2000. As they have throughout their history, these papers typically offer oppositional viewpoints to the mainstream press and record the daily activities of black communities by listing weddings, births, deaths, graduations, meetings, and religious functions.

Frederick Douglass helped found the *North Star* in 1847. Under his leadership, the paper came out weekly until 1860, addressing problems facing blacks around the country and offering a forum for Douglass to debate his fellow black activists.

Spanish Language

Bilingual and Spanish-language newspapers have long served a variety of Mexican, Puerto Rican, Cuban, and other Hispanic readerships. By 2010, the United States had more than a thousand Spanish-language papers, which reached more than seventeen million readers nationwide—an increase of five million since 1984.[7] The oldest Hispanic daily in the United States, New York's *El Diario-La Prensa,* has been catering to Spanish-language readers since 1913, while Los Angeles's *La Opinión*, founded in 1926, is the nation's largest Spanish-language daily, with a circulation of a hundred thousand (down 20 percent from 2007). These two papers merged in 2004 to create

The *Sing Tao Daily* newspaper is one of the largest Chinese-language media operations in the United States.

ImpreMedia.[8] Serving the large Cuban and Cuban American population in the Miami area, *El Nuevo Herald* has a circulation of over seventy-seven thousand.

Asian American

In the 1980s, hundreds of small papers published in various languages arose to serve immigrants from the Philippines, Pakistan, Laos, Cambodia, and China. About four hundred online and print Asian American papers are published in the United States, serving the more than sixteen million Asians and Asian Americans. For example, more than fifty small U.S. papers are now printed in Vietnamese. Serving many Chinese immigrants, the *Sing Tao Daily*, founded in 1938 in Hong Kong, is among the largest Chinese-language U.S. media operations. Ethnic papers like these help readers both adjust to foreign surroundings and retain ties to their traditional heritage. In addition, these papers often cover stories that are downplayed in the mainstream press but that hold interest for Asian populations.

Native American

An activist Native American press has provided oppositional voices to mainstream American media since 1828, when the *Cherokee Phoenix* appeared in Georgia. The Native American Press Association has documented more than 350 different Native American papers, most of them printed in English but a few in tribal languages. Currently, national papers serving this audience include the *Native American Times*, which offers a Native American perspective on "sovereign rights, civil rights, and government-to-government relationships with the federal government," and *Indian Country Today*, which is owned by the Oneida Nation in New York State and has the largest circulation of any Native American paper. These smaller papers provide a forum for debates on tribal conflicts and concerns. They also often signal the mainstream press on issues—such as gambling or hunting and fishing rights—that have significance for larger American society.

Arab American

According to the Pew Project for Excellence in Journalism's "State of the News Media 2009," the number of Arab American newspapers grew to eighty-five by 2009 (up from seventy-seven in 2007). Based in Dearborn, Michigan, the *Arab*

American News is the oldest U.S. Arab American newspaper, founded in 1984. It is a free paper, supported only by advertising, and has reported a weekly circulation of thirty thousand. In the Eastern United States, *Aramica* is among the largest Arab American newspapers. A bilingual paper, it began in Brooklyn in 2002 and has reported a nationwide weekly circulation of fifty thousand.

The Underground Press

The mid to late 1960s saw an explosion of alternative newspapers—the *underground press*—that questioned mainstream political policies and conventional values. Springing up on college campuses and in major cities, underground papers were inspired by the writings of socialists and intellectuals active in the 1930s and 1940s and by a new wave of thinkers and artists including Allen Ginsberg, Jack Kerouac, LeRoi Jones, Bob Dylan, and Joan Baez. In criticizing social institutions, alternative papers questioned the official reports distributed by public relations agents, government spokespeople, and the conventional press. These publications often featured the voices of students, women, blacks, Native Americans, gay men, lesbians, and others whom the mainstream press had sidelined. The first and most enduring underground paper, the *Village Voice*, was founded in Greenwich Village in 1955. Though its circulation started to decrease by 2010 (as its online reach grows), it is still distributed free, surviving solely through advertising. Reflecting the consolidation now reshaping the newspaper industry, even the *Village Voice* has acquired other papers located in Los Angeles, Denver, Miami, Minneapolis, and other major cities. (See Figure 3.1 on page 80 for other alternative newspapers.)

Founded in 1955 as the nation's first alternative newspaper, the *Village Voice* has earned numerous accolades for its writing and reporting on the life, culture, arts, and politics within New York City.

The Economics of Newspapers

Regardless of how frequently a newspaper is published, which readers it serves, and how it approaches reporting, all papers need to take in money (whether it's from deep-pocketed owners, subscriptions, street sales, or advertising) as well as spend money (for example, on journalists' salaries, newsprint, and wire services) to survive.

FIGURE 3.1 // SELECTED
ALTERNATIVE NEWSPAPERS
IN THE UNITED STATES

Willamette Week
Portland, Ore.

City Pages
Minneapolis/
St. Paul, Minn.

*Pittsburgh
City Paper*

Westword
Denver, Colo.

Chicago Reader

Boston Phoenix

*San Francisco
Bay Guardian*

Village Voice
New York City

*Washington
City Paper*

LA Weekly

Independent Weekly
Durham, N.C.

Salt Lake City Weekly

Creative Loafing
Atlanta, Ga.

Austin Chronicle
Austin, Tex.

Riverfront Times
St. Louis, Mo.

Gambit Weekly
New Orleans, La.

Miami New Times

*Source: Association of Alternative
Newsmedia, www.AltWeeklies.com*

Yet these economic realities are in flux today. Ever since the rise of television network evening news programs helped kill the afternoon daily, newspapers have faced a difficult competitive marketplace. In recent years, the twin challenges of the Internet and the economic crisis starting in late 2008 sent many papers into bankruptcy. The Internet had already ended newspapers' long hold on classified ads, but the economic crisis saw ad revenues from car dealers, realtors, and retail businesses cut in half, and new lows are still expected. On top of this, many newspaper corporations like the Tribune Company, which declared bankruptcy in 2008, became *overleveraged.* That is, once advertising revenues fell, many media conglomerates that previously borrowed lots of money in an effort to consolidate business in the 1980s and 1990s were incapable of paying back their debts, causing them to sell their businesses or declare bankruptcy. As a result, many papers have had to cut staffing to the bone to lower expenses in the hopes of remaining profitable. But this has often backfired as they try to expand their online operations with fewer reporters and editors.

Money In

For most newspapers, the majority of their revenues derive from selling advertising space. For some papers, ads provide the *only* source of revenue. Indeed, the majority of large daily papers devote as much as one-half to two-thirds of their pages to advertisements. What remains after the advertising department places the ads in the paper is called the **newshole**, the space not taken up by ads and devoted to front-page news reports, special regional or topical sections, horoscopes, advice columns, crossword puzzles, and letters to the editor. Accounting for about 15 percent of all ad dollars spent annually in the United States, newspaper advertising—in print and online—can take forms ranging from expensive full-page spreads for department stores to classifieds, which individual consumers can purchase for a few dollars to sell everything from used cars to furniture to exercise equipment. Of course, one of the biggest problems for print newspapers is that consumers can now place most of these ads online free of charge. Some papers are attempting to make up the difference by charging for online access to their news content after readers exceed a number of free monthly visits.

Money Out

Like any other enterprise, a newspaper has to spend money to fulfill its mission. Its costs include overhead (such as rent and utilities), salaries and wages, marketing and sales, and any investments in wire services or feature syndication required to offer content for readers.

Salaries and Wages

A major expense for most newspapers comes in the form of salaries and wages paid to the various editors and reporters working for the paper, though in the last five to ten years newspapers have shrunk not only their newshole but the size of their reporting staffs. By various estimates, depending on the newspaper, 20 to 40 percent fewer reporters worked in newsrooms in 2010 than in 1990. Most large papers have a publisher and an owner, an editor in chief and a managing editor in charge of the daily news-gathering and writing processes, and assistant editors and news managers running different news divisions. These key divisions include features, sports, photos, local news, state news, and wire service containing much of the day's national and international news reports.

Reporters work for editors. *General assignment reporters* handle all sorts of stories that might emerge—or "break"—in a given day. *Specialty reporters* are assigned to particular beats (police, courts, schools, local and national government) or topics (education, religion, health, environment, technology). On large dailies, *bureau reporters* also file reports from other major cities. In addition,

The digitization of news content means that online newspapers routinely include audio and video components. These reporters are covering the Occupy Wall Street protests of 2011.

large daily papers feature columnists and critics who cover various aspects of culture, such as books, television, movies, and food.

By the early 2000s, when digitization of news content was in full swing, many newspapers employed a separate staff for their online operations, even though most of these operations were losing money. Nowadays, the economic downturn and industry consolidation has led to reductions in newsroom headcount, as merging papers laid off redundant personnel and cut additional staff to reduce costs. In 2001, the American Society of Newspaper Editors (ASNE) reported 56,400 reporters in newsrooms; only about 41,600 were working by late 2011.[9] Fewer and fewer papers now maintain bureaus outside their own city limits. Some smaller daily papers have even quit sending reporters to cover state government. The *Los Angeles Times*, the *Chicago Tribune*, the *Baltimore Sun*, and the *Hartford Courant*—all owned by the Tribune Company—all closed their independent bureaus in 2008.[10]

All these trends have put a strain on the remaining reporters and editors, who are increasingly being asked to develop stories in multiple formats with fewer personnel. The downside of this money-saving technique means that far fewer versions of stories are being produced as readers become more reliant on a single version of a news report.

Wire Services and Feature Syndication

To provide adequate coverage of important events and deliver high-quality reporting, many newspapers rely on wire services and syndicated feature services to supplement local coverage by their own reporters and writers. A few major dailies, such as the *New York Times*, run their own wire services, selling their stories to other papers to reprint. Other agencies, such as the Associated Press (AP), United Press International (UPI), and Reuters (based in London) have hundreds of staffers stationed throughout major U.S. cities and world capitals. They submit stories, photos, and videos each day for distribution to newspapers, newscasts, and online sites across the country and sometimes internationally.

Daily papers generally pay monthly fees for access to all wire stories. Although they use only a fraction of what's available over the wires, editors carefully monitor wire services each day for important stories and ideas for local angles.

In addition, newspapers may contract with **feature syndicates**, such as United Features and Tribune Media Services, to provide work from the nation's best political writers, editorial cartoonists, comic-strip artists, and self-help columnists.

These companies serve as brokers, distributing horoscopes and crossword puzzles as well as the columns and comic strips that appeal to a wide audience; however, with the downsizing of newspapers in terms of space, most papers today offer far fewer syndication services than in the 1990s.

Challenges Facing Newspapers

As we've seen, newspapers today face a host of challenges—including declines in readership, the inability of most cities to support competing newspapers, the cost of newsprint, and competition from Web sites like craigslist.com for lucrative classified advertising. These problems have raised pressing questions, such as what role newspapers will play in our lives in the coming years and whether this medium can even survive. Given that newspapers are still the most reliable source of investigative reporting and analysis, and that TV and other news sources still rely heavily on them, the image of a world without newspapers is troubling indeed.

Declining Readership

Although more people than ever before look at newspaper content each day (much of this online), the decline in actual newspaper readership in the United States began during the Great Depression, with the rise of radio. It continued in the late 1960s through the 1970s with the rise in network television viewing. "The State of the News Media 2011" report showed that daily circulation since 1990 had declined 30 percent. Readership was found to be particularly low among eighteen-to-twenty-four-year-olds; by 2010, only 27 percent reported they had read a newspaper the day before.[11]

Decreasing Competition

With the decline in readership, many newspapers have gone out of business. Others have been bought up by larger media companies, which have then merged the acquired publications and streamlined reporting to reduce redundancy. These developments have led to a decrease in newspaper competition. For example, although the overall U.S. population increased between 1950 and 2008, the number of daily papers in the United States dropped from 1,772 to around 1,400 in those same years. Back in the mid-1920s, about five hundred American cities had two or more newspapers with separate owners. By 2010, fewer than fifteen cities had more than one independent, competing paper. This situation doesn't bode well for a society that values open debate of ideas and interpretation of important events through a free press. How informed can we be if we have access to just one viewpoint on any particular issue or seek out only like-minded opinions on blog sites? And how can we make smart decisions—about crucial matters such as whom to vote for, where to send our children to school, or how to invest our hard-earned savings—if we're not as informed by newspaper reporting at the same level as earlier generations?

Joint Operating Agreements

In 1970, a worried Congress passed the Newspaper Preservation Act, which enabled failing papers to continue operating through a **joint operating agreement**

(JOA). Under a JOA, two competing papers keep separate news divisions while merging business and production operations for a specific number of years. Although JOAs and mergers encourage monopolistic tendencies, they have sometimes been seen as the best way to maintain some editorial competition between newspapers. After passage of the act, twenty-eight cities adopted JOAs. In 2011, however, just six JOAs remained—once again raising questions about newspapers' likelihood of surviving. Since 1991, sixteen newspapers that were once part of a JOA have folded.

In this photo of the *Seattle Post-Intelligencer* newsroom, employees stopped to watch a press conference on a dispute over its JOA with the *Seattle Times*. The *Post-Intelligencer* was started in 1863 and became an online-only paper in 2009 as the JOA ended. Hearst bought the print paper in 1921, and the online operation remains part of the Hearst Corporation today.

Newspaper Chains

Newspaper chains, companies that own several papers throughout the country, have played a part in the consolidation that's reshaping print journalism. With the rise of chains, the power to control information conveyed through the printed word has become concentrated in fewer and fewer hands. Edward Wyllis Scripps founded the first newspaper chain in the 1890s. By the 1920s, there were about thirty chains in the United States, each owning an average of five papers. By 2004, the top ten chains controlled more than one-half of the nation's total daily newspaper circulation. Around 2005, the consolidation trend in newspaper ownership had leveled off. Despite the fact that most newspapers still generated up to 20 percent profit margins even in 2006 and 2007, the decline in newspaper circulation and ad sales sparked panic among investors, and newspapers saw their stock prices plummet as the market showed little faith that newspapers had a future. Many newspaper chains responded by further slashing newsroom jobs.

About the same time, some large chains started to break up their holdings, selling unprofitable individual newspapers to private individuals and equity firms. Ownership of one of the three national U.S. newspapers—the *Wall Street Journal*—also changed hands, as the paper was bought up by media mogul

Rupert Murdoch's News Corp. in 2007 (see "Media Literacy Case Study: Covering Business News" on page 72). The move raised serious concerns among critics, who warned that papers weren't likely to conduct high-quality journalism if they were owned by large entertainment conglomerates. By 2009, Congress held the first hearings on the future of newspapers and considered the possibility of nonprofit models—like that used to support public radio and television. One such model already exists: The *St. Petersburg Times*, Florida's largest newspaper, is owned by the nonprofit Poynter Institute, which specializes in training journalists.

Going Digital

One of the biggest challenges facing newspapers has been the digital revolution. Newspapers struck back by developing online editions of their papers, charging subscription fees for access to these versions or relying solely on online ads to stay in business. By 2010, more and more newspapers were moving the bulk of their operations online while dramatically decreasing their news staffs. For example, the *Seattle Post-Intelligencer* folded its print paper in 2009 and went online only. In this transformation, the reporting staff shrank from 165 to 20.

Though slow to evolve, online newspapers are now taking advantage of the flexibility the Internet offers by posting stories and reader letters online that they didn't have room to print in their paper editions. They can also run longer stories with more in-depth coverage, often with hyperlinks to other information sources for readers who want to know more. And they can provide free video and audio links, as well as offer immediate updates to breaking news. Also, most stories appear online before they appear in print, so they can be posted at any time and updated several times a day.

Despite these advances, print newspapers still collect more advertising revenue than any other medium except television, although that amount has been declining since the late 1980s (see Figure 3.2 on page 87). To boost online revenue, more than four hundred daily newspapers struck business deals with Yahoo! and Google—the Web sites most readers use to search for news—in 2008, to launch an ad venture promising to raise online papers' revenue by 10 to 20 percent. Google also established contracts with the Associated Press wire service to carry news, though some newspapers argued that Google was making money on advertising by linking readers and users to newspaper Web sites that were then receiving little compensation from Google.

Some better-known papers, such as the *Wall Street Journal* and the *New York Times*, have experimented with charging online readers. The *Wall Street Journal* has placed content behind a subscriber-only **paywall** since 1997, while the *Times* has experimented with varying levels of access. The most recent model, implemented in 2011, allows readers to view up to twenty articles per month, while

VideoCentral ©
bedfordstmartins.com /mediaessentials

Newspapers and the Internet: Convergence
This video discusses the ways newspapers are adapting to online delivery of news.
Discussion: What different kinds of skills are needed to be effective in the new online world? What skills might remain the same?

CONVERGING MEDIA
Case Study

News Aggregation

"Frankly, the *New York Times* is a bore. As are actually most news organizations which continue to write for an older world. I mean, the *New York Times* writes as though one is only reading the *New York Times*."[1]

These fighting words were spoken by Michael Wolff, editorial director of *Adweek* and founder of *Newser*. Like the *Drudge Report* and the *Huffington Post*, *Newser* thrives on a new type of content convergence called *news aggregation*, in which a site packages news summaries, usually providing links to the sources from which it draws (such as online versions of a newspaper, magazine, or wire service). The *Drudge Report* is the oldest and most famous of these sites. With a Web 1.0 look, the *Drudge Report* presents links to news reports, opinion pieces, and blogs with a general conservative bent. The *Huffington Post* (bought by AOL in 2011), though claiming to be independent, often reverses *Drudge*'s partisanship with a liberal slant. *Newser* steers clear of partisanship, branding itself as "a news curator with a kick." The site reduces the long, "boring" stories from, say, the *New York Times* to summaries with links to the original reports, intended to be readable in a variety of formats: desktop, laptop, mobile device.

In recent years, news aggregators have come under public attack for promoting a form of journalism that only takes and gives nothing back. In September 2009, media entrepreneur Mark Cuban took aim at *Newser*, declaring that major media companies should use software that blocks links, thus preventing hyperlink access to the offending sites.[2] Wolff's response, "Mark Cuban is a Big Fat Idiot—News Will Stay Free," claimed *Newser* should be thanked, not condemned, because some readers click through to the original stories.[3]

A year later, it was Arianna Huffington's time to deflect the barbs of an Old News representative. In a

lecture, former executive editor of the *Washington Post* Len Downie named the *Huffington Post* as an example of a news media "parasite," condemning news aggregation as thievery.[4] Huffington dismissed his concerns: "Once again, some in the old media have decided that the best way to save, if not journalism, at least themselves, is by pointing fingers and calling names."[5]

As the name-calling feuds suggest, media convergence often arouses passion and arrogance on both sides of the new/old media divide. But we don't have to pick sides to recognize the paradox of Wolff's declaration that "the news will stay free." Despite his argument that he provides a service to his hosts, Wolff doesn't pay any newsroom salaries. As such, it's possible that news aggregation could help hasten the demise of businesses that do actually pay reporters—after all, if there's no one to report and write up the news, there will be nothing for the aggregators to aggregate. Clearly audiences are seeking new forms of journalism, and many media companies are working to find a model that makes financial sense. What's not yet clear is where this process will leave organizations like *Newser*— or their audiences.

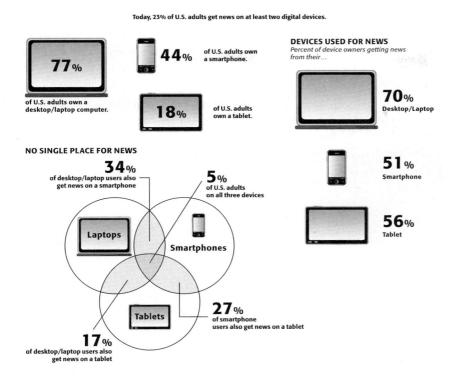

Today, 23% of U.S. adults get news on at least two digital devices.

77%
of U.S. adults own a desktop/laptop computer.

44% of U.S. adults own a smartphone.

18% of U.S. adults own a tablet.

DEVICES USED FOR NEWS
Percent of device owners getting news from their…

70% Desktop/Laptop

51% Smartphone

56% Tablet

NO SINGLE PLACE FOR NEWS

34% of desktop/laptop users also get news on a smartphone

5% of U.S. adults on all three devices

Laptops

Smartphones

Tablets

27% of smartphone users also get news on a tablet

17% of desktop/laptop users also get news on a tablet

FIGURE 3.2 // DIGITAL DEVICES AND THE NEWS

How do you consume your news? A 2012 study found that more and more people are using smartphones and tablets for news consumption, and are accessing news media throughout the day. However, these positive developments for news sites are complicated by the fact that they must compete with many mobile and social media apps vying for users' attention.

Source: "Mobile Devices and News Consumption," in Pew Research Center's Project for Excellence in Journalism, State of the News Media 2012. *March 19, 2012. http://stateofthemedia.org/2012 /mobile-devices-and-news -consumption-some-good-signs-for -journalism/*

subscribers get unlimited access. This version has been deemed a success so far,[12] showing some hope for a new online-inclusive path toward profitability—at least for papers with strong name recognition and loyal readership.

Other news companies are finding ways to cater to readers' increasingly digital lifestyles, developing material for new digital platforms like the touchscreen tablet. In 2011, for example, Rupert Murdoch's News Corp. launched the *Daily*—the first "newspaper" designed especially for an iPad. The *Daily* offers readers who download the app free content for two weeks, and then asks them to subscribe for 99 cents a week or $39.99 for a year. News Corp. invested $30 million in the project, started with a staff of a hundred, and featured six sections, including news, gossip, opinion, arts and life, apps and games, and sports.

Blogs

The rise of blogs has presented yet another challenge for newspapers. What started out in the late 1990s and early 2000s as amateur, sideline journalism has become a major source of news—one that has begun calling papers' authority into

The *Huffington Post*, a news blog founded in 2005, offers original content as well as aggregated headlines.

question. Widely read blogs like *Daily Kos*, the *Huffington Post*, Andrew Sullivan's the *Dish.com*, the *Drudge Report*, *Talking Points Memo*, and *POLITICO* have moved this Internet feature into the realm of traditional journalism. In fact, many reporters now write a blog in addition to their regular newspaper, television, or radio work. And some big-name newspapers such as the *Washington Post* and the *New York Times* even hire journalists to blog exclusively for their Web sites.

While blogging has grown in popularity, it has also raised concerns among critics who point out that, unlike print journalists, bloggers aren't required to check their sources rigorously. A blogger merely has to post his or her opinion about an issue or event, yet many readers swallow this content whether or not it has been backed by rigorous reporting practices. The rise of blogs has also triggered turmoil in many news organizations, as established journalists have left to begin new careers in the blogosphere. For example, top journalists John Harris and Jim VandeHei departed the *Washington Post* to launch *POLITICO* in 2007, a national blog (and, secondarily, a local newspaper) about Capitol Hill politics.

Indeed, some blogs have won respect as viable information sources. In 2008, the *Talking Points Memo* blog, headed by Joshua Micah Mitchell, won a George Polk Award for legal reporting. Today some blog sites stand alongside printed papers as trusted, authoritative sources of news (see "Converging Media Case Study: News Aggregation" on page 86).

Citizen Journalism

A final development influencing newspapers' survival is **citizen journalism**, also known as *citizen media* or *community journalism*. Through citizen journalism, people who are not professional journalists—such as activists concerned about a specific issue—use the Internet and blog sites to disseminate information and opinions about their favorite issues. With steep declines in newsroom staffs, numerous news media organizations—like CNN (iReport) and many regional newspapers—are increasingly drawing on citizen journalists' work to make up for the loss of professional journalists through newsroom "downsizing." By some estimates, more than twelve hundred community-based Web sites had emerged by 2010, well over twice the number from 2007.

Newspapers in a Democratic Society

While pondering the future of the newspaper—and of our democracy—we must recognize that a free press isn't free, nor is its survival certain.

As newsroom cutbacks accelerate, as state, national, and foreign bureaus close down, and as industry consolidation continues apace, we must ask ourselves where we will get the thorough reporting we need to make informed choices and present well-considered viewpoints—two hallmarks of a vibrant democracy. Since the days of Nellie Bly, Americans have depended on journalists to hunt down the facts and either present them or analyze them. As our world becomes even smaller and the issues confronting us even more perilous, a press devoted to serving the diverse interests of the common good is crucial to the health of our democracy.

However, a host of current developments in print journalism undermine the newspaper's role as bulwark of democracy. Many cities now have just one newspaper, which tends to cover only issues and events of interest to middle- and upper-middle-class readers. The experiences and events affecting poorer and working-class citizens get short shrift, and with the rise of newspaper chains, the chances that mainstream daily papers will publish a diversity of opinions, ideas, and information will likely decrease. Moreover, chain owner-ship—often concerned first about the bottom line and saving money—has tended to discourage watchdog journalism, the most expensive type of report-ing. This means that we, as citizens, must remain ever mindful of our news sources and consider the motivations and interests concealed behind the news we're receiving and ask ourselves why we're receiving it.

As news increasingly reaches us through a wide range of digital distribution channels, print journalism is losing readers and advertisers and may eventually cease to exist. Editor John Carroll described the situation in no uncertain terms. Having presided over thirteen Pulitzer Prize–winning reports at the *Los Angeles Times* as editor from 2000 to 2005, Carroll left the paper to protest deep cor-porate cuts to the newsroom. He lamented the apparently imminent demise of newspapers, proclaiming: "Newspapers are doing the reporting in this country. Google and Yahoo! and those people aren't putting reporters on the street in any numbers at all. Blogs can't afford it. Network television is taking reporters off the street.... Newspapers are the last ones standing, and newspapers are threatened.... Reporting is absolutely an essential thing for democratic self-government. Who's going to do it? Who's going to pay for the news? If newspapers fall by the wayside, what will we know?"[13]

CHAPTER ESSENTIALS

Now that you have finished reading this chapter, you can use the following tools:

REVIEW

Explain Major Developments in Newspapers' Early History

- The social impact of **news**—the process by which people gather and create information and reports to make sense of events surrounding them—accelerated with the invention of the printing press, leading to the creation of the first colonial newspapers in the late seventeenth century. Known as the **partisan press**, these papers critiqued government, spread the views of different political parties, and offered commercial information to businessmen of that era (pp. 64–65).

- Paper and production advances made during the Industrial Revolution as well as a rising middle class set the stage for a more inclusive press, leading to the creation of **penny papers**—priced at an affordable one cent—which enabled papers to become a mass medium. The first penny papers included Day's *New York Sun*, which favored **human-interest stories**, and Bennett's *New York Morning Herald* (pp. 65–67).

- The proliferation of penny papers caused many papers to begin accepting ads, which further expanded the industry and led six New York newspapers in 1848 to form the Associated Press, the first news **wire service**, a commercial and cooperative organization that relayed news stories and information around the country and the world using telegraph lines (pp. 67–68).

- In the late 1800s, a new brand of papers arose, ushering in an era of **yellow journalism**, which emphasized sensational stories and also established the foundation for investigative journalism (pp. 68–69).

Track the Evolution of the Modern Era of Print Journalism

- In the late 1800s, as readership expanded nationwide, many papers, such as the *New York Times*, began presenting so-called **objective journalism**, or factual, balanced coverage, via the **inverted-pyramid style**, a story form that packaged and presented reports based on answering who, what, when, and where (pp. 71, 74–75).

- Amid the complex national and global events of the early 1900s, **interpretive journalism** grew out of the public's need to put events and issues in context. Later, by the 1960s, many Americans questioned traditional authority and key institutions, causing an exploration into new types of journalism such as **literary journalism**, which adapts fictional techniques to nonfiction material and reporting (pp. 71, 74).

- In the early 1980s, an emphasis on color printing and brevity of content (thanks to *USA Today*) as well as the digitization of news content ushered in a new brand of journalism (pp. 74–75).

Understand the Types of Newspapers in Existence Today

- A variety of papers have arisen to meet different readers' needs. Small local papers, mostly weeklies, feature **consensus-oriented journalism** by promoting social and economic harmony in the towns they serve. Larger regional papers, sometimes called metro dailies, and national papers focus on **conflict-oriented journalism** by featuring events or issues that often highlight experiences that deviate from social norms. Ethnic and minority newspapers feature interpretations of developments and events from the perspective of people outside of white, mainstream readers (pp. 76–78).

- Rising in the 1960s, the *underground press* refers to alternative newspapers that have often questioned mainstream political policies and conventional values (p. 79).

Discuss the Economics behind Newspapers

- The majority of newspapers' revenue comes from selling advertising space, which can take up as much as one-half to two-thirds of large newspapers' pages. The **newshole**, which has shrunk in most newspapers today, refers to the space left over in a newspaper for news content after all the ads are placed (p. 81).

- Newspapers spend money on salaries and wages for their employees—from the publisher to various editors and reporters—and on wire services and **feature syndicates**, commercial outlets or brokers that contract with newspapers to provide work from well-known political writers, editorial cartoonists, comic-strip artists, and self-help columnists (pp. 81–83).

Consider the Challenges Facing Newspapers Today

- Newspapers have been dealing with a decline in readership since the rise of television. In an effort to maintain competition, the government sanctioned **joint operating agreements (JOAs)** in the early 1970s, which permitted competing papers to operate separate editorial divisions while merging business and production units. But this has had limited success. The Internet and the economic crisis of 2008–09 have made matters much worse for newspapers. Furthermore, the formation and rise of **newspaper chains**, companies that own several papers throughout the country, left power over news in fewer hands. But many of these big media companies, some now in bankruptcy, have taken on too much debt and seen their stock prices drop (pp. 83–85).

- The digitization of news content has called the survival of print journalism into question as well as shifted advertising patterns. Some newspapers are experimenting with placing digital content behind a subscriber-only **paywall** in an attempt to raise online profitability. In addition, the rise of blogs has raised concerns among critics about the loss of reporting and documentation in journalism and the validity of some blogs as a reliable news source. Similarly, **citizen journalism**, where individual citizens, not professional journalists, use the Internet and blogs to disseminate news and information, has become an issue (pp. 85, 87–88).

Explore How Newspapers' Existing Challenges Pose a Threat to Sustaining a Democratic Society

---

- As the fate of print journalism is called into question, we must ask ourselves where we will get the best information, based on strong reporting, that we need to make informed choices and receive multiple points of view (p. 89).

STUDY QUESTIONS

1. How did newspapers emerge as a mass medium during the penny press era? How did content changes make this happen?
2. What different forms of journalism developed? What are their characteristics? What are their strengths and limitations?
3. What is the difference between consensus- and conflict-oriented newspapers? What role have ethnic, minority, and oppositional newspapers played in the United States?
4. Describe and discuss some of the business challenges faced by newspapers today.
5. What are the major reasons for the decline in U.S. newspaper circulation figures?
6. What is a newspaper's role in a democracy?

MEDIA LITERACY PRACTICE

The toughest issue facing newspapers today is their survival—either in print or online or both. To investigate this economic and social problem, consider a newspaper in your community.

DESCRIBE the current financial situation of your local newspaper, including its circulation and advertisers, and the online version of the paper. Ask others to comment on the current problems facing newspapers.

ANALYZE trends and patterns in the data. What problems are noted most often? What do people seem to like and/or dislike about your local paper? What are the main points people make about your local paper and its online edition?

INTERPRET what these patterns mean. For example, who is being best served by the newspaper in your community? Are there people in your community who are not served well by the newspaper?

EVALUATE what you have discovered. Which criticisms and ideas are good or bad, and why?

ENGAGE with your community on your findings. What problems and solutions are noted most often? What new business models are suggested? Ask the people you have been talking to about two or three specific good ideas to improve the news in your community.

⊙ ONLINE RESOURCES

Go to **bedfordstmartins.com/mediaessentials** for review quizzes, links, and more.

Visit the site's **VIDEOCENTRAL: MASS COMMUNICATION** section for videos like the one on page 76. There, you can find additional exclusive videos related to Chapter 3, including:

THE MEDIA AND DEMOCRACY
This video traces the history of media's role in democracy from newspapers and television to the Internet.

NEWSPAPERS NOW: BALANCING CITIZEN JOURNALISM AND INVESTIGATIVE REPORTING
Reporters explain the value of investigative journalism and debate how citizen journalism fits within the spectrum of traditional reporting.

Helen Gurley Brown
in her office at
Cosmopolitan in
the 1960s.

4

Magazines in the Age of Specialization

Cosmopolitan, like the magazine industry in general, has demonstrated a remarkable ability to change with the times in order to sustain circulation and attract advertisers. When it was first launched in 1886, it was an illustrated monthly focusing on childcare and household decoration. After almost going out of business, a new owner gave it a second chance as an illustrated magazine of literature. In 1905, *Cosmopolitan* got another new owner (famed newspaper publisher William Randolph Hearst), who made it into a progressive muckraking magazine focusing on exposing corruption in business, government, and social institutions. But by the next decade, it was back to an illustrated monthly targeting women and featuring short stories and serialized novels. In the 1960s, the magazine had its most radical makeover. Helen Gurley Brown, a talented advertising copywriter and author of the best-selling book *Sex and the Single Girl*, was hired to reinvent the magazine modeled on her vision of strong, sexually liberated women. The new *Cosmopolitan* both reflected and fueled the sexual revolution erupting during the 1960s and was marketed to the "Cosmo Girl": a woman age eighteen to thirty-four with an interest in love, sex, fashion, and a career.

Brown's vision of *Cosmo* lives on in the magazine's "fun, fearless female" slogan. Today, it's the top-selling women's fashion magazine—surpassing competitors like *Glamour*, *InStyle*, and *Vogue*. It also maintains a popular Web site and a mobile version for reading on smartphones. *Cosmopolitan*'s ability to reinvent itself repeatedly over the last 125 years testifies to the remarkable power of magazines as a mass medium to both adapt to and shape American society and culture.

SINCE THE 1740s, magazines have played a key role in America, becoming a national mass medium even before newspapers (which at the time were mainly local and regional in scope). Magazines provided venues for political leaders and thinkers to offer their views on the broad issues and events of the age, including public education, abolition, women's suffrage, and the Civil War. Many leading literary figures also used magazines to gain public exposure for their essays or stories. Readers consumed the articles and fictional accounts offered in magazines and snapped up the products and services advertised in each issue—hastening the rise of a consumer society. As consumerism grew, magazines themselves changed, with the most popular titles often focusing less on news and essays, and more on fashion, celebrities, advice, and entertainment.

Today, more than nineteen thousand magazines are published in the United States annually. And like newspapers, radio, movies, and television, these magazines, including *Cosmopolitan*, both reflect and create what's going on in American life.

In this chapter, we track the shifting role of magazines in the United States by:

- tracing the early history of magazines, including their highly politicized purpose in colonial and early America and their transformation into the country's first national medium

- examining turning points in the evolution of modern American magazines, such as the emergence of muckraking as a magazine-reporting style and the rise and fall of general-interest magazines

- taking stock of the many different types of magazines specialized for particular audiences (including men, women, sports fans, young people, and minorities)

- discovering how magazines operate economically, including how they make money and what they spend money on to fulfill their mission and surmount challenges

• considering how magazines today are affecting the health of our democratic society

The Early History of Magazines

Magazines have changed extensively during their journey to mass-medium
status. They started out in Europe as infrequently published periodicals that
looked like newspapers and contained mostly political commentary. These
caught on slowly in colonial America and served mostly as vehicles for politicians (such as John Adams and Thomas Jefferson) and thinkers (including
Thomas Paine) to convey their views. It wasn't until the nineteenth century
that magazines really took off in America. During the 1800s, magazines
took the form of specialized and general-interest periodicals that appealed
to an increasingly literate populace, that could be published quickly through
improved printing technologies, and that boasted arresting illustrations.

Today, the word **magazine** broadly refers to any collection of articles,
stories, and advertisements published on a nondaily cycle (such as weekly
or monthly) in the smaller tabloid style rather than larger broadsheet
newspaper style.

The First Magazines: European Origins

The first magazines appeared in seventeenth-century France in the form of bookseller catalogues and notices that book publishers inserted in newspapers.
(In fact, the word *magazine* derives from the French term *magasin*, meaning
"storehouse.") In Europe, magazines then became channels for political commentary and argument. They looked like newspapers of the time, but they were
published less frequently. The first political magazine, called the *Review*,
appeared in London in 1704 and was printed sporadically until 1713.

Regularly published magazines or pamphlets, such as the *Tatler* and the
Spectator, also appeared in England around this time. Offering poetry, politics,
and philosophy for London's elite, they served small readerships of a few thousand. The first publication to use the term *magazine* was *Gentleman's Magazine*,
which appeared in London in 1731 and consisted of articles reprinted from newspapers, books, and political pamphlets.

The first issue of Benjamin Franklin's *General Magazine and Historical Chronicle* appeared in February 1741. While it lasted only six months, Franklin found success in other publications, like his annual *Poor Richard's Almanac*, starting in 1732 and lasting twenty-five years.

Magazines in Eighteenth-Century America: The Voices of Revolution

Without a substantial middle class, widespread literacy, or advanced printing technology, magazines took root slowly in America. Like the partisan newspapers of the time, colonial magazines served politicians, the educated, and the merchant class. However, they also served the wider purpose of conveying colonial leaders' thoughts about the big questions percolating during their era—such as how taxation should work, how much self-rule the colonies should have, how Indians should be treated, and who should have access to public education. Magazines thus gave voice to the people who ultimately decided to break away from England and create a new, independent nation.

The first colonial magazines appeared in Philadelphia in 1741, about fifty years after the earliest newspapers. Andrew Bradford started it all with *American Magazine, or A Monthly View of the Political State of the British Colonies*. Three days later, Benjamin Franklin launched his *General Magazine and Historical Chronicle*.

Though neither of these experiments was successful, they inspired other publishers to launch magazines in the remaining colonies, beginning in Boston in the 1740s. The most successful of these periodicals simply reprinted articles from leading London newspapers to keep readers abreast of European events.

Magazines in Nineteenth-Century America: Specialization and General Interest

As the nineteenth century dawned, the magazine industry remained somewhat unstable in the newly created United States. During 1800–1825, about five hundred such periodicals had cropped up and then withered. However, as the century progressed, the idea of specialized magazines devoted to certain categories of readers gained momentum—leading to the creation of religious magazines, literary

---

CHAPTER 4 // TIMELINE

1741 Colonial Magazines
First appearing in Philadelphia and Boston, these magazines mainly reprinted material from London newspapers.

1821 National Magazines
The *Saturday Evening Post* is launched, becoming the first major magazine to appeal directly to women and the longest-running magazine in U.S. history.

1850s Engravings and Illustrations
Drawings, woodcuts, and other forms of illustration begin to fill the pages of magazines.

1879 Postal Act of 1879
Both postal rates and rail transportation costs plummet, allowing magazine distribution to thrive.

periodicals publishing the works of important writers of the day, and magazines devoted to professions such as law and medicine.

The nineteenth century also saw the birth of the first general-interest magazine aimed at a large national audience: the *Saturday Evening Post*, launched in 1821. Like most magazines of the day, the early *Post* included a few original essays but reprinted many pieces from other sources. Eventually, however, the *Post* grew to incorporate news, poetry, essays, play reviews, and the writings of popular authors such as Nathaniel Hawthorne and Harriet Beecher Stowe.

The *Post* was also the first major magazine to appeal directly to women, through its "Lady's Friend" advice column. This new device may have served as an inspiration. In 1828, Sarah Josepha Hale started the first magazine directed exclusively to a female audience: *Ladies' Magazine*. In addition to general-interest pieces including essays and criticism, the periodical advocated for women's education, work, and property rights. Other women's magazines—including the hugely successful *Godey's Lady's Book*—would soon follow.

Colorful illustrations first became popular in the fashion sections of women's magazines in the mid-1800s. The color for this fashion image from *Godey's* was added to the illustration by hand.

Going National as the Twentieth Century Approaches

Thanks to increases in literacy and public education, the development of faster printing technologies, and improvements in mail delivery (through rail transportation), demand for national (versus local) magazines soared. Whereas in 1825, a mere one hundred magazines struggled for survival, by 1850 nearly six hundred magazines were being published regularly, many of them with national readerships. Magazines were on their way to becoming a mass medium. Significant national magazines of this era included *Graham's Magazine* (1840–1858), *Knickerbocker* (1833–1864), the *Nation* (1865–present), and *Youth's Companion* (1826–1929).

The advent of illustration further moved magazines toward mass-medium status. By the mid-1850s, drawings, engravings, woodcuts, and other forms of

**Early 1900s
Muckraking Magazines**
McClure's, Collier's, Ladies' Home Journal, and *Cosmopolitan* push progressive social reforms with their investigative reports.

1903 *Ladies' Home Journal*
The magazine reaches a circulation of one million.

1922 *Reader's Digest*
The pocket-size monthly becomes the leading magazine in the nation.

1923 *Time*
Time is launched and develops a new brand of journalism where stories are written in narrative form.

illustration had become a major feature of magazines and greatly heightened their appeal for readers. During the 1890s, magazines (and newspapers) also began including photographs with printed articles, helping to launch an entirely new profession: photojournalism.

The Evolution of Modern American Magazines

As the sun set on the nineteenth century, decreases in postage costs made it cheaper for publishers to distribute magazines, and improvements in production technologies lowered the costs of printing them. Now accessible and affordable to ever larger audiences, magazines became a true mass medium. They also began reflecting the social, demographic, and technological changes unfolding within the nation as the twentieth century progressed. For example, a new interest in social reform sparked the rise of muckraking, or investigative journalism designed to expose wrongdoing. The growth of the middle class initially heightened receptivity to general-interest magazines aimed at broad audiences, but then television's rising popularity put many general-interest magazines out of business. Some magazines struck back by focusing their content on topics not covered by TV programmers and by featuring short articles heavily illustrated with photos.

Distribution and Production Costs Plummet

In 1870, about twelve hundred magazines were produced in the United States; by 1890, that number reached forty-five hundred. By 1905, the nation boasted more than six thousand magazines. Part of this surge in titles and readership was

CHAPTER 4 // TIMELINE continued

1936 *Life*
Life is launched and pioneers fashion spreads and advances in photojournalism.

1953 *TV Guide*
TV Guide becomes an overnight success as a niche publication.

1965 *Cosmopolitan*
Editor Helen Gurley Brown turns *Cosmopolitan* into a leading magazine by targeting women ages eighteen to thirty-four with an interest in love, sex, fashion, and careers.

1969–1972 Shutdowns
The *Saturday Evening Post*, *Look*, and *Life* shut down; competition from television is a chief factor.

facilitated by the Postal Act of 1879, which had assigned magazines lower postage rates—putting them on an equal footing with newspapers delivered by mail. This vastly reduced distribution costs. Meanwhile, advances in mass-production printing, conveyor systems, assembly lines, and printing-press speeds lowered production costs and made large-circulation national magazines possible.[1]

This combination of reduced distribution and production costs enabled publishers to slash magazine prices. As prices dropped from thirty-five cents to fifteen and then to ten cents, people of modest means began subscribing to national publications. Magazine circulation skyrocketed, attracting new waves of advertising revenues. Even though publishers had dropped the price of an issue below the actual cost to produce a single copy, they recouped the loss through ad revenue—guaranteeing large readerships to advertisers eager to reach more customers. By the turn of the twentieth century, advertisers increasingly used national magazines to capture consumers' attention and build a national marketplace.

Muckrakers Expose Social Ills

The rise in magazine circulation coincided with major changes in American society in the early 1900s. Hundreds of thousands of Americans were moving from the country to the city in search of industrial jobs, and millions of people from foreign lands were immigrating to the United States hoping for new opportunities. Many newspaper reporters interested in writing about these and other social changes turned to magazines, where they could write longer, more analytical pieces on topics such as corruption in big business and government, urban problems faced by immigrants, labor conflicts, and race relations. Some of these writers built their careers on crusading for social reform on behalf of the public good—often openly criticizing long-standing American institutions.

Booth Tarkington's serial "The Two Vanrevels" enhances the value of this issue of "McClure's Magazine."

Muckraking magazines like *McClure's* were the first to publish investigative stories on American institutions.

1974 *People*
The first successful mass market magazine in decades is published.

1998 *ESPN The Magazine*
The magazine launches, successfully capitalizing on the growing ESPN sports media empire.

2008 *AARP Bulletin* and *AARP The Magazine*
These subscription-only publications continue to boast the highest circulations of any magazine in the United States.

2009 Recession
The economic recession leads to the closing of several leading magazines, including *Country Home, Domino, Nickelodeon Magazine, Gourmet, Modern Bride, Portfolio, Teen, Vibe,* and *Blender.*

First of C. S. FORESTER'S NEW NAVY STORIES

Norman Rockwell's 322 cover illustrations for the *Saturday Evening Post* between 1916 and 1963 included a series of 11 covers featuring a young World War II GI named Willie Gillis. The character was modeled after a Vermont neighbor of Rockwell's who posed for the artist and later went to war himself.

able to compete w/ radio

In 1906, President Theodore Roosevelt dubbed these investigative reporters **muckrakers**, because they were willing to crawl through society's muck to uncover a story. Although Roosevelt wasn't always a fan of it, muckraking journalism led to some much-needed reforms. For example, influenced in part by exposés at *Ladies' Home Journal* and *Collier's* magazines, Congress in 1906 passed the Pure Food and Drug Act and the Meat Inspection Act. Reports in *Cosmopolitan, McClure's,* and other magazines led to laws calling for increased government oversight of business, a progressive income tax, and the direct election of U.S. senators.

General-Interest Magazines Hit Their Stride

The heyday of the muckraking era lasted into the mid-1910s, when America was drawn into World War I. During the next few decades and even through the 1950s, **general-interest magazines** gained further prominence. These publications offered occasional investigative articles but also covered a wide variety of topics aimed at a broad national audience—such as recent developments in government, medicine, or society. A key aspect of these magazines was **photojournalism**—the use of photographs to augment editorial content (see "Media Literacy Case Study: The Evolution of Photojournalism" on pages 104–105). High-quality photos gave general-interest magazines a visual advantage over radio, which was the most popular medium of the day. In 1920, about fifty-five magazines fit the general-interest category; by 1946, more than a hundred such magazines competed with radio networks for the national audience. This genre of magazine was dominated by four giants: the *Saturday Evening Post*, *Reader's Digest, Time,* and *Life*.

Saturday Evening Post

Although the *Post* had been around since 1821, Cyrus Curtis (who bought it in 1897) transformed it into the first widely popular general-interest magazine by printing popular fiction and romanticizing American virtues through words and pictures. During the 1920s, Curtis also featured articles celebrating the business boom of the decade. This reversed the journalistic direction of the muckraking era, in which magazines focused on exposing corruption in business. By the 1920s, the *Post* had reached two million in circulation, the first magazine to hit that mark.

Reader's Digest

Reader's Digest championed one of the earliest functions of magazines: printing condensed versions of selected articles from other magazines. With its inexpensive production costs, low price, and popular pocket-size format, the magazine saw its circulation climb to more than one million even during the depths of the Great Depression. By 1946, it was the nation's most popular magazine, with a circulation of more than nine million. By the mid-1980s, it was the most popular magazine in the world.

Time

During the general-interest era, national newsmagazines such as *Time* also scored major commercial successes. Begun in 1923, *Time* developed a magazine brand of interpretive journalism, assigning reporter-researcher teams to cover newsworthy events while a rewrite editor would shape the teams' findings into articles presenting a point of view on the events covered. Newsmagazines took over photojournalism's role in news reporting, visually documenting both national and international events. Today, *Time's* circulation stands at about 2.6 million.

Life

More than any other magazines of its day, *Life*, an oversized pictorial weekly, struck back at radio's popularity by advancing photojournalism. Launched in 1936, *Life* satisfied the public's fascination with images (invigorated by the movie industry) by featuring extensive photo spreads with its researched articles, lavish advertisements, and even fashion photography. By the end of the 1930s, *Life* had a **pass-along readership**—the total number of people who come into contact with a single copy of a magazine—of more than seventeen million. This rivaled the ratings of even the most popular national radio programs.

General-Interest Magazines Decline

In the 1950s, weekly general-interest magazines began to lose circulation after dominating the industry for thirty years. Following years of struggle, the *Saturday Evening Post* finally folded in 1969; *Look* (another oversized pictorial weekly), in 1971; and *Life*, in 1972. All three at the time were in the Top 10 in paid circulation. Although some critics blamed the problem on poor management, general-interest magazines were victims of several forces—high production costs, increased postal rates, and television in particular. As families began spending more time gathered around their TVs instead of reading magazines, advertisers started spending more money on TV spots,

Margaret Bourke-White was a photojournalist of many "firsts": first female photographer for *Life* magazine, first western photographer allowed into the Soviet Union, first to shoot the cover photo for *Life*, and first female war correspondent. Bourke-White was well known for her photos of WWII—including concentration camps—but she also captured images reflecting the economic realities of her time, including the photo "At the Time of the Louisville Flood" (1937), which shows African Americans waiting in line for food against the backdrop of a billboard featuring a happy white family driving in a car.

MEDIA LITERACY
Case Study

The Evolution of Photojournalism
By Christopher R. Harris

What we now recognize as photo-journalism started with the assignment of photographer Roger Fenton, of the *Sunday Times* of London, to document the Crimean War in 1856. Since then—from the earliest woodcut technology to halftone reproduction to the flexible-film camera—photojournalism's impact has been felt worldwide, capturing many historic moments and playing an important political and social role. For example, Jimmy Hare's photoreportage on the sinking of the battleship *Maine* in 1898 near Havana, Cuba, fed into growing popular support for Cuban independence from Spain and eventual U.S. involvement in the Spanish-American War; the documentary photography of Jacob Riis and Lewis Hine at the turn of the twentieth century captured the harsh working and living conditions of the nation's many child laborers. Reaction to these shockingly honest photographs resulted in public outcry and new laws against the exploitation of children. In addition, *Time* magazine's coverage of the Roaring Twenties to the Great Depression and *Life's* images from World War II and the Korean War changed the way people viewed the world.

With the advent of television, photojournalism continued to take on a significant role, bringing to the public live coverage of the assassination of President Kennedy in 1963 and its aftermath as well as visual documentation of the turbulent 1960s, including aggressive photographic coverage

Eddie Adams's Pulitzer Prize–winning photo of a general executing a suspected Vietcong terrorist during the Vietnam War is said to have turned some Americans against the war. Adams (1933–2004) later regretted the notoriety the image brought to the general, as the man he shot had just murdered eight people (including six children).

of the Vietnam War and shocking images of the Civil Rights movement.

Into the 1970s and onward, new computer technologies emerged which have brought about new technological ethical concerns with photojournalism. These new concerns primarily deal with the ability of photographers and photo editors to change or digitally alter the documentary aspects of a news photograph. By the late 1980s, computers could transform images into digital form, easily manipulated by sophisticated software programs. In addition, any photographer can now transmit images around the world almost instantaneously by using digital transmission, and the Internet allows publication of virtually any image, without censorship. Because of the absence of physical film, there is a resulting loss of proof, or veracity, of the authenticity of images. Digital images can be easily altered, but such alteration can be very difficult to detect.

A recent example of image-tampering involved the *Men's Health* cover photo of tennis star Andy Roddick. Roddick, who is muscular but not bulky, didn't consent to the digital enhancement of his arms and later joked on his blog: "Little did I know I had 22-inch guns," referring to the size of his arms in the photo. (A birthmark on his right arm had also been erased.) A *Men's Health* spokesman said "I don't see what the big issue is here."[1]

Have photo editors gone too far? Photojournalists and news sources are now confronted with unprecedented concerns over truth-telling. In the past, trust in documentary photojournalism rested solely on the verifiability of images as they were used in the media. Just as we must evaluate the words we read, at the start of a new century we must also view with a more critical eye these images that mean so much to so many.

Source: Christopher R. Harris is a professor in the Department of Electronic Media Communication at Middle Tennessee State University.

APPLYING THE CRITICAL PROCESS

DESCRIPTION Select three different types of magazines (for example, national, political, alternative) that contain photojournalistic images. Look through these magazines, taking note of what you see.

ANALYSIS Document patterns in each one. What kinds of images are included? What kinds of topics are discussed? Do certain stories or articles have more images than others? Are the subjects generally recognizable, or do they introduce readers to new people or places? Do the images accompany an article, or are they stand-alone, with or without a caption?

INTERPRETATION What do these patterns mean? Talk about what you think the orientation is of each

magazine based upon the images. How do the photos work to achieve this view? Do the images help the magazine in terms of verification or truth-telling? Or, are the images mainly to attract attention? Can images do both?

EVALUATION Do you find the motives of each magazine to be clear? Can you see any examples where an image may be framed or digitally altered to convey a specific point of view? What are the dangers in this? Explain.

ENGAGEMENT If you find evidence that a photo has been altered, or has framed the subject in a manner that makes it less accurate, e-mail the magazine's editor and explain why you think this is a problem.

With large pages, beautiful photographs, and compelling stories on celebrities, *Look* entertained millions of readers from 1939 to 1971, emphasizing photojournalism to compete with radio. By the late 1960s, however, TV lured away national advertisers, postal rates increased, and production costs rose, forcing *Look* to fold despite a readership of more than eight million.

which were less expensive than magazine ads and reached a larger audience.

While some of the most venerated general-interest magazines sputtered, new types of publications—notably *TV Guide* and *People*—cropped up to take advantage of Americans' shifting preferences.

TV Guide

Launched in 1953 to exploit the nation's growing fascination with television, *TV Guide*, which published TV program listings, took its cue from the pocket-size format of *Reader's Digest* and the supermarket sales strategy used by women's magazines. By filling a need (many newspapers were not yet listing TV programs), the magazine by 1962 had become the first weekly to reach a circulation of eight million. It had seventy regional editions. (See Table 4.1 for the circulation figures of the Top 10 U.S. magazines.)

When local newspapers began listing TV program schedules, they undermined *TV Guide*'s regional editions, and the magazine saw its circulation decline. But it has transformed itself to survive. Today, *TV Guide* is a full-size, single-edition, national magazine, having dropped its smaller digest format and its 140 regional editions in 2005. It now focuses on entertainment and lifestyle news and carries only limited listings of cable and network TV schedules. The brand name also lives on in the TV Guide Network, an on-screen cable and satellite TV program guide, and TVGuide.com.

People

People (launched by Time Inc. in March 1974) capitalized on the celebrity-crazy culture that accompanied the rise of television. And like *TV Guide*, it crafted a distribution strategy emphasizing supermarket sales. These moves helped it become the first successful mass-market magazine to be introduced in decades. With an abundance of celebrity profiles and human-interest stories, *People*

TABLE 4.1 // THE TOP 10 MAGAZINES (RANKED BY PAID U.S.
CIRCULATION AND SINGLE-COPY SALES, 1972 vs. 2011)

1972		2011	
Rank/Publication	**Circulation**	**Rank/Publication**	**Circulation**
1 Reader's Digest	17,825,661	1 AARP The Magazine	22,407,421
2 TV Guide	16,410,858	2 AARP Bulletin	22,171,632
3 Woman's Day	8,191,731	3 Better Homes and Gardens	7,617,844
4 Better Homes and Gardens	7,996,050	4 gameinformer	7,514,460
5 Family Circle	7,889,587	5 Reader's Digest	5,560,046
6 McCall's	7,516,960	6 National Geographic	4,480,788
7 National Geographic	7,260,179	7 Good Housekeeping	4,341,426
8 Ladies' Home Journal	7,014,251	8 Woman's Day	3,886,853
9 Playboy	6,400,573	9 Family Circle	3,872,671
10 Good Housekeeping	5,801,446	10 People	3,569,811

Source: Magazine Publishers of America, http://www.magazine.org, 2012.

showed a profit in just two years and reached a circulation of more than two million within five years. Instead of using a bulky oversized format and relying on subscriptions, *People* downsized and generated most of its circulation revenue from newsstand and supermarket sales. It also uses plenty of photos, and its articles are about one-third the length of those in a typical newsmagazine. *People*'s success has inspired the launching of other similar magazines specializing in celebrities, human-interest stories, and fashion, such as *InStyle* and *Hello*, and has influenced competing webzines like *TMZ* and *Wonderwall*.

Types of Magazines: Domination of Specialization

As television has commanded more of Americans' attention, magazines have had to switch tactics to remain viable. General-interest publications have given way to highly specialized magazines appealing to narrower audiences that can be guaranteed to advertisers seeking to tap into niche markets. These narrow groups of readers might be defined by profession (*CIO, Progressive Grocer*), lifestyle (*Dakota Farmer, Game Informer Magazine*), gender (*Men's Health/O, The Oprah Magazine*), age (*AARP The Magazine, Highlights for Children*), or ethnic group (*Ebony, Latina*). There are even specialty magazines appealing to fans of specific interests and hobbies—such as hand spinning, private piloting, antique gun restoration, and poetry. These niche markets can be categorized in a few broader areas of specialization.

Men's and Women's Magazines

One way the magazine industry competed with television was to reach niche audiences who were not being served by TV, including people interested in adult subject matter. *Playboy*, started in 1953 by Hugh Hefner, was the first magazine to address this audience by emphasizing previously taboo topics. Now less popular than before, perhaps because people can freely access soft pornography on the Internet, *Playboy* and comparable publications nevertheless continue to publish. But newer men's magazines have broadened their focus to include health (*Men's Health*) and lifestyle (*Details* and *Maxim*) in addition to provocative photos and stories.

Women's magazines had long demonstrated that targeting readers by gender was highly effective. Yet as the magazine industry grew more specialized, publishers stepped up their efforts to capture even more of the enormous market of women readers. *Better Homes and Gardens, Good Housekeeping, Ladies' Home Journal*, and *Woman's Day* focused on cultivating the image of women as homemakers and consumers in the conservative 1950s and early 1960s. As the women's movement advanced in the late 1960s and into the 1970s, such magazines began including articles on sexuality, careers, and politics—topics previously associated primarily with men.

Entertainment, Leisure, and Sports Magazines

The television age spawned not only *TV Guide* but also a number of specialized entertainment, leisure, and sports magazines. These periodicals' executives have developed multiple magazines for fans of everything from soap operas, running, tennis, golf, and hunting, to quilting, antiquing, surfing, and gaming. Within categories, magazines specialize further, targeting (for instance) older or younger

Specialized magazines target a wide range of interests from mainstream sports to hobbies like making model airplanes. Some of the more successful specialized magazines include *Vogue, Popular Science,* and *AARP The Magazine.*

runners, men or women golfers, duck hunters or bird-watchers, and midwestern or southern antique collectors.

The most popular sports and leisure magazine is *Sports Illustrated*, which took its name from a failed 1935 publication. Launched in 1954 by Henry Luce's Time Inc., *Sports Illustrated*'s circulation rose to more than 3.2 million by 2010. It is now the most successful general sports magazine in history.

Another popular magazine type that fits loosely into the leisure category includes magazines devoted to music—everything from the *Source* (hip-hop) to *Country Weekly*. The all-time circulation champ in this category is *Rolling Stone*, started in 1967. Once considered an alternative magazine, by 1982 *Rolling Stone* had become mainstream with a circulation approaching 800,000. By 2010, that number had expanded to more than 1.4 million.

National Geographic is another successful publication in this category. Founded in 1888, it promoted "humanized geography" and began featuring color photography in 1910. *National Geographic*'s circulation reached 1 million in 1935 and 10 million in the 1970s. Starting in the late 1990s, its circulation of paid subscriptions began slipping somewhat. Still, many of *National Geographic*'s televised nature and culture specials, which began airing back in 1965, rank among the most popular programs in the history of public TV.

Age-Specific Magazines

Magazines have sliced their target markets even more finely by appealing to ever-narrower age groups often ignored by mainstream television. For example, magazines such as *Youth's Companion*, *Boy's Life* (the Boy Scouts' national publication since 1912), *Highlights for Children*, and *Ranger Rick* have successfully targeted preschool and elementary-school children. The ad-free and subscription-only *Highlights for Children* topped the children's magazine category in 2011, with a circulation of more than 2 million.

Leading female teen magazines have also shown substantial growth; the top magazine for thirteen- to nineteen-year-olds is *Seventeen*, with a circulation of 2 million in 2010.

Maxim, launched in 1997, targeted young men in their twenties and was one of the fastest-growing magazines of the late 1990s. Its covers boast the magazine's obsession with "sex, sports, beer, gadgets, clothes, fitness." But by 2010, the "lad fad" had worn off; ad revenues declined, although *Maxim* still had about 2.5 million subscribers.

Magazines that have had the most success with targeting audiences by age have set their sights on readers over fifty, America's fastest-growing age demographic. These publications have tried to meet the interests of older Americans, whom mainstream culture has historically ignored. By 2010, *AARP The Magazine*, the American Association of Retired Persons' publication, founded in 1958, had a circulation of 23.7 million, far surpassing those of all other magazines. (Its sister publication, *AARP Bulletin*, has a similar circulation.) *AARP The Magazine* articles cover a range of topics related to lifestyle, travel, money, health, and entertainment, such as the effects of Viagra on relationships, secrets for spectacular vacations, and how playing poker can sharpen your mind (see Table 4.1 on page 107).

Latina, launched in 1996, has become the largest magazine targeted to Hispanic women in the United States. It counts a readership of two million bilingual, bicultural women and is also the top Hispanic magazine in advertising pages.

Elite Magazines

Although they had long existed, *elite magazines* gained popularity as magazines began specializing. Elite magazines are characterized by their combination of literature, criticism, humor, and journalism and by their appeal to highly educated audiences, often living in urban areas. The most widely circulated elite magazine is the *New Yorker*. Launched in 1925 by Harold Ross, the *New Yorker* became the first city magazine aimed at a national upscale audience. Over the years, it featured many prominent biographers, writers, reporters, and humorists and introduced some of the finest literary journalism of the century. By the mid-1960s, the *New Yorker's* circulation hovered around 500,000; by 2010, it stood at 1 million.[2]

Minority Magazines

Minority-targeted magazines, like newspapers, have existed since before the Civil War. One of the most influential early African American magazines, the *Crisis*, was founded by W. E. B. Du Bois in 1910 and is the official magazine of the National Association for the Advancement of Colored People (NAACP).

Since then, the major magazine publisher for African Americans has been John H. Johnson, a former Chicago insurance salesman. Johnson started *Negro Digest* in 1942, *Ebony* in 1945 (a picture text magazine modeled on *Life* but serving black readers), and *Jet* in 1951 (a pocket-size supermarket magazine). *Essence*, the first major magazine geared toward African American women, debuted in 1969, and by 2010 had a circulation of more than 1 million.

Other magazines have served additional minority groups. For example, the *Advocate*, founded in 1967 as a twelve-page newsletter, was the first major magazine to address issues of interest to gay men and lesbians. Since its founding, it has published some of the best journalism on topics not covered by the mainstream press.

Magazines appealing to Spanish-speaking readers have also proliferated since the 1980s, reflecting the growth of Hispanic populations in the United States. Today, *People en Español*, *Latina*, and *Glamour en Español* rank as the top three Hispanic magazines by ad revenue. Although national magazines aimed at other minority groups were slow to arrive, there are now magazines targeting virtually every race, culture, and ethnicity, including *Asian Week*, *Native Peoples*, *Tikkun* (published for Jewish readers), and many more.

Variety, a trade magazine covering the entertainment industry, was founded in 1933 and remains a widely read source of news and reviews.

Trade Magazines

Trade and professional magazines represent one of the most stable segments in the magazine industry. **Trade publications**—specialty magazines aimed at narrowly defined audiences—supply news, spot trends, share data, and disseminate expert insights relevant to specific manufacturing trades, professional fields, and business sectors. The trade press includes such diverse magazines as *Organic Matters* for organic farmers, *Packaging Machinery Technology* for packaging engineers, and *Coach and Bus Week*. Media industries, too, have relied on trade magazines like *Advertising Age* and *Variety*. In addition to narrowly targeted advertising content, trade publications provide an invaluable venue for job notices related to the specific field. The health of the trade press is evident in findings of a media usage study conducted by Readex Research and released in October 2011. According to the study, when professionals were asked which media they used regularly in their work, print trade magazines came in second (tied with e-newsletters) at 74 percent. Only search engines ranked higher.[3]

Alternative Magazines

About 90 of the almost 20,600 American magazines now in existence reach circulations of 1 million or more. That means most magazines serve relatively small groups of readers. Of these, many are alternative magazines: They focus their articles on topics that lie far outside the mainstream—from punk rock to hobby farming to spouse-swapping. At any given time, there are more than 2,000 of these alternative periodicals in circulation, with many failing and others starting up every month.

Numerous alternative magazines have defined themselves in terms of politics—published either by the Left (the *Progressive, In These Times*, the *Nation*) or the Right (the *National Review, American Spectator, Insight*). Though their circulations may be relatively small, they often exert significant influence on politics by stimulating public debate and affecting citizens' political choices.

Supermarket Tabloids

With headlines like "Angelina Walks in on Brad & Jen," "Extraterrestrials Follow the Teachings of Oprah Winfrey," and "Al-Qaeda Breeding Killer Mosquitoes," **supermarket tabloids** push the limits of credibility. Although they are published on newsprint, the Audit Bureau of Circulations, which checks newspaper and magazine circulation figures to determine advertising rates, counts weekly tabloids as magazines. Tabloids have their historical roots in newspapers' use of graphics and pictorial layouts in the 1860s and 1870s. But the modern U.S. tabloid began with the founding of the *National Enquirer* by William Randolph Hearst in 1926. Its popularity inspired the founding of other tabloids like *Globe* (1954) and *Star* (1974) as well as the adoption of a tabloid style by some general-interest magazines, such as *People* and *Us Weekly*. Today, tabloid magazine sales are down from their peak in the 1980s, but these publications continue to have a devoted following.

Online Magazines

With nearly two-thirds of Americans linked to a broadband Internet connection, the Internet has become the place where specialized magazines can further extend their reach to their target audiences. Some magazines are now published in both print and online versions. Others have moved to online-only format after their print version ended. Still other magazines—**webzines**—started up online and have remained there. Respected webzines include *Slate* (claiming 8 million monthly unique visitors in 2012) and *Salon* (with 6.4 million monthly unique visitors). These online-only publications have made the Web a legitimate arena for reporting breaking news and encouraging public debate about culture and politics. In 2011, one blog post from a magazine even jump-started a social movement. Inspired by the Arab Spring uprisings in Tunisia and Egypt that were facilitated by the revolutionary use of social media, an anti-consumerist print and online magazine called *Adbusters* intitiated, mobilized, and orchestrated the Occupy Wall Street protests.

Online magazines like *Slate* (pictured) have made the Web their exclusive home. Since launching in 1996, *Slate* has won many awards, such as the National Magazine Award for General Excellence Online.

Although many observers initially viewed the Internet as the death knell for print magazines, the industry now embraces it. Numerous magazines that have moved online now carry blogs, original video and audio podcasts, social-networking features, and other interactive components that could never work in print. For example, the online version of *Popular Mechanics* offers interactive 3-D models for do-it-yourself projects: Readers can use the 3-D models to construct a piece of furniture, for instance, by examining joints and parts from every angle.

In fact, new print magazines often publish with brand-extending synergies in mind. In 1998, for example, cable network ESPN launched *ESPN The Magazine*. The brand familiarity helped the new print periodical find readers in a segment already crowded with *Sports Illustrated*, the *Sporting News*, and dozens of niche sports publications. The magazine also drives cross-promotion of ESPN's growing business empire, including its cable channels, ESPN radio, the ESPN Web site, ESPN Zone restaurants, and the X Games. As magazines create apps for smartphones and tablets, editorial content will be even more tightly woven with advertising. Readers can now, for example, read *Entertainment Weekly*'s music recommendations on their devices and then click through to buy the song or album mentioned. The publication gets a cut of the sale, and the reader gets music almost instantly.

VideoCentral ▶
**bedfordstmartins.com
/mediaessentials**

Ernie Rideout

Narrowcasting in Magazines
Magazine editors explain the benefits and consequences of narrowcasting.
Discussion: Think of magazines that might be considered a good example of narrowcasting. What makes them a good example, and would you consider them successful? Why or why not?

CONVERGING MEDIA
Case Study

Print, Web, and Synergy

Media convergence has led to a number of high profile mergers—some successful, others less so. One recent merger may stand as a sign of the times in the magazine industry—*Newsweek*'s 50/50 joint venture with the Web-based *Daily Beast*. The merger paired a heritage newsmagazine that had been around since 1933 with a veritable toddler in the news business. But sometimes mergers don't work out as expected.

The *Daily Beast*, launched in October 2008, was barely two years old when the merger was announced in November 2010. But the people behind the Webzine could hardly be called upstarts. IAC/Inter ActiveCorp, the parent company of the *Daily Beast*, was chaired by Barry Diller, an experienced mass-media executive whose accomplishments include launching two national television networks (Fox and USA).

Tina Brown, a founding partner of the *Daily Beast*, also had considerable media experience. After filling similar positions of authority at *Vanity Fair* and the *New Yorker*, she earned a reputation for rejuvenating established magazines. Her exploits in the magazine industry resulted in her being named editor in chief of both *Newsweek* and the *Daily Beast* after the merger. In this merging (and converging) of traditional print and emergent digital newsmagazines, Brown had expected to forge an inventive and profitable new model: "I see *Newsweek* and the *Beast* as a marriage between *Newsweek*'s journalistic depth and the vibrant versatility the *Daily Beast* has realized on the Web. . . . The two entities together offer writers, photographers and marketers a powerful dual platform."[1]

In her capacity as editor in chief, Brown was responsible for perhaps the most controversial magazine cover of 2011: an unflattering photo of presidential

candidate Michele Bachmann, attracting Web-like attention to a newsweekly at a time when so much media attention was devoted elsewhere. Unfortunately, despite high expectations, the *Daily Beast* seemed unable to lend its momentum to the print publication, at least in part because *Newsweek* failed to integrate its more traditional editorial content with the pace and relevance of the Webzine's. In October 2012, Tina Brown announced that after nearly eighty years of print publication, *Newsweek* would transition into a digital newsmagazine by the year's end.*

Though the merger failed, a key idea behind it has since proven successful online: linking the power of news aggregators with the solid reporting of traditional news outlets, as practiced by such Webzines as the *Huffington Post*, *Buzzfeed*, *Media Bistro*, and others.

*Source: Christine Haughney and David Carr, "At Newsweek, Ending Print and a Blend of Two Styles," Media Decoder, nytimes.com, October 18, 2012, http://mediadecoder.blogs.nytimes.com/2012/10/18/newsweek-will-cease-print-publication-at-end-of-year/.

As more publications migrate over to digital and mobile platforms, these partnerships have become more important than ever, as have the brand identities of magazines themselves. With so many magazines appearing in a variety of formats, publishers want to create the sense that names like ESPN, *Cosmopolitan*, or *Entertainment Weekly* can be trusted all across the media landscape.

The Economics of Magazines

Whatever their circulation size, specialty, or format (print or online), magazines must bring in money (for example, from advertising revenues and subscription fees) to fulfill their mission and compete with other media. For instance, to combat loss of ad dollars to TV, many magazines publish special editions that guarantee advertisers access to their target markets. These competitive strategies fueled the massive growth of magazines despite competition from television, but now magazines face new challenges from Web sites, blogs, and social media, all competing for audiences and ad dollars. Magazines must also invest money to carry out the business processes essential to their operations—such as content development, production, sales and marketing, and distribution. To extend their reach, lower their costs, and beef up their budgets, many magazines have merged into large chains, often backed financially by major media conglomerates. Even large chains, however, are not immune to the economic reality that many well-known magazine titles continue to cease production entirely.

Money In

Magazine publishers make money through two primary means: advertisers and newsstand/subscription sales.

Advertising

Consumer magazines rely heavily on advertising revenue. The more successful the magazine (that is, the higher its circulation), the more it can charge for ad space. A top-rated consumer magazine might charge as much as $320,000 for a full-page color ad and $89,000 for a one-third-page, black-and-white ad. The average magazine contains about 50 percent ad copy and 50 percent editorial content, a ratio that has remained fairly constant for the past twenty-five years.

In some cases, advertisers can strongly influence editorial content. For example, some companies have canceled their ads after a magazine printed articles that were unflattering toward or critical of the firm or its industry.[4] For editors, the specter of a major advertiser bringing its business elsewhere can present a dilemma: Should the magazine shift its editorial point of view to avoid offending advertisers and thus retain much-needed ad revenues? Or should it continue publishing the same types of articles, hoping that if some advertisers are driven away, others that agree with the magazine's viewpoint will come in and take their place?

In addition to grappling with this dilemma, magazines have developed innovative strategies for retaining advertisers. For instance, as television stations began generating more national ad revenues in the 1950s, magazines started introducing different editions to guarantee advertisers a specific audience—and thus win them back. There are several types of special editions:

- **Regional editions** are national magazines whose content is tailored to the interests of different geographic areas. For example, *Sports Illustrated* often prints five different regional versions of its College Football Preview and March Madness Preview editions, picturing a different local star on each of the five covers.
- In **split-run editions**, the editorial content remains the same, but the magazine includes a few pages of ads purchased by local or regional companies. Most editions of *Time*, *Newsweek*, and *Sports Illustrated*, for instance, contain a number of pages reserved for regional ads.
- **Demographic editions** target particular groups of consumers. In this case, market researchers identify subscribers primarily by occupation, class, and zip code. *Time* magazine, for example, developed special editions of its magazine for top management, high-income zip-code areas, and ultrahigh-income professional/managerial households.

Newsstand and Subscription Sales

Magazines also make money from single-copy sales at newsstands and from subscription sales. (Some online magazines charge a subscription fee in addition to making money from advertisers.) Toward the end of the general-interest magazine era in 1950, newsstand sales accounted for about 43 percent of magazine sales, and subscriptions constituted 57 percent. Today, newsstand sales have fallen to 12 percent, while subscriptions' contribution to sales has risen to 88 percent.

One tactic used by magazine circulation departments to increase subscription sales is to encourage consumers to renew well in advance of the date by which their subscription is set to expire. Another strategy is the **evergreen subscription**—which is automatically renewed on a credit card unless subscribers request that the automatic renewal be stopped.

Controlled circulations can boost revenue from ad sales. Here's how it works: A business or other type of organization (such as an airline or a professional association) sponsors the magazine, and the published issues are given free to readers (such as airline passengers or members of the professional associations). Advertisers are often interested in buying ad space in such magazines, attracted by the captive audiences.

Money Out

To operate, magazines must spend money on resources essential to their business, such as development of content (including staff writers' salaries and freelance writers' fees), desktop-publishing technology needed for designing and laying out each issue, production (which includes paper and printing costs for print versions of magazines and IT-related costs for online-only periodicals), sales and marketing, and distribution (including postage for printed periodicals).

Content Development

The lifeblood of any magazine is the *editorial department*, which produces the periodical's content, excluding advertisements. Like newspapers, most magazines have a chain of command that begins with a publisher and extends down to the editor in chief, the managing editor, and a variety of subeditors. These subeditors oversee such editorial functions as photography, illustrations, reporting and writing, and copyediting. Magazine writers generally include contributing staff writers, who are specialists in certain fields, and *freelance writers*, self-employed professionals assigned to cover particular stories or regions. Many magazines, especially those with small budgets, also accept unsolicited articles from freelancers to fill their pages—often paying the writers a flat fee or an honorarium in return for their work.

Production

A magazine's *production and technology department* maintains the computer hardware and software necessary to design each issue of the magazine (that is, to select typefaces and styles) and to lay out the issue (place the text and graphics together on each page spread). Staff or freelance subeditors specializing in design and layout are often assigned to these tasks.

Ms. magazine, founded in 1972 as the first magazine to take the feminist movement seriously, made another bold move when it stopped carrying advertisements in 1990 (except for ads from nonprofit and cause-related organizations). Unfortunately, while that choice has allowed the magazine to publish more thought-provoking articles, it has led to continued financial instability.

A small newsletter or magazine can be launched quite cheaply with the use of computer-based **desktop publishing**, which enables an aspiring publisher/editor to write, design, lay out, and print the publication or post it online. Yet despite the rise of inexpensive desktop publishing, most large commercial magazines still operate several departments, which employ hundreds of people.

Production costs also include paper and printing for those magazines published in print format. Because such magazines are on a weekly, monthly, or bimonthly publication cycle, instead of daily, it is not economically practical for their publishers to maintain expensive print facilities. Instead, many national magazines digitally transport files containing their print-ready issues to regional printing sites for the insertion of local ads and for faster distribution.

Sales and Marketing

Magazine publishers must also maintain a sales force and a marketing staff to focus on increasing subscriptions and attracting more advertisers. These professionals' responsibilities might include gathering and analyzing subscriber data to see who's renewing their subscriptions (and why) and who's letting their subscriptions lapse (and why), as well as designing marketing campaigns to attract new readers.

Distribution

Magazines also have to spend money on distribution. This function includes maintenance of subscriber mailing lists, postage for shipping published issues of print-version magazines to subscribers, and possibly fees for displaying and selling published issues through newsstands or at supermarket checkout lines. This is an area where online versions of magazines have an advantage, although hosting, maintaining, and promoting an online magazine introduces its own set of new distribution challenges (see "Converging Media Case Study: Print, Web, and Synergy" on page 114).

Major Magazine Chains

To survive in an increasingly competitive marketplace, many magazines have merged into large, powerful chains often backed by deep-pocketed media conglomerates. This strategy provides

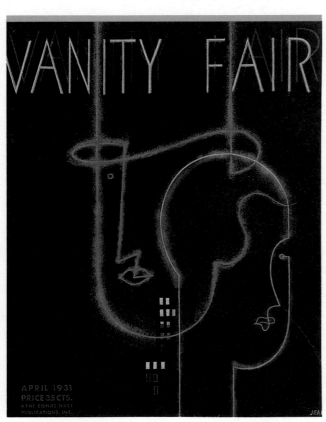

Originally launched in the United States in 1914 by Condé Nast, *Vanity Fair* featured top writers such as Dorothy Parker and P. G. Wodehouse. Known for its mix of social and political commentary, celebrity profiles, fiction, and arts coverage, *Vanity Fair* today includes contributions by noted photographer Annie Leibovitz and writers James Wolcott and Bethany McLean.

more funding for magazines and enables them to lower their costs; for example, by centralizing basic functions such as content development or production.

In the commercial magazine industry, large companies or chains have come to dominate the business. Condé Nast is one example. A division of Advance Publications, which operates the Newhouse newspaper chain, the Condé Nast group controls several upscale consumer magazines, including *Vanity Fair*, *GQ*, and *Vogue*. Time Warner, one of the world's largest media conglomerates, also runs a magazine subsidiary, Time Inc. This top player among magazine-chain operators boasts about thirty major titles, including *People* and *Sports Illustrated* (see Table 4.2 on page 120).

Many large publishers, including the Hearst Corporation, the Meredith Corporation, Time Inc., and Rodale Press, have also generated additional revenue by creating custom-publishing divisions. These divisions produce limited-distribution publications sometimes called **magalogs** for client companies that combine the style of glossy magazines with the sales pitch of retail catalogs. For example, a large, international corporation might pay a publisher to produce a magalog on "how to manage your 401(k)" for its employees.

A number of major magazines (*Reader's Digest*, *Cosmopolitan*, *Newsweek*, and *Time* are good examples) have further boosted revenues by launching international editions in several languages. However, most U.S. magazines are local, regional, or specialized and therefore aren't readily exportable to other countries. Of the approximately twenty thousand magazines now published in the United States, only about two hundred circulate routinely in the world market. Moreover, even the best-known and most-circulated magazines, backed by the largest companies, may not survive in the marketplace. For example, Condé Nast shut down the popular *Gourmet* and *Modern Bride* magazines at the end of 2009, though the *Gourmet* brand name continues to be used for occasional online and print publications.

Magazines in a Democratic Society

In earlier days of the industry, individual magazines had a powerful national voice and united separate communities around important political and social issues such as abolition and suffrage. Muckrackers promoted social reform in the pages of general-interest magazines. Today, with so many specialized magazines appealing to ever-narrower groups of consumers, magazines no longer foster such a strong sense of national identity.

TABLE 4.2 // MAJOR MAGAZINE CHAINS
Selected magazine titles for each major chain.

Advance Publications (Staten Island, N.Y.)

Allure	*Glamour*	*Teen Vogue*
Architectural Digest	*GQ*	*Vanity Fair*
Bon Appétit	*Lucky*	*Vogue*
Brides	*New Yorker*	*W*
Condé Nast Traveler	*Parade*	*Wired*
Details	*Self*	

Hearst Corporation (New York, N.Y.)

Car and Driver	*Good Housekeeping*	*Redbook*
Cosmopolitan	*Harper's Bazaar*	*Road & Track*
Country Living	*House Beautiful*	*Seventeen*
Elle	*Marie Claire*	*Town & Country*
Elle Decor	*O, The Oprah Magazine*	*Woman's Day*
Esquire	*Popular Mechanics*	

Meredith Corporation (Des Moines, Ia.)

American Baby	*Fitness*	*Ready Made*
Better Homes and Gardens	*Ladies' Home Journal*	*Scrapbooks*
Family Circle	*Parents*	*Successful Farming*

Time Inc., A Subsidiary of Time Warner (New York, N.Y.)

Cooking Light	*InStyle*	*Sports Illustrated*
Entertainment Weekly	*Money*	*Sports Illustrated for Kids*
Essence	*People*	*Sunset*
FORTUNE	*Real Simple*	*This Old House*
Health	*Southern Living*	

Source: Advance.net, Hearst.com, meredith.com, TimeInc.com, accessed January 2012.

To be sure, contemporary commercial magazines still provide essential information about politics, society, and culture. Thus they help us to form opinions about the big issues of the day and to make decisions—key activities in any democracy. However, owing to their increasing dependence on advertising revenue, some publications view their readers as consumers first (viewers of displayed products and purchasers of material goods) and citizens second. To keep advertising dollars flowing in, editorial staffs may decide to keep controversial content out of their magazine's pages—which constrains debate and thus hurts the democratic process.

At the same time, magazines have arguably had more freedom than other media to encourage and participate in democratic debate. More magazines circulate in the marketplace than do broadcast or cable television channels. And many new magazines are uniting dispersed groups of readers by, for example, giving cultural minorities or newly arrived immigrants a sense of membership in a broader community.

In addition, because magazines are distributed weekly, monthly, or bimonthly, they are less restricted by deadline pressure than are newspaper publishers and radio and television broadcasters. Journalists writing for magazines can thus take time to offer more rigorous and thoughtful analyses of the topics they cover. The biweekly *Rolling Stone*, for example, often mounts more detailed, comprehensive political pieces than you might find in a daily news source.

Amid today's swirl of images, magazines and their advertisements certainly contribute to the commotion. But good magazines—especially those offering carefully researched, thoughtful, or entertaining articles and photos—have continued to inspire lively discussion among readers. And if they're also well designed, they maintain readers' connection to words—no small feat in today's increasingly image-driven world.

CHAPTER ESSENTIALS

Now that you have finished reading this chapter, you can use the following tools:

REVIEW

Track Main Points of Magazines' Early History

- The first **magazines**—collections of articles, stories, and advertisements published on a nondaily cycle in a smaller tabloid style—were influenced by European newspapers of the seventeenth century. As the eighteenth century unfolded, a rising middle class, increased literacy, and advancements in printing technology helped magazines spread to America, where colonial leaders and thinkers used the medium to discuss important issues of the day (pp. 97–98).

- Due to even greater increases in literacy and education, faster printing technology, and improvements in mail delivery, the demand for national (as opposed to local) magazines soared in the twentieth century. The advent of illustration in magazines, such as woodcuts, drawings, and engravings, heightened their appeal to readers. These factors helped move magazines to a mass medium status (pp. 98–100).

Understand Key Events in the Evolution of Modern American Magazines

- As distribution and production costs declined, magazines were able to reach a wider audience, and advertisers began to turn to them to capture consumer attention. The rise in magazine circulation caused the growth of different kinds of newspaper reporting, such as **muckraking**—inspired by an interest in advocating social reform and exposing wrongdoing (pp. 101–102).

- The growth of the middle class created a market for **general-interest magazines**, which covered a wide variety of topics aimed at a broad national audience, such as recent developments in government, medicine, or society. A key aspect of these magazines was **photojournalism**, the use of photographs to augment editorial content. The popularity of these magazines was marked by their high **pass-along readership**, the total number of readers of a single issue. Four of the most notable general-interest magazines of the twentieth century include the *Saturday Evening Post*, *Reader's Digest*, *Time*, and *Life* (pp. 102–103).

- Television's rising popularity put many general-interest magazines out of business in the 1950s. Some magazines fought back by focusing their content on topics not covered by TV programmers and by featuring short articles heavily illustrated with photos. Two early examples include *TV Guide* and *People* (pp. 103, 106–109).

Outline the Many Different Types of Magazines

- General-interest magazines have now given way to highly specialized magazines appealing to narrower audiences and niche markets. Some areas of specialization include men's and women's magazines; entertainment, leisure, and sports magazines; age-specific magazines; elite magazines; minority magazines; and alternative magazines (pp. 107–112).

- Another type of magazine, the **supermarket tabloid**, features bizarre human-interest stories, gruesome murder tales, violent accident accounts, unexplained phenomena stories, and malicious celebrity gossip (p. 112).

- Recently, the Internet has become a place where specialized magazines can extend their reach to target audiences. Some magazines are published in both print and online versions; others have moved to online-only formats. Still others, **webzines**, started up online and have remained there (pp. 113–115).

Explain How Magazines Operate Economically

- Magazine publishers make money through advertisers. As a result, many magazines have developed different editions to target specific audiences and guarantee advertising revenue. For example, **regional editions** are national magazines whose content is tailored to the interests of different geographic areas; **split-run editions** contain the same editorial content, but the magazines have a few pages of ads purchased by local or regional companies; **demographic editions** target particular groups of consumers (pp. 115–116).

- Magazine publishers also take in revenue from newsstand and subscription sales. One subscription strategy, the **evergreen subscription**, automatically renews a consumer's subscription on a credit card unless subscribers request that the automatic renewal be stopped (pp. 116–117).

- Magazine publishers spend money on the development of content, production (such as **desktop publishing**, which enables the publisher/editor to write, design, lay out, and print the publication or post it online), sales and marketing, and distribution (pp. 117–118).

- To survive in an increasingly competitive marketplace, many magazines have merged into large chains often backed by media conglomerates. This strategy provides more funding for magazines and enables them to lower their costs by centralizing basic functions. Many large publishers have also generated revenue by producing limited-distribution publications—**magalogs**—that combine glossy magazines with the sales pitch of retail catalogs (pp. 118–119).

Discuss the Effect of Magazines on Our Democratic Society

- Early magazines had a powerful national voice and united separate communities around significant political and social issues. Magazines provided an important venue for muckrakers in the early 1900s: Reporters investigated social problems, and their stories often led to much-needed reforms (p. 119).

- Today, with so much specialization, magazines no longer foster a strong sense of national identity, though they continue to have a strong influence on society (pp. 120–121).

STUDY QUESTIONS

1. How did magazines become national in scope?
2. What role did magazines play in social reform at the turn of the twentieth century?
3. What triggered the move toward magazine specialization?
4. What are the major magazine chains, and what is their impact on the mass media industry in general?
5. How do magazines serve a democratic society?

MEDIA LITERACY PRACTICE

An ongoing conflict in the magazine industry exists between the desire for editorial independence and the drive for advertising revenue. Investigate the so-called firewall between the editorial and business side by comparing at least two magazines.

DESCRIBE the magazines by charting the placement and kinds of ads that appear in the magazines and the magazines' editorial content, including stories, photographs, and other features.

ANALYZE the information by looking for patterns: How similar are the ads and editorial content in style and subject matter? Are ads placed in proximity to content on related subjects (e.g., sunglasses advertised next to an article on beach vacations)? Are there ads at odds with the content (e.g., cigarette ads in youth-oriented magazines)?

INTERPRET what these patterns mean. Is there a clear firewall between editorial and business content, or do the ads seem to influence magazine content?

EVALUATE your findings and consider whether there can be a desirable balance between ads and editorial content.

ENGAGE with the magazine industry by writing letters to the editors of magazines that seem to shape editorial copy for advertisers or ignore important issues that might offend advertisers.

⊙ ONLINE RESOURCES

Go to **bedfordstmartins.com/mediaessentials** for review quizzes, links, and more.

Visit the site's **VIDEOCENTRAL: MASS COMMUNICATION** section for videos like the ones on pages 108 and 113.

5

Sound Recording and Popular Music

Of all mass media, sound recording has arguably been most immediately transformed by recent technological advances. This transformation both enables and invigorates the lasting popularity of Gregg Gillis—more commonly known as Girl Talk. Gillis in performance resembles a mad scientist on a manic mission to make people dance. He's not a vocalist or rapper, however, nor is he a virtuoso guitarist—and he is adamant about not being labeled a deejay. He is, instead, a master of laptop remixing: of digitally sampling and reassembling bits and pieces of popular songs into something strange and new called a *mashup*. Even at his live shows, the music comes together by triggering samples from a computer. This repurposed music can be incredibly dense and inspires much attention from his fans: in November 2010, Girl Talk released *All Day*, his fifth album, as a free download, and within twenty-four hours, fans had identified and catalogued 373 samples in the new album.[1]

Whether honored as an artist or condemned as a thief, Girl Talk amplifies a list of provocative questions that confront music lovers during the age of digital reproduction: How will we "consume"—or "appropriate," poach, pirate, remix, and mashup—popular recorded music in the future? What role will the Internet, cell phones, iPods, and laptops play in our relationship to recorded music? Who will control the sound recording industry in the years to come, as new competitors like Gregg Gillis step up to challenge the industry leaders? What messages will songwriters, singers, and musicians convey to us through their work? And how will artists profit from their efforts?

THE INVENTION OF SOUND RECORDING TECHNOLOGY transformed our relationship with popular music and made sound recording a mass medium. Before recording, people had one way to listen to music: attend a live performance. With the advent of sound recording, people could also buy recordings and listen to their favorite music wherever and as often as they wanted. As technological advances made it cheaper and easier for everyone to gain access to sound recordings, music began reshaping society and culture. But the recording industry itself has also changed with the times. Consider what happened in the 1950s after TV began capturing a bigger share of Americans' attention and time: Record labels and radio stations—previously adversaries—joined forces to create Top 40 or "hit song" programming to attract more listeners and stimulate music sales. Many years later, the industry was forced to shift again in the face of technology, as the MP3 format made recorded music more accessible (and easier to duplicate) than ever.

In this chapter, we assess the full impact of sound recording and popular music on our lives by:

- examining the early history and evolution of sound recording, including the shift from analog to digital technology and the shifting relationship between record labels and radio stations

- shining a spotlight on the rise of popular music (including jazz, rock, and country) in the United States

- tracing changes in the American popular-music scene, such as rock's move into the mainstream and the proliferation of rock alternatives (including folk and grunge)

- analyzing the economics of the sound recording industry, including how music labels, artists, and other participants make and spend money

- considering sound recording's impact on our democratic society today by exploring questions such as whether the recording industry is broadening participation in democracy or constraining it

The Early History and Evolution of Sound Recording

Early inventors' work helped make sound recording a mass medium and a product that enterprising businesspeople could sell. The product's format changed with additional technology advances (for example, moving from records and tapes to CDs and then to online downloads). Technology also enhanced the product's quality. (For example, many people praised CDs' digital clarity over "scratchy" analog recording.) However, the latest technology—online downloading of music—has drastically reduced sales of CDs and other physical formats, forcing industry players to look for other ways to survive.

From Cylinders to Disks: Sound Recording Becomes a Mass Medium

In the development stage of sound recording, inventors experimented with sound technology. In sound recording's entrepreneurial stage, people sought to make money from the technology. Finally, sound recording reached the mass medium stage when entrepreneurs figured out how to quickly and cheaply produce and distribute many copies of sound recordings.

The Development Stage

In the 1850s, the French printer Edouard-Leon Scott de Martinville conducted the first experiments with sound recording. Using a hog's-hair bristle as a needle, he tied one end to a thin membrane stretched over the narrow part of a funnel. When he spoke into the wide part of the funnel, the membrane vibrated, and the bristle's free end made grooves on a revolving cylinder coated with a thick liquid. Although de Martinville never figured out how to play back the sound, his experiments ushered in the *development stage* of sound recording.

The Entrepreneurial Stage

In 1877, Thomas Edison helped move sound recording into its *entrepreneurial stage* by determining how to play back sound and market the machine to do it. He recorded his own voice by concocting a machine that played foil cylinders, known as the *phonograph* (derived from the Greek terms for "sound" and "writing"). Edison then patented his phonograph in 1878 as a kind of answering machine. In 1886, Chichester Bell and Charles Sumner Tainter patented an improvement on the phonograph, known as the *graphophone*, that played more durable wax cylinders.[2] Both Edison's phonograph and Bell and Tainter's graphophone had only marginal success as a voice-recording office machine. Yet these inventions laid the foundation for others to develop more viable sound recording technologies.

A graphophone and a collection of prerecorded wax cylinders.

The Mass Medium Stage

Adapting ideas from previous inventors, Emile Berliner, a German engineer who had immigrated to America, made sound recording into a *mass medium*. Berliner developed a turntable machine that played flat disks, or "records," made of shellac. He called this device a *gramophone* and patented it in 1887. He also discovered how to mass-produce his records by making a master recording from which many copies could be easily duplicated. In addition, Berliner's records could be stamped in the center with labels indicating song title, performer, and songwriter.

By the early 1900s, record-playing phonographs were widely available for home use. Early record players, known as Victrolas, were mechanical and had to be primed with a crank handle. Electric record players, first available in 1925, gradually replaced Victrolas as more homes were wired for electricity.

Recorded music initially had limited appeal, owing to the loud scratches and pops that interrupted the music, and they contained only three to four minutes of music. However, in the early 1940s, when shellac was needed for World War II munitions, the record industry began manufacturing records made of polyvinyl plastic. The vinyl recordings (called 78s because they turned at seventy-eight revolutions per minute, or rpms) were less noisy and more durable than shellac records. Enthusiastic about these new advantages, people began buying more records.

In 1948, CBS Records introduced the 33⅓-rpm *long-playing record* (LP), which contained about twenty minutes of music on each side. This created a

CHAPTER 5 // TIMELINE

1850s de Martinville
The first experiments in sound recording are conducted using a hog's-hair bristle as a needle; de Martinville can record sound but is unable to play it back.

1877 Phonograph
Edison invents the phonograph by figuring out how to play back sound.

1888 or 1889 Flat Disk
Berliner invents the flat disk and develops the gramophone to play it. The disks are easily mass-produced, and sound recording becomes a mass medium.

1910 Victrolas
Music players enter living rooms as elaborate pieces of furniture, replacing pianos as musical entertainment.

market for multisong albums and classical music, which is written primarily for ballet, opera, ensemble, or symphony and continues to have a significant fan base worldwide. The next year, RCA developed a competing 45-rpm record featuring a quarter-size hole in the middle that made it easy to play the records in jukeboxes. The two new recording configurations could not be played on each other's machines, so a marketing battle erupted. In 1953, CBS and RCA compromised. The LP became the standard for long-playing albums, the 45 became the standard for singles, and record players were designed to accommodate both formats (as well as 78s, for a while).

From Records to Tapes to CDs: Analog Goes Digital

The advent of magnetic **audiotape** and tape players in the 1940s paved the way for major innovations such as cassettes, stereophonic sound, and, most significantly, digital recording. Audiotape's lightweight magnetized strands made possible sound editing and multiple-track mixing, in which instrumentals or vocals could be recorded at one location and later mixed onto a master recording in a studio. This vastly improved studio recordings' quality and boosted sales, though recordings continued to be sold primarily in vinyl format until the late 1970s.

By the mid-1960s, engineers had placed miniaturized (reel-to-reel) audiotape inside small plastic cases and developed portable cassette players. Listeners could now bring recorded music anywhere, which created a market for prerecorded cassettes. Audiotape also permitted "home dubbing," which began eroding record sales.

Some people thought audiotape's portability, superior sound, and recording capabilities would mean the demise of records. However, vinyl's popularity continued, in part thanks to the improved fidelity that came with stereophonic sound. Invented in 1931 by Alan Blumlein, but not put to commercial use until 1958, **stereo** permitted the recording of two separate channels, or tracks, of sound.

1925 Radio Threatens the Sound Recording Industry
"Free" music can be heard over the airwaves.

1940s Audiotape
Developed in Germany, the audiotape enables multitrack recording.

1950s Music Industry
As television threatens radio, radio turns to the music industry for salvation and becomes a marketing arm for the sound recording industry.

1950s Rock and Roll
This new music form challenges class, gender, race, geographic, and religious norms in the United States.

Recording-studio engineers, using audiotape, could now record many instrumental or vocal tracks, which they "mixed down" to two stereo tracks, creating a more natural sound.

The biggest recording advancement came in the 1970s, when electrical engineer Thomas Stockham made the first digital audio recordings on standard computer equipment. In contrast to **analog recording**, which captures the fluctuations of sound waves and stores those signals in a record's grooves or a tape's continuous stream of magnetized particles, **digital recording** translates sound waves into binary on-off pulses and stores that information in sequences of ones and zeros as numerical code. Drawing on this technology, in 1983 Sony and Phillips began selling digitally recorded **compact discs** (CDs), which could be produced more cheaply than vinyl records and even audiocassettes. By 2000, CDs had rendered records and audiocassettes nearly obsolete except among deejays, hip-hop artists (who still used vinyl for scratching and sampling), and some audiophile loyalists (see Figure 5.1).

From CDs to MP3s: Sound Recording in the Internet Age

In 1992, the **MP3** file format was developed as part of a video compression standard. As it turns out, MP3 also enables sound, including music, to be compressed into small, manageable digital files. Combined with the Internet, MP3 revolutionized sound recording. By the mid-1990s, computer users were swapping MP3 music files online. These files could be uploaded and downloaded in a fraction of the time it took to exchange noncompressed music. And the files used up less memory.

In 1999, Napster's now infamous free file-sharing service brought MP3 to popular attention. By then, music files were widely available on the Internet—some for sale, some available legally for free downloading, and many traded in

VideoCentral ◉
bedfordstmartins.com /mediaessentials

....
Recording Music Today
Composer Scott Dugdale discusses technological innovations in music recording.
Discussion: What surprised you the most about the way a song was produced, as was shown in the video?

CHAPTER 5 // TIMELINE continued

1953 A Sound Recording Standard
This is established at 33⅓ rpm for long-playing albums (LPs), 45 rpm for two-sided singles.

1960s Cassettes
This new format makes music portable.

1970s Hip-Hop
This musical art form emerges.

1983 CDs
The first format to incorporate digital technology hits the market.

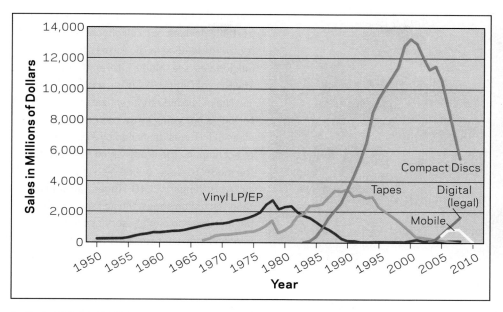

Source: Recording
Industry Association of
America, 2010 year-end
statistics.

Note: "Digital" includes
singles, albums, music videos, and kiosk sales.
Cassette tapes fell under
$1 million in sales in 2008.

**FIGURE 5.1 //
ANNUAL VINYL,
TAPE, CD,
MOBILE, AND
DIGITAL SALES**

violation of copyright laws. Losing countless music sales to free downloading, the music industry initiated lawsuits against file-sharing companies and individual downloaders.

In 2001, the U.S. Supreme Court ruled in favor of the music industry and against Napster—declaring free music file-swapping illegal because it violated music copyrights held by recording labels and artists. Yet even today, illegal swapping continues at a high level—in part because of how difficult it is to police the decentralized Internet. Music MP3s (some acquired legally, some not) are now played on

2000 MP3
A new format compressing music into digital files shakes up the industry as millions of Internet users share music files on Napster.

2001 File-Sharing
A host of new peer-to-peer Internet services make music file-sharing more popular than ever.

2008 Online Music Stores
Apple's iTunes becomes the No. 1 retailer of music in the United States.

Apple's iPod, the leading portable music and video player, began a revolution in digital music.

computers, home stereo systems, car stereos, portable devices, and cell phones. In fact, MP3 is now the leading music format. (For more on music sales, see "Media Literacy Case Study: The Rise of Digital Music" on pages 136–137.)

The music industry, realizing that the MP3 format is not going away, has embraced services like iTunes (launched by Apple in 2003 to accompany the iPod), which has become the model for legal online distribution of music. As of January 2010, iTunes had sold more than ten billion songs. Music fans have also begun to use streaming services like Spotify, Grooveshark, Last.fm, and Pandora, which cross a playlist-like aesthetic with elements of classic radio.

Records and Radio: A Rocky Relationship

We can't discuss the development of sound recording without also discussing radio (covered in detail in Chapter 6). Though each industry developed independently of the other, radio constituted recorded sound's first rival for listeners' attention. This competition triggered innovations in sound recording technology *and* in the business relationship between the two industries.

It all started in the 1920s when, to the recording industry's alarm, radio stations began broadcasting recorded music—without compensating the music industry. The American Society of Composers, Authors, and Publishers (ASCAP), founded in 1914 to collect copyright fees for music publishers and writers, accused radio of hurting sales of records and sheet music. By 1925, ASCAP established music-rights fees for radio, charging stations between $250 and $2,500 a week to play recorded music. Many stations couldn't afford these fees and had to leave the air. Other stations countered by establishing their own live, in-house orchestras, disseminating music free to listeners. Throughout the late 1920s and 1930s, record sales continued plummeting as the Great Depression worsened.

In the early 1950s, as television became popular, it began pilfering radio's programs, its advertising revenue, and its audience. Seeking to reinvent itself, radio turned to the record industry. Brokering a deal that gave radio a cheap source of content and record companies greater profits, many radio stations adopted a new "hit songs" or Top 40 format, named for the number of records that a jukebox could store. Now when radio stations aired songs, record sales soared.

In the early 2000s, though, the radio and recorded-music industries were in conflict again. Upset by online radio stations' decision to stream music on the Internet, the recording industry began pushing for high royalty charges, hindering the development of Internet radio. The most popular online streaming services have developed separately from the traditional radio stations.

U.S. Popular Music and the Rise of Rock

As sound recording became a mass medium, it fueled the growth of popular or **pop music**, which appeals to large segments of the population or sizable groups distinguished by age, region, or ethnic background. Pop music today includes numerous genres—rock and roll, jazz, blues, country, Tejano, salsa, reggae, punk, hip-hop, and dance—many of which evolved from a common foundation. For example, rock splintered off from blues (which originated in the American South), and hip-hop grew out of R&B, dance music, and rock. This proliferation of music genres created a broad range of products that industry players could package and sell—targeted to increasingly narrow listener groups.

Among these genres, rock turned out to exert a major influence on American society, culture, and even politics. For instance, it infused southern culture into the North and challenged cultural constraints on sexuality. It also blurred racial lines, as many of the blues artists who helped create the music that evolved into rock were black. But this blurring and shifting of boundaries also came through the fans—the many black and white young listeners who shared a passion for the new music.

The Rise of Pop Music

Though technological advancements made sound recording a mass medium and sparked the proliferation of pop music genres, this music had its earliest roots in something far less technical: sheet music. With mass production of sheet music in the nineteenth and early twentieth centuries, pop developed into a business fed by artists who set standards for the different genres—including jazz, rock, blues, and R&B.

Back in the late nineteenth century, a section of Broadway in Manhattan known as Tin Pan Alley began selling sheet music for piano and other instruments. (The name Tin Pan Alley referred to the way these quickly produced tunes supposedly sounded like cheap pans clanging together.) Songwriting along Tin Pan Alley

MEDIA LITERACY
Case Study

The Rise of Digital Music
By John Dougan

It is a success story that could have only happened in the hyperspeed of the digital age. Since its debut in April 2003, iTunes has gone from an intriguing concept to the number-one music retailer (surpassing retail giant Walmart) in the United States. Boasting a customer base of fifty million, a library of six million songs, and sales in excess of ten billion dollars, iTunes has conclusively proven that consumers, irrespective of age, have readily and happily adapted to downloading, preferring it to purchasing CDs. Frustrated by escalating CD prices and convinced that most releases contained only a few good songs and too much filler—not to mention the physical clutter created by CDs—many consumers have begun to shop on digital music sites, which offer them an à la carte menu where they can cherry-pick their favorite tracks and build a music library that is easily stored on a hard drive, transferable to an MP3 player, and, increasingly, accessible from other computers or devices via a cloud drive —a third-party server that stores files outside of personal devices.

The move toward digital music has also forever altered the way music fans locate and access nonmainstream music and recordings by unsigned bands. If iTunes resembles a traditional retailer with a deep catalogue, then a competitor such as eMusic is the online equivalent of a specialty record store, designed for connoisseurs who are uninterested in mass-marketed pop. The success of social-networking sites and music blogs has made them important gathering places for virtual communities of fans for thousands of bands in dozens of genres. The Internet is changing not only how consumers are exposed to music, but how record

label A&R (artist & repertoire) departments scout talent. A&R reps, who no longer travel as much to locate talent, are searching for acts who do their own marketing and come with a built-in fan following.

The digital age has also made the album-length CD increasingly obsolete. While digital downloading allows consumers greater and more immediate access to music, aesthetically it harkens back to the late 1950s and early 1960s when the 45-rpm single was dominant and the most reliable indicator of whether a song was a hit. Downloading a variety of tracks means that consumers build their own collection of virtual 45s that, when taken as a whole, becomes a personalized greatest-hits collection. Some artists imagine a future where they no longer release full albums but rather a series of individual tracks that consumers can piece together however they please.

But if the death knell has been sounded for the compact disc, what of the digital download? In 2010, there were those who claimed that, after only seven years, iTunes was showing its age and would face a stiff challenge from Google's Android mobile operating system at some point. With Android, users are able to purchase music from any computer and have the files appear instantly on their phones. Users are able to send the music on their hard drive to the Internet, so they can access it on their phone as long as they have an Internet connection—a cloud drive that detaches music from a personal, physical device. However, in 2011 Apple developed a Web-based iTunes (iTunes in the Cloud) and went further with iTunes Match, which allows users to upload all their music (even if not purchased through iTunes) to the cloud and play it on all their devices. Perhaps, then, the future means accessing music from anywhere at any time.

John Dougan is an associate professor in the Department of the Recording Industry at Middle Tennessee State University.

APPLYING THE CRITICAL PROCESS

DESCRIPTION Arrange to interview four to eight friends or relatives about how they purchase music today. Where do they buy most of their music—online through sites like iTunes, or in a retail store? When is the last time they bought a CD from a retail store? Devise questions about what makes them decide where to purchase music.

ANALYSIS Chart and organize your results. Do you recognize any patterns emerging from the data? What influences your friends' purchasing behaviors? Have their actions changed over time?

INTERPRETATION Based on the patterns you have charted, determine what they mean. Over time, have the changes in buying been significant? Why or why not? Why do you think people's buying preferences developed as they did?

EVALUATION Do you think the influences of MP3 and other new digital technology forms help or hurt musical artists? Why do so many contemporary musical performers differ in their opinions about the Internet?

ENGAGEMENT To expand on your findings and see how they match up with industry findings, go to your local retail store and speak with a customer service representative about what the buying patterns are in their store. Have they noticed a shift in retail buying in the last five years? Share your findings with them and discuss whether your data matches theirs. Speculate about ways retail stores can survive against the digital community.

Louis Armstrong (1901–1971) transformed jazz with astonishing improvised trumpet solos and scat singing.

helped transform pop music into big business. At the turn of the twentieth century, improvements in printing technology enabled song publishers to mass-produce sheet music for a growing middle class. Previously a novelty, popular music now became a major enterprise. With the emergence of the phonograph and recorded tunes, interest in and sales of sheet music soared. (Eventually, these sales would decline with the rise of radio in the 1920s, making audiences more into listeners in their music habits rather than active participants who were playing instruments from sheet music in their living rooms.)

As sheet music gained popularity and phonograph sales rose, **jazz** developed in New Orleans. An improvisational and mostly instrumental musical form, jazz absorbed and integrated a diverse array of musical styles, including African rhythms, blues, and gospel. Groups led by Louis Armstrong, Tommy Dorsey, and others counted among the most renowned of the "swing" jazz bands, whose rhythmic sound also dominated radio, recording, and dance halls.

The first pop vocalists of the twentieth century came out of vaudeville—stage performances featuring dancing, singing, comedy, and magic shows. By the 1930s, Rudy Vallée and Bing Crosby had established themselves as the first "crooners" singing pop standards. Bing Crosby also popularized Irving Berlin's "White Christmas," which became one of the most covered songs in recording history. (A song recorded or performed by another artist is known as **cover music**.) Meanwhile, the bluesy harmonies of a New Orleans vocal trio, the Boswell Sisters, influenced the Andrews Sisters, whose boogie-woogie style sold more than sixty million records in the late 1930s and 1940s. Helped by radio, pop vocalists like Frank Sinatra in the 1940s were among the first singers to win the hearts of a large national teen audience. Indeed, Sinatra's early performances incited the kinds of audience riots that would later characterize rock-and-roll concerts.

Rock and Roll Is Here to Stay

Pop music's expanding appeal paved the way for **rock and roll** to emerge in the mid-1950s. Rock both reflected and shaped powerful societal forces (such as blacks' migration from South to North and the growth of youth culture) that had begun transforming American life. Rock also stirred controversy. Like the word *jazz*, the phrase *rock and roll* was a blues slang expression meaning sex—which offended some people with more conservative tastes in music and worried them about what their children were listening to. Finally, rock grew out of a blending of numerous different music styles. For instance, early rock combined the vocal and instrumental traditions of pop with the rhythm-and-blues sounds of Memphis and the country twang of Nashville.

Blues and R&B Set the Stage for Rock

The migration of southern blacks to northern cities in search of better jobs during the first half of the twentieth century had helped disseminate different popular music styles to new places. In particular, **blues** music traveled north. Blues became the foundation of rock and roll and was influenced by African American spirituals, ballads, and work songs from the rural South.

Influential blues artists included Robert Johnson, Ma Rainey, Bessie Smith, Muddy Waters, Howlin' Wolf, and Charley Patton. After the introduction of the electric guitar in the 1930s, blues-based urban black music began to be marketed under the name **rhythm and blues (R&B)**. This new music appealed to young listeners fascinated by the explicit (and forbidden) sexual lyrics in songs like "Annie Had a Baby," "Sexy Ways," and "Wild Wild Young Men." Although banned on some stations, R&B continued gaining popularity into the early 1950s. Still, black and white musical forms were segregated, and trade magazines in the 1950s tracked R&B record sales on "race" charts separate from the white "pop" charts.

Young People Flock to Rock

Young people embraced rock and roll, further helping to secure this pop-music genre's place in American society and eventually around the world. The popularity of rock stemmed in part from the repressive and uneasy atmosphere of the 1950s. To cope with the backdrop and uncertainty of the atomic bomb, the Cold War, and communist witch hunts, young people sought escape from the menacing world created by adults. Rock's driving beat and danceable quality offered distraction and a cultural form that young people could call their own.

Black and White Come Together through Rock

A blending of white and black cultures, arising from key social and political events, also fueled rock's popularity. By the early 1950s, President Truman's 1948 executive order integrating the armed forces was fully in practice, bringing young men from very different ethnic and economic backgrounds together. Then, in 1954, the Supreme Court's *Brown v. Board of Education* decision declared unconstitutional the "separate but equal" laws that had segregated blacks and whites for decades. Mainstream America began to wrestle seriously with the legacy of slavery and the unequal treatment of its African American citizens. As both blacks and whites embraced rock and roll, their shared experience began chipping away at the wall of racial division that had long characterized the nation.

Rock Blurs Additional Boundaries

While rock and roll was molded by powerful social, cultural, and political forces, it also shaped them in return. As we've seen, it began blurring the boundaries between black and white. But it broke down additional divisions as well—between high and low culture, masculinity and femininity, country and city, North and South, and the sacred and the secular.

High and Low Culture

Rock challenged the long-standing distinction between high and low culture initially through its lyrics and later through its performance styles. In 1956, Chuck Berry's song "Roll Over Beethoven" merged rock and roll (which many people considered low culture) with high culture through lyrics that included references to classical music: "You know my temperature's risin' / the jukebox is blowin' a fuse.... Roll over Beethoven / and tell Tchaikovsky the news." Rock artists also defied norms governing how musicians should behave: Berry's "duck walk" across the stage, Elvis Presley's tight pants and gyrating hips, and Bo Diddley's use of the guitar as a phallic symbol shocked elite audiences—and inspired additional antics by subsequent artists.

Masculinity and Femininity

Rock and roll was also the first pop-music genre to overtly challenge assumptions about sexual identity and orientation. Although early rock and roll largely attracted males as performers, the most fascinating feature of Elvis Presley, according to the Rolling Stones' Mick Jagger, was his androgynous appearance.[3] Little Richard (Penniman) took things even further, sporting a pompadour hairdo, decorative makeup, and feminized costumes during his performances.[4]

Country and City

Rock and roll also blended cultural borders between black urban rhythms and white country & western music. Early white rockers such as Buddy Holly and Carl Perkins combined country or hillbilly music, southern gospel, and Mississippi delta blues to create a sound called **rockabilly**. Conversely, rhythm and blues spilled into rock and roll. Many songs such as "Rocket 88," first popular on R&B labels, crossed over to the pop charts during the mid to late 1950s, though many of these songs were performed by more widely known white artists.

Rock lyrics in the 1950s may not have been especially provocative or overtly political by today's standards. But soaring record sales and the crossover appeal of the music itself represented an enormous threat to long-standing racial and class divisions defined by geography. Distinctions between traditionally rural white music and urban black music dissolved, as some black artists (like Chuck Berry) strived to "sound white" to attract Caucasian fans, and some white artists (such as Elvis Presley) were encouraged by record producers to "sound black."

A major influence on early rock and roll, Chuck Berry, born in 1926, scored big hits between 1955 and 1958, writing "Maybellene," "Roll Over Beethoven," "School Day," "Sweet Little Sixteen," and "Johnny B. Goode." At the time, he was criticized by some black R&B artists for sounding white and by some white conservative critics for his popularity among white teenagers. Today, young guitar players routinely imitate his style.

North and South

Not only did rock and roll blur the line between urban and rural, it also mixed northern and southern influences together. As many blacks migrated north during the early twentieth century, they brought their love of blues and R&B with them. Meanwhile, musicians and audiences in the North had claimed blues music as their own, forever extending its reach beyond its origins in the rural South. Some white artists from the South—most notably Carl Perkins, Elvis Presley, and Buddy Holly—further carried southern musical styles to northern listeners.

Sacred and Secular

Many mainstream adults in the 1950s complained that rock and roll's sexual overtones and gender-bending constituted an offense against God—even though numerous early rock figures (such as Elvis Presley, Jerry Lee Lewis, and Little Richard) had strong religious upbringings. In the late 1950s, public outrage over rock proved so great that even Little Richard and Jerry Lee Lewis, both sons of southern preachers, became convinced that they were playing the "devil's music." Throughout the rock era and even today, boundaries between the sacred and secular continue to blur through music. For example, some churches are using rock and roll to appeal to youth, and some Christian-themed rock groups are recording in seemingly incongruous musical styles, such as heavy metal.

Although his unofficial title, "King of Rock and Roll," has been challenged by Little Richard and Chuck Berry, Elvis Presley remains among the most popular solo artists of all time. From 1956 to 1962, he recorded seventeen No. 1 hits, from "Heartbreak Hotel" to "Good Luck Charm."

Rock and Roll Embattled

Rock's blurring of racial and other lines alarmed enough Americans that performers and producers alike worried that fans would begin defecting. They used various tactics to get people to accept the music. Cleveland deejay Alan Freed played original R&B recordings from the race charts and black versions of early rock on his program, while Philadelphia deejay Dick Clark took a different tactic—playing white artists' cover versions of black music. Still, problems persisted that further eroded rock's acceptance. These included black artists' frustration with being undermined by white cover music, payola scandals signaling corruption in the industry, and censorship by officials convinced that rock turned wholesome young people into juvenile delinquents.

White Cover Music Undermines Black Artists

Despite rock's ability to blend black and white culture and musical styles, racial tensions continued to simmer in the rock-music industry. These tensions developed in part from white musicians' covering black artists' work to capitalize on successful songs from the R&B race charts and transform them into hits on the white pop charts. Often, white producers would give cowriting credit to white performers like Elvis Presley (who never wrote songs himself) for the tunes they covered. Many producers also bought the rights to potential hits from black songwriters, who seldom saw a penny in royalties or received songwriting credit.

By 1955, R&B hits regularly crossed over to the pop charts, but for a time the white cover versions were more popular and profitable. For example, Pat Boone's cover of Fats Domino's "Ain't That a Shame" shot to No. 1 and stayed on the Top 40's pop chart for twenty weeks. Domino's original made it only to No. 10. A turning point, however, came in 1962, when Ray Charles covered "I Can't Stop Loving You," a 1958 country song by the Grand Old Opry's Don Gibson. This marked the first time that a black artist, covering a white artist's song, had notched a No. 1 pop hit.

Fear of Delinquents Fuels Censorship

One particularly difficult battle rock faced was the perception among mainstream adults that the music caused juvenile delinquency. Such delinquency was statistically on the rise in the 1950s, owing to contributing factors such as parental neglect, the rising consumer culture, and the burgeoning youth population after World War II. But adults sought an easier culprit to blame. It was far simpler to point the finger at rock—especially artists who blatantly defied rules governing proper behavior. Authorities responded by censoring rock lyrics.

Rattled by this and other developments, the U.S. recording industry decided it needed a makeover. To protect the enormous profits the new music had been generating, record companies began practicing some censorship of their own. In the early 1960s, the industry introduced a new generation of clean-cut white singers, including Frankie Avalon, Connie Francis, Ricky Nelson, Lesley Gore, and Fabian. Rock's explosive violations of racial, class, and other boundaries gave way to simpler generation-gap problems, and the music—for a time—developed a milder reputation.

With 1950s hits like "I've Got a Woman," "Hallelujah, I Love Her So," and "What'd I Say," Ray Charles (1930–2004) merged the sounds of rhythm and blues, gospel, country, jazz, and pop.

The Evolution of Pop Music

As the volatile decade of the 1960s unfolded, pop music (including rock) changed to reflect additional social, cultural, and political shifts—while continuing to influence these aspects of American life as well. Authorities made further attempts to "tame" rock, concerned about its influence on teenagers. These attempts sparked resistance from defiant young people, many of whom embraced rock musicians from Great Britain who hadn't

toned down their style. Two British groups in particular—the Beatles and the Rolling Stones—developed such unique and contrasting styles that rock split into distinctive types. Moreover, as pop music adapted to the times, it spun off several additional genres over the next few decades. These included soul, folk, and psychedelic music as well as country, punk, grunge, alternative, and hip-hop.

British rock groups like the Beatles and the Rolling Stones first invaded American pop charts in the 1960s. While the Beatles broke up in 1970, each member went on to work on solo projects. The Stones are still (mostly) together and touring nearly fifty years later.

The British Are Coming!

Rock and roll proved so powerful that it transformed pop music across national borders. For instance, in England during the late 1950s, the young members of the Rolling Stones covered blues songs by American artists Robert Johnson and Muddy Waters. And the young Beatles imitated Chuck Berry and Little Richard.

   Until 1964, rock-and-roll recordings had traveled on a one-way ticket to Europe. Even though American artists regularly reached the tops of charts overseas, no British performers had yet appeared on any Top 10 pop lists in the States. This changed virtually overnight in 1964, when the Beatles came to America with their mop haircuts and delivered pop reinterpretations of American blues and rock. Within the next few years, more British bands—the Kinks, the Who, the Yardbirds—produced hits that climbed the American Top 40 charts. Ed Sullivan, who booked the Beatles several times on his TV variety show in the mid-1960s, helped promote the group's early success.

With the British invasion, the rock industry split into two styles of music. The Rolling Stones developed a style emphasizing gritty, chord-driven, high-volume rock, which would influence bands that later created glam rock, hard rock, punk, heavy metal, and grunge. Meanwhile, the Beatles presented a more accessible, melodic, and softer sound, which would eventually inspire new genres such as pop-rock, power-pop, new wave, and alternative rock. The British groups' success also demonstrated to the recording industry that older American musical forms, especially blues and R&B, could be repackaged as rock and exported around the world.

Motown: The Home of Soul

As rock attracted more and more devotees, it resurrected interest in styles of music from which it had originated. Throughout the 1960s, black singers like James Brown, Aretha Franklin, Wilson Pickett, Otis Redding, and Ike and Tina Turner picked up on this interest—transforming the rhythms and melodies of older R&B, pop, and early rock and roll into what became known as **soul**. These artists attracted large and racially diverse audiences, countering the British invaders with powerful vocal performances.

The most prominent independent label supporting black songwriters' and performers' work was Motown, started in 1959 by former Detroit autoworker and songwriter Berry Gordy. Motown signed many successful black artists and groups, including the Four Tops ("Baby I Need Your Loving"), the Marvelettes ("Please Mr. Postman"), Marvin Gaye ("What's Going On"), and the Jackson 5 ("I'll Be There"). But the label's most successful group was the Supremes, featuring Diana Ross, who scored as many as twelve No. 1 singles between 1964 and 1969 (including "Where Did Our Love Go" and "Stop! In the Name of Love"). The Supremes' success showed Motown producers that songs emphasizing romance and featuring a danceable beat won far more young white fans than those trumpeting rebellion and political upheaval.

One of the most successful groups in rock-and-roll history, the Supremes recorded twelve No. 1 hits between 1964 and 1969, including "Where Did Our Love Go," "Baby Love," "Come See About Me," and "Stop! In the Name of Love." The group was inducted into the Rock and Roll Hall of Fame in 1988.

Folk and Psychedelic: Protest and Drugs

Popular music has always been both a product of and a shaper of its time. So it's not surprising that the social upheavals of the 1960s and early 1970s—over Civil Rights, women's rights, environmental protection, the Vietnam War, and the use of recreational drugs—found their reflections in rock music during these decades. By the late 1960s, many songwriters and performers spoke to their generation's social and political concerns through two music genres: folk and psychedelic rock.

Folk Inspires Protest

The musical genre that most clearly expressed pivotal political events of the time was folk, which had long served as a voice for social activism. **Folk music** exists in all cultures; it's usually performed by untrained musicians and passed down mainly through oral traditions. With its rough edges and amateur quality, folk is considered a democratic and participatory musical form. During the 1930s, the work of Woody Guthrie ("This Land Is Your Land") set a new standard for American folk music. Later, in the 1960s and 1970s, groups such as the Weavers, featuring labor activist and songwriter Pete Seeger, carried on Guthrie's legacy. These newer groups inspired yet another crop of singer-songwriters—Joan Baez; Arlo Guthrie; Peter, Paul, and Mary; Phil Ochs; Bob Dylan—who took a stand against worrisome developments of the day, including industrialization, poverty, racism, and war.

Rock Turns Psychedelic

With the increasing use of recreational drugs by young people and the availability of LSD (not illegal until the mid-1960s), more and more rock musicians experimented with and sang about drugs during rock's *psychedelic* era. Defining groups and performers of this era included newcomers like Jefferson Airplane, Big Brother and the Holding Company (featuring Janis Joplin), the Jimi Hendrix Experience, the Doors, and the Grateful Dead, as well as established artists like the Beatles and the Rolling Stones. These musicians believed they could enhance their artistic prowess by taking mind-altering drugs. They also saw drug-taking as a form of personal expression and an appropriate response to the government's failure to deal with social and political problems such as racism and America's involvement in the Vietnam War.

After a surge of optimism that culminated in the historic Woodstock concert in August 1969, the sun set on the psychedelic era. In particular, some of psychedelic rock's greatest stars died from drug overdoses, including Janis Joplin, Jimi Hendrix, and Jim Morrison of the Doors.

Punk, Grunge, and Alternative Rock: New Genres on the Horizon

As rock and roll moved from the edges of the American music scene into the mainstream, other genres arose to take its place on the fringes. While many people had

Born Robert Allen Zimmerman in Minnesota, Bob Dylan took his stage name from Welsh poet Dylan Thomas. He led a folk music movement in the early 1960s with engaging, socially provocative lyrics, but later infused folk with the electric sounds of rock.

considered rock a major part of the rebel counterculture in the 1960s, in the 1970s they increasingly viewed it as part of consumer culture. With major music acts earning huge profits, rock had become just another product for manufacturers and retailers to promote, package, and profit from. According to critic Ken Tucker, this situation produced "faceless rock" performed by bands with "no established individual personalities outside their own large but essentially discrete audiences" of young white males.[5] These "faceless" groups—REO Speedwagon, Styx, Boston, Journey, Kansas—filled stadiums and entertained the maximum number of people while stirring the minimum amount of controversy. It was only a matter of time before new types of music—punk, grunge, and alternative rock—arose to challenge rock's mainstream once more. Concurrently, an older genre, country music, rose to greater prominence, crossing over to gain more mainstream acceptance.

Punk Revives Rock's Rebellious Spirit

Punk rock arose in the late 1970s to defy the orthodoxy and commercialism of the record business. Punk attempted to revive rock's basic defining characteristics: simple chord structures that anyone with a few guitar lessons could master, catchy melodies, and politically or socially defiant lyrics. Emerging in New York City around bands such as the Ramones, Blondie, and Talking Heads, punk quickly spread to England, where a soaring unemployment rate and growing class inequality ensured the success of socially critical rock. Groups like the Sex Pistols, the Clash, the Buzzcocks, and Siouxsie and the Banshees sprang up and even scored Top 40 hits on the U.K. charts. Despite their popularity, the Sex Pistols, one of the most controversial groups in rock history, was eventually banned for offending British decorum.

Punk didn't succeed commercially in the United States, in part because it was so hostile toward the commercialization of the mainstream music industry. However, it did help to break down the "boys' club" mentality of rock, launching unapologetic and unadorned front women like Patti Smith, Joan Jett, Debbie Harry, and Chrissie Hynde. It also introduced all-women bands whose members not only wrote but also performed their own music. Many of these female groups made it into the mainstream. Through these and other innovations, punk reopened the door to experimentation at a time when the industry had turned music into a purely commercial enterprise.

Joan Jett, of the punk-rock group the Runaways and later Joan Jett and the Blackhearts, was influential in breaking down the boys' club mentality of rock and roll.

Grunge and Alternative Reinterpret Rock

Building on the innovative spirit of punk, the **grunge** genre further transformed rock in the 1990s. Grunge got its name from its often messy guitar sound and the torn jeans and flannel shirts worn by its musicians and fans. Its lineage traced back to 1980s bands like Sonic Youth, the Minutemen, and Hüsker Dü. In 1992, after years of limited commercial success, this younger cousin of punk finally broke into the American mainstream with the success of Nirvana's "Smells Like Teen Spirit," the hit single from their album *Nevermind*.

Some critics view punk and grunge as subcategories or fringe movements of **alternative rock**, even though grunge was far more commercially successful than punk. This vague label encompasses many types of experimental rock music that offered departures from the staged extravaganzas of 1970s glam rock. Such music appealed chiefly to college students and twenty-somethings and set itself apart from the sounds of Top 40 and commercial FM radio. The same is true of **indie rock**, a broad category of independent-minded rock music, usually distributed by smaller record labels; this genre can also be traced to 1980s punk and post-punk acts, and has achieved greater commercial success in recent years.

Nirvana's lead singer, Kurt Cobain, during his brief career in the early 1990s. The release of Nirvana's *Nevermind* in September 1991 bumped Michael Jackson's *Dangerous* from the top of the charts and signaled a new direction in popular music. Other grunge bands soon followed Nirvana on the charts, including Pearl Jam, Alice in Chains, Stone Temple Pilots, and Soundgarden.

Hip-Hop Redraws Musical Lines

Hip-hop was another genre demonstrating pop music's ability to change with the times and move from the edge of the music scene into the mainstream. Just as punk arose to challenge commercial rock, **hip-hop** emerged to defy the polished, professional, and often unpoliticized world of soul. By the 1980s, the pop-music scene was dominated by "safe" dance disco performed by white bands (such as the Bee Gees), black artists (including Donna Summer), and integrated groups (for example, the Village People). This left a vacuum for a new sound.

Hip-hop drew on features of urban culture including *rapping*, *cutting* (or music *sampling*) by deejays, break dancing, street clothing, poetry slams, and graffiti art. Initially, the music industry saw it as a novelty destined to go nowhere. But by 1985, hip-hop had become a popular genre with the commercial successes of groups and artists like Run-DMC, the Fat Boys, LL Cool J, and Queen Latifah. Soon, white groups like the Beastie Boys, Limp Bizkit, and Kid Rock were combining hip-hop and hard rock, and some white artists (such as Eminem) attracted huge followings by emulating black rap artists.

Artists like Kanye West (*left*) and Nicki Minaj (*right*) have found a place in the world of hip-hop. Kanye West, born in Atlanta in 1977, is an American rapper, producer, and singer/songwriter who has received many awards and won critical acclaim for his work, often introducing controversy along the way. Born in Trinidad in 1982, Minaj began her career with mixtapes and guest appearances before releasing her debut album *Pink Friday* featuring the hit single "Super Bars" in 2010.

Although hip-hop encompasses many different styles, its most controversial subgenre is probably **gangster rap**. In seeking to describe gang violence in America, gangster rap has been accused of inciting violence through its lyrics and the illegal activities of some of its performers. Gangster rap drew widespread condemnation in 1996 with the shooting death of Tupac Shakur, a rapper and convicted sex offender. Criticism mounted in 1997 after a drive-by shooter killed the Notorious B.I.G., who had dealt drugs as a youngster before becoming a rapper. Under pressure, the hip-hop industry softened its hard edges. Most prominently, artist Sean "Diddy" Combs developed a more danceable hip-hop that combined singing and rapping with musical elements of rock and soul. Today, hip-hop stars include artists such as 50 Cent, who emulates the gangster drama, and artists like Kanye West, Lupe Fiasco, Drake, and Talib Kweli, who often bring an old-school social consciousness to their performances.

From its origins in an urban American subculture, hip-hop has become a major part of mainstream global culture. Today, it's big business, and its most successful practitioners have diversified from record labels to clothing lines, restaurants, and movie production companies.

The Country Road

Country music has attracted enough loyal listeners in its various forms to survive as a profitable sector of the recording industry since the early days of pop music. Though the many styles of **country** represent significant variations in the development of this musical form, they all share one element: the country voice, inflected by a twang or drawl. In the late 1950s, the wilder honky-tonk sounds of country were tamed by a smoother style inspired by the mellower songs of Elvis Presley. Replacing the fiddles, electric guitars, and nasal vocals of honky-tonk with symphonic

strings, pitch-perfect background vocalists, and croon-
ing stars like Jim Reeves and Patsy Cline, the emergent
style would become known as the "Nashville Sound."
This laid-back and toned-down form of country music
reigned throughout the 1960s.[6] In the 1970s, some
singers and producers aimed for more mainstream
acceptance. Lynn Anderson ("I Never Promised You a
Rose Garden"), Charlie Pride ("Behind Closed Doors"),
and Marie Osmond ("Paper Roses") belted out hits
that made the country idiom well liked in suburban
America.[7] By the late 1970s, this movement had
spawned "pop country," a form dedicated to generating hits that would score on both the pop and country
charts, launching the careers of superstars Glen

Faith Hill became one of
country's most popular stars
in the 1990s.

Campbell, John Denver, and Kenny Rogers. However, the genre would not peak
until the 1990s when "New Country" attracted fresh throngs of fans. In 1989,
Clint Black perfected the New Country sound in his *Killin' Time* album, and in
1992 Billy Ray Cyrus followed up Black's triumph with the massive hit "Achy
Breaky Heart." Shania Twain and Faith Hill went on to sell platinum country
albums in the 1990s—but Garth Brooks would be the star to break sales and
concert attendance records during the decade, establishing a huge country
market for years to come.

The Economics of Sound Recording

Sound recording is a complex business, with many participants playing
many different roles and controlling numerous dimensions of the industry. Songwriters, singers, and musicians create the sounds. Producers
and record labels sign up artists to create music and often own the
artists' work. Promoters market artists' work, managers handle bands'
touring schedules, and agents seek the best royalty deals for their
artist-clients.

   Ever since sound recording became a mass medium, there's been a lot
of money to be had from the industry—primarily through sales of records
and CDs. But with more and more music available for digital download,
the traditional business model has broken down. Control of the industry
became concentrated in the hands of a few giant music labels like Time

CONVERGING MEDIA
Case Study

360 Degrees of Music

As digital innovations change the music industry and major record labels continue to consolidate, artists have begun looking for new ways to establish themselves—or to simply stay afloat. In 2007, the British alternative rock group Radiohead sold its new album *In Rainbows* on the Internet—for whatever price fans wished to pay, including nothing. While many downloaders took the album for free, many others paid. One study estimated that Radiohead made an average of $2.26 on each download. If that's true, it may have raked in more money per recording than the royalties typically earned by an artist on a major label release.[1]

This direct-distribution model sent shock waves through the recording industry. But while Radiohead's self-released album confirmed the band's autonomy, not all artists can afford that degree of independence. As Radiohead themselves have pointed out, it was their preexisting popularity, arguably assisted by their time on a major label, that allowed them their experiment.[2]

As such, many acts still look for support when it comes to increasing their revenue in the face of declining album sales. This search for new methods of distribution and money-making has led to the adoption of a new paradigm for contracting recording artists: the 360-degree deal. Defined by legal scholar Sara Karubian as "a legal contract between a musical artist and one company incorporating components of an artist's career that have traditionally been handled by separate contracts with different companies," the 360-degree deal gives a single corporation control over everything from merchandising and publishing to endorsements and touring.[3] This multiplatform convergence is contractual, turning music distribution companies into publishers, merchandisers, and event bookers.

Such 360-degree deals could give artists a chance to centralize and maximize their revenue at a time when they can no longer depend on album royalties alone. But these deals are not unambiguously good; they could also shift power back to conglomerates at a time when more indie labels have gained traction. As with the decision to sign to a major label, artists will need to decide whether the potential benefits outweigh the risks. Some artists may be content to become "middle-class" touring bands, making a little money off albums and singles but using them primarily to promote their live shows and accompanying merchandise. Media convergence has made this middle-class existence a more viable alternative for many acts that would have, in more label-dominated years, been forced to produce a huge hit or face obscurity.

Other music acts with large enough fan bases may follow Radiohead's lead and handle their career without contracted label backing (though physical CD distribution is usually handled through a third party regardless—while Radiohead self-released their 2011 album *King of Limbs*, it, like *In Rainbows*, was released as a CD via the label TBD Records). In these cases, artists are allowing multiple media to converge into their own hands. Whether through 360-degree deals, middle-class touring careers, or a self-releasing strategy, convergence is changing the way many musicians make money.

Warner, even as independent production houses began cropping up. Then illegal downloading presented a particularly difficult hurdle for the industry. Money comes in today primarily from sources other than CD sales—such as download fees and touring. In fact, North American ticket sales from tours and concerts rose 7 percent from 2007 to 2008, generating $4.2 billion (average ticket price in 2008: $67).[8] In the end, industry players and musical artists must rethink how they're spending money and using their time to remain commercially viable (see "Converging Media Case Study: 360 Degrees of Music" on page 150).

A Shifting Power Structure

Over the years, the U.S. recording industry has experienced dramatic shifts in its power structure. From the 1950s through the 1980s, the industry consisted of numerous competing major labels as well as independent production houses, or **indies**. Over time, the major labels began swallowing up the indies and then buying each other. By 1998, only six big labels remained: Universal, Warner, Sony, BMG, EMI, and Polygram. That year, Universal acquired Polygram; in 2003 BMG and Sony merged; and in late 2011, EMI was auctioned off to Universal. Today, only three major music corporations exist: Sony BMG Music Entertainment, Universal Music Group, and Warner Music Group. Together, these firms control more than 85 percent of the recording industry in the United States. Critics, consumers, and artists alike complain that this consolidation of power in the hands of a few resists new sounds in music that may not have traditional commercial appeal and supports only those major artists and sounds that have large mainstream appeal.

Arcade Fire, signed to independent music label Merge Records, won a Grammy for Album of the Year in 2011. Indie acts have become increasingly prominent as music audiences become more fragmented.

Still, about five thousand U.S. indies (some large, some small) have managed to survive. For example, Fat Wreck Chords, a punk label, and Merge Records, an indie rock label with recent Album of the Year Grammy winners Arcade Fire as well as smaller bands like She & Him, the Mountain Goats, and Spoon, continue to provide outlets for new music and nonmainstream sounds. These companies record less commercially viable music, established older artists now ignored by the major labels, or music they hope will become profitable. Many indies also reissue forgotten artists and record new innovative performers. They thus play a major role as the industry's risk-takers, since major labels are reluctant to invest in forgotten or commercially unproven artists. Producing 12 to 15 percent of America's music in a typical year, indies often ink deals with majors to gain wider distribution for their artists.

Indies tend to struggle financially, and many have turned to the Internet as a tool for lowering their costs. Through personal Web sites and social-networking sites like Facebook and MySpace, indies sell recordings and merchandise, list tour schedules, and provide other promotional information about their company's offerings. Bands that previously would have had no choice but to sign with a major label now have another path to success, thanks to the Internet and other independent alternatives.

Making and Spending Money

Like most mass media, the recorded-music business consists of several components. Money today comes in as revenue earned mostly from sales of CDs and song downloads. It goes out in forms such as royalties paid to artists, production costs, and distribution expenses.

Money In

In the recording industry, the product that generates revenue is the music itself. However, selling in the music business has become more challenging than ever. Revenues for the recording industry started shrinking in 2000 as file-sharing began undercutting CD sales. By 2008, U.S. music sales had fallen to $8.5 billion—down from a peak of $14.5 billion in 1999.[9] CD sales alone declined 23 percent between 2009 and 2010, although digital performance royalties increased by 60 percent in that time.[10] In 2011, digital sales surpassed physical CD sales for the first time.

In previous decades, the primary sales outlets for music were direct-retail record stores (independents or chains such as the now-defunct Tower) and general retail outlets like Walmart, Best Buy, and Target. Another 10 percent of recording sales came from music clubs, which operated like book clubs (see Chapter 2). But during the past decade, the Internet became a major music retailer. Online stores like Amazon and Barnes & Noble, along with independents like Insound, sell recordings as just part of their media product mix. Moreover, digital downloading now constitutes the fastest-growing segment of music sales. Since Apple opened the first successful online music store, iTunes, in 2003, the legal music download business (which includes other online stores like eMusic) has flourished. Indeed, by 2011 digital sales (which include mobile telephone downloads for songs and ringtones) accounted for more than 50.3 percent of the music market in the United States,[11] up from just 9 percent in 2005.

As digital sales have climbed, CD sales have plummeted, hurting retailers badly. Unauthorized recordings (particularly those produced illegally in China) that skirt official copyright permissions are further eating into retailers' and music labels' profits. Finally, "free" illegal downloads far outpace paid legal downloads like Apple's iTunes, which have yet to make up for plunging CD sales—down from 867 million units sold in 1999 to just 348 million CDs sold in 2008.[12] Altogether about 1.265 billion songs were legally downloaded worldwide in 2010.[13]

Money Out

In the recording industry, major labels and indies must spend money to produce the product, including employing people with the right array of skills. They must also invest in the equipment and other resources essential for recording and duplicating songs and albums. The process begins with **A&R (artist & repertoire) agents**, who are the talent scouts of the music business. They work to discover, develop, and sometimes manage artists. A&R executives at the labels listen to demonstration tapes, or *demos*, from new artists, deciding what music to reject, whom to sign, and which songs to record.

Recording is complex and expensive. A typical recording session involves the artist, the producer, the session engineer, and audio technicians. In charge of the overall recording process, the producer handles most nontechnical elements of the session, including reserving studio space, hiring session musicians if necessary, and making final decisions about the recording's quality. The session engineer oversees the technical aspects of the recording session—everything from choosing recording equipment to managing the audio technicians.

Dividing the Profits

The complex relationship between artists and businesspeople in the recording industry (including label executives and retailers) becomes especially obvious in the struggle over who gets how much money. To see how this works, let's consider the costs and profits from a typical CD that retails at $14 to $15. The wholesale price for that CD (the price paid by the store that sells it) is about $9 to $10, leaving the remainder as profit for the retailer. The more heavily discounted the CD, the less profit the retailer earns. The wholesale price represents the actual cost of producing and promoting the recording, plus the recording label's profits. The record company reaps the highest profit (about $4 to $5 on a typical undiscounted CD). But, along with the artist, the record label also bears the bulk of the expenses: manufacturing costs, CD packaging design, advertising and promotion, and artists' royalties. The actual physical product—the CD itself—costs less than 25 cents to manufacture.

Solomon Linda (on far left, pictured with his singing group, the Original Evening Birds), the writer of the frequently covered hit song "The Lion Sleeps Tonight," signed over the copyright for his song for 10 shillings—the equivalent of 87 cents today—in 1952. After his death in 1962, with only $22 to his name, his family fought for the royalties Mr. Linda should have received, resulting in a successful financial settlement for the family in 2006.

New artists usually negotiate a royalty rate of 8 to 12 percent on the retail price of a CD, while more established performers might bargain for 15 percent or higher. An artist who has negotiated a typical 10-percent royalty rate would earn about $1.50 for every CD sold at a price of $15. So, a CD that "goes gold"—sells 500,000 units—would net the artist around $750,000. But out of this amount, artists must repay the record company the money they have been advanced to cover the costs of recording, making music videos, and touring. Artists must also pay their band members, managers, and attorneys.

In addition to sales royalties, there are also performance and mechanical royalties that go to various participants in the industry. A *performance royalty* is paid to artists and music publishers whenever a song they created or own is played in any money-making medium or venue—such as on the radio, on television, in a film, or in a restaurant. Performance royalties are collected and paid out by the three major music performance rights organizations: the American Society of Composers, Authors, and Publishers (ASCAP); the Society of European Stage Authors and Composers (SESAC); and Broadcast Music, Inc. (BMI). Songwriters also receive a *mechanical royalty* each time a recording of their song is sold. The mechanical royalty is usually split between the music publisher and the songwriter. However, songwriters sometimes sell their copyrights to publishers to make a short-term profit. In these cases, they forgo the long-term royalties they would have received by retaining the copyright.

Profits are divided somewhat differently in digital download sales. A 99-cent iTunes download generates about 31 cents for iTunes and a standard 9.1-cent mechanical royalty for the song publisher and writer, leaving about 57 cents for the record company.[14] This doesn't sound like much, but without CD printing and packaging costs, record companies can retain more of the revenue on download sales. Artists typically get royalties for downloads, but the percentage depends on how online sales are defined. In the early 2000s, the rules for dividing the profits for online sales were in great flux, but late in 2008, for the first time, three Copyright Royalty Board judges, appointed by the Librarian of Congress, set the mechanical royalty rate for downloaded music at a standard 9.1 cents per song.

Sound Recording in a Democratic Society

Of all the developments that have unfolded since sound recording became a mass medium, controversies sparked by some forms of popular music have raised the most provocative questions about music's role in our democracy. Battles over what artists should be allowed to say in a song and how they should behave on stage or in a video speak to the heart of democratic expression. Are songs that express violent intent toward gay people, women, or ethnic or racial groups hate crimes? Are songs protected as free speech under the First Amendment of the U.S. Constitution? Moreover, will the ongoing consolidation of the industry by a few powerful music labels encourage them to "approve" lyrics and other forms of musical expression only to achieve maximum profits? Will the Internet continue to create more spaces for independent music to grow and for alternative voices to be heard? Popular musical forms that push at cultural boundaries face a dilemma: how to uphold the right to free expression while resisting control by companies bent on maximizing profits. Since the 1950s, forms of rock music have arisen to break through boundaries, then have been reined in to create a successful commercial product, then have reemerged as new agents of rebellion—and on and on, repeating the cycle.

Still, this dynamic between popular music's innovation and capitalism's profit motive seems like an ongoing dance that has sustained—at least until the age of the Internet—the economic structure of the music industry. The major labels need indies to identify and develop new and fresh talent. And talent is fresh only if it seems alternative or less commercial and comes from nonmainstream origins, such as ethnic communities, backyard garages, dance parties, and neighborhood clubs. For a long time, it was taken as a given that musicians need the major labels if they want to distribute their work widely, become famous, and reach large audiences. But examination of major label practices, both in terms of business and artist relations, may not reinforce this belief any longer, especially given the considerable success of several musical acts that have never been on a major label. A major component of media literacy as related to popular music involves evaluating the usefulness and pitfalls of the conglomerates that attempt to lead the industry. The interdependence of artists and businesses presents alluring opportunities (and potential trade-offs) for participants in the industry as well as those who watch and analyze it.

CHAPTER ESSENTIALS

Now that you have finished reading this chapter, you can use the following tools:

REVIEW

Trace the Early History and Evolution of Sound Recording

- In the development stage of sound recording, early inventors experimented with sound technology; in the entrepreneurial stage, people sought to make money from this technology; finally, in the mass medium stage, entrepreneurs learned how they could cheaply produce and distribute recorded music to large audiences (pp. 129–131).

- The introduction of magnetic **audiotape** (which made possible sound editing and multiple-track mixing, with vocals or instrumentals recorded at one location and later mixed onto a master recording in a studio) and tape players in the 1940s paved the way for innovations such as cassettes in the mid-1960s; the commercial use in the 1950s of **stereo** (more specifically, stereophonic sound, which created a more natural sound by improving on this 1930s invention); and **digital recording** in the 1970s, which stands in contrast to **analog recording**. Using digital technology, the first **compact discs** (CDs)—produced more cheaply than vinyl and audiocassettes—were first sold in 1983 (pp. 131–132).

- In 1992, the **MP3** file format was developed as part of a video compression standard, enabling sound to be compressed into small, manageable digital files. This allowed people to easily download music, thereby reducing sales of CDs and other physical formats, revolutionizing the sound recording industry, and shifting the rocky relationship between record labels and radio stations (pp. 132–134).

Understand the Rise of Popular Music and Rock in the United States

- As sound recording became a mass medium, it fueled the growth of **pop music**, which arose out of sheet-music sales. Pop music became a major enterprise with numerous genres evolving from a common foundation, the first of which were blues and **jazz** (whose early artists often performed **cover music**) (pp. 135, 138).

- Pop music's appeal grew quickly, ushering in **rock and roll** in the mid-1950s. Rock's strongest influences can be traced back to **blues** (whose roots come from African American songs from the rural South) and **rhythm and blues**, or **R&B** (blues-based urban black music that emerged with the introduction of the electric guitar) (pp. 138–139).

- Rock both reflected and shaped powerful social forces, such as blacks' migration from South to North and the growth of youth culture. It also blurred the boundaries between black and white, and broke down divisions between high and low culture, masculinity and femininity, country and city (white rockers combined country or hillbilly music, southern gospel, and Mississippi delta blues to create a sound called **rockabilly**), North and South, and the sacred and the secular (pp. 139–141).

- Due to rock's social and cultural influence, it stirred controversies that eroded its acceptance. These controversies included black artists' frustration with being undermined by white cover music and censorship by officials who thought rock turned young people into delinquents (pp. 141–142).

Explain the Evolution of Pop Music

- Despite authorities' attempts to "tame" rock, it would continue to grow even across national borders, influenced by the emergence of the Rolling Stones and the Beatles in the 1960s, all the while reflecting social, cultural, and political shifts of the time (pp. 143–144).

- As pop adapted to the times, it led to the creation of numerous genres over the next few decades, including **soul**, **folk music**, psychedelic music, and eventually **punk rock**, **grunge**, **alternative rock**, **indie rock**, **hip-hop**, **gangster rap**, and **country** (pp. 144–149).

Outline the Economics of the Sound-Recording Industry

- Over the years, the recording industry has undergone a shift in its power structure—from numerous competing labels and independent production houses, or **indies**, to a few major labels swallowing up the indies and buying each other out (pp. 151–152).

- The recording industry makes money through music sales, though selling music has become increasingly challenging in the digital age as file-sharing has undercut CD sales and online retailers and digital downloading has undermined music stores and cut into the sale of CDs (pp. 152–153).

- Recording-industry executives and workforce spend money on producing music (including the employment of people and the investment in equipment and other resources to get the job done). The process begins with **A&R (artist & repertoire)** agents, who are the talent scouts of the business (p. 153).

- Artists and businesspeople divide profits based on CD prices, manufacturing costs, CD packaging and design, advertising and promotion, and royalties. As of 2008, the rules for dividing digital download profits became more standardized (pp. 153–154).

- Popular music has raised many questions about music's role in our democracy, such as what people should be allowed to say in a song and whether or not they are protected under the First Amendment (p. 155).

- The challenge becomes how to support freedom of expression while resisting powerful control by companies whose profit motives are usually paramount (p. 155).

STUDY QUESTIONS

1. How did sound recording survive the advent of radio and the Great Depression?
2. How did rock and roll significantly influence two mass media industries?
3. Why did hip-hop and punk rock emerge as significant musical forms in the late 1970s and 1980s? What do their developments have in common, and how are they different?
4. What accounts for the cost of a typical CD recording? Where do the profits go? Where does the revenue from an iTunes download go?
5. Why do so many forms of alternative music become commercially successful? Explain this in economic terms.

MEDIA LITERACY PRACTICE

Take on the investigation of a recording company/music label—preferably a smaller one. Visit the label's Web site, and/or e-mail or call the company for information and background.

DESCRIBE what kind of music the label specializes in. Is the label limited to one genre or type of music? What/who are some of the groups or artists that the label produces? How does the label distribute its recordings to consumers?

ANALYZE the patterns. Does the variety of groups and artists the label produces suggest a type of fan the label is targeting? What methods does the label use to promote artists and reach its listeners? Is the label independent or part of a larger recording industry company?

INTERPRET your research. What do you see as the major problems facing your label specifically and the industry in general? How do smaller labels overcome these problems?

EVALUATE the impact of the current industry system on the quality of music produced by your label (and by the industry in general).

ENGAGE with your community. Try to contact someone from the label—an artist, a producer, or an executive—and pose some of these questions to that person. From this exercise, you are trying to get a sense of the obstacles musicians and artists face in trying to make careers from their talent and performances.

⊙ ONLINE RESOURCES

Go to **bedfordstmartins.com/mediaessentials** for review quizzes, links, and more.

Visit the site's **VIDEOCENTRAL: MASS COMMUNICATION** section for videos like the ones on pages 132 and 153.

6

Popular Radio and the Origins of Broadcasting

A few years ago, a young woman named Kristin* took an entry-level position running the audio board for on-air radio personalities at an AM radio station. She loved radio, and hoped that this job would jump-start her career in the industry. She won a regular microphone shift while just a college student, and because the station was owned by Atlanta-based Cumulus Media, one of the largest radio groups in the country with 350 stations in 68 markets, there were opportunities for Kristin to grow within the company. She was transferred to a group of three FM stations owned by Cumulus at a larger city nearby, and started hosting a show on the popular contemporary hits station, playing the latest songs. "I was so excited to be living my dream," Kristin said, so much so that she didn't mind that she was earning only minimum wage.

That dream soon revealed its darker side—the realities of today's homogenized radio industry. Kristin was asked to do voice-tracking, a cost-saving measure in which a radio deejay prerecords voice breaks that are then inserted into an automated shift. To the listeners, it may have seemed like they were getting three different deejays on Cumulus's contemporary hits station, rock station, and country station. After all, they were hearing three different

---

Name has been changed for confidentiality reasons.

names, with three slightly different names, with three slightly different personalities. In reality, Kristin was the midday deejay on the contemporary hits radio station; she was the evening deejay on the rock format station; and she was also the weekend voice of the company's country format station.

Eventually, Kristin left the radio station and went to grad school. "I wouldn't be able to pay my college loans with the money I was making," she said. But more than the low wages, her biggest disappointment was that the kind of commercial radio she grew up listening to was being phased out by the time she went to work in the business. The consolidation of stations into massive radio groups like Cumulus and Clear Channel in the 1990s and 2000s resulted in budget-cutting demands from the corporate offices and, ultimately, stations with less connection

to their local audience. Kristin's contemporary hits station had five full-time on-air deejays when she started. Today, it has just one.

Kristin's story raises provocative questions: As radio has morphed from small, locally owned broadcasting to national networks and large radio conglomerates, what has happened to the economics driving this business? Do technological innovations like the Internet give more power to consumers, who can now listen to any format or message from any part of the world based on their preferences? Is localism still an important concept for the radio industry? Does nonprofit radio bring different kinds of voices to the airwaves (or Internet)? To find clues to possible answers, let's first trace how radio has evolved since its emergence as a full-blown mass medium.

THE STORY OF RADIO—from its invention in the late nineteenth century to its current incarnation as a multi-technology mass medium is one of the most remarkable in media history. In the United States, the early days of network radio gave Americans "a national identity" and "a chance to share in a common experience."[1] Even with the arrival of TV in the 1950s, the recent "corporatization" of broadcasting, and the demographic segmentation of radio today, this medium has continued to play a powerful role in our lives. For people throughout the nation, the music and talk emanating every day from their radios, PCs, and handheld devices powerfully shape political opinions, social mores, and (owing to advertisements) purchasing decisions. In this chapter, we will explore these themes by:

- examining radio's early history, including how its evolution from one-to-one to one-to-many communication led to new regulations and innovations in programming

- looking at how technological advances such as transistors and FM sparked the rise of format radio

- familiarizing ourselves with the array of characteristics defining radio today, such as format specialization, nonprofit business models, and digital radio technologies

- exploring the economics behind modern radio, including advertising and consolidation of ownership over the public airwaves

- considering radio's influence on American culture in an age when control of the public airwaves lies in fewer hands than ever

The Early History of Radio

Radio did not emerge as a full-blown mass medium until the 1920s, though it had been evolving from technology developed in the 1840s. As with most media, inventors tinkered in these earliest years with the technologies of the day to address practical needs. These technologies (including the telegraph and the first forays into wireless communication) set the stage for future advances in radio as a communication medium.

Inventors Paving the Way: Morse, Maxwell, and Hertz

The **telegraph**—the precursor of radio technology—was invented in the United States in the 1840s and was the first technology to enable messages to move faster than human travel. Through the telegraph, messages (such as news) could be transmitted from coast to coast within minutes, rather than the days required by ships and other modes of conveyance. American artist and inventor Samuel Morse initially developed this practical system of sending electrical impulses from a transmitter through a cable to a reception device. To send messages, telegraph operators used what became known as **Morse code**—a series of dots and dashes that stood for letters in the alphabet and that interrupted the electrical current along a wire cable. By 1844, Morse had set up the first telegraph line, which linked Washington, D.C., and Baltimore, Maryland. By 1861, telegraph lines stretched coast-to-coast. Just five years later, the first transatlantic cable, capable of transmitting about six words a minute, ran between Newfoundland and Ireland along the ocean floor.

Though revolutionary, the telegraph had significant limitations. For one thing, it couldn't transmit the human voice. Moreover, because it depended on wires, it was no help for anyone seeking to communicate with commercial or military ships at sea.

Guglielmo Marconi (1874–1937) transmitted the first radio signal across the Atlantic Ocean in 1901. He shared the 1909 Nobel Prize for Physics for his contributions to wireless telegraphy, soon required on all seagoing ships and credited with saving more than seven hundred lives when the *Titanic* sank in 1912.

The world needed a telegraph *without* wires. A promising theory came from James Maxwell, a Scottish physicist who in the mid-1860s postulated the existence of **radio waves** that could be harnessed to send signals from a transmission point to a reception point. In the 1880s, German physicist Heinrich Hertz tested Maxwell's theory—with interesting results. Hertz conducted an experiment using electrical sparks that emitted **electromagnetic waves**, invisible electronic impulses similar to light. The experiment was the first recorded transmission and reception of radio waves, and would dramatically advance the development of wireless communication.

Innovators in Wireless: Marconi, Fessenden, and De Forest

As the nineteenth century unfolded, inventors building on the earlier technologies continued improving wireless communication. New developments took wireless from **narrowcasting** (person-to-person or point-to-point transmission of messages) to **broadcasting** (transmission from one point to multiple listeners; also known as one-to-many communication).

Marconi: The Father of Wireless Telegraphy

In 1894, a twenty-year-old, self-educated Italian engineer named Guglielmo Marconi read Hertz's work. He swiftly realized that developing a way to

CHAPTER 6 // TIMELINE

1844 Samuel Morse
First telegraph line is set up between Washington, D.C., and Baltimore, Maryland.

1894 Guglielmo Marconi
The Italian inventor begins experiments on wireless telegraphy, seeing his invention as a means for point-to-point communication.

1906 Lee De Forest
American inventor develops the Audion vacuum tube for amplifying radio sound.

1910 Wireless Ship Act
Congress passes this act, requiring that all major ships be equipped with wireless radio.

1917 Amateur Radio Shutdown
The navy closes down all amateur radio stations to ensure military security as the United States enters World War I.

send high-speed messages over great distances would transform communication, commercial shipping, and the military. The young engineer set out to make wireless technology practical. After successfully figuring out how to build a wireless communication device that could send Morse code from a transmitter to a receiver, Marconi traveled to England in 1896. There, he received a patent on **wireless telegraphy**, a form of voiceless *point-to-point communication*.

In London the following year, the Italian inventor formed the Marconi Wireless Telegraph Company, later known as British Marconi. He began installing wireless technology on British naval and private commercial ships. This left other innovators to explore the wireless transmission of voice and music, later known as **wireless telephony** and eventually radio. In 1899, Marconi opened a branch in the United States nicknamed American Marconi. That same year, he sent the first wireless Morse code signal across the English Channel to France. In 1901, he relayed the first wireless signal from Cornwall, England, across the Atlantic Ocean to St. John's, Newfoundland. History often cites Marconi as the "father of radio," but a Russian scientist, Alexander Popov, accomplished similar feats in St. Petersburg at the same time, and Nikola Tesla, a Serbian Croatian inventor who immigrated to the United States, invented a wireless electrical device in 1892.

Fessenden: The First Voice Broadcast

Marconi had taken major steps in London and the United States. But it was Canadian engineer Reginald Fessenden who transformed wireless telegraphy into *one-to-many communication*. Fessenden is credited with providing the first voice broadcast. Formerly a chief chemist for Thomas Edison, he went to work for the U.S. Navy and eventually for General Electric (GE), where he focused on improving the frequency of wireless signals. Both the navy and GE were interested in the potential for voice transmission. On Christmas Eve in 1906, after GE built Fessenden a powerful transmitter, he gave his first public demonstration, sending his performance of "O Holy Night" on the violin and a reading of a Bible passage through the airwaves from his station at Brant

1922 Commercial Radio
The first radio advertisements cause an uproar as people question the right to pollute the public airwaves with commercial messages.

1926 David Sarnoff
NBC is created, the first lasting network of radio stations; connected by AT&T long lines, the network broadcasts nationally and plays a prominent role in unifying the country.

1927 Radio Act of 1927
Radio stations are required to operate in the "public interest, convenience, or necessity."

1928 William Paley
CBS is founded and becomes a competitor to NBC.

1930s The Golden Age of Radio
Living rooms are filled with music, drama, comedy, variety and quiz shows, and news.

Inventor Lee De Forest's (1873–1961) lengthy radio career was marked by incredible innovations, missed opportunities, and poor business practices. In the end, De Forest was upset that radio content had stooped, in his opinion, to such low standards. With a passion for opera, he had hoped radio would be a tool for elite culture.

Rock, Massachusetts, to an unknown number of shipboard operators off the Atlantic Coast.

De Forest: Birthing Modern Electronics

American inventor Lee De Forest improved the usefulness of broadcasting by greatly increasing listeners' ability to hear dots and dashes, and later speech and music, on a receiver. In 1906, he developed the Audion vacuum tube, which detected and amplified radio signals. The device was essential to the development of voice transmission, long-distance radio, and (eventually) television. Although De Forest had the patent for the Audion, he was accused in court and by fellow engineers of stealing others' ideas, even when the court ruled in his favor.[2] Many historians consider the Audion—which powered radios until the arrival of transistors and solid-state circuits in the 1950s—the origin of modern electronics.

In 1907, De Forest demonstrated his invention's power and practical value by broadcasting a performance by Metropolitan opera tenor Enrico Caruso to his friends in New York. The next year, he and his wife, Nora, played records into a microphone from atop the Eiffel Tower in Paris. The signals were picked up by receivers up to five hundred miles away.

Early Regulation of Wireless/Radio

By the turn of the twentieth century, radio had become a new force in American life. U.S. lawmakers—recognizing radio's power to shape political opinion, economic dynamics, and military strategy and tactics—moved to ensure U.S. control over the fledgling industry. With this goal in mind, legislators first defined radio

---

CHAPTER 6 // TIMELINE continued

1934 Federal Communications Act of 1934
This act allows commercial interests to control the airwaves.

1941 ABC
ABC is formed when RCA is forced to sell NBC-Blue.

1950 Radio Suffers
In the wake of TV's popularity, radio suffers but is resurrected via rock-and-roll music formats and transistor radios.

1960s FM
Invented by Edwin Armstrong in the 1920s and 1930s, a new format finally gains national popularity.

1990 Talk Radio
Talk radio becomes the most popular format, especially on AM stations.

as a shared resource for the public good. Then they passed laws regulating how the public airwaves could be used and in what manner private businesses could take part in the industry.

Providing Public Safety

Because radio waves crossed state and national borders, legislators determined that broadcasting constituted a "natural resource"—a kind of interstate commerce. Therefore, radio waves could not be owned; they were the collective property of all Americans, just like national parks. And as collective property, they should provide a benefit to society. To that end, U.S. lawmakers enacted rules focused on national security and public safety, but which also set the stage for the emergence of radio as a public mass medium.

The first came in 1910, when Congress passed the **Wireless Ship Act**. The law mandated that all major U.S. seagoing ships carrying more than fifty passengers and traveling more than two hundred miles off either coast be equipped with wireless equipment with a one-hundred-mile range. The importance of this act was underscored by the *Titanic* disaster in 1912, when radio distress signals called rescue ships, enabling them to save more than seven hundred lives. In the wake of the *Titanic* tragedy, Congress passed the **Radio Act of 1912**, which required all radio stations on land or at sea to be licensed and assigned special call letters, and for each station to be operated only by a licensed person. The act helped to bring some order to the airwaves, which had been increasingly jammed with amateur radio operators. This act also formally adopted the SOS Morse-code distress signal that other countries had been using for several years.

Ensuring National Security

The government also took steps to ensure that radio contributed to national security. By 1915, more than twenty American companies sold wireless point-to-point communication systems, primarily for use in ship-to-shore communication. American Marconi (a subsidiary of British Marconi) was the biggest of these

1996 Telecommunications Act of 1996	**1990s** Internet Radio	**2002** Satellite Radio	**2004** Podcasts	**2011** Streaming Advances
This law effects a rapid, unprecedented consolidation in radio ownership across the United States.	In the second half of the decade, Internet radio—either streaming the content of an on-air station or an exclusive Webcast—takes hold.	A new format begins service.	The combination of iPods and broadcasting creates podcasts, downloadable audio file programs posted to the Internet.	The popular Spotify service comes to the United States.

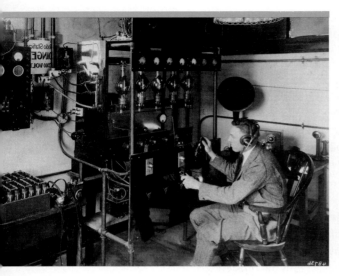

A radio operator at the controls in Minnesota, in October 1923. In that year, only about a half million U.S. households had a radio receiver to hear the signals. Within two years, more than five million households would own radios.

companies. But in 1914, with World War I erupting in Europe, the U.S. Navy questioned the wisdom of allowing a foreign-controlled company to wield so much power over communication. When the United States entered the war in 1917, the government closed down all amateur radio operations, took control of key radio transmitters, and blocked British Marconi from purchasing alternators from General Electric. These moves addressed concerns about national security. They also enabled the United States to reduce Britain's influence over communication and tightened U.S. control over the emerging wireless infrastructure—key steps in safeguarding U.S. interests.

RCA: The Formation of an American Radio Monopoly

Some members of Congress, along with some business leaders, opposed federal legislation granting the government or the navy a radio monopoly. To secure a place in the fast-evolving industry, General Electric proposed a plan by which it would create a *private-sector monopoly*—a privately owned company that would have the government's approval to dominate the radio industry. In 1919, the plan was accepted by the powers that be at both General Electric and the U.S. Navy, the government branch most prominently fighting for control of the radio industry in America. GE swiftly broke off negotiations to sell key radio technologies to European-owned companies such as British Marconi, thereby limiting those companies' global reach. In 1919, it founded a new company, **Radio Corporation of America (RCA)**, which soon acquired American Marconi as well as radio patents of other U.S. companies and wireless patents from AT&T. Having pooled the necessary technology and patents to monopolize the wireless industry, RCA was poised to expand American communication technology throughout the world.[3]

KDKA: The First Commercial Radio Station

With the advent of the United States' global dominance in mass communication, many people became intrigued by radio's potential. Amateur stations popped up in places like San Jose, California; Medford, Massachusetts; New York; Detroit; and Pierre, South Dakota. The best-known early station was started by an engineer named Frank Conrad, who worked for GE's rival, Westinghouse Electric Company. In 1916, he set up a radio studio above his Pittsburgh garage by placing a microphone in front of a phonograph. Conrad broadcast music and news to his friends (whom he supplied with receivers) two evenings a week on experimental station 8XK. When a Westinghouse executive got wind of Conrad's activities in 1920, he established KDKA, generally regarded as the first commercial (profit-based) broadcast station. The following year, the U.S. Commerce Department officially licensed five radio stations for operation; by early 1923, more than six hundred commercial and noncommercial stations were operating. Just two years later, a whopping 5.5 million radio sets were in use across America—made by companies such as GE and Westinghouse and costing about $55 ($664 in today's dollars). Radio was officially a mass medium.

The Networks

With the establishment of the private sector's involvement in radio, the groundwork was laid for radio to take off as a business—which would enable commercial station owners (and the advertisers that funded them) to reach more listeners more efficiently than ever. The radio **network** arose: a cost-saving operation that links a group of affiliate or subsidiary broadcast stations that share programming produced at a central location. (At that time, stations were linked through special phone lines; today, it's through satellite relays.)

A network enables stations to control program costs and avoid unnecessary duplication of content creation. Simply put, it was cheaper to produce programs at one station and broadcast them simultaneously over multiple owned or affiliated stations than for each station to generate its own programs. Networks thus brought the best musical, dramatic, and comedic talent to one place, where programs could be produced and then distributed all over the country. This new business model concentrated control of radio in the hands of a few corporate players, all of whom jockeyed for additional power.

AT&T: Making a Power Grab

The shift toward networks began in 1922 when RCA's partnership with AT&T started to unravel. In a major power grab, AT&T, which already had a government-sanctioned monopoly in the telephone business, decided to break its RCA agreements in an attempt to monopolize radio. Identifying the new medium as the "wireless telephone," AT&T argued that broadcasting was merely an extension of its control over the telephone. The corporate giant complained that RCA had gained too much power. In violation of its early agreements with RCA, AT&T began making and selling its own radio receivers.

That same year, AT&T started WEAF (now WNBC) in New York, the first radio station to regularly sell commercial time to advertisers. Advertising (company executives reasoned) would ensure profits long after radio-set sales had saturated the consumer market. AT&T claimed that under the RCA agreements, it had the exclusive right to sell ads, which AT&T called *toll broadcasting*. Most people in radio at the time recoiled at the idea of using the medium for advertising, viewing the medium instead as a public information service. But executives remained riveted by the potential of radio ads to enhance profits.

Still, the initial motivation behind AT&T's toll broadcasting idea was to dominate radio. Through its agreements with RCA, AT&T retained the rights to interconnect the signals between two or more radio stations via telephone wires. By the end of 1924, AT&T had interconnected twenty-two stations in a network to air a talk by President Calvin Coolidge. Some of these stations were owned by AT&T, but most simply consented to become AT&T "affiliates," agreeing to air the phone company's programs.

Seeing AT&T's success, GE, Westinghouse, and RCA launched a competing network. AT&T promptly denied them access to its telephone wires, so GE, Westinghouse, and RCA used inferior telegraph lines to connect its network stations. In 1925, the Justice Department, irritated by AT&T's power grab, redefined patent agreements. AT&T received a monopoly on providing the wires, known as *long lines*, to interconnect stations nationwide. In exchange, AT&T agreed to sell its network to RCA for $1 million and promised not to reenter broadcasting for eight years.

David Sarnoff, creator of NBC and network radio, demonstrated calculated ambition in the radio industry, which can easily be compared to Bill Gates's drive to control the computer software and Internet industries.

NBC: RCA Forms a Network

The commercial rewards of the network and affiliate system continued to excite executives' imaginations. For example, after RCA bought AT&T's telephone network, David Sarnoff, RCA's general manager, created a new subsidiary in September 1926 called the National Broadcasting Company (NBC). NBC's ownership was shared by RCA (50 percent), General Electric (30 percent), and Westinghouse (20 percent). The subsidiary became known as the NBC-Red network. The network created by RCA, GE, and Westinghouse became a sister network named NBC-Blue. By 1933, NBC-Red would have twenty-eight affiliates; NBC-Blue, twenty-four.

CBS: A Rival Network Challenges NBC

The network and affiliate system under RCA/NBC thrived throughout most of the 1920s and brought Americans together as never before to participate in the big events of the day. For example, when aviator Charles Lindbergh returned from the first solo transatlantic flight in 1927, an estimated twenty-five to thirty million people listened to his welcome-home party on the six million radio sets then in use. At the time, it was the largest shared audience experience in the history of any mass medium.

During this decade, competition also stiffened further within the industry. For instance, in 1928, William Paley, the twenty-seven-year-old son of a Philadelphia cigar company owner, bought the Columbia Phonograph Company and built it into a network later renamed the Columbia Broadcasting System (CBS). Unlike NBC, which actually charged its affiliates up to $96 a week for having the privilege of carrying its programming, CBS paid affiliates as much as $50 an hour to carry its programs. By 1933, Paley's efforts had netted CBS more than ninety affiliates, many of which had defected from NBC. Paley also concentrated on developing news programs and entertainment shows, particularly soap operas and comedy-variety series. To that end, CBS raided NBC not just for affiliates but for top talent such as comedian Jack Benny and singer Frank Sinatra. In 1949, CBS finally surpassed NBC as the highest-rated network on radio.

The Radio Act of 1927

The growing concentration of power in the network and affiliate system raised a red flag for government leaders. Throughout the 1920s to early 1940s, lawmakers would enact many regulations aimed at regaining control over the industry. In particular, by the late 1920s, the government had become alarmed by RCA/NBC's growing influence over radio content. Moreover, as radio moved from narrowcasting to broadcasting, battles among various players over issues such as more frequency space and less channel interference heated up. Manufacturers, engineers, station operators, network executives, and the listening public demanded action to address their conflicting interests. Many wanted more sweeping regulation than the simple licensing function granted under the Radio Act of 1912, which gave the Commerce Department little power to deny a license or to unclog the airwaves.

To restore order, Congress passed the **Radio Act of 1927**, which introduced a pivotal new principle: Licensees did not *own* their channels but could use them only as long as they operated to serve the "public interest, convenience, or necessity." To oversee licenses and negotiate channel problems such as too many stations trying to air on too few frequencies, the 1927 act created the **Federal Radio Commission (FRC)**, whose members were appointed by the president.

Although the FRC was intended as a temporary committee, it grew into a powerful regulatory agency. In 1934, with passage of the **Federal Communications Act of 1934**, the FRC became the **Federal Communications Commission (FCC)**. Its jurisdiction covered not only radio but also the telephone and the telegraph (and later television, cable, and the Internet). More significantly, by this time Congress and the president had sided with the already-powerful radio networks and acceded to a system of advertising-supported commercial broadcasting as best serving "public interest, convenience, or necessity," overriding the concerns of educational, labor, religious, and citizen broadcasting advocates.

William S. Paley (*shown standing*), president of Columbia Broadcasting System for more than fifty years, makes the contact that opens up the world's largest regular hook-up of radio stations in 1928. Known for his early support of quality programming and network news, Paley was also criticized for undermining his news division to sidestep controversy or to increase profits.

In 1941, an activist FCC set out to break up what it saw as overly large and powerful networks, which led to a Supreme Court ruling forcing RCA to sell NBC-Blue. The divested enterprise became the American Broadcasting Company (ABC). Such government crackdowns brought long-overdue reform to the radio industry. However, they came too late to prevent considerable damage to noncommercial radio.

The Golden Age of Radio

From the late 1920s to the 1940s, radio basked in a golden age marked by a proliferation of informative and entertaining programs (such as weather forecasts, farm reports, news, music, dramas, quiz shows, and comedies). This diversity of programming shaped—and was shaped by—American culture. It also paved the way for programs that Americans would later enjoy on television, as NBC, CBS, and ABC created television networks in the late 1940s and 1950s.

Early Radio Programming

In the early days of radio, only a handful of stations operated in most large radio markets. Through the networks they were affiliated with, these stations broadcast a variety of programs into listeners' homes (and in some cases, into their cars).

This giant bank of radio network microphones makes us wonder today how President Franklin D. Roosevelt managed to project such an intimate and reassuring tone in his famous fireside chats. Conceived originally to promote FDR's New Deal policies amid the Great Depression, these chats were delivered between 1933 and 1944 and touched on national topics. Roosevelt was the first president to effectively use broadcasting to communicate with citizens.

People had favorite evening programs, usually fifteen minutes long. After dinner, families gathered around the radio to hear comedies, dramas, public service announcements, and more. Popular programs included *Amos 'n' Andy* (a serial situation comedy), *The Shadow* (a mystery drama), *The Lone Ranger* (a Western), *The Green Hornet* (a crime drama), and *Fibber McGee and Molly* (a comedy), as well as the "fireside chats" regularly presented by President Franklin Roosevelt.

Variety shows featuring musical performances and comedy skits planted the seeds for popular TV variety shows that would come later, such as the *Ed Sullivan Show. Quiz shows* (including *The Old Time Spelling Bee*) introduced Americans to the thrill of competition. These radio programs set the stage for later competition-based TV shows ranging from *The Price Is Right* and *Who Wants to Be a Millionaire* to reality-based shows such as *Survivor, Fear Factor, Project Runway*, and *Top Chef*.

Dramatic programs, mostly radio plays broadcast live from theaters, would later inspire TV dramas, including "soap operas." (The term came into use after Colgate-Palmolive began selling its soap products on dramas it sponsored.) Another type of program—the *serial show*—introduced the idea of continuing story lines from one day to the next. This format was soon copied by soap operas and some comedy programs.

Radio as Cultural Mirror

Radio programs powerfully reflected shifts in American culture, including attitudes about race and levels of tolerance for stereotypes. For example, the situation comedy *Amos 'n' Andy* was based on the conventions of the nineteenth-century minstrel show and featured black characters stereotyped as shiftless and stupid. Created as a blackface stage act by two white comedians, Charles Correll and Freeman Gosden, the program was criticized as racist by some at the time. But NBC and the program's producers claimed that *Amos 'n' Andy* was as popular among black audiences as among white listeners.[4]

Early radio research estimated that the program aired in more than half of all radio homes in the nation during the 1930–31 season, making it the most popular radio series in history. In 1951, *Amos 'n' Andy* made a brief transition to television, after Correll and Gosden sold the rights to CBS for $1 million. It became the first TV series to have an all-black cast. But amid a strengthening Civil Rights movement and a formal protest by the National Association for the Advancement of Colored People (NAACP), which argued that "every character is either a clown or a crook," CBS canceled the program in 1953.[5]

The Authority of Radio

In addition to reflecting evolving cultural beliefs, radio increasingly shaped them— in part by being perceived by listeners as the voice of authority. The adaptation of science-fiction author H. G. Wells's *War of the Worlds* (1898) on the radio series

On Halloween eve in 1938, Orson Welles's radio dramatization of *War of the Worlds* (*left*) created a panic up and down the East Coast, especially in Grover's Mill, New Jersey—the setting for the fictional Martian invasion that many listeners assumed was real. A seventy-six-year-old Grover's Mill resident (*right*) guarded a warehouse against alien invaders.

Mercury Theatre on the Air provides the most notable example of this. Considered the most famous single radio broadcast of all time, *War of the Worlds* was produced and hosted by Orson Welles, who also narrated it. On Halloween eve in 1938, the twenty-three-year-old Welles aired the Martian invasion story in the style of a contemporary radio news bulletin. For people who missed the opening disclaimer, the program sounded like an authentic news report, with apparently eyewitness accounts of battles between Martian invaders and the U.S. Army.

The program triggered a panic among some listeners. In New Jersey, some people walked through the streets with wet towels wrapped around their heads for protection against deadly Martian heat rays. In New York, young men reported to their National Guard headquarters to prepare for battle. Across the nation, calls from terrified citizens jammed police switchboards. The FCC called for stricter warnings both before and during programs imitating the style of radio news.

The Evolution of Radio

In the 1950s, a new form of mass media—television—came on the scene. TV snatched radio's advertisers, program genres, major celebrities, and large evening audiences. The TV set even physically displaced the radio as the living-room centerpiece around which families gathered. To survive, players in the radio industry transformed their business model so they could provide new forms of value for listeners.

Transistors: Making Radio Portable

The portability of radio proved to be a major advantage in the medium's struggle for survival. In the late 1920s, car radios had existed but were considered a luxury. But when the transistor was invented by Bell Laboratories in 1947, radios became more accessible and portable than before. **Transistors** were small electrical devices that, like vacuum tubes, could receive and amplify radio signals. However, they used less power and heat than vacuum tubes, and were more durable and less expensive. Best of all, they were tiny. The development of transistors let radio go where television could not—to the beach, to the office, into bedrooms and bathrooms, and into nearly all new cars.

The FM Revolution

To replace the shows radio had lost to TV, many people in radio switched the medium's emphasis to music, turning to the recording industry for content. However, making music sound better on radio required some technological innovation. Until then, radio technology had centered on **AM** (amplitude modulation). AM affected the volume of radio waves to enable transmission and reception. This type of modulation was sufficient for radio content such as talk but it wasn't ideal for music. For that, radio needed **FM** (frequency modulation), which provided greater clarity as well as static-free radio reception.

FM radio had existed for decades. American inventor Edwin Armstrong had discovered and developed it during the 1920s and early 1930s. Between 1930 and 1933, he filed five patents on FM. The number of FM stations grew to 700 but then fell to 560 by the 1950s, as Armstrong was pulled into legal skirmishes over patents with heavy hitters such as David Sarnoff. (The RCA executive had initially supported Armstrong's explorations into FM but then opted to throw his weight behind the development of TV.) In 1954, weary from years of legal battles, Armstrong wrote a note apologizing to his wife, removed the air conditioner from his thirteenth-story New York apartment, and jumped to his death. It wasn't until the early 1960s, when the FCC opened up more spectrum space for the superior sound of FM, that FM began to grow into the preferred radio band for music.

The Rise of Format Radio

Once radio became portable and FM was introduced, music began to dominate the medium more than ever. This eventually led to the creation of **format radio**, by which station managers (rather than disc jockeys) control the station's hour-by-hour music programming. Of course, in the late 1930s, music had been radio's single biggest staple, accounting for 48 percent of all programming. However, most music was live, which many people considered superior to recorded music. The first disc jockeys demonstrated that recorded music could attract just as many listeners as live music.

As early as 1949, station owner Todd Storz in Omaha, Nebraska, had experimented with format radio and music. When Storz and his program manager noticed that bar patrons and waitresses repeatedly played certain favorite songs from the forty records available in a jukebox, they began researching record sales to identify the most popular tunes. Drawing from jukebox culture, Storz hit on the idea of **rotation**: playing the top songs many times during the day. By the mid-1950s, the management-control idea combined with the rock-and-roll explosion—and the *Top 40 format* was born. Although the term *Top 40* derived from the number of records stored in a jukebox, this format came to refer to the forty most popular hits in a given week as measured by record sales.

As format radio grew, program managers combined rapid deejay chatter with the best-selling songs of the day and occasional oldies—popular songs from a few months earlier. In these early days of format radio, managers created a program log that deejays followed and sectioned off blocks of roughly four hours throughout the day and night. Management would vary the format for each block to appeal to listeners' interests, and thus attract more advertising dollars. For instance, a Top 40 station would feature its best deejays in the morning and afternoon periods, during listeners' commutes to school or work. Management also made savvy use of re-search. For example, if statistics showed that teenagers tended to listen to the radio mostly during evening hours and preferred music to news, then stations marketing to teens avoided scheduling news breaks during those hours.

The expansion of FM in the mid-1960s created room for stations to experi-ment, particularly with classical music, jazz, blues, and non–Top 40 rock songs. Many noncommercial stations broadcast from college campuses, where student deejays and managers rejected the commercialism associated with Top 40 tunes and began playing lesser-known alternative music and longer album cuts.

The Characteristics of Contemporary Radio

Contemporary radio differs markedly from its predecessor. In contrast to the few stations per market in the 1930s, most large markets today include more than forty stations that vie for listener loyalty. With the exception of national network-sponsored news segments and nationally syndicated pro-grams, most programming is locally produced and heavily dependent on the music industry for content. In short, stations today are more specialized. Listeners are loyal to favorite stations, music formats, and even radio per-sonalities, rather than to specific shows, and they generally listen to only four or five stations. About fifteen thousand radio stations now operate in the United States, customizing their sounds to reach niche audiences through format specialization and alternative programming.

Format Specialization

Radio stations today use a variety of formats to serve diverse groups of listeners. (See Figure 6.1.) To please advertisers, who want to know exactly who is listening, formats usually target audiences according to their age, income, gender, or race/ethnicity. Radio's specialization enables advertisers to reach smaller target audiences at costs much lower than those for television. The most popular formats include the following:

• **News and talk radio.** As the most popular format in the nation, news and talk ra-dio has been buoyed by the popularity of personalities like Howard Stern, Tavis Smiley, and Rush Limbaugh. This format tends to cater to adults over age

FIGURE 6.1 // MOST POPULAR RADIO FORMATS IN THE UNITED STATES

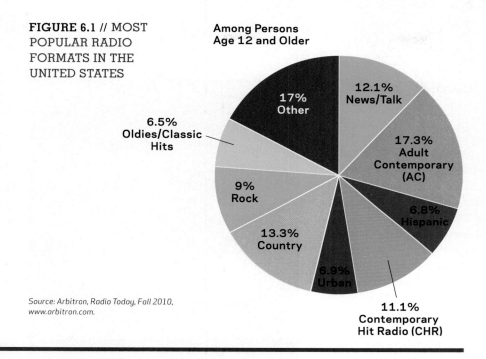

Among Persons Age 12 and Older

- 12.1% News/Talk
- 17.3% Adult Contemporary (AC)
- 6.8% Hispanic
- 11.1% Contemporary Hit Radio (CHR)
- 6.9% Urban
- 13.3% Country
- 9% Rock
- 6.5% Oldies/Classic Hits
- 17% Other

Source: Arbitron, Radio Today, Fall 2010, www.arbitron.com.

thirty-five (except for sports talk programs, which draw mostly male sports fans of all ages). Though more expensive to produce than a music format, it appeals to advertisers seeking to target working and middle-class adult consumers (see "Media Literacy Case Study: Host: The Origins of Talk Radio" on page 178).

- **Adult contemporary (AC).** This format, also known as middle-of-the-road, or MOR, is among radio's oldest and most popular formats. It reaches over 17 percent of all listeners, most of them older than forty, with an eclectic mix of news, talk, oldies, and soft rock music. *Broadcasting* magazine describes AC as "not too soft, not too loud, not too fast, not too slow, not too hard, not too lush, not too old, not too new."

- **Top 40/contemporary hit radio (CHR).** Encompassing everything from rap to pop rock songs, this format appeals to many teens and young adults. Since the mid-1980s, however, these stations have lost ground steadily as younger generations have followed music first on MTV and now online rather than on radio.

- **Country.** Claiming the most stations, this format consists of tiny markets where country is traditionally the default format for communities with only one radio station. Country music has old roots in radio, starting in 1925 with the influential Grand Ole Opry program on WSM in Nashville.

MEDIA LITERACY
Case Study

Host: The Origins of Talk Radio
By David Foster Wallace

The origins of contemporary political talk radio can be traced to three phenomena of the 1980s. The first of these involved AM music stations' getting absolutely murdered by FM, which could broadcast music in stereo and allowed for much better fidelity on high and low notes. The human voice, on the other hand, is midrange and doesn't require high fidelity. The eighties' proliferation of talk formats on the AM band also provided new careers for some music deejays —e.g., Don Imus, Morton Downey Jr.—whose chatty personas didn't fit well with FM's all-about-the-music ethos.

The second big factor was the repeal, late in Ronald Reagan's second term, of what was known as the Fairness Doctrine. This was a 1949 FCC rule designed to minimize any possible restrictions on free speech caused by limited access to broadcasting outlets. The idea was that, as one of the conditions for receiving an FCC broadcast license, a station had to "devote reasonable attention to the coverage of controversial issues of public importance," and consequently had to provide "reasonable, although not necessarily equal" opportunities for opposing sides to express their views. Because of the Fairness Doctrine, talk stations had to hire and program symmetrically: If you had a three-hour program whose host's politics were on one side of the ideological spectrum, you had to have another long-form program whose host more or less spoke for the other side. Weirdly enough, up through the mid-eighties it was usually the U.S. Right that benefited most from the Doctrine.

The Fairness Doctrine's repeal was part of the sweeping deregulations of the Reagan era, which

aimed to liberate all sorts of industries from government interference and allow them to compete freely in the marketplace. After 1987, though, just another industry is pretty much what radio became, and its only real responsibility now is to attract and retain listeners in order to generate revenue.

More or less on the heels of the Fairness Doctrine's repeal came the West Coast and then national syndication of *The Rush Limbaugh Show* through Mr. McLaughlin's EFM Media. Limbaugh is the third great progenitor of today's political talk radio partly because he's a host of extraordinary, once-in-a-generation talent and charisma—bright, loquacious, witty, complexly authoritative—whose show's blend of news, entertainment, and partisan analysis became the model for legions of imitators. But he was also the first great promulgator of the Mainstream Media's Liberal Bias idea. This turned out to be a brilliantly effective rhetorical move, since the MMLB concept functioned simultaneously as a standard around which Rush's audience could rally, as an articulation of the need for right-wing (i.e., unbiased) media, and as a mechanism by which any criticism or refutation of conservative ideas could be dismissed (either as biased or as the product of indoctrination by biased media). Boiled way down, the MMLB thesis is able both to exploit and to perpetuate many conservatives' dissatisfaction with extant media sources—and it's this dissatisfaction that cements political talk radio's large and loyal audience.

Source: Excerpted from David Foster Wallace, "Host: The Origins of Talk Radio," Atlantic, April 2005, 66–68.

APPLYING THE CRITICAL PROCESS

DESCRIPTION Check your local listings and find a typical morning or late afternoon hour of a popular right-wing talk-news radio station and an hour of a typical left-wing talk-news radio station from the same time period. Listen to each program over a two-to-three-day period. Keep a log of what topics are covered and what news stories are reported.

ANALYSIS Look for patterns. What kinds of stories are covered? What kinds of topics are discussed? Create a chart to categorize the stories. How much time is given to *reporting* (clearly verified information) compared to time devoted to *opinion*? What kinds of interview sources are used?

INTERPRETATION What do these patterns mean? Is there a balance between reporting and opinion? Do you detect any bias, and if so, how did you determine this?

EVALUATION Do you agree with the 1949–1987 FCC Fairness Doctrine rule that broadcasting should provide "reasonable, although not necessarily equal" attention to "controversial issues of public importance"? Why or why not? From which station did you learn the most, and which station did you find most entertaining? Explain. What did you like and dislike about each station?

ENGAGEMENT Contact the local general manager, program director, or news director at the stations you analyzed. Ask them what their goals are for the daily news/talk programming and what audience they are trying to reach. Incorporate their comments into a report on your findings. Finally, offer suggestions on how to make the programming at each station better.

Eddie "Piolin" Sotelo is a popular Los Angeles radio personality on KSCA (101.9 FM), which has a regional Mexican format and is the highest-rated station in the market. Sotelo is a major supporter of immigrant rights and helped to organize a huge rally in 2006.

- **Urban.** In 1947, WDIA in Memphis was the first station to program exclusively for black listeners. This format targets a wide variety of African American listeners, primarily in large cities. Urban typically plays popular dance, rap, R&B, and hip-hop music (featuring performers like Rihanna and Tyga).
- **Spanish-language radio.** One of radio's fastest-growing, this format is concentrated mostly in large Hispanic markets such as Miami, New York, Chicago, Las Vegas, California, Arizona, New Mexico, and Texas. Besides talk shows and news segments in Spanish, this format features a variety of Spanish, Caribbean, and Latin American musical styles.

In addition to the formats above, today some stations specialize their formulas by focusing on **album-oriented rock (AOR)**, which features album cuts from mainstream rock bands. There are even several spin-offs from AOR. *Classic rock* serves up rock oldies from the mid-1960s through the 1980s to the baby-boom generation and other listeners who have outgrown the Top 40. The *oldies* format serves adults who grew up on rock and roll from the 1950s through the 1970s. The *alternative music* format recaptures some of the experimental approach of the FM stations of the 1960s, although with much more controlled playlists, and has helped to introduce artists such as the Black Keys and Arcade Fire. Research indicates that most people identify closely with the music they listened to as adolescents and young adults. This tendency partially explains why oldies and classic rock stations combined have surpassed Top 40 stations today. It also helps to explain the recent nostalgia for music from the 1980s and 1990s.

Nonprofit Radio and NPR

Although commercial radio dominates the radio spectrum, nonprofit radio maintains a voice. In the 1930s, the Wagner-Hatfield Amendment to the 1934 Communications Act intended to set aside 25 percent of radio for a wide variety of nonprofit stations. In addition, two government rulings, both in 1948, aided nonprofit radio. Through the first ruling, the government began authorizing noncommercial licenses to stations not affiliated with labor, religion, education, or civic groups. The first license went to Lewis Kimball Hill, a radio reporter and pacifist during World War II who started the **Pacifica Foundation** to run experimental public stations. Pacifica stations have often challenged the status quo in radio and in government. In the second ruling, the FCC approved 10-watt FM stations. Before 1948, radio stations had to have at least 250 watts to get licensed. A 10-watt station with a broadcast range of only about seven miles took very little capital to operate, so the ruling enabled many more people to participate in radio. Many of these tiny stations became training sites for students interested in a broadcasting career.

During the 1960s, nonprofit broadcasting found a new friend in Congress, which proved sympathetic to an old idea: using radio and television as educational tools. In 1967, Congress created the first noncommercial networks: **National Public Radio (NPR)** and the **Public Broadcasting Service (PBS)**. Under the provisions of the **Public Broadcasting Act of 1967** and the **Corporation for Public Broadcasting (CPB)**, NPR and PBS were mandated to provide alternatives to commercial broadcasting. With almost one thousand member stations, NPR draws 26.8 million listeners a week to popular news and interview programs like *Morning Edition* and *All Things Considered*. NPR and PBS stations rely on a blend of private donations, corporate sponsorship, and a small amount of public funding. Today, more than thirty-six hundred nonprofit radio stations operate in the United States.

Steve Inskeep is one of the hosts of NPR's *Morning Edition*, a daily news show with breaking stories, in-depth reports, and features.

Radio Goes Digital

Over the past decade or so, four alternative radio technologies have helped bring more diverse sounds and options for listening to radio audiences: the Internet, satellite, podcasts, and HD (digital) radio.

- **Internet radio.** Emerging in the 1990s with the popularity of the Web, Internet radio stations come in two types: An existing station may "stream" a simulcast version of its on-air signal over the Web, or a station may be created exclusively for the Internet. Some of the most popular Internet radio stations are those that carry music formats unavailable on local radio, such as jazz, blues, and New Age music. This allows traditional stations to reach beyond their borders; however, recent rulings regarding royalty fees for streaming copyrighted songs have made this difficult at times. For now, small commercial Webcasters continue to operate under lower royalty rates than larger Webcasters like

VideoCentral ◎
bedfordstmartins.com /mediaessentials

Going Visual: Video, Radio, and the Web
This video looks at how radio adapted to the Internet by providing multimedia on their Web sites to attract online listeners.
Discussion: If video is now important to radio, what might that mean for journalism and broadcasting students who are considering a job in radio?

Howard Stern's broadcast radio show holds the record for FCC indecency fines, a fact that he and his cohost, Robin Quivers, use for material on the show. Stern avoided further indecency fines when he moved to satellite radio in 2006.

Pandora (see "Converging Media Case Study: Streaming Music" on page 183).

- **Satellite radio.** Another alternative radio technology added a third band—satellite radio—to AM and FM. Two services, XM and Sirius, completed their national introduction by 2002 and offered more than one hundred digital music, news, and talk channels to the continental United States via satellite, and automakers (investors in the satellite radio companies) began equipping most new cars with a satellite band, in addition to AM and FM, helping to ensure the adoption of satellite radio. In 2008, XM and Sirius, which struggled to make a profit as they built competing satellite systems and battled for listeners, merged and became Sirius XM Radio. The service ranges from $7.99 to $19.99 a month. In 2009, Liberty Media, the company that owns DirecTV, became the largest shareholder of Sirius XM.

- **Podcasting.** Developed in 2004, *podcasting* (the term marries "iPod" and "broadcasting") refers to the practice of making audio programs available on the Internet so listeners can download and listen to them on their computers or transfer them to MP3 players, smartphones, or other portable devices with audio capabilities. This popular distribution method quickly went mainstream. Mass media companies created commercial podcasts to promote and extend existing content, such as news and reality TV. Meanwhile, independent producers kept pace with their own podcasts on niche topics like knitting, fly-fishing, and learning Russian.

- **HD Radio.** Approved by the FCC in 2002, HD radio is a digital technology that enables AM and FM radio broadcasters to multicast two to three additional compressed digital signals within their traditional analog frequency. For example, KNOW, a public radio station at 91.1 FM in Minneapolis–St. Paul, runs its National Public Radio news format on 91.1 HD1, BBC News on 91.1 HD2, and the BBC Mundo Spanish-language news service on 91.1 HD3. About two thousand radio stations now broadcast in digital HD.

The Economics of Commercial Radio

Radio today remains one of the most-used mass media, reaching 93 percent of all Americans age twelve or older every week.[6] Because of this continued

CONVERGING MEDIA
Case Study

Streaming Music

Broadcast and satellite radio draw in most of their listeners because being wireless enables them to be mobile. Online music streaming services like Pandora, Spotify, Rdio, MOG, and Turntable.fm have gained fans as they've enabled listeners to customize their experience. More recently, streaming's ability to also be wireless—particularly as the services are accessed via WiFi and mobile phones—puts them in direct competition with radio broadcasters.

One of the oldest of these services, Pandora Radio, launched in 2005 and provides an experience similar to broadcast and satellite radio, but without a human DJ. Pandora selects songs based on an analysis of up to four hundred attributes that company employees index and categorize. Listeners can create up to a hundred personalized stations with key words (Outlaw Country), artists' names (Johnny Cash), or even a song ("Someone Like You"). After creating the station, Pandora streams music with genomes that match the station's name. The service has more than 900,000 tracks available to listeners. By 2012, Pandora had more than 125 million users and a 68 percent market share of Internet radio listening (and, a number of cars are now built with Pandora applications).[1] Like its broadcast counterparts, Pandora licenses its songs from music rights organizations like ASCAP and BMI, and pays royalty fees on the songs it streams.

The radio industry has responded to the Internet radio start-ups with its own streaming start-up. Leading radio corporation Clear Channel Communications unveiled its iHeartRadio service (www.iheart.com) in 2008, putting more than 850 of its stations from around the country on a free streaming service, and also allowing listeners to create their own custom stations by artist, song, or genre. In 2011, Clear Channel signed an agreement with Cumulus Radio to add its 570 stations to the iHeartRadio lineup.

With social media such as Facebook and Twitter, listening to music on the Internet has become a social experience. By 2011, with Turntable.fm, Internet radio listeners could share music and listen simultaneously in chat rooms. Then, in 2012, Facebook created its "Listen to Music With Your Friends" feature that identifies the songs a user's friends in chat are listening to on streaming services like Spotify and invites that user to listen simultaneously.[2]

Radio's technological convergence puts it in a unique position. On one hand, it remains the most local of media, where DJs can break into the playlist to provide live traffic, weather, and news updates, or broadcast live from a community event. On the other hand, radio now can be the most global of media, streaming programs around the world, while still enabling far-flung friends to share a song together. As such, music can become more social without listeners going to a club or a concert; in many ways, convergent media are not only reinventing traditional forms of entertainment, but also changing what it means to be social in the twenty-first century.

broad reach, the airwaves are still desirable real estate for advertisers and content programmers, who want to target people in and out of their homes; for record labels, who want their artists' songs played; and for radio station owners, who want to attract large groups of diverse listeners to dominate multiple markets.

Money In and Money Out

As in any other enterprise, money flows both into and out of radio. Commercial stations take in money from advertisers and spend it on assets such as content programming, often purchasing programming from national network radio. Noncommercial stations are funded by donations, which are then used to cover expenses, including content.

Revenues from Local and National Advertising

VideoCentral◉
**bedfordstmartins.com
/mediaessentials**

....
Radio: Yesterday, Today,
and Tomorrow
Scholars and radio producers
explain how radio adapts to
and influences other media.
Discussion: Do you expect
that the Internet will be the
end of radio, or will radio
stations still be around
decades from now?

About 8 percent of all U.S. spending on media advertising goes to radio stations. Like newspapers, radio generates its largest profits by selling local and regional ads. Thirty-second radio ads range from $1,500 in large markets to just a few dollars in the smallest markets. Today, gross advertising receipts for radio are about $19.4 billion (about three-quarters of the revenues from local ad sales, with the remainder in national spot and network sales), down from about $21.7 billion in 2006. The industry consists of approximately 15,029 stations (4,762 AM stations, and 10,267 commercial and educational FM stations).

Spending for Radio Content

Local radio stations get much of their music content free from the recording industry (although by 2009, the music industry—which has seen a shortfall in its own revenues—was proposing to charge radio for playing music on the air). Therefore, only about 20 percent of a typical radio station's budget goes to cover music programming costs. When radio stations want to purchase additional programming, they often turn to national network radio, which generates more than $1.1 billion in ad sales annually by offering dozens of specialized services (such as news features, entertainment programs, and music formats). The companies providing these programming services to local stations receive time slots for national ads in return.

Buying Influence with Payola

In the world of radio, record labels play a central role in the relationship between money and content. Just as advertisers want to target specific audiences, record labels want specific people to hear their artists' songs. **Payola**, the questionable practice by which record promoters pay deejays to play particular records, was rampant during the 1950s as record companies sought to guarantee record sales. In response, radio management took control of programming. Managers argued that if individual deejays had less impact on which records were played, they would be less susceptible to bribery. Despite congressional hearings and new regulations, payola persisted. Record promoters showered their favors on a few influential, high-profile deejays, whose backing could make or break a record nationally, or on key program managers in charge of Top 40 formats in large urban markets. Recently, the FCC has stepped up enforcement of payola laws.

Radio Ownership: From Diversity to Consolidation

From the 1950s through the 1980s, the FCC tried to encourage diversity in broadcast ownership—and thus programming—by limiting the number of stations a media company could own. The **Telecommunications Act of 1996** introduced a new age of consolidation in the industry, as the FCC eliminated most ownership restrictions on radio. As a result, some 2,100 stations and $15 billion changed hands that year alone. From 1995 to 2005, the number of radio station owners declined by one-third, from 6,600 to about 4,400.[7]

Comedian Marc Maron hosts the popular podcast *WTF*, featuring detailed interviews with famous comedians like Amy Poehler, Conan O'Brien, Ben Stiller, and Sarah Silverman.

The 1996 act allows individuals and companies to acquire as many radio stations as they want, with relaxed restrictions on the number of stations a single broadcaster may own in the same city. The larger the market or area, the more stations a company may own within that market. With few exceptions, for the past two decades the FCC has embraced the consolidation schemes pushed by the powerful National Association of Broadcasters (NAB) lobbyists in Washington, D.C., under which fewer and fewer owners control more and more of the airwaves.

The 1996 act and other pushes for deregulation have reshaped the industry once more. Consider the cases of Clear Channel Communications and CBS Radio, the two largest radio chain owners in terms of total revenue. Combined, Clear Channel and CBS own roughly one thousand radio stations—about 8 percent of all commercial U.S. stations—and control about 25 percent of the entire radio industry's $17.3 billion revenue.

When large corporations regained control of America's radio airwaves in the 1990s, activists in hundreds of communities across the United States protested by starting up their own noncommercial "pirate" radio stations capable of broadcasting over a few miles with low-power FM signals of 1 to 10 watts. The major complaint of pirate radio station operators was that the FCC had long ago ceased licensing low-power community radio stations. In 2000, the FCC responded to tens of thousands of inquiries about the development of a new local radio broadcasting service: It approved a new noncommercial **low-power FM (LPFM)** class of 10 and 100-watt stations to give voice to local groups lacking access to the public airwaves. LPFM station licensees included mostly religious groups but also high schools, colleges and universities, Native American tribes, labor groups, and museums. William E. Kennard, then-FCC chairman who fostered the LPFM initiative, explained: "This is about the haves—the broadcast industry—trying to prevent many have-nots—small community and educational organizations—from having just a little piece of the pie. Just a little piece of the airwaves which belong to all of the people."[8]

The Coalition of Immokalee Workers (CIW) launched its 100-watt low-power FM station, WCIW-LP, 107.9 FM, in December 2003. The CIW is a community-based organization, composed mostly of immigrant farm workers in Florida. The station covers a fifteen-mile radius and broadcasts news, educational programs, and music in Spanish, Haitian Creole, and indigenous languages of Mexico and Guatemala.

Radio in a Democratic Society

As the first national electronic mass medium, radio has powerfully molded American culture. It has given us soap operas, situation comedies, and broadcast news. And it helped to popularize rock and roll, car culture, and the politics of talk radio. Yet for all of its national influence and recent move toward consolidation, broadcast radio is

still a supremely local medium. For decades, listeners have tuned in to hear the familiar voices of their community's deejays and talk show hosts, and to enjoy music popular in their cultural heritage.

The early debates over how radio should be used produced one of the most important and enduring ideas in communication policy for any democracy: a requirement to operate in the "public interest, convenience, or necessity." But as we've seen, the broadcasting industry has long chafed at this policy. Executives have maintained that because radio corporations invest heavily in technology, they should have more control over the radio frequencies on which they operate—as well as own as many stations as they want.

Deregulation in the past few decades has moved the industry closer to that corporate vision. Today, nearly every radio market in the nation is dominated by a few owners, and those owners are required to renew their broadcasting licenses only every eight years.

This trend has begun moving radio away from its localism, as radio groups often manage hundreds of stations from afar. Given broadcasters' reluctance to openly discuss their own economic arrangements, public debate regarding radio as a natural resource has dwindled. Looking to the future, we face a big question: With a few large broadcast companies now permitted to dominate radio ownership nationwide, how much will the number and kinds of voices permitted to speak over the public airwaves be restricted? If restriction occurs, what will happen to the democracy we live in—which is defined by local communities' having a say in how they're governed? To ensure that mass media, including radio, continue to serve democracy, we—the public—must play a role in developing the answers to these questions.

CHAPTER ESSENTIALS

Now that you have finished reading this chapter, you can use the following tools:

REVIEW

Understand Key Aspects of Radio's Early History

- The **telegraph**, invented in the 1840s, sent electrical impulses through a cable from a transmitter to a reception point and was the first technology to enable communication to exceed the speed of human transportation. To send messages, telegraph operators used **Morse code**—a series of dots and dashes that stood for letters in the alphabet. The telegraph's limitations caused others to experiment without wires, leading to the discovery of **radio waves** and **electromagnetic waves** (pp. 163–164).

- New developments in the nineteenth century improved wireless communication, taking it from **narrowcasting** (point-to-point communication) to **broadcasting** (one-to-many communication). Marconi is credited with developing **wireless telegraphy**, a form of voiceless point-to-point communication, in the 1890s, leaving others such as Lee De Forest and Reginald Fessenden to experiment with producing **wireless telephony** (voice transmissions) and amplifying radio sound (pp. 164–165).

- Early regulation of wireless/radio focused on providing public safety and national security; in 1910 Congress passed the **Wireless Ship Act**, which required all major ships to be equipped with wireless equipment, and two years later it passed the **Radio Act of 1912**, which required all radio stations on land or at sea to be licensed and assigned special call letters, and for each station to be operated only by a licensed person (p. 167).

- During World War I, radio moved into the private sector with the formation of **Radio Corporation of America (RCA)**—a privately owned company that had the government's approval to acquire radio patents and dominate the radio industry (p. 168).

- Radio's development as a business was solidified with the creation of the first lasting **network**, NBC, in 1926. Backed by David Sarnoff and connected by AT&T long lines, the network broadcast programs nationally and played a prominent role in unifying the country (pp. 169–170).

- The growth of the network and affiliate system alarmed government leaders, who banded together to pass the **Radio Act of 1927**, which began the process of issuing radio licenses and created the **Federal Radio Commission (FRC)** to oversee radio licenses and negotiate channel problems. The Radio Act introduced a pivotal new principle: Licensees did not *own* their channels but could only use them as long as they operated to serve the "public interest, convenience, or necessity." With the passage of the **Federal Communications Act of 1934**, which allowed commercial interests to control the airwaves, the FRC became the **Federal Communications Commission (FCC)**, an independent U.S. government agency charged with regulating interstate and international communications (pp. 171–172).

- By 1930, the Golden Age of Radio was in full force; living rooms were filled with music, drama, comedy, variety and quiz shows, and news (pp. 172–174).

Outline the Evolution of Radio

- In the wake of TV's development and massive popularity in the 1950s, radio suffered but was resurrected via portable **transistor** radios and the shift to music formats that relied on the recording industry for content (p. 174).

- The rise of **FM** (frequency modulation) brought greater clarity and reception to radio, and became the dominant band for music by the 1980s. Until then, radio technology had centered on **AM** (amplitude modulation) (pp. 174–175).

- The rise of **format radio**, whereby music and talk programs developed and played specific styles (or formats) geared to specific listeners, solidified music as radio's single biggest staple and also introduced the idea of **rotation**: playing the top songs many times during the day (pp. 175–176).

Explain the Characteristics of Contemporary Radio

- Radio stations use a variety of formats to serve a diverse group of listeners, including **news and talk radio** (the most popular format of the 1990s, especially on AM stations) and music, which is often categorized by **adult contemporary (AC), Top 40/contemporary hit radio (CHR), country, urban, Spanish-language** (sometimes in both talk and music formats), and **album-oriented rock (AOR)** (pp. 176–177, 180).

- Nonprofit radio stations, such as those in the **Pacifica Foundation** network, and noncommercial networks, such as **National Public Radio (NPR)** and the **Public Broadcasting Service (PBS)**—the latter two of which were mandated under federal provisions of the **Public Broadcasting Act of 1967** and the **Corporation for Public Broadcasting (CPB)**—were created to provide alternatives to commercial broadcasting (pp. 180–181).

- Over the past decade or so, four alternative radio technologies have helped bring more diverse sounds and options for listening to radio audiences: **Internet radio, satellite radio, podcasting,** and **HD radio** (pp. 181–182).

Discuss the Economics behind Modern Radio

- Commercial radio stations take in revenue from advertisers and spend money on assets such as content programming, often purchasing programming from national network radio (p. 184).

- A radio station's musical content can be influenced by **payola**, the unethical practice of record promoters paying deejays or radio programmers to favor particular songs over others (pp. 184–185).

- The **Telecommunications Act of 1996** introduced a new age of consolidation in radio ownership across the United States (p. 185).

- In response to large corporations' control over the airwaves, **low-power FM (LPFM)** was approved by the FCC in 2000 as a new class of noncommercial radio stations that aimed to give voice to local groups lacking access to the public airwaves (pp. 185–186).

Consider Radio's Influence on Our Democratic Society

- Radio has shaped trends in music, news, and entertainment while also still remaining a supremely local medium, yet the trend has begun moving radio away from its localism, as radio groups often manage hundreds of stations from afar (p. 186).

- In an age when control of the public airwaves lies in fewer hands than ever, it is important to think about the impact this has on the number of voices permitted to speak and how this affects democracy (pp. 186–187).

STUDY QUESTIONS

1. How did broadcasting, unlike print media, come to be federally regulated?
2. What is the significance of the Radio Act of 1927 and the Federal Communications Act of 1934?
3. How did radio adapt to the arrival of television?
4. What has been the main effect of the Telecommunications Act of 1996 on radio station ownership?
5. What is the relevance of localism to debates about ownership in radio?

MEDIA LITERACY PRACTICE

One of the most contentious issues in radio today involves diversity of owner-ship, which might influence diversity in sound and formats. To investigate this issue, explore the radio stations in your community.

DESCRIBE the ownership of stations in your (or a nearby) radio market, their formats, and their ratings by creating a list. (See www.arbitron.com /radio_stations/home.htm for an archive of Arbitron radio ratings.)

ANALYZE the information in your list, looking for patterns and trends: How many station groups attract the majority of the market's ratings? Are there multiple stations serving the same formats? What formats are missing?

INTERPRET what these patterns mean. For example, what does your market profile suggest about diversity in ownership and station formats? Are there people in your community who are underserved by all of the on-air options?

EVALUATE radio in your community. Do newer developments like Internet radio, satellite radio, podcasts, and HD radio offer better alternatives, or are they poor substitutes for broadcast radio?

ENGAGE with your community by writing to a local station. Tell the manager what the station is doing right or what could be done better to serve the community.

◉ ONLINE RESOURCES

Go to **bedfordstmartins.com/mediaessentials** for review quizzes, links, and more.

Visit the site's **VIDEOCENTRAL: MASS COMMUNICATION** section for videos like the ones on pages 181 and 184.

7

Movies and the Impact of Images

Though Trudy Chacon (Michelle Rodriguez) ranks as a secondary character in *Avatar*, the tough combat pilot delivers one of the most memorable lines from the highest grossing movie of all time. The moment comes after Chacon's aircraft breaks through a bank of clouds to reveal a breathtaking view of the Hallelujah Mountains. As her passengers gasp at the sight of floating peaks, Chacon remarks "You should see your faces." Resonating with Al Jolson's "You ain't heard nothin' yet," Chacon's words are directed both to characters within the world of the story and to those strangers gathered in dark auditoriums mesmerized by the spectacle of *Avatar*. Like Georges Méliès' *A Trip to the Moon*, Warner Brothers' *The Jazz Singer*, and Orson Welles's *Citizen Kane*, James Cameron's *Avatar* stands as a benchmark movie—a movie that represents a new way to use motion picture technology to delight and challenge audiences hungry for compelling and involving experiences. Where Méliès pioneered the use of fantasy in film, Warner Brothers ushered in the sound era, and Welles developed deep-focus cinematography and other technical milestones, Cameron masterfully deployed the innovation of digital performance-capture technology to transform the 3-D movie from gimmick to potential art form. Two years later, Martin Scorsese was using 3-D and other digital tricks to tell a story about the early days of filmmaking with *Hugo*.

The movies, then, have always been a technological spectacle, a grand illusion that—like a magic act—uses smoke, light, and trickery to make marvelous illusions come to life. Since the early twentieth century, when Méliès took delighted audiences to the moon and back, the movies have operated as one of the world's chief storytellers, excavating the past, commenting on the present, and fantasizing about the future, while visiting people and places both familiar and extraordinary. These movie narratives create community, too. We attend theaters or watch at home with family and friends. Our movie experiences also touch our interactions with other groups and can affect how we discuss topics like war (e.g., *The Hurt Locker*, 2009), think about people struggling with desperate situations (e.g., *Precious*, 2009), or even play games (e.g., the *Scene It?* game brand built around the Harry Potter, James Bond, and *Pirates of the Caribbean* movie series). Of course, as cultural products, movies are subject to the same economic constraints as other mass media forms. For example, there is a tendency for the major studios to roll out standardized big-budget blockbusters in hopes of finding the next *Avatar*, while narratives that break the mold can sometimes languish for lack of major studio backing. But in the emerging terrain of digital video and Internet distribution, the ability for moviemakers to find audiences without major studio support is increasing.

GIVEN THE FILM INDUSTRY'S LENGTHY AND COMPLEX ROLE in Americans' lives, along with its steady transformation in response to new technologies, cultural change, and other developments, it's vital to take a closer look at this unique mass medium. In particular, we need to ask big questions such as what purposes movies serve for us today, compared to the past; how strong an impact the U.S. film industry has on society and culture in our own country and in others; and where the film industry may be headed in the future.

To these ends, we use this chapter to examine the rich legacy and current role of movies by:

• considering film's early history, including the technological advances that made movies possible

• tracing the evolution of the Hollywood studio system that arose to dominate the global film industry

• exploring how narrative styles developed in moviemaking, including the transition from silent film to "talkies" and the emergence of different camera techniques and movie genres

- examining the transformation of the Hollywood studio system in response to new forces such as the birth of television and the rise of home entertainment

- analyzing the economics of the movie business; specifically, how it makes money and what it invests in to stay profitable

- weighing movies' role in our democracy today and in the diverse world around us

The Early History of Movies

Filmmaking has passed through several stages on its way to mass medium status. In the following pages, we trace those stages—including development (when inventors first made pictures move), entrepreneurship (when experimenters conducted movie demonstrations for a small number of paid viewers), and finally true mass media (when movies began telling coherent stories with specific meanings for viewers and became widely accessible). Throughout all these stages, creative and bold innovators have worked together to constantly advance the medium—revealing the strongly collaborative nature of this industry.

Advances in Film Technology

The concept of film goes back as early as Leonardo da Vinci, who theorized in the late 1400s that a device could be created to reproduce reality. There were other early precursors to film as well. For example, in the 1600s, the *magic lantern* projected images painted on glass plates using an oil lamp as a light source. In 1824, the *thaumatrope* consisted of a two-sided card with different images on each side that appeared to combine the images when twirled. And the *zoetrope*, created in 1834, was a cylindrical device that rapidly twirled images inside and appeared to make the images move.

Eadweard Muybridge's studies of horses in motion, like the one shown, proved that a horse gets all four feet off the ground during a gallop. In his various studies of motion, Muybridge could use twelve cameras at a time.

But the true development stage of filmmaking began when inventors discovered a process for making a series of photographs appear to move while projected on a screen.

Muybridge and Goodwin Make Pictures Move

Eadweard Muybridge, an English photographer living in America, is credited with being the first person to make images move. He studied motion by using multiple cameras to take successive photographs of humans and animals in motion. By 1880, he had developed a method for projecting the photographic images on a wall for public viewing.

Meanwhile, other inventors were also capturing moving images and projecting them. In 1884, George Eastman (founder of Eastman Kodak) developed the first roll film—a huge improvement over the heavy metal and glass plates previously used to make individual photos. Louis Aimé Augustin Le Prince, a Frenchman living in England, invented the first motion-picture camera using roll film. Le Prince, who disappeared mysteriously on a train ride to Paris in 1890, is credited with filming the first motion picture, *Roundhay Garden Scene*, in 1888. Recorded at twelve frames per second, the film depicts several people strolling on a lawn and runs for just a few seconds.

In 1889, a New Jersey minister, Hannibal Goodwin, improved Eastman's roll film by using thin strips of transparent, pliable material called **celluloid** that could hold a coating of chemicals sensitive to light. Goodwin's breakthrough enabled a strip of film to move through a camera and be photographed in rapid succession, producing a series of pictures.

Edison and the Brothers Lumière Create Motion Pictures

The early developers of film laid the groundwork for a shift to the entrepreneurial stage. During this stage, inventors came up with new projection and distribution technologies enabling people to come together in a public place to view movies. The action began in the late 1800s, when American inventor and businessman

---

CHAPTER 7 // TIMELINE

1889 Celluloid
U.S. minister Hannibal Goodwin develops celluloid, which enables motion pictures to be created.

1894 Kinetoscope Parlors
Thomas Edison's team opens the first such parlor of coin-operated machines.

1896 The Vitascope
Edison's vitascope invention popularizes large-screen film projection in the United States.

1907 Nickelodeons
Storefront movie theaters with a five-cent admission price begin to flourish in the United States.

1914 Movie Palaces
The first of a national trend of opulent movie palaces opens in New York.

Thomas Edison (with the help of his assistant, William Kennedy Dickson) combined his incandescent light bulb, Goodwin's celluloid, and Le Prince's camera to create another early movie camera, the **kinetograph**, and a single-person viewing system, the **kinetoscope**. This small projection system required individual viewers to look through a small hole to see images moving on a tiny plate.

Meanwhile in France, brothers Louis and Auguste Lumière developed the *cinematograph*, a combined camera, film development, and projection system. The projection system was particularly important, as it enabled more than one person at a time to see the moving images on a large screen.

With inventors around the world now dabbling in moving pictures, Edison continued innovating in film. He patented several inventions and manufactured a new large-screen system called the **vitascope**, through which longer filmstrips could be projected without interruption. This device hinted at the potential of movies as a future mass medium. Staged at a music hall in New York in April 1896, Edison's first public showing of the vitascope featured shots from a boxing match and waves rolling onto a beach. Some members of the audience were so taken with the realism of the images that they stepped back from the screen's crashing waves to avoid getting their feet wet.

At this point, movies consisted of movement recorded by a single continuous camera shot. Early filmmakers had not yet figured out how to move the camera itself or how to edit film shots together. Moreover, movies' content consisted of simply people or objects in motion, without conveying any story. Nonetheless, various innovators had spotted the commercial possibilities of

Kinetoscopes allowed individuals to view motion pictures through a window in a cabinet that held the film. The first kinetoscope parlor opened in 1894 and was such a hit that many others quickly followed.

film. By 1900, short movies had become a part of the entertainment industry, used as visual novelties in amusement arcades, traveling carnivals, wax museums, and vaudeville theaters.

Telling Stories: The Introduction of Narrative

With the introduction of **narrative films**—movies that tell stories through the series of actions depicted (later matched with sound)—the industry advanced from the entrepreneurial stage to mass medium status. And it promised to offer a far richer experience than other storytelling media—specifically, books and radio. Unlike those media, narrative films provided realistic moving images and compelling stories in which viewers became so immersed that they sometimes forgot they were watching a fictional representation.

Some of the earliest narrative films (which were silent) were produced and directed by French magician and inventor Georges Méliès, who opened the first public movie theater in France in 1896. Méliès began producing short fantasy and fairy-tale films—including *The Vanishing Lady* (1896), *Cinderella* (1899), and *A Trip to the Moon* (1902). He increasingly used editing and existing camera tricks and techniques, such as slow motion and cartoon animation, that would become key ingredients in future narrative filmmaking.

The first American filmmaker to adapt Méliès' innovations to narrative film was Edwin S. Porter. He shot narrative scenes out of order (for instance, some in a studio and some outdoors) and reassembled, or edited, them to tell a story. In 1902, he made what is regarded as America's first narrative film, *The Life of an American Fireman*, which included the first recorded close-up. Porter also introduced the western genre and the first chase scene in *The Great Train Robbery* (1903).

The Great Train Robbery (1903) may have introduced the western genre, but it was actually filmed in New Jersey. The still above shows a famous scene in which a bandit shoots his gun at the audience.

CHAPTER 7 // TIMELINE continued

1967 Ratings System
The Motion Picture Association of America initiates the first ratings system for age appropriateness.

1977 Video Transforms the Industry
VHS-format videocassette recorders (VCRs) hit the consumer market, creating the movie rental and purchase industry.

1990s The Rise of the Indies
Independent films become an important source for identifying new talent.

1995 Megaplex Mania
A wave of giant movie complexes are built.

The Arrival of Nickelodeons

Another turning point in film's development as a mass medium was the arrival of **nickelodeons**—a type of movie theater whose name combines the admission price (five cents) with the Greek word for "theater." According to media historian Douglas Gomery, these small and uncomfortable makeshift theaters often consisted of converted storefronts redecorated to mimic vaudeville theaters.[1] Nickelodeons showed silent films that usually transcended language barriers and that provided workers and immigrants with an inexpensive escape from the challenges of urban life. Not surprisingly, they flourished during the great European immigration at the dawn of the twentieth century. Between 1907 and 1909, the number of nickelodeons in the United States skyrocketed from five thousand to ten thousand. The craze peaked by 1910, when entrepreneurs began seeking more affluent spectators, attracting them with larger and more lavish movie theaters.

The Evolution of the Hollywood Studio System

By the 1910s, movies had become a major industry, and entrepreneurs developed many tactics for controlling it—including monopolizing patents on film-related technologies and dominating the "three pillars" of the movie business: production (making movies), distribution (getting films into theaters), and exhibition (playing films in theaters). Controlling those three parts of an industry achieves **vertical integration**. In the film business it means managing the moviemaking process all the way from the development of an idea to

1997 DVDs
The new format is quickly adopted as superior to the VHS cassette.

2000 Digital Film Production
The digital production and distribution format gains strength in Hollywood and with independents.

Early 2000s IMAX Experience
Select Hollywood films are digitally remastered and exhibited in the larger IMAX format.

2008 Blu-ray
Hollywood settles on the Blu-ray format to succeed the DVD, but home exhibition also moves toward Internet streaming.

2012 3-D
Over two dozen movies are released in digital 3-D, including several converted classics.

the screening of the final product before an audience. The resulting concentration of power gave rise to the **studio system**, by which creative talent was firmly controlled by certain powerful studios. Five vertically integrated movie studios made up this new film **oligopoly** (a situation in which an industry is controlled by just a few firms): Paramount, MGM, Warner Brothers, Twentieth Century Fox, and RKO. An additional three studios—Columbia, Universal, and United Artists—did not own chains of theaters but held powerful positions in movie production and distribution.

Edison's Attempt to Control the Industry

Among the first to try his hand at dominating the movie business and reaping its profits, Thomas Edison formed the Motion Picture Patents Company, known as the Trust, in 1908. A cartel of major U.S. and French film producers, the company pooled film-technology patents, acquired most major film distributorships, and signed an exclusive deal with George Eastman, who agreed to supply stock film only to Trust-approved theater companies.

However, some independent producers refused to bow to the Trust's terms. They abandoned film-production centers in New York and New Jersey and moved to Cuba, Florida, and ultimately Hollywood, California. In particular, two Hungarian immigrants—Adolph Zukor (who would eventually run Paramount Pictures) and William Fox (who would found the Fox Film Corporation, later named Twentieth Century Fox)—wanted to free their movie operations from the Trust's tyrannical grasp. Zukor's early companies figured out ways to bypass the Trust. A suit by Fox, a nickelodeon operator turned film distributor, resulted in the Trust's breakup for restraint of trade violations in 1917.

A Closer Look at the Three Pillars

Ironically, film entrepreneurs like Zukor who fought the Trust realized they could control the film industry themselves through vertical integration. The three pillars of vertical integration occur in a specific sequence: First, movies are produced. Next, copies are distributed to people or companies who get them out to theaters. Finally, the movies are exhibited in theaters. But even as power through vertical integration became concentrated in just a few big studios, other studios sought to dominate one or another of the three pillars. This competition sparked tension between the forces of centralization and those of independence.

Production
A major element in the production pillar is the choice of actors for a particular film. This circumstance opened an opportunity for some studios to gain control by

tactics other than Edison's pooling of patents. Once these companies learned that audiences preferred specific actors to anonymous ones, they signed exclusive contracts with big-name actors. In this way, the studio system began controlling the talent in the industry. For example, Adolph Zukor hired a number of popular actors and formed the Famous Players Company in 1912. One Famous Players performer was Mary Pickford, who became known as "America's Sweetheart" for her portrayal of spunky and innocent heroines. Pickford so elevated film actors' status that in 1919 she broke from Zukor to form her own company, United Artists. Actor Douglas Fairbanks (her future husband) joined her, along with comedian-director Charlie Chaplin and director D. W. Griffith.

Although United Artists represented a brief triumph of autonomy for a few powerful actors, by the 1920s the studio system had solidified its control over all creative talent in the industry. Pioneered by director Thomas Ince and his company, Triangle, the system constituted a kind of assembly line for moviemaking talent: actors, directors, editors, writers, and others all worked under exclusive contracts for the major studios. Ince also designated himself the first studio head: He appointed producers to handle hiring, logistics, and finances so he could more easily supervise many pictures at once. The studio system proved so efficient that major studios were soon producing new feature films every week. Pooling talent, rather than patents, turned out to be a more ingenious tactic for movie studios seeking to dominate film production.

Distribution

Whereas there were two main strategies for controlling the production pillar of moviemaking (pooling patents or pooling talent), studios seeking power in the industry had more options open to them for controlling distribution. One early effort to do so came in 1904, when movie companies provided vaudeville theaters with films and projectors on a *film exchange* system. In return for their short films, shown between live acts in the theaters, movie producers received a small percentage of the vaudeville ticket-gate receipts.

Edison's Trust used another tactic: withholding projection equipment from theater companies not willing to pay the Trust's patent-use fees. However, as with the production of film, independent film companies looked for distribution strategies outside of the Trust. Again, Adolph Zukor led the fight, developing **block booking**. Under this system, movie exhibitors who wanted access to popular films with big stars like Mary Pickford had to also rent new or marginal

With legions of fans, Mary Pickford became the first woman ever to make a salary of $1 million in a year and gained the freedom to take artistic risks with her roles. She launched United Artists, a film distribution company, with Douglas Fairbanks, Charlie Chaplin, and D. W. Griffith. No woman since has been as powerful a player in the movie industry. Here she is seen with Buddy Rogers in *My Best Girl*.

films featuring no stars. Although this practice was eventually outlawed as monopolistic, such contracts enabled the studios to test-market possible up-and-coming stars at little financial risk.

As yet another distribution strategy, some companies marketed American films in Europe. World War I so disrupted film production in Europe that the United States stepped in to fill the gap—eventually becoming the leader in the commercial movie business worldwide. After the war, no other nation's film industry could compete economically with Hollywood. By the mid-1920s, foreign revenue from U.S. films totaled $100 million. Even today, Hollywood dominates the world market for movies.

Exhibition

Companies could gain further control of the movie industry by finding ways to get more people to buy more movie tickets. Innovations in exhibition (such as construction of more inviting theaters) transformed the way people watched films and began attracting more middle- and upper-middle-class viewers.

Initially, Edison's Trust tried to dominate exhibition by controlling the flow of films to theater owners. If theaters wanted to ensure they had films to show their patrons, they had to purchase a license from the Trust and pay whatever price it asked. But after the Trust collapsed, emerging studios in Hollywood came up with their own ideas for controlling exhibition and making certain the movies they produced were shown. When industrious theater owners began forming film cooperatives to compete with block-booking tactics, producers like Zukor conspired to buy up theaters. Zukor and the heads of several major studios understood that they did not have to own all the theaters to ensure that their movies were shown. Instead, the major studios only needed to own the first-run theaters (about 15 percent of the nation's theaters). First-run theaters premiered new films in major downtown areas in front of the largest audiences, and generated 85 to 95 percent of all film revenue.

The studios quickly realized that to earn revenue from these first-run theaters, they would have to draw members of the middle and upper-middle classes to the movies. With this goal in mind, they built **movie palaces**, full-time single-screen theaters that provided a more enjoyable and comfortable movie-viewing environment. In 1914, the three-thousand-seat Strand Theatre, the first movie palace, opened in New York.

The historic Fox Movie Palace, located in Detroit, was originally built in the late 1920s and later restored in 1990.

Another major innovation in exhibition was the development of *mid-city movie theaters*. These were built in convenient locations near urban mass-transit stations. They attracted city dwellers as well as the initial wave of people who had moved to city outskirts in the 1920s and commuted into work from the suburbs. This strategy is alive and well today, as **multiplexes** and **megaplexes** featuring many screens (often fourteen or more), upscale concession services, stadium-style seating, digital projection and sound, 3-D capabilities, and giant IMAX screens lure middle-class crowds to interstate highway crossroads (see "Converging Media Case Study: Movie Theaters and Live Exhibition" on page 217).

Hollywood's Golden Age: The Development of Style

Once the Hollywood studio system was established as a profitable business model, studios had the luxury of developing a distinctive moviemaking style that ultimately marked Hollywood's Golden Age. This style began taking shape in 1915—characterized by the use of new narrative techniques (such as close-up camera shots and multiple story lines) in the silent era, the later introduction of sound, and the rise of movie genres. Hollywood's monopolization of this style produced numerous films that have since become treasured classics. Yet during Hollywood's Golden Age, other moviemaking models—including foreign films, documentaries, and independent films—provided alternatives to the classic style and shaped the medium just as powerfully.

Narrative Techniques in the Silent Era

Though telling stories in films occurred early on, moviemaking hit its stride as a viable art form when studios developed innovative narrative techniques including the use of varied camera distances, close-up shots, multiple story lines, fast-paced editing, and symbolic imagery to tell a story—even before sound was introduced. As these techniques evolved, making a movie became more than just telling a story; it became all about *how* to tell the story. For example, the same sequence of events filmed from different camera angles could have totally different impacts on viewers.

D. W. Griffith, among the earliest "star" directors, used nearly all of these techniques at the same time in *The Birth of a Nation* (1915)—the first *feature-length film* (more than an hour long) produced in America. Although considered a technical masterpiece and an enormous hit, the film glorified the Ku Klux Klan and stereotyped southern blacks. The National Association for the Advancement of Colored People (NAACP) campaigned against the film, and protests and riots broke out at many screenings.

Other popular films created during the silent era were historical and religious epics, including *Napoleon, Ben-Hur,* and *The Ten Commandments.* But the era also produced pioneering social dramas, mysteries, comedies, horror films, science fiction movies, war films, crime dramas, and westerns.

Augmenting Images with Sound

Hollywood's Golden Age also saw the introduction of sound in 1927, which further established a distinctive narrative style and set new commercial standards in the industry. The availability of movies with sound pushed annual movie attendance in the United States from sixty million a week in 1927 to ninety million a week just two years later. By 1931, nearly 85 percent of America's twenty thousand theaters accommodated **talkies** (sound pictures). And by 1935, the rest of the world had adopted talking films as the commercial standard.

Earlier attempts at creating talkies had failed; however, technical breakthroughs in the 1910s at AT&T's research arm, Bell Labs, produced prototypes of loudspeakers and sound amplifiers. Experiments with sound continued during the 1920s, particularly at Warner Brothers. In 1927, the studio produced *The Jazz Singer,* a feature-length silent film interspersed with musical numbers and brief dialogue. Starring Al Jolson, a charismatic and popular vaudeville singer who wore blackface makeup as part of his act, the movie further demonstrated racism's presence in the film industry. Warner Brothers' 1928 release *The Singing Fool,* which also starred Jolson, became the real breakthrough for talkies. Costing $200,000 to make, the film raked in a whopping $5 million and "proved to all doubters that talkies were here to stay."[2]

Warner Brothers was not the only studio exploring sound technology. Five months before *The Jazz Singer* opened, Fox premiered sound-film **newsreels** (weekly ten-minute compilations of news events from around the world). Fox's newsreel company, Movietone, captured the first film footage with sound of the takeoff and return of Charles Lindbergh, who piloted the first solo, nonstop flight across the Atlantic Ocean in May 1927. The Movietone sound system eventually became the industry standard.

Al Jolson in *The Singing Fool* (1928). The film was the box-office champ for more than ten years until 1939, when it was dethroned by *Gone with the Wind.*

Inside the Hollywood System:
Setting the Standard for Narrative Style

By the time talkies had transformed the film industry, Hollywood had established firm control over narrative style, the recognizable way in which directors told stories through the movies they made. Hollywood had set the example for most moviemaking style worldwide, and continues to dominate American filmmaking style today. The model it developed serves up three ingredients that give Hollywood movies their distinctive flavor: the narrative (or story), the genre (type of story), and the author (or director). The right blend of these ingredients—combined with timing, marketing, and luck—has enabled Hollywood to create a long string of movie hits, from 1930s and 1940s classics like *Gone with the Wind* and *Casablanca* to recent successes like *The Avengers* and *Moonrise Kingdom*.

Hollywood Narratives

As we've seen, storytelling had long existed in movies, even in the silent era. But it was Hollywood's Golden Age that saw the emerge`nce of a distinctive narrative style that movie viewers soon associated with American filmmaking. *Narrative* always includes a story (what happens to whom) and discourse (how the story is told). Most movies feature a number of stories that play out within the film's larger, overarching narrative. These narratives also present recognizable character types (protagonist, antagonist, romantic interest, sidekick) and have a clear beginning, middle, and end. The plot is usually propelled by the main character's decisions and actions to resolve a conflict by the end of the movie. Nowadays, filmmakers also use computer-generated imagery (CGI) or digital remastering to augment narratives with special effects—providing a powerful experience that satisfies most audiences' appetite for both the familiar and the distinctive.

Hollywood genres help us categorize movies. The 1942 film *Casablanca* is considered a drama whereas Woody Allen's *Annie Hall* is a popular comedy made in 1977 and *Alice in Wonderland* is a 2010 fantasy film.

Hollywood Genres

In addition to establishing a unique narrative style in its Golden Age, Hollywood gave birth to movie **genres**, categories in which conventions regarding characters, scenes, and themes recur in combination. Familiar genres include comedy, drama, romance, action/adventure, mystery/suspense, gangster, westerns, horror, fantasy/science fiction, musicals, and film noir (French for "black film")—a genre developed in the United States after World War II that explores unstable characters and the sinister side of human nature.

Grouping films by category enabled the movie industry to achieve both *product standardization* (a set of formulas for producing genres) and *product differentiation* (a diverse set of movie-watching experiences for viewers to choose from).

Hollywood "Authors"

As another defining characteristic of Hollywood's Golden Age, movie directors gained significant status. In commercial filmmaking, the director serves as the main "author" of a film. Sometimes called by the French term, *auteurs*, successful directors develop a particular cinematic style or an interest in specific topics that differentiates their narratives from those of other directors. During Hollywood's Golden Age, great directors included Alfred Hitchcock, Howard Hughes, Sam Goldwyn, and Busby Berkeley—each famous for his defining moviemaking style. Today, directors are just as distinctive: When you hear that a new movie is a "Spielberg film," a "Tarantino project," or "the latest from the Coen brothers," you have a good idea of what to expect.

As the 1960s and 1970s unfolded, the films of Francis Ford Coppola (*The Godfather*), Brian De Palma (*Carrie*), William Friedkin (*The Exorcist*), George Lucas (*Star Wars*), Martin Scorsese (*Taxi Driver*), and Steven Spielberg (*Jaws*) signaled the start of a period that Scorsese has called "the deification of the director." Through this development, a handful of talented directors gained the kind of economic clout and celebrity standing that had previously belonged to top movie stars. Though directors lost power in the 1980s and 1990s, the tradition carries on with well-known directors like Tim Burton, Quentin Tarantino, and Christopher Nolan.

Even today, most well-known film directors are white men. Only four women have ever received an Academy Award nomination for directing a feature film: Lina Wertmüller in 1976 for *Seven Beauties*, Jane Campion in 1994 for *The Piano*, Sofia Coppola in 2004 for *Lost in Translation,* and Kathryn Bigelow who won

Female directors have long struggled in Hollywood. However, some, like Nancy Meyers (*shown*), are making a name for themselves. Meyers has written, produced, and directed such hits as *Something's Gotta Give* (2003) and *It's Complicated* (2009).

Best Director for *The Hurt Locker* in 2010. Directors from other groups have also struggled for recognition in Hollywood—and a few have become success-ful. Well-regarded African American directors include Kasi Lemmons (*Talk to Me*, 2007), John Singleton (*Abduction*, 2011), and Spike Lee (*Red Hook Summer*, 2012). (For more see "Media Literacy Case Study: Breaking through Hollywood's Race Barrier" on page 208.) Asian Americans M. Night Shyamalan (*The Last Airbender*, 2010), Ang Lee (*Life of Pi*, 2012), and Wayne Wang (*Snow Flower and the Secret Fan*, 2011) have also built accomplished directing careers.

Outside the Hollywood System: Providing Alternatives

Despite Hollywood's dominance of the film industry, viewers have long had alter-natives to the feature-length, hugely attended, big-budget movies offered by the studio system. These alternatives include foreign films, documentaries, and independent films.

The Secret World of Arrietty, a Japanese animated film adapted from the novel *The Borrowers,* was first released in Japan in 2010 and came to North America in early 2012.

Foreign Films

Films made in other countries constitute less than 2 percent of motion pictures seen in the United States today. Yet foreign films did well in 1920s America, espe-cially in diverse neighborhoods in large cities. These films' popularity has waxed and waned since the Great Depression, in response to developments such as assimilation of immigrants, postwar prosperity, and the rise of home-market video.

To be sure, the modern success in the United States of movies like *Crouching Tiger, Hidden Dragon* (Taiwan, 2000), *Amélie* (France, 2001), and *The Lives of Others* (Germany, 2006) suggest that American audiences are willing to watch subtitled films with non-Hollywood perspectives. But foreign films have continued losing screen space to the expanding independent American film market. Today, the largest foreign-film industry is in India, which aficionados call "Bollywood" (a play on words combining Bombay and Hollywood). Bollywood produces as many as one thousand films every year, most of them romances or adventure musicals showing a distinct style.

There are other avenues for U.S. audiences seeking access to international cinema. The Global Film Initiative, for example, selects and distributes an annual film series to more than thirty-five locations in the United States, including many college campuses. Global Lens 2012 includes films from Albania, Argentina, Brazil, Colombia, Iran, Iraq, Morocco, and Rwanda.

Documentaries

Documentaries, through which directors interpret reality by recording real people and settings, evolved from several earlier types of nonfictional movies: *interest films* (which contained compiled footage of regional wars, political leaders,

MEDIA LITERACY
Case Study

Breaking through Hollywood's Race Barrier

Despite inequities and discrimination, a thriving black cinema existed in New York's Harlem district during the 1930s and 1940s. Usually bankrolled by white business executives who were capitalizing on the black-only theaters fostered by segregation, independent films featuring black casts were supported by African American moviegoers, even during the Depression. But it was a popular Hollywood film, *Imitation of Life* (1934), that emerged as the highest-grossing film in black theaters during the mid-1930s. The film told the story of friendship between a white woman and a black woman whose young daughter denied her heritage and passed for white, breaking her mother's heart.

Despite African Americans' long support of the film industry, their moviegoing experience has not been the same as that of whites. From the late 1800s until the passage of Civil Rights legislation in the mid-1960s, many theater owners discriminated against black patrons. In large cities, blacks often had to attend separate theaters where new movies might not appear until a year or two after white theaters had shown them. In smaller towns and in the South, blacks were often only allowed to patronize local theaters after midnight. In addition, some theater managers required black patrons to sit in less desirable areas of the theater.[1]

Changes took place during and after World War II, however. When the "white flight" from central cities began during the suburbanization of the 1950s, many downtown and neighborhood theaters began catering to black customers in order to keep from going out of business. By the late 1960s and early 1970s, these theaters had become major venues for popular commercial films such as *Guess Who's*

Spike Lee.

Coming to Dinner? (1967) and *In the Heat of the Night* (1967).

Based on the popularity of these films, black photographer-turned-filmmaker Gordon Parks, who directed *The Learning Tree* (1969), adapted from his own novel, went on to make commercial action/ adventure films, including *Shaft* (1971), remade by John Singleton in 2000. Popular in urban theaters, especially among black teenagers, the movies produced by Parks and his son—Gordon Parks Jr. (*Super Fly*, 1972)—spawned a number of commercial imitators, labeled blaxploitation movies. These films were the subject of heated cultural debates in the 1970s; like some rap songs today, they were both praised for their realistic depictions of black urban life and criticized for glorifying violence. Nevertheless, these films reinvigorated urban movie attendance, reaching an audience that had not been well served by the film industry until the 1960s.

Although opportunities for black film directors expanded in the 1980s and 1990s, mainstream Hollywood is still a formidable place for outsiders to crack. Even acclaimed director Spike Lee has had difficulty in getting large budgets from the studios, even after several critical and commercial successes. For example, in making *Get on the Bus* (1996), Lee asked a number of wealthy black men to bankroll $2 million for the film, which depicted the October 1995 Million Man March on Washington, D.C., celebrating the kind of black self-reliance that Lee's own moviemaking has long illustrated. And in 2004, director and playwright Tyler Perry split the $5.5 million budget with Lionsgate Films for *Diary of a Mad Black Woman*, which went on to gross more than $50 million. Its success allowed Perry to become an industry unto himself, writing, directing, and producing a series of successful films. These films consistently demonstrate the appeal of themes and narratives brought to the screen by black directors.

APPLYING THE CRITICAL PROCESS

DESCRIPTION Consider a list of the top twenty-five all-time highest-grossing movies in the United States, such as the one on the Internet Movie Database, http://us.imdb.com/boxoffice/alltimegross.

ANALYSIS Note patterns in the list. For example, of these twenty-five top-grossing films, pay attention to how many films are from African American directors, or have major roles with African American actors. Note what the most popular genres are.

INTERPRETATION What do the patterns mean? It's clear, economically, why Hollywood likes to have successful blockbuster movie franchises. But what kinds of films and representations get left out of the mix?

EVALUATION It is likely that we will continue to see an increase in youth-oriented, animated/action movie franchises that are heavily merchandised and intended for wide international distribution. Indeed, Hollywood does not have a lot of motivation to put out other kinds of movies that don't fit these categories. Is this a good thing?

ENGAGEMENT Watch a film by an African American director and consider what's missing from most theater marquees. Visit aafca.com or browse imdb.com to find more films that feature African American directors and actors. See if Netflix, Hulu Plus, or your campus libraries carry any of these titles, and request them if they don't. Spread the word on notable African American films by reviewing them online or in a college newspaper.

industrial workers, and agricultural scenes), *newsreels*, and *travelogues* (depictions of daily life in various communities around the world).

Over time, documentaries developed a unique identity. As educational, noncommercial presentations, they usually required the backing of industry, government, or philanthropy to cover production and other costs. By the late 1950s and early 1960s, the development of portable cameras led to a documentary style known as **cinema verité** (French for "truth film"). Portable cameras enabled documentarians (such as Robert Drew, for *Primary*, 1960) to go where cameras could not go before and record fragments of everyday life unobtrusively.

Perhaps the major contribution of documentaries has been their willingness to tackle controversial subject matter. For example, American documentary filmmaker Michael Moore often targets corporations or the government in his films, which include *Fahrenheit 9/11* (2004), a critique of the Bush administration's Middle East policies and the Iraq war, and *Sicko* (2007), an investigation into the flaws of the U.S. health-care system. Former Vice President Al Gore used the film version of his presentation *An Inconvenient Truth* (2006) to spearhead environmental advocacy; there have also been a number of other successful recent nature documentaries, including *March of the Penguins* (2005) and *Chimpanzee* (2012).

Independent Films

The success of some documentary films dovetails with the rise of **indies**, another alternative to the Hollywood system. As opposed to directors who work within the Hollywood system, independent filmmakers typically operate on a shoestring budget and show their movies in campus auditoriums, small film festivals, and—if they're lucky—independent theaters. Successful independents like Kevin Smith (*Clerks, Dogma*), Todd Haynes (*Far from Heaven, I'm Not There*), and Mira Nair (*Monsoon Wedding, The Namesake*) continue to find substantial audiences in theaters and through online services like Netflix, which promote work produced outside the studio system.

The Transformation of the Hollywood Studio System

Starting in the late 1940s, a number of forces began reshaping how people viewed movies and what they expected to see when they watched a film. These forces stemmed from new regulations seeking to break up studios' hold over the film industry, social developments (for example, massive migrations of city dwellers to the suburbs), and competing mass media (namely, increasing popularity of TV). Together, these changes forced the Hollywood studio system to adapt in an effort to remain viable and profitable, even after national weekly movie attendance peaked in 1946.

The Paramount Decision

An important force reshaping the Hollywood system took form in the wake of the **Paramount decision**. This 1948 court ruling (fueled by the government's discomfort with the movie industry's power) forced the big, vertically integrated studios to break up their ownership of movie production, distribution, and exhibition. The studios eventually gave up their theater businesses.

The ruling never really changed the oligopoly structure of the Hollywood film industry, because it failed to weaken the industry's control over movie distribution. However, it did open up opportunities in the exhibition pillar of the industry for new players outside Hollywood. For instance, art houses began showing more documentaries or foreign films, and thousands of new drive-in theaters sprang up in farmers' fields—all of which offered alternative fare to moviegoers.

Flight to the Suburbs

After World War II, waves of Americans experienced a severe case of pent-up consumer demand after years of wartime frugality. They migrated from cities to the suburbs to purchase their own homes and spend their much-increased discretionary income on all manner of newly available luxuries. These changes badly hurt the Hollywood studio system: Suburban neighborhoods were located far from downtown movie theaters, and people's leisure-time preferences had shifted from watching movies to shopping for material goods such as cars, barbecues, and furniture.

To make matters worse for studios, after the war the average age of couples entering marriage dropped from twenty-four to nineteen. Thus there were significantly fewer young couples going to the movies on dates.

Television

As Hollywood responded to the political, regulatory, and social changes transforming 1940s and 1950s America, it also sought to strike back at the major technological force emerging at that time: television. Studios used several strategies to try competing against TV.

First, with growing legions of people gathering around their living-room TV sets, studios shifted movie content toward more serious themes—including alcoholism (*The Lost Weekend*, 1945), racism (*Pinky*, 1949), sexuality (*Peyton Place*, 1957; *Butterfield 8*, 1960; and *Lolita*, 1962), and other topics television

The controversial subject of interracial marriage in *Guess Who's Coming to Dinner* (1967) combined with the explicit language and situations in other films led to the formation of the current ratings system in 1967.

steered clear of. Ironically, such films challenged the authority of the industry's own Motion Picture Production Code, adopted in the early 1930s to restrict film depictions of violence, crime, drug use, and sexual behavior. (For more on the Code, see Chapter 14.) In 1967, the Motion Picture Association of America initiated the current ratings system, which rates films for age appropriateness, rather than censoring all adult content.

Second, the film industry introduced a host of technological improvements designed to lure Americans away from their TV sets. These innovations included "Technicolor," a series of color film processes (alluring in a world where TV screens showed only black-and-white images). Movie theaters also began offering wide screens, stereophonic sound, and extra-clear film that was a huge improvement over previously fuzzy images. But while these developments may have drawn some people back to downtown movie theaters, they weren't enough to surmount the studios' core problem: the middle-class flight to the suburbs, away from downtown movie theaters.

Home Entertainment

Things got even more challenging for the studio system in the 1970s, when the introduction of cable television and the videocassette gave rise to the home-entertainment movement. Despite advances in movie exhibition, many people prefer the convenience of watching movies at home. Though home theater looked like the final blow to the studio system at the time, Hollywood managed to adapt, and developed a new market for renting and selling movies, first on VHS, and then DVD. Currently, almost 50 percent of domestic revenue for Hollywood studios comes from the video/DVD rental and sales markets, leaving box-office receipts accounting for just 20 percent of total film revenue.

Today, as many audiences augment their high-definition television sets with surround sound audio systems, home movie exhibition is again in transition, now incorporating Internet delivery. As DVD sales began to decline, Hollywood endorsed the high-definition format Blu-ray in 2008 to revive sales, but the format hasn't grown quickly enough to help the flagging video store business. Meanwhile, online rental company Netflix became a success delivering DVDs by mail to millions of subscribers; however, Netflix predicts that the future of its business is in video streaming. Initially, its customers could watch part of the Netflix movie collection by streaming it via the Internet for free. But as streaming became more common among its users, Netflix decided to charge extra for that service. Currently, Netflix customers can subscribe to a streaming-only service, the traditional mail-only option, or a combination of the two. Movie fans can also download and stream videos through Xbox and Apple TV devices, or watch a selection of streaming movies through services like Amazon Instant or Hulu Plus, available via a traditional computer or through devices like the Roku.

The Economics of the Movie Business

Despite the many changes transforming the movie business, the Hollywood studio system has managed to adapt. The industry continues to make money, whether it's through producing movies, distributing them (through channels such as movie theaters and home-video sales), or exhibiting them (for example, in theaters or through downloads from the Internet). But to remain profitable, industry players must also invest money—including paying for creative talent, postproduction tasks such as editing, and construction of theaters.

Money In

Film-industry players make money through a variety of means. In the Hollywood commercial film business, these **Big Six** players are Warner Brothers, Paramount, Twentieth Century Fox, Universal, Columbia Pictures, and Disney—all owned by large parent conglomerates (see Figure 7.1). Together, the Big Six account for more than 90 percent of the revenue generated by commercial films. They also control more than half the movie market in Europe and Asia.

Nevertheless, the cost of producing films has risen, and studios have had to find ways to generate more revenues to produce movies profitably. They have six major revenue sources to draw from:

1. **Box-office sales.** Studios get about 40 percent of the theater box-office take in this first "window" for movie exhibition (the theater gets the rest).
2. **DVD/video sales and rentals.** This release window accounts for almost 50 percent of all domestic-film income for major studios. A small percentage of this market includes "direct-to-DVD" films.
3. **Cable and television outlets.** These windows comprise pay-per-view, video-on-demand, premium cable (such as HBO), and network and basic cable. The syndicated TV market also pays the studios on a negotiated film-by-film basis.

FIGURE 7.1 //
MARKET
SHARE OF U.S.
FILM STUDIOS
AND DISTRIB-
UTORS, 2011
(IN $ MILLIONS)

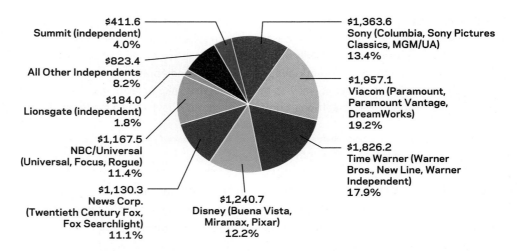

$411.6
Summit (independent)
4.0%

$823.4
All Other Independents
8.2%

$184.0
Lionsgate (independent)
1.8%

$1,167.5
NBC/Universal
(Universal, Focus, Rogue)
11.4%

$1,130.3
News Corp.
(Twentieth Century Fox,
Fox Searchlight)
11.1%

$1,363.6
Sony (Columbia, Sony Pictures
Classics, MGM/UA)
13.4%

$1,957.1
Viacom (Paramount,
Paramount Vantage,
DreamWorks)
19.2%

$1,826.2
Time Warner (Warner
Bros., New Line, Warner
Independent)
17.9%

$1,240.7
Disney (Buena Vista,
Miramax, Pixar)
12.2%

Note: Based on gross box-office revenue, January 1, 2011–December 31, 2011. Overall gross for period: $10.174 billion.

Source: Box Office Mojo, Studio Market Share, www.boxofficemojo .com/studio/.

4. **Foreign distribution.** Studios earn profits from distributing films in foreign markets. In fact, international box-office gross revenues are almost double the U.S. and Canadian box-office receipts.

5. **Independent-film distribution.** Studios make money by distributing the work of independent producers and filmmakers, who hire the studios to gain wider circulation. Independents pay the studios 30–50 percent of the box-office and video-rental money they make from their movies.

6. **Licensing and product placement.** Studios earn revenues from merchandise licensing (for example, licensing sales of action-figure toys representing characters from a particular movie) to retailers. Companies that make cars, snacks, and other products also pay studios to place their products in movies—showing actors and characters using those products. Famous product placements include Reese's Pieces in *E.T.: The Extra-Terrestrial* (1982) and Pepsi-Cola in *Back to the Future II* (1989). The James Bond movie *Skyfall* (2012) reportedly contains a new record amount of product placement, accounting for almost a third of the movie's budget.

Blockbusters like *Transformers: Dark of the Moon* (2012) are sought after despite large budgets because they can potentially bring in twice that much in box-office sales, DVDs, merchandising, and licensing fees.

Synergy—the promotion and sale of a product throughout the various subsidiaries of a media conglomerate—has further driven revenues in the film industry. Companies like Disney promote not only the new movies produced by its studio division but also books, soundtracks, calendars, T-shirts, and toys based on these movies.

Money Out

Just as film-industry participants generate revenues through an array of sources, they must also spend money on various expenditures to provide the kinds of moviegoing experiences viewers want. Major expenditures include the following:

- **Production**—such as fees paid to stars, directors, and other personnel, and costs associated with special-effects technology, set design, and musical-score composition. In recent years, production costs amount to about 65 percent of the cost to make a movie.
- **Marketing, advertising, and print** costs. For typical Hollywood films, these expenses can amount to 35 percent of the movie's overall cost[3]. Heavy advance promotion can double the cost of a commercial film.
- **Postproduction** activities such as film editing and sound recording.
- **Distribution** expenses; for example, screening a movie for prospective buyers representing theaters.
- **Exhibition** costs, such as the significant expenses involved in constructing theaters and purchasing projection equipment.

• **Acquisitions.** Many big studios buy up other media-related companies (such as firms making media equipment that consumers use in their homes or enterprises providing animation services) to gain the technologies and competencies needed to stay in business. For example, in 2006, Disney bought its animation partner, Pixar, and in 2009 signed a long-term distribution deal with Steven Spielberg's DreamWorks Studios. Likewise, Time Warner's purchase of basic and premium cable channels like TBS and HBO has enabled it to distribute its own films on cable channels for home viewing.

To cut costs, many professional filmmakers have begun seeking less expensive ways of producing movies. **Digital video** has become a major alternative to celluloid film, allowing filmmakers to replace expensive and bulky 16-mm and 35-mm film cameras with cheaper, lightweight digital-video cameras. Digital video also lets filmmakers see the results of their camera work immediately instead of having to wait until film is developed. Moreover, they can capture additional footage cheaply, compared with costlier film stock and processing expenses. In fact, few new film cameras are being manufactured in the United States as they recede in favor of the digital models.

With digital-video equipment and computer-based desktop editors, people can now make movies for just a few thousand dollars—a tiny fraction of what the cost would be on film. More and more films every year are made digitally. And nonprofessionals are jumping into the action—producing their own films through accessible tools such as FinalCutPro and posting them on venues such as YouTube and Vimeo.

Digital video is now common in Hollywood films. One of the latest digital cameras, the Red, is considered affordable at $17,500, making digital equipment more accessible to new or lower-budget filmmakers.

New Uncertainties in the Digital Age

The dawn of the Digital Age has vastly changed the economics driving the film industry—presenting new uncertainties, bringing in new entities that are now competing for movie viewers' attention, and forcing studios to radically rethink their business models. For instance, as broadband Internet service connects more households, movie fans are more likely to download movies from the Web than drive to a theater or buy or rent a DVD. In 2008, Apple's iTunes Store began offering new movie rentals from all of the major studios for just $3.99 per movie. That same year, online DVD rental service Netflix began offering their streaming service, while the parent companies of

CONVERGING MEDIA
Case Study

Movie Theaters and Live Exhibition

Adaptation or extinction. This Darwinian law has helped the business of movie exhibition survive into the twenty-first century. Since the arrival of the nickelodeon, the first permanent locations devoted to screening motion pictures, the exhibition branch has witnessed several profound transformations, from the development of drive-ins in the 1950s to the proliferation of multiplex screens in the 1970s and 1980s. As home viewing becomes an increasingly viable option, movie theaters are still on the lookout for opportunities to fill seats, especially on weeknights when business is slow.

Media convergence has provided just such an opportunity. In 2011, the transition to digital cinema reached what industry analysts consider a tipping point. With more than sixty thousand screens converted to digital projection technology (roughly half the exhibition facilities worldwide), movie exhibition is taking the next step in its technological evolution: the addition of live programming. Until recently, the use of theaters for the presentation of live events was limited, but not unheard of. According to legend, the *Amos 'n' Andy* radio show was so popular in the 1930s that many theaters halted their screenings for fifteen minutes to play the program over loudspeakers to the gathered audience.[1] But until recently, television and radio have been the media devoted to the presentation of live events.

The repurposing of movie theaters, enabled by the conversion to digital projection, began as early as 2002, but did not attract national attention until December 2006 when National CineMedia's programming division, NCM Fathom, presented *The Magic Flute*, the first installment of its *Metropolitan Opera—Live in HD* series.[2] Fathom now boasts a

network of five hundred screens; Cinedigm, another player in this fledgling field, specializes in distributing live 3-D sporting events to its eighty-eight-theater network.[3] Cinedigm's 3-D presentation of the 2009 BCS National Championship football game sold out nineteen of the eighty theaters then in its network and generated four times the per-screen revenue of any film that night, and more than a hundred thousand customers paid $20 a ticket to watch Fathom's live operatic presentation of *Carmen*.[4]

In addition to using this technology for sports, concerts, and opera, Fathom is also exploring and cultivating corporate and religious markets. This convergence may help movie theaters survive even as more people opt to watch movies at home; just as audiences have a greater range of choices in how, when, and where they choose to watch a movie than just a theatrical engagement, movie theaters can offer a greater range of choices in communal experiences than just new films. The movie theater of the twenty-first century could potentially be the destination for professional conventions, worship services, political rallies, and electronic gaming tournaments, as well as watching movies in the dark with strangers.

Universal Studios and Twentieth Century Fox launched Hulu. Even some mobile phone makers are muscling into the movie business—positioning their phones as devices for playing short movies and distributing them to friends throughout users' online social networks.

Digitizing movies for the big screen has posed additional challenges for studios. As Hollywood began making more 3-D films (the latest form of product differentiation), studios have had to subsidize theater chains' installations of new projection systems. More than 12,620 3-D screens had been installed in the United States by 2012.[4]

The Movies in a Democratic Society

Movies function as **consensus narratives**, popular cultural products that provide us with shared experiences. Whether they are dramas, romances, westerns, or mysteries, movies communicate values, hopes, and dreams through accessible language and imagery that often bridge cultural differences. As the American film industry has continued dominating the movie-watching experience in many other nations, observers have begun asking questions about this phenomenon. Some have wondered whether American-made films are helping to create a kind of global village where people around the world share a universal culture. Others have asked whether these films stifle local cultures worldwide.

With the rise of international media conglomerates, public debate over such questions has ebbed. This is worrisome, as movies exert such a powerful impact on people's beliefs, values, and even actions. As other nations view the American film industry as an interloper in their people's culture, they may develop a resentment against the United States overall.

Likewise, the continuing power of the movie industry within our own nation raises questions about movies' role in our democracy. It's vital that those of us who consume movies do so with a critical eye and a willingness to debate these larger questions about this mass medium's cultural, political, and social significance. For instance, most mainstream audiences see Disney's movies as harmless forms of entertainment. But a critical look at the images of femininity in Disney films from *Snow White* to *Pirates of the Caribbean* reveals a consistent view of beauty that hews close to a Barbie-doll ideal—and that inner beauty is typically reflected by attractive outward appearances. Other Disney films (like the *Lion King* and *Pocahontas*) verge on racial stereotyping—or xenophobia, as when the

VideoCentral ◉
**bedfordstmartins.com
/mediaessentials**

More than a Movie: Social Issues and Film
Independent filmmakers are using social media to get moviegoers involved.
Discussion: Do you think digital media converging with social-issue movies helps those films make a larger impact? Why or why not?

heroes of *Aladdin* look less Middle Eastern than the villains. A media literate viewer, then, must recognize that part of the cultural power of broad entertainments like Disney movies is bound up in packaging potentially questionable messages about gender, race, and class in stories that seem transparently wholesome. Given the expanded viewing options and the increasing access to independent, foreign, and otherwise nonmainstream films, viewers can also seek out various alternatives to massmarketed Hollywood films. With an entity as large as the U.S. film industry producing compelling messages about what we should value, how we should live, and how we should act, it's vital for those of us who consume movies to do so with a critical, media-literate eye—and to seek out other cinematic voices.

CHAPTER ESSENTIALS

Now that you have finished reading this chapter, you can use the following tools:

REVIEW

Understand Main Events in Movies' Early History

- Major advances in film technology took place in the late nineteenth century when Muybridge created a method for making images move while Eastman developed the first roll film, capable of capturing moving images and projecting them. Soon after, Goodwin improved roll film by using strips of transparent, pliable material called **celluloid**, enabling a strip of film to move through a camera and be photographed in rapid succession, producing a series of pictures (pp. 195–196).

- Film moved to the entrepreneurial stage when inventors such as Thomas Edison created an early movie camera—the **kinetograph**, a single-person viewing system, the **kinetoscope**, and the **vitascope**, a new large-screen system through which longer film strips could be projected without interruption. During this time, others dabbled in film development, and movies first began to be seen by the public—although they consisted of movement recorded by a single continuous camera shot (pp. 196–198).

- Movies advanced to the mass medium stage in the late 1890s with the introduction of **narrative films**—movies that tell stories through a series of actions, offering audiences a realistic movie experience. In addition, the arrival of **nickelodeons**, a type of movie theater whose name combines the admission price with the Greek word for "theater," made movies accessible to everyone—from struggling immigrants to affluent people (pp. 198–199).

Trace the Evolution of the Hollywood Studio System

- By the 1910s movies had become a major industry due to the creation of monopolies and entrepreneurs jockeying for power over the "three pillars" of the film business: production (making movies), distribution (getting films into theaters), and exhibition (playing films in theaters). Controlling these three parts achieved **vertical integration**. The resulting concentration of power gave rise to the **studio system**, by which creative talent was firmly controlled by studios. Five film studios made up this new film **oligopoly**, where industry is dominated by just a few firms (pp. 199–200).

- By monopolizing patents, inventor Thomas Edison tried to dominate the business by forming in 1908 the Motion Picture Patents Company, known as the Trust, to the dismay of many early film producers. Edison's monopoly was later broken up, but movie studios emerged and gained power through a variety of tactics, such as **block booking**, or pressuring theater operators to accept marginal films with no stars in order to get access to films with the most popular stars and drawing in members of the middle and upper class with **movie palaces** and later city dwellers with **multiplexes** and modern **megaplexes** (pp. 200–203).

Discuss the Development of Style in Hollywood's Golden Age

- Once the Hollywood studio system established itself as a profitable business, it ushered in a Golden Age beginning in 1915 whereby distinct moviemaking styles were developed and standards were set, including narrative techniques like innovative use of camera angles to tell stories; the introduction of sound pictures (**talkies**) and later sound-film **newsreels**; a Hollywood narrative style with recognizable plots and character types; movie **genres**, or categories in which conventions regarding characters, scenes, and themes recur in combination; and the rise in status of the movie director, who developed a particular cinematic style or specific interest in a topic (pp. 203–207).

- Outside the Hollywood system, many alternatives to the feature-length film exist, such as foreign films, **documentaries** (sometimes developed with portable cameras in a style known as **cinema verité**), and independent films, or **indies** (pp. 207, 210).

Explain the Transformation of the Studio System

- Beginning in the 1940s, a number of political, social, and cultural forces reshaped how people viewed movies, forcing the Hollywood studio system to adapt. For example, the **Paramount Decision** in 1948—a court ruling forcing the big, vertically integrated studios to break up their ownership of the three pillars—and the migration of Americans from the cities to the suburbs (and away from movies to new luxuries) changed the way movies were consumed (pp. 210–211).

- While many people thought the introduction of television and home entertainment (such as the rise of cable and the videocassette) would be the end of film, studios used several strategies to compete, such as covering more serious themes in movies and using technological improvements like "Technicolor" in film while also capitalizing on video/DVD sales and rentals (pp. 211–213).

Analyze the Economics of the Movie Business

- In the commercial film business, players such as the **Big Six** (Warner Brothers, Paramount, Twentieth Century Fox, Universal, Columbia Pictures, and Disney) make money from box-office sales, DVD/video sales and rentals, cable and television outlets, foreign distribution, independent film distribution, and licensing and product placement. **Synergy**—the promotion and sale of a product through various subsidiaries of a media conglomerate—further drives revenue (pp. 213–215).

- The film industry spends money on production, marketing, advertising and print costs, postproduction fees, distribution, exhibition, and acquisitions. To cut costs, many filmmakers have sought less expensive ways of producing movies with **digital video**. However, the dawn of the Digital Age presents new uncertainties and is forcing studios to rethink their business models (pp. 215–216, 218).

Consider How Movies Function in Our Democratic Society

- Movies act as **consensus narratives**, popular cultural products that provide us with shared experiences and communicate values, hopes, and dreams (p. 218).

- The continuing power of the movie industry raises questions about movies' role in society—both internationally and within the United States. Therefore, it's vital to consume movies with a critical eye (pp. 218–219).

STUDY QUESTIONS

1. How did film go from the novelty stage to the mass medium stage?
2. Why did Thomas Edison and the patents Trust fail to shape and control the film industry, and why did Adolph Zukor of Paramount succeed?
3. Why are genres and directors important to the film industry?
4. What political and cultural forces changed the Hollywood system in the 1950s?
5. What are the various ways in which major movie studios make money from the film business?
6. Do films contribute to a global village in which people throughout the world share a universal culture? Or do U.S.-based films overwhelm the development of other cultures worldwide? Discuss.

MEDIA LITERACY PRACTICE

Although American-made films may create a kind of global village where people around the world share a universal culture, there has long been concern about whether American films stifle local cultures worldwide, creating a cultural imperialism in which U.S. stories and images dominate. But what do *we* learn from American movies about people outside of our own borders? Consider a few movies to investigate this question.

DESCRIBE the representations of "foreign" people and places in the ten U.S. films you have seen most recently.

ANALYZE the information in your list: Do the movie narratives treat the foreigners as friends or foes, fellow humans or strange curiosities? How are foreign environments treated—as friendly, alienating, or otherwise?

INTERPRET what these patterns mean. For example, does language, skin color, or gender of the foreign characters make a difference? Is a foreign love interest "exotic" while a foreign official is "threatening"?

EVALUATE the portrayal of international characters and places in American movies. Do American movies enable us to see the foreign characters as they might see themselves, or do we interpret them through an "American" gaze (or, more specifically, a white, middle-class, male American gaze)?

ENGAGE with your community by reviewing the portrayal of foreign people and places for an online site or a college newspaper, and submitting your review for online posting or publication.

◉ ONLINE RESOURCES

Go to **bedfordstmartins.com/mediaessentials** for review quizzes, links, and more.

Visit the site's **VIDEOCENTRAL: MASS COMMUNICATION** section for videos like the one on page 218.

8

Television, Cable, and Specialization in Visual Culture

Whether we watch traditional broadcast TV, cable, or even direct broadcast satellite TV, we use this visual/audio medium for multiple purposes—like viewing a presidential press conference, catching up on the latest sports scandal, or watching a cooking demonstration given by a first-rate chef. That's been true for Americans ever since TV sets first became popular in U.S. homes in the 1950s. Yet like radio and magazines, television has changed dramatically over time, reinventing itself to stay relevant in the face of competition from the Internet and video games—which deliver entertainment and information in a more immediate and interactive way.

Consider ABC's award-winning sitcom *Modern Family*. Adopting a documentary style similar to that used in *The Office, Modern Family* blends traditional sitcom stories with film-style comedy and even hints of reality programming. As a mockumentary, it lacks the familiar "laugh track" that accompanies many TV situation comedies (sitcoms), and the characters sometimes even look uncomfortably into the camera. Yet the plot lines and dialogue are tightly scripted. *Modern Family* has won a wide following that includes many families as well as young, affluent professionals—the key demographic group sought by advertisers.

Though most Americans now get their stories and news from many sources in addition to television, such as radio, the Internet, cell phones, iPods, and video game consoles, the popularity of *Modern Family* illustrates that this once-dominant medium still plays a central role in U.S. society. Viewership may be half of what it was in the 1970s and 1980s, but programs like *Modern Family, NCIS*, or *American Idol* can still command a greater audience than many popular movies, books, or albums. At the same time, even with thirteen or fourteen million viewers each week, the way that some audiences watch shows like *Modern Family* has changed dramatically.

FOR A LONG TIME AFTER ITS INCEPTION, TV brought millions of American viewers together to share major turning points in U.S. history. For example, people gathered around their sets to watch coverage of Civil Rights struggles, the moon landing, the Watergate scandal, the explosion of a space shuttle, a war in the Middle East, the 9/11 attacks, Hurricane Katrina, and President Obama's inauguration. TV also united people around more enjoyable activities. Throughout the country, Americans watched the latest episode of their favorite TV comedy or drama at home, then discussed it with friends and colleagues the next day.

With the invention of cable and then satellite TV, we now have more channels and programming options than ever to choose from, each of them appealing, like magazines, to narrow niches of viewers. New platforms keep attracting more users as the ways we experience television continue to change. In 1977, only 14 percent of all American homes received cable services (which at that time carried just twelve channels). In 1999, that number had grown to 70 percent (with many times more channels). However, by 2011 it dipped below 50 percent because of competition from the Internet and direct broadcast satellite (DBS) services like DirecTV. Even traditional cable television customers no longer rely on the same services, with digital cable, DVR, and video-on-demand giving us more options for what we watch and how we watch it.

These technologies and business models, then, have changed the way we watch TV and modified the role it plays in our lives. It's become easier to watch only what we want—when and where we want. But it's also harder to capture that sense of community that comes from watching a program together in our living rooms and talking about it with others afterward.

In this chapter, we examine television's impact on American life—yesterday, today, and tomorrow—by:

- considering TV's early history, including its foundational technological innovations, the development of program content, and the arrival of cable

- tracing turning points in the evolution of network programming, such as the development of daily news broadcasts, the arrival of new entertainment forms (comedy, drama, reality TV), and the creation of public television

- exploring the evolution of cable and satellite programming, including the emergence of basic and premium services

- assessing the regulatory challenges TV and cable have faced, such as the government's attempts to decrease networks' control over content and limit cable's growth

- examining TV and cable in the Digital Age, including the impact of home video, the Internet, direct broadcast satellite, and now cell phones, mobile video, and WiMax

- analyzing the economics of television by considering how industry players make money and what they spend it on to stay in business

- raising questions about TV's role in our democratic society, such as whether it is uniting us or fragmenting us and whether it's giving a greater or fewer number of people a voice

The Early History of Television

In 1948, only 1 percent of American households had a television set. By 1953, more than 50 percent had one, and by the early 1960s, the number rose past 90 percent. During these early years, several major developments shaped television and helped turn it into a dominant mass medium. Others, especially an infamous scandal over corrupt TV quiz shows, brought its potential and promise into question.

Philo Farnsworth, one of the inventors of television, experiments with an early version of an electronic TV set.

Becoming a Mass Medium

Inspired by the ability to transmit audio signals from one place to another, inventors had long sought to send "tele-visual" images. For example, in the 1880s, German inventor Paul Nipkow developed the *scanning disk*, a large flat metal disk perforated with small holes organized in a spiral pattern. As the disk rotated, it separated pictures into pinpoints of light that could be transmitted as a series of electronic lines. Subsequent inventors improved on this early electronic technology. Their achievements pushed television from the development stage to the entrepreneurial stage and then to the mass medium stage—complete with technical standards, regulation, and further innovation (such as the move from black-and-white to color TV).

The Development Stage: Establishing Patents

Television's development and commercialization were fueled by a battle over patents between two independent inventors—Vladimir Zworykin and Philo Farnsworth—each seeking a way to send pictures through the air over long distances. In 1923, after immigrating to America and taking a job at RCA, the Russian-born Zworykin invented the *iconoscope*, the first TV camera tube to convert light rays into electrical signals. He received a patent for his device in 1928.

Around the same time, Farnsworth, an Idaho teenager, transmitted the first electronic TV picture by rotating a straight line scratched on a square of painted glass by 90 degrees. RCA accused Farnsworth of patent violation. But in 1930, after his high school teacher provided evidence of his original drawings from 1922, Farnsworth received a patent for the first electronic television and later licensed his patents to RCA and AT&T, which used them to commercialize the

---

CHAPTER 8 // TIMELINE

Late 1880s
Cathode
Ray Tube
The cathode ray tube—forerunner of the TV picture tube—is invented.

1927 First TV Transmission
Philo Farnsworth transmits the first TV picture electronically.

1934 First Public TV Demo
Farnsworth conducts the first public demonstration of television in Philadelphia.

1940s Cable TV
CATV systems originate in Oregon, Pennsylvania, New York City, and elsewhere to bring in TV signals blocked by mountains and tall buildings.

1951 *I Love Lucy*
I Love Lucy becomes the first TV program filmed in front of a live studio audience.

1952–54 *Today* and *Tonight Show*
NBC introduces *Today* and the *Tonight Show*, helping to wrest control of programming away from advertisers.

technology. He also conducted the first public demonstration of television at the Franklin Institute in Philadelphia in 1934—five years before RCA's much more famous public demonstration at the 1939 World's Fair.

The Entrepreneurial Stage: Setting Technical Standards

Turning TV into a business required creating a coherent set of technical standards for product manufacturers. In the late 1930s, the National Television Systems Committee (NTSC), a group representing engineers, inventors, network executives, and major electronics firms, began outlining industry-wide manufacturing practices and defining technical standards. In 1941 the Federal Communications Commission (FCC) adopted an **analog** standard (a 525-line image) for all U.S. TV sets (which at that time could show only black-and-white images). About thirty countries adopted this system, though most of Europe and Asia eventually adopted a system with slightly better image quality and resolution.

The Mass Medium Stage: Assigning Frequencies and Introducing Color

TV signals are part of the same electromagnetic spectrum that carries light waves and radio signals. In the early days of television, and before the advent of cable, the number of TV stations a city or region could support was limited because airwave frequencies interfered with one another (so you could have a Channel 5 but not a Channel 6 in the same market). In the 1940s, the FCC began assigning certain channels in specific geographic areas to prevent interference. In 1952, after years of licensing freezes due to World War II, the FCC created a national map and tried to distribute all available channels evenly throughout the country. By the mid-1950s, the nation had more than four hundred television stations in operation. TV had become a mass medium.

Television's new status led to additional standards. In 1952, the FCC tentatively approved an experimental color system developed by CBS. But its signal could not be received by black-and-white sets. In 1954, RCA's color system, which sent TV

1954 Color TV Standard	**1958–59** Quiz-Show Scandal	**1960** Telstar	**1967** PBS	**1968** *60 Minutes*	**1975–76** Consumer VCRs
RCA's color system is approved by the FCC as the industry standard.	Investigations into rigged quiz shows force networks to cancel twenty programs.	The first communication satellite relays telephone and television signals.	Congress creates the Corporation for Public Broadcasting, which establishes PBS and begins funding nonprofit radio and public TV stations.	CBS premiers *60 Minutes*, establishing the standard for TV newsmagazines.	Beta and VHS videocassette recorders begin to be sold to consumers.

On the assembly line, this 1954 RCA CT-100 was the first mass-produced electronic color TV set. Only affluent customers could afford these early sets, priced at $1,000 or more.

images in color but allowed older sets to receive the images as black-and-white, became the color standard.

Controlling TV Content

As a mass medium, television had become big business, and broadcast networks began jockeying for increased control over its content. As in radio during the 1930s and 1940s, early television programs were developed, produced, and supported by a single sponsor—often a company, such as Goodyear, Colgate, or Buick. This arrangement gave the companies that controlled brand-name products extensive power over what was shown on television. But then newly emerging broadcast networks wanted more control and, using several strategies, set out to diminish sponsor and ad agency control.

One strategy involved lengthening program showing times. Sylvester "Pat" Weaver, president of NBC, took the lead. A former advertising executive used to controlling radio content for his clients, Weaver increased TV program length from fifteen minutes (standard for radio programs) to thirty minutes and even longer. This substantially raised program costs for advertisers, discouraging some from sponsoring programs.

In addition, NBC introduced two TV program types to gain more control over content. The first type—the magazine format—featured multiple segments, including news, talk, comedy, and music. These early 1950s programs—*Today* and the *Tonight Show*—are still attracting morning and late evening audiences. By running daily rather than weekly, they made studio production costs much more prohibitive for a single sponsor. Instead of sponsoring, an advertiser paid the network for thirty- or sixty-second time slots during the show. The network, not the sponsor, now owned such programs or bought them from independent producers. In the second new

CHAPTER 8 // TIMELINE continued

1975 HBO Uplinks to Satellite
The first premium channel is launched in the United States.

1976 Cable Takes Off
Ted Turner beams a signal from WTBS, his Atlanta broadcast station, creating the first superstation.

Late 1970s Franchising Frenzy
Cable companies rush to win local cable franchises across the United States.

1979 *Midwest Video Case*
A U.S. Supreme Court decision grants cable companies the power to select the content they carry.

1980 CNN
Ted Turner's 24-hour news network premiers and grows to revolutionize the news business.

1981 MTV
Warner Communications launches the influential music television channel, which is acquired by Viacom in 1985.

program type—the "television spectacular"—networks bought programs on special topics from producers and sold ad spots to multiple advertisers. Early "spectaculars" (which came to be called "specials") included decades of Bob Hope Christmas shows and the 1955 TV version of *Peter Pan*, which drew over sixty-five million viewers—more than triple the audience for an episode of *American Idol*.

Staining TV's Reputation

In the late 1950s, corruption in an increasingly popular TV program format—quiz shows—tainted TV's reputation and further altered the power balance between broadcast networks and program sponsors. Quiz shows had become huge business. By the end of the 1957–58 TV season, twenty-two of them aired on network television. They were (and remain) cheap to produce, with inexpensive sets and amateurs as guests. For each show the corporate sponsor—like Revlon or Geritol—prominently displayed its name on the set throughout the program.

But as it turned out, many quiz shows were rigged. To heighten the drama and get rid of unappealing guests, sponsors pressured TV executives to give their favorite contestants answers to the quiz questions and allow them to rehearse their responses. The most notorious rigging occurred on *Twenty-One*, a quiz show owned by Geritol, whose profits had climbed by a whopping $4 million a year after it began sponsoring the program in 1956.

When investigations exposed the rigging, the networks further decreased their use of sponsors to create programming. Even more important, the fraud undermined Americans' belief in TV's democratic promise—to bring inexpensive, honest information and entertainment into every household. The scandals had

In 1957, the most popular contestant on the quiz show *Twenty-One* was college professor Charles Van Doren (*left*). Congressional hearings on rigged quiz shows revealed that Van Doren had been given some answers that helped him defeat opponents that the show's producers and sponsors deemed less appealing than Van Doren.

1987 Fox and *The Simpsons*
The Australian media giant News Corp. launches the Fox network, the first network launch in more than thirty-five years.

1994 DBS
The direct broadcast satellite (DBS) industry offers full-scale services, growing at a rate faster than cable.

1996 Telecommunications Act of 1996
The act abolishes most TV ownership restrictions, paving the way for consolidation. Cable is again deregulated.

2003 VOD
Digital video-on-demand (VOD) service is tested in several cable systems in the United States.

2009 Digital TV Standard
The FCC ends a TV set's ability to receive analog broadcast signals through the airwaves with an antenna.

magnified the separation between the privileged, powerful few (wealthy companies) and the general public. For the next forty years, the broadcast networks kept quiz shows out of **prime time**—the block of time (7–11 P.M. EST) with large viewer audiences.

Introducing Cable

Despite the quiz-show scandals, broadcast television continued to grow in popularity in the late 1950s; however, some communities were unable to receive traditional over-the-air TV signals, often because of their isolation or because mountains or tall buildings blocked transmission. To solve this problem, the first small cable systems—called **CATV**, or community antenna television—originated in Oregon, Pennsylvania, and New York City in the late 1940s. New cable companies ran wires from relay towers that brought in broadcast signals from far away. The cable companies then strung wire from utility poles and sent the signals to individual homes, stimulating demand for TV sets in those communities.

These early systems served only about 10 percent of the country and usually contained only twelve channels because of early technical and regulatory limits. Yet cable offered big advantages. First, it routed each channel in a separate wire, thereby eliminating the over-the-air interference that sometimes happened with broadcast transmissions. Second, it ran signals through *coaxial cable*, a core of

FIGURE 8.1 //
A BASIC CABLE TELEVISION SYSTEM

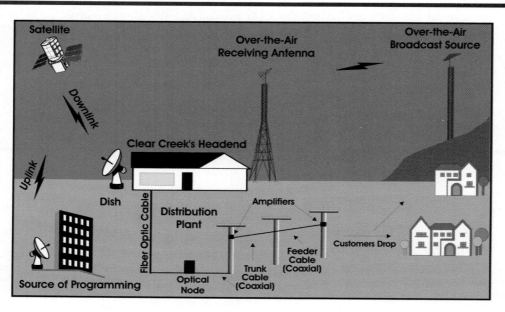

Source: Clear Creek Telephone & TeleVision, www.ccmtc.com.

aluminum wire encircled by braided wires that provided the option of adding more channels. Initially, many small communities with CATV received twice as many channels as were available over the air in much larger cities. Eventually, the cable industry would pose a major competitive threat to conventional broadcast television. But cable would also encounter new challenges (and opportunities) with the invention of satellite TV, which uses large dishes to "downlink" signals from communication satellites in order to transmit new cable TV services like HBO and CNN (see Figure 8.1).

The Evolution of Network Programming

Even with the emergence of mostly small-town cable operations, broadcast networks still controlled most TV programming in the 1950s. They began specializing in many types of programming (much of it "borrowed" from radio), including early evening newscasts, variety shows, sitcoms, and soap operas. Eventually, additional genres and services emerged, including talk shows, newsmagazines, reality TV, and public television.

Information: Network News

Over time, many Americans abandoned their habit of reading an afternoon newspaper and began following the network evening news to catch coverage of the latest national and international events. By the 1960s, NBC, CBS, and ABC offered different thirty-minute versions of the evening news and dominated national TV news coverage until the emergence of CNN and the 24/7 cable news cycle began in the 1980s. The network news divisions have been responsible for a number of milestones. *The CBS-TV News*, which premiered on CBS in May 1948, in 1956 became the first news show videotaped for rebroadcast in central and western time zones on **affiliate stations** (i.e., local TV stations that contract with a network to carry its programs; each network has roughly two hundred affiliates around the country), while NBC's weekly *Meet the Press* (1947–) remains the oldest show on television.

By early 2012, NBC's nightly newscast drew about nine million viewers, ABC's attracted about eight million, and CBS drew between six and seven million, all skewing on the older side. Faced with increasing competition from Internet news, bloggers, and 24/7 cable, audience numbers have eroded. In 2003, NBC and ABC attracted between ten and eleven million viewers each with CBS drawing about eight million viewers for each evening broadcast—and even these numbers were less than half the audience size that network evening news programs pulled in

back in the 1980s. Nonetheless, all three network newscasts routinely draw more viewers than many prime-time programs.

Entertainment: Comedy

Originally many new programs on TV were broadcast live and are therefore lost to us today. The networks sometimes did manage to "save" early 1950s shows through poor quality **kinescopes** made by using a film camera to record live TV shows off a studio monitor. However, the producers of *I Love Lucy* decided to preserve their comedy series by filming each episode, like a movie. This produced a high quality version of each show that was far superior to any kinescope (which today would be like saving an *American Idol* episode by shooting the TV screen in our living room with a video camera). In 1956 videotape was invented, and many early comedies were preserved this way, allowing networks to create a rerun season in late spring and summer, thereby reducing the number of episodes produced each year from thirty-nine live broadcasts to about twenty-four taped programs.

In 1968, after the popular CBS news anchor Walter Cronkite visited Vietnam, CBS produced the documentary "Report from Vietnam by Walter Cronkite." Most political observers said that Cronkite's opposition to the war—along with his reputation as "the most trusted man in America"—influenced President Johnson's decision not to seek reelection.

In capturing *I Love Lucy* on film for future generations, the program's producers understood the enduring appeal of comedy. While a number of comedy programs and ideas were stolen from radio, television eventually developed its own long history with comedy, which became a central programming strategy for both the networks and cable. TV comedy has been delivered to audiences through sketch comedy and situation comedy (sitcom).

Sketch Comedy

Sketch comedy was a key element in early TV variety shows, which also included singers, dancers, acrobats, animal acts, stand-up comics, and ventriloquists. Vaudeville performers, such as Milton Berle and Sid Caesar, were among television's earliest sketch comedy stars. But sketch comedy had drawbacks. The hour-long variety series in which many of these skits appeared—such as the *Perry Como Show* (1948–63) and the *Carol Burnett Show* (1967–79)—were harder to sustain than half-hour sitcoms. Unlike the stability of a sitcom with its recurring characters and reusable sets, sketch comedy often required a whole new concept each week, with new characters and new, expensive sets. Today, however, the legacy of sketch comedy endures in programs like NBC's long-running *Saturday Night Live* (1975–).

Situation Comedy

Until recently, the most dependable entertainment program on television has been the half-hour **situation comedy (sitcom)**, such as *I Love Lucy*, *Seinfeld*, and *How I Met Your Mother*. Unlike many sketch comedy routines, a sitcom features a recurring cast (in fact, an early popular sitcom, *The Honeymooners*, developed first as a sketch comedy on a 1951 variety show). Each episode typically establishes a situation, complicates it, develops increasing confusion among its characters, and then usually resolves the complications.[1] In some sitcoms, character development is downplayed in favor of zany plots; others will feature a personal problem or family crisis that characters must solve—and through which they develop. In addition to the traditional workplace or domestic sitcoms, some comedies today may also mix dramatic and comedic elements. This blurring of serious and comic themes has created a hybrid, sometimes called *dramedy*, which includes such series as *The Wonder Years*, *Northern Exposure*, and *Desperate Housewives* on the traditional networks, *Royal Pains* on basic cable, and *Weeds* on premium cable.

Comedies are often among the most popular shows on television. *I Love Lucy* was the top-ranked show from 1952 to 1955 and influenced other shows such as the *Dick Van Dyke Show*, *Laverne & Shirley*, *Roseanne*, and *Will & Grace*.

Entertainment: Drama

Television's drama programs, which also came from radio, developed as another key genre of entertainment programming. Because production of TV entertainment was centered in New York in its early days, many of their sets, technicians, actors, and directors came from New York theater. Young stage actors often worked in the new television medium if they couldn't find stage work. The TV dramas that grew from these early influences fit roughly into two categories: anthology dramas and episodic series.

Anthology Drama

In the early 1950s, television programming served relatively wealthy viewers who could afford to buy TV sets. **Anthology dramas** brought live dramatic theater to these viewers. Influenced by stage plays, anthologies offered new, artistically significant *teleplays* (scripts written for television) from one week to the next.

But the anthology's run as a dramatic staple on television proved brief. For one thing, advertisers started to avoid anthologies because they often presented complex, hard-to-solve human problems. Ads displayed during these programs routinely touted quick fixes through products such as deodorant or floor wax. The competing messages of the dramatic portrayal of life's complexities interrupted by the ad world's simple thirty-second solutions through consumption seemed out of sync. Moreover, the growing numbers of working- and middle-class people, not accustomed to New York theater but who eventually could afford TV sets, found anthology dramas unfamiliar or unappealing. The shows were also expensive to produce, with each week requiring a whole new story, cast, and sets. Finally, anthologies that explored complex issues such as racial tensions or social-class differences were sometimes labeled politically controversial, scaring off some sponsors and networks.

By the early 1960s, this dramatic genre had virtually disappeared from network television. However, its legacy continues on American public television, especially with the imported British program *Masterpiece Theatre* (1971–), now known as *Masterpiece Mystery!* and *Masterpiece Classic*.

Episodic Series

Abandoning anthologies, network producers and writers developed **episodic series**, first used on radio in the late 1920s. In this format, main characters continue from week to week, sets and locales remain the same, and technical crews stay with the program. Story concepts are broad enough to accommodate new adventures each week, establishing ongoing characters with whom viewers can regularly identify. Such episodic series come in two general types: chapter shows and serial programs.

Chapter shows are self-contained stories that feature a problem, a series of conflicts, and a resolution. Often reflecting Americans' hopes, fears, and values, this structure has been used in a wide range of dramatic genres, including network westerns like *Gunsmoke*; network medical dramas like *House* or cable's *Hawthorne*; police/crime network shows like *CSI: Crime Scene Investigation* or cable's *The Closer*; network family dramas like *Little House on the Prairie*; and fantasy/science fiction like network's *Once Upon a Time* or cable's *Battlestar Galactica*.

Serial programs are open-ended episodic shows; that is, most story lines continue from episode to episode. Cheaper to produce than chapter shows, employing just a few indoor sets, and running five days a week, daytime *soap operas* are among the longest-running and most familiar serial programs in TV history. Audiences watch every day to keep track of the multiple story lines. Prime-time serials include *miniseries* like *Roots*—which run over a two-day to two-week period, usually on consecutive nights—and *hybrids* like *Hill Street Blues* and *The X-Files*, which mixed comic situations with more serious plot lines.

Serial programs like ABC's popular fantasy series *Once Upon a Time* feature continuing story lines over many episodes, though they may feature chapter elements as well, like *Once Upon a Time's* individual character flashbacks.

Talk Shows and TV Newsmagazines

Many other programming genres have arisen in TV's history, both inside and outside prime time. Talk shows like the *Tonight Show* (1954–) emerged to satisfy viewers' curiosity about celebrities and politicians, and to offer satire on politics and business. Game shows like *Jeopardy* (which has been around in some version since 1964) provide people with easy-to-digest current-events fare and history quizzes that families can enjoy together. Variety programs like the *Ed Sullivan Show* (1948–1971) have introduced new comedians as well as music artists, including Elvis Presley and the Beatles. **TV newsmagazines** like CBS's long-running *60 Minutes* usually feature three stories per episode, alternating hard-hitting investigations of corruption or political intrigue with "softer" feature stories about Hollywood celebrities and cultural trends.

Reality TV

Among the newer evolutions in programming, reality-based shows such as network's *The Bachelor* and cable's *Project Runway* introduce viewers to characters and people who seem more like us and less like celebrities. Featuring non-actors, cheap sets, and no extensive scripts, reality shows (like quiz shows) are much less expensive to produce than sitcoms and dramas. While reality programs have dominated network prime time since the late 1990s with Fox's *American Idol*, the nation's No. 1–rated TV show from 2004–2009, the genre was inspired by a cable TV program: *The Real World*, which began in 1992 and is MTV's longest-running program.

The most influential children's show in TV history, *Sesame Street* (1969–) has been teaching children their letters and numbers for more than forty years.

Public Television

In the 1960s public TV was created by Congress to serve viewers whose interests were largely ignored by ad-driven commercial television. Much of this noncommercial TV was targeted to children, older Americans, and the well educated. Under President Lyndon Johnson, Congress passed the Public Broadcasting Act of 1967, which established the Corporation for Public Broadcasting (CPB) and Public Broadcasting Service (PBS). The act led to the creation of children's series like *Mister Rogers' Neighborhood*, *Sesame Street*, and *Barney*. Public TV also broadcast more adult fare such as *Masterpiece Theater* and other imported British programs.

In the early 2000s, the future of PBS and public television remained cloudy, despite the continued success of some

staples such as *Sesame Street*. Government funding of public television was slashed during the Bush administration, although the Obama administration restored some of it. However, with the rise of cable and satellite, people who have long watched PBS now get their favorite kinds of content from sources other than network and public TV. For example, the BBC—historically a major provider of British programs to PBS—also sells its shows to cable channels. The expensive nature series *Planet Earth*, once a natural fit for PBS, started appearing on the Discovery Channel, which could better afford to carry it. In addition, the cable channel Nickelodeon, popular among children and teens for its reruns of older network family-oriented comedies, has been carrying more educational programming for children.

The Evolution of Cable Programming

As network programming evolved, so did cable programming—offering greater variety of content and services thanks in part to satellite technology. For instance, in 1975, the HBO (originally called Home Box Office) premium cable service began delivering uncut, commercial-free movies and exclusive live coverage of major boxing matches for a monthly fee. The following year an independent Atlanta broadcast station, WTBS, owned then by eventual media mogul Ted Turner, was uplinked to a satellite and made available to cable companies, becoming the first cable "superstation." In 1980, Turner, who had become a major player in cable, established CNN (originally the Cable News Network) as a 24/7 news operation. Such efforts gave more people greater and more convenient TV access to movies, news, sports, and other content—presenting a direct challenge to traditional over-the-air broadcast TV.

With the advent of satellite TV, cable companies could excel at **narrowcasting**—the delivery of specialized programming like the History Channel or the Food Network for niche viewer groups—which cut into broadcasting's large mass audience. Narrowcasting in turn gave rise to different types of cable stations offering different types of content and service options: Viewers could choose basic cable services for a modest monthly fee or add premium cable services for a higher monthly or per-use fee. (See "Media Literacy Case Study: The United Segments of America: Niche Marketing in Cable" on page 240.)

Basic Cable

Basic cable offers numerous channels appealing to specific audiences' interests that the broadcast networks don't offer—such as ESPN (sports), CNN (news), MTV and VH1 (music), Nickelodeon (new children's programs and older TV series reruns), Lifetime (movies), BET (Black Entertainment Television), the Weather Channel, and QVC (home shopping). Basic cable also offers **superstations** (independent broadcast TV stations uplinked to a satellite) such as WGN (Chicago) or WPIX (New York).

Typically, local cable companies pay each satellite-delivered service anywhere from less than $1 per month per subscriber for low-cost, low-demand channels to as much as $3 or $4 per month per subscriber for high-cost, high-demand channels like ESPN, which is available in two hundred countries worldwide. A standard basic cable channel may negotiate a fee somewhere between 25¢ and $1 per subscriber per month, usually demanding more in areas serving larger populations. That fee is passed along to consumers as part of their basic monthly fee.

In 1992, 87 cable networks were in business. By 2012 that number had grown to nearly 900, including cable and satellite television services.[2] With the advent of high-bandwidth fiber-optic cable and *digital cable* in the late 1990s, cable systems could expand their offerings beyond the basic analog channels. Digital cable typically uses set-top cable boxes to offer on-screen program guides and dozens of additional premium, pay-per-view, and audio music channels, increasing total cable capacities to between 150 and 500 channels. Even more than broadcast network programming, cable services evolved far beyond the old limited categories of news information and fictional entertainment. Satisfied with smaller niche audiences, cable became much more specialized than its broadcast counterpart.

Specialized Information: CNN

CNN, the first 24/7 cable TV news channel, quickly mastered continuous coverage of breaking news events and early on avoided presenting news anchors as celebrities (like network anchors). With around-the-clock programming, it began delivering up-to-the-minute news in great detail and featuring live, unedited coverage of news conferences, press briefings, and special events. Through its commitment to maintaining international bureaus (although cutbacks occurred during the 2008–2009 economic crisis), CNN today dominates international TV news coverage. It operates in more than two hundred territories and countries where many viewers use it to practice their English; more than two billion people have access to a CNN service. Since CNN's emergence, 24/7 cable news stations, including MSNBC, Fox News, and several financial news channels (like CNBC and Bloomberg), have proliferated, stealing even more viewers from broadcast network news.

MEDIA LITERACY
Case Study

The United Segments of America: Niche Marketing in Cable

Individually, most cable television programs don't generate very impressive audience numbers. A top network television program like *NCIS* on CBS delivers about eighteen million television viewers for an episode. A top cable television program like *Jersey Shore* on MTV delivers more than six million viewers; many cable hits draw closer to three or four million.

Yet taken together, cable television now attracts a larger total audience than the traditional television networks (ABC, CBS, NBC, Fox, and the CW). Moreover, a number of top advertisers such as General Motors are putting the majority of their television advertising budget into cable, not broadcast network television. The key to cable's success is its ability to attract highly specific audiences, which may explain why some cable shows are gaining in popularity despite competition from the Internet and other media, while network shows continue to dip. Cable can still offer advertisers attractive demographics that may not be as focused on a particular network series or online program.

For example, Bravo, home of *Real Housewives* and *Top Chef*, bills itself as the best cable network to reach adult viewers ages 25 to 54 who have a household income greater than $150,000, hold top management positions, and have a graduate degree. Also, the Food Network is a top choice for reaching what it calls "upscale" women in this age bracket. These viewers are likely to be working women with a household income of $75,000 or more who have a Visa or MasterCard Gold card. Even news channels

have niche audiences—Fox News Channel is known for being politically to the right of CNN and draws more male viewers, whereas CNN draws slightly more female viewers.

MTV offers itself to advertisers as the one channel that "owns the young adult demographic." MTV says that it is the "best way to connect" with the 12-to-34 age group, which at ninety-one million strong and growing represents 33 percent of the population and more than $250 billion in spending power. The median age of MTV's viewers is 20.4.

Similarly, Black Entertainment Television (BET) markets itself as the best way to reach African Americans, who spend more than $500 billion on consumer products annually. BET's main focus, especially in prime time, is the demographic of African Americans ages 18 to 34.

Where do you find the older demographics? Flip between the History Channel and the Weather Channel (median age 46) and A&E (median age 47). To reach children, advertisers can look to the

Cartoon Network, where the audience is composed of 70 percent kids and teens. However, Nickelodeon is the king of this demographic, delivering more children under 12 than any other basic cable network. Its shows *SpongeBob SquarePants* and *iCarly* are the two leading children's programs on cable. Overall, 62 percent of Nickelodeon's audience is ages 2 to 11, 12 percent ages 12 to 17, and 26 percent adults 18 and above. Even more specifically, Nickelodeon claims to deliver more women ages 18 to 49 who have children under 12 years of age than any other basic cable network (apparently, the moms are watching with their children).

For women, Lifetime (with an audience of 76 percent women) is the top cable network, with Oxygen, SoapNet, and HGTV competing for the same audience. For men, ESPN (with an audience of 75 percent men) is the leader, and it claims more high-income male viewers than any other ad-supported network. Other cable networks that skew heavily male include the Speed Channel (85 percent men), the Golf Channel (74.5 percent men), ESPN2 (72.3 percent men), and Comedy Central (its hit series *South Park* "out-delivers all cable programs among men 12–34").

APPLYING THE CRITICAL PROCESS

DESCRIPTION Arrange to interview four to eight friends or relatives about their cable program tastes. Devise questions about the shows they watch. Note how their preferences have changed over time. Collect demographic and consumer information: age, gender, occupation, educational background, place of birth, and current place of residence.

ANALYSIS Compose a chart comparing the viewing preferences among these people. Do you recognize any patterns emerging from the data? What kinds of shows do people of different ages and genders watch?

INTERPRETATION Based on what you have discovered and the patterns you have charted, determine what the patterns mean. Does age, gender, geographic location, or education matter in programming tastes?

Why or why not? Why do you think various people's television preferences developed as they did?

EVALUATION Determine how your interview subjects came to like the particular programs. What constitutes "good" and "bad" shows for them? Did their ideas change over time? How? Do you think their criteria are a valid way for cable companies to target audiences?

ENGAGEMENT To expand on your findings and see how they match up with industry findings, track down a cable company representative and ask whom they are trying to target with their shows. How does the company find out about the program tastes of its consumers? Share your findings with the representative and discuss whether they match the company's practices.

Anderson Cooper has been the primary anchor of *Anderson Cooper 360°* since 2003. Although the program is mainly taped and broadcast from his New York City studio and typically features reports of the day's main news stories with added analyses from experts, Cooper is one of the few "talking heads" who still report live fairly often from the field for major news stories. Most recently and notably, he has done extensive coverage of the 2010 BP oil spill in the Gulf of Mexico (above), the February 2011 uprisings in Egypt, and the devastating earthquake in Japan in 2011.

Specialized Entertainment: MTV

Started in 1981, MTV (originally the Music Television Network) and its global offspring reach more than four hundred million homes worldwide. MTV initially played popular music videos from mainstream white artists for white suburban teens; however, the popularity of Michael Jackson's *Thriller* album in late 1982 opened MTV up to black artists and more diverse music forms. Then, in the late 1980s and early 1990s, MTV began providing more original programming with shows like *The Real World* and *Beavis and Butt-head* and more recently *Jersey Shore* and *MADE*. Since MTV's inception critics have worried that much of MTV's programming has encouraged vulgarity and overt sexism. Advocates maintain that MTV (and cable overall) has created a global village by giving people around the world a common language and cultural bond. They also applaud MTV's special programs on important social issues such as drug addiction, racism, and social/political activism, especially with its Rock the Vote campaigns that encourage young people to participate in national elections.

Premium Cable

Besides basic programming, cable offers special **premium channels** featuring recent and classic Hollywood movies as well as original movies and popular series like HBO's *Entourage* and Showtime's *Dexter*—all with no advertising. Premium services have also proved innovative. They include pay-per-view (PPV) programs; video-on-demand (VOD); and interactive services through which consumers can bank, shop, play games, and access the Internet. Subscribers pay fees in addition to charges for basic cable.

Innovative Content: HBO

HBO—the oldest premium cable channel—pioneered original, uncut movies and series on cable. Its most successful and acclaimed shows include *The Sopranos*, *The Wire*, *Curb Your Enthusiasm*, and *True Blood*. Since the late 1990s, HBO has regularly garnered more Emmy nominations each year for its original programs than any of the traditional networks. Its widespread appeal and acclaim have even inspired basic cable services to produce original programming, such as Bravo's *Project Runway*, USA's *Burn Notice*, TNT's *The Closer*, and AMC's *Mad Men*. HBO remains the dominant premium channel, selling monthly subscriptions to more than twenty-eight million homes as of 2009. HBO and Cinemax (the second-highest rated premium channel) bring more than thirty-eight million premium subscribers to parent corporation Time Warner.

Innovative Viewing Options: Pay-per-View and Video-on-Demand

In addition to presenting fresh types of programming, premium cable has introduced innovative viewing options to customers. **Pay-per-view (PPV)** channels came first. These offered recently released movies or special one-time sporting events (such as a championship boxing match) to subscribers who paid a designated charge to their cable company. In the early 2000s, U.S. cable companies introduced a new pay-per-view option for their digital customers: **video-on-demand (VOD)**. Through VOD, customers choose among hundreds of titles, then download a selection from the cable operator's server onto their cable TV box hard drive for free (for access to older TV series or movies) or up to four dollars (for more popular recent movies). They watch the movie the same way they would watch a video, pausing and fast-forwarding when desired. Now, the largest cable companies and DBS services also offer digital video recorders (DVRs) to their customers.

Boardwalk Empire is the latest crime drama from HBO's renowned original programming division. With its mix of violence, sex, human drama, and dark comedy, it is a successor to HBO's influential hit *The Sopranos*.

Regulatory Challenges Facing Television and Cable

Though cable cut into broadcast TV's viewership, both types of programming came under scrutiny from the U.S. government. Initially, thanks to extensive lobbying efforts, cable growth was suppressed to ensure that local broadcasters and traditional TV networks' ad-revenue streams were not harmed by the emergence of cable. Later, as cable developed, FCC officials worried that power and profits were growing increasingly concentrated in fewer and fewer industry players' hands. Therefore, the commission set out to mitigate the situation through a variety of other rules and regulations.

Restricting Broadcast Networks' Control

From the late 1950s to the end of the 1970s—the **network era**—CBS, NBC, and ABC dominated prime-time TV programming. By the late 1960s, the FCC, viewing the three networks as a quasi-monopoly, passed a series of regulations to under-cut their power. The Prime Time Access Rule (PTAR), introduced in April 1970, re-duced networks' control of prime-time programming from four to three hours in an effort to encourage more local news and public-affairs programs, usually slated

Infotainment, a type of television program that packages human-interest and celebrity stories in TV news style

Major merger deals, such as Disney's acquisition of ABC in 1995, have caused many independent companies to argue that a few corporations have too much control over broadcast content.

for the 6–7 P.M. (EST) time block. However, most stations simply ran thirty minutes of local news at 6 P.M. and then acquired syndicated quiz shows (*Wheel of Fortune*) or **infotainment** programs (*Entertainment Tonight*) to fill up the remaining half-hour.

In 1970, the FCC also created the Financial Interest and Syndication Rules—called **fin-syn**—which banned the networks from running their own syndication companies and thus reduced their ability to reap profits from syndicating old TV series. Five years later, the Department of Justice limited the networks' production of non-news shows, requiring them to seek most of their programming from independent production companies and film studios.

With the rise of cable and home video in the 1990s, the FCC gradually phased out fin-syn, arguing that by then the TV market had grown more competitive. Beginning in 1995, the networks were once again allowed to syndicate and profit from rerun programs, but only those they had produced in-house.

Buoyed by the spirit of deregulation in the 1980s and 1990s, the elimination of fin-syn and other rules opened the door for major merger deals (such as Disney's acquisition of ABC in 1995) that have constrained independent producers from creating new shows and competing for prime-time slots. Many independent companies and TV critics complain that the corporations that now own the networks—Disney, CBS, News Corp., and GE/Comcast—have historically exerted too much power and control over broadcast television content.

Reining in Cable's Growth—for a While

Throughout the 1950s and 1960s (before the broadcast networks accumulated extensive power), the FCC blocked cable companies from bringing distant TV stations into cities and towns that had local channels. The National Association of Broadcasters (NAB), the main trade organization for over-the-air television, lobbied Congress to restrict cable's growth so that it would not interfere with broadcast station interests and local TV ad sales. However, by the early 1970s, particularly with the advent of communication satellites, cable had the capacity for more channels and better reception—and the potential to expand beyond small, isolated communities. In 1972 new FCC rules began to allow cable to start expanding while still protecting broadcasters.

Through the **must-carry rules**, the FCC required all cable operators to carry all local TV broadcasts on their systems. This ensured that local network affiliates, independent stations (those not carrying network programs), and public television channels would benefit from cable's clearer reception. The FCC also mandated **access channels** in the nation's top one hundred TV markets, requiring cable systems to provide free nonbroadcast channels that local citizens, educators, and governments could use. In addition, the FCC called for **leased channels**, on which citizens could buy time and produce longer programs or present controversial views.

Because the Communications Act of 1934 had not anticipated cable, the industry's regulatory status was unclear at first. As a result, in the 1970s, there was uncertainty about whether cable should be treated like print and broadcast media (with cable receiving First Amendment protections of its content choices). Cable operators argued that they should be considered **electronic publishers** able to choose which channels and content to carry. However, some FCC officials and consumer groups maintained that cable systems were really more like **common carriers**—services, like phone companies, that do not get involved in monitoring channel content. Access to content should be determined by whoever paid the money to lease or use the channel (like a telephone company that does not interfere with the content of a phone call). In 1979, this debate ended in the landmark *Midwest Video* case, in which the U.S. Supreme Court upheld cable companies' right to dictate their own content and defined the industry as a form of electronic publishing.[3] With cable's regulatory future secured, competition to obtain franchises to supply local cable services intensified.

Through the 1980s and early 1990s, Congress approved several cable acts until rewriting the nation's communications laws in the **Telecommunications Act of 1996**, which took away a number of ownership restrictions from radio and television and also brought cable fully under federal oversight, treating the industry like broadcasting. In its most significant move, Congress used the Telecommunications Act to knock down regulatory barriers. By allowing regional phone companies, long-distance carriers, and cable companies to enter one another's markets, lawmakers hoped to spur competition and lower rates for consumers. Instead, cable and phone companies have merged operations in many markets, keeping prices at a premium. In fact, broadcast networks now own or co-own cable services. As the broadcast TV audience eroded throughout the 1990s and 2000s, the major networks also began acquiring or developing cable channels to recapture viewers. Thus, what appears to be competition between TV and cable is sometimes an illusion. NBC, for example, operates cable news services MSNBC (with Microsoft), CNBC, and entertainment channel Bravo. ABC owns the successful ESPN sports franchise, along with portions of Lifetime, A&E, History, and E! CBS was the slowest to develop cable holdings. Its once successful TNN (now Spike TV) and CMT (Country Music TV) channels are now controlled by its former parent company, Viacom. Such business practices and ownership combinations have continued in the digital era, as broadcast TV and cable seek to maintain their position in the face of new technologies that are changing the way Americans view and use TV content.

Television in the Digital Age

Thanks to new technologies—from home video, the Internet, and DBS to cell phones, mobile video, and WiMax—Americans can now watch the visual content they want (whether it's movies, broadcast TV shows, or cable programming), when they want, and where they want (on a TV set, on their laptop, on a handheld mobile device).

Home Video and Recording

The emergence of home recording technology, such as Sony's Betamax VCR in 1975, changed American viewing. Today's home recording is dominated by the use of DVRs, which store saved or recorded TV shows in digitized computer form rather than on the cassette tapes required by VCRs.

Home-video technologies have evolved over the past few decades. In 1975–1976, the introduction of videocassettes and **videocassette recorders (VCRs)** enabled viewers to tape-record TV programs and play them back later. The VHS (Video Home System) introduced by JVC quickly became the consumer standard (while Sony's Beta system became the industry and news standard). Today, however, analog VHS has surrendered to digital DVD—which in turn has expanded to include Internet downloading, **high-definition** DVD pictures and players, and Blu-ray DVDs.

In 2010, more than 90 percent of American homes were equipped with DVD players. Nearly 40 percent of U.S. homes also had **DVRs (digital video recorders)**, which let users download onto the DVR's computer memory specific shows or even types of shows that appear on any channel. The newest versions of DVRs are also recordable—like VCRs—and allow users to make DVD collections of their favorite shows. Some critics argue that DVRs have shattered our notion of prime-time television because viewers can now watch whatever show they like at any time.

While offering greater flexibility for viewers, DVRs also provide a means for advertisers to watch the watchers—by feeding information to corporations about what each household is viewing. This has changed the ways TV ratings are compiled and advertising dollars are divided. A.C. Nielsen Market Research, which provides the main audience ratings service for television, is trying to figure out how to track Americans' TV habits—including what they watch, when, and where (such as on their cell phones, TV sets, or computer monitors). In 2009, the DVR pioneer company, TiVo, challenged Nielsen's service by offering not only its own data from national TV audiences but daily "second-by-second" information about the shows and ads that people watch on a TiVo brand DVR. This kind of technology does raise concerns among some lawmakers and consumer groups over having our personal viewing and buying habits tracked by advertisers and marketers.

The Internet and Improved On-Demand Technology

The Internet has further transformed the way we watch TV and has fueled convergence of the different technologies. For example, many people now have access to the Internet through their cable companies. On the Internet, we can download traditional TV shows and watch them on computer monitors, iPods, or cell phones—for fees of around $2 to $3 per episode. On some Web sites like hulu.com, full episodes are available for free (with ads) for a limited time, with more programming and viewing options offered through the fee-based Hulu Plus. In addition, cable TV giants like Comcast and Time Warner are making traditional network programs available as part of their video-

Hulu.com allows viewers to watch TV shows, both current and old favorites, for free, and is supported by ad breaks before and within the shows. Some networks, however, do not place their shows on Hulu right away or at all, hoping viewers will tune in live or pay to download episodes.

CONVERGING MEDIA
Case Study

Television Online

During the 2007–2008 Writers Guild of America strike, writer-director Joss Whedon decided to do something more productive than waiting for an agreement between the studios and the guild. Whedon teamed up with two brothers and a sister-in-law to create low-budget but high-quality entertainment for Internet-only distribution. In many ways, the effort was meant to demonstrate that creative people no longer have to cave in to unfair demands by the industry: Broadcast and cable networks are not the only distribution options for televised entertainment content.

The name of the now-legendary production, *Dr. Horrible's Sing-Along Blog*, speaks to the emergent power of Web 2.0, in which users interact as creators (or "prosumers") of user-generated content in a virtual community. Neil Patrick Harris stars as Dr. Horrible, whose unrequited love for Penny (played by Felicia Day, herself a Web-production veteran) drives him toward super-villainy. Part musical, part comedy, and part tragedy, *Dr. Horrible* was originally distributed as a miniseries in three parts. The experiment was a success; the production garnered a Hugo Award, a Golden Globe Award, and the first ever Emmy for a Web series.

A number of other Web series could rightly be considered original online television. Felicia Day has found a loyal following for *The Guild*, her comedy series about an addicted group of online gamers; and a large number of electronic gaming fans watch installments of a machinima-animated series called *Red vs. Blue*, now in its ninth season. Another notable Web TV success is *Between Two Ferns*, a faux talk show hosted by Zach Galifianakis and appearing on the Funny or Die Web site, featuring comic interviews with such prominent media stars as Natalie Portman, Charlize Theron, Ben Stiller, Bruce Willis, and Will Ferrell. Netflix has announced that new episodes of

the canceled TV series *Arrested Development* will premiere on the streaming service exclusively in 2013. Without the scheduling or content restrictions of a typical television channel—or the kind of budgets that require a large audience to stay on the air—these programs have a creative freedom that matches or exceeds many traditional cable channels.

In fact, some media-savvy consumers have canceled their contracts with cable and satellite providers because of the flood of readily available online television programming, which includes these original productions as well as series that air on network and cable TV. Thanks to devices like the Roku and the Apple TV box, as well as wireless-enabled Blu-ray players, viewers are not restricted to laptop or tablet viewing; online television content can now be easily piped onto big-screen television sets.

Such developments in online television production and distribution will, of course, have a dramatic impact on the cable and broadcast industries. Already, low-rated shows have better odds of survival. While some beloved TV series are still canceled too soon, the variety of production and distribution options makes this unfortunate fate far less likely than it was ten or fifteen years earlier. Broadcast network audiences may be down, but convergence allows for new and more varied definitions of success.

on-demand (VOD) services, through which we can buy TV shows and watch them when we want. (See also "Converging Media Case Study: Television Online" on page 248.)

As a result, television programs are no longer restricted by network scheduling, which for many years meant that to watch a particular show, viewers needed to be in front of their television sets at a particular time and on a particular day. Now, TV ratings try to account for "timeshifting"—a process facilitated by VOD and DVRs that allows people to watch a show outside of its broadcast time slot. Timeshifting data can reveal fan loyalty to particular shows that might not have been noticed in the past, but it presents other problems for broadcasters. Streaming, digital recording, and on-demand programming can limit the exposure of advertising; viewers can fast-forward through the ads in a matter of seconds, or open another browser window to ignore even the shorter ad breaks included in many streaming broadcasts.

The Internet has also opened the door to alternative forms of TV programming. Web series like *Quarterlife*, *The Guild*, and *Web Therapy* take advantage of the Internet's ability to showcase short-form programming. Some online series have made the jump to cable television; the absurdist comedy *Childrens' Hospital*, for example, moved to Cartoon Network in 2010.

DBS

Of all the emerging technologies, **direct broadcast satellite (DBS)** has had the biggest direct impact on cable in particular. In the early days, DBS transmission was especially efficient in regions with rugged terrain or isolated farm regions where it's difficult or cost prohibitive to install cable wiring. DBS differs from cable in that it allows individual consumers to downlink satellite-transmitted signals into their homes without having them relayed through cable companies that process these same signals and then send them out to homes via wires.

Japanese companies launched the first DBS system in Florida in 1978, but the early receiving dishes, which used to dot the rural landscape in the 1980s, were ten to twelve feet in diameter and expensive ($3,000). By 1994, however, full-scale DBS service was available, and consumers soon could buy satellite dishes the size of a large pizza. Today, there are two U.S.-based DBS companies: DirecTV, with close to twenty million U.S. customers, and the DISH Network (formerly known as EchoStar Communication), which has around fourteen million subscribers. These companies can offer consumers most of the same channels and tiers of service that cable companies carry, often at a slightly lower monthly cost.

DBS systems can carry between 350 and 500 basic, premium, and pay-per-view channels, which customers can purchase in various packages. In addition, DBS gives subscribers nationwide access (in packages that cost between $10 and

Creating mobile video for cell phones is one of the goals of emerging technology like WiMax.

$40 per month) to more professional sports leagues than most premium cable services—including hockey, football, baseball, soccer, and men's and women's basketball—that aren't carried locally on broadcast networks or basic cable channels. Finally, DBS systems have the same ability as cable to bundle high-speed Internet and telephone service with their video programming so consumers pay one bill for phone, TV, and Internet needs.

Cell Phones, Mobile Video, and WiMax

Changes in how visual content is delivered have forced broadcast TV and cable to further reinvent themselves to remain relevant. Consider the expanding capacities of the cell phone—we can now download music, TV programs, and movies to cell phones as easily as to laptops. In addition, wireless technology called **WiMax** (Worldwide Interoperability for Microwave Access) conveys data over long distances through traditional cell-phone connections as well as by linking mobile phones to traditional mass media. In 2008, major cable, phone, and Internet companies all began talks to create a U.S. wireless network to link computers, televisions, and cell phones using WiMax technology. For some companies in the wired cable industry, a WiMax deal would provide a wireless strategy for competing against DBS systems.

The Economics of Television and Cable

The economics of TV and cable differ in certain ways, as we'll see in the pages that follow. However, like all other industries, both TV and cable must bring in revenue from specific sources and then invest that money in the business processes that are crucial to their operations.

Money In

Sources of revenue differ in some respects between TV and cable. Both broadcast network and cable programming make money from syndication and from advertising, but only cable also makes money from subscriptions—monthly fees charged to consumers for different tiers of service.

Syndication

Syndication—leasing TV stations the exclusive right to air older TV series—is a critical source of revenue for broadcast networks and cable companies. Early each year, executives from thousands of local TV stations gather at the world's largest "TV supermarket" convention, the National Association of Television Program Executives (NATPE), to acquire programs that broadcast networks (and, more recently, cable channels) have put up for syndication. Networks might make cash deals—selling shows to the highest-bidding local station—or give a program to a local station in exchange for a split in the advertising revenue, usually called a **barter** deal, as no money changes hands. Through this process, the stations obtain the exclusive local market rights, usually for two- or three-year periods, to network-created game shows, talk shows, and **evergreens**—popular reruns such as the *Andy Griffith Show*, *I Love Lucy*, or *Seinfeld*. Buying syndicated programs is usually cheaper for local TV stations than producing their own programs, and it provides a familiar lead-in show to the local news.

Many local stations show syndicated programs during **fringe time**—immediately before the evening's prime-time schedule and following the local evening news or the network's late-night talk show. Syndicated shows filling these slots are either "off-network" or "first-run." In **off-network syndication**, older programs, such as *Everybody Loves Raymond*, that no longer run during network prime time are made available as reruns to local stations, cable operators, online services, and foreign markets. **First-run syndication** is any non-network program specifically produced for sale only into syndication markets, such as the *Oprah Winfrey Show* or *Wheel of Fortune*.

The highest-rated daytime talk show in American history, the *Oprah Winfrey Show* was made for first-run syndication and independently produced by Oprah's Harpo company. Approximately forty-eight million people a week watched *Oprah*, which first aired in 1986 but came to a close in May 2011.

Advertising

Advertising is another major source of revenue for the industry. TV shows live or die based on how satisfied advertisers are with the quantity and quality of the viewing audience. Since 1950, the major organization tracking and rating prime-time viewing has been Nielsen, which estimates what viewers are watching in the nation's major markets. Ratings services provide advertisers, networks, and local stations with considerable detail about viewers—from race and gender to age, occupation, and educational background.

In TV measurement, a **rating** is a statistical estimate, based on a random sample, expressed as the percent of households tuned to a program in the total market being sampled. Another audience measure is the **share**, which gauges the percent of homes tuned to a program compared with those actually using their sets at the time of the sample. Prime-time advertisers want to reach relatively affluent 18- to 49-year-old viewers, who account for most consumer spending.

**FIGURE 8.2 //
PRIME-TIME
NETWORK TV
PRICING**

The average costs in 2011
for a thirty-second com-
mercial during popular
prime-time programs on
network television for a
Monday and Thursday night.

MONDAY 8 P.M. (ET)		9 P.M.		10 P.M.	
ABC	Dancing with the Stars $233,482	The Bachelor $177,150			Castle $121,914
CBS	How I Met Your Mother $168,829	2 Broke Girls $166,678	Two and a Half Men $252,418	Mike & Molly $196,497	Hawaii Five-0 $130,514
NBC	The Sing-Off $81,541	The Voice $206,500	Awake $117,550	Playboy Club (cancelled) $74,273	Smash $154,000
FOX	Terra Nova $167,854	House $236,500	House $184,051	Alcatraz $160,000	
CW	Gossip Girl $50,304		Hart of Dixie $47,406		

THURSDAY 8 P.M. (ET)		9 P.M.		10 P.M.	
ABC	Charlie's Angels (canceled) $69,640		Grey's Anatomy $203,078	Private Practice $129,266	Scandal $92,800
CBS	Big Bang Theory $198,348	How To Be a Gentleman (canceled) $128,147	Person of Interest $174,574		The Mentalist $154,781
NBC	Community $93,533	Parks and Recreation $116,883	The Office $178,840	Whitney $120,604	30 Rock $133,000	Prime Suspect $93,092
FOX	The X-Factor Results $283,034	American Idol Results $468,100	Bones $145,721	The Finder $152,100	
CW	Vampire Diaries $54,016		The Secret Circle $45,970		

*Source: Brian Steinberg, "'American Idol,' NFL Duke It Out for Priciest TV Spot," AdAge Mediaworks, October 24, 2011,
http://adage.com/article/mediaworks/chart-american idol-nfl-duke-priciest-tv-spot/230547/*

If a show is attracting those viewers, advertisers will compete to buy time during
that program (see Figure 8.2). Traditionally, shows that did not reach enough of
the "right" viewers wouldn't attract advertising dollars—and thus risked being
canceled. But in the age of niche markets and Internet competition, smaller
audience ratings and shares are tolerated, especially in cable programming.

Advertising also brings in money for cable. Most basic cable channels block
out time for local and regional ads from, for example, restaurants, clothing stores,
or car dealerships in the area. These ads are cheaply produced compared with national network ads, and they reach a smaller audience.

Subscriptions

In addition to making money from syndication and from selling local ads, cable companies also earn revenue through monthly subscriptions for basic service, pay-per-view
programming, and premium movie channels. Cable companies charge the customer a
monthly fee—on average between $40 and $50 per month in 2009—and then pay
cable channels like CNN or ESPN 35¢ to more than $3 per customer per month for
these basic cable services. Whereas a cable company might pay HBO or Showtime $4
to $6 per month per subscriber to carry one of these premium channels, the company
can charge each customer $10 or more per month—reaping a nice profit.

Money Out

For both TV and cable, primary costs include production (creation of programming). TV networks also invest heavily in distribution (airing of the programs they've created) by paying affiliate stations a fee to show their content. Cable operators distribute their programs most often by downlinking them from communication satellites and transmitting them to their various communities.

Production

Key players in the TV and cable industry—networks, cable stations, producers, and film studios—spend fortunes creating programs that they hope will keep viewers captivated for a long time. Roughly 40 percent of a new program's production budget goes to "below-the-line" costs such as equipment, special effects, cameras and crews, sets and designers, carpenters, electricians, art directors, wardrobe, lighting, and transportation. The remaining 60 percent covers the creative talent—or "above-the-line" costs—such as actors, writers, producers, editors, and directors. In highly successful long-running series (like *Friends* or *ER*), actors' salary demands can drive these above-the-line costs from 60 percent to more than 90 percent.

Many prime-time programs today are developed by independent production companies owned or backed by a major film studio such as Sony or Disney. In addition to providing and renting production facilities, these studios serve as a bank, offering enough capital to carry producers through one or more seasons. In television, after a network agrees to carry a program, it's kept on the air through **deficit financing**: The production company leases the show to a network for a license fee that is less than the cost of production, assuming it will recoup this loss later in lucrative rerun syndication.

To save money and control content, many networks and cable stations create their own programs, including TV newsmagazines and reality programs. For example, NBC's *Dateline* requires only about half the outlay (between $600,000 and $800,000 per episode) demanded by a new hour-long drama. In addition, by producing projects in-house, the networks avoid paying license fees to independent producers.

Distribution

Whereas cable companies rely on subscriptions to fund distribution of content, the broadcast networks must pay their affiliate stations a fee to show the programs the networks have created or have licensed from independent production companies. In return for this fee, networks have the right to sell the bulk of advertising time (and run promotions of its own programs) during the shows—which helps them recoup their investments in these programs. Through this arrangement, local stations not only receive income, they also get national programs that attract large local audiences to the local ad slots they retain as part of their affiliation contracts with their network.

The networks themselves don't usually own their affiliated stations, except in major markets like New York, Los Angeles, and Chicago. Instead, they sign contracts with local stations (one each from the two-hundred-plus top regional TV markets) to rent time on these stations to air their network programs.

Ownership and Consolidation

To broaden their offerings, expand their market share, and lower expenses, many players in the TV and cable industry have consolidated. Others (such as the major broadcast networks) have been acquired by media conglomerates or large corporations. For example, Disney owns ABC; General Electric owns NBC; News Corp. owns Fox; Time Warner and CBS jointly own the newer CW network; and in 2009, Comcast struck a deal to buy 51 percent of NBC from GE.

The world of cable has also seen extensive consolidation. In 2010, there were about 7,500 U.S. cable systems, down from 11,200 in 1994. Increasingly, these systems are being bought by **multiple-system operators (MSOs)**, large corporations eager to cash in on the infrastructure of high-bandwidth wires connecting households across the country. In 1998, the twelve biggest MSOs controlled the lines into 70 percent of all households wired for cable. By 2009, the five top MSOs served more than 80 percent of all U.S. cable subscribers (see Figure 8.3 on page 255). As with other media, this trend suggests a move toward **oligopoly**, in which a handful of media megafirms control cable and DBS programming.

AT&T, TCI, and Comcast

Facing increasing competition and declining long-distance revenues, AT&T, the nation's leading long-distance phone company, purchased cable giant TCI (Tele-Communications, Inc.) in 1998. At that time, TCI was the leading cable MSO, boasting thirteen million households. AT&T renamed the cable division AT&T Broadband & Internet Services. In 2000, AT&T acquired MediaOne, the third-largest cable firm, a move that boosted its direct subscriber base to sixteen million.

Ultimately, AT&T's appetite for acquisitions gave it a bad case of debt. In late 2001, only three years after it had ventured into the cable and broadband industry, AT&T got out of the business by merging its cable division in a $72 billion deal with Comcast. The new Comcast instantly became the cable industry behemoth. Ironically, AT&T later returned to the business by delivering video service through its telephone lines.

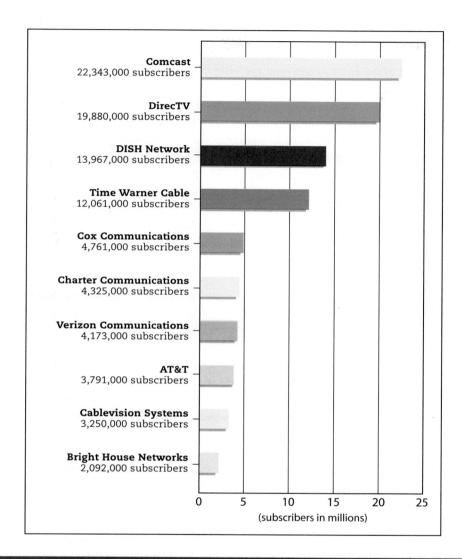

FIGURE 8.3 // TOP 10 U.S. VIDEO PROGRAMMING DISTRIBUTORS (RANKED BY NUMBER OF SUBSCRIBERS), 2011

Comcast
22,343,000 subscribers

DirecTV
19,880,000 subscribers

DISH Network
13,967,000 subscribers

Time Warner Cable
12,061,000 subscribers

Cox Communications
4,761,000 subscribers

Charter Communications
4,325,000 subscribers

Verizon Communications
4,173,000 subscribers

AT&T
3,791,000 subscribers

Cablevision Systems
3,250,000 subscribers

Bright House Networks
2,092,000 subscribers

0   5   10   15   20   25
(subscribers in millions)

Note: Unless otherwise noted, counts include owned and managed subscribers.

Source: National Cable & Telecommunications Association; September 2011, www.ncta.com. ©2011 SNL Kagan, a division of SNL Financial LC.

Time Warner, AOL, and Turner

Time Warner Cable is a division of the world's largest media company, Time Warner. In 1995, Time Warner bought Cablevision Systems—the eighth-largest MSO—and by 2011, Time Warner had around twelve million cable subscribers.

Beyond its cable-subscriber base, Time Warner is also a major provider of programming services. In 1995, it secured its position as the world's largest media corporation by offering $6.5 billion to acquire Ted Turner's Turner Broadcasting, which included superstation WTBS, CNN, Headline News, TNT, and CNN Radio.

DirecTV and DISH Network

In the 2000s, the two rival DBS companies DirecTV and DISH Network vaulted onto the list of major players in what the industry calls the *multi-channel video programming distributor (MVPD)* market (see Figure 8.3). DirecTV was established in 1977, and its DBS system debuted in 1994. News Corp., owner of several media properties (including the first DBS service in Europe, Sky Television), acquired DirecTV in 2003. In 2008, the FCC approved a deal to transfer the controlling interest in DirecTV from News Corp. to cable service provider Liberty Media, which also owns the Starz Entertainment movie channel.

The independently owned DISH Network was founded as EchoStar Communications in 1980. Originally a distributor of big-dish television systems, the company later refocused on the emerging DBS market and launched its DISH Network service in 1995. Each of the two DBS companies operates between eight and ten satellites.

Television in a Democratic Society

By offering a huge array of increasingly specialized programming, cable television, along with newer innovations like DVRs and the Internet, has frayed the common social bonds born of shared experiences that network TV had once established. The appearances of MTV, ESPN, and Nickelodeon in the early days of the cable boom drew stronger demographic lines than their network counterparts, and this niche prospecting has continued as the cable landscape has evolved. Take, for example, the Spike channel. A rebranding of the Nashville Network (TNN), Spike joined MTV's family of cable channels in 2003. In seeking to expand the appeal of the network beyond TNN's southern-rural-male market share, Spike is now branded as a digitally savvy channel for men, not unlike the audience for a magazine like *Maxim*.

Because of their specialization, cable channels are more susceptible to this kind of rebranding than the broadcast networks, which must appeal to a broader segment of the audience. This means that just as cable channels can adopt a particular niche, as Spike did, they can gradually move away from their initial mission in an attempt to change (or increase) their audience. MTV, for example, spent years dealing only with music-related programming, but has become better known for reality shows like *Jersey Shore* and *Teen Mom*. Similarly, AMC made the transition from its initial identity as American Movie Classics to a major destination for original programming that happens to show older movies in its off-hours. Even a channel with a niche as seemingly simple as Cartoon Network has drifted away from its animation-only beginnings and adopted plenty of live-action programming.

Broadcasting, then, has become both broader as a whole and more niche-driven and adaptive in terms of individual channels. Certainly new generations that grow up on cable and/or the Internet rarely make a distinction between a broadcast network, a cable service, or an online streaming service. But these niche channels still tend to come from a limited number of service and content providers, with little input from citizens, just as the most-watched shows on Hulu tend to come from the subset of shows broadcast on networks and cable. The mergers and consolidations in TV and cable have worried critics who think these trends will ultimately limit political viewpoints, programming options, and technical innovation—and thus damage our democracy. Some even fear that giant companies merging cable, DBS, computer, and phone services will fix prices—preventing consumers from getting the lower prices that come when companies compete for business. Industry players have argued that given the tremendous capital investments needed to run these enterprises, conglomerates are necessary to buy up struggling companies and keep them afloat.

As such, television as it stands today can still unite a large audience, for better or for worse. For example, despite the fragmentations and specialization of post-cable television, one annual television event still captures the attention of almost every segment of the American public: the Super Bowl. One of the few surviving institutions of television's network era, the Super Bowl still routinely draws a massive audience; the 2010 and 2011 games were two of the most-viewed programs in history, with over 100 million viewers each. The Internet, rather than detracting from a mass audience, may actually increase it, as viewers may tune in with their laptops open, watching the game, the ads, and the accompanying commentary on Twitter, Facebook, and elsewhere. Social networking and multiple TV platforms have only solidified Super Bowl Sunday's place celebrating the contradictions of our democracy and economy. The game itself remains a sports competition, but since the 1980s (when lavish advertising campaigns and extravagant half-time shows became part of the ritual), the Super Bowl broadcast has become a showcase for superstars and superconsumerism. Now alongside the competition ethic that defines professional football, the Super Bowl also upholds the countervalues associated with consuming at all costs. For media-literate students, then, what does the Super Bowl tell us about what matters in broadcasting? And, by extension, American society?

MTV began with primarily music-related programming, but has become better known for reality shows like *Teen Mom*, which follows young mothers dealing with the consequences of unplanned pregnancies.

CHAPTER ESSENTIALS

Now that you have finished reading this chapter, you can use the following tools:

REVIEW

Trace the Early History of Television

- In the development stage of television, early inventors (Zworykin and Farnsworth) competed to establish a patent for the first electronic TV. In the entrepreneurial stage, TV developed technical standards and turned into a business; the FCC adopted **analog** (broadcast signals made of radio waves) for all U.S. TV sets. In the mass medium stage, the FCC began assigning channels throughout the country and later introduced the color standard (pp. 228–230).

- Television soon became a big business, and broadcast networks competed for control over its content, mainly by setting out to diminish sponsors' influence on and ownership of programming. Spot advertising developed (pp. 230–231).

- In the late 1950s, the rigging of quiz shows, in particular *Twenty-One*, tainted TV's reputation and caused networks to further minimize the control of sponsors. For the next forty years, quiz shows were kept out of **prime time**, the all-important 7–11 P.M. (EST) time slot with large audiences (pp. 231–232).

- The introduction of cable provided access for communities that couldn't receive airwave-based broadcast signals, but it also posed a major competitive threat to broadcast television. The first small cable systems—**CATV**, or community antenna television—originated in the late 1940s (pp. 232–233).

Consider the Evolution of Network Programming

- In the 1950s broadcast networks began specializing in different types of programming. Information, in the form of news, became popular with the major networks: ABC, NBC, and CBS (the first to run a news show videotaped for rebroadcast on **affiliate stations**, which contract with a network to carry its programs) (pp. 233–234).

- The networks also experimented with entertainment programming—sometimes preserving shows with **kinescopes** made by using a film camera to record live shows off a monitor. Comedies became popular and came in two varieties: **sketch comedy** and **situation comedy (sitcom)** (pp. 234–235).

- Drama arose as another genre of entertainment programming. **Anthology dramas** brought live dramatic theater to viewers; **episodic series** showed central characters appearing every week. Episodic series come in two types: **chapter shows** and **serial programs** (pp. 235–237).

- Other programming genres that have arisen in TV's history include talk shows, **TV newsmagazines**, reality TV, and public television (pp. 237–238).

Discuss the Evolution of Cable Programming

- With the advent of satellite TV, cable companies could excel at **narrowcasting**—delivery of specialized programming for niche viewer groups (thereby cutting into broadcasting's large audiences) (pp. 238, 240).

- **Basic cable** is composed of local broadcast signals, nonbroadcast access channels, a few regional PBS stations, and a variety of cable channels (including **superstations**—independent broadcast stations uplinked to a satellite). **Premium channels** include movie channels and interactive services, such as **pay-per-view (PPV)** and **video-on-demand (VOD)** (pp. 239, 242–243).

Explain the Regulatory Challenges Facing Television and Cable

- From the late 1950s to the end of the 1970s—the **network era**—CBS, NBC, and ABC dominated prime-time TV programming. To undercut the networks' power, the FCC passed a series of regulations, such as the **fin-syn** rules in 1970 that banned the networks from running their own syndication companies. (This was in response to the networks' acquisition of syndicated shows and **infotainment programs**—those that package human-interest and celebrity stories.) These rules have since been eliminated (pp. 243–244).

- Through the **must-carry rules**, the FCC required all cable operators to assign channels to and carry all local TV broadcasts on their systems. It also mandated **access channels**, requiring cable systems to provide free nonbroadcast channels for education, local government, and the public; and **leased channels**, on which citizens could buy time. In response, cable operators maintained they operated like **electronic publishers** (and, as such, they should carry whatever channels and content they wanted); however, some FCC officials claimed cable should be treated like **common carriers**—services like traditional phone companies that do not get involved in channel content. The *Midwest Video* case settled this in 1978, declaring cable operated like electronic publishers. Congress eventually rewrote the nation's laws in the **Telecommunications Act of 1996**, bringing cable fully under federal jurisdiction (pp. 244–246).

Describe Television in the Digital Age

- Home-video technologies challenged traditional television, starting with the introduction of **videocassette recorders (VCRs)** in 1975–1976. Today, viewers turn to DVDs, **high-definition** DVD players, cell-phone services, Internet downloading, and **DVRs (digital video recorders)**, which let users download specific shows to the DVR's computer memory (pp. 246–247).

- **Direct broadcast satellite (DBS)** allows individual consumers to downlink hundreds of satellite channels and services for a monthly fee (pp. 249–250).

- Cell phones, mobile video, and **WiMax**, which conveys data through traditional cell-phone connections to services that link mobile phones to traditional mass media, change how visual content is delivered (p. 250).

Outline the Economics of Television and Cable

- Both broadcast networks and cable programmers make money from **syndication**—leasing rights to air reruns or **first-run** programs during **fringe time**. The networks and cable programmers also make money from advertising, which is based on **ratings** and **shares**; only cable and DBS earn revenue from subscriptions (pp. 250–252).

- Broadcast networks and cable companies spend money on production and distribution of programs. This often involves **deficit financing**, in which the company leases the show to a network for a license fee that is less than the cost of production (pp. 253–254).

- Cable systems are being bought up by **multiple-system operators (MSOs)**—large corporations eager to cash in on the infrastructure of high-bandwidth wires connecting households across the country; this trend suggests a move toward **oligopoly**, in which a handful of megafirms control programming (pp. 254–256).

Answer Questions about TV's Role in Our Democratic Society

- Many people argue that cable hasn't fully realized its potential and that its specialization has frayed the common shared experiences network programs once offered. Questions of access emerge as cable giants control content and cost (pp. 256–257).

- Regardless, television provides a forum where people gather to participate in cultural or sociological events like the Super Bowl, which can have both positive and negative effects on broadcasting and society (p. 257).

STUDY QUESTIONS

1. What were the major factors that shaped the early history of television?
2. Why did cable and its programming pose a challenge to broadcasting?
3. What role has the FCC taken in regulating networks and cable?
4. What are the technological challenges that network television and cable face?
5. How has television served as a national cultural center or reference point?

MEDIA LITERACY PRACTICE

Interview two or three people who are a generation or two ahead of you about their experiences with television and cable news.

DESCRIBE the impact televised news has had on their lives. What network and cable news shows do they watch? Have their attitudes toward TV news changed?

ANALYZE the patterns and common themes that emerge from your interviews. What kinds of TV news experiences stick with your interview subjects?

INTERPRET what these patterns mean. What does it say about TV news if your subjects have shifted in their attitudes toward it? What does it say about TV and cable that your subjects remember certain news events?

EVALUATE what they think about the quality of news on traditional networks (ABC, NBC, CBS) vs. cable news programs (Fox, MSNBC, CNN) vs. print forms of news.

ENGAGE with your peers by comparing your findings. Is there any common ground? Look for a place to publish these in an online forum.

◉ ONLINE RESOURCES

Go to **bedfordstmartins.com/mediaessentials** for review quizzes, links, and more.

Visit the site's **VIDEOCENTRAL: MASS COMMUNICATION** section for videos like the ones on pages 233 and 238. There, you can find additional exclusive videos related to Chapter 8, including:

CHANGES IN PRIME TIME

Television industry experts discuss shifts in programming, including the fading influence of the prime-time block.

WIRED OR WIRELESS: TELEVISION DELIVERY TODAY

This video explores the switch to digital TV signals in 2009 and how it is changing television delivery.

9

The Internet and New Technologies: The Media Converge

The first political turmoil tagged with the name of "Twitter Revolution" occurred in April 2009. In Moldova, protesters angry about parliamentary elections that gave a majority of seats to the Communist Party used social media to organize anti-government demonstrations. Later that year, a contentious election in Iran prompted what was called the Green Revolution, another antigovernment movement that, again, exploited the use of the Internet and new media. These two events would be harbingers of 2011 "Arab Spring" uprisings in Tunisia and Egypt. In both, videos taken by cell phones and disseminated by Facebook played key roles in successfully accomplishing the goal of regime change. Closer to home, this same combination of devices prompted public outrage over a viral video on YouTube depicting police casually pepper-spraying seemingly peaceful protesters at University of California–Davis.

Though it is too simplistic to say the new media "caused" these events, there is still ample evidence to suggest that we have entered a new era in global politics in which mobile communication devices coupled with social media apps are changing the way ideas are disseminated and bodies are mobilized.

Social media theorist Nathan Jurgenson terms these events "augmented revolutions."

For people whose actions are augmented by this technology, the primary interface with the virtual world is the cell phone. At the end of 2007, *New York Times* technology columnist David Pogue deemed that year (in which the iPhone was introduced) "The Year of the Cellphone." As Pogue said, 2007 was the year that "all kinds of interesting phones and services were made interesting because they married Internet data with the phones in our pocket."[1] Since that time, it seems that every year has seen greater developments in cell phone change and growth. Beginning in 2008, the iPhone has spawned the creation of more than 500,000 apps— applications made by companies and independent programmers alike. These apps represent the software created for the cell phone hardware that was deployed so effectively in the Moldovan, Iranian, Tunisian, and Egyptian uprisings. But the apps also enable smartphone users to do things like play games, travel efficiently, or do business. By early 2012, more than ten billion apps had been downloaded.

What apps do you have on your mobile phone? Which do you consider to be essential to conducting your everyday life? In what ways has the mobile, wireless digital experience augmented and even defined your life? As we explore media convergence in the newest communication technologies, think about how these ever-present interfaces with the virtual world are changing, from the political to the personal.

THE INTERNET —the vast network of telephone and cable lines, wireless connections, and satellite systems that link and carry computer information worldwide—was described early on as the *information superhighway*. This description suggests that people envisioned a new system for conveying information that would replace the old one (books, newspapers, television, and radio). Created in the 1950s, the Internet was a government-sponsored technology enabling military and academic researchers in different locations to share information and findings by computer. Drawing on the technology used to build the first computer (the ENIAC, invented in 1946), the Internet exploited the power of digitization. Through **digitization**, information in analog form (such as text or pictures) is translated into binary code—a series of ones and zeros that can be encoded in software and transmitted between computers.

In many ways, the original description of the Internet has turned out to be accurate: This medium has expanded dramatically from its initial incarnation to a vast entity that encompasses all other media today (video and audio content in addition to text). Since becoming a mass medium in the mid-1990s, the Internet has transformed the way we do business, communicate, socialize, entertain ourselves, and get information—in short, it has profoundly touched the way most of us interact with media across all aspects of our lives.

Unlike other mass media, the Internet seems to have no limits: More and more content is being made accessible on it, more and more people are gaining access to it, and more and more types of media are converging on it. But one thing *is* certain: As governments, corporations, and public and private interests vie to shape the Internet so it suits their needs, the questions of who will have access to it and who will control it are taking on more urgency.

In this chapter, we explore these questions, along with the Internet's impact on various aspects of our lives by:

- examining the early history of the Internet, including its initial uses as a military-government communication tool

- tracing the evolution of the Internet to a mass medium with multimedia capability

- analyzing the economics of the Internet, including the new business models it has inspired as well as the noncommercial entities that use it

- considering concerns that have arisen regarding the security of personal information on the Internet and the appropriateness of content now accessible through this medium

- weighing the negative and positive implications of the Internet for our democratic society

The Early History of the Internet

After World War II, the United States entered the Cold War against the Soviet Union, pitting the two great powers in a decades-long battle of military and economic superiority. The space race was a symbolic part of the Cold War, and when the Soviet spacecraft *Sputnik* became the first to orbit the earth in 1957, the United States was shocked at being beaten. The event ushered in a new era of great U.S. government spending on technological, scientific, and military developments. The United States would later make its first successful rocket launch with *Explorer* in 1958, but perhaps more important to our world today was the creation that same year of a new U.S. Defense Department research agency that would eventually develop the Internet. In the decades that followed, new technology like microprocessors and fiber-optic cable increased the commercial viability of data transmission, paving the way for the Internet to become a mass medium.

Unveiled on April 7, 1964, the IBM 360 was considered one of the most influential computer rollouts. Programmers could use the special typewriter to talk to the mainframe.

Military Functions, Civic Roots

Created in 1958, the U.S. Defense Department's Advanced Research Projects Agency (ARPA) assembled a team of computer scientists around the country to develop and test technological innovations. Computers were relatively new at this time, and there were only a few expensive mainframe computers, each big enough to fill an entire room. Yet, the scientists working on ARPA projects wanted access to these computers. A solution to the problem was proposed: First, share computer processing time by creating a wired network system in which users from multiple locations could log onto a computer whenever they needed it. Second, to prevent logjams in data communication, the network used a system called packet switching, which broke down messages into smaller pieces to easily route through the network, and reassembled them on the other end. This system provided multiple paths linking computers to one another, thereby allowing communication to continue if

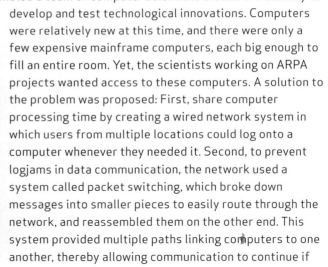

CHAPTER 9 // TIMELINE

1960s ARPAnet
U.S. Defense Department begins research on a distributed network—ARPAnet—the groundwork for the Internet.

1971 E-mail
E-mail is invented, revolutionizing modes of communication.

1971 Microprocessors
These circuits enable personal computers (PCs) to be born.

1980s Fiber-Optic Cable
These bundles of fiber enable the transmission of thousands of messages at once.

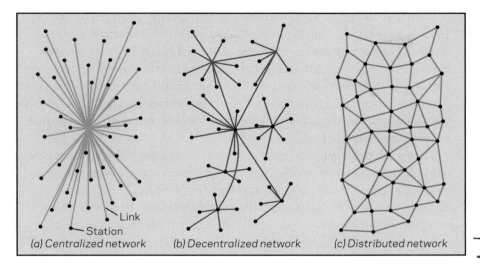

(a) Centralized network   (b) Decentralized network   (c) Distributed network

Link
Station

FIGURE 9.1 //
DISTRIBUTED
NETWORKS

Paul Baran, a computer scientist at the Rand Corporation during the Cold War era, worked on developing a national communications system. Centralized networks (a) lead all the paths to a single nerve center. Decentralized networks (b) contain several main nerve centers. In a distributed network (c), which resembles a net, there are no nerve centers; if any connection is severed, information can be immediately rerouted and delivered to its destination. But is there a downside to distributed networks when it comes to the circulation of network viruses?

Source: Katie Hafner and Matthew Lyon, Where Wizards Stay Up Late (New York: Simon & Schuster, 1996).

one of the paths got clogged or disrupted—much like the national highway system supported by President Eisenhower. This computer network became the original Internet—called **ARPAnet** and nicknamed the Net—and it enabled military and academic researchers to communicate on a distributed network system (see Figure 9.1).

With only a few large, powerful research computers in the country, many computer scientists were suddenly able to access massive (for that time) amounts of computer power. The first Net messages ever were sent in 1969, when ARPAnet connections linked four universities: the University of California–Los Angeles, the

1980s Hypertext
This data-linking feature enables users to link one Web page to another, creating the World Wide Web.

1985 AOL
The company is launched, becoming the most successful ISP over the next decade.

1986 NSF
The National Science Foundation bankrolls a high-speed communications network, connecting computers across the country.

1993 Web Browsers
The Internet becomes navigable and user-friendly.

University of California–Santa Barbara, Stanford, and the University of Utah. By 1970, another terminal was in place in Cambridge, Massachusetts, at computer research firm Bolt, Beranek and Newman (BBN), and by late 1971 there were twenty-three Internet hosts at university and government research centers across the United States. This same year, Ray Tomlinson of BBN came up with an essential innovation to help researchers communicate—**e-mail**—and decided to use the "@" sign to separate the user's name from the computer name, a convention that has been used ever since.

During this development stage, the Internet (still called ARPAnet at this time) was used primarily by universities, government research labs, and corporations involved in computer software and other high-tech products. These users exchanged e-mail and posted information on computer *bulletin boards*, sites that listed information about particular topics such as health, technology, or employment services.

This advertisement for the Commodore 64, one of the first home PCs, touts the features of the computer. The Commodore was heralded in its time, but today's PCs far exceed its abilities.

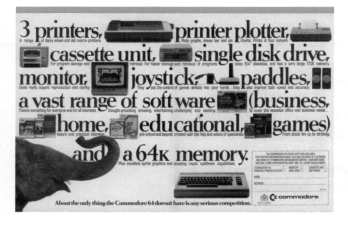

The Net Widens

From the early 1970s to the late 1980s, the Internet moved from the development stage to the entrepreneurial stage, in which it became a marketable medium. The first signal of the Net's imminent marketability came in 1971 with the introduction of **microprocessors**, which led to the introduction of the first *personal computers* (PCs), which were smaller, cheaper, and more powerful than the bulky systems that had occupied entire floors of buildings during the 1960s. In 1986, the

---

CHAPTER 9 // TIMELINE continued

1999 Blogging
Blogging software is created, helping to popularize this form of communication.

2000 Cookies
Information profiles on users enable data-mining to flourish.

2000s Broadband
Users switch from dial-up to broadband with cable modem or DSL connections.

National Science Foundation developed a high-speed communication network (NSFNET) as well as five new supercomputer centers (at Princeton, the University of Illinois, the University of California–San Diego, Cornell, and in Pittsburgh—a center jointly operated by Carnegie-Mellon, the University of Pittsburgh, and Westinghouse), which were designed to speed up access to research data and encourage private investment in the Net. This government investment triggered a dramatic rise in Internet use and opened the door to additional commercial possibilities.

Also in the mid-1980s, **fiber-optic cable**, capable of transmitting thousands of messages simultaneously (via laser light), became the standard for conveying communication data speedily—making the commercial use of computers even more viable than before. Today, thanks to this increased speed, the amount of information that digital technology can transport is nearly limitless.

In 1990, ARPAnet officially ended, and in 1991 the NSF opened its network fully to commercial use. By this time, a growing community of researchers, computer programmers, amateur hackers, and commercial interests had already tapped into the Internet. These tens of thousands of participants in the network became the initial audience for the Internet's emergence as a mass medium.

The Evolution of the Internet: From Web 1.0 to Web 2.0 and Beyond

During the 1990s and early 2000s, the Internet's primary applications were e-mail (one-to-one communication) and Web page display (one-to-many communication). By 2005 it had evolved into a far more powerful social network. In other words, the Web became a many-to-many tool as

2001 Instant Messaging
The fastest growing area of the Internet.

2002 Social Networking
Friendster is founded as the first major social networking site, inspiring MySpace (2003) and Facebook (2004).

2007 Smartphones
The iPhone is introduced, creating a trend toward Internet-accessing smartphones.

2010 iPad
Apple releases a multipurpose touchscreen tablet.

an increasing number of applications on it led to the creation of new content and navigational possibilities for users. Through social networks, users can engage in real-time conversations with others; write, read, and comment on blogs and wikis; share photos and videos; and interact within virtual 3-D environments. People commonly describe these two phases in the Internet's evolution as Web 1.0 and Web 2.0.

Web 1.0

Internet use before the 1990s mostly consisted of people transferring files, accessing computer databases from remote locations, and sending e-mails through an unwieldy interface. The **World Wide Web** (or the Web) changed all of that. Developed in the late 1980s by software engineer Tim Berners-Lee at the CERN particle physics lab in Switzerland to help scientists better collaborate, the Web enabled users to access texts through clickable links rather than through difficult computer code. Known as *hypertext*, the system allowed computer-accessed information to associate with, or link to, other information on the Internet—no matter where it was located. **HTML (HyperText Markup Language)**, the written code that creates Web pages and links, can be read by all computers. Thus computers with different operating systems (Windows, Macintosh, Linux) can communicate easily through hypertext. After CERN released the World Wide Web source code into the public domain in 1993, many people began to build software to further enhance the Internet's versatility.

The GUI (graphical user interface) of the World Wide Web changed overnight with the release of Mosaic in 1993. As the first popular Web browser, Mosaic unleashed the multimedia potential of the Internet. Mosaic was the inspiration for the commercial browser Netscape, which was released in 1994.

The release of Web **browsers**—software applications that help users navigate the Web—brought the Web to mass audiences for the first time. Computer programmers led by Marc Andreessen at the University of Illinois (a supercomputer center that was part of NSFNet) released Mosaic in 1993, the first user-friendly browser to load text and graphics together in a magazine-like layout. With its attractive fonts and easy-to-use navigation buttons, Mosaic was a huge improvement over previous technology. In 1994, Andreessen joined investors in California's Silicon Valley to introduce another major advance—a commercial browser called Netscape. Together, the World Wide Web, Mosaic, and Netscape gave the Internet basic multimedia capability, enabling users to transmit pictures, sound, and video.

Web 2.0

The shift to Web 2.0 has encouraged a deeper trend toward *media convergence*: different types of content (video, text, audio) created by all sorts of sources (users, corporations, nonprofit organizations) coming together. While the Internet was primarily a medium for computer-savvy users to deliver text-and-graphic content during its Web 1.0 stage, it's now a place where people can access and share all manner of media content: music on Spotify, video on YouTube, journalism on Blogspot, eBooks on Amazon, mountains of collective intelligence on *Wikipedia*, gossip on Twitter, and relationships on Facebook. Where the signature products of Web 1.0 were increased content access and accompanying dot-com consumerism, the iconic achievement of Web 2.0 is social networking.

Clearly, the Internet is much more interactive, collaborative, and ungovernable than before: People use it not only for uploading and downloading content, but also for chatting with friends and colleagues; for social, political, and professional networking; and for spreading, processing, and challenging information with blogs and wikis. Consider the following defining applications of Web 2.0.

Instant Messaging (IM)

One of the Internet's fastest-growing features in the late 1990s, **instant messaging (IM)** services allow users to assemble personalized "buddy lists" of friends, build personal profiles, and chat in real time with any of their buddies online (a type of one-to-one communication). Major IM services—many of which now offer voice and video chat capabilities as well—include AOL Instant Messenger (AIM), Microsoft's MSN Messenger Service, Yahoo!'s Messenger, Apple's iChat, Skype (owned by eBay), and Google's GChat. The rapid growth of some IM services has slowed in recent years as mobile phone text-messaging and IM tools on Facebook and MySpace have become popular.

Social Networking Sites

Social networking sites—including Facebook, MySpace, Friendster, LiveJournal, hi5, Bebo, and Xanga—have become among the most popular places on the Internet. The largest of these sites, Facebook, has become a global phenomenon. Facebook empowers users to create personal profiles; upload photos; create lists of their favorite movies, books, and music; and post messages to connect with old friends and meet new ones. A subcategory of social networking sites contains sites more specifically devoted to professional networking, such as LinkedIn.

Social networking sites have given a huge boost to one-to-many communication. They've also raised some thorny privacy questions: Should we post highly personal information about ourselves, including pictures and messages about our political views? (Potential—or current—employers routinely visit these sites to examine job candidates' or employees' profiles.) Should information in our profiles be considered public for some eyes but off-limits to others?

VideoCentral◎
bedfordstmartins.com /mediaessentials

The Rise of Social Media
Media experts discuss how social media are changing traditional media.
Discussion: Some consider the new social media an extension of the very old oral form of communication. Do you agree or disagree with this view? Why or why not?

Talking Points Memo began in 2000 and has grown into one of the most popular political blogs, with an average of 21 million pageviews per month.

Blogs

Weblogs, more commonly known as **blogs**, are sites containing user-generated articles in chronological, journal-like form, often including reader comments and links to other sites. There are also video blogs, in which bloggers deliver their message on screen, usually captured by a Webcam.

Like IM and social networking sites, blogs have reshaped the way people consume and use information. Some blogs are simply an individual's online journal or personal musings. Others provide information, analysis, or commentary that isn't presented in the more traditional news media. Many blogs, including *TMZ* (celebrity gossip), *Talking Points Memo* (investigative news), *Engadget* (electronics), and *Crooks and Liars* (politics) have become highly visited sites. Although some are written by journalists, the vast majority of the Web's approximately 200 million blogs are written by individuals who don't use established editorial practices to check their facts.

Wikis

Wikis are informative Web sites that anyone can edit and contribute to (*wiki* means "quick" in Hawaiian). Large wikis include Wikitravel (a global travel guide), WikiMapia (combining Google Maps with wiki comments), FluWiki (a clearinghouse for influenza pandemic preparation), and of course, *Wikipedia*, the online encyclopedia that is constantly being updated by interested volunteers. In *Wikipedia*, all previous page versions of each entry are stored, enabling users to see how the entry has evolved.

Although *Wikipedia* has become one of the most popular resources on the Web, some people have expressed concern that its open editing model compromises its accuracy.[2] When accessing any wiki, the user may not knows for certain who has contributed which parts of the information found there, who is changing the content, and what their motives are. (For example, politicians and other well-known individuals who are particularly concerned about their public image may distort information in their *Wikipedia* entries to improve their image—or their supporters may do the same.) This worry has led *Wikipedia* to lock down topic pages that are especially contested, which has inevitably led to user protests about information control. At the same time, *Wikipedia* generally offers a vibrant forum where information unfolds, where debates happen, and where controversy over topics can be documented.

Web 3.0

Controversy abounds regarding what the next era of the Web will be like. Certainly, the Internet will boast even greater bandwidth for faster, more graphically rich 3-D applications. Many Internet visionaries claim that in the coming age of Web 3.0, information databases will be layered and connected in new ways that enable software agents to sift through the data and process it automatically for users. For instance, the search engines of Web 2.0 provide us with relevant Web pages when we submit a search query. The software agents of Web 3.0 will reputedly gather information about our interests based on our Web-usage patterns and automatically send us updates on topics they have concluded are important to us. Amazon.com does a basic version of this, sending customers e-mails describing books and other products that may be of interest, given customers' previous purchases. Indeed, some observers argue that we're already living in the age of Web 3.0.

Web 3.0 will also likely involve ever-increasing mobile connectivity and convergence. Thanks to smartphones and PDAs, Internet connections have been freed from desktops and laptops, further solidifying the Internet as a major vehicle for delivering media content of all kinds—movies, television, books, news, and more—to increasingly converged devices. Much of this content is still created by traditional industries, but how the content is consumed (and paid for) continues to evolve with Internet technology, bringing about the popularity of sites, services, and devices like iTunes, Hulu, Netflix Streaming, Spotify, Amazon's Kindle, and so on. These changes in consumption and distribution cannot always be predicted, but they will almost certainly render Web 3.0 even more central to other media industries—and to our daily media experiences.

The Economics of the Internet

One of the unique things about the Internet is that no one owns it—but that hasn't stopped some corporations from trying to control it. Companies have realized the potential of dominating the Internet through access to phone and broadband wires, browser software, search engines, and, perhaps most important, advertising; however, throughout the Internet's relatively short history, several companies have risen and fallen trying to control a medium characterized by few regulations and a strong entrepreneurial ethic.

MEDIA LITERACY
Case Study

Net Neutrality

For every mass medium, there comes a pivotal time where society must decide whether it will be a democratic medium or not. Now is that time for the Internet. The issue is called "net neutrality," and it refers to the principle that every Web site—one owned by a multinational corporation or one owned by you—has the right to the same Internet network speed and access. The idea of an open and neutral network has existed since the origins of the Internet, but it has never been written into law.

But now major telephone companies and cable companies, which control 98 percent of broadband access in the United States (through DSL and cable modem service), would like to dismiss net neutrality and give faster connections and greater priority to clients willing to pay higher rates. The companies who want to eliminate net neutrality, including AT&T, Verizon, Comcast, Time Warner, and Qwest, explain that the money they could make with multi-tier Internet access will give them the incentive they need to build expensive new networks; however, many think it is a scheme to make more money.

One of the main groups in favor of preserving net neutrality is SavetheInternet.com, a nonprofit coalition of more than one million people, mostly bloggers, video gamers, educators, religious groups, unions, and small businesses. Even large Internet corporations like Google, Yahoo!, Amazon.com, eBay, Microsoft, and Facebook support net neutrality, because their business depends on their millions of customers having equal access to the Web. SavetheInternet outlined some of the threats posed by an Internet without network neutrality rules:

- **Small businesses.** The little guy will be left in the "slow lane" with inferior Internet service, unable to compete.

- **Innovators with the next big idea.** Start-ups and entrepreneurs will be muscled out of the marketplace by big corporations that pay Internet providers for the top spots on the Web.
- **iPod listeners.** A company like Comcast could slow access to iTunes, steering users to a higher-priced music service it owns.
- **Political groups.** Political organizing could be slowed by a handful of dominant Internet providers who ask advocacy groups to pay "protection money" for their Web sites and online features to work correctly.
- **Nonprofits.** A charity's Web site could open at snail-like speeds, and online contributions could grind to a halt if nonprofits don't pay Internet providers for access to "the fast lane."

There is some hope for net neutrality. The SavetheInternet coalition is petitioning Congress to make a free and open Internet permanent with a net neutrality act. The movement has bipartisan support, but the telecommunications industry has already spent more than $175 million in lobbying, campaign contributions, and phony grassroots organizations to kill net neutrality, so passage is not a certainty.

In the meantime, Internet rights advocates have faced other challenges. In 2012, Congress considered both the Stop Online Piracy Act (SOPA) and the Protect IP Act (PIPA), bills designed to give the government and rights-holders greater power to enforce copyright laws—power some advocates worried could damage the freedom of the Internet, as well as free speech. To protest this bill, many popular Web sites, including *Wikipedia* and Reddit, went "dark" on January 18, 2012, replacing their content with an anti-SOPA message. Shortly thereafter, votes on both bills were postponed, and SOPA will be redrawn. But the fights over net neutrality and copyright protection are far from over.

APPLYING THE CRITICAL PROCESS

DESCRIPTION Interview a sample of people about their views on net neutrality. Would they be willing to pay higher rates for faster connections? Do they think every Web site should have the same network speed and access?

ANALYSIS What sort of patterns emerge from your interviews? Are there common views on the way the Internet should be accessed? Do the interviewees seem to be concerned, or unconcerned, about the issue of net neutrality? Do your questions make them think about this issue for the first time?

INTERPRETATION What do these patterns mean? Is the idea of net neutrality better or worse for democracy? Would eliminating net neutrality undercut the usefulness and accessibility of the medium?

EVALUATION Is net neutrality a benefit of the Internet? What should the standards of speed and access to it be? How should they be enforced?

ENGAGEMENT Learn about and take action for or against net neutrality. Visit SavetheInternet.com to learn how to prevent net neutrality's elimination. Share your knowledge with your peers.

Money In and Money Out

The Internet's quick commercialization in the 1990s led to battles between corporations vying to attract the most users. In the beginning, commercial entities like AOL (America Online) and Microsoft sought to capture business as Internet service providers and Web browsing software companies, respectively. What no one anticipated was the emergence of search engines as a key advertising force, and the influence a small Internet start-up—Google—would have over Internet content within less than a decade. The main commercial services of the Web fall into four areas: Internet service providers, Web browsers, and directories and search engines.

Internet Service Providers

Since the early 1990s, **Internet service providers (ISPs)** have competed to provide consumers with access to the Internet. The earliest ISPs offered dial-up access. Today, the preferred access method is through **broadband** connections—which can quickly download multimedia content via high-speed service from cable, telephone, or satellite companies—making those companies the top ISPs.

AOL initially tried to dominate the ISP industry, connecting millions of home users to its proprietary Web system through dial-up access. The company was so successful that media giant Time Warner merged with AOL in 2000. However, AOL's dial-up ISP business sharply declined as its customers shifted to broadband. The company adapted to the broadband environment by dropping its monthly membership service charge, making its content free, and attempting to capture more customers and thus attract more advertisers. Today, AOL's sites—including AOL Instant Messenger, ICQ, CitySearch, Moviefone, and MapQuest—are among the most visited properties on the Internet, but AOL itself is a much smaller company. Time Warner finally split from AOL in 2009, as the promise of controlling the Internet through the merger nine years earlier never materialized. AOL worked to reinvent itself as a content company with the acquisition of Patch.com and community news sites in 2009, and the purchase of the *Huffington Post* in 2011.

Web browsers like Mozilla's Firefox, an open-source and free browser, compete with Microsoft's dominant Internet Explorer.

Web Browsers

In the early 1990s, as the Web became the most popular part of the Internet, companies like Microsoft thought that the key to commercial success on the Net would be through a Web browser, since it is the most common interface with the Internet.

Beginning in 1995, Microsoft, at that time with a near-monopoly over computer operating systems with its Windows software, built a near-monopoly over the Internet by strategically bundling its Windows 95 operating system with its new Internet Explorer browser software. The release of Windows 95, which made Internet Explorer the preferred browser for computers using Windows, devastated Netscape, the most popular browser at the time. Alarmed by the company's growing power, the U.S. Department of Justice brought an antitrust lawsuit against Microsoft in 1997, arguing that it had used its operating-system dominance to sabotage competing browsers. In 2001, the Department of Justice dropped its efforts to break Microsoft into two independent companies. In Europe, though, the European Union ruled that Microsoft committed antitrust violations and fined Microsoft a total of about $2.5 billion.[3] Web browsers never became huge revenue-generating portals, and today companies like Microsoft, Apple, and Google release free browsers as a way to familiarize users with their other software. (Firefox, a nonprofit open-source browser, is an exception.) Although Internet Explorer continues to be the dominant Web browser, there is increasing competition from Firefox, Google Chrome, Safari, and Opera.

Directories and Search Engines

As Web sites rapidly proliferated on the Internet throughout the early 1990s, entrepreneurs seized the opportunity to help users navigate this vast amount of information. Two types of companies emerged—directories and search engines.

Directories rely on people to review and catalogue Web sites, creating categories with hierarchical topic listings that can be browsed. Yahoo! was one of the first companies to successfully provide such a service. Established in 1994, Yahoo!'s directory quickly dominated the Web-directory market by acting as an all-purpose entry point, or **portal**, to the Internet.

Search engines offer a different route for finding content on the Web: a complicated algorithm and an enormous database of Web pages compiled and regularly updated by the search-engine company. Users type in key words, and the algorithm is then applied to the company's massive database, gleaning a list of Web pages ranked in order of relevance. Beyond its directory, Yahoo! began syndicating with the search-engine service Inktomi to bring algorithmic search to its very popular portal.

In 1998, Google introduced the first algorithm to mathematically rank a page's "popularity" based on how many other pages link to it—and immediately became the megastar search engine. Even Yahoo! switched to Google, along with many other portals, as its main search provider. However, search-engine syndication provided only so much revenue. The application that made search engines (and Google especially) such important Web properties in the early 2000s was the ability to connect advertisers to the same key words users were typing into the search box. Ad sites soon appeared alongside (and in some cases, within) an algorithmic search list—an advertising strategy that was far more effective than banner ads. Google transformed almost overnight from a syndicated search-engine service into an advertising firm. Yahoo! and Microsoft have heavily invested in competing search-engine initiatives to reap some of the advertising profits but have not been able to match Google's superior search engine. By 2011, Google had more than 65 percent of the search-engine market in the United States, while Yahoo!'s share was about 15 percent. Microsoft's share had hit about 15 percent, just behind Yahoo!, with their Bing search engine.

Today, Google generates billions of dollars of revenue each year through the pay-per-click advertisements that accompany key-word searches. (Each time a user clicks on an online ad, Google gets money.) The company now also offers other Internet services, including shopping (Froogle), mapping (Google Maps), e-mail (Gmail), blogging (Blogger), and browsing (Chrome), and has begun to experiment with behavioral advertising and the placement of TV ads. Google has even begun challenging Microsoft's Office programs with Google Apps software. In its most significant investments to date, Google acquired YouTube for $1.64 billion and purchased DoubleClick, one of the Internet's leading advertising placement companies.

E-mail

Because sending and receiving e-mail is still one of the most popular uses of the Internet, major Web corporations such as Yahoo!, AOL, Google, and Microsoft continue to offer free e-mail accounts to draw users to their sites; even Facebook

introduced e-mail accounts in 2010. Each of these companies, some with millions of users, generates revenue through advertisements in subscribers' e-mail messages, with Google's Gmail ads tailored to keywords contained in the message.

A Closer Look at Advertising on the Internet

As previously noted, in the early years of the Web, advertising consisted of traditional display ads placed on pages. These reached small, general audiences and thus weren't very profitable. In the late 1990s, Web advertising began shifting to search engines. Paid links appeared as "sponsored links" at the top, bottom, and side of a search-engine result list. Every time a user clicks on a sponsored link, the advertiser pays the search engine for the click-through. However, even though search engines insist on the relevance of their search results, the increasingly commercial nature of the Web and ability of commercial sites to buy advertisements on popular sites (thus making more links) means that search-engine results are biased toward commercial sites.

Advertising has also spread from Web pages to the newer, more interactive elements of the Internet, including social networking sites in which computer users reveal something about themselves and their interests. This information has made Internet advertising the most targeted kind of advertising in the history of mass communication. For example, Yahoo! gleans information from the search terms, Google scans the contents of Gmail messages, for keywords and Facebook uses profile information (age, gender, location, interests) to deliver individualized ads to users' screens.

Overhead: Building the Infrastructure

We've just explored ways in which companies make money by attracting users—and thus advertisers—to the Internet. But what about money they have to spend to build their Internet businesses? "Money out" takes the form of investments in infrastructure needed for the Internet to operate. This infrastructure includes software, facilities, and equipment such as fiber-optic networks and bandwidth.

The Noncommercial Web

Despite powerful commercial forces dictating much of the content we access online, the pioneering spirit of the Internet's independent early days endures; the Internet continues to be a participatory medium where anyone can be involved. Two of the most prominent areas in which alternative voices continue to flourish are in open-source software and digital archiving.

Open-Source Software

Microsoft has long dominated the software industry—requiring users to pay for both its applications and its upgrades, and keeping its proprietary code protected from changes by outsiders. Yet independent software creators persist in making alternatives through **open-source software**, in which code can be updated by anyone interested in modifying it. One example is the open-source operating system Linux, introduced in 1991 by Linus Torvalds and shared with computer programmers and hobbyists around the world who have avidly participated to improve it. Today, even Microsoft acknowledges that Linux is a credible alternative to expensive commercial programs.

Digital Archiving

Librarians have worked tirelessly to build digital archives that exist outside of any commercial system. One of the biggest and most impressive digital-preservation initiatives is the Internet Archive

Linus Torvalds, the Finnish software developer, holds a license plate bearing the name of his invention, the Linux computer operating system. Since Torvalds's first version of Linux in 1991, hundreds of other developers around the world have contributed improvements to this open-source software rival of Microsoft's Windows.

(www.archive.org), established in 1996. The Internet Archive aims to ensure that researchers, historians, scholars, and all U.S. citizens have access to digitized content. This content comprises all the text, moving images, audio, software, and more than eighty-five billion archived Web pages reaching back to the earliest days of the Internet.

The Internet Archive has also partnered with the Open Content Alliance to digitize every book in the public domain (generally, those published before 1922). This book-scanning effort is the nonprofit alternative to Google's Library Project, which has the colossal goal of digitizing every book ever printed. The Open Content Alliance, which works with the Boston Public Library, several university and international libraries, and a few corporate sponsors, aims to keep as much online information as possible in the "commons"—a term that refers to the collective ownership of certain public resources, like the broadcast airwaves, the Internet, and public parks. The alliance's concern is that online content like digital books might otherwise become solely the property of commercial entities.

Security and Appropriateness on the Internet

When we watch television, listen to the radio, read a book, or go see a movie, we don't need to provide personal information to get access to the media content we're consuming. However, when we use the Internet— whether it's to sign up for an e-mail account, comment on a blog, or shop online—we give away personal information, even if we don't mean to. This has raised concerns about the security of information, personal safety, and the appropriateness of content available on the Web.

Information Security: What's Private?

Government surveillance, online fraud, and unethical data-gathering methods have become common, making the Internet a potentially treacherous place.

- *Government Surveillance.* Since the inception of the Internet, government agencies around the world have obtained communication logs, Web-browser histories, and the online records of users who thought their Internet activities were private. In a traditional wiretap, a police agency gets court permission to listen in on a single telephone line. When investigating Internet communications, an agency captures the communications of *every* user of an Internet service provider. While agencies use this information to target criminals and terrorists, the scope of Internet surveillance procedures raises questions about just how far into our private lives the government should be allowed to reach.

• *Online Fraud.* The Internet has increasingly become a conduit for online robbery and *identity theft*, the illegal obtaining of someone's credit and identity information to fraudulently spend his or her money. One particularly costly form of Internet identity theft is **phishing**. Through this tactic, scammers send phony e-mail messages that appear to be from official Web sites—e.g., eBay, PayPal, AOL—asking customers to update their credit card details and other personal information (such as bank account numbers). Once scammers have this information, they can go on a shopping spree using the victim's credit card or siphon funds out of the victim's bank account.

Several cookies from visiting the *Minneapolis Star Tribune's* Web site will reside on this user's computer until 2023, tracking every subsequent visit to the newspaper Web site unless the user manually removes the cookies.

• *Unethical Data Gathering.* Millions of people, despite knowing that shopping online can make them vulnerable to online fraud, have embraced the convenience of **e-commerce**: the buying and selling of products and services on the Internet. What many people *don't* know is that a company may use their personal information without their knowledge for commercial purposes, such as developing targeted advertisements. One way companies do this is through **cookies**, information profiles that are automatically collected and transferred between computer servers whenever users access Web sites. Companies doing business on the Net use cookies to tailor their marketing messages to niche groups of users, which many people view as intrusive and even unethical. Even more frustrating is **spyware**, information-gathering software that's often secretly bundled with free downloaded software and that sends pop-up ads to users' computer screens. Spyware has also made it possible for unauthorized parties (such as hackers) to collect personal or account information about users and to plant viruses and malicious click-fraud programs on computers.

In 1998, the U.S. Federal Trade Commission (FTC) developed fair-information principles to combat the unauthorized collection of personal data online. Unfortunately, the FTC has no power to enforce these principles, and most Web sites either don't self-enforce them or say they do when they really don't.[4] Consumer and privacy advocates are calling for stronger regulations, such as requiring Web sites to adopt **opt-in policies**. Opt-in policies require a Web site to obtain explicit permission from consumers before it can collect their browsing-history data.

Personal Safety: Online Predators

In some cases, predators have used access to Internet users to cause harm. For instance, child molesters have used social networking sites to pose as friendly people, with the goal of forming relationships with naïve underage youngsters. Once a relationship takes root online, the predator suggests a face-to-face meeting, with the intent of exploiting the youngster sexually. These incidents have provoked an outcry from parents and demands for better mechanisms for protecting Internet users' safety.

Appropriateness: What Should Be Online?

The question of what constitutes appropriate content has been part of the story of every mass medium, from debates over the morality of lurid pulp-fiction books in the nineteenth century to arguments over the appropriateness of racist, sexist, and homophobic content in films and music. But, the biggest topic of debate has centered on sexually explicit content.

Public objection to indecent and obscene Internet content has led to various legislative efforts to tame the Web. For example, the Children's Internet Protection Act of 2000 was passed and upheld in 2003. This act requires schools and libraries that receive federal funding for Internet access to use software that filters out any visual content deemed obscene, pornographic, or harmful to minors, unless disabled at the request of adult users. Yet regardless of laws, pornography continues to flourish on commercial sites, individuals' blogs, and social networking pages.

Although the "back alleys of sex" of the Internet have caused considerable public concern, sites that carry potentially dangerous information (such as bomb-building instructions and hate speech) have also incited calls for Internet censorship. The terrorist attacks of September 11, 2001, along with tragic incidents where armed, disturbed high school students massacred fellow students, have intensified debate about whether such information should be available on the Net.

The Internet in a Democratic Society

Despite concerns over some online content, many tout the Internet as the most democratic social network ever conceived. (See also "Converging Media Case Study: Fragmentation, Polarization, and Convergence" on page 283.) But this same medium has also presented threats to our democracy—in the form of a division between people who can afford to use the Internet and those who can't, and in the form of the Internet's increasing commercialization.

CONVERGING MEDIA
Case Study

Fragmentation, Polarization, and Convergence

The greatest irony of the emerging Internet-driven media convergence is that it coincides with a period of increasing cultural fragmentation and political polarization in the United States. The same conditions that have enabled the user-generated collective intelligence of the wikis have also facilitated the opposing mobilizations of both the Tea Party and the Occupy Wall Street movements.

With the help of two national conservative organizations, the Tea Party succeeded in using Web resources and online social networks to connect local groups to the national leadership. These well-financed operations trained local Tea Party organizations in using new media and also enlisted the local membership as focus groups to test political messaging. The midterm elections of 2010 saw the defeat of enough Democrats by Tea Party–approved candidates to place the House of Representatives firmly in Republican hands.[1]

The same technologies augmented a competing movement attempting to shift the political agenda in a different direction. Energized by the digitally augmented revolutions in Tunisia and Egypt, an anti-consumerism Web site in Canada called Adbusters planned, organized, and mobilized the first Occupy Wall Street (OWS) protests on September 17, 2011, in New York City. OWS activism quickly spread to other major cities and has resulted in rising media coverage and political discussion of income inequality, financial accountability, and unemployment.

This convergence of the online and "real" worlds can affect personal lives as well as political movements. Though social media can be terrifically empowering, some users can also become overreliant on them (as is the case with almost any technology). The smartphone, for example, has not only augmented the revolutionary changes of the Arab Spring, but has also enabled the existence of "helicopter" parents who remain overly involved in the daily lives of their children long after they depart home for college. Similarly, Facebook users may feel self-conscious about projecting different, potentially fragmented images to different groups of friends—or finding a single identity that fits all of them. Online identities have begun to feel less virtual, more integrated into our everyday experiences.

Whether the aims are political, personal, or a mixture of the two, Internet users can now find friends, news sources, music, movies, and other media that challenge their thoughts, ideas, and opinions—or reinforce them. This fragmentation combined with the blurring of boundaries between online and "real" identity has the potential to affect behavior throughout the world—for better, for worse, or perhaps both. It also makes the process of becoming media literate more necessary than ever.

Access: Closing the Digital Divide

Coined to echo the term "economic divide" (the disparity of wealth between the rich and poor), the term **digital divide** refers to the contrast between the "information haves" (those who can afford to pay for Internet services) and the "information have-nots" (those who can't).

Access to the Internet has increased among groups that were once poorly represented online, such as Americans over the age of 65 and people who did not graduate from high school. But gaps still exist: One digital divide has developed in the United States as Americans have switched from slow dial-up connections to the more expensive high-speed broadband service. Though the majority of all Internet users in the United States now use broadband connections, those in lower-income households are much less likely to have this high-speed service.

One way of closing the digital divide is to make Internet access available in public libraries. The Bill and Melinda Gates Foundation has led the charge to provide networked computers in libraries since 1997. Another way to bridge the digital divide is for cities and other municipalities to offer inexpensive **Wi-Fi**, or wireless Internet access, which enables users of laptops, tablets, and other devices to connect to the Internet wherever they are. Entire cities, such as Corpus Christi, Texas; St. Cloud, Florida; San Francisco, California; and Washington, D.C., are developing Wi-Fi mesh systems. The growing popularity of Internet-enabled smartphones has also made online access more common; many Internet-ready phones are less expensive than laptop or desktop computers, though smartphone use, despite its popularity, is by no means universal.

Globally, though, the have-nots face an even greater obstacle crossing the digital divide. Although the Web claims to be worldwide, in some countries—Jordan, Saudi Arabia, Syria, and Myanmar (Burma)—governments limit or forbid access to the Web. In other nations—Argentina, Colombia, Brazil, Mexico—an inadequate telecommunications infrastructure means some people must wait hours or even days to get online. And in some developing countries, phone lines and computers are almost nonexistent.

The question remains: Does someone who lacks access to the Internet also lack access to the rights, freedoms, and responsibilities that come with living in a democratic society?

Ownership and Customization

Some people have argued that the biggest threat to democracy on the Internet is its increasing commercialization.

Despite the Iranian government's crackdown on traditional media after the country's 2009 disputed election, many tech-savvy Iranians turned to their cell phones and made use of Twitter to capture the events. How does Internet access play out in this political equation?

(See "Media Literacy Case Study: Net Neutrality" on page 274.) Similar to what happened with radio and television, the growth of commercial "channels" on the Internet has far outpaced the emergence of viable nonprofit channels, as a few corporations have gained more control over this medium. Although there was much buzz about lucrative Internet start-ups in the 1990s, it was the largest corporations (Microsoft, Yahoo!, Google) that weathered the crash of the "dot-coms" in the early 2000s and maintained their dominance.

As we've seen, the Net's booming popularity has tempted commercial interests to gain even more control over the medium. It has also sparked debate between defenders of the Digital Age and those who want to regulate the Net. Defenders argue that newer media forms—digital music files, online streaming of films and TV shows, blogs—have made life more satisfying and enjoyable for Americans than any other medium. Further, they maintain that **mass customization**, whereby individual consumers can tailor a Web page or other media form, has enabled us to express our creativity more easily and conveniently than ever. For example, if we use a service like Facebook, we get the benefits of creating our own personal Web space without having to write the underlying Web code. On the other hand (dissenters point out), we're limited to the options, templates, and automated RSS feeds provided by the media company. So (the dissenters ask), how free are we, really, to express our true creative selves? And how much are we being controlled by the big Internet firms?

VideoCentral ◉

bedfordstmartins.com /mediaessentials

Net Neutrality
Experts discuss Net neutrality and privatization of the Internet.
Discussion: Do you support Net neutrality? Why or why not?

CHAPTER ESSENTIALS

Now that you have finished reading this chapter, you can use the following tools:

REVIEW

Understand Key Points of the Internet's Early History

- The **Internet**—the vast central network of high-speed telephone lines designed to link and carry computer information worldwide—was initially modeled after the highway system. Begun in the late 1960s, the original Internet, **ARPAnet**, was created by the U.S. Defense Department's Advanced Research Project Agency (ARPA) and used as a military-government communication tool. **E-mail** enabled military personnel and researchers to communicate with ease from separate locations (pp. 264–268).

- Innovations in the 1970s and 80s took the Internet from the development stage to the entrepreneurial stage as a growing community of researchers, computer programmers, amateur hackers, and commercial interests tapped into the Net. **Microprocessors**—miniature circuits that could process and store electronic signals—led to the introduction of the first personal computers (PCs); **fiber-optic cable**—thin glass bundles of fiber capable of transmitting thousands of messages at once—helped make the commercial use of computers even more viable (pp. 268–269).

Outline the Evolution of the Internet

- Though limited to text browsing (content-only) and e-mailing capabilities (Web 1.0), the Internet reached the masses for the first time in the 1980s with the creation of the **World Wide Web**—a free and open data-linking system for organizing and standardizing information on the Internet that is made accessible through **HTML (HyperText Markup Language)**, the written code that connects Web pages and links, and Web **browsers**, software that helps users navigate the Web (p. 270).

- The rise of faster microprocessors, high-speed broadband networks, and the proliferation of digital content in the 2000s have pushed the Internet into a new phase (Web 2.0) whereby multimedia, interactive, user-generated functions and media convergence abound. People use the Web for **instant messaging (IM)**, **social networking**, and writing and reading **blogs** and **wikis**. (pp. 270–272).

- Though some people claim we are currently in Web 3.0, many Internet visionaries say that in the coming age information databases will be layered and connected in ways that enable software agents to sift through and process data automatically for users (p. 273).

Explain the Economics of the Internet

- Commercial entities on the Web strive to bring in money by selling advertising or services for fees. **Internet service providers (ISPs)** compete to provide consumers with Web access via **broadband** connections; **browsers** make it easy for users to navigate the Web; **directories** and **search engines** make money by providing users access (by acting as an all-purpose entry point or **portal**) to desired content, and then placing relevant ads with the content; **e-mail** companies offer a variety of services as a way to gain additional users, who are also targets of advertising (pp. 273, 276–279).

- Noncommercial entities on the Web do not make a profit from the Internet but still strive to innovate in their operations. **Open-source software** is shared freely and developed collectively on the Internet, while digital archiving aims to ensure that data is stored and preserved digitally so all people have access to it (p. 279).

Discuss Issues of Security and Appropriateness on the Internet

- Government surveillance, online fraud (such as **phishing** or sending phony e-mail messages that appear to be from official Web sites), questionable data gathering via **e-commerce, cookies** (information profiles that are collected and transferred between computer servers), and **spyware** have raised questions of information security on the Web and what should be considered private (pp. 280–281).

- At the same time, the issues of protecting people from online predators and figuring out what constitutes appropriate content on the Web, particularly regarding sexually explicit material, have sparked public concern (p. 282).

Consider the Internet's Influence on Our Democratic Society

- The Internet has made it easier for more people to voice opinions and become involved in a wide range of topics, but it has also revealed a **digital divide** regarding those who have access to information and those who do not. One way to bridge the gap is for cities and other municipalities to offer inexpensive **Wi-Fi**, or wireless Internet access, allowing users to connect wherever they are (pp. 282, 284).

- Questions over commercial ownership and **mass customization**, whereby individual consumers can tailor a Web page or other media form, have raised doubts about the true participatory nature of the Internet (pp. 284–285).

STUDY QUESTIONS

1. How did the Internet originate? What does its development have in common with earlier mass media?
2. Trace the evolution of the Internet from Web 1.0 to Web 2.0. What are the key differences between these two phases of Internet growth?
3. How have major companies tried to control the Internet? Which failed, and why?
4. What are the central concerns about the Internet regarding security and appropriateness?
5. How can the Internet make democracy work better? What are the key challenges to making the Internet itself more democratic?

MEDIA LITERACY PRACTICE

As media consumers, we are virtually anonymous to the people who make the television we watch; the films we see; the music and radio we listen to; and the books, magazines, and newspapers we read. But on the Internet, all of that has changed. How much do media companies follow our habits as we navigate the Web? To help figure this out, look at the computer you regularly use. Go to the Web browser, and select "Preferences." Find where the cookies are stored (depending on your browsing software, it might be under "Privacy" or "Security"). Have the browser show the cookies.

DESCRIBE what you see. Set the browser preferences to always ask you if you wish to accept cookies, or, alternately, to never accept cookies. Then, when you use your computer, note how often you need a cookie to advance to the next Web page.

ANALYZE your findings by looking for patterns. Can you identify which companies set cookies on your browser? What is the expiration date for most cookies? In your "cookie-less" browser run, how often did you get stopped because the site wanted to set cookies?

INTERPRET what all of this means. Were you aware that so many cookies were tracking your visits to certain sites? Did you give those sites explicit permission? Do you have any idea what the cookie information was being used for? What does this say about privacy and ethics on the Web?

EVALUATE whether this kind of data collection is good or bad.

ENGAGE with your community by writing to the FCC (see the FCC "Consumer Complaints" Web page) to register your concerns, and/or communicate directly with one of the Web sites and ask your contact there exactly what kind of information the site is collecting.

◉ ONLINE RESOURCES

Go to **bedfordstmartins.com/mediaessentials** for review quizzes, links, and more.

Visit the site's **VIDEOCENTRAL: MASS COMMUNICATION** section for videos like the ones on pages 271 and 285. There, you can find additional exclusive videos related to Chapter 9, including:

USER-GENERATED CONTENT
Editors, producers, and advertisers discuss the varieties of user-generated content and how it can contribute to the democratization of media.

INTERNET MEDIA ENTREPRENEURS: NEWSY.COM
Jim Spencer, creator of Newsy.com, describes his news service that delivers multiple sources on individual stories straight to laptops, mobile phones, and other devices.

10

Electronic Gaming and the Media Playground

Electronic gaming no longer appeals only to a cult of enthusiasts. For the first few decades after these games were invented, that cult tended to be identified as young and male. But recently, advances in technology and a broader range of games—from massively multiplayer online role-playing games like *World of Warcraft* to so-called casual games like *Angry Birds*—have made electronic gaming appealing to a wider spectrum of players. Today, the average gamer age is thirty, 47 percent of gamers are female, and there are as many avid gamers over age thirty-six as under eighteen.[1] And with increased Internet access worldwide, gaming has become a truly global phenomenon—in fact, in some places it's become even more culturally central than it is in the United States. South Korea, for example, has become the epicenter of electronic sports (or eSports), with gaming stars held in esteem comparable to that of NASCAR legends in the United States.

One of the world's most wired societies, South Korea is home to nearly thirty thousand PC *bangs*, or Internet gaming cafés. Most of them are open twenty-four hours a day and serve food, giving their customers no reason to leave. These cafés generate an estimated $6 billion a year in revenue. One of South Korea's most popular eSports players, Lim Yo-Hwan, began his career at PC bangs because he couldn't afford his own computer. Eventually, his creative play of real-time strategy games like *StarCraft: Brood War* fueled the popularity of two South Korean broadcast channels devoted to eSports. Lim won more than four hundred televised matches and became the first professional Korean gamer to be signed to a salaried corporate sponsorship contract when South Korea's largest cell phone company hired him to captain its now legendary gaming team, SK Telecom T1.[2]

Lim Yo-Hwan also claimed two gold medals at the World Cyber Games (WCG), a competitive gaming event that now includes finalists from ninety countries spread across six continents. The existence of the WCG and the stardom of players like Lim Yo-Hwan speak to gaming's new status. Electronic gaming's history, range of genres, and level of fandom today rival older mass media like books and film.

ELECTRONIC GAMES offer play, entertainment, and social interaction. Like the Internet, they combine text, audio, and moving images. But they go even further than the Internet by enabling players to interact with aspects of the medium in the context of the game—from deciding when an on-screen character jumps or punches to controlling the direction of the "story" in games such as *World of Warcraft*. This creates an experience so compelling that vibrant communities of fans have cropped up around the globe. And the games have powerfully shaped the everyday lives of millions of people worldwide.

Players can now choose from a massive range of games designed to satisfy almost any taste. Today, electronic gaming and the media playground encompass classic video games like *Super Mario Bros.*, virtual sports-management games like ESPN's *Fantasy Football*, and more physically interactive games like those found on the Wii Fit—to say nothing of massively multiplayer online role-playing games and casual games like *Angry Birds*. Indeed, for players around the world, electronic gaming has become a social medium—as compelling and distracting as other social media. The U.S. Supreme Court has even granted electronic gaming First Amendment freedom of speech rights, ensuring its place as a mass medium.

In this chapter, we take a look at the evolving mass medium of electronic gaming by:

- examining the early history of electronic gaming, including its roots in penny arcades

- tracing the evolution of electronic gaming from arcades and bars into living rooms and our hands

- discussing the rise of gaming as a social medium that forms communities of play

- analyzing the economics of gaming, including the industry's various revenue streams

- raising questions about the role of electronic gaming in our democratic society

The Early History of Electronic Gaming

When the Industrial Revolution swept Western civilization two centuries ago, the technological advances involved weren't simply about mass production. They also promoted mass consumption and the emergence of *leisure time*—both of which created money-making opportunities for media makers. By the late nineteenth century, the availability of leisure time sparked the creation of mechanical games like pinball. Technology continued to grow, and by the 1950s computer science students in the United States had developed early versions of the video games we know today.

Mechanical Gaming

In the 1880s, the seeds of the modern entertainment industry were planted by a series of coin-operated contraptions devoted to cashing in on idleness. First appearing in train depots, hotel lobbies, bars, and restaurants, these leisure machines (also called "counter machines") would find a permanent home in the first thoroughly modern indoor playground: the **penny arcade**.[3]

Arcades were like nurseries for fledgling forms of amusement that would mature into mass entertainment industries during the twentieth century. They offered fun even as they began shaping future media technology. For example, automated phonographs used in arcade machines evolved into the jukebox, while the kinetoscope (see Chapter 7) set the stage for the coming wonders of the movies. But the machines most relevant to today's electronic gaming were more interactive and primitive than the phonograph and kinetoscope. Some were strength testers that dared young men to show off their muscles by punching a boxing bag or arm-wrestling a robot-like Uncle Sam. Others required more refined

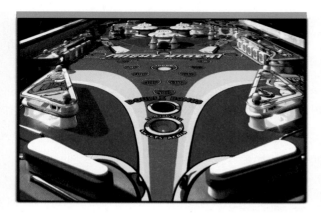

The modern pinball machine with flipper bumpers

skills and sustained play, such as those that simulated bowling, horse racing, and football.[4]

Another arcade game, the bagatelle, spawned the **pinball machine**, the most prominent of the mechanical games. In pinball, players score points by manipulating the path of a metal ball on a playfield in a glass-covered case. In the 1930s and 1940s, players could control only the launch of the ball. For this reason, pinball was considered a sinister game of chance that, like the slot machine, fed the coffers of the gambling underworld. As a result, pinball was banned in most American cities, including New York, Chicago, and Los Angeles.[5] However, pinball gained mainstream acceptance and popularity after World War II with the addition of the **flipper bumper**, which enables players to careen the ball back up the play table. This innovation transformed pinball into a challenging game of skill, touch, and timing—all of which would become vital abilities for video game players years later.

The First Video Games

The postwar popularity of pinball set the stage for the emergence of video games; the first video game patent was issued on December 14, 1948. It went to Thomas T. Goldsmith and Estle Ray Mann for what they described as a "Cathode-Ray Tube Amusement Device." The invention, which was never marketed or sold, featured the key component of the first video games: the **cathode-ray tube** (CRT).

CRT-type screens provided the images for analog television and for early computers' displays, where the first video games appeared a few years later. Computer science students developed these games as novelties in the 1950s

CHAPTER 10 // TIMELINE

1880s Penny Arcades
Penny arcades become popular, showing off automated phonographs, kinetoscopes, and mechanical games like strength testers and sports simulations.

1931 Pinball Machines
The first coin-operated pinball machine is invented by Automatic Industries.

1947 Flipper Bumpers
The flipper bumper is introduced by the D. Gottlieb Company, giving pinball players more control.

1948 First Video Game Patent
Thomas T. Goldsmith and Estle Ray Mann patent a "Cathode-Ray Tube Amusement Device," featuring the cathode-ray tube (CRT).

and 1960s. But because computers consisted of massive mainframes at the time, the games were not readily available to the general public.

However, more and more people owned televisions, and this development provided a platform for video games. The first home television gaming system, called Odyssey, was developed by German immigrant and television engineer Ralph Baer. Released by Magnavox in 1972 and sold for a whopping $100, the Odyssey used player controllers that moved dots of light around the screen in a twelve-game inventory of simple aiming and sports games. From 1972 until Odyssey's replacement by a simpler model (the Odyssey 100) in 1975, Magnavox sold roughly 330,000 of the consoles.[6]

In the next decade, a ripped-off version of one of the Odyssey games brought the delights of video gaming into modern **arcades**, establishments gathering multiple coin-operated games together in a newer version of the penny arcade. The same year that Magnavox released the Odyssey system, a young American computer engineer named Nolan Bushnell and a friend formed a video game development company called **Atari**. The enterprise's first creation was *Pong*, a simple two-dimensional tennis-style game with two vertical paddles that bounced a white dot back and forth. Unlike the Odyssey version, *Pong* made blip noises when the ball hit the paddles or bounced off the sides of the court. *Pong* quickly became the first video game to hit it big in arcades.

In 1975, Atari began successfully marketing a home version of *Pong* through an exclusive deal with Sears. The arrangement established the home video game

A later model of the Odyssey console, The Odyssey², was released in 1978 and featured a full keyboard that could be used for educational games.

| **1972** First Home Television Gaming Console
Magnavox releases the Odyssey, sold for $100 and featuring a twelve-game inventory. | **1972** *Pong*
Atari releases the first commercially successful arcade video game. | **1977** 8-bit Processing and Cartridge System
The Atari 2600, using an 8-bit processor and interchangeable game cartridges, is introduced. | **1983** Nintendo
The first Nintendo Entertainment System is released in Japan. | **1984** Atari's Demise
Warner Communications shuts down its Atari division. |

market. Just two years later, Bushnell (who also started the Chuck E. Cheese pizza-arcade restaurant chain) sold Atari to Warner Communications for an astounding $28 million. Although Atari folded in 1984, plenty of companies—including Nintendo, Sony, and Microsoft—followed its early lead, transforming the video game business into a full-fledged industry.

The Evolution of Electronic Gaming

In their most basic form, electronic games involve users in an interactive computerized environment where they strive to achieve a desired outcome. These days, most electronic games go beyond a simple competition like *Pong*; they often entail sweeping narratives and offer imaginative and exciting adventures, sophisticated problem-solving opportunities, and multiple possible outcomes.

But the boundaries were not always so varied. Electronic games evolved from their simplest forms in the arcade into four major formats: television, handheld devices, computers, and finally the Internet. As these formats evolved and graphics advanced, distinctive types of games emerged and became popular. These included classically structured games played in arcades and on consoles and mobile devices, online role-playing games, computerized versions of card games, fantasy sports leagues, and

Gaming has undergone enormous changes since the days of Atari and *Pong*.

CHAPTER 10 // TIMELINE continued

1989 16-bit Processing
Sega releases the Genesis, the first 16-bit console.

1989 Handheld Consoles
Nintendo releases the Game Boy, a popular handheld console.

1993 Entertainment Software Rating Board
The ESRB institutes a rating system for video games.

1995 PlayStation
With its CD-ROM technology and emphasis on 3-D gaming, the PlayStation becomes the first console to ship 100 million units.

virtual social environments. Together, these varied formats constitute an industry that now generates more than $45 billion in annual revenues worldwide—and that has become a socially driven mass medium.

Arcades and Classic Games

By the late 1970s and early 1980s, games like *Asteroids*, *Pac-Man*, and *Donkey Kong* filled arcades and bars, competing with traditional pinball machines. In a way, arcades signaled electronic gaming's potential as a social medium, because many games allowed players to compete with or against each other, standing side by side. To be sure, arcade gaming has been superseded by the console and computer. But the industry still attracts fun-seekers to amusement parks, malls, and casinos, as well as to businesses like Dave & Buster's, a gaming/restaurant chain operating in more than fifty locations.

To play the classic arcade games, and many of today's popular console games, players use controllers like joysticks and buttons to interact with graphical elements on a video screen. With a few notable exceptions (puzzle games like *Tetris*, for instance), these types of video games require players to identify with a position on the screen. In *Pong*, this position is represented by an electronic paddle; in *Space Invaders*, it's an earthbound shooting position. After *Pac-Man*, the **avatar** (a graphic interactive "character" situated within the world of the game) became the most common figure of player control and position identification. In the United States, the most popular video games today assume a "first-person" perspective in which the player "sees" the virtual environment through the eyes of an avatar. In contrast, players in South Korea often favor real-time strategy games with an elevated "three-quarters" perspective, which affords a grander and more strategic vantage point on the field of play.

1999 Online Consoles
Sega Dreamcast becomes the first home console to feature a built-in modem boosting online play.

2001 Xbox
Microsoft enters the console market providing new competition for Sony and Nintendo.

2004 Rise of the MMORPG
Blizzard releases *World of Warcraft*, which brings the MMORPG to a mass audience of 11 million.

2006 Motion Controllers
Nintendo's Wii reinvents video gaming with an innovative motion controller.

2011 First Amendment Protection
The U.S. Supreme Court grants electronic gaming freedom of speech protections.

Though home consoles have become widespread, some gaming fans still enjoy playing in arcades, which provide a different social experience from today's Internet-enabled home systems.

Consoles and Advancing Graphics

Today, many electronic games are played on home **consoles**, devices people use specifically to play video games. These systems have become increasingly more powerful since the appearance of the early Atari consoles in the 1970s. One way of charting the evolution of consoles is to track the number of bits (binary digits) that they can process at one time. The bit rating of a console is a measure of its power at rendering computer graphics. The higher the bit rating, the more detailed and sophisticated the graphics. The Atari 2600, released in 1977, used an 8-bit processor, as did the wildly popular Nintendo Entertainment System, first released in Japan in 1983. Sega Genesis, the first 16-bit console, appeared in 1989. In 1992, 32-bit computers appeared on the market; the following year, 64 bits became the new standard. The 128-bit era dawned with the marketing of Sega Dreamcast in 1997. With the current generation of consoles, 256-bit processors are the standard.

But more detailed graphics have not always replaced simpler games. Nintendo, for example, offers many of its older, classic games for download onto its newest consoles even as updated versions are released, for nostalgic gamers as well as new fans. Perhaps the best example of enduring games is the *Super Mario Bros.* series. Created by Nintendo mainstay Shigeru Miyamoto in 1983, the original *Mario Bros.* game began in arcades. The 1985 sequel, *Super Mario Bros.*, developed for the 8-bit Nintendo Entertainment System, became the best-selling video game of all time. It held this title until as recently as 2009, when it was unseated by Nintendo's *Wii Sports*. Graphical elements from the *Mario Bros.* games, like the "1-Up" mushroom that gives players an extra life, remain instantly recognizable to gamers of many ages. Some even appear on nostalgic T-shirts, as toys and cartoons, and in updated versions of newer games.

Through decades of ups and downs in the electronic gaming industry (Atari closing down, Sega no longer making video consoles), three major home console makers emerged: Nintendo, Sony, and Microsoft. Nintendo has been making consoles since the 1980s; Sony and Microsoft came later, but both companies were already major media conglomerates and thus well positioned to support and promote their interests in the video game market. Veteran electronics manufacturer Sony has the second most popular console, its PlayStation series, introduced in 1994. Its current console, the PlayStation 3 (PS3), boasts more than forty million users on its online PlayStation Network. Microsoft's first foray into video game consoles was the Xbox, released in 2001 and linked to the Xbox Live online service in 2002. Xbox Live lets its twenty million subscribers play online and enables users to download new content directly to the console—the Xbox 360. In 2010, this was the world's third most popular console.

Nintendo released its most recent console, the Wii, in 2006. The device supports traditional video games like the *New Super Mario Bros.* However, its unique wireless motion-sensing controller takes the often-sedentary nature out of video gameplay. Games like *Wii Sports* require the user to mimic the full-body motion of bowling or playing tennis, while *Wii Fit* uses a wireless balance board for interactive yoga, strength, aerobic, and balance games. Although the Wii has lagged behind Xbox and PlayStation in establishing an online community, it is now the best-selling of the three major console systems.

Advances in graphics and game play have also enhanced smaller handheld consoles. Nintendo's Game Boy, a two-color handheld console introduced in 1989, was one early success, selling far more than the competing Sega Game Gear and Atari Lynx, even though those two systems included full-color graphics. For many players, cutting-edge graphics on handheld consoles were—and remain—second in importance to convenience and simplicity. Nonetheless, the early handhelds gave way to later generations of devices offering more advanced graphics and wireless capabilities. These include the Nintendo DS and the PlayStation PSP, as well as simpler games played on smartphones and other mobile devices. Handheld video games have made the medium more accessible and widespread. Even people who wouldn't identify themselves as gamers may kill time between classes or waiting in line by playing *Angry Birds* on their phones. (See "Converging Media Case Study: Consoles, Portables, and Entertainment Centers" on page 305.)

ATARI® SPACE INVADERS*

These images trace gaming graphics from 8-bit (*Space Invaders*) to 16-bit (*Super Mario World*) to 64-bit (*Mario Kart 64*) to a modern 256-bit entry in the *Tomb Raider* series.

Computers and Related Gaming Formats

Early home computer games, like the early console games, often mimicked (and sometimes ripped off) popular arcade games like *Frogger*, *Centipede*, *Pac-Man*, and *Space Invaders*. But for a time in the late 1980s and much of the 1990s, personal computers held some clear advantages over console gaming. The versatility of keyboards, compared with the relatively simple early console controllers, allowed for ambitious puzzle-solving games like *Myst*. Moreover, faster processing speeds gave some computer games richer, more detailed three-dimensional (3-D) graphics. Many of the most popular, early, first-person shooter games like *Doom* and *Quake* were developed for home computers rather than traditional video game consoles. As consoles caught up with greater processing speeds and disc-based games in the late 1990s, elaborate computer games attracted less attention.

But computer-based gaming survives in the form of certain genres not often seen on consoles. Examples include the digitization of card and board games.

In video games, players identify with a playing position on the screen; in digital versions of card and board games, players remain positioned outside the field of play.

The early days of the personal computer saw the creation of electronic versions of *Solitaire*; electronic versions of games like *Hearts*, *Spades*, and *Chess* followed. Currently, players can build their skills by playing against the computer and then test their skills by competing in online matches with other people. Sometimes players start online and then transfer their skills to traditional environments. For example, in 2003, Chris Moneymaker (his real name), an accountant from Tennessee, paid $39 to enter a qualifying tournament at PokerStars.com. He moved from online poker to the face-to-face gaming tables of Las Vegas, where he ended up taking home the $2.5 million grand prize of the World Series of Poker. One of the largest and most vibrant types of electronic gaming performs the reverse action, transferring real-world action into a gaming environment: online fantasy sports. Fantasy sports games eventually became a key component of Internet-connected social gaming.

The Internet and Social Gaming

With the introduction of the Sega Dreamcast in 1999, the first console to feature a built-in modem, game playing emerged as an online, multiplayer social activity. The Dreamcast didn't last, but online connections are now a normal part of console video games. Internet-connected players oppose one another in combat, fight together against a common enemy, or team up to achieve a common goal (like sustain a medieval community). With multiple players joining in electronic games through the Internet, this form of gaming has become a contemporary social medium.

Some of the biggest social-gaming titles have been first-person shooter games like *Counter-Strike*, an online spin-off of the popular *Half-Life* console game. Each player views the game from the first-person perspective but also plays in a team as terrorists or counterterrorists. The ability to play online has added a new dimension to other, less combat-oriented games, too. For example, football and music enthusiasts playing already-popular console games like *Madden NFL* and *Rock Band* can now engage with others in live online multiplayer play. And young and old alike can compete against teams in other locations in Internet-based bowling tournaments using the Wii.

The increasingly social nature of video games has made them a natural fit for social networking sites. Many online games like *Lexulous* (inspired by the board game *Scrabble*) and *Farmville* are now embedded in these sites. **Online**

INNOVATIONS IN TRADITIONAL VIDEO GAMES

Innovation	Description	Examples	
Avatars	On-screen figures of player identification	Pac-Man, the Mario Bros. (right), Sonic the Hedgehog, Link from *Legend of Zelda*	
Bosses	Powerful enemy characters that represent the final challenge in a stage or the entire game	Bowser from the *Mario* series, Hitler in *Castle Wolfenstein*, Donkey Kong (right)	
Vertical and Side Scrolling	As opposed to a fixed screen, scrolling that follows the action as it moves up, down, or sideways in what is called a "tracking shot" in the cinema	Platform games like *Jump Bug*, *Jungle King*, and *Super Mario Bros.*; also integrated into the design of *Angry Birds* (right)	
Isometric Perspective (also called **Three-Quarters Perspective**)	An elevated and angled perspective that enhances the sense of three-dimensionality by allowing players to see the tops and sides of objects	*Zaxxon* (right), real-time strategy games like *StarCraft*, god games like *Civilization* and *Populous*	

Innovation	Description	Examples	
First-Person Perspective	Presents the gameplay through the eyes of your avatar	First-person shooter (FPS) games like *Castle Wolfenstein*, *Doom* (right), *Halo*, and *Call of Duty*	
Third-Person Perspective (or **Over-the-Shoulders Perspective**)	Enables you to view your heroic avatar in action from an external viewpoint	*Tomb Raider* (right), *Assassin's Creed*, and the default viewpoint on *World of Warcraft*	
Cut Scenes (also called **In-Game Cinematic** or **In-Game Movie**)	Narrative respite from gameplay, providing cinematic scenes that advance the story. They often appear at the beginning of games and between levels.	A well-known early example appears in *Maniac Mansion* (1987). Cut scenes from games like the *Grand Theft Auto* series (right) have become increasingly vivid and complex.	

fantasy sports games also reach a mass audience with a major social component. Players—real-life friends, virtual acquaintances, or a mix of both—assemble teams and use actual sports results to determine scores in their online games. But rather than experiencing the visceral thrills of, say, *Madden NFL 11*, fantasy football participants take a more detached, managerial perspective on the game—a departure from the classic video game experience. Fantasy sports' managerial angle makes it even more fun to watch almost any televised game. That's because players focus more on making strategic investments in individual performances scattered across the various professional teams than they do in rooting for local teams. In the process, players become statistically savvy aficionados of the game overall, rather than rabid fans of a particular team. In 2011, about thirty-five million Americans played fantasy sports, according to the Fantasy Sports Trade Association.[7]

This kind of online community-building has also enabled a fairly recent form of gaming: the **massively multiplayer online role-playing games** (MMORPGs). These games are set in virtual worlds that require users to play through an avatar of their own design. The fantasy adventure game *World of Warcraft* is the most popular MMORPG, boasting more than eleven million players around the globe. Users can select from ten different types of avatars, including dwarves, gnomes, night elves, orcs, trolls, and humans. To succeed in the game, many players join with other players to form guilds or tribes, working together toward in-game goals that can be achieved only by teams. *Second Life*, a 3-D social simulation set in real time, also features social interaction. Players build human avatars, selecting from an array of physical characteristics and clothing. Then they use real money to buy virtual land and to trade in virtual goods and services.

Simulations like *Second Life* and MMORPGs like *World of Warcraft* are aimed at teenagers and adults. But one of the biggest areas in online gaming is the children's market. Club Penguin, a moderated virtual world purchased by Disney, enables kids to play games and chat as colorful penguins. Similarly, the toy maker Ganz developed the online Webkinz World to revive its stuffed animal sales. Each Webkinz stuffed animal comes with a code that lets players access the online world, play games, and care for the virtual version of their plush pets.

Online games have further fostered media convergence. *World of Warcraft*, for instance, is now a comic book series, a quarterly magazine, and a feature film in development with director Sam Raimi. The "massively multiplayer" aspect of MMORPGs also indicates that electronic games—once designed for solo or small-group play—have expanded to reach large groups, similar to traditional mass media.

CONVERGING MEDIA
Case Study

Consoles, Portables, and Entertainment Centers

In the earlier days of video games, their most prominent media crossovers came when a movie or perhaps a TV cartoon was derived from a popular game. Increasingly, though, games can be consumed the same way so much music, television, and film are consumed: just about anywhere, in a number of shapes, sizes, and styles. Video game consoles, once used exclusively for games, now work as part computer, part cable box. They've become powerful entertainment centers, with multiple forms of media converging in a single device. For example, Xbox 360 and PS3 can function as DVD players and digital video recorders (with hard drives of up to 250 gigabytes) and offer access to Twitter, Facebook, blogs, and video chat. PS3 can also play Blu-ray discs, and all three console systems offer connections to stream Netflix movies. Portable players like the top-selling Nintendo DS, released in 2004, and PlayStation Portable (PSP), released in 2005, are additional examples of converged gaming devices. Both are Wi-Fi capable, so players can interface with other DS or PSP users to play games or even browse the Internet.

Portable players remain immensely popular; Nintendo DS sold more than 130 million units through 2010. However, they face competition from the widespread use of smartphones and touchscreen tablets like iPads. These devices are not typically designed principally for games, but their capabilities bring casual gaming to customers interested in the handheld consoles of the past. Manufacturers of these devices are catching on to their gaming potential: After years of relatively little interest in video games, Apple introduced Game Center in 2010. This social gaming network allows users to invite friends or find others for multiplayer gaming, track their scores, and view high scores on a leader board—which the DS and PSP do as well. With more than 86 million iPhone, iPod

Touch, and iPad devices in circulation, plus more than 50,000 games (like *Bejeweled* and *Angry Birds*) available in its App Store, Apple has all the elements in place to transform the portable video game business. Gaming on smartphones will gather steam as well, especially with Xbox Live access on Microsoft's Windows Phone 7.

This convergence is changing the way people look at video games and their systems. The games themselves are no longer confined to arcades or home television sets, while the latter have gained power as entertainment tools, reaching a wider and more diverse audience. Many phones and PDAs operate as de facto handheld consoles, and many home consoles serve as comprehensive entertainment centers. Thus gaming has become an everyday form of entertainment, rather than the niche pursuit of hard-core enthusiasts.

With its increased profile and flexibility across platforms, the gaming industry has achieved a mass medium status on par with film or television. This rise in status has come with stiffer and more complex competition, not just within the gaming industry but across media. Rather than Sony competing with Nintendo, or TV networks competing among themselves for viewers, or new movies facing off at the box office, media must now compete against other media for an audience's attention.

The Media Playground

To fully explore the larger media playground, we need to look beyond electronic gaming's technical aspects and consider the human faces of gaming. The attractions of this interactive playground validate electronic gaming's status as one of today's most powerful social media. Players can interact socially within the games themselves; they can also participate in communities outside of the games, organized around gaming-related interests.

Communities of Play: Inside the Game

Virtual communities often crop up around online video games and fantasy sports leagues. Indeed, players may get to know one another through games without ever meeting in person. They can interact in two basic types of groups. PUGs (short for "Pick-Up Groups") are temporary teams usually assembled by matchmaking programs integrated into the game. The members of a PUG may range from elite players to noobs (clueless beginners) and may be geographically and generationally diverse. PUGs are notorious for harboring ninjas and trolls—two universally despised player types (not to be confused with ninja or troll avatars). Ninjas are players who snatch loot out of turn and then leave the group; trolls are players who delight in intentionally spoiling the gaming experience for others.

Because of the frustration of dealing with noobs, ninjas, and trolls, most experienced players join organized groups called guilds or clans. These groups can be small and easygoing or large and demanding. Guild members can usually avoid PUGs and team up with guildmates to complete difficult challenges requiring coordinated group activity. As the terms *ninja*, *troll*, and *noob* suggest, online communication is often encoded in gamespeak, a language filled with jargon, abbreviations, and acronyms relevant to gameplay. The typical codes of text messaging (OMG, LOL, ROFL, and so forth) form the bedrock of this language system.

Players communicate in two forms of in-game chat—voice and text. Xbox LIVE, for example, uses three types of voice chat that allow players to socialize and strategize, in groups or one-on-one. Other in-game chat systems, like *World of Warcraft*'s, are text based, with chat channels for trading in-game goods or coordinating missions within a guild. These methods of

The first *Warcraft* game was released in 1994; the first MMORPG version, *World of Warcraft*, followed in 2004. In this version, players can compete and cooperate within an online game; they can also participate in text-based chatting.

communicating with fellow players who may or may not know one another outside the game create a sense of community around the game's story. Some players have formed lasting friendships or romantic relationships through game playing. Avid gamers have even held in-game ceremonies, like weddings or funerals—sometimes for game-only characters, sometimes for real-life events.

Communities of Play: Outside the Game

Communities also form outside games, through Web sites and even face-to-face gatherings dedicated to electronic gaming in its many forms. This is similar to when online and in-person groups form to discuss other mass media like movies, TV shows, and books. These communities extend beyond game play, enhancing the social experience gained through the game. Sites that cater to communities of play fit into three categories. Some collect and share user-generated **collective intelligence** on game play.[8] Others are independent sites that operate as community organizers for gamers. Still others are maintained by the industry and focus on distributing promotional material provided by hardware manufacturers and game publishers.

Collective Intelligence

Gamers looking for tips and cheats provided by fellow players need only Google what they want. The largest of the sites devoted to sharing **collective intelligence** is the *World of Warcraft* wiki (http://wowwiki.com). Similar user-generated sites are dedicated to a range of electronic games including *Age of Conan*, *Assassin's Creed*, *Grand Theft Auto*, *Halo*, *Super Mario Bros.*, *Metal Gear*, *Pokémon*, *Sonic the Hedgehog* , and *Spore*.

Independent Sites

Penny-arcade.com is perhaps the best known of the independent community-building sites. Founded by Jerry Holkins and Mike Krahulik, the site started out as a Web comic focused on video game culture. It has since expanded to include forums and a Webcast called PATV that documents behind-the-scenes work at Penny Arcade. Penny Arcade organizes a live festival for gamers called the Penny Arcade Expo (PAX), a celebration of gamer culture, and a children's charity called Child's Play.

Industry Sites

GameSpot.com and IGN.com are apt examples of the giant industry sites. GameSpot serves all the major gaming platforms and provides reviews, news, videos, cheats, and forums. It also has a culture section that features interviews

The Penny Arcade Expo (PAX) has expanded to include festivals held on the West Coast, in Seattle, and on the East Coast, in Boston. First held in 2004, the events now routinely sell out all of their passes on both coasts.

with game designers and other creative artists. In 2011, GameSpot launched Fuse, a social networking service for gamers that is designed to be "your personal gaming dashboard." IGN.com has most of the same services, as well as the regular Webcast of a news show about games called *The Daily Fix*.

Immersion and Addiction

As games and their communities have grown more elaborate and alluring, many players have spent more and more time immersed in them. This can feed addictive behavior in some people. These deep levels of involvement are not always considered negative, especially within the media playground, but they are nonetheless issues to consider as gaming continues to evolve.

Immersion

For better or worse, gaming technology of the future promises experiences that will be more immersive, more portable, and more inclusive. As gaming matures as a mass medium, the industry will use its potential for immersion to attract different audiences seeking diverse experiences.

For example, the Wii's system has successfully harnessed more user-friendly motion-control technology to open up gaming to nontraditional players—women, senior citizens, and technophobes of all ages. More motion-controlled gaming is expected, with wireless controls to detect more of players' body movements and even facial expressions. One version of this technology is Microsoft's Kinect system, which uses a sensor camera to capture full-body player motion. The Kinect will also recognize players' voices and faces, making on-screen avatars more accurate likenesses of the players. With Xbox LIVE, players can interact in full video or avatar form with friends online.

Another form of immersion has been imported from an older mass medium: In light of Hollywood's great success with 3-D movies, television set production and video games have moved toward 3-D experiences. PlayStation rolled out 3-D games in the summer of 2010, while Nintendo has released the 3DS, a 3-D version of its popular handheld console that doesn't require special glasses.

These technological enhancements are being applied to existing entertainment brands, but video games in the future will also continue to move beyond entertainment. Games are already being used in workforce training, in military recruiting, for social causes, in classrooms, and as part of multimedia journalism. For instance, to accompany related news stories, the *New York Times* developed an interactive game called *Gauging Your Distraction*. The game demonstrates how distractions like cell phones affect a person's driving ability. All of these developments continue to make games an ever-larger part of our media experiences— even for people who may not consider themselves avid gamers.

VideoCentral ◎
**bedfordstmartins.com
/mediaessentials**

Tablets, Technology, and the Classroom
Students and teachers discuss how portable electronics are replacing textbooks in the classroom.
Discussion: This video discusses classroom use of devices like tablet computers. Could handheld gaming systems be used like this? Do you ultimately think it would be distracting or helpful? Why or why not?

Addiction

No serious—and honest—gamer can deny the addictive qualities of electronic gaming. In a Harris Poll in 2007, 8.5 percent of respondents between the ages of eight and eighteen could be classified as video game addicts. And a study conducted by Stanford University Medical School in 2008 found that males are two to three times more likely than females to become addicted to video games. These findings are not entirely surprising, given that many electronic games are not addictive by accident, but rather by design. Just as "habit formation" is a primary goal of virtually every commercial form of electronic media, from newspapers to television to radio, cultivating obsessive play is the aim of most game designs. From recognizing high scores to offering a variety of difficulty settings (encouraging players to try easy, medium, and hard versions) to embedded levels that gradually increase in difficulty, designers provide constant in-game incentives for obsessive play. This is especially true of multiplayer online games—like *Halo*, *Call of Duty*, or *World of Warcraft*—that make money from long-term engagement by selling expansion packs or charging monthly subscription fees. These games have elaborate achievement systems with hard-to-resist rewards that include military ranks like "General" or fanciful titles like "King Slayer," as well as special armor, weapons, and mounts (creatures your avatar can ride, including bears, wolves, or even dragons), all aimed at turning casual players into habitual ones.

This strategy of promoting habit formation may not differ from the cultivation of other media obsessions like watching televised sporting events. Even so, real-life stories, such as that of the South Korean couple whose three-month-old daughter died of malnutrition while the negligent parents spent ten-hour overnight sessions in an Internet café raising a virtual daughter, bring up serious questions about video games and addiction. South Korea, one of the world's most Internet-connected countries, is already sponsoring efforts to battle Internet addiction.[9] Meanwhile, industry executives and others cite the positive impact of digital games, such as the learning benefits of games like *SimCity* and the health benefits of Wii Fit.

The Economics of Electronic Gaming

Thanks largely to the introduction of the Wii, today's audience for video games extends beyond the young male gamer stereotype. Though the obsessive gamers who frequent GameSpot and IGN.com are largely youthful and male, the population of casual gamers has grown much more diverse. According to the video and computer game industry's main trade group, the Entertainment Software Association, the average game player is thirty years old and has been playing games for twelve years. Women constitute 47 percent of game players, and 36 percent of Americans over age thirty-six play video games; 72 percent of American households play computer or video games.[10] These numbers speak to the economic health of the electronic gaming industry, which has proved recession-proof so far. Electronic gaming companies can make money selling not just consoles and games but also online subscriptions, companion books, and movie rights.

Money In

The primary source of revenue in the electronic gaming industry is the sale of games and the consoles on which they can be played. By 2010, about 60 percent of U.S. households owned a video game console.[11] Although a higher percentage of households have computers, console games (which play on the usually larger screens of a television) and portable handheld games constitute 95 percent of the $10.5 billion video game market, while computer games are just about 5 percent of the market. The entire video game market, including portable and console hardware and accessories, adds up to $20.2 billion a year.[12]

Beyond the immediate industry, electronic games have had a pronounced effect on media culture. Fantasy league sports have spawned a number of draft specials on ESPN as well as a regular podcast, *Fantasy Focus*, on ESPN Radio. On FX, fantasy football has even inspired an adult comedy called *The League*. Like television shows, books, and comics before them, electronic games have also inspired movies, such as *Super Mario Bros.* (1993), *Lara Croft: Tomb Raider* (2001), and the *Resident Evil* series (2002–present, including a fifth installment in 2012). For many Hollywood blockbusters today, a video game spin-off is a must-have item. Recent box–office hits like *Avatar* (2009), *Transformers: Dark of the Moon* (2011), *Up* (2009), *Inception* (2010), and *Fast Five* (2011) have companion video games for consoles and portable players. The video game–inspired *Tron* (1982) was revived with a sequel (*Tron: Legacy*) in 2010 and accompanying game and TV series. Japanese manga and animé (comic books and animation) have also inspired video games, such as *Akira*, *Astro Boy*, and *Naruto*.

Milla Jovovich stars as Alice in the popular *Resident Evil* film series, including *Resident Evil: Afterlife* (2010) and *Resident Evil: Retribution* (2012). Not all game adaptations have been so successful; film versions of *Super Mario Bros.*, *Doom*, and *Prince of Persia* disappointed at the box office—though gaming companies were still paid for the rights.

The commercial nature of the entertainment media has influenced video games as well. Like television's infomercials and newspaper and magazines' advertorials, "advergames" are video games created for purely promotional purposes. In 1992, Chester Cheetah, the official mascot for Cheetos snacks, starred in two video games for the Sega Genesis and Super Nintendo systems—*Chester Cheetah: Too Cool to Fool* and *Chester Cheetah: Wild Wild Quest*. In late 2006, Burger King sold three advergame titles for Xbox and Xbox 360 consoles for $3.99 each with value-meal purchases. One title, *Sneak King*, required the player to have the Burger King mascot deliver food to other characters before they faint from hunger.

While the commercial objectives of the Burger King games are clear, in-game product placement is often more subtle. In-game advertisements are ads for companies and products that appear as billboards or logos on products in the game environment, or as screen-blocking pop-up ads. In-game ad specialist agency IGA claims to put "hundreds of millions of impressions per week" in video games played on PS3, Wii, and Xbox 360 for clients like McDonald's, T-Mobile, Geico, AT&T, and Red Bull.[13]

One of many games in the *Grand Theft Auto* series, *Grand Theft Auto: San Andreas* (2004) takes place in a fictional state based on both California and Nevada.

Money Out

AAA game titles (games that represent the current standard for technical excellence) can cost as much as a blockbuster film to make and promote. With a budget of $100 million, *Grand Theft Auto 4* (*GTA4*) currently ranks as the most expensive console game ever made. During three and half years of production, more than one thousand people worked on the game. Just obtaining rights for the hundreds of music tracks in *GTA4* involved contacting more than two thousand people.[14]

Development, licensing, and marketing constitute the major expenditures in game publishing. The largest part of the **development budget**—the money spent designing, coding, scoring, and testing a game—goes to paying talent, digital artists, and game testers. Each new generation of gaming platforms doubles the number of people involved in designing, programming, and mixing digitized images and sounds.

Independent game makers must also deal with two types of licensing. First, they have to pay royalties to console manufacturers (Microsoft, Sony, or Nintendo) for the right to distribute a game using their system. These royalties vary from $3 to $10 per unit sold. The other form of

MEDIA LITERACY
Case Study

Writing about Games

A host of opportunities await talented writers interested in pursuing a career in gaming journalism. Gaming publications provide information on news, games, and peripherals associated with a popular platform. Some, like *PlayStation: The Official Magazine* and the *Official Xbox Magazine*, are sanctioned by console manufacturers. Others, like *Edge* and *gameinformer*, report on a broader spectrum of the electronic gaming industry. Almost all follow a reveal/preview/review cycle, whereby periodicals announce, promote, and evaluate new consoles and games.

Like traditional journalistic domains, reporting on the electronic playground requires that a writer master several skills and ethical concepts. The game journalist must be able to translate jargon into plain English and conduct interviews with a variety of gaming professionals. Perhaps most important, game journalists have an obligation to gamers to report with integrity and accuracy in the face of pressure from game and console developers to misrepresent the facts. Journalists who fail the integrity test can lose their credibility. Game journalists also share much in common with other types of specialty reporters. Just as science and medical reporters must be familiar with the histories of their respective fields, a competent game journalist should possess detailed knowledge about the origin and evolution of electronic gaming. In addition, game journalism requires a good deal of technical knowledge, business savvy, and familiarity with the legal and ethical contexts of gaming.

Though much of gaming journalism focuses on hardware, software, and economics, a relatively small group of writers who take gaming seriously have followed a decidedly different path. This group practices what they call New Game Journalism. An

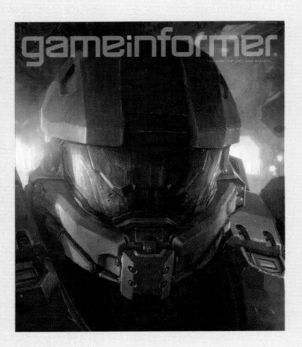

article published in *PC Gamer*, a British magazine, provided the inspiration for the movement. In the piece, Ian Shanahan (who uses the screen name always_black) relates the story of how a random online opponent opened a saber duel with a racial slur because he assumed Shanahan to be a player of color. Shanahan then transports the reader into a fleeting gaming moment when, for him, winning a routine match carried special meaning and significance beyond the fantasy of the game he was playing at the time of the challenge, *Jedi Knight II*.[1]

Kieron Gillen, a fellow British writer, found Shanahan's article so compelling that he wrote a widely read blog post calling for the establishment of New Game Journalism—an intensely personal form of game writing that would embrace the human side of gaming. The idea of writing about games in the manner of the New Journalism of the 1960–1970s attracted the attention of game writers on both sides of the Atlantic. Citing the examples of Tom Wolfe, Truman Capote, Norman Mailer, and Hunter S. Thompson, Gillen argued that "the worth of a video game lies not in the game, but in the gamer." If done correctly, New Game Journalism would resemble travel journalism, but would take readers to imaginary places instead of real ones. "Our job is to describe what it's like to visit a place that doesn't exist outside of the gamer's head . . . ," writes Gillen, and to "go to a place, report on its cultures, foibles, distractions and bring it back to entertain your readers."[2]

Video game fans may be prepared to write professional articles that follow the reveal/preview/review rituals of traditional game journalism. However, all media students have something to say about their own experiences with electronic gaming and the electronic playground. New Game Journalism thus counts as a provocative development. With its focus on the player experience, it gives a voice to anyone who wants to comment on this emergent medium.

APPLYING THE CRITICAL PROCESS

DESCRIPTION Investigate New Game Journalism by reading the reputedly seminal tract on the movement at www.alwaysblack.com/blackbox/bownigger.html. For purposes of comparison, also read a game review posted on GameSpot or IGN.com.

ANALYSIS Does always_black address you as a consumer, a citizen, or a fellow gamer? What part of the gaming dynamic is important to always_black? How does the standard game review address the reader? What part of the gaming dynamic is emphasized at GameSpot or IGN.com? What type of reader would be attracted to New Game Journalism? What type of reader would be alienated by it? Why?

INTERPRETATION Which form of game journalism—traditional or new—seeks to discover what it means to play electronic games? Which form is devoted to reporting information about electronic games?

EVALUATION Discuss the strengths and weaknesses of New Game Journalism.

ENGAGEMENT Write your own New Game Journalism article. Report on a particularly meaningful experience you had with electronic gaming. Or go to a video arcade on a busy night and record your opinions about what arcade gaming means today.

licensing involves **intellectual properties**—stories, characters, personalities, and music that require licensing agreements. In 2005, for instance, John Madden reportedly signed a $150 million deal with EA Sports that allowed the company to use his name and likeness for the next ten years.[15]

The marketing costs of launching an electronic game often equal or exceed the development costs. The successful launch of a game involves online promotions, banner ads, magazine print ads, in-store displays, and the most expensive of all: television advertising. In many ways, the marketing blitz associated with introducing a major new franchise title, including cinematic television trailers, resembles the promotional campaigns surrounding the debut of a blockbuster movie. Just as avid fans line up for the midnight release of a new *Batman* or *Twilight* movie, devoted gamers mob participating retail outlets during the countdown to the midnight launch of a hotly anticipated new game.

Electronic Gaming in a Democratic Society

Though many people view gaming as a simple leisure activity, the electronic gaming industry has sparked controversy. Parents and politicians have expressed concern about the content of some games, while the gaming industry has argued that it qualifies for free-speech protection, and that the ratings and regulations should not necessarily bear the force of law.

Self-Regulation

Back in 1976, an arcade game called *Death Race* prompted the first public outcry over violence in electronic gaming. The primitive graphics of the game depicted a blocky car running down stick-figure gremlins that, if struck, turned into grave markers. Described as "sick and morbid" by the National Safety Council, *Death Race* inspired a *60 Minutes* report on the potential psychological damage of playing video games. In the next thirty-five years, violent video games would prompt citizen groups and politicians to call for government regulation of electronic games' content.

In 1993, after the violence of *Mortal Kombat* and *Night Trap* attracted the attention of religious and educational organizations, U.S. Senator Joe Lieberman conducted a hearing that proposed federal regulation of the gaming industry. Following a pattern established in the movie and music industries, the gaming industry implemented a self-regulation system enforced by an industry panel. The industry founded the **Entertainment Software Rating Board (ESRB)** to institute a labeling system designed to inform parents of sexual and violent content that might not be suitable for younger players. Currently the ESRB sorts games into six categories: EC (Early Childhood), E (Everyone), E 10+, T (Teens), M 17+, and AO (Adults Only 18+).[16]

Free Speech and Video Games

Though 80 percent of retail outlets voluntarily chose to observe the ESRB guidelines and not sell M and AO rated games to minors, the ratings did not have force of law. That changed in 2005, when California tried to make renting or selling an M-rated game to a minor an offense enforced by fines. The law was immediately challenged by the industry and struck down by a lower court as unconstitutional. California petitioned the Supreme Court to hear the case. In a landmark decision handed down in 2011, the Supreme Court granted electronic games speech protections afforded by the First Amendment. According to the opinion written by Justice Antonin Scalia, video games communicate ideas worthy of such protection:

Though unrealistic by today's standards, the violence in *Mortal Kombat* attracted the ire of some parents in the early nineties.

> Like the protected books, plays, and movies that preceded them, video games communicate ideas—and even social messages—through many familiar literary devices (such as characters, dialogue, plot, and music) and through features distinctive to the medium (such as the player's interaction with the virtual world).[17]

Scalia even mentions *Mortal Kombat* in footnote 4 of the decision:

> Reading Dante is unquestionably more cultured and intellectually edifying than playing *Mortal Kombat*. But these cultural and intellectual differences are not constitutional ones. Crudely violent video games, tawdry TV shows, and cheap novels and magazines are no less forms of speech than *The Divine Comedy*. . . . Even if we can see in them "nothing of any possible value to society" . . . they are as much entitled to the protection of free speech as the best of literature.

However, as in the music, television, and film industries, First Amendment protections will not make the rating system for the gaming industry go away. Parents continue to have legitimate concerns about the games their children play. Game publishers and retailers understand it is still in their best interests to respect those concerns even though the ratings cannot be enforced by law.

CHAPTER ESSENTIALS

Now that you have finished reading this chapter, you can use the following tools:

REVIEW

Track Main Points of Electronic Gaming's Early History

- In the 1880s, the seeds of the modern entertainment industry were planted in coin-operated contraptions. First appearing in train depots, hotel lobbies, bars, and restaurants, these leisure machines would find a permanent home in the **penny arcade** (pp. 293–294).

- The most prominent of mechanical machines, **pinball**, gained mainstream acceptance and popularity after World War II with the addition of the flipper bumper, an innovation that transformed it into a challenging game of skill, touch, and timing (p. 294).

- **CRT** screens provided the images for analog television as well as the displays for early computers, where the earliest video games first appeared. These games were developed as novelties by computer science students in the 1950s and 1960s. However, because computers were massive mainframes at the time, distributing the games was difficult (pp. 294–295).

- Magnavox released the Odyssey, the first home gaming system, in 1972. The same year, Noah Bushnell formed a video game development company called **Atari**. Atari's first creation was *Pong*, a simple two-dimensional tennis-style game with two vertical paddles bouncing a white dot back and forth. *Pong* quickly became the first big **arcade** video game (p. 295). In 1975, Atari began successfully marketing a home version of *Pong* through an exclusive deal with Sears, thus establishing the home video game market (pp. 295–296).

Understand Key Events in the Evolution of Electronic Gaming

- By the late 1970s and early 1980s, games like *Asteroids*, *Pac-Man*, and *Donkey Kong* filled arcades and bars, competing with traditional pinball machines. After *Pac-Man*, the **avatar** became the most popular figure of player control in a video game. Though arcade gaming has been superseded by the console and computer, the industry still attracts fun-seekers to chains, malls, and casinos (pp. 296–297).

- Through decades of ups and downs in the electronic gaming industry, three major

console makers emerged: Nintendo, Sony, and Microsoft. Nintendo's Wii is now the best-selling of the three major console systems (pp. 299–300).

- With multiple players joining in electronic gaming through the Internet, gaming has become a contemporary social medium (pp. 301–304). The social dimension of gaming is especially apparent in **online fantasy sports** and **massively multiplayer online role-playing games (MMORPGs)**. In fantasy sports leagues, real-life friends, virtual acquaintances, or a mixture of both, draft teams and use actual sports results to determine team standings. *World of Warcraft*, the most popular MMORPG, counts more than 11 million players around the globe (pp. 301, 304).

- Many players get to know one another without ever meeting in person. Most online games facilitate player interaction by enabling two types of groups: PUGs (short for "Pick-Up Groups") and guilds or clans (pp. 306–307).

Map the Media Playground

- Sites that cater to communities of play fit into three categories. Some collect and share user-generated **collective intelligence** on gameplay. Others are independent and operate as community organizers for gamers. Still others are maintained by the industry and are primarily devoted to distributing promotional material provided by hardware manufacturers and game publishers (pp. 307–308).

- As gaming technology continues to develop, future experiences will likely be more immersive, portable, and inclusive. Games are still largely considered entertainment, but they are also being used in workforce training, military recruiting, classrooms, and as part of multimedia journalism (p. 308).

- In a 2007 poll, 8.5 percent of respondents between the ages of eight and eighteen could be classified as video game addicts. These findings are not entirely surprising, given that many electronic games are addictive by design. Just as habit formation is a primary goal of virtually every commercial form of electronic media, cultivating obsessive play is the aim of most game designs (p. 309).

Explain How Electronic Gaming Operates Economically

- The primary source of revenue in the electronic gaming industry is the sale of games and the consoles on which they can be played. Although a higher percentage of households have computers, console games (which play on the usually larger screens of a television) and portable handheld games constitute 95 percent of the $10.5 billion video game market, while computer games are just about 5 percent of the market. The entire video game market, including portable and console hardware and accessories, adds up to $20.2 billion a year (pp. 309–310).

- Development, licensing, and marketing constitute the major expenditures in game publishing. The largest part of the **development budget** (the money spent designing, coding, scoring, and testing a game) goes to paying talent, digital artists, and game testers (pp. 311, 314).

- Independent gamemakers deal with two types of licensing. First, they must pay royalties to console manufacturers (Nintendo, Sony, or Microsoft) for the right to distribute a game that uses the manufacturers' systems. They also pay licenses for **intellectual properties**—stories, characters, personalities, and music used in their games (pp. 311, 314).

- The marketing costs of launching an electronic game often equal or exceed the development costs. The successful launch of a game involves online promotions, banner ads, magazine print ads, in-store displays, and the most expensive of all: television advertising (p. 314).

Discuss the Place of Electronic Gaming in Our Democratic Society

- In 1993, Senator Joe Lieberman conducted a hearing that proposed federal regulation of the gaming industry. In response to this threat, the industry founded the **Entertainment Software Rating Board (ESRB)** to institute a labeling system designed to inform parents of sexual and violent content that might not be suitable for younger players (pp. 314–315).

- Though most retail outlets voluntarily chose to observe the ESRB guidelines, the ratings did not have force of law until 2005, when California tried to make renting or selling an M-rated game to a minor an offense enforced by fines. The law was immediately challenged by the industry and struck down by a lower court as unconstitutional. California petitioned the Supreme Court to hear the case. In a landmark decision handed down in 2011, the Supreme Court granted electronic games First Amendment freedom of speech protections (p. 315).

STUDY QUESTIONS

1. Why were the first video games developed at major research universities?
2. Why is bit rate useful for charting the evolution of gaming consoles?

3. How does online fantasy football differ from the classic video game?
4. What is an example of a Web site that addresses gamers as citizens of a virtual community?
5. On what grounds did the Supreme Court grant video games First Amendment protection?

MEDIA LITERACY PRACTICE

Can you judge a video game by its cover? Game covers, like book covers, serve the important function of informing customers about the content and the pleasures of the entertainment experience. In short, game covers tell players what to expect. They can also tell a potential customer that "this game is not for you."

DESCRIBE the treatment of female figures on the covers of the top 10-selling video game titles at your local gaming store.

ANALYZE the information by looking for patterns: Do the game covers represent an invitation or a warning to potential female gamers? Which consoles seem more female friendly? Female neutral? Female hostile?

INTERPRET these patterns' meaning. What do these images say about gamers' values and attitudes?

EVALUATE your findings. Consider how problems with the treatment of women on game covers might be addressed. Who is to blame for troubling depictions of women?

ENGAGE with the media playground. Participate in blogs and forums on gender relations in the gaming community. Share what you discovered in your study of gaming covers.

⊙ ONLINE RESOURCES

Go to **bedfordstmartins.com/mediaessentials** for review quizzes, links, and more. Visit the site's **VIDEOCENTRAL: MASS COMMUNICATION** section for videos like the one on page 308.

11

Advertising and Commercial Culture

Set in the male-dominated advertising world of Madison Avenue in the 1960s, the critically acclaimed AMC series *Mad Men* has honed product placement into an art. Focusing on the lives of executives at the Sterling Cooper advertising agency, the show's storylines overtly integrate an array of consumer products. In one episode, Don Draper, the main character, shops for a Cadillac. In another, the agency hires a well-known comedian to hawk Utz's potato chips. In yet another, the characters debate strategy for their Heineken ad campaign. This integration makes sense, given the show's setting, but many products featured on the show are brands from the 1960s that are still available today and whose companies have fostered partnerships with AMC— bringing product integration to a whole new level.

Building ads into TV shows and movies has become standard practice— not surprising in an age when advertising is everywhere, from roadside billboards to T-shirt logos to gas-station pump handles. But as advertising has proliferated and become such a taken-for-granted part of our daily lives, it has come to look very different today than it did in its infancy. Compare the carved stone signs merchants placed outside their shops in ancient Babylonia with product placement in TV shows or Google's AdWords system, which enables individuals and small companies to develop cheap online ads tailored to ever-narrower audiences.

Regardless of how its forms may have changed, advertising has long played a prominent role in contemporary life. For consumers, ads shape our purchasing decisions: Have you ever thirsted for a carbonated beverage after viewing a TV ad for the product? Ads fuel our hopes: "Maybe if I buy that cologne, I'll get more dates." They spark debate about companies' trustworthiness: "Hey! The ad said this hair spray would give my hair body, but it's still limp. What a rip-off!" And they get us identifying with particular brands: "This Lexus SUV really captures my style."

For companies, savvy advertising can drive sales, putting a firm far ahead of its competitors. Advertising has also given rise to whole new industries and lucrative business models—from the Madison Avenue ad agencies that produce slick campaigns for high-end clients to the most basic classified ads created by individuals on craigslist to the search-engine industry now led by Google and fueled by online ads. Even industries that were once less advertising-dependent have joined in: Musicians, for example, now stand to make more money from licensing their music to commercials than from traditional album sales.

Indeed, for all players in the realm of advertising, the economic rewards can be huge. About 96 percent of Google's $37.9 billion revenue in 2011 came from advertising, and they recently bought AdMob, a company that serves ads to mobile screens, to expand their advertising reach. As big players like Google take advantage of these technological advances, the advertising business itself is evolving. Only time will reveal what direction this multibillion-dollar support system for mass media industries will take.

ADVERTISING COMES IN MANY FORMS—from classifieds to business-to-business ads to those providing detailed information on specific consumer products. However, in this chapter, we concentrate on the more conspicuous consumer advertisements that shape product images and brand-name identities. Because so much consumer advertising intrudes into daily life, many people routinely complain about it. And they increasingly find ways to avoid ads; for example, by using digital DVRs to zip through them or by blocking pop-ups with Web browsers. However, because advertising shows up in most media—the Internet, TV, radio, books, newspapers, magazines, movies—it serves as a kind of economic glue holding these industries together. Without consumer advertisements, most media businesses would cease to function in their present forms.

In this chapter, we take a close look at advertising's evolving role in our lives by:

- examining the early history of American advertising, including the rise of ad agencies, brand-name recognition, advertising's power to create new markets and build a consumer culture, and regulation to control that power

- tracing the evolution of U.S. advertising, including the shift to emphasizing visual design in ads, specialization and restructuring of advertising agencies, and the impact of the Internet on this medium

- assessing persuasive techniques in contemporary advertising, such as using testimonials, playing on people's fears, and placing products on movie sets or on TV shows

- considering the nature of "commercial speech" and regulation of such speech; for example, to combat deception in advertising

- exploring advertising's impact on our democracy

The Early History of American Advertising: 1850s to 1950s

Before the Industrial Revolution, most Americans lived in isolated areas and produced much of what they needed—tools, clothes, food—themselves. There were few products for sale, other than by merchants who offered additional goods and services in their own communities, so anything like modern advertising simply wasn't necessary.

All that began changing in the 1850s, with the Industrial Revolution and linking of American villages and towns through railroads, the telegraph, and new print media. Merchants (such as patent medicine makers or cereal producers) wanted to advertise their wares in newspapers and magazines—giving rise to advertising agencies that managed these deals. These first national ads introduced the notion that it was important for sellers to differentiate their product from competing goods. And it inspired more and more businesspeople to adopt advertising to drive sales.

Over the coming decades, all this fueled the growth of a consumer culture, in which Americans began desiring specific products and giving their loyalty to particular brands. Critics began decrying advertising's power to seemingly dictate values and create needs in people—triggering the formation of watchdog organizations and careful consumers.

The First Advertising Agencies

The first American advertising agents were newspaper **space brokers**: individuals who purchased space in newspapers and then sold it to various merchants. Newspapers, accustomed to advertisers' not paying their bills (or paying late), welcomed the space brokers, who paid up front. Brokers usually received discounts of 15 to 30 percent, then sold the space to advertisers at the going rate. In 1841, Volney Palmer opened the first ad agency in Philadelphia; for a 25 percent commission from newspaper publishers, he sold space to advertisers.

The first full-service modern ad agency, N. W. Ayer, introduced a different model: Instead of working for newspapers, the agency worked primarily for companies—or clients—that manufactured consumer products. Opening in 1869 in Philadelphia, N. W. Ayer helped develop, write, produce, and place ads in selected newspapers and magazines for its clients. The agency collected a fee from its clients for each ad placed that covered the price that each media outlet charged for placement of the ad, plus a 15 percent commission. According to this model, the more ads an agency placed, the larger its revenue. Today, while the commission model still dominates, some advertising agencies now work for a flat fee, and some are paid on how well the ads they create drive sales for the client.

Retail Stores: Giving Birth to Branding

During the mid-1800s, most manufacturers sold their goods directly to retail store owners, who usually set their own prices by purchasing products in large quantities. Stores would then sell these loose goods—from clothing to cereal—in large barrels and bins, so customers had no idea who made them. This arrangement shifted after manufacturers started using newspaper advertising to create

Originally called the Joseph A. Campbell Preserve Company back in 1869, the Campbell Soup Co. introduced its classic red-and-white soup can labels in 1897. Today, the label is updated, but Campbell's red-and-white cans remain one of the most recognized brands in the country.

CHAPTER 11 // TIMELINE

1704 First Newspaper Ad
The first newspaper ads in colonial America run in the *Boston News-Letter*.

1841 First Ad Agency
Representing newspaper publishers, Volney Palmer opens the first ad agency in Philadelphia.

1869 First Modern Agency
The N. W. Ayer agency, working for advertisers and product companies rather than publishers, opens in Philadelphia.

1906 Food and Drugs Act
To monitor misleading patent medicine claims in newspaper and magazine ads, the Federal Food and Drugs Act is passed.

brand names—that is, to differentiate their offerings and their company's image from those of their competitors in the minds of consumers and retailers—even if the goods were basically the same. For example, one of the earliest brand names, Quaker Oats (the first cereal company to register a trademark in the 1870s) used the image of William Penn, the Quaker who founded Pennsylvania in 1681, in its ads to project a company image of honesty, decency, and hard work.

Consumers, convinced by the ads, began demanding certain products. And retail stores felt compelled to stock the desired brands. This enabled manufacturers, not the retailers, to begin setting the prices of their goods—confident that they'd prevail over the stores' anonymous, bulk items. Indeed, product differentiation in brand-name packaged goods represents advertising's single biggest triumph. Though most ads don't trigger a large jump in sales in the short run, over time they create demand by leading consumers to associate particular brands with qualities and values important to them.

Patent Medicines: Making Outrageous Claims

As the nineteenth century marched on, patent-medicine makers, excited by advertising's power to differentiate their products, invested heavily in print ads developed and placed by ad agencies. But many patent medicines (which consisted of mostly water and high concentrations of ethyl alcohol) made outrageous claims about the medical problems they could cure. The misleading ads spawned public cynicism. As a result, advertisers began to police their own ranks and developed industry codes to restore consumers' confidence. Partly to monitor patent medicine claims, Congress passed the Federal Food and Drugs Act in 1906.

Unregulated patent medicines, such as the one represented in this ad for Armour's Vigoral, created a bonanza for nineteenth-century print media in search of advertising revenue. After several investigative (or "muckraking") magazine reports about deceptive patent medicine claims, Congress created the Food and Drug Administration (FDA) in 1906.

1914 FTC
The Federal Trade Commission (FTC) is established by the federal government to help monitor advertising abuses.

1940s The War Advertising Council
A voluntary group of agencies and advertisers organizes war bond sales, blood donor drives, and food rationing.

1971 TV Tobacco Ban
Tobacco ads are banned on TV following a government ruling.

1988 Joe Camel
Joe Camel is revived as a cartoon character from an earlier print media campaign; the percentage of teens smoking Camels rises.

Department Stores: Fueling a Consumer Culture

Along with patent medicine makers, department stores began advertising heavily in newspapers and magazines in the late nineteenth century. By the early 1890s, more than 20 percent of ad space in these media was devoted to department stores.

By selling huge volumes of goods and providing little individualized service, department stores saved a lot of money—and passed these savings on to customers in the form of lower prices (as Target and Walmart do today). The department stores thus lured customers away from small local stores, making even more money that they could reinvest in advertising. This development helped further fuel the growth of a large-scale consumer culture in the United States.

Transforming American Society

By the dawn of the twentieth century, advertising had become pervasive in the United States. As it gathered force, it began transforming American society. For one thing, by stimulating demand among consumers for more and more products, advertising helped manufacturers create whole new markets. The resulting brisk sales also enabled companies to recover their product-development costs quickly. In addition, advertising made people hungry for technological advances by showing how new machines—vacuum cleaners, washing machines, cars—might make daily life easier or better. All this encouraged economic growth by increasing sales of a wide range of goods.

Advertising also began influencing Americans' values. As just one example, ads for household-related products (mops, cleaning solutions, washing machines) conveyed the message that "good" wives were happy to vanquish dirt from their homes. By the early 1900s, business leaders and ad agencies believed that women, who constituted as much as 70 to 80 percent of newspaper and magazine readerships, controlled most household purchasing decisions. Agencies developed simple ads tailored to supposedly feminine characteristics—ads featuring emotional and even irrational content.

CHAPTER 11 // TIMELINE continued

1989 Channel One
Channel One is introduced into thousands of schools, offering "free" equipment in exchange for ten minutes of news programming and two minutes of commercials.

1998 Billboard Tobacco Ban
The tobacco industry agrees to a settlement with several states, and tobacco ads are banned on billboards.

1990s Beer Ads on TV
Budweiser uses cartoonlike animal characters to appeal to young viewers.

For instance, many such ads portrayed cleaning products and household appliances as "heroic" and showed grateful women gushing about how the product "saved" them from the shame of a dirty house or the hard labor of doing laundry by hand.

Early Regulation of Advertising

During the early 1900s, advertising's growing clout—along with revelations of fraudulent advertising claims and practices—catalyzed the formation of the first watchdog organizations. For example, advocates in the business community in 1913 created the nonprofit Better Business Bureau, whose mission included keeping tabs on deceptive advertising. The following year, the government established the Federal Trade Commission (FTC), in part to further help monitor advertising abuses. Alarmed by government's willingness to step in, players in the advertising industry urged self-regulation to keep government interference at bay.

At the same time, advertisers recognized that a little self-regulation could benefit them in other ways as well. They especially wanted a formal service that tracked newspaper and magazine readership, guaranteed accurate audience measures, and ensured that newspapers didn't overcharge agencies and their clients. To that end, publishers formed the Audit Bureau of Circulation (ABC) in 1914 to monitor circulation figures.

But it wasn't until the 1940s that the industry began to deflect the long-standing criticisms that advertisers created needs that consumers never knew they had, that advertisers dictated values, and that they had too strong a hand in the economy. To promote a more positive self-image, the ad industry developed the War Advertising Council. This voluntary group of ad agencies and advertisers

During World War II, the federal government engaged the advertising industry to create messages to support the U.S. war effort. Advertisers promoted the sale of war bonds, conservation of natural resources such as tin and gasoline, and even saving kitchen waste so it could be fed to farm animals.

2002 Mega-Agencies
Four international mega-agencies—Omnicom, Interpublic, WPP, and Publicis—control more than one-half of the world's ad revenues.

2007 TV Ad Time
Fifteen minutes of each hour of prime-time network TV contains ads.

2012 Super Bowl Record
The cost of a thirty-second spot during the Super Bowl reaches $3.5 million for the first time.

began organizing war bond sales, blood donor drives, and the rationing of scarce goods. Known today by a broader mission and its postwar name, the Ad Council chooses a dozen worthy causes annually and produces pro bono *public service announcements* (PSAs) aimed at combating social problems such as illiteracy, homelessness, drug addiction, smoking, and AIDS.

In the 1950s, with the advent of television, advertisers had a brand-new visual medium for reaching consumers. Critics complained about the increased intrusion of ads into daily family life. They especially decried what was then labeled **subliminal advertising**. Through this tactic, TV ads supposedly used hidden or disguised print and visual messages (often related to sex, like the shape of a woman's body in an ice cube for a vodka ad) that allegedly register only in viewers' subconscious minds, fooling them into buying products they don't need. However, research has reported over the years that subliminal ads are no more powerful than regular ads. Demonstrating a willingness to self-regulate, though, the National Association of Broadcasters banned the use of anything resembling a subliminal-type ad in 1958.

The Evolution of U.S. Advertising: 1950s to Today

As the twentieth century progressed, U.S. advertising changed in several ways. Visual design began to play a more prominent role in ads, reflecting people's growing interest in imagery. This trend helped spark the growth of new types of ad agencies that began dominating the field—large, global firms serving a broad range of clients, and small companies working for a select group of clients. Ad agencies of all types developed a distinctive organizational structure, which included specialized departments responsible for activities such as account planning and creative development. But that, too, began changing with the advent of the Internet in the 1990s. The new medium presented fresh possibilities for designing and placing ads, giving rise to entirely new types of players in the advertising sector, including search-engine giant Google.

Visual Design Comes to the Fore

Visual design began playing a more central role in advertising during the 1960s and 1970s. This revolution was influenced in part by overseas design schools and European designers—whom agencies hired as art directors and who were not tied to word-driven print and radio advertising. The new emphasis on imagery also drew inspiration from changes in television and cable content. By the early 1970s, agencies had developed teams of writers and visual artists, thus granting equal status to images and words in the creative process. Video-style ads featuring prominent performers (Ray Charles, Michael Jackson, Madonna) soon saturated TV.

Today, thanks to technologies such as mobile phones, tablet computers, and incredibly crisp digital displays, visual design has reached new levels of sophistication. For example, ads on mobile phones feature full-motion, 3-D animation and high-quality audio. At the same time, designers have also had to simplify the imagery they create, so ads and logos can show up clearly and scroll vertically on small digital screens. Finally, to appeal to the global audience, many ad agencies are hiring graphic designers who can capture a diversity of visual styles from around the world.

New Breeds of Advertising Agencies Are Born

The increasing prominence of visual design in advertising led to the development of two specialized types of advertising agencies: **mega-agencies**, large firms that are formed from the merging of several individual agencies and that maintain worldwide regional offices, and **boutique agencies**, smaller companies that devote their talents to just a handful of select clients. Both types of agencies wield great control over the type of advertising we see daily.

Mega-Agencies

Mega-agencies provide a full range of services—from advertising and public relations to operating their own in-house radio and TV production studios. In 2012, the top four mega-agencies were WPP, Omnicom, Interpublic, and Publicis.[1] (See Figure 11.1.)

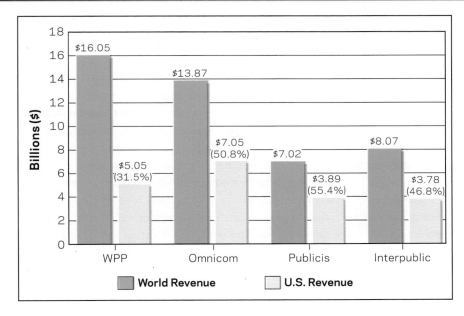

**FIGURE 11.1 //
REVENUE FOR THE
WORLD'S FOUR
LARGEST AGENCIES**

Source: "Advertising Age's Agency Family Trees 2011," http://adage.com /images/random/datacenter/2011 /agencyfamilytrees11.pdf, Accessed on August 16, 2012.

The mega-agency trend has stirred debate among consumer and media watchdog groups. Some have considered large agencies a threat to the independence of smaller firms, which were slowly bought up in the 1990s. Others warn against having a few firms control much of the distribution of advertising dollars globally. According to these critics, with such concentration of power, the cultural values depicted in U.S. and European ads (such as an obsession with youth or appearance) could unduly influence people in developing countries or regions who have markedly different values. Such critics decry the supposed intrusion of American culture into these other cultures.

Boutique Agencies

The visual revolutions in advertising during the 1960s elevated the standing of the creative side of the ad business, particularly the designers, writers, and graphic artists who became closely identified with the look of specific ads. Breaking away from bigger agencies, many of these individuals formed small boutique agencies. Offering more personal services, the boutiques prospered—thanks to the innovative ad campaigns they developed to popularize brands like Nike, ESPN, and Target.

Throughout the 1980s and 1990s, large agencies bought up many of the boutiques. Nevertheless, some boutiques continue to operate as fairly independent subsidiaries of multinational corporations. With the economic crisis, both types of ad agencies suffered revenue declines in 2008 and 2009 but slowly improved in 2010 and 2011.

Ad Agencies Develop a Distinctive Structure

Regardless of type (mega or boutique), most ad agencies have a similar organizational structure comprising four main functions: account planning, creative development, media buying, and account management.

Account Planning

The account planner's role is to develop an effective advertising strategy by combining the views of the client, creative team, and consumers. Consumers' views are the most difficult to understand, so account planners coordinate **market research** to assess consumers' behaviors and attitudes regarding particular products long before the agency develops any ads. Researchers might test consumers' preferences regarding a wide range of things—including possible names for a new product, size of text in a possible print ad, and potential features of a product in development.

Agencies have increasingly employed scientific methods to study consumer behavior. The earliest type of market research, **demographics**, mainly documented audience members' age, gender, occupation, ethnicity, education, and income—and then looked for patterns between these characteristics and consumers' purchasing choices. (For example, what types of clothing and skin-care products do high-earning women over forty years of age generally purchase?) Today, demographic data have become even more specific, enabling marketers to identify consumers' economic status and geographic location (usually by zip code) and compare their consumption behaviors, lifestyles, and attitudes.

By the 1960s and 1970s, advertisers and agencies began using **psychographics**, a research approach that attempts to categorize consumers according to their attitudes, beliefs, interests, and motivations. Psychographic analysis often relies on **focus groups**, a small-group interview technique in which a moderator leads a discussion about a product or an issue, usually with six to twelve participants. For instance, a focus group moderator may ask participants what they think of several possible names for a new brand of beer, why they like or dislike particular names proposed, and what role beer plays in their lives.

In 1978, this research grew even more sophisticated when Strategic Business Insights (formerly SRI International) developed its **Values and Lifestyles (VALS)** strategy. Using questionnaires, VALS researchers today divide respondents into eight types—thinkers, innovators, achievers, strivers, survivors, believers, makers, experiencers—associated with certain behaviors and preferences of interest to clients. For example, an automaker considering which vehicle models to advertise in which types of TV shows might be told that *achievers* watch a lot of sports programs and prefer luxury cars, while *thinkers* enjoy TV dramas and documentaries and like minivans and hybrids.

VALS research assumes that not every product suits every consumer, and encourages advertisers to pitch various sales slants to particular market niches. VALS (and similar research techniques) ultimately provides advertisers with microscopic details suggesting which consumers may be most likely to buy which products, but it also stereotypes people as consumers, reduced to eight manageable categories.

As a leading consumer group, teens are often one of the most targeted demographics for large companies advertising their products. Here we see young women shopping for dresses in Macy's department store.

Creative Development

Teams of writers and artists—many of whom regard ads as a commercial art form—make up the nerve center of the advertising business. They outline the rough sketches for print and online ads and then develop the words and graphics. For radio, "creatives" prepare a working script, generating ideas for everything from choosing the narrator's voice to determining background sound effects. For television, they develop a **storyboard**, a roughly drawn comic-strip version showing each scene in the potential ad. For digital media, the creative team may

Lemon.

The New York ad agency Doyle Dane Bernbach created a famous series of print and television ads for Volkswagen beginning in 1959 and helped to usher in an era of creative advertising that combined a single-point sales emphasis with bold design, humor, and apparent honesty.

develop Web sites, interactive tools, games, downloads, social media campaigns, and **viral marketing**—short videos or other forms of content that they hope will swiftly capture an ever-widening circle of attention as users share the content with friends online or by word of mouth.

Creatives often lock horns with researchers over what will appeal most to consumers and how best to influence target markets. However, both sides acknowledge that they can't predict with absolute certainty which ads will succeed, especially in a competitive economy where eight out of ten new products introduced to market typically fail. Agencies say ads are at their best if they slowly create and then hold brand-name identities by associating certain products over time with quality and reliability in the minds of consumers. Famous brands like Coca-Cola, Budweiser, Toyota, and Microsoft spend millions of dollars each year just to maintain their brand-name aura. However, some economists maintain that much of the money spent on advertising, especially to promote new products, is ultimately wasted, since it just encourages consumers to change from one well-known brand name to another.

Media Buying

An ad agency's media coordination department is staffed by media planners and **media buyers**: people who choose and purchase the types of media that are best suited to carry a client's ads and reach the targeted audience. For instance, a company like Procter & Gamble, always among the world's top purchasers of advertising, displays its hundreds of major brands—most of them household products like Crest toothpaste, Ivory soap, and Pampers diapers—on TV shows viewed primarily by women, who still do the majority of household cleaning.

Client companies usually pay an ad agency a commission or fee for its work. But they might also add incentive clauses to their contracts with the agency. For example, they may pay a higher fee if sales reach a specific target after an ad is aired—or pay a lower fee if sales fall short of the target. Incentive clauses can sometimes encourage agencies to conduct repetitive **saturation advertising**, by which they inundate a variety of media with ads aimed at target audiences. The initial Miller Lite beer campaign ("Tastes great, less filling"), which used humor and retired athletes to reach its male audience, ran from 1973 to 1991 and became one of the most successful saturation campaigns in media history.

Of course, such efforts are expensive. And indeed, the cost of advertising—especially on network television—increases each year. The Super Bowl remains the most expensive program for purchasing television advertising, but running a thirty-second ad during a national prime-time TV show can cost from $100,000 to more than $600,000 depending on the program's popularity and ratings. Cost thus strongly influences where and when media buyers place ads.

Account Management

An agency's **account executives** are responsible for bringing in new business. For example, if a potential new client has requested bids for an upcoming ad campaign, the account executive might coordinate the presentation of a proposed campaign, complete with cost estimates. Account executives also manage relationships with established clients, including overseeing project budgets, market research, creative work, and media planning done on their campaigns. Account executives thus function as liaisons between the client firm and the agency's creative team.

The advertising business is volatile, and account-management departments are especially vulnerable to upheavals. Clients routinely conduct **account reviews**—assessing an existing ad agency's campaign or inviting several new agencies to submit new campaign strategies. If they're dissatisfied, they may switch agencies, something that has occurred more and more frequently since the late 1980s.[2]

The Internet Alters the Ad Landscape

When the Internet made its appearance as a new mass medium in the 1990s, it presented a host of new decisions for companies to grapple with—such as what kinds of ads to invest in and where to place them. It also opened the door for new giants (such as Google) to dominate the online-advertising industry.

The Rise of Web Advertising

The earliest form of Web advertising showed up in the mid-1990s and featured banner ads, the print-like display ads that load across the top or side of a Web page. Since that time, Web advertising has grown in sophistication. Other formats have emerged, including pop-up ads, pop-under ads, multimedia ads, and—ironically—the classic thirty-second video ad. Internet advertising now also includes classified ads—the most prominent is Craigslist—and unsolicited e-mail ads known as **spam**. In fact, a number of companies have emerged in the past few years, several in India, devoted simply to producing spam ads for various clients.

Today, paid search advertising dominates sites such as Google, Yahoo!, and Bing. These search engines have quietly morphed into online advertising companies, selling sponsored links associated with search terms and distributing online ads to affiliated Web pages.[3] This type of advertising is far more precise than the

VideoCentral ◉
bedfordstmartins.com /mediaessentials

Richard Campbell
Author, Media and Culture

Advertising in the Digital Age
This video discusses how ads evolve to overcome resistance to advertising.
Discussion: Do you recall many ads from the last few times you used the Internet? What do you think this might mean for advertisers?

Online ads are mostly placed with large Internet companies like Google, Yahoo!, Facebook, and Twitter. Such services have allowed small businesses access to more customers than traditional advertising because the online ads are cheaper and only shown to targeted users. Social media sites have become particularly popular for advertisers.

earlier Web ads, enabling companies to reach target customers defined in ever-narrower terms, such as where they live and what key words they use while searching the Web. Some observers claim that clients in the near future will pay only for highly targeted ads and proven results.

Currently, online companies pose a real threat to traditional advertising agencies. In recent years, Internet ads have accounted for at least 9 percent of all advertising spending in the United States, and by 2012, Internet advertising was estimated to be a $36.8 billion industry.

How Online Ads Work

Online ads are generally placed by advertising agencies and served to hundreds of client sites by the agencies' computers. The agencies track **ad impressions** (how often ads are seen) and **click-throughs** (how often users land briefly on a site before clicking through to the next site). They also develop consumer profiles that direct targeted advertisements to Web site visitors. Online agencies gather information about Internet users through "cookies" (code that tracks users' activity on the Web) and online surveys.

Mobile phones and tablets have provided a "third screen" (in addition to TV and personal computers) for online advertisers. These devices present the possibility for advertisers to tailor ads to phone users' specific geographic location. For example, a restaurant chain can display a special promotional ad on the mobile phone of someone driving a car or walking in the area of its nearest location. Google has also developed unique applications for mobile advertising and search. For example, the Google Goggles smartphone app enables users to take a photo of an object such as a book cover, a landmark, or a logo and then have Google return related search results. Google's Voice Search app lets users speak their search terms. Such apps are designed to maintain Google's dominant Web search-engine position (which generates most of its profits) on the increasingly important mobile platform. Other mobile ad technologies include **QR (Quick Response) codes**, square bar codes that are easily scannable by mobile phone cameras and link to videos and Web pages. Mobile phone cameras can also be used to launch "augmented reality" views (not unlike the effect of the digital "first down" line in football television broadcasts), which can layer advertising and other sorts of information over a camera's real-time image of a product or shopping district. Google has put that same augmented reality technology into eyeglasses, which have small cameras that "see" what we see, then layer information (and ultimately advertising) in the small screens for each eye. Dubbed "Project Glass," the glasses interface with Google apps and allow users to send e-mail via dictation, take pictures and upload them, and get directions.

Advertising Invades Social Media

Social media, such as Facebook, Twitter, and Foursquare, provide a wealth of data for advertisers to mine. These sites and apps create an unprecedented public display of likes, dislikes, locations, and other personal information; advertisers use such information to further refine their ability to send targeted ads. Facebook and other sites like Hulu go even further by asking users if they liked the ad or not. The information users provide goes straight back to advertisers so they can revise their advertising and better engage their viewers. Most social media also encourage advertisers to create their own online identity, with a Facebook page that users can "like" and share with one another. Despite appearances, such profiles and identities still constitute advertising and serve to promote products to an online audience for virtually no cost.

Companies and organizations also buy traditional paid advertisements on social media sites. A major objective of their paid media is to get earned media, or to convince online consumers to promote products on their own. If you "like" a particular ad or product on Facebook, your friends may view it, knowing that you like it. Social media are helping advertisers use such personal endorsements to further their own products and marketing messages.

Web Advertising's Growing Power

The leading Internet companies aggressively expanded into the advertising market by acquiring smaller Internet advertising agencies. For example, in the past few years Google bought DoubleClick, the biggest online ad server, and AdMob, a mobile advertising company. Yahoo! purchased Right Media, which auctions online ad space. Microsoft acquired aQuantive, an online ad server and network that enables potential advertisers to place ads on many Web sites with a single buy. Apple purchased Quattro Wireless, a mobile ad company, while Facebook bought Rel8tion, another mobile advertising firm. Amazon.com didn't purchase an ad agency, but partnered with San Francisco-based online advertiser Triggit to sell ads to Amazon users based on their browsing history. This kind of micro-targeted advertising—based on the data mining of browsing or buying history, social media contacts, and other personalized information—is becoming ever more common as mass media (and other aspects of life) converge onto the Internet.

With their deep pockets and broad reach, these companies also began to move beyond the multi-billion-dollar Internet ad market and have become ad brokers for other mass media. Meanwhile, the traditional advertising agencies have struck back by expanding their Internet capabilities.

Persuasive Techniques in Contemporary Advertising

In addition to using a similar organizational structure, most ad agencies employ a wide variety of persuasive techniques in the ad campaigns they create for their clients. Indeed, persuasion—getting consumers to buy one company's products and services and not another's—lies at the core of the advertising industry. Persuasive techniques take numerous forms, ranging from conventional strategies (such as having a famous person endorse a product) to not-so-conventional (for instance, showing video game characters using a product).

Do these tactics work; that is, do they boost sales? This is a tough question, because it's difficult to distinguish an ad's impact on consumers from the effects of other cultural and social forces. But companies continue investing in advertising on the assumption that without the product and brand awareness that advertising builds, consumers just might go to a competitor.

Celebrities can be used to endorse brands; they can also use endorsements to promote their own brands. Here Lady Gaga promotes MAC cosmetics, as well as a pet social cause.

Using Conventional Persuasive Strategies

Advertisers have long used a number of conventional persuasive strategies.

1. **Famous-person testimonial:** A product is endorsed by a well-known person. For example, Serena Williams has become a leading sports spokesperson, having appeared in ads for companies including Nike, Kraft Foods, and Procter & Gamble.
2. **Plain-folks pitch:** A product is associated with simplicity. For instance, General Electric ("Imagination at work") and Microsoft ("Your potential. Our passion.") have used straightforward slogans stressing how new technologies fit into the lives of ordinary people.
3. **Snob appeal:** An ad attempts to persuade consumers that using a product will maintain or elevate their social status. Advertisers selling jewelry, perfume, clothing, and luxury automobiles often use snob appeal.

4. **Bandwagon effect:** The ad claims that "everyone" is using a particular product. Brands that refer to themselves as "America's favorite" or "the best-selling" imply that consumers will be "left behind" if they ignore these products.

5. **Hidden-fear appeal:** A campaign plays on consumers' sense of insecurity. Deodorant, mouthwash, and shampoo ads often tap into people's fears of having embarrassing personal hygiene problems if they don't use the suggested product.

6. **Irritation advertising:** An ad creates product-name recognition by being annoying or obnoxious. (You may have seen one of these on TV, in the form of a local car salesman loudly touting the "UNBELIEVABLE BARGAINS!" available at his dealership.)

Associating Products with Values

In addition to the conventional persuasive techniques described above, ad agencies draw on the **association principle** in many campaigns for consumer products. Through this technique, the agency associates a product with a positive cultural value or image—even if that value or image has little connection to the product. For example, many ads displayed visual symbols of American patriotism in the wake of the 9/11 terrorist attacks in an attempt to associate products and companies with national pride.

Yet this technique has also been used to link products with stereotyped caricatures of targeted consumer groups, such as men, women, or specific ethnic groups. For example, many ads have sought to appeal to women by portraying men as idiots who know nothing about how to use a washing machine or how to heat up leftovers for dinner. The assumption is that portraying men as idiots will make women feel better about themselves—and thus be attracted to the advertised product (see "Media Literacy Case Study: Idiots and Objects: Stereotyping in Advertising" on page 338).

Another popular use of the association principle is to claim that products are "real" and "natural"—possibly the most common adjectives used in advertising. For example, Coke sells itself as "the real thing." The cosmetics industry offers synthetic products that make us look "natural." And "green" marketing touts products that are often manufactured and not always environmentally friendly.

In the 1950s and 1960s, Philip Morris used the association principle to transform the image of its Marlboro filtered cigarette brand (considered a product for women in the 1920s) into a product for men. Ad campaigns featured images of active, rugged males, particularly cowboys. Three men, however, who appeared in these ad campaigns died of lung cancer caused by cigarette smoking. But that

MEDIA LITERACY
Case Study

Idiots and Objects: Stereotyping in Advertising

Over the years, critics and consumers alike have complained about stereotyping in main-stream advertising. *Stereotyping* refers to the process of assigning people to abstract groups, whose members are assumed to act as a single entity—rather than as individuals with distinct identities—and to display shared characteristics, which often have negative connotations.

Today, particularly in beer ads, men are often stereotyped as inept or stupid, incapable of negotiating a routine day or a normal conversation unless fortified—or dulled—by the heroic product. Throughout advertising history, men have often been portrayed as doofuses and idiots when confronted by ordinary food items or a simple household appliance.

On the other hand, in the early history of product ads on television, women were often stereotyped as naïve or emotional, needing the experienced voice of a rational male narrator to guide them around their own homes. Ads have also stereotyped women as brainless or helpless or offered them as a man's reward for drinking a

particular beer, wearing cool jeans, or smoking the right cigarette. Worst of all, women, or even parts of women—with their heads cut from the frame—have been used as objects, merely associated with a particular product (e.g., a swimsuit model holding a new car muffler or wrapped around a bottle of Scotch). Influenced by the women's movement and critiques of advertising culture, such as Betty Friedan's *The Feminine Mystique* (1963), ads depicting women have changed. Although many sexist stereotypes still persist in advertising, women today are portrayed in a variety of social roles.

In addition to ads that have stereotyped men and women, there is also invisible stereotyping.

This occurs when whole segments of the population are ignored—particularly African, Arab, Asian, Latin, and Native Americans. Advertising—especially in its early history—has often faced criticism that many segments of the varied and multicultural U.S. population have been missing or underrepresented in the ads and images that dominate the landscape. In the last several years, however, conscious of how diverse the United States has become, many companies have been doing a better job of representing various cultures in their product ads.

APPLYING THE CRITICAL PROCESS

DESCRIPTION Gather four to six advertisements from various newspapers, magazines, or Internet sites that feature individuals (and not just products).

ANALYSIS Examine the content of each ad—what product is being sold? What are the profiles of the people who appear in the ad, or what are they doing? Note the publication or Web site each ad comes from. What patterns emerge, and what do these patterns suggest to you?

INTERPRETATION What do the patterns mean? How are the people in the ads helping to sell the product? What is the message that the ad is trying to portray?

Why did the advertiser choose the specific newspaper, magazine, or Internet site to advertise the product?

EVALUATION Do any of the ads foster existing stereotypes? Explain how they do or do not. Do you think these ads are effective? How might the stereotypes in these ads convey a distorted or mixed message to the consumer?

ENGAGEMENT Choose one ad from your selection to revise. How might you redesign this ad to remove existing stereotypes? Compose a draft. Do you think your ad is more, or less, effective? Explain your answer.

apparently hasn't blunted the brand's impact. By 2011, the branding consultancy BrandZ had named Marlboro the world's eighth "most powerful [memorable] brand," having an estimated worth of $67.5 billion. (Apple, Google, and IBM were the top three rated brands; see Table 11.1.)

Telling Stories

Many ads also tell stories that contain elements found in myths (narratives that convey a culture's deepest values and social norms). For example, an ad might take the shape of a minidrama or sitcom, complete with characters, settings, and plots. Perhaps a character might experience a conflict or problem of some type. The character resolves the situation by the end of the ad, usually by purchasing or using the product. The product and those who use it emerge as the heroes of the story.

For instance, in the early 2000s, ads for GEICO car insurance featured TV commercials that looked like thirty-second sitcoms. The ad's plot lines told the story of cavemen trying to cope in the modern world but who found themselves constantly ridiculed—for being cavemen ("so easy a caveman can do it"). The point of the ads included associating the product with humor, making the audience feel slightly superior to slightly dim-witted prehistoric guys. The ads were funny and

TABLE 11.1 // THE TOP 10 GLOBAL BRANDS

Rank	Brand	Brand Value ($Millions)	Brand Value Change, 11 vs. 10 (%)
1	Apple	153,285	84
2	Google	111,498	-2
3	IBM	100,649	17
4	McDonald's	81,016	23
5	Microsoft	78,243	2
6	Coca-Cola*	73,752	8
7	AT&T	69,916	N/A
8	Marlboro	67,522	18
9	China Mobile	57,326	9
10	GE (General Electric)	50,318	12

Coca-Cola includes Diet Coke, Coke Light, and Coke Zero.

Source: "BrandZ Top 100 Most Powerful Brands 2011." Millward Brown Optimor. http://www.millwardbrown.com/brandz/2011/report/.

popular, and ABC actually commissioned a short-lived sitcom called *Cavemen* based on the ads' characters.

Although most of us realize that ads telling stories create a fictional world, we often can't help but get caught up in them. That's because they reinforce our values and assumptions about how the world works. And they reassure us that by using familiar brand names—packaged in comforting ministries—we can manage the everyday tensions and problems that confront us.

Placing Products in Media

Product placement—strategically placing ads or buying space in movies, TV shows, comic books, and video games so they appear as part of a story's set environment—is another persuasive strategy ad agencies use. For example, the 2010 movie *Iron Man 2* features product placements from over sixty brands, almost triple the number shown in the original 2008 film, which itself included prominent use of brands like Burger King, Audi, and LG mobile. The NBC sitcom *30 Rock* even makes fun of product placement, satirizing how widespread it has become. In one scene, the actors talk about how great Diet Snapple is. Then an actual commercial for Snapple appears.

Many critics argue that product placement has gotten out of hand. In 2005, watchdog organization Commercial Alert asked both the FTC and the FCC to mandate that consumers be warned about product placement in television shows. The FTC rejected the petition, and by 2008 the FCC had still made no formal response to the request. Most defenders of product placement argue there is little or no concrete evidence or research that this practice harms consumers. The 2011 documentary *POM Wonderful Presents: The Greatest Movie Ever Sold* takes a satirical look at product placement—and filmmaker Morgan Spurlock financed the film's entire budget with that very process.

The James Bond film franchise has long been home to a variety of product placements, especially when showcasing cars (as in this scene from 2008's *Quantum of Solace*). The 2012 Bond film *Skyfall* follows suit.

Commercial Speech and Regulating Advertising

Advertisements are considered **commercial speech**—defined as any print or broadcast expression for which a fee is charged to organizations and individuals buying time or space in the mass media. Though the U.S. Constitution's First Amendment protects freedom of speech and of the press, it doesn't specify whether advertisers can say anything they want in

Less cars, more world. **Drivers wanted.**

Adbusters Media Foundation is a nonprofit organization that aims to criticize the consumerist nature of global culture. Based in Canada, the organization likes to create spoof ads that endorse "a better product and beat the corporations at their own game."

VideoCentral ▣
bedfordstmartins.com /mediaessentials

Advertising and Effects on Children
Scholars and advertisers analyze the effects of advertising on children.
Discussion: In the video, some argue that using cute, kid-friendly imagery in alcohol ads can lead children to begin drinking; others dispute this claim. What do you think, and why?

their commercial speech, so the question of whether commercial speech is protected by the Constitution is tricky. In some critics' view, certain forms of advertising can have destructive consequences and therefore should be regulated. These include ads that target children, that tout unhealthy products (such as alcohol and tobacco), that prompt people to adopt dangerous behaviors (such as starving themselves to look like models in magazines), and that hawk prescription medications directly to consumers instead of to doctors.

To be sure, no one has figured out just how much power such ads have to actually influence target consumers. Indeed, studies have suggested that 75 to 90 percent of new consumer products fail because the buying public doesn't embrace them—suggesting that advertising isn't as effective as some critics might think.[4] Nevertheless, serious concerns over the impact of advertising persist.

Targeting Children and Teens

Because children and teenagers may influence billions of dollars each year in family spending—on everything from snacks to cars—advertisers have increasingly targeted them, often viewing young people as "consumers in training." When ads influence youngsters in a good way (for example, by getting them interested in reading books), no one complains about advertising's power. It's when ads influence kids and teens in a dangerous way (such as tempting them with unhealthy foods) that concerns arise.

For years, groups such as Action for Children's Television (ACT) worked to limit advertising aimed at children (especially ads promoting toys associated with a show). In addition, parent groups have pushed to limit the heavy promotion of unhealthy products like sugar-coated cereals during children's TV programs. Congress has responded weakly, hesitant to question the First Amendment's protection of commercial speech and pressured by determined lobbying from the advertising industry. The Children's Television Act of 1990 mandated that networks provide some educational and informational children's programming, but the act has been difficult to enforce and has done little to restrict advertising aimed at kids.

CONVERGING MEDIA
Case Study

Naming Rights as Convergent Advertising

Selling naming rights to sporting venues is as old as Boston's Fenway Park. When the park was christened in 1912, the name paid tribute to Fenway Realty, a local enterprise linked to the stadium's owner. Chicago's Wrigley Field and St. Louis's Busch Stadium are also vintage examples of corporate names being stamped onto ball parks. However, the digital age has reinvigorated this type of high-profile advertising. Many businesses have found that branding sports facilities is a cost-effective way of waving their flag across a broad range of platforms.

For some professional sports franchises, this type of sponsorship represents a major funding stream; as a convergent media strategy, naming rights to a sports setting can be an expensive, long-term investment. In 2001, for instance, PNC Bank agreed to a twenty-year, $30 million deal to affix its name to the Pittsburgh Pirates' new stadium, and the H. J. Heinz Company inked a twenty-year contract with the Pittsburgh Steelers for naming rights to another new stadium. This strategy has spread to nonprofessional sports as well: college football bowl games have increased from just five in 1940 to over thirty-five today, all with branded sponsors. As advertising costs go, sponsoring even a small bowl game may make sense. In 2012, the Idaho Potato Commission paid $375,000 for naming rights to the Famous Idaho Potato Bowl; compare this to the cost of a thirty-second spot on the Super Bowl the same year: $3.5 million.

This branding ensures the sponsor regular mention in print or digital media reports on events that take place in the facility, elevating the awareness of a company both locally and nationally. Etching a name on a landmark results in the brand appearing free-of-charge on maps, tourist Web sites, and road signs.

Name placement does not always turn out as hoped, as the once and present Candlestick Park

demonstrates. The original and current name was selected in 1959 from a write-in contest. In 1995, 3Com paid $4 million to San Francisco for naming rights to the stadium. Fans received the name change with a mixture of hostility and indifference. At the end of seven years, 3Com chose not to renew and the name was changed to Monster Park after Monster Cable paid $6 million for four years of naming rights. The citizens of San Francisco had had enough and in 2004 passed a referendum mandating that the original name be restored after the end of the Monster deal in 2008.

The current prominence of naming rights is a symptom of the postconvergence challenges facing advertisers. Advertisers once enjoyed a more captive audience; viewers tended to stay tuned to the same station for multiple hours of programming and accompanying ads. In today's media environment, viewers can watch shows on their DVRs, computers, and phones—platforms that make skipping or ignoring advertising comparably easier. Advertisers, then, must be more resourceful in finding ways to raise consumer awareness and enhance a company's brand. Naming rights make a sponsor unavoidable even to those who may record a game and fast-forward the commercials. This sort of built-in advertising will likely become even more common; as different media continue to converge, so will advertising and entertainment.

In addition to trying to control TV advertising aimed at young people, critics have complained about advertising that has encroached on school property. The introduction of Channel One into thousands of schools during the 1989–1990 school year has been one of the most controversial cases of in-school advertising. The brainchild of advertising firm Whittle Communications, Channel One offered free video and satellite equipment (tuned exclusively to Channel One) in exchange for a twelve-minute package of current-events programming that included two minutes of commercials.

Over the years, the National Dairy Council and other organizations have also used schools to promote products—for example, by providing free filmstrips, posters, magazines, folders, and study guides adorned with member companies' logos. Many teachers, especially in underfunded districts, have been grateful for these free materials. However, many parent and teacher groups have objected to Channel One (now in about eight thousand middle and high schools in the United States), which in their view requires teens to watch commercial messages in a learning environment.

Triggering Anorexia and Overeating

Some critics accuse ads of contributing to anorexia among girls and women; others, of contributing to obesity among young and adult Americans. To be sure, companies have long marketed fashions and cosmetics by showing ultrathin female models using their products. Through such campaigns, advertising strongly shapes standards of beauty in our culture. Many girls and women apparently feel compelled to achieve those standards—even if it means starving themselves or having repeated cosmetic surgeries.

Critics argue that toothpick-sized models set unattainable standards that can lead to eating disorders among women.

At the same time, advertising has also been blamed for the tripling of obesity rates in the United States since the 1980s. Corn-syrup-laden soft drinks, fast food, junk food, and processed food are the staples of media advertising. Critics maintain that advertisements for fattening products have directly contributed to widespread obesity in the United States. The food and restaurant industry has denied this connection. Industry advocates claim that people have the power to decide what they eat—and many individuals are making poor choices, such as eating too much fast food.

Promoting Smoking

One of the most sustained criticisms of advertising is its promotion of tobacco consumption. Each year, an estimated 438,000 Americans die from diseases related to nicotine addiction and poisoning. Still, for a long time, tobacco companies kept cranking out ad campaigns designed to win over new customer segments, which often included teenagers.

The government's position regarding the tobacco industry began changing in the mid-1990s. At that time, new reports revealed that tobacco companies had known that nicotine was addictive as far back as the 1950s and had withheld that information from the public. Recent settlements between the industry and states have put significant limits on advertising and marketing of tobacco products. For example, ads cannot use cartoon characters such as Joe Camel, because such characters appeal to young people. And companies can't show ads on billboards or in subway or commuter trains, where young people might be vulnerable to them. In June 2009 President Obama, himself a professed addicted smoker since his teen years, signed the Family Smoking Prevention and Tobacco Control Act. The act allows the Food and Drug Administration (FDA) to lessen the nicotine in tobacco products and block misleading cigarette packaging labels that say "low tar" and "light." Despite these restrictions, tobacco companies still spend about $13.1 billion annually on U.S. advertisements—more than twenty times the amount spent on antitobacco public service spots.

Promoting Drinking

Every year, more than 100,000 people in the United States die from alcohol-related diseases; another 16,000 to 17,000 lose their lives in car crashes involving drunk drivers. Many of the same complaints regarding tobacco advertising are also being leveled at alcohol ads. For example, critics have protested that one of the most popular beer campaigns of the late 1990s—featuring a trio of frogs croaking Budweis-errrr—used cartoonlike animal characters to appeal to young viewers. Some alcohol ads, such as Pabst Brewing Company's ads featuring Snoop Dogg for Blast by Colt 45 (a strong flavored malt beverage that the Massachusetts Attorney General called "binge-in-a can"), have targeted young minority populations specifically.

The alcohol industry has also heavily targeted college students with ads, especially for beer. The images and slogans in alcohol ads often associate the products with power, romance, sexual prowess, or athletic skill. In reality, though, alcohol is a depressant: It diminishes athletic ability and sexual performance, triggers addiction in as much as 10 percent of the U.S. population, and factors into many domestic-abuse cases. Thus many ads present a false impression of what alcohol products can do for consumers.

Hawking Drugs Directly to Consumers

New advertising tactics by the pharmaceutical industry—such as marketing directly to consumers instead of to doctors—have also drawn fire from critics worried about vulnerable groups of consumers. According to a study by the Kaiser Family Foundation, from 1994 to 2005, spending on direct-to-consumer advertising for prescription drugs soared from $266 million to $4.7 billion. About two-thirds of such ads are shown on television, and they've proved effective for the pharmaceutical companies that invest in and use them. A survey found that nearly one in three adults has talked to a doctor about a particular drug after seeing an ad for it on TV, and one in eight subsequently has received a prescription. The tremendous growth of prescription-drug ads brings with it the potential for misleading or downright false claims. That's because a brief TV advertisement can't communicate effectively all of the cautionary information consumers need to know about these medications.

Monitoring the Advertising Industry

Worried about advertising's power over vulnerable consumers, a few nonprofit watchdog and advocacy organizations, such as Commercial Alert and the American Legacy Foundation, have emerged. Such groups strive to compensate for some of the shortcomings of the Federal Trade Commission (FTC) and other government agencies in monitoring false and deceptive ads and the excesses of commercialism. At the same time, the FTC is still trying to combat the negative impact of advertising, though its effectiveness remains questionable, especially in light of cutbacks at the agency that have been going on since the 1980s.

Commercial Alert

Since 1998, Commercial Alert has worked to "limit excessive commercialism in society." Founded in part with help from longtime consumer advocate Ralph Nader, Commercial Alert became a project of Public Citizen, a nonprofit consumer protection organization based in Washington, D. C. In addition to trying to check commercialism, Commercial Alert has challenged specific marketing tactics that allow corporations to intrude into civic life. For example, in 2012 Commercial Alert objected to the state of Kentucky's proposal to sell advertising on school buses. The group argued that "children need a sanctuary from a world where everything seems to be for sale." In constantly questioning the role of advertising in our democracy, Commercial Alert has aimed to strengthen noncommercial culture and limit the amount of corporate influence on publicly elected government officials and organizations.

The American Legacy Foundation

Some nonprofit organizations have used innovative advertising of their own to offset the effects of ads for dangerous products. For example, in 2000, the American Legacy Foundation launched an antismoking/antitobacco–industry ad campaign called "Truth." The campaign's mission has been to counteract tobacco marketing and reduce tobacco use among young people. The "Truth" project uses print and television ads that contradict the images that have long been featured in cigarette ads. For example, one spot shows a giant rat expiring on a city sidewalk, clutching a cardboard sign saying that cigarettes contain the same chemical found in rat poison. All "Truth" spots prominently reference the foundation's Web site, www.thetruth.com, which offers statistics, discussion forums, and outlets for teen creativity, such as games.

In 2005, "Truth," the national youth smoking prevention campaign, won an Emmy Award in the National Public Service Announcement category. Here a "Truth" ad reinterprets a common image found in Marlboro cigarette ads.

The FTC

Through its truth-in-advertising rules, the FTC has played an investigative role in substantiating the claims of various advertisers. Thus the organization contributes to some regulation of the ad industry. The FTC usually permits a certain amount of *puffery*—ads featuring hyperbole and exaggeration—particularly when an ad describes a product as "new and improved." However, the FTC defines ads as deceptive when they are likely to mislead reasonable consumers through statements made, images shown, or omission of certain information. (For example, in some Campbell Soup ads once featuring images of a bowl of soup, marbles had been placed in the bottom of the bowl to push bulkier ingredients to the surface. This was deceptive advertising because it made the soup look less watery than it really was.) Moreover, when an advertiser makes comparative claims for a product, such as it's "the best," "the greatest," or "preferred by four out of five doctors," FTC rules require statistical evidence to back up the claims.

When the FTC discovers deception in advertising, it usually requires advertisers to change or remove the ads from circulation. The FTC can also impose monetary civil penalties, which are paid to consumers. And it occasionally requires an advertiser to run spots correcting the deceptive ads.

Advertising in a Democratic Society

Advertising has had both creative and destructive impacts on our democratic society. With its ability to "produce" not products, but actual consumers, it became the central economic support system for American mass media industries. It has thus powerfully fueled our economy. Yet in creating a consumerist society, the ad

Politicians have been employing advertising techniques for years. During the 2008 presidential campaign, Barack Obama logos, like this one, provided his campaign with a successful way to brand itself.

industry has also widened divisions between those who can afford to buy all the alluring products it promotes and those who cannot (or, alternately, those who go into debt buying the alluring products on credit). When some people can participate in an economy and others are unable to, democracy is undermined. Moreover, advertising's ubiquity intrudes on our privacy and subjects us to corporate efforts to gather personal information about us (such as income and spending habits).

Equally worrisome, fewer and fewer large media conglomerates are controlling more and more commercial speech, especially in mainstream, traditional media. This raises the question of whether we're getting all the information we need to make well-reasoned choices—a key characteristic of any democratic society.

Advertising's role in politics offers an apt example. Since the 1950s, political consultants have adopted market-research and advertising techniques to "sell" their candidates to the electorate. **Political advertising**, the use of ad techniques to promote a candidate's image and persuade the public to adopt a particular viewpoint, is the most popular form of this. (During the 2008 election year, a record $2.6 billion was reportedly spent on all political advertising up to Election Day in November.[5])

Many political ads are shown on television in the form of thirty-second spots paid for by candidates from the two main parties (or largely unregulated political action committees and Super PACs, made legal by the 2010 Supreme Court case *Citizens United v. Federal Elections Commission*). However, only very wealthy candidates, or those with the wealthiest patrons, can typically afford these expensive promotional strategies. So, many citizens don't get exposure to information about less affluent candidates who may actually be better qualified for the job despite their lack of wealth. Citizens who rely on TV for their information thus don't get a complete picture of the options available and may never learn about obscure but qualified third-party candidates who can't afford to pay for TV spots. The present political environment, in which the most affluent can flood the commercial media with their paid messages, has become a situation in which free speech really isn't "free."

Moreover, critics have raised probing questions about the unintended consequences of political ads aired on TV. For example, can serious information about complex political issues really be conveyed in a thirty-second spot? If not, viewers aren't getting a full understanding of the issues and can't make informed voting decisions. And do repeated attack ads, which assault another candidate's character, undermine citizens' confidence in the electoral process? If so, people may stop voting entirely—a *really* bad thing for a democracy. As it is, about 62 percent of eligible voters turned out in the 2008 national election, which means that 38 percent of us chose not to vote. And that 62 percent was the highest national voter turnout percentage since the 1960s.

Political ads most often appear during traditional televised commercial breaks, but other forms of advertising can be more subtle, especially in the digital world of promotion-paid Twitter accounts, product placement, and ads woven into search engine results. As advertising becomes more niche-targeted, it's important for citizens to remain media literate about how and when they're being targeted as consumers. Thus, we need to be aware that simple activities in our daily lives—such as clicking "like" on a Facebook page, searching on Google, or shopping on Amazon—are also part of the data collection system that profiles our behavior and targets us with ever more advertising.

Despite these and other concerns about advertising's potential negative consequences for our democracy, it maintains its hold on American culture—for several reasons. Without advertising, many mass media industries—television, the Internet, movies, magazines—would have to entirely reinvent their business models, as newspapers and magazines are doing right now in the face of losing so much of their ad revenue sources over the last decade. Leaders in these industries continue to embrace advertising as an economic necessity. Consumers themselves hold conflicting views of the ad industry: Some dismiss advertising as trivial and ineffective. These individuals don't really support strong monitoring of the industry. Others find ads entertaining, decorating their rooms or clothing with their favorite product posters or company logos and happily identifying with the images certain products convey. They, too, remain oblivious to advertising's less-than-positive effects on our society. Advertising can be enjoyable—think of the viewers who watch the Super Bowl to see new ads that are often hyped just as heavily as the products they hawk, or even the game itself—but if we consider it just entertainment, we misunderstand its ultimate purpose.

What does all this mean for advertising's future in the United States? As with any other mass medium, it's important that we all remember what advertising's purpose is, understand how it both benefits and costs our society, and "consume" commercial culture and its ads with a critical eye.

Think about it: In what ways are our own behaviors, values, and decisions—in all aspects of our life—affected by advertising? How might we consume and respond to ads more critically? And in what ways could we all participate in efforts to monitor the advertising landscape?

CHAPTER ESSENTIALS

Now that you have finished reading this chapter, you can use the following tools:

REVIEW

Outline the Early History of American Advertising

- The first American advertising agents were newspaper **space brokers**, individuals who purchased space in newspapers and then sold it to various merchants. The first modern ad agencies worked mainly for companies that manufactured consumer products, not for the newspapers (p. 324).

- As a result of manufacturers using newspaper stories and ads to create brand names, consumers began demanding specific products and retail stores started stocking desired brands, ushering in product differentiation (pp. 324–325).

- Patent medicine makers in the nineteenth century embraced advertising as a way to differentiate their products, sometimes making outrageous claims or covering up a product's harmful effects. Such behaviors sparked cynicism and the development of industry codes. At the same time, department stores began advertising heavily in newspapers and magazines, luring people away from small local stores (pp. 325–326).

- By the twentieth century, advertising had transformed American society, creating new markets, shaping values, and influencing the rising consumer culture. This influence catalyzed the first watchdog organizations, such as the Better Business Bureau and the Federal Trade Commission (FTC). To create a more positive image, the advertising industry developed the War Advertising Council, known today as the Ad Council, to support worthy causes. However, with the advent of TV in the 1950s, the industry faced criticism again for its use of **subliminal advertising** (pp. 326–328).

Track the Evolution of U.S. Advertising

- Beginning in the 1960s and 1970s, visual design played a more prominent role in advertising. This trend sparked the growth of new types of advertising agencies: **mega-agencies**—large firms that are formed from the merging of several individual agencies and that maintain worldwide regional offices—and **boutique agencies**—smaller companies that devote their talents to just a handful of select clients (pp. 328–330).

- Regardless of the type of ad agency, most have similar organizational structures consisting of account planning departments (where planners coordinate **market research** to assess consumer behaviors and attitudes by studying **demographics** and **psychographics**—often relying on **focus groups**—and conducting **Values and Lifestyles [VALS]** research); creative development (where writers and artists develop **storyboards** that show each scene of a potential ad or a **viral marketing** campaign to be shared online); media buying (staffed by media planners and **media buyers** who choose and purchase the types of media that are best suited to carry a client's ads and reach the targeted audience, sometimes by engaging in repetitive **saturation advertising**); and account management (staffed with **account executives** who are responsible for bringing in new business and are most vulnerable to **account reviews** or client assessments of an existing ad campaign) (pp. 330–333).

- The growth of the Internet in the 1990s has changed the advertising industry considerably. New forms of Internet advertising include pop-up ads, and ad **spam**. Internet ad companies pose a threat to traditional advertising agencies. Ad agencies can track **ad impressions** and **click-throughs** and develop consumer profiles. Mobile ad technologies include **QR codes** (pp. 333–335).

Explain Persuasive Techniques in Contemporary Advertising

- Ad agencies use a number of persuasive strategies, such as **famous-person testimonial** (a product endorsed by a well-known person); **plain-folks pitch** (a product associated with simplicity); **snob appeal** (an ad that claims using a product will elevate one's status); **bandwagon effect** (an ad that claims "everyone is using it"); **hidden-fear appeal** (a campaign that plays on a consumer's insecurities); **irritation advertising** (an ad that creates product-name recognition by being annoying or obnoxious) (pp. 336–337).

- In addition, advertisers also draw on the **association principle** in which a product is linked with a positive cultural value or image. Others tell stories or narratives that convey a culture's deepest values and social norms. Still other advertisers focus on **product placement**—strategically placing ads or buying space in movies, TV shows, comic books, and video games so they appear as part of a story's environment (pp. 337, 340–341).

Discuss Commercial Speech and the Regulation of Advertising

- Advertisements consist of **commercial speech**, any print or broadcast expression for which a fee is charged to organizations and individuals buying time or space in the mass media. The question of whether advertisers are fully protected by the First Amendment remains controversial (pp. 341–342).

- Serious concerns exist over the impact of advertising on children, teens, and people susceptible to eating disorders, smoking, alcoholism, or inappropriate prescription-drug use, which has led to the creation of nonprofit watchdog and advocacy organizations, such as Commercial Alert and the American Legacy Foundation (pp. 342, 344–347).

Consider Advertising's Impact on Our Democratic Society

- Advertising has helped fuel the economy while also creating a consumer society with divisions between those who can afford to buy and those who cannot. It has also raised concerns about the impact of a handful of large media conglomerates controlling commercial speech. **Political advertising**—the use of ad techniques to promote a candidate's image and persuade the public to adopt a particular viewpoint—makes us question whether or not we're getting unbiased information (pp. 347–349).

- Despite these issues, without advertising, many mass media industries would not survive. Given advertising's pervasiveness, it's important for the public to be critical consumers of advertising (p. 349).

STUDY QUESTIONS

1. What role did advertising play in transforming the United States into a consumer society?
2. What are the major divisions at most ad agencies? What is the function of each department?
3. How do the common persuasive techniques used in advertising work?
4. What are four serious contemporary issues regarding health and advertising? Why is each issue controversial?
5. What are the effects of advertising on a democratic society?

MEDIA LITERACY PRACTICE

TV advertising functions to promote an advertiser's goods or services, but ads always mean more than advertisers intend. Investigate this issue by examining some familiar ads.

DESCRIBE ads that are from similar product categories—clothing or accessories, automobiles, computers or cell phones, etc.—that run during your favorite shows on TV or streamed via the Internet . Take notes on the stories told and the techniques used to make the products appealing, and write up your notes in a three- to four-page paper.

ANALYZE the patterns. What kind of stories are the ads telling in order to sell their products? Are there any product placement ads that also coincide with the "regular" TV spots from your category?

INTERPRET what these ads mean and the values or attitudes being sold. What does it mean if product placement ads are prevalent during your TV program?

EVALUATE whether you think your ads do a good or a poor job of selling their product. If there are product placement ads, how effective are they?

ENGAGE with your community by contacting someone from the company that advertised the products you studied. What is that person's general view of the ad industry and product placement?

⊙ ONLINE RESOURCES

Go to **bedfordstmartins.com/mediaessentials** for review quizzes, links, and more.

Visit the site's **VIDEOCENTRAL: MASS COMMUNICATION** section for videos like the ones on pages 333 and 342. There, you can find additional exclusive videos related to Chapter 11, including:

BLURRING THE LINES: MARKETING PROGRAMS ACROSS PLATFORMS

An executive for MTV New Media explores how recent television programs blur the line between scripted and reality shows—and how MTV markets online to reach today's younger viewers.

12

Public Relations and Framing the Message

About a hundred years ago, in the second decade of the twentieth century, media stardom emerged as both the subject of public fascination and a human resource to be exploited by the movie business. Interest in the private lives of stars spawned gossip columns and fan magazines that usually relayed information provided by press agents employed by the stars' studios. Today, Hollywood's public relations (PR) machinery continues to construct images, often emphasizing the ordinary aspects of its extraordinary people; stars are depicted as regular folks who enjoy sports, love their children and pets, and go grocery shopping. However, even the most visible stars have traditionally been insulated from direct contact with their adoring fans by armies of bodyguards, publicists, and other industry functionaries.

For many popular performers, the layers of PR professionals protecting them from both their fans and themselves have been peeled away by the social networking site Twitter. Twitter, which began in 2006, is a "micro-blogging" site where users can post status updates and follow feeds that display the updates of friends, acquaintances, and, increasingly, celebrities—a converged form of mass communication that can be used to reach dozens of friends or thousands (or millions) of fans. In 2012, Lady Gaga edged out Justin Bieber as the star with the largest Twitter following, with twenty-four million fans and counting.

These enormous followings allow Gaga, Kanye West, and other stars to engage in public relations beyond magazines like *Us Weekly* or gossip shows like *Entertainment Tonight*; rather than funneling PR through agents, press releases, and articles, it can come straight from a celebrity (or a celebrity's handler) to the fans. Some celebrities even use Twitter to conduct Q&As or to interact with individual fans, making a converged media experience feel personal.

But while the method of crafting their image has changed, some stars still wind up needing public relations help, especially when given a mass-media platform like Twitter. Ashton Kutcher, for example, built an enormous Twitter following—far larger than some bigger stars—but discovered the dangers of spontaneous, unfiltered broadcasting when he reacted to the firing of Joe Paterno, the head football coach at Penn State. He lambasted the decision without fully understanding that it was connected to the coach's implication in the cover-up of a child sex-abuse scandal. Kutcher later deleted the tweet, but not before prompting a flood of responses that attacked the star for supporting the disgraced football legend. The event so rattled Kutcher that he issued a statement announcing that he was turning the management of his account over to his PR team at Katalyst Media as a "secondary editorial measure."[1]

Clearly, much of the popularity of stars like Lady Gaga, Kanye West, and Ashton Kutcher has been cultivated and nurtured by Twitter-based connections with their publics. But it seems likely that this newfound interactivity will, if anything, increase the need for PR professionals, be it the formal approvals of Kutcher's media team or less regulated consulting for celebrities who want to keep control of their feed. With media platforms converging and stars made more accessible than ever, public relations work will continue to expand beyond traditional events, comments, and press releases.

AS THE STORY OF CELEBRITY TWITTER ACCOUNTS REVEALS, the field of public relations continues to grow and change with the media industries it depends on. An effective public relations effort involves numerous activities, including shaping the public image of a product (or a person or an organization), establishing or restoring communication between consumers and companies, and promoting particular individuals or organizations. Broadly defined, **public relations** refers to the total communication strategy conducted by a person, a government, or an organization attempting to reach an audience and persuade it to adopt a point of view.[2] Or, in the brief definition offered by the Public Relations Society of America (PRSA), "Public relations helps an organization and its publics adapt mutually to each other."

While public relations may sound very similar to advertising, which also seeks to persuade audiences, it differs in important respects. Advertising uses discrete, simple, and fixed messages ("Our appliance is the most efficient and affordable") transmitted directly to the public through the purchase of ads for specific products or services. Whereas advertising focuses mainly on sales, public relations develops or reshapes an image for a person, an organization, a product, a service, or an issue to make it more marketable, popular, important, compelling, or accessible, among other desired outcomes. In doing so, public relations creates more complex messages that may evolve over time (for example, a political campaign, or a long-term strategy to dispel unfavorable reports about "fatty processed foods"). PR may be transmitted to the public indirectly, often through articles and reports in the news media. Finally, public relations messages often reflect larger trends and ideas that are percolating through society—such as the notion that it is good to recycle, or that smoking is bad for you. Even broad ideas like "liberty" or "fairness" often take on connotations based on public relations efforts. PR thus shapes and is shaped by what is going on in society at large.

Since its inception, PR has exerted a huge influence on American society and culture. For example, after the Industrial Revolution, when people began purchasing (rather than making) many goods they needed, manufacturers used PR to emphasize how various industries benefited consumers. By helping to drive economic activity, the public relations profession thus contributed to an improvement in standards of living in the United States. PR also set the tone for the corporate image-building that characterized the twentieth century—and for the debates over today's environmental, energy, labor, and other public policy issues. However, PR's most significant impact is probably on the political process: Politicians and organizations hire PR professionals to shape their image in the media, which influences how people vote. No matter what issue you care about, there is undoubtedly someone doing PR on its behalf, on all sides.

Today, there are more than twenty-nine hundred PR firms worldwide, including nineteen hundred in the United States. Many organizations also have in-house departments devoted to PR. Moreover, since the 1980s, the formal study of public relations has grown significantly at colleges and universities. By 2012, the Public Relations Student Society of America (PRSSA) boasted more than ten thousand members and more than three hundred chapters in colleges and universities.

In this chapter, we examine the workings and the impact of public relations in more detail by:

- looking at the early days of public relations, including the emergence of press agents and the birth of modern PR

- considering how the PR profession has evolved in terms of how public relations firms are structured and what functions PR practitioners perform (such as formulating messages about their clients and conveying those messages to the public)

- exploring the tensions that have arisen between public relations professionals and the press, and the causes behind those tensions

- considering the role PR plays in our democratic society, by focusing on the impact of public relations on the political process in particular

Early History of Public Relations

Public relations traveled an interesting path in its journey toward becoming a profession. The first PR practitioners were **press agents**, people who conveyed favorable messages to the public about their clients, often by staging stunts that reporters described in newspapers. As the United States became industrialized and people began purchasing more goods and services, larger companies—impressed by press agents' power to shape public opinion—began hiring them to further their interests. Some PR tactics proved

CHAPTER 12 // TIMELINE

1840–1880 Early Promotions through Media
Theatrical agent P. T. Barnum employs early PR tactics to promote his many acts.

1880 The Railroads
The PR practice of bribing reporters for positive news stories and deadheading reaches its height.

1914 "Poison Ivy" Lee
After opening one of the first PR firms in New York in the early 1900s, "Poison Ivy" Lee works for the wealthy Rockefeller family.

1923 Edward Bernays
Bernays teaches the first public relations course at New York University and writes the first PR textbook.

1948 PRSA
To better its standing among the public and the news media, the PR industry forms the Public Relations Society of America (PRSA) to function as an international watchdog.

deceitful, but when journalists and citizens complained, PR agencies began policing themselves to foster more ethical practices in the profession.

Age of the Press Agent: P. T. Barnum and Buffalo Bill

The earliest press agents excelled at **publicity**—a type of PR communication that uses various media messages to spread information and interest (or "buzz") about a person, a corporation, an issue, or a policy. The most effective publicity efforts not only excited people's imagination but also helped establish enduring national values.

In the 1800s, some publicity tactics could also border on outrageous. Consider press agent Phineas Taylor (P. T.) Barnum, who used gross exaggeration, fraudulent stories, and staged events to secure newspaper coverage for his clients, for his American Museum, and (later) for his circus, which he dubbed "The Greatest Show on Earth."

William F. Cody was another notorious publicity hound. From 1883 to 1916, Cody, who once killed buffalo for the railroads, used press agents to promote himself and his traveling show: "Buffalo Bill's Wild West and Congress of Rough Riders of the World." The show employed sharpshooter Annie Oakley and Lakota holy man Sitting Bull, whose legends were partially shaped by Cody's press agents. These agents were led by John Burke, one of the first to use an array of media channels to generate publicity. Burke promoted Cody's show through a heady mix of newspaper stories, magazine articles and ads, dime novels, theater marquees, poster art, and early films. Burke and Buffalo Bill fired up Americans' love of rugged individualism and frontier expansion—a national mythology that later showed up in books, radio programs, and Hollywood films about the American West.

"Buffalo Bill's Wild West and Congress of Rough Riders of the World" show, depicted here, was internationally popular as a touring show for more than thirty years.

1982 Tylenol Scare
After a criminal laces Tylenol capsules with cyanide, Johnson & Johnson responds with rapid and ethical PR crisis management, saving the Tylenol brand.

1989 *Exxon Valdez* Disaster
Exxon's initial denials of responsibility and slow response to the *Exxon Valdez* oil spill severely damage its reputation.

1996 Walmart and Sweatshop Labor
Human-rights groups bring attention to sweatshop labor when they expose the production conditions of Walmart's Kathie Lee Gifford clothing line.

2005 Video News Releases (VNRs)
Responding to citizen pressure, the FCC mandates that the source of a video news release (VNR) must be clearly disclosed when broadcast.

Business Adopts Press Agent Methods

The successes enjoyed by P. T. Barnum, Buffalo Bill, John Burke, and others demonstrated that publicity not only could stimulate business, it also could help any individual or organization (such as not-for-profit groups and government agencies) spread the word about its value and fulfill its mission. For businesses, press agentry became an important mechanism for generating the profits and (in some cases) bringing in the government funding needed to achieve their mission. However, in these early days of press agents, some tactics used were especially deceptive.

Around 1850, for example, the railroads began hiring press agents to help them obtain federal funds—which hinged on positive public perceptions of the railroads' value. These agents' tactics included bribing journalists to write favorable news stories about rail travel. Agents also engaged in **deadheading**—giving reporters free rail passes with the tacit understanding that they would write glowing reports about traveling by rail. Finally, larger railroads used **lobbyists**—professionals who seek to influence lawmakers' votes—to gain federal subsidies and establish policies (such as rate reductions) that made it harder for smaller regional lines to compete. Thanks to such efforts, a few large rail companies gained dominance over the industry.

Utility companies such as Chicago Edison and AT&T also used press agent strategies in the late 1800s for similar ends. Again, some of their tactics were deceptive. For instance, they, too, bought votes of key lawmakers, and they hired third-party editorial services to produce written pieces in their favor. For example, these services sent articles touting the utilities to newspapers, produced ghostwritten articles lauding the utilities' value, and influenced textbook authors to write historical accounts that put the utilities in a positive light.[3]

Professional Public Relations Emerges

By the early 1900s, some journalists began investigating and reporting on the questionable promotional practices businesses were using. Their efforts helped increase awareness of these tactics among the public. Facing a more informed citizenry, businesses found it harder to buy favorable press and use it to mislead people. Two PR pioneers—Ivy Ledbetter Lee and Edward Bernays—realized that public relations needed to be more professional. They ushered in new approaches that emphasized honesty, directness, and an understanding of psychology and sociology.

Ivy Ledbetter Lee: Two Sides to Every Story

Press agent Ivy Ledbetter Lee counseled his corporate clients that honesty and directness were better PR devices than the deceptive practices of the 1800s, which had given big business a bad name. Lee opened one of the first PR firms in the early 1900s with George Parker. A few years later, Lee quit the firm to work for the Pennsylvania Railroad. Following a rail accident, Penn Railroad had hired him to help downplay the resulting unfavorable publicity. Lee advised Penn

Ivy Lee, a founding father of public relations, did innovative crisis work with John D. Rockefeller Jr., staging photo opportunities at the Ludlow mines.

Railroad to admit its mistake, vow to do better, and let newspapers in on the story—rather than trying to cover up the accident or deny responsibility.

In 1914, Lee went to work for John D. Rockefeller Jr., who by the 1880s controlled 90 percent of the nation's oil industry. Rockefeller and his Standard Oil company had image problems, especially after journalists published a powerful muckraking series about his business tactics and after his company's strikebreakers and members of the state militia battled striking coal miners trying to win recognition for their union. Fifty-three workers and their family members were killed in Ludlow, Colorado. The oil magnate hired Lee to contain the damaging publicity fallout. Lee immediately distributed a series of "fact sheets" to the press, telling the company's side of the story and discrediting the tactics of the United Mine Workers, who had organized the strike. Lee clearly recognized that there are several sides to every story, and that decisions about which facts to present to the public, and which to leave out, could strongly shape public perceptions. Lee also brought in the press and staged photo opportunities at Rockefeller's company, which helped rehabilitate the Rockefeller family's image.

Edward Bernays: Public Relations Counselor

Edward Bernays opened his own PR office in 1919. He was the first person to apply the findings of psychology and sociology to the public relations profession. Bernays described the shaping of public opinion through PR as the "engineering of consent." That is, he believed that skilled experts, leaders, and PR professionals could shape messages and ideas in ways people could rally behind.[4]

Indeed, Bernays referred to himself as a "public relations counselor" rather than a "publicity agent." Over the years, his client list included such big-name companies as the American Tobacco Company (now R. J. Reynolds Tobacco), General Electric, and General

Edward Bernays and his business partner and wife, Doris Fleischman, creatively influenced public opinion. Bernays worked on behalf of a client, the American Tobacco Company (who owned Lucky Strike and other brands), to make smoking socially acceptable for women.

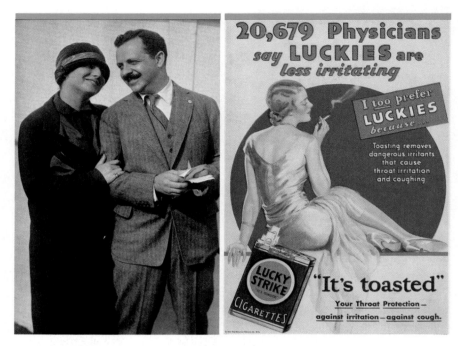

Motors. Bernays also worked for the Committee on Public Information (CPI) during World War I. In that role, he developed propaganda that supported the U.S. entry into the war and promoted the image of President Woodrow Wilson as a peacemaker.

Bernays also demonstrated that women could work in the PR profession. His business partner and later his wife, Doris Fleischman, collaborated with him on many of his campaigns as a researcher and coauthor. PR later became one of the few professions accessible to women who chose to work outside the home. Today, women outnumber men by more than three to one in the profession.

The Evolution of Public Relations

As the PR profession evolved, two major types of public relations organizations took shape: PR agencies and in-house PR services. Practitioners in this field began excelling at specific functions, such as researching target audiences and formulating messages conveyed to them.

PR Agencies and In-House PR Services

Almost two thousand U.S. companies identify themselves as public relations agencies today. Many large ones are owned by, or are affiliated with, multinational communications holding companies like WPP, Omnicom, and Interpublic. (See Figure 12.1.) Two of the largest PR agencies—Burson-Marsteller and Hill & Knowlton—generated part of the $16.05 billion in PR

FIGURE 12.1 // THE TOP SIX HOLDING FIRMS, WITH MAJOR PUBLIC RELATIONS SUBSIDIARIES, 2011 (BY WORLDWIDE REVENUE IN U.S. DOLLARS)

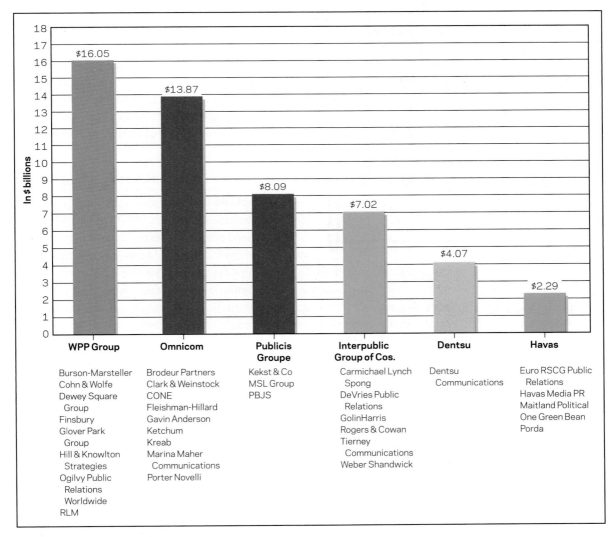

Source: "Agency Report 2012," Advertising Age, *April 30, 2012.*

Note: Revenue represents total company income including advertising and PR agencies.

I WANT YOU FOR U.S. ARMY

NEAREST RECRUITING STATION

World War II was a time when the U.S. government used propaganda, such as Uncle Sam, and other PR strategies to drum up support for the war.

revenue for their parent corporation, the WPP Group, in 2011. Other PR firms are independent. These companies tend to be smaller than the conglomerate-owned ones and have just local or regional operations. New York–based Edelman, the largest independent PR agency, is an exception, boasting global operations and clients from around the world.

Many corporations, professional organizations, and nonprofit entities retain PR agencies to provide a range of services. Large organizations of all types—particularly in the manufacturing and service industries—often have their own in-house PR staffs as well. These departments handle numerous tasks, such as writing press releases, managing journalists' requests for interviews with company personnel, and staging special events.

A Closer Look at Public Relations Functions

Regardless of whether they work at a PR agency or on staff at an organization's in-house PR department, public relations professionals pay careful attention to the needs of their clients and to the perspectives of their targeted audiences. They provide a multitude of services, including developing publicity campaigns and formulating messages about what their clients are doing in areas such as government relations, community outreach, industry relations, diversity initiatives, and product or service development. Some PR professionals also craft **propaganda.** This is communication that is presented as advertising or publicity and that is intended to gain (or undermine) public support for a special issue, program, or policy—such as a nation's war effort (see "Converging Media Case Study: YouTube and Wartime PR" on page 365). In addition, PR practitioners might produce employee newsletters, manage client trade shows and conferences, conduct historical tours, appear on news programs, organize damage control after negative publicity, or analyze complex issues and trends affecting a client's future.

Research: Formulating the Message
Like advertising, PR makes use of mail, telephone, Internet surveys, and focus groups to get a fix on an audience's perceptions of an issue, a policy, a program, or

CONVERGING MEDIA
Case Study

YouTube and Wartime PR

The Vietnam War was also known as the "Television War" because the seemingly unending river of images of American casualties and strategic futility appearing on newscasts played a key role in undermining public support. In 1992, and again in 2003, the U.S. military developed and deployed ways of managing the press, including the use of embedded reporters, to avoid repeating the public relations mistakes of Vietnam and to generate more favorable journalistic coverage of military actions in Iraq and Afghanistan. But these strategies could not contain a new public relations threat on the battlefield—the presence of digital cameras. Just as Twitter has complicated relations between VIPs and their publics, the widespread use of digital cameras, included in so many smartphones and other mobile devices, has had a terrific impact on the waging of war.

The new realities of waging war in the face of converged media was the subject of a 2009 report by Cori E. Dauber that was published by the Strategic Studies Institute of the U.S. Army War College. Titled *YouTube War: Fighting in a World of Cameras in Every Cell Phone and Photoshop on Every Computer*, the report argues that "Terrorist attacks ought to be understood as consciously crafted *media events*": "Their true target is not that which is blown up—that item or those people—for that is merely a stage prop. The goal, after all, is to have a psychological effect (to terrorize), and it isn't possible to have such an effect on the dead."[1] The report finds that mainstream television journalism often uses footage released by insurgents because of the visual power of the imagery—even though this practice essentially expanded the audience for the enemy propaganda while actually encouraging more attention-getting "newsworthy" actions.

There's an even more daunting and devastating threat to waging war in a world saturated with digital cameras: Images from the cameras of U.S. service members which, at worst, can become the public-relations equivalent of the damage caused by friendly fire. The most damaging of these incidents involved photographs taken by military police personnel of the U.S. Army documenting torture of prisoners held at the Abu Ghraib prison in Iraq. First reported in 2004 by CBS, the photos were believed to have circulated via e-mail before being seized by military authorities. More recently, in January 2012, a video surfaced on the Internet documenting four U.S. Marines urinating on Taliban corpses in Afghanistan. Prompting a flurry of media stories, the video has complicated U.S. efforts at winning the trust and respect of the population in that war-torn part of the globe.

The U.S. military, then, must contend with the way converged and viral media makes public relations trickier and more difficult to control. Part of fighting a war in an era of global and converged media involves recognizing that public perceptions matter and because of this, images matter—images that are more accessible and easier to disseminate than ever before. Soldiers and military leaders should be made aware of a major consequence of the inevitable spread of these images: Their actions and attitudes undermine their terrorism-fighting mission.

a client's image. This research also helps PR firms focus their campaign messages. For example, the Liz Claiborne Foundation has tried to combat domestic violence (specifically, teen dating abuse) by using survey results from 683 teens to develop its "Love Is Not Abuse" campaign.

Communication: Conveying the Message

Once a PR group has formulated a message, it conveys the message through a variety of channels. With advances in digital technology, these channels have become predominantly Internet-based in recent years. **Press releases**, or news releases, are announcements written in the style of news reports that provide new information about an individual, a company, or an organization, now typically issued via e-mail. In issuing press releases, PR agents hope that journalists will pick up the information and transform it into news reports about the agents' clients.

Since the introduction of portable video equipment in the 1970s, PR agencies and departments have also been issuing **video news releases (VNRs)**—thirty- to ninety-second visual press releases designed to mimic the style of a broadcast news report. Although networks and large TV news stations do not usually broadcast VNRs, news stations in small TV markets regularly use material from these releases, which can also be sent to editors of well-trafficked blogs and other Web sites, or displayed independently online. As with press releases, VNRs give PR firms some control over what constitutes "news" and a chance to influence the public's opinions about an issue, a program, or a policy, although the FCC requires that the source of a VNR be disclosed if video from the VNR is broadcast in a news program.

PR firms can also bring attention to nonprofits by creating **public service announcements (PSAs)**: usually fifteen- to sixty-second audio or video reports that promote government programs, educational projects, volunteer agencies, or social reform.

The Internet has also become an essential avenue for transmitting PR messages. Public relations practitioners use the Internet to send electronic press releases and VNRs, make press kits available for downloading, post YouTube videos, and host PR-based Web sites (for instance, the official Web sites of political candidates).

The Web also enables PR professionals to have their clients interact with audiences on a more personal, direct basis through social media tools like Facebook, Twitter, Wikipedia, and blogs. Executives, celebrities, and politicians can seem more accessible and personable through a Twitter feed. The immediacy of social media also means that public relations professionals might be forced to respond more quickly and decisively to a message or an image once it goes viral. The Internet and social media also complicate the traditional PR relationship of an organization to its publics: Now potentially anyone connected to the Internet can be one of the "publics" that interact with the organization.

Managing Media Relations

Some PR practitioners specialize in media relations. They promote a client or an organization by securing publicity or favorable coverage in the various news media. In an in-house PR department, media-relations specialists will speak on behalf of their organization or direct reporters to experts inside and outside the company who can provide information about whatever topic the reporter is writing about.

Media-relations specialists may also recommend advertising to their clients when it seems that ads would help focus a complex issue or enhance a client's image. In addition, they cultivate connections with editors, reporters, freelance writers, and broadcast news directors to ensure that their press releases or VNRs are favorably received. (See "Media Literacy Case Study: Improving the Credibility Gap" on page 368.)

If a client company has had some negative publicity (for example, one of its products has been shown to be defective or dangerous, or a viral video on the Internet quickly spreads disinformation about the company), media-relations specialists also perform damage control or crisis management. In fact, during a crisis, these specialists might be the sole source of information about the situation for the public. How PR professionals perform this part of their job can make or break

I CAN'T MISS WORK BECAUSE OF THE FLU.

For more information, visit
http://www.cdc.gov/flu

Every year, I get my flu vaccine to protect myself, my coworkers, and my family from getting sick from the flu.

Even healthy people can get the flu, and it can be serious. This season, protect yourself and those around you by getting a flu vaccine.

FOR OFFICE USE

CDC U.S. Department of Health and Human Services
Centers for Disease Control and Prevention

Public service announcements also include print and Web components (not just TV or radio ads). The Centers for Disease Control and Prevention created the ad above to spread awareness of the flu vaccine.

MEDIA LITERACY
Case Study

Improving the Credibility Gap

In the 1990s, a growing tide of Americans focused on the problems of outsourcing: using the production, manufacturing, and labor resources of foreign companies to produce American brand-name products, sometimes under deplorable working conditions. Outsourcing was pushed into the public eye in 1996 after major media attention focused on morning talk-show host Kathie Lee Gifford when investigations by the National Labor Committee revealed that part of her clothing line, made and distributed by Walmart (then branded as Wal-Mart), came from sweatshops in New York and Honduras. The sweatshops paid less than minimum wages, and some employed child laborers. Human-rights activists claimed that in overseas sweatshops in particular, children were being exploited in violation of international child-labor laws.

Many leading clothing labels and retailers continue to ignore pressure from consumer and labor groups, and still tolerate sweatshop conditions in which workers take home minimal pay. Gap Inc.—one of the world's largest clothing retailers with more than thirty-one hundred Gap, Banana Republic, Old Navy, and Forth & Towne stores (and an online shoe store)—made a huge statement in the industry by publicizing its efforts to watch over labor conditions at its overseas factories. The move was an enormous policy shift from the company's past defensiveness against allegations of worker exploitation. Gap issued its first Social Responsibility Report in 2004—the first time any company has ever publicly detailed the production and labor information of the factories with which it contracts.

The report is Gap's effort for improved transparency and better communication with its employees,

shareholders, and those concerned about garment industry operations. The company now employs a team of more than ninety people to inspect and improve working conditions in its approximately three thousand contracted garment factories in fifty countries, and continues to issue progress reports. In most cases, Gap is able to improve labor conditions, but it also cancels contracts when needed. Gap terminated seventy factory contracts in 2004 and another sixty-two in 2005. Typical violations include lack of compliance with child-labor laws, pay below minimum wage, work weeks in excess of sixty hours, psychological coercion and verbal abuse, locked or inaccessible exits, and lack of access to potable water.

Gap's social responsibility efforts also involve cosponsorship of the global (PRODUCT) RED campaign, founded in part by rock singer Bono to raise awareness of and money for HIV/AIDS in Africa.

Gap's role includes spending millions in advertising dollars to sell (PRODUCT) RED clothing to support HIV/AIDS relief, and helping to develop a sustainable garment industry in Lesotho. The campaign also includes other consumer products manufacturers, such as Converse, Giorgio Armani, American Express, Motorola, and Apple. Social responsibility has sprung up in entire new clothing lines as well.

Edun, for example, is a collection established by Bono; his wife, Ali Hewson; and designer Rogan Gregory to create fair, sustainable microindustries in developing countries, particularly in Africa. As Hewson says, "People are reading the labels on their clothes. They're asking themselves if they want to wear something that was made out of someone else's despair."[1]

APPLYING THE CRITICAL PROCESS

DESCRIPTION Select three clothing retailers—for example, chains like Target, Macy's, Dillard's, JCPenney, J. Crew, Ann Taylor, Limited Brands, or Abercrombie & Fitch.

ANALYSIS Go to each retailer's corporate Web site, and (often under investor relations) find its social responsibility statement or guidelines. (If there is not a category like this, look for its code of ethics or business practices.) Look for the patterns—similarities and differences—among the three. Do their ethics apply to only the corporate environment of the company, or do they also consider the environmental impact and labor conditions of their suppliers in the United States and developing countries?

INTERPRETATION How comprehensive and transparent should a corporation's ethical and social responsibility

guidelines be? (In other words, how broadly should a corporation define its "publics"—its employees, its customers, the local communities, the entire world—and what should the corporation promise to do?)

EVALUATION Which of the three companies has the most comprehensive and transparent corporate social/ethical policy? What made it the best of the three?

ENGAGEMENT Engage directly with the business by writing or e-mailing the one(s) you were most impressed with, and telling it why. Contact the one(s) with deficient policies, and tell it how it could improve. You can also connect with a number of other groups, such as the National Labor Committee, to learn more about corporate labor records.

Hurricane Katrina slammed into the Gulf Coast on August 29, 2005, creating the worst natural disaster in the nation's history and an unimaginable opportunity for crisis communications.

an organization. The handling of the *Exxon Valdez* oil spill and Tylenol tampering deaths in the 1980s offer two contrasting examples.

In 1989, the *Exxon Valdez* oil tanker spilled eleven million gallons of crude oil into Prince William Sound. The accident contaminated fifteen hundred miles of Alaskan coastline and killed countless birds, otters, seals, and fish. In one of the biggest PR blunders of that century, Exxon reacted to the crisis grudgingly and accepted responsibility slowly. Although the company's PR advisers had advised a quick response, Exxon failed to send any of its chief officers immediately to the site—a major gaffe. Many critics believed that Exxon was trying to duck responsibility by laying the burden of the crisis on the shoulders of the tanker's captain. Even though the company changed the name of the tanker to *Mediterranean* and implemented other strategies intended to salvage the company's image, the public continued to view Exxon in a negative light. BP had a similar public relations failure following a deadly oil rig explosion and massive oil leak in the Gulf of Mexico in 2010.

A decidedly different approach was taken in the 1982 tragedy involving Tylenol pain-relief capsules. Seven people in the Chicago area died after consuming capsules that someone had laced with poison. The parent company, Johnson & Johnson, and its PR representatives discussed whether to pull all Tylenol capsules from store shelves. Some participants in these discussions worried that this move might send the message that corporations could be intimidated by a single deranged person. Nevertheless, Johnson & Johnson's chairman and the company's PR agency, Burson-Marsteller, opted to fully disclose the tragedy to the media and to immediately recall all Tylenol capsules across the nation. The recall cost the company an estimated $100 million and cut its market share in half.

Burson-Marsteller tracked public opinion about the crisis and about its client nightly through telephone surveys. It also organized satellite press conferences to debrief the news media. In addition, it set up emergency phone lines to take calls from consumers and health-care providers who had questions about the crisis. When the company reintroduced Tylenol three months later, it did so with tamper-resistant bottles that almost every major drug manufacturer soon copied. According to Burson-Marsteller, which received PRSA awards for its handling of the crisis, the public thought Johnson & Johnson had responded admirably to the situation and did not hold Tylenol responsible for the deaths. In fewer than three years, Tylenol recaptured its dominant share of the market.

Coordinating Special and Pseudo Events

Another public relations practice involves coordinating *special events* to raise the profile of corporate, organizational, or government clients. Through such events, a corporate sponsor aligns itself with a cause or an organization that has positive stature among the public. For example, John Hancock Financial has been the primary sponsor of the Boston Marathon since 1986 and provides the race's prize money.

In contrast to a special event, a **pseudo event** is any circumstance created for the sole purpose of gaining coverage in the media. Pseudo events may take the form of press conferences, TV and radio talk-show appearances, or any other staged activity aimed at drawing public attention and media coverage. Clients and sometimes paid performers participate in these events, and their success is strongly determined by how much media attention the event attracts. For example, during the 1960s, antiwar and Civil Rights activists staged protest events only if news media were assembled.

Fostering Positive Community and Consumer Relations

Another responsibility of PR practitioners is to sustain goodwill between their clients and the public. Many public relations professionals define "the public" as consisting of two distinct audiences: communities and consumers. Thus they carefully manage relations with both groups.

PR specialists let the public know that their clients or companies are valuable members of the communities in which they operate. They design opportunities for their clients to demonstrate that they are good citizens. For example, they arrange for client firms to participate in community activities such as hosting plant tours and open houses, making donations to national and local charities, participating in town events like parades and festivals, and allowing employees to take part in local fund-raising drives for good causes.

PR strategists also strive to show that their clients care about their customers. For example, a PR campaign might send the message that the business has established product-safety guarantees, or that the company will answer all calls and mail from customers promptly. These efforts result in satisfied customers,

The intense media coverage at awards shows drums up ad revenue for broadcasts and seemingly endless magazine coverage. Can we consider the Oscars or Golden Globes a pseudo event?

Public relations also works for nonprofits such as the Rainforest Action Network, which has worked to protect millions of acres of forests in North and South America, and has convinced companies like Home Depot and Boise Cascade to change their practices.

which translates into repeat business and new business, as customers spread the word about their positive experiences with the organization.

Cultivating Government Relations

PR groups working for or in corporations also cultivate connections with the government agencies that have some say in how companies operate in a particular community, state, or nation. Through such connections, these groups can monitor the regulatory environment and determine new laws' potential implications for the organization's they represent. For example, a new regulation might require companies to provide more comprehensive reporting on their environmental-safety practices, which would represent an added responsibility.

Government PR specialists monitor new and existing legislation, look for opportunities to generate favorable publicity, and write press releases and direct-mail letters to inform the public about the pros and cons of new regulations. In many industries, government relations has developed into **lobbying**: the process of trying to influence lawmakers to support legislation that would serve an organization's or industry's best interests. In seeking favorable legislation, some lobbyists contact government officials on a daily basis. In Washington, D.C., alone, there are about twelve thousand registered lobbyists, and lobbying expenditures targeting the federal government rose to $3.5 billion in 2010, up from $1.56 billion ten years earlier.[5]

The millions of dollars that lobbyists inject into the political process—treating lawmakers to special events and campaign contributions in return for legislation that accommodates their clients' interests—is viewed by many as unethical. Another unethical practice is **astroturf lobbying**, which consists of phony grassroots public-affairs campaigns engineered by unscrupulous public relations firms. Through this type of lobbying, PR firms deploy blogs, social media campaigns, massive phone banks, and computerized mailing lists to drum up support and create the impression that millions of citizens back their client's side of an issue—even if the number is much lower.

Just as corporations use PR to manage government relations, some governments have used PR to manage their image in the public's mind. For example, following the September 11, 2001, terrorist attacks on the United States, the Saudi Arabian government hired the PR firm Qorvis Communications to help repair its image with American citizens after it was revealed that many of the 9/11 terrorists were from Saudi Arabia.[6]

Tensions between Public Relations and the Press

The relationship between PR and the press has long been antagonistic. This tension has several sources, including the complex interdependence of the two professions as well as the press's skepticism about PR practices. Some of the press's complaints about PR have led public relations practitioners to take steps to enhance their profession's image.

Elements of Interdependence

Journalists have historically viewed themselves as independent professionals providing a public service: gathering and delivering the facts about current events to the public. Some have accused PR professionals of distorting the facts to serve their clients' interests. Yet journalists rely heavily on public relations practitioners to provide the information used in creating news reports. Many editors, for instance, admit that more than half of their story ideas each day originate from PR work such as press releases. In the face of newspaper staff cutbacks and television's growing need to cover local news events, professionals in the news media need PR story ideas more than ever. This doesn't sit comfortably with some journalists.

As another example of the two professions' interdependence, PR firms often raid news media's workforces for new talent. Because most press releases are written in the style of news reports, the PR profession has always sought skilled writers who are well connected to sources and knowledgeable about the news business. But although many reporters move into the PR profession, few public relations practitioners—especially those who started their careers as journalists—move back into journalism.

PR practitioners, for their part, maintain that they make reporters' jobs easier—supplying the kinds of information reporters used to gather themselves. Some members of the news media criticize their own ranks for being lazy. Others, grateful for the help, have hesitated to criticize a particular PR firm's clients— which brings up questions of journalistic ethics.

VideoCentral ◉
bedfordstmartins.com /mediaessentials

Give and Take: Public Relations and Journalism
This video debates the relationship between public relations and journalism. Discussion: Are the similarities between public relations and journalism practices a good thing for the public? Why or why not?

Journalists' Skepticism about PR Practices

In addition to the uncomfortable interdependence characterizing the journalism and PR professions, several specific complaints about PR from journalists have heightened the tension between the two groups. Specifically, some journalists maintain that PR professionals undermine the facts and block reporters' access to information. Journalism's most prevalent criticism of public relations is that it counters the truths reporters seek to bring to the public by selectively choosing which facts to communicate or by delivering deceptive information. To be sure, outright deception is unethical, and the PR profession has worked to eradicate it in its own ranks. But deciding which facts to present is something that journalists do, too. After all, a reporter cannot say everything about a particular event, so he or she must choose which information to include and which to leave out. Journalists have also objected that PR professionals block the press's access to business leaders, political figures, and other newsworthy people. This blocking, reporters explain, can manipulate reporters by giving exclusives to those most likely to write a favorable story, or by cutting off a reporter's access to a newsworthy figure if the reporter has written unfavorably about that client.

Others dislike the PR field's tendency to present publicity as news. Journalists critical of the PR profession claim that PR thus takes media space and time away from organizations and individuals who do not have the money or sophistication required to attract the public eye. These critics also complain that by presenting client information in a journalistic context, PR gains credibility for its clients that the purchase of advertising does not offer.

The manipulation of scientific facts by "experts" trying to promote a specific agenda is addressed in a series of books by John Stauber and Sheldon Rampton.

Shaping PR's Image

Questionable PR moves in the past and journalism's hostility toward PR prompted some public relations practitioners to direct their skills toward improving their profession's image. In 1948, the PR industry formed its own professional organization, the PRSA (Public Relations Society of America). The PRSA functions as an internal watchdog group that accredits PR agents and firms, maintains a code of ethics, and probes its own practices, especially those pertaining to its influence on the news media.

TABLE 12.1 // PUBLIC RELATIONS SOCIETY OF AMERICA ETHICS CODE

In 2000, the PRSA approved a completely revised Code of Ethics, which included core principles, guidelines, and examples of improper conduct. Here is one section of the code.

PRSA Member Statement of Professional Values

This statement presents the core values of PRSA members and, more broadly, of the public relations profession. These values provide the foundation for the Member Code of Ethics and set the industry standard for the professional practice of public relations. These values are the fundamental beliefs that guide our behaviors and decision making process. We believe our professional values are vital to the integrity of the profession as a whole.

Advocacy

We serve the public interest by acting as responsible advocates for those we represent. We provide a voice in the marketplace of ideas, facts, and viewpoints to aid informed public debate.

Honesty

We adhere to the highest standards of accuracy and truth in advancing the interests of those we represent and in communicating with the public.

Expertise

We acquire and responsibly use specialized knowledge and experience. We advance the profession through continued professional development, research, and education. We build mutual understanding, credibility, and relationships among a wide array of institutions and audiences.

Independence

We provide objective counsel to those we represent. We are accountable for our actions.

Loyalty

We are faithful to those we represent, while honoring our obligation to serve the public interest.

Fairness

We deal fairly with clients, employers, competitors, peers, vendors, the media and the general public. We respect all opinions and support the right of free expression.

Source: The full text of the PRSA Code of Ethics is available at http://www.prsa.org.

Note: Adherence to the PRSA Code of Ethics is voluntary; there is no enforcement mechanism.

In addition to the PRSA, independent organizations devoted to uncovering shady or unethical public relations activities publish their findings in periodicals like *PR Week* and *PR Watch*. In particular, the Center for Media and Democracy's *PR Watch* seeks to serve the public by discussing and investigating PR practices. Indeed, ethical issues have become a major focus of the PR profession (see Table 12.1).

PR practitioners have also begun using different language—such as *institutional relations*, *corporate communications*, and *news and information services*—to describe what they do. Their hope is that the new language will signal a more ethically responsible industry. Public relations' best strategy, however, may be to point out the shortcomings of the journalism profession itself. Journalism organizations only occasionally examine their own practices, and journalists have their own vulnerability to manipulation by public relations. Thus, by not publicly revealing PR's strategies to influence their news stories, many journalists have allowed PR professionals to interpret "facts" to their clients' advantage.

Public Relations in a Democratic Society

PR's most significant impact on our democracy may be its involvement in the political process, especially when organizations hire public relations specialists to favorably shape or reshape a candidate's image. Consider PR's role in national election campaigns. During these immense efforts, all candidates have an extensive PR and strategy staff. Sometimes things go well; other times, they don't. For example, in the 2008 presidential contest, Democratic nominee Barack Obama's team was headed by David Axelrod, founder of Chicago-based political and media consulting firm AKPD Message and Media, who smoothly guided Obama to the White House. By contrast, Republican nominee John McCain and his running mate Sarah Palin went through numerous campaign and PR strategists in their more tumultuous bid for the Oval Office.

Political public relations efforts don't end after an election, however. PR is in play when candidates take office, govern, or participate in or react to political movements like the Tea Party or Occupy Wall Street. Just as many journalism outlets cover the news in permanent twenty-four-hour cycles, so must PR agencies stay involved with political, social, and media processes.

Though public relations often provides political information and story ideas, the PR profession bears only part of the responsibility for "spun" news; after all, it is the job of a PR agency to get favorable news coverage for the individual or group it represents. PR professionals police their own ranks for unethical or irresponsible practices,

David Axelrod was the chief strategist for Obama's 2008 campaign and was later appointed the president's senior adviser.

but the news media should also monitor the public relations industry, as they do other government and business activities. Journalism itself also needs to be more conscious of how its own practices play into the hands of spin strategies.

As a positive example of change on this front, many major newspapers and TV networks now offer regular assessments of the facts and falsehoods contained in political advertising. This media vigilance should be on behalf of citizens, who are entitled to robust, well-rounded debates on important social and political issues.

Like advertising and other forms of commercial speech, PR campaigns that result in free media exposure raise a number of questions regarding democracy and the expression of ideas. Large companies and PR agencies, like well-financed politicians, have money to invest in figuring out how to obtain favorable publicity. The question is not how to prevent that but how to ensure that other voices, less well financed and less commercial, also receive an adequate hearing. To that end, journalists need to become less willing conduits in the distribution of publicity. PR agencies, for their part, need to show clients that participating as responsible citizens in the democratic process can serve them well and enhance their image. But in the end, all citizens bear the responsibility of understanding that the public relations industry surrounds us, regardless of what issues or sides we favor. It is a part of the media experience and, as such, part of our daily lives. As such, media literacy must also include awareness and knowledge of PR, and all of that ways it can affect us.

CHAPTER ESSENTIALS

Now that you have finished reading this chapter, you can use the following tools:

REVIEW

Understand the Early History of Public Relations

- **Public relations** refers to the total communication strategy conducted by a person, a government, or an organization attempting to reach and persuade its audience to adopt a point of view. The first PR practitioners in the 1800s were **press agents**, such as P. T. Barnum and John Burke, who conveyed favorable messages to the public about their clients, often by staging stunts that reporters described in newspapers. These agents focused on **publicity**, using various media messages to spread information and interest about a person, a corporation, an issue, or a policy (pp. 356–359).

- As the United States became more industrialized and moved toward a consumer society, larger companies, such as railroads and utility organizations like AT&T, began hiring press agents to generate profits and spread the word on whatever they were promoting.

However, in these early days of press agents, some tactics used were deceptive. Agents bribed journalists to write favorable stories and engaged in **deadheading**, or giving reporters free rail passes. Larger railroads and utility companies used **lobbyists**, professionals who seek to influence lawmakers' votes—to gain federal subsidies and establish policies (p. 360).

- By the early 1900s journalists began investigating some of the questionable PR practices being used, precipitating the professionalization of public relations. This professionalization effort was spearheaded by two pioneers of PR, Ivy Ledbetter Lee and Edward Bernays. Lee counseled his clients that honesty and directness were better PR devices and later worked with John D. Rockefeller. Bernays was the first to apply the findings of psychology and sociology to the PR profession (pp. 360–362).

Track the Evolution of Public Relations

- As the PR profession grew, two major types of public relations organizations took shape: PR agencies and in-house PR services (p. 362).

- Many large PR agencies are owned by or affiliated with multinational holding companies like WPP, Omnicom, and Interpublic. Other firms are independent and have local or regional operations, such as Edelman (pp. 362–364).

- Both PR agencies and in-house services have many functions. They sometimes craft **propaganda**, or communication that is presented as advertising or publicity intended to gain or undermine public support (p. 364).

- In addition, PR professionals research or formulate the message for a given product, policy, program, or issue. They are responsible for conveying the message, often via **press releases** (news releases), **video news releases (VNRs)**, or **public service announcements (PSAs)**, which are press releases for nonprofits (pp. 364, 366).

- Some PR practitioners manage media relations. This includes responding to negative images or crisis situations (pp. 369, 370).

- PR agents may also coordinate special and **pseudo events** (staged activities aimed at drawing public attention and media coverage) in an effort to raise the profile of a corporate, organizational, or business client (p. 371).

- PR practitioners foster positive community and consumer relations and cultivate government relations, which is sometimes accomplished via **lobbying** (the process of trying to influence lawmakers to support legislation that would serve an organization or industry's best interest). **Astroturf lobbying** is a kind of lobbying that consists of phony grassroots public-affairs campaigns engineered by unscrupulous PR firms (pp. 371–372).

Discuss the Tensions between Public Relations and the Press

- The tense relationship between PR and the press consists of a complex interdependence of the two professions as well as journalists' skepticism about some PR practices (p. 373).

- PR practitioners maintain they make journalists' jobs easier by supplying information, while journalists argue that PR agents selectively choose which facts to bring forward (p. 374).

- Some of the complaints from the press about PR have led some public relations practitioners to take steps to improve the profession's image. The industry formed its own professional organization (the Public Relations Society of America) in 1948, which functions as a watchdog group. PR practitioners have also begun using different language to describe what they do (pp. 374–376).

- PR's impact on the political process is significant as many organizations hire public relations specialists to shape or reshape a candidate's image (p. 376).

- The fact that most affluent people and corporations can afford the most media exposure through PR raises questions about whether this restricts the expression of ideas from other, less affluent sources (p. 377).

STUDY QUESTIONS

1. Who were the individuals who conducted the earliest type of public relations in the nineteenth century? How did they contribute to the development of modern public relations in the twentieth century?
2. What are the two organizational structures for a PR firm? What are some of the ways these structures conduct business for their clients?
3. Explain the antagonism between journalism and public relations. Can and should the often hostile relationship between the two be mended? Why or why not?
4. In what ways does the profession of public relations serve the process of election campaigns? In what ways can it impede election campaigns?

MEDIA LITERACY PRACTICE

As noted earlier, public relations and journalism are extremely interdependent. To investigate this relationship, examine the public relations practices of an organization that interests you.

DESCRIBE the list of the most recent ten or twelve press releases from a local/regional business or organization large enough to have its own PR department (your own college or university might be a worthy subject).

ANALYZE the resulting patterns: How many of the releases resulted in stories in the local city or university newspaper? (Alternatively, you could use another local news organization.) Were the releases published in the newspaper verbatim, or were the stories just loosely based on the press releases?

INTERPRET what these patterns mean. For example, do press releases from this organization make an impact in the local news? Do you think the size of the newspaper and its staff makes a difference in how press releases are handled?

EVALUATE the relationship between public relations and journalism in your community. Based on this case study, is the level of the newspaper's reliance on public relations a good thing or bad thing for the people in your community? Are the press releases promoting a healthy dialogue in the community or trying to publicize something not worthy of the news?

ENGAGE with the community by writing to the newspaper's editor and letting her or him know about your case study and conclusions.

◉ ONLINE RESOURCES

Go to **bedfordstmartins.com/mediaessentials** for review quizzes, links, and more.

Visit the site's **VIDEOCENTRAL: MASS COMMUNICATION** section for videos like the one on page 373. There, you can find additional exclusive videos related to Chapter 12, including:

FILLING THE HOLES: VIDEO NEWS RELEASES
Television and PR experts explain the increasing use of video news releases as networks continue to cut costs.

GOING VIRAL: POLITICAL CAMPAIGNS AND VIDEO
Online video has changed political campaigning forever. In this video, Peggy Miles of Intervox Communications discusses how politicians use the Internet to reach out to voters.

Dustin Hoffman and Robert Redford in the 1976 adaptation of *All the President's Men*.

13

The Culture of Journalism: Values, Ethics, and Democracy

The scandal erupted on June 17, 1972, when five men were arrested for breaking and entering into the Democratic National Committee headquarters at the Watergate office complex in Washington, D.C. The burglary turned out to be just one of many illegal activities that President Richard Nixon had authorized and that were carried out by Nixon's staff. These activities included campaign fraud, political espionage, illegal wiretapping, and a secret slush fund laundered in Mexico to pay those who conducted the operations and to buy their silence.

The break-in spurred intense media coverage, most notably by the *Washington Post*. Reporters Bob Woodward and Carl Bernstein uncovered information suggesting that knowledge of the break-in, and attempts at a cover-up, extended into the Justice Department, the FBI, the CIA—and even the White House. During their investigation, Woodward and Bernstein came under immense pressure from the *Post* to keep producing accurate stories while being challenged by skeptics to reveal the names of their anonymous sources—which they resolutely refused to do. They protected the identity of their main source—Mark Felt, known only as "Deep Throat"—for more than thirty years. Felt, the former associate director of the FBI, admitted shortly before his death in 2005 that he had been the reporters' key source.

The two journalists, working under editor Ben Bradlee, won renown for being the first to report on the political "dirty tricks" used by the committee managing Nixon's reelection campaign. After publishing a book about the scandal—*All the President's Men*, which was made into a movie in 1976—the reporters became celebrities and inspired widespread interest in investigative journalism.

Investigations into the scandal by various oversight bodies eventually forced the president to ask for the resignations of key aides, including H. R. Haldeman and John Ehrlichman, who were both indicted and sent to prison. Nixon also fired White House Counsel John Dean, who had testified before the Senate and who eventually became the key witness against the president.

As Nixon's position eroded, the House of Representatives began formal investigations into possible impeachment. On August 8, 1974, the president (apparently bowing to the inevitable) announced his resignation.

Woodward and Bernstein's accomplishments reveal journalism's power—to contribute to the downfall of a U.S. president, fuel the creation of new works in other media (including books and movies), and reshape young people's career aspirations. The two reporters' experiences also illuminate the tough constraints journalists operate under—including pressure to produce timely stories, to follow strict criteria for determining what's newsworthy, to reveal their sources, and to challenge authority figures. In fact, in terms of public trust of news media performance, the coverage of Watergate by the print and TV news in the 1970s is considered a high point for U.S. journalism. Since the mid-1970s, public confidence in the news media has eroded and declined steadily.

JOURNALISM IS THE ONLY MEDIA ENTERPRISE that democracy absolutely requires—and is the only media practice and business specifically protected by the U.S. Constitution. However, with the decline in traditional news audiences, mounting criticism of "celebrity" journalists, the growth of partisanship in politics, and the rise of highly opinionated twenty-four-hour cable news and Internet news blogs, mainstream journalists have begun losing their credibility with the public.

In this chapter, we examine the changing landscape of journalism and explore its role in our lives today by:

- looking at journalism in the Information Age, including changing definitions of "news" and the evolution of journalism's values

- exploring ethics and the news media, including dilemmas journalists face (such as whether to invade someone's privacy to get information) and approaches to resolving ethical questions

- taking stock of reporting rituals (such as focusing on the present and relying on experts)

- considering journalism in the age of TV and the Internet, by comparing print and TV news and assessing the opportunities and challenges that the Internet poses for journalism

- gaining familiarity with alternative models of journalism, such as public journalism, fake news, and satiric journalism

- asking what role journalism might play in our democracy as a force for social responsibility and for greater public discourse

Modern Journalism in the Information Age

In modern America, journalism's highest role has been to provide information that enables citizens to make intelligent decisions. Today, this guiding principle has been partially derailed. Why? First, the media may be producing *too* much information through too many communication channels, making it harder to confirm facts and engage in thoughtful discussion about them. Second, the information the media now provide apparently has not improved the quality of public and political life—a core mission of journalism. For example, many people feel disconnected from the stories about the major institutions and political processes that serve as the foundation of democratic society.

For these reasons, it's important to revisit what we mean by "news," why well-practiced and accurate journalism is so important, and how the values that have long characterized journalism have helped create the profession's strengths as well as its weaknesses.

Journalists, such as those shown here at a White House press conference, report on the issues, events, and prominent figures of the day and consider themselves information-gatherers.

What Is News?

Many journalists today view themselves as information-gatherers. **News** (as we saw in Chapter 3) is the process of gathering information and making reports that use a narrative framework; that is, news reports tell stories. News reports (whether in print, on TV, or on the Internet) help the public make sense of prominent people, important events, and unusual happenings in everyday life. Over time, journalists have developed a set of criteria for determining whether information is **newsworthy**—that is, whether it merits transformation into news stories. These criteria include timeliness, proximity, conflict, prominence, human interest, consequence, usefulness, novelty, and deviance.[1] For example:

- Most issues and events that journalists cover are *timely* or *new*. Reporters, for instance, cover speeches, meetings, crimes, and court cases that have just happened.
- The bulk of these events usually occur close by, or in *proximity* to, the readers and viewers who will consume the news stories. Although local papers used to offer a broader range of national and international news stories, readers and viewers have usually expected to find the bulk of news devoted to their own communities.
- In developing news narratives, reporters often seek contentious quotes from those with opposing views, creating a sense of *conflict*. For example, stories on the fight against terrorism almost always feature opposing viewpoints on how our country should make trade-offs between freedom and national security.
- Surveys indicate that most people identify more closely with an individual than with an abstract issue. Therefore, the news media tend to report stories that feature *prominent*, powerful, or influential people.
- However, reporters also look for the *human-interest* story: extraordinary incidents that happen to "ordinary" people. In fact, reporters often relate a story about a complicated issue (such as unemployment, health care, or homelessness) by illustrating its impact on one "average" person or "typical" family.
- Many editors and reporters believe that some news must also be of *consequence* to a majority of their readers or viewers. For example, they might include stories about new business regulations that affect credit cards or home mortgages.
- Likewise, many people look for *useful* stories: for instance, those offering hints on how to buy a used car or choose a college.
- When events happen that are outside the routine of daily life—that is, they are *novel*—they will likely generate news coverage. Examples might include a

seven-year-old girl who tries to pilot a plane across the country or a fading celebrity who gets arrested for drunk driving.

- Reporters also cover events that appear to *deviate* from social norms, including murders, rapes, fatal car or plane crashes, fires, political scandals, and wars.

In producing news stories that meet many of these criteria, journalists influence our interpretations of what is going on around us and thus the decisions we make. For example, if we read a newsmagazine article filled with contentious quotations from various experts, we may conclude that life is all about conflict and argument. If we read a story in the newspaper emphasizing consequences of failing to save for retirement, we may conclude that such saving is important—and that we'd better do more of it. And if we watch several TV news segments on plane crashes, we might decide that air travel simply is not safe—and choose a nearby destination (reachable by car) for our next vacation.

Values in American Journalism

Although newsworthiness criteria reveal how journalists define news, they do not tell us much about the wide range of values that have emerged in American journalism. Perhaps the most prominent and obvious of these values is neutrality, or the apparent lack of bias, a quality that remains prized even in a more polarized environment that has given rise to more opinionated forms of news.

Neutrality

Journalists generally believe that they are—and should be—neutral observers who present "facts" and information without judging them. Neutrality, they maintain, lends them greater credibility. Conventions such as the inverted-pyramid news lead (starting reports with the most important information), the careful attribution of sources (favoring quoted interview subjects rather than the reporter's analysis), the minimal use of adverbs and adjectives (getting rid of ornate, flowery language in order to look "factual"), and a detached third-person point of view (using the omniscient or all-knowing authorial point of view favored by many novelists) all help reporters present their findings in a supposedly neutral way.

Yet the desire to be neutral also stems from a less noble goal: to reach as many readers and viewers as possible. In addition, neutrality is an unreachable ideal. Merely by deciding which information and experience to include in a news story, journalists cannot help but present a point of view on the story's topic. Indeed, surveys have shown that while journalists may work hard to claim neutrality, most people regard them as politically biased. (See "Media Literacy Case Study: Bias in the News" on page 388.)

MEDIA LITERACY
Case Study

Bias in the News

All news is biased. News, after all, is primarily selective storytelling, not objective science. Editors choose certain events to cover and ignore others; reporters choose particular words or images to use or reject. The news is also biased in favor of storytelling, drama, and conflict; in favor of telling "two sides of a story"; in favor of powerful and connected sources; and in favor of practices that serve journalists' space and time limits.

In terms of overt political bias, public perception says that mainstream news media operate mostly with a liberal bias. A June 2006 Harris Poll found 38 percent of adults surveyed detected a liberal bias in news coverage while 25 percent sensed a conservative bias (31 percent were "not sure" and 5 percent said there was "no bias"; see Table 13.1).[1]

Given the primary dictionary definitions of liberal (adj., "favorable to progress or reform, as in political or religious affairs") and conservative (adj., "disposed to preserve existing conditions, institutions, etc., or to restore traditional ones, and to limit change"), it is not surprising that a high percentage of liberals and moderates gravitate to mainstream journalism.[2] A profession that honors documenting change, checking power, and reporting wrongdoing would attract fewer conservatives, who are predisposed to "preserve existing conditions" and to "limit change." As sociologist Herbert Gans demonstrated in *Deciding What's News*, his 1970s landmark study of newsroom values, most reporters are socialized into a set of work rituals—especially getting the story first and telling it from "both sides" to achieve balance.[3] In fact, this commitment to "balance" mandates that if journalists interview someone on the Left, they must also interview someone on the Right. Ultimately, such a balancing act makes conventional news a middle-of-the-road proposition. In fact, most mainstream journalists (and 50 percent of Americans) identify themselves chiefly as political moderates.

Still, the "liberal bias" narrative persists. In 2001 Bernard Goldberg, a former producer at CBS News, published *Bias*. Using anecdotes from his days at CBS, he maintained that national news slanted to the left.[4] In 2003, Eric Alterman, a writer for the *Nation*, countered with *What Liberal Media?* Alterman admitted that mainstream news media do reflect more liberal views on social issues, but that they have become more conservative on politics and economics—displayed in their support for deregulated media and concentrated ownership.[5] Alterman says the liberal bias tale persists because conservatives keep repeating that story in the major media.

Since journalists are primarily storytellers, and not scientists, searching for liberal or conservative bias should not be the main focus of our criticism. As *The Daily Show*'s Jon Stewart told Bill Moyers in 2003 on PBS's *NOW*, much of the highest-profile "noise" in the public sphere is made by 10 percent of the population—5 percent on the Left and 5 percent on the Right, while most of us remain somewhere in between. Under time and space constraints, most journalists serve the routine process of their profession, which calls on them to moderate their own political agendas. News reports, then, are always "biased," given human imperfection in storytelling and in communicating events/issues through the lens of language, images, and institutional values. Rather, fully critiquing news stories—whether they are fair, whether they represent an issue's complexity, whether they provide verification and documentation, whether they represent multiple views, and whether they serve democracy—should be our focus.

TABLE 13.1 // IS THERE A BIAS IN REPORTING THE NEWS?

| | **Political Party Affiliation** | | | | **Political Philosophy** | | |
	Total %	Republican %	Democrat %	Independent %	Conservative %	Moderate %	Liberal %
There is a liberal bias in the media.	38	66	18	36	62	35	10
There is no bias in the media.	5	1	8	7	3	5	9
There is a conservative bias in the media.	25	13	37	26	13	24	47
Not at all sure.	31	20	36	31	22	36	34

Note: Percentages add up to more than 100 percent due to multiple responses accepted.

Source: Harris Poll® #52, "News Reporting Perceived as Biased . . . ," Harris Interactive, June 30, 2006, www.harrisinteractive.com/harris_poll.

APPLYING THE CRITICAL PROCESS

DESCRIPTION Find print news stories on the same subject from two different sources. Make copies of each story, and note the pictures chosen to tell the story.

ANALYSIS Find patterns in the coverage. How are the stories treated differently in the two sources? Are there similarities in the words chosen or images used? What kinds of details are presented? Who are the sources the reporters use to verify their information?

INTERPRETATION What do these patterns suggest? Can you make any interpretations or arguments based on the kinds of details included, sources used, or words/images chosen? How are the stories told in relation to their importance to the entire community or nation? How complex are the stories?

EVALUATION Which story has the strongest bias? Why? Make a judgment on how this story serves as a representation of a particular view or opinion.

ENGAGEMENT In an e-mail or letter report your findings to relevant editors. How did they respond?

Small-town pastoralism is about stories that feature the "goodness" of small-town America, like communities pulling together to sandbag riverbanks during the floods in the Midwest in 2008.

Other Values in Journalism

Neutral journalism is a selective process and is governed by a deeper set of subjective beliefs that are not neutral. Some sociologists, including Herbert Gans, who studied the newsroom cultures of CBS, NBC, *Newsweek*, and *Time* in the 1970s, generalize that several basic "enduring values" have been shared by most American reporters and editors. These values include ethnocentrism (viewing other cultures through an American "lens"), responsible or benign capitalism (the assumption that the main goal of business is to enhance prosperity for everyone), small-town pastoralism (favoring small, rural communities over big cities), and a major emphasis on individualism and personal stories over the operations of large institutions or organizations.[2] Many of these beliefs are still prevalent in today's more fragmented news culture, though they are undergoing shifts along with the rest of the industry.

- **Ethnocentrism.** By ethnocentrism, Gans means that reporters judge other countries and cultures on the basis of how "they live up to or imitate American practices and values." This remains true of many news outlets, although the ubiquity of the Internet has greatly increased the diversity of news sources available in some countries, making other perspectives more accessible to many Americans.
- **Responsible capitalism.** Another value Gans described as held by American journalists, responsible capitalism, assumes that the purpose of business is not to maximize profits but "to create increased prosperity for all." Gans points out that although most reporters and editors condemn monopolies, they provide "little implicit or explicit criticism of the oligopolistic nature of much of today's economy."[3] This continues today, complicated by the fact that many news outlets are owned by large, multinational corporations. In the wake of the 2008–09 financial crisis, more news outlets began to report on businessworld wrongdoing, but conflicts of ownership remain.
- **Small-town pastoralism.** Another value that Gans identified was small-town pastoralism, whereby journalists tend to favor the small over the large and the rural over the urban. Many journalists continue to frame stories about rustic communities with

crime or drug problems—like illegal meth labs springing up in isolated rural areas—as country life being contaminated by corrupt big city values.

- **Individualism.** According to Gans, many reporters have been attracted to the journalism profession because it has tended toward or praised an individualistic, rugged tenacity for confronting and exposing corruption. This value is further revealed in the many news stories that focus on individuals who have overcome personal adversity. Yet such stories neglect to acknowledge or analyze the role of large social organizations and institutions in individual and personal achievements.

Ethics and the News Media

Just as journalists grapple with guidelines about what is considered newsworthy and whether they embody the right values in their profession, they also frequently face ethical dilemmas. For example, they must decide when to protect government secrets and when to reveal those secrets to the public. They must consider whether it is ethically acceptable to use deception or to invade someone's privacy to get information the public deserves to know, and they must guard against accepting gifts or favors in return for producing a news story or presenting a story's subject in a favorable light. These and other predicaments have prompted members of the journalism profession to establish policies and guidelines for resolving such dilemmas.

Ethical Predicaments

The importance of national security can present ethical challenges for large news organizations, as journalists struggle to determine whether publishing a story about, say, military activities in a war zone would put American soldiers in danger. But the most common ethical dilemmas encountered in most newsrooms across the United States involve deception, privacy invasions, and conflicts of interest.

Deception

Ever since Nellie Bly faked insanity to get inside a corrupt asylum in the 1880s (see Chapter 3), some investigative journalists have used deception to gain access to the information they need to create news stories. For example, they might pose as a desperately ill client to expose a suspected fraudulent clinic.

The ethical question about deception is: Does the end justify such means? A person could take a number of different positions on this question. At one extreme, *absolutist ethics* suggests that a moral society has laws and codes, including "be honest" or "don't lie," that everyone must live by at all times and in all cases. At the other end is *situational ethics,* which say that we must make decisions on a case-by-case basis about how we can best serve the greater public good—even if doing so requires deception or dishonesty.

Just as outright lying constitutes deception, so can withholding certain information. For example, should a journalist conceal his or her professional identity to get a quote or a story from an interview subject? Most newsrooms frown on this. In particular situations, though, they might condone the practice if reporters and their editors believe that the public needs the information the act of deception could produce. The ethics code adopted by the Society of Professional Journalists (SPJ) is fairly silent on issues of deception. The code instead calls on journalists to "seek truth and report it," "minimize harm" (i.e., show compassion and sensitivity toward individuals in news stories), "act independently" (i.e., "be free of obligation to any interest other than the public's right to know"), and "be accountable . . . to their readers, listeners, viewers, and each other." The preamble to the SPJ code asks journalists to provide "a fair and comprehensive account of events and issues."[4]

Privacy Invasion

To gather information for new stories, journalists routinely straddle a line between "the public's right to know" and a person's right to privacy. For example, reporters may rush to a hospital to gather quotes from people who have been injured in a train derailment. Although the U.S. Constitution contains no explicit right to privacy that would protect people from reporters who want to question them, the Bill of Rights does protect specific aspects of what has become "privacy law" in various court cases through the years, such as the "privacy" of our beliefs and speech (First Amendment), the privacy of protecting personal possessions against unreasonable search and seizure (Fourth Amendment), and the privilege against self-incrimination, which provides some protection of personal information (Fifth Amendment). In instances where the news media want access to personal information pertaining to a story, do journalists responsibly weigh the protection of individual privacy against the public's right to know? Indeed, there is also no constitutional guarantee that the public has "a right to know."

One infamous example of this conflict is the recent phone hacking scandal involving News Corp.'s now-shuttered British newspaper, *News of the World.* In 2011, the *Guardian* reported that *News of the World* reporters had hired a private investigator to hack into the voice mail of thirteen-year-old murder victim Milly Dowler and had deleted some of her messages. This revelation, on top of past allegations of private voice mail hacking by *News of the World* reporters, caused a huge scandal and led to the arrests and resignations of several senior executives.

Today, when reporters can gain access to private e-mail messages, Twitter accounts, and Facebook pages as well as voicemail, such practices raise serious questions about how far a reporter should go to get information.

To resolve these issues, reporters and editors can ask themselves such questions as: What public good would be served if I invaded someone's privacy to get information for this story? What significant knowledge will the public gain? Journalism's code of ethics says "only an overriding public need can justify intrusion into anyone's privacy," but this could clash with another part of the code: "Journalists should be free of obligation to any interest other than the public's right to know." When these two ethical standards collide, reporters often err on the side of the public's right to know because it is usually in journalism's interest to get the best quotes and information for the story.

Conflicts of Interest

Journalism's code of ethics also warns reporters and editors not to place themselves in positions that create a **conflict of interest**—that is, situations in which journalists may stand to benefit personally from producing a story or from presenting the subject in a certain light. "Journalists should refuse gifts, favors, fees, free travel and special treatment," the code states, "and shun secondary employment, political involvement, public office and service in community organizations if they compromise journalistic integrity."[5]

Many news outlets attempt to protect journalists from getting into compromising positions. For instance, in most cities, journalists do not actively participate in politics or support social causes. Some journalists will not reveal their political affiliations, and some have even declined to vote. If a journalist has a tie to any organization, and that organization is later suspected of involvement in shady or criminal activity, the reporter's ability to report fairly on the organization would be compromised—along with the credibility of the news outlet for which he or she works. Conversely, other journalists believe that not participating in politics or social causes means abandoning one's civic obligations.

Resolving Ethical Dilemmas

With the crush of deadlines and daily duties, most media professionals deal with ethical situations as they arise, claiming "I'm just doing my job." However, examining some established ethical theories may help journalists develop a general framework for ethical behavior, rather than continuing to use a situational approach. Although we cannot address all major moral codes here, insights from a few great philosophers can provide some direction. Using these insights, journalists have occasionally developed sound ethical policies that guide them whenever a dilemma arises.

Consulting the Great Philosophers

The Greek philosopher Aristotle offered an early ethical concept, the "golden mean," as a guideline for seeking balance between competing positions. For Aristotle, the golden mean referred to the desirable middle ground between extreme positions. For example, Aristotle saw ambition as the golden mean between sloth and greed.

Another ethical principle entails the "categorical imperative," developed by German philosopher Immanuel Kant (1724–1804). This idea suggests that a society must adhere to moral codes that are universal and unconditional, applicable in all situations at all times. For example, the Golden Rule ("Do unto others as you would have them do unto you") is articulated in one form or another in most of the world's major religious and philosophical traditions, and operates as an absolutist moral principle.

British philosophers Jeremy Bentham (1748–1832) and John Stuart Mill (1806–1873) promoted another general ethics principle derived from "the greatest good for the greatest number." This principle directs us "to distribute a good consequence to more people rather than to fewer, whenever we have a choice."[6]

Making Ethics Decisions

To decide how to handle an ethical dilemma, journalists can draw from the great philosophers' insights, adapting those insights to the realities facing them today. For example, consider how the press handled the case of Richard Jewell, the Atlanta security guard whom the FBI suspected of setting off a bomb at the 1996 Olympics. The FBI never actually charged Jewell with a crime. However, the news media competed to report developments in the case, camping out daily in front of Jewell's mother's house (where he lived) and clamoring to interview them. The case pitted the media's right to tell stories and earn profits against a person's right to be left alone.

Jewell later successfully sued several news organizations for libel. The lawsuit and its decision suggest that journalists mishandled the situation.

Security guard Richard Jewell, the FBI's main suspect in the July 1996 Olympic Park bombing, was formally exonerated three months later. In 2005, serial bomber Eric Rudolph pleaded guilty to the Olympics bombing and three other bomb attacks.

To avoid this unpleasant outcome while working on other stories, journalists might look to the major philosophers for guidance on how to behave. For instance, if reporters invoked the Golden Rule, perhaps they might conclude that since they would not want reporters camped out at *their* homes, they should look for alternative means to interview their subjects. If they invoked Aristotle's notion of the golden mean, perhaps they would seek a way to balance a source's interests and those of the news media. For example, they might invite an interview subject to suggest a neutral site, away from his or her private dwelling, and then give interviews to a small group—or "pool"—of reporters who could then report back to the larger media contingent.

Reporting Rituals

While reporters are perfectly comfortable questioning others to get stories, they are rarely questioned themselves. Thus, many are uncomfortable discussing the strategies they use to gather information. Nevertheless, over the decades, journalists have developed specific reporting rituals that are derived from two somewhat contradictory desires: to make news interesting and to demonstrate fairness (or what became known in the twentieth century as "objectivity"). These rituals have included focusing on the present, relying on experts, creating and balancing story conflict, and challenging leaders and institutions.

Focusing on the Present

In the 1840s, when the telegraph first enabled news to crisscross America instantly, modern journalism was born. To seize advantage of the new technology's immediacy, newspaper editors began to encourage reporters to focus on the present in their stories. Over time, editors asked journalists to accent the new and the now, while downplaying the historical developments that led up to a current event (and took up more space in the report). "Get a good story—and get it first" became the goal for reporters.

Treating Events as Momentary Sensations
As a result of this focus on the present, the press began treating (and still treats) many hot-button topics (crime, immigration, abortion) as momentary sensations rather than the complex, long-term issues and experiences that they really are.

An event related to one of these topics erupts—for instance, an abortion provider is murdered—and news media crank out stories about it, but without providing any historical context or nuanced analysis. Citizens get fired up by the sensational coverage, forming and exchanging heated opinions. Then news media move on to other attention-grabbing events, and people forget about the latest one, even though it remains an important and complex issue. Through this process, news decisions and choices help set the agenda about what gets regarded or constructed as important and significant on any given day—even though what passes for news on some days is neither particularly important nor significant but merely dramatic or sensational.

Getting a Good Story

In addition to causing journalists to treat complex issues as momentary sensations, the profession's focus on the present puts immense pressure on reporters to tell compelling stories for readers and viewers. But some media critics have raised the question of whether "getting a good story" should be the end result of reporters' responsibilities.

In May 2003, the *New York Times* revealed that one of its reporters, twenty-seven-year-old Jayson Blair (*left*), made up facts; invented sources; stole quotes from other newspapers; and, in short, plagiarized dozens of articles. Both the chief editor and managing editor of the *Times* resigned shortly after Blair's dismissal.

Consider Janet Cooke, a former *Washington Post* reporter, who in the 1980s was fired for fabricating an investigative report for which she initially won a Pulitzer Prize. (It was later revoked.) To develop her fake report, Cooke had created a cast of characters, including a woman who supposedly contributed to the heroin addiction of her eight-year-old son.

When the hoax was exposed, Chicago columnist Mike Royko criticized conventional journalism for allowing the imperative of getting a good story to trump the importance of being a responsible citizen: "There's something more important than a story here. This eight-year-old kid is being murdered. The editors should have said forget the story, find the kid.... People in any other profession would have gone right to the police."[7] Had editors at the *Post* demanded such help, Cooke's hoax would not have gone as far as it did. Fabricated stories have continued to turn up occasionally, including the cases of Jayson Blair of the *New York Times*, Stephen Glass of the *New Republic*, and Jonah Lehrer who was fired from the *New Yorker* for falsely attributing quotes to Bob Dylan.

Getting a Story First

The imperative to not only get a good story but also get it first has, for some journalists, turned the profession into a highly competitive game. It has become routine for local TV stations and newspapers to brag about how they beat competitors to a story. During major elections, for example, news outlets that project winners in particular races have often hyped their projections when they are able to forecast results before the competition does.

In some ways, the news cycle, enhanced by cable and the Internet, has intensified the race to get the story first. With a fragmented audience and more media competing for news, mainstream news outlets can feel pressured to resort to exclusive, often sensational, stories to lure readers and viewers away from rivals. Yet the earliest reports are not necessarily better, more accurate, or as complete as stories written later that provide more context and perspective.

On occasion, the drive to get exclusive stories—and to feed the ever-hungry "news hole" created by today's world of 24/7 news—also triggers **pack journalism**: reporters desperate for material stake out someone's house, chase celebrities in herds or packs, or follow a story with such unoriginal single-mindedness that the entire profession seems to lose its bearings. For example, in spring 2008, after Barack Obama clinched the Democratic presidential nomination, his wife Michelle gave him an affectionate "fist bump" that was caught on camera. Though many people recognized it as a congratulatory gesture signifying a task well done, some cable news reports sought to turn the fist bump into big, scary news. For example, one pundit, E. D. Hill of Fox News, speculated: "A fist bump? A pound? A terrorist fist jab? The gesture everyone seems to interpret differently?" Treating this particularly insignificant event as a meaningful spectacle, cable news analysts and reporters kept this story alive for weeks simply because other unimaginative reporters and news channels deemed the story newsworthy.

Pack journalism often leads to the overexposure of a story or an incident that should not merit extreme amounts of attention, such as the fist bump between Barack Obama and his wife, Michelle.

Relying on Experts

Another ritual of modern print journalism—relying on outside sources—has made reporters heavily dependent on experts. To be sure, use of experts can lend credibility and balance to a news report as well as help reporters translate specialized knowledge into accessible language for readers and viewers. However, some journalists use quotes from experts merely to back up the focus or "angle" they want to present in their report. Others use them to create narrative conflict—pitting quotes from one expert against rebuttals from another.

To use experts, journalists must contact them directly—by phone or e-mail or in person. In selecting experts, they do not usually cite other reporters' work, since that would reveal they did not get a story first or on their own. Yet some journalists have ended up presenting *themselves* as experts, in part to fill the news vacuum that arose in the late 1990s with the boom in 24/7 cable news programs. The vacuum began filling with talk shows and interviews with journalists willing to give their views on topics they wrote about. For example, during events in this decade that garnered intense media coverage, such as the 9/11 terrorist attacks, the Iraq and Afghanistan wars, and recent presidential elections, many print journalists appeared regularly on cable programs acting as experts on the story. Sometimes they provided factual information, but often they offered opinion and speculation. This trend reflects a corporate need to use pundits—supposed experts who can cheaply feed the cavernous news hole with knowledge and opinions—and avoid the expense of sending reporters out to document key events and investigate significant issues. Pundits also promote their own media outlets when they routinely appear on TV talk shows.

Creating and Balancing Story Conflict

For most journalists, *balance* means presenting all sides of an issue without appearing to favor any one position. The quest for balance presents challenges for journalists. For one thing, time and space constraints do not always permit representing *multiple* sides of a story. So journalists have simplified things by "telling *both* sides of a story." Recounting news stories as two-sided dramas not only takes less time, it also enables journalists to set up conflicts in their reports. Conflict usually sells, as it simplifies real-world experiences and under-represents the complexity of social problems.

For example, reporters may treat the abortion controversy as a war between two extreme positions: One side advocates no abortion at all, ever, while the other calls for abortion on demand for everyone. In presenting the two sides, a reporter might select the most incendiary quotations he or she can find from representatives of both positions—further enhancing the drama. In fact, though, the majority of Americans' views on abortion fall somewhere between the two extremes. Yet these more moderate or nuanced perspectives seldom are reflected in news reports.

Other journalists take a different approach to dealing with the problem of balance. They stake out a moderate or middle-of-the-road position between the two sides they have presented in a story. By offering a third-person, seemingly all-knowing point of view (a narrative device preferred by many novelists), they appear to transcend judgment of the issue in the story and thus give the impression of neutrality. This can further backfire, though, when journalists give coverage to fringe views; even if journalists treat an extreme point of view as an outlier, the attention paid to those views can shift the conversation in that fringe direction—reorienting the perceived middle of the road to a different, skewed middle. For example, although the vast majority of the scientific community agrees that climate change is real and caused by humankind, journalists sometimes give voice to climate change deniers on the fringes in order to maintain a sense of "balance."

Acting as Adversaries

Many journalists adopt an adversarial stance toward the prominent leaders and major institutions they cover. They use tough questioning to confront wrongdoers, then expose their misdeeds to the public through stories in the news. This approach is particularly prominent in political reporting. Numerous journalists assume that leaders are hiding something and that a reporter's main job is to ferret out the truth through tenacious fact-gathering and "gotcha" questions. An extension of the search for balance, this stance locates the reporter in the middle—between "them" (our leaders) and "us" (the people our leaders are elected to represent).

Critics of the tough-question style of reporting argue that while it can reveal significant information, it also fosters a cynicism among journalists (if it is overused) that actually harms the democratic process. After all, if reporters are constantly searching for what politicians may be hiding, they risk missing other important issues that also merit coverage in the press.

Journalism in the Age of TV and the Internet

Television (starting in the 1950s) and now the Internet have profoundly reshaped both American journalism and the national culture with which it is closely intertwined. Most important, these technologies have made it possible for people to get information not only by reading newspapers but also by viewing live footage and watching news reporters deliver the latest updates. Thus TV and the Internet have helped transform American culture from a print-oriented one to a popular culture landscape built on visual imagery. The Internet, especially, introduced an immediacy to journalism—through real-time reporting—that newspapers did not offer (but would eventually provide in their online incarnations).

The rules and rituals governing American journalism began shifting in the 1950s. In the early days, the most influential and respected news program was CBS's *See It Now*, coproduced by Edward R. Murrow. The show practiced a kind of TV journalism lodged between the neutral and narrative traditions.

But despite these differences, TV and the Internet also show some similarities to print journalism. For example, like some newspapers, many TV news programs and Web sites foreground a dramatic narrative approach (pitting two sides in conflict) to delivering news, then use video footage to help tell and sell stories. And some Internet sites, like Politico.com, have begun specializing in investigative journalism, although local TV news stations have largely abandoned this kind of in-depth reporting in recent years.

Comparing Print, TV, and Internet News

Although TV news reporters share many values and conventions with their print counterparts, they also differ from them in significant ways. First, while print editors fit stories around ads on the printed page, TV news directors have to time stories to fit between commercials, which can make the ads seem more intrusive to viewers. Second, while modern print journalists derive their credibility from their apparent neutrality, TV news reporters gain credibility from providing live, on-the-spot reporting; believable imagery; and an earnest, personable demeanor that makes them seem more approachable, even more trustworthy, than the detached, faceless print reporters. As TV news reporting evolved, it developed a style of its own, one defined by attractive, congenial newscasters skilled at perky banter (sometimes called "happy talk") and short, seven- to eight-second quotes (or "sound bites") from interview subjects. Print and TV reporters also must compete with Internet-only outlets, which combine elements of both television and print journalism.

Pretty Faces and Happy Talk

In the 1970s, TV news program directors learned that more people watched the news if it was delivered by attractive men and women with upbeat personalities who exchanged apparently spontaneous banter. News anchors who didn't fit these criteria—they looked too old, too fat, or (in women's cases) too aggressive—were replaced. This development helped create a stereotype of the unintelligent but physically attractive news anchor, reinforced by popular culture images (from Ted Baxter on TV's *Mary Tyler Moore Show* to Ron Burgundy in the film *Anchorman*). Although the situation has improved slightly, national news consultants set the agenda for what local reporters should cover (lots of crime) as well as how they should look and sound (young, attractive, pleasant, and with little or no regional accent).

Another news strategy favored by news consultants has been *happy talk*: the ad-libbed or scripted banter that goes on among local news anchors, reporters, meteorologists, and sports reporters before and after news reports. During the 1970s, consultants often recommended such chatter to create a more relaxed feeling on the news set and to foster the illusion of conversational intimacy with viewers. A strategy still used today, happy talk often appears forced and may create awkward transitions when anchors move from bantering to reporting on sad or tragic events. However, this tactic may continue to look ever more dated, as it's less often a component of Internet news reporting.

Sound Bites

In the 1980s, when stations began devoting more time to commercials during news programs, people being interviewed by reporters had less time to answer questions and explain their views. The **sound bite** was born. The TV equivalent of a quote in print news, a sound bite is the part of a broadcast news report in which an expert, a celebrity, a victim, or a "person on the street" responds to some aspect of an event or issue with a short, memorable comment.

Some reporters have sought to use sound bites to create dramatic tension and satisfy the "both sides of a story" ritual by editing competing bites together as if the interviewees had been in the same location speaking to one another. This tactic has drawn criticism from some observers. Of course, print news also pits one quote against another in a story, even though the actual interview subjects may never have met. However, in a TV news story, the visual images added to the spoken word make the resulting sound bites more memorable for viewers. On the Internet, the brevity and accessibility of a memorable sound bite can help it go viral, circulating to people who may not be reached by traditional articles or TV broadcasts.

Adapting to the Internet

The Internet has opened new doors for journalists and citizens alike. For example, print and TV reporters can now continually update breaking stories online. Today, many reporters post online versions of their stories first and then work on the traditional versions. Readers and viewers no longer have to wait for the morning paper or for the local evening newscast to stay current with important stories. Online reports can also be augmented with video or audio as well as additional information that would not fit in a printed article or a TV news story. Readers and viewers can thus see full interviews rather than just the selected quotes in the paper or the sound bites on the TV report.

However, the Internet has also presented new problems. For instance, it has encouraged print reporters to do e-mail interviews rather than leave the office to question a subject in person. Many editors worry that e-mail interviews lack the surprise or spontaneity that phone or in-person interviews have. Sources have time to think about their responses and thus may deliver less-than-honest comments. Often, some editors will allow e-mail interviews only when a phone or live interview is impossible.

The enormous amount of information available on the Internet has also made it all too easy for journalists to unwittingly copy work that other journalists have done. In addition, access to databases and other informational sites can keep reporters at their computers rather than out tracking down certain kinds of information, cultivating sources, and staying in touch with their communities. Blogging has become another double-edged sword. While blog posts enable journalists (and nonjournalists) to provide their opinions and analysis (thus freeing them from the constraints of neutrality), blogs often do not demonstrate much actual reporting or documenting stories with evidence. The immediacy of the Internet has moved some audiences away from print news, but it has also emphasized what newspapers can still do well: produce well-researched and fact-checked articles that go into greater depth than quick updates about breaking stories.

Perhaps most notable for journalists in the digital age are the demands that convergence has made on their reporting and writing. Print journalists are expected to carry digital cameras so they can post video along with the print versions of their stories (see "Converging Media Case Study: Digital Camera Journalism," page 403). TV reporters are expected to write print-style news reports for their station's Web site to supplement the streaming video of their original TV stories. And both print and TV reporters are often expected to post the Internet versions of their stories first, before the versions they do for the morning paper or the evening news. Increasingly, journalists today are also expected to blog and tweet.

The Power of Visual Language

The shift from a print-dominated culture to an electronic-digital culture brings up the question of how the power of the visual imagery so prominent in TV and Internet news compares with the power of the printed word. For the second half of

CONVERGING MEDIA
Case Study

Digital Camera Journalism

One side effect of converging media is the ubiquity of digital cameras, which have become smaller and easier to use on their own and also integrated into many computers, phones, and other mobile devices. Journalism has been shaken up by the prevalence of these cameras, which represent both an opportunity and a danger to news producers and audiences alike.

Some of the thorniest professional and ethical issues surround the use of hidden cameras. Though hidden cameras as a gimmick on television have been around as long as Alan Funt's *Candid Camera* (which began as the radio show *Candid Microphone*), today's smaller and more versatile digital video cameras make it even easier to conduct the deceptions, invasions, and entrapments of this technique. The program *To Catch a Predator*, a *Dateline NBC* series that has worked with an online watchdog group to bust adults who contact minors on the Internet for sexual purposes, became popular by using hidden-camera techniques, but has drawn criticism (and at least one successful lawsuit) for blurring the lines between journalism, police work, and entertainment. The widespread availability of affordable digital video also means that citizens can make their own hidden-camera reports, for better or for worse. The late Andrew Breitbart's site BigGovernment.com specialized in hidden-camera footage, like a segment shot undercover at the Association of Community Organizations for Reform Now (ACORN), purporting to show ACORN workers giving illicit advice on avoiding taxes and hiding prostitution. Though the videos did immense damage to ACORN, the BigGovernment.com reporters were criticized for editing the videos to mislead viewers.

But despite the controversy that often comes with the newfound freedom to create journalistic video, digital cameras also have provided some of the most compelling news coverage of the last decade. Footage generated by amateurs using smartphones provided the first glimpses of the devastation wrought by the 2004 tsunami in Indonesia and the standoff at Norris Hall during the 2007 Virginia Tech Massacre; in previous chapters we have explored how images gathered by smartphones and distributed by social media played key roles in the Arab Spring uprisings and the Occupy Wall Street movement. We have also considered the ethical problems of using visually compelling footage provided by terrorist organizations. As these contrasting cases suggest, digital footage—now so easy to shoot and distribute—gathered by non-journalists constitutes an ethical minefield for professional journalists. For news consumers, this material also demands a high level of critical engagement—the engagement that comes with being media literate.

Al-Jazeera, the Arab satellite news service originating in the small Persian Gulf nation of Qatar, launched its English-language Web site at http://english.al-jazeera.net in 2003, and in 2006 started an English-language TV station. Some have charged al-Jazeera with an anti-U.S. bias, but it is actually the most independent news service in the Arab world.

the twentieth century, TV news dramatized America's key events visually. Civil Rights activists, for instance, acknowledge that the movement benefited enormously from televised news that documented the plight of southern blacks in the 1960s in evocative moving images. Many people find visual images far more compelling and memorable than written descriptions of events or individuals.

Today, the Internet functions as a repository for news photos as well as film and audio. When broadcast repeatedly by TV news stations or radio stations, these digitized recordings can now extend a message farther and spread it much faster than in previous eras. For example, on the 2008 campaign trail in Philadelphia, then presidential candidate Barack Obama delivered a speech on U.S. race relations and his biracial heritage, titled "A More Perfect Union," that critics and supporters alike compared favorably to Martin Luther King Jr.'s famous 1964 "I Have a Dream" speech. While Obama's speech drew relatively small audiences on cable when he delivered it live, millions viewed it later on YouTube. Digital broadcasting and rebroadcasting can have more negative effects, too: In 2010, as Donald Trump toyed briefly with running for president in 2012, he resurrected an old accusation, suggesting that President Obama was born in Kenya, not Hawaii. This story spread across the Internet—on Twitter, blogs, and forums—and traditional news outlets also covered the "controversy," even doing stories about *not* covering the completely unfounded rumors. In late April 2011, President Obama released his long-form birth certificate just to curtail the resilient (and baseless) story.

Alternative Models: Public Journalism and Fake News

Today, most American journalism relies heavily on the *informational* model, which emphasizes describing events and issues from a seemingly neutral stance. For example, front-page stories in newspapers strive for this detachment, confining obvious opinions to the editorial pages.

However, alternative models have emerged to challenge this approach. The alternatives include the public and citizen (or "participatory") journalism movements, whereby citizens more actively participate in the news process, and fake news forms, exemplified by TV shows like *The Daily Show with Jon Stewart* and *The Colbert Report* and by publications like the *Onion*, which satirize the limitations of mainstream news at the same time they provide often original, if idiosyncratic, news and analysis. These newer models generate lively discussion among observers today about what constitutes news, what's wrong with it, and how news might be produced to better serve democracy.

One way technology has allowed citizens to become involved in the reporting of news is through cell phone photos and videos. Witnesses can now pass on what they have captured to major mainstream news sources.

Public Journalism

From the late 1980s through the 1990s, a number of newspapers experimented with ways to involve readers more actively in creating news. These experiments in what has become known as **public journalism** surfaced primarily at midsized daily papers in Kansas, Minnesota, and North Carolina. Davis Merritt, editor and vice president of the *Wichita Eagle*, one paper that conducted such experiments, described public journalism with these words:

- It moves beyond the limited mission of "telling the news" to a broader mission of helping public life go well, and acts out that imperative. . . .
- It moves from detachment to being a fair-minded participant in public life. . . .
- It moves beyond only describing what is "going wrong" to also imagining what "going right" would be like. . . .
- It moves from seeing people as consumers—as readers or nonreaders, as bystanders to be informed—to seeing them as . . . actors in arriving at democratic solutions to public problems.[8]

Public journalism emerged as a way to involve citizens and journalists more centrally in civic and political life. Newspaper editors and reporters interested in addressing citizen alienation—and reporter cynicism—began devising ways to engage both groups in conversation about the news. To draw the public into discussions about community priorities, these journalists began sponsoring forums where citizens were invited to have a voice in the news that directly affected them. Reporters then published stories framed from the citizens' perspectives and created citizen task forces to keep the conversation going about the issues most important to the community.

Public journalism did not directly transform the industry, but an extension of the movement, citizen or community journalism (see Chapter 3), has changed the role of some in the news audience from readers and viewers to actual participants in journalism. As members of a grassroots movement, activist amateurs and concerned citizens use the Internet and blog sites to disseminate news and information. In fact, with devastating cutbacks in newsroom staffs in recent years, many professional news organizations are now using some of their readers/viewers and prominent community citizens to do work that journalists used to do.

Fake News

In addition to public journalism, fake news emerged as a response to increasing cynicism about the political process and other issues covered by journalists. This cynicism is not surprising in a nation where two political parties control the government and where many incumbent lawmakers get reelected each year because they have done favors for the lobbyists who helped get them elected initially.

Following in the tradition of *Saturday Night Live*'s "Weekend Update" sketches, which began in 1975, two half-hour cable satires, *The Daily Show with Jon Stewart* and *The Colbert Report*, are today attracting large audiences. On these shows, the hosts tell audiences something that seems truthful about politicians and explain how political leaders try to manipulate the media and public opinion. They often expose hypocrisy by comparing what a politician said "yesterday" in the news with the opposite position held and articulated by the same politician months or years earlier. They also use humor to skewer the news media's often superficial treatment of politics.

Often the hosts mock the formulas that real TV news programs have long used—everything from the distinctive way news anchors talk to the canned sound bites the reporters present. The more people watch TV news satire, the staler and more irrelevant these formulas seem. Indeed, many Americans have admitted that they watch satires such as *The Daily Show* not only to be entertained but also to stay current with what is going on in the world. In fact, a prominent Pew Research Center study in 2007 found that people who watched these satiric shows were more often "better informed" than most other news consumers, usually because these viewers tended to get their news from multiple sources and a cross section of news media.[9]

The Colbert Report satirizes cable news hosts and the opinion-argument culture promoted by their programs.

These developments suggest that journalism—especially TV news—needs to break free from tired formulas and create fresh ways to tell stories. After all, in fictional TV, storytelling has evolved over time, becoming increasingly complex and nuanced. And the Internet has introduced new models of journalism. To remain viable, especially as younger people abandon traditional news media, TV news will need to be just as innovative.

Journalism in a Democratic Society

Journalism is central to democracy: Citizens must have access to information the news media provide to make important decisions on when to go to war or whether every citizen should have health care. And gaining this information often involves reporting in-depth and questioning our top politicians, government officials, and business leaders. But this questioning can prompt a backlash. For example, after the 9/11 attacks, some government officials claimed that reporters who asked whether the United States should invade Iraq were being unpatriotic. And during the 2008–09 economic crisis, some leaders on Wall Street criticized news media for questioning whether capitalism was working well for the majority or just a privileged and wealthy minority.

Conventional journalists will fight ferociously for the basic tenets that underpin their profession: freedom of the press, the importance of challenging leaders, the public's right to know, and the notion that there are two sides to every story. These are all worthy ideals, but they do have limitations. For example, they do not acknowledge that journalists also can—and perhaps should—take some responsibility for improving the quality of daily life. Most reporters leave such responsibility to political groups, nonprofit organizations, business philanthropists, and citizens.

Over the years, some journalists have bucked this trend. Among them was James Agee in the 1930s. In his book *Let Us Now Praise Famous Men*, which was accompanied by the Depression-era photography of Walker Evans, Agee criticized conventional journalists for intruding on people's

In *Let Us Now Praise Famous Men*, which begins with haunting photos taken by Walker Evans, author James Agee questioned the basic honesty of daily journalism in the late 1930s.

personal lives and turning them into story characters that newspapers and magazines then exploited for profit.

Others have pointed to public journalism as a way for reporters to fulfill their social responsibility. According to advocates of this model, reporters chiefly concerned with challenging political leaders are less willing and able to improve political discourse themselves. News *and* democracy pay the price. *Washington Post* columnist David Broder confesses that national journalists like him—who enjoy big salaries, prestige, and formal education—have distanced themselves "from the people that we are writing for and have become much, much closer to [the prominent] people we are writing about."[10] Broder believes that journalists need to become activists, not for a particular party but for the political process itself and in the interest of reenergizing public life.

The Internet offers a way to realize this ideal because it gives citizens the opportunity to participate in more discussions and debates, serves perhaps as an extension of the public journalism movement, and gives more experienced reporters the opportunity to cover those interactions. This kind of journalism fosters a *deliberative democracy* in which citizen groups, local government, and the news media work together to actively shape social, economic, and political agendas. In a deliberative democracy, a large segment of the community discusses public life and social policy before advising or electing officials who represent the community's interests. Of course, this ideal of the Internet and digital media has not always been realized; it can also lead to increased fragmentation and polarization when audiences seek out journalism that conforms only to their beliefs and expectations.

In 1989, historian Christopher Lasch argued that "the job of the press is to encourage debate, not to supply the public with information."[11] Although he overstated his case—journalism does both and more—Lasch made a cogent point about how conventional journalism sometimes lost its bearings in chasing supposed objectivity. That early mission of journalism—to advocate opinions and encourage public debate—today is carried out by news blogs and cable news channels, which increasingly target specific audience segments, as with certain left-leaning shows on MSNBC or the right-slanting Fox News. Indeed, as we enter what may be a postobjectivity age of journalism, there is now a danger of turning too much attention over to talking-head debates, sound bites, and unresearched viral stories.

Yet some degree of debate is needed, and the Internet could pave the way for more diverse, more media-literate news coverage. As advocates of public journalism acknowledge, people have grown accustomed to letting their representatives think and act for them, and to letting the press feed them information that they passively ingest. Converged journalism offers citizens an opportunity to influence their leaders. The increasing variety of news sources may allow for journalism that uses techniques like paying more attention to the historical and economic contexts of stories; doing more investigative reports that analyze news conventions and social issues; participating more fully in the public life of their own communities; and admitting to their cultural biases and occasional mistakes. Media-literate audiences, then, should demand media-literate journalists.

CHAPTER ESSENTIALS

Now that you have finished reading this chapter, you can use the following tools:

REVIEW

Discuss Modern Journalism in the Information Age

- We define **news** as the process of gathering information and making reports that use a narrative framework. A key part of a journalist's job is determining what information is **newsworthy**—that is, what merits transformation into news stories (pp. 386–387).

- A number of values underscore American journalism. These include neutrality (which leads to greater credibility), **ethnocentrism** (which involves judging other countries and cultures according to how they live up to or imitate American practices and ideals), **responsible capitalism** (which assumes that businesspeople compete with one another to increase prosperity for all), **small-town pastoralism** (which causes journalists to favor the small over the large and the rural over the urban), and **individualism** (which favors individual rights and responsibilities over group needs or institutional mandates) (pp. 387, 390–391).

Explain Ethics and the News Media

- Journalists face a variety of ethical dilemmas. For example, they must decide whether or not to use deception to gain information or whether to invade someone's privacy, all the while trying to avoid situations that present **conflicts of interest** or situations in which journalists may benefit personally (pp. 391–393).

- In an effort to resolve their dilemmas, journalists have developed policies and guidelines (pp. 395–396).

Understand Reporting Rituals

- In order to produce good stories that will attract readers, reporters have a set of rituals they follow. These include focusing on the present (which sometimes leads to **pack journalism**, where reporters stake out a house or follow a story in such large groups that the entire profession comes under attack for invading people's privacy or exploiting their personal tragedies); relying on experts; creating and balancing story conflict; and developing an adversarial stance toward leaders and institutions (pp. 397–399).

Describe Journalism in the Age of TV and the Internet

- Television and the Internet have transformed journalism by introducing live coverage and visual imagery. As TV evolved, it developed its own conventions with its use of the **sound bite** (the part of a news report in which a person is interviewed about some aspect of an event or issue) and attractive, personable newscasters (pp. 400–401).

- The Internet has presented new opportunities for journalists and citizens, but it also raises questions about how to best interview sources, deal with the abundance of information on the Web, sort through opinion versus fact, and use the power of visual imagery (pp. 401–402, 404).

Outline Alternative Models of Journalism

- Aside from the informational model of journalism, which advocates describing events from a neutral stance, other types have emerged. **Public journalism** is driven by citizen forums and goes beyond telling the news to embrace a broader mission of improving the quality of public life. In addition, fake news is a response to increasing cynicism about the political process and other issues covered by journalists (pp. 405–407).

Contemplate Journalism's Role in Our Democratic Society

- Journalism is essential to democracy in that it provides people with access to information, much of which comes from news media, needed to make important decisions (p. 407).

- Many believe public journalism is a way for reporters to fulfill their social responsibility to citizens (pp. 408–409).

STUDY QUESTIONS

1. What are some of the key values that underlie modern journalism?
2. How do issues such as deception and privacy present ethical problems for journalists?
3. Why do many conventional journalists (and citizens) believe firmly in the idea that there are two sides to every story?
4. In what ways has the Internet influenced traditional forms of journalism?
5. What is public journalism? In what ways is it believed to make journalism better?
6. What is deliberative democracy, and what does it have to do with journalism?

MEDIA LITERACY PRACTICE

Explore the effects of an increasingly visual culture on news reporting. Select *one* recent issue of *Time* or *Newsweek*. Your focus will be on all the visual images in the magazine—both the news images and the ad images.

DESCRIBE all the images. Look at what percentage of the magazine is devoted to ads, to printed/written news content, and to news photos/images. Make a list of what is in the images, particularly what kinds of people are represented. Make a list about the ads, too, again noting who or what is represented/featured.

ANALYZE the information. What are the major differences and/or similarities between the news photos and ad images?

INTERPRET what the information means. What do the magazine's editors believe are the most important kinds of news images for their readers? What can you tell about the target audience from the ads?

EVALUATE the images. Do you think there is any disconnect or discontinuity between the ad images and the news photos?

ENGAGE with your community by contacting an editor or the news director or an ad person from the magazine you investigated. Discuss your findings and concerns with this person.

▶ ONLINE RESOURCES

Go to **bedfordstmartins.com/mediaessentials** for review quizzes, links, and more.

Visit the site's **VIDEOCENTRAL: MASS COMMUNICATION** section for videos like the ones on pages 387 and 406. There, you can find additional exclusive videos related to Chapter 13, including:

JOURNALISM ETHICS: WHAT NEWS IS FIT TO PRINT?
Journalism and legal scholars discuss the ethical considerations inherent to the news industry.

THE OBJECTIVITY MYTH
Pulitzer Prize–winning journalist Clarence Page and the *Onion* editor Joe Randazzo explore how objectivity began in journalism and how reporter biases may nonetheless influence news stories.

SHIELD LAWS AND NONTRADITIONAL JOURNALISTS
Reporters and media critics explain what shield laws are and how they apply to both professional and citizen journalists.

MURKY WATERS: DEBATING THE ROLE OF CITIZEN JOURNALISM
Media experts look at the role of citizen journalism and the potential complications it causes for traditional reporting.

DOUBLE PLAY: THE NEW ERA OF SPORTS REPORTING
Sports journalist Chris Haft discusses how his job is changing with the rise of social media.

14

Legal Controls and Freedom of Expression

On January 18, 2012, anyone visiting the popular Web site *Wikipedia* was met with a blackout: An estimated 160 million visitors saw none of the site's usual encyclopedic entries or search function, only a message asking people to "Imagine a world without free knowledge." Internet users looking for access to sites like Reddit, Twitpic, and Mozilla found similar messages; they were just a few of the more than 115,000 Web sites that participated in protesting the Stop Online Piracy Act (SOPA), a bill under consideration in Congress that would expand governmental powers to combat copyright infringement on the Internet. The centerpiece of the protest was *Wikipedia*'s blacking out of its English-language site for twenty-four hours, advocating that users consider the consequences of this bill. The protest resulted in 3 million people e-mailing Congress to register opposition to SOPA and a similar bill being considered in the Senate—the Protect Intellectual Property Act (PIPA).[1]

Both SOPA and PIPA were pushed by old media powers that comprise the copyright lobby (including the Motion Picture Association of America, the Recording Industry Association of America, and an array of other companies in the music, television, film, and publishing industries). Supporters of the legislation claimed they were only trying to go after foreign sites that sell pirated copies of software, videos, and music.

The new media opponents of the bill, many associated with popular sites featuring a mix of preexisting and user-generated content, took issue with how the old media hoped to strengthen the law's enforcement. The proposed law would have enabled copyright holders to block Web sites, censor search results, and cut off advertising revenue without even going through a judge. Some feared that the language of the law was so vague that one violation could result in the shutting down of an entire domain. Others argued the costs of complying with the law would have a chilling effect on the Internet economy by discouraging investors from developing new businesses.

The most relevant opposition to SOPA involved questions of censorship. Lawrence H. Tribe, a professor of constitutional law at Harvard University, wrote in a letter to Congress that SOPA's "very existence would dramatically chill protected speech by undermining the openness and free exchange of information at the heart of the internet."[2] International responses also condemned the legislation as a form of censorship. The European Union Parliament adopted a resolution that stressed "the need to protect the integrity of the global internet and freedom of communication by refraining from unilateral measures to revoke IP addresses or domain names."[3]

SUCH DEBATES OVER WHAT CONSTITUTES "FREE SPEECH" or "free expression" have intensified as technological advances enable easy creation of new types of media content. The questions explored in such debates center on two themes: economics and politics. For example, arguments about what constitutes copyright violation revolve around who should be allowed to make money from the creation, distribution, and ownership of media content—and who should shoulder the expense of enforcing copyright law. Meanwhile, debates about the particular messages in a piece of media content raise questions about politics. For instance, do teenagers have a right to use social media to bully a person because of his or her sexual orientation? Do military secrets published on the Internet prevent the government from protecting the citizenry?

Such arguments also raise questions regarding the variation in regulatory standards that has evolved across different mass media. For example, print media have the least regulation, as the First Amendment clearly protects freedom of the press. Broadcast has the strictest regulation, as lawmakers have defined the airwaves as a shared public resource. And regulation regarding the Internet is contested, as the technology (and the different ways in which people and organizations use it) is still comparatively new.

In this chapter, we examine these themes more closely by:

- exploring the origins of free expression and a free press, identifying four models of free expression, taking a closer look at the First Amendment to the U.S. Constitution, tracing the emergence of censorship, and comparing the First Amendment with the Sixth Amendment

- shining a spotlight on film and the First Amendment, assessing social and political pressures affecting moviemaking, self-regulation in the film industry, and the emergence of the film-ratings system

- taking stock of free expression in the broadcast and online media, including examining the Federal Communications Commission (FCC) regulation of broadcasting, definitions and regulation of indecent speech, laws governing political broadcasts, the impact of the Fairness Doctrine, and communication policy regarding the Internet

- considering the First Amendment's role in our democracy today, including questions such as who (journalists? citizens? both?) should fulfill the civic role of watchdog

The Origins of Free Expression and Free Press

In the United States, freedom of speech and freedom of the press are protected by the First Amendment in the Bill of Rights developed for our nation's Constitution. Roughly interpreted, these freedoms suggest that anyone should be able to express his or her views, and that the press should be able to publish whatever it wants, without prohibition from Congress. But there's always been a tension between the notion of free expression and the idea that some expression (such as sexually explicit words or images) should perhaps be prohibited or censored. Many people have wondered what free expression really means.

In this section, we examine several aspects of free speech and freedom of the press. We explore the roots of the First Amendment and different interpretations of *free expression* that have arisen in modern times. We look at evolving notions of censorship and forms of expression that are not protected by the U.S. Constitution. And we consider ways in which the First Amendment has clashed with the Sixth Amendment, which guarantees accused individuals the right to speedy and public trials by impartial juries.

A Closer Look at the First Amendment

To understand how the idea of free expression has developed in the United States, we must understand how the notion of a free press came about. The story goes back to the 1600s, when various national governments in Europe controlled the circulation of ideas through the press by requiring printers to obtain licenses from them. Their goal was to monitor the ideas published by editors and writers and swiftly suppress subversion. However, in 1644, English poet John Milton published his essay *Areopagitica*, which opposed government licenses for printers and defended a free press. Milton argued that in a democratic society, all sorts of ideas—even false ones—should be allowed to circulate. Eventually, he maintained, the truth would emerge. In 1695, England stopped licensing newspapers, and most of Europe followed suit. In many democracies today, publishing a newspaper, magazine, or newsletter requires no license.

Less than a hundred years after 1695, the writers of the U.S. Constitution were ambivalent about the idea of a free press. Indeed, the version of the Constitution ratified in 1788 did not include such protection. The states took a different tack, however. At that time, nine of the original thirteen states had charters defending freedom of the press. These states pushed to have federal guarantees of free speech and the press approved at the first session of the new Congress. Their efforts paid off: The Bill of Rights, which contained the first ten amendments to the Constitution, won ratification in 1791.

However, commitment to freedom of the press was not yet tested. In 1798, the Federalist Party, which controlled the presidency and the Congress, passed the

AREOPAGITICA

A

SPEECH

OF

Mr *JOHN MILTON*

For the Liberty of UNLICENSED

PRINTING

To the PARLIAMENT of ENGLAND

Τοὐλεύθερον δ᾽ ἐκεῖνο· εἴ τις θέλει πόλει
Χρηστόν τι βούλευμ᾽ εἰς μέσον φέρειν ἔχων.
Καὶ ταῦθ᾽ ὁ χρῄζων λαμπρὸς ἐσθ᾽, ὁ μὴ θέλων
Σιγᾷ. τί τούτων ἐστ᾽ ἰσαίτερον πόλει;

Euripid. Hicetid.

*This is true Liberty when free born men
Having to advise the public may speak free,
Which he who can, and will, deserves high praise,
Who neither can nor will, may hold his peace;
What can be juster in a State than this?*

Euripid. Hicetid.

THEY who to states and governors of the commonwealth direct their speech, high court of parliament, or wanting such access in a private condition, write that which they foresee may advance the public good; I suppose them, as at the beginning of no mean endeavour, not a little altered and moved inwardly in their minds; some with doubt of what will be the success, others with fear of what will be the censure; some with hope, others with confidence of what they

M.   I

John Milton's *Areopagitica* is one of the most significant early defenses of freedom of the press.

Sedition Act to silence opposition to an anticipated war against France. The act was signed into law by President John Adams and resulted in the arrest and conviction of several publishers. But, after failing to curb opposition, the Sedition Act expired in 1801 during Thomas Jefferson's presidency. Jefferson, a Democratic-Republican who had challenged the act's constitutionality, pardoned all defendants convicted under it.[4] Ironically, the Sedition Act—the first major attempt to constrain the First Amendment—ended up solidifying American support behind the notion of a free press.

Interpretations of Free Expression

Americans are not alone in debating what constitutes free expression and whether constraining expression is ever appropriate. Over time, four models have emerged that capture the widely differing interpretations of what "free expression" means.[5] We can think of these as the authoritarian, state, social responsibility, and libertarian models. These models are distinguished by the degree of freedom their proponents advocate, and by ruling classes' attitudes toward the freedoms granted to average citizens.

The Authoritarian Model

The **authoritarian model** developed around the time the printing press first arrived in sixteenth-century England. Under this model, criticism of government and public dissent were not tolerated, especially if such speech undermined "the common good"—an ideal that elites and rulers defined. The government actively censored any expression it found threatening, and it issued printing licenses only to those publishers willing to say positive things about the government. Today, this model persists in many developing countries that have authoritarian governments. In these nations, journalism's job is to support government and business efforts to foster economic growth, minimize political dissent, and promote social stability.

Government control of the press under the state model has led to protests like the Burmese monk's opposition shown here.

The State Model

Under the **state model**, the government controls the press and what it reports. Leaders believe that the press should serve the goals of the state. Although the government tolerates some criticism, it suppresses ideas that challenge the basic premises of state authority. Today, a few countries use this model, including Myanmar (Burma), China, Cuba, and North Korea.

The Social Responsibility Model

The **social responsibility model** captures the ideals of mainstream journalism in the United States and most other democracies. The concepts and assumptions behind this model were outlined in 1947 by the Hutchins Commission, which was formed to examine the press's increasing influence. The commission's report first called for the development of press watchdog groups, on the assumption that the mass media had grown too powerful. Second, the report concluded, the press needed to take more responsibility for improving American society through actions like news forums for the exchange of ideas and better coverage of social groups and society's range of economic classes.

The social responsibility model has roots in revolutionary Europe. This model calls for the press to be privately owned, so that newspapers operate independently of government. The press functions as a **Fourth Estate**—an unofficial branch of government that watches for abuses of power by the legislative, judicial, and executive branches. The press supplies information about such abuses to citizens so they can make informed decisions about political and social issues.

In 1971, Daniel Ellsberg, a former Pentagon researcher, turned against America's military policy in Vietnam and leaked information to the press. The federal case against him was dropped in 1973 when illegal government-sponsored wiretaps of Ellsberg's psychoanalyst came to light during the Watergate scandal.

The Libertarian Model

The **libertarian model** is the flip side of both the state and authoritarian models and an extension of the social responsibility model. This model encourages vigorous criticism of government and supports the highest degree of individual and press freedoms. Proponents of the libertarian model argue that *no* restrictions should be placed on the mass media or on individual speech. In North America and Europe, many alternative newspapers and magazines operate on such a model. They often emphasize the importance of securing rights for sidelined populations (such as gay men and lesbians), and follow an ethic that absolute freedom of expression is the best way to fight injustice and arrive at the truth.

The Evolution of Censorship

In the United States, the First Amendment theoretically prohibits censorship. Over time, Supreme Court decisions have defined censorship as **prior restraint**—meaning that courts and governments cannot block any publication or speech before it actually occurs. The principle behind prior restraint is that a law has not been broken until an illegal act has been committed. However, the Court left open the idea that the judiciary could halt publication of news in exceptional cases—for example, if such publication would threaten national security. In the 1970s, two pivotal court decisions tested the idea of prior restraint.

The Pentagon Papers Decision

In 1971, with the Vietnam War still raging, Daniel Ellsberg, a former Defense Department employee, stole a copy of the forty-seven-volume report, "History of U.S. Decision-Making Process on Vietnam Policy." A thorough study of U.S. involvement in Vietnam since World War II, the report was classified by the government as top secret. Ellsberg and a friend leaked the report—nicknamed the Pentagon Papers—to the *New York Times* and the *Washington Post*. In June 1971, the *Times* began publishing articles based on the report. To block any further publications, the Nixon administration applied for and received a federal court injunction against the *Times* to halt publication of the stories, arguing that the publication of these documents posed "a clear and present danger" to national security by revealing military strategy to the enemy.

In a 6–3 vote, the Supreme Court sided with the newspaper. Justice Hugo Black, in his majority opinion, attacked the government's attempt to suppress publication: "Both the history and language of the First Amendment support the view that the press must be left free to publish news, whatever the source, without censorship, injunctions, or prior restraints."[6]

The *Progressive* Magazine Decision

The conflict between prior restraint and national security surfaced again in 1979, when the U.S. government issued an injunction to block publication of the *Progressive*, a national left-wing magazine. The editors had planned to publish an article titled "The H-Bomb Secret: How We Got It, Why We're Telling It." The dispute began when the magazine's editor sent a draft to the Department of Energy to verify technical portions of the article. Believing that the article contained sensitive data that might damage U.S. efforts to halt the proliferation of nuclear weapons, the Energy Department asked the magazine not to publish it. When the magazine said it would proceed anyway, the government sued the *Progressive* and asked a federal district court to block publication.

In an unprecedented action, Justice Robert Warren sided with the government, deciding that "a mistake in ruling against the United States could pave the way for thermonuclear annihilation for us all. In that event, our right to life is extinguished and the right to publish becomes moot."[7] Warren was seeking to balance the *Progressive*'s First Amendment rights against the possibility that the article, if published, would spread dangerous information and undermine national security. During appeals, several other publications printed their own stories about the H-bomb, and the U.S. government eventually dropped the case. None of the articles, including one ultimately published by the *Progressive*, contained precise details on how to design a nuclear weapon. But Warren's decision represented the first time in American history that a prior-restraint order imposed in the name of national security stopped initial publication of a news report.

Unprotected Forms of Expression

Despite the First Amendment's provision that "Congress shall make no law" restricting speech and the press, the federal government, state laws, and even local ordinances have on occasion curbed some forms of expression. And over the years, the U.S. court system has determined that some kinds of expression do not merit protection under the Constitution. These forms include sedition, copyright infringement, libel, obscenity, and violation of privacy rights.

Sedition

For more than a century after the Sedition Act of 1798, Congress passed no laws prohibiting the articulation or publication of dissenting opinions. But sentiments that fueled the Sedition Act resurfaced in the twentieth century, particularly in times of war. For instance, the Espionage Acts of 1917 and 1918, enforced during the two world wars, made it a federal crime to utter or publish "seditious" statements, defined as anything expressing opposition to the U.S. war effort.

For example, in the landmark *Schenck v. United States* (1919) appeal case, held during World War I, the Supreme Court upheld the conviction of a Socialist Party leader, Charles T. Schenck, for distributing leaflets urging American men to protest the draft. Justices argued that Schenck had violated the recently passed Espionage Act.

In supporting Schenck's sentence—a ten-year prison term—Justice Oliver Wendell Holmes noted that the Socialist leaflets were entitled to First Amendment protection, but only during times of peace. In establishing the "clear and present danger" criterion for expression, the Supreme Court demonstrated the limits of the First Amendment.

Copyright Infringement

Appropriating a writer's or an artist's words, images, or music without consent or payment is also a form of expression not protected by the First Amendment. A

copyright legally protects the rights of authors and producers to their published or unpublished writing, music, lyrics, TV programs, movies, or graphic-art designs. Congress passed the first Copyright Act in 1790, which gave authors the right to control their published works for fourteen years, with the opportunity to renew copyright protection for another fourteen years. After the end of the copyright period, the work would enter the **public domain**, which would give the public free access to the work. (For example, a publisher could reprint a written work that had entered the public domain.) The idea was that a period of copyright control would give authors financial incentive to create original works, and that moving works into the public domain would give others incentive to create works derived from earlier accomplishments.

In a 1994 landmark case, the Supreme Court ruled that the rap group 2 Live Crew's 1989 song "Pretty Woman" was a legitimate parody of the 1964 Roy Orbison song and was thus covered by the fair use exception to copyright.

But in time, artists, as they began to live longer, and corporations, which could also hold copyrights, wanted to prolong the period in which they could profit from creative works. In 1976 Congress extended the copyright period to the life of the author plus fifty years (seventy-five years for a corporate copyright owner). In 1998 (as copyrights on works such as Disney's Mickey Mouse were set to expire), Congress again extended the copyright period for twenty additional years.

Today, nearly every innovation in digital culture creates new questions about copyright law. For example, is a video remix that samples copyrighted sounds and images a copyright violation or a creative accomplishment protected under the concept of *fair use* (the same standard that enables students to legally quote attributed text in their research papers)? One of the laws that tips the debates toward stricter enforcement of copyright is the Digital Millennium Copyright Act of 1998, which outlaws technology or actions that circumvent copyright systems. In other words, it may be illegal merely to create or distribute technology that enables someone to make illegal copies of digital content, such as a movie DVD.

The copyright lobby continues to pressure lawmakers to enact measures that would criminalize infringement. Legislation first proposed in 2011 would hold online service providers like YouTube, Internet search engines like Google, and payment service providers like Paypal accountable for policing their users and enforcing U.S. intellectual property law globally. As manifested in the Stop Online Piracy Act (SOPA) and Protect Intellectual Property Act (PIPA), this legislation has prompted recent worldwide protests, which have, as mentioned in the opening of this chapter, derailed the proposed bills—at least temporarily.

Both sides of the piracy struggle recognize that the SOPA/PIPA conflict is just a skirmish in a much longer engagement over the future of free expression on the Internet.

Libel

The biggest legal worry haunting editors and publishers today is the possibility of being sued for libel, a form of expression that, unlike political speech, is not protected under the First Amendment. **Libel** is defamation of someone's character in written or broadcast form. It differs from **slander**, which is spoken defamation.

This is the 1960 *New York Times* advertisement that triggered one of the most influential and important libel cases in U.S. history.

THE NEW YORK TIMES, TUESDAY, MARCH 29, 1960.

"The growing movement of peaceful mass demonstrations by Negroes is something new in the South, something understandable.... Let Congress heed their rising voices, for they will be heard."
—*New York Times* editorial
Saturday, March 19, 1960

Heed Their Rising Voices

Your Help Is Urgently Needed . . . NOW ! !

We in the south who are struggling daily for dignity and freedom warmly endorse this appeal

COMMITTEE TO DEFEND MARTIN LUTHER KING and THE STRUGGLE FOR FREEDOM IN THE SOUTH
312 West 125th Street, New York 27, N. Y.

Please mail this coupon TODAY!

Inherited from British common law, libel is generally defined as a false statement that holds a person up to public ridicule, contempt, or hatred or that injures a person's business or livelihood. Examples of potentially libelous statements include falsely accusing someone of professional incompetence (such as medical malpractice); falsely accusing a person of a crime (such as drug dealing); falsely stating that someone is mentally ill or engages in unacceptable behavior (such as public drunkenness); and falsely accusing a person of associating with a disreputable organization or cause (such as being a member of the Mafia or a neo-Nazi military group). (See "Media Literacy Case Study: A False *Wikipedia* 'Biography'" on page 426.)

Since 1964, *The New York Times v. Sullivan* case has served as the standard for libel law. The case stems from a 1960 full-page advertisement placed in the *New York Times* by the Committee to Defend Martin Luther King and the Struggle for Freedom in the South. Without naming names, the ad criticized the law-enforcement tactics used in southern cities to break up Civil Rights demonstrations. The city commissioner of Montgomery, Alabama, L. B. Sullivan, sued the *Times* for libel, claiming the ad defamed him indirectly. Alabama civil courts awarded Sullivan $500,000, but the *Times'* lawyers appealed to the Supreme Court. The Court reversed the ruling, holding that Alabama libel law violated the *Times'* First Amendment rights.[8]

Private individuals (such as city sanitation employees, undercover police informants, or nurses) must prove three things to win a libel case: (1) that the public statement about them was false; (2) that damages or actual injury occurred (such as loss of a job, or mental anguish); and (3) that the publisher or broadcaster was negligent in failing to determine the truthfulness of the statement.

In the *Sullivan* case, the Supreme Court asked future civil courts to distinguish whether plaintiffs in libel cases are "public officials" or "private individuals." To win libel cases, the Court said, public officials (such as movie or sports stars, political leaders, or lawyers defending a prominent client) are held to a tougher standard, and must prove falsehood, damages, negligence, and **actual malice** on the part of the news media. Actual malice means that the reporter or editor knew the statement was false and printed or broadcast it anyway, or acted with a reckless disregard for the truth. Because actual malice against a public official is hard to prove, it is difficult for public figures to win libel suits.

Historically, the best defense against libel in American courts has been the truth. In most cases, if libel defendants can demonstrate that they printed or broadcast true statements, plaintiffs will not recover any damages—even if their reputations were harmed. There are other defenses against libel as well. For example, prosecutors (who would otherwise be vulnerable to accusations of libel) are granted *absolute privilege* in a court of law so they can freely make accusatory statements toward defendants—a key part of their job. Reporters who print or broadcast statements made in court are also protected against libel.

Another defense against libel is the rule of **opinion and fair comment**, the notion that libel consists of *intentional* misstatements of factual information, not expressions of opinion. However, the line between fact and opinion is often blurry. For instance, one of the most famous tests of opinion and fair comment came with a case pitting conservative minister and political activist Jerry Falwell against Larry Flynt, publisher of *Hustler*, a pornographic magazine. The case developed after a spoof ad in the November 1983 issue of *Hustler* suggested that Falwell had had sex with his mother. Falwell sued for libel, demanding $45 million in damages. The jury rejected the libel suit but found that Flynt had intentionally caused Falwell emotional distress—and awarded Falwell $200,000. Flynt's lawyers appealed, and the U.S. Supreme Court overturned the verdict in 1988, explaining that the magazine was entitled to constitutional protection.

MEDIA LITERACY
Case Study

A False *Wikipedia* "Biography"
By John Seigenthaler

> "John Seigenthaler Sr. was the assistant to Attorney General Robert Kennedy in the early 1960's. For a brief time, he was thought to have been directly involved in the Kennedy assassinations of both John, and his brother, Bobby. Nothing was ever proven."
>
> *–Wikipedia*

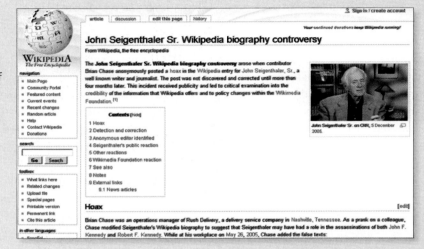

This is a highly personal story about Internet character assassination. It could be your story. I have no idea whose sick mind conceived the false, malicious "biography" that appeared under my name for 132 days on *Wikipedia*, the popular, online, free encyclopedia whose authors are unknown and virtually untraceable.

At age 78, I thought I was beyond surprise or hurt at anything negative said about me. I was wrong. One sentence in the biography was true. I was Robert Kennedy's administrative assistant in the early 1960s.

At my request, executives of the website now have removed the false content about me. I phoned Jimmy Wales, *Wikipedia*'s founder, and asked, "Do you . . . have any way to know who wrote that?"

"No, we don't," he said. Naturally, I want to unmask my "biographer." But searching cyberspace for the identity of people who post spurious information can be frustrating. I traced the registered IP (Internet Protocol) number of my "biographer" to a customer of BellSouth Internet and left two e-mails with the company's "Abuse Team."

After three weeks, hearing nothing further about the Abuse Team investigation, I phoned BellSouth's Atlanta corporate headquarters, which led to conversations between my lawyer and BellSouth's counsel. My only remote chance of getting the name, I learned, was to file a "John or Jane Doe" lawsuit against my "biographer." Major communications Internet companies are bound by federal privacy laws that protect the identity of their customers, even those who defame online. Only if a lawsuit resulted in a court subpoena would BellSouth give up the name.

Federal law also protects online corporations— BellSouth, AOL, MCI, Wikipedia, etc.—from libel lawsuits. Under the Communications Decency Act, passed in 1996—and unlike print and broadcast companies—online service providers cannot be sued for disseminating defamatory attacks on citizens posted by others.

Wikipedia's Web site acknowledges that it is not responsible for inaccurate information, but Wales, in a C-Span interview with Brian Lamb, insisted that his website is accountable and that his community of thousands of volunteer editors (he said he has only one paid employee) corrects mistakes within minutes.

My experience refutes that. My "biography" was posted May 26 [2005]. For four months, *Wikipedia* depicted me as a suspected assassin before Wales erased it from his website's history Oct. 5. And so we live in a universe of new media with phenomenal opportunities for worldwide communications and research—but populated by volunteer vandals with poison-pen intellects. Congress has enabled them and protects them.

Note: In 2006 Seigenthaler, with the help of some intrepid reporters, tracked down the man who posted the libelous content. Seigenthaler, however, chose not to sue him, deciding instead to speak out about the experience and to call on *Wikipedia* to require those who post entries to sign their names and take responsibility for their work. The controversy is now a part of his online *Wikipedia* bio and also has its own entry (pictured).

Source: Excerpted from John Seigenthaler, "A False Wikipedia 'Biography,'" USA Today, November 30, 2005, p. 11A.

APPLYING THE CRITICAL PROCESS

DESCRIPTION Go to *Wikipedia* and look up entries for three topics with which you are familiar. (For example, they could be entries on movies, a musical act, or your hometown.)

ANALYSIS Look for patterns: Are the entries accurate, with sufficient footnoted sources for verification? Is there significant information missing from the entries? When was the entry last updated (see the bottom of the entry page)? Is there an active debate about the topic?

INTERPRETATION What makes a good *Wikipedia* entry? Why might some topics receive more editing attention than others?

EVALUATION Is the mostly open editing process of *Wikipedia* a good thing or a bad thing?

ENGAGEMENT Become a registered user of Wikipedia and correct or update a *Wikipedia* entry yourself.

Libel laws also protect satire, comedy, and opinions expressed in reviews of books, plays, movies, and restaurants. However, such laws do not protect malicious statements in which plaintiffs can prove that defendants used their free-speech rights to mount an uncalled-for damaging personal attack.

Obscenity

For most of this nation's history, legislators have argued that **obscenity** is not a form of expression protected by the First Amendment. However, experts have not been able to agree on what constitutes an obscene work, especially as definitions of obscenity have changed over the years. For example, during the 1930s, novels (such as James Joyce's *Ulysses*) were judged obscene if they contained "four-letter words."

The current legal definition of obscenity, derived from the 1973 *Miller v. California* case, states that obscene materials meet three criteria: (1) the average person, applying contemporary community standards, finds the material as a whole appeals to prurient interest (i.e., incites lust); (2) the material depicts or describes sexual conduct in a patently offensive way; and (3) the material, as a whole, lacks serious literary, artistic, political, or scientific value. The *Miller* decision acknowledged that different communities and regions of the country have different standards with which to judge obscenity. It also required that a work be judged *as a whole*. This was designed to keep publishers from simply inserting a political essay or literary poem into pornographic materials to demonstrate that their publication contained redeeming features.

Since the *Miller* decision, major prosecutions of obscenity have been rare, and most battles now concern the Internet, where the concept of community standards has been eclipsed by this medium's global reach. The most recent incarnation of the Child Online Protection Act—originally formed in 1998 to make it illegal to post "material that is harmful to minors"—was found unconstitutional in 2007 because it infringed on the right to free speech online. The presiding judge in this decision also stated that the act would be ineffective, as it wouldn't apply to pornographic Web sites from overseas, which account for up to half of such sites. The ruling suggested that parents and software filters offer the best protection for children against harmful content on the Web.

Violation of Privacy Rights

Whereas libel laws safeguard a person's character and reputation, the right to privacy protects an individual's peace of mind and personal feelings. In the simplest terms, the **right to privacy** addresses a person's right to be left alone, without his or her name, image, or daily activities becoming public property.

The most common forms of privacy invasion are unauthorized tape recording, photographing, and wiretapping of someone; making someone's personal records such as health and phone records available to the public; disclosing personal information such as religious or sexual activities; and appropriating (without authorization) someone's image or name for advertising or other commercial purposes.

In general, the news media have been granted wide protections under the First Amendment to do their work even if it approaches or constitutes violation of privacy. For instance, journalists can typically use the names and pictures of private individuals and public figures without their consent in their news stories. Still, many local municipalities and states have passed "anti-paparazzi" laws protecting public individuals from unwarranted scrutiny and surveillance on their private property. A number of laws also protect regular citizens' privacy. For example, the Privacy Act of 1974 protects individuals' records from public disclosure unless they give written consent. In some cases, however, private citizens become public figures—for example, rape victims who are covered in the news. In these situations, reporters have been allowed to record these individuals' quotes and use their images without permission.

Right to privacy is different for public and private individuals. However, the recent trend of oppressive paparazzi has led to laws protecting some personal activities for celebrities.

The Electronic Communications Privacy Act of 1986 extended the law regarding private citizens to computer-stored data and the Internet, including employees' e-mails composed and sent through their employer's equipment. However, subsequent court decisions ruled that employees have no privacy rights in electronic communications conducted on their employer's equipment. The USA PATRIOT Act of 2001 further weakened the earlier laws, giving the federal government more latitude in searching private citizens' records and intercepting electronic communications without a court order.

Congress made a step toward bringing more Internet privacy to Americans by proposing the Do Not Track Me Online Act of 2011. It would give consumers the ability to opt out of having their online activity collected by private companies without their permission. But in a society that is both fiercely defensive of its privacy and widely engaged in sharing more personal information than in any other period in history, it remains unclear how individual privacy will be legally controlled in the digital age.

First Amendment versus Sixth Amendment

First Amendment protections of speech and the press have often clashed with the Sixth Amendment, which guarantees an accused individual in "all criminal prosecutions . . . the right to a speedy and public trial, by an impartial jury." Gag orders, shield laws, and laws governing use of cameras in a courtroom all put restrictions on speech and other forms of expression for the sake of Sixth Amendment rights.

Gag Orders

In recent criminal cases, some lawyers have used the news media to comment publicly on cases that are pending or in trial. This can make it difficult to assemble an impartial jury, thus threatening individuals' Sixth Amendment rights. In the 1960s, the Supreme Court introduced safeguards for ensuring fair trials in heavily publicized cases. These included placing speech restrictions, or **gag orders**, on lawyers and witnesses. In some countries, courts have issued gag orders to prohibit the press from releasing information or giving commentary that might prejudice jury selection or cause an unfair trial. But in the United States, especially since a Supreme Court review in 1976, gag orders have been struck down as a prior-restraint violation of the First Amendment.

Shield Laws

Shield laws state that reporters do not have to reveal their sources of information used in news stories. The news media have argued that protecting sources' confidentiality maintains reporters' credibility, protects sources from possible retaliation, and serves the public interest by providing information citizens might not otherwise receive. Thirty-five states and the District of Columbia now have some type of shield law. There is no federal shield law in the United States, though, leaving journalists exposed to subpoenas from federal prosecutors and courts.

Laws Regarding Use of Cameras in Courtrooms

Debates over limiting electronic broadcast equipment and photographers in courtrooms date back to the Bruno Hauptmann trial in the mid-1930s. Hauptmann was convicted and executed for the kidnap-murder of the nineteen-month-old son of Anne and Charles Lindbergh (the aviation hero who made the first solo flight across the Atlantic Ocean in 1927). During the

An early 1980s Supreme Court ruling opened the door for the debut of court TV in 1991 and the televised O. J. Simpson trial of 1994 (the most publicized case in history).

trial, Hauptmann and his attorney complained that the circus atmosphere fueled by the presence of radio and flash cameras prejudiced the jury and turned the public against him. After the trial, the American Bar Association amended its professional ethics code, stating that electronic equipment in the courtroom detracted "from the essential dignity of the proceedings." For years after the Hauptmann trial, almost every state banned photographic, radio, and TV equipment from courtrooms.

But as broadcast equipment became more portable and less obtrusive, and as television became the major news source for most Americans, courts gradually reevaluated the bans. In the early 1980s, the Supreme Court ruled that the presence of TV equipment did not make fair trials impossible. The Court then left it up to each state to implement its own system. Today, all states allow television coverage of cases, though most also allow presiding judges to place certain restrictions on coverage of courtrooms. The Supreme Court continues to ban TV from its proceedings, although in 2000, it broke its anti-radio rule by permitting delayed broadcasts of the hearings on the Florida vote recount case that determined the winner of the 2000 presidential election.

The First Amendment and Film

Back when the Bill of Rights was ratified, our nation's founders could not have predicted the advent of visual media. Film, which came into existence in the late 1890s, presented new challenges for those seeking to determine whether expression in film should be protected. The First Amendment said nothing explicit about film. So, until the Supreme Court ruled it was protected speech in 1952, movies were subject first to censorship by citizen groups and lawmakers, and then to the film industry's self-censorship.

Citizens and Lawmakers Control the Movies

During the early part of the twentieth century, movies were enormously popular with European immigrants and others of modest means. This, in turn, spurred the formation of local *review boards* by civic leaders who screened movies to

Jack Johnson (1878–1946) was the first black heavyweight boxing champion, from 1908 to 1914. His stunning victory over white champion Jim Jeffries in 1910 resulted in race riots across the country and led to a ban on the interstate transportation of boxing films.

Will Hays, the president of the Motion Picture Producers and Distributors of America, promoted self-regulation of the movie industry.

determine their moral suitability for the community. By 1920, more than ninety cities in the United States had such boards, which were comprised of vice-squad officers, politicians, or citizens. By 1923, twenty-two states had such boards.

Meanwhile, lawmakers seeking to please their constituencies introduced legislation to control films. For example, after African American Jack Johnson won the heavyweight championship in 1908, the federal government outlawed transportation of boxing movies across state lines. The move reflected racist attitudes more than distaste for violent imagery, as legislators pandered to white constituents who saw Johnson as a threat.

The first Supreme Court decision regarding film's protection under the First Amendment came in 1915 (*Mutual v. Ohio*), and reflected the prevailing attitudes toward film. The Court declared that motion pictures were not a form of speech but "a business pure and simple" and thus not protected by the First Amendment. The Court further described the film industry as a circus, a "spectacle" for entertainment with "a special capacity for evil."

The Movie Industry Regulates Itself

In the early 1920s, a series of scandals rocked Hollywood and pressured the movie industry to regulate itself. The scandals included the rape and murder of an aspiring actress at a wild party in a San Francisco hotel, allegedly by the party's host, silent-film comedian Fatty Arbuckle. Concerned that such scandals could turn Americans away from watching movies, industry leaders began putting their own regulations and watchdog groups in place to monitor movies' content and ensure that industry players (such as actors) had squeaky-clean reputations. These efforts unfolded over the next few decades, and included the formation of the Motion Picture Producers and Distributors of America watchdog group as well as the Motion Picture Production Code. Eventually, the industry also set up a ratings system.

The Motion Picture Producers and Distributors of America

In the 1920s, industry leaders hired Will Hays, a former Republican National Committee chair, as president of the Motion Picture Producers and Distributors of America (MPPDA). Hays blacklisted promising actors or movie extras who had even minor police records. He also developed a public-relations division for the

MPPDA, which promptly squelched a national movement to create a federal law censoring movies.

The Motion Picture Production Code

In the early 1930s, the Hays Office established the Motion Picture Production Code. The code stipulated that "no picture shall be produced which will lower the moral standards of those who see it. Hence the sympathy of the audience shall never be thrown to the side of crime, wrong-doing, evil or sin." The code also dictated which phrases, images, and topics producers and directors had to avoid. For example, "excessive and lustful kissing" and "suggestive postures" were not allowed. The code also prohibited negative portrayals of religion or religious figures.

Almost every executive in the industry adopted the code, viewing it as better than regulation coming from the government, and it influenced most commercial movies for the next twenty years. Things changed in 1952, when the Supreme Court decided in *Burstyn v. Wilson* that New York could not ban the Italian film *The Miracle* under state regulations barring "sacrilegious" films. The Court had decided that movies were an important vehicle for public opinion, and put American movies on the same footing as books and newspapers in terms of protection under the First Amendment.

The Rating System

In the wake of the 1952 *Miracle* case and the demise of the production code, renewed discontent over sexual language and imagery in movies pushed the MPPDA (renamed the Motion Picture Association of America, or MPAA) in the late 1960s to establish a movie-rating system to help concerned viewers avoid offensive material. Eventually, G, PG, R, and X ratings emerged as guideposts for films' suitability for various age groups. In 1984, the MPAA added the PG-13 rating to distinguish slightly higher levels of violence or adult themes in movies that might otherwise qualify as PG (see Table 14.1).

The MPAA trademarked all rating designations except for X, which the pornographic film industry gradually appropriated as a promotional tool. The MPAA, to avoid inadvertently supporting pornography, stopped issuing the X rating between 1972 and 1989. In 1990, however, filmmakers protested that some movies containing adult sexual themes were not necessarily pornographic and called for a new rating to distinguish such films. The industry copyrighted the NC-17 rating—no children age seventeen or under. But many theater chains avoided showing NC-17 films, fearing these films' strong content would drive customers away. Lacking support from theaters, few NC-17 films have succeeded commercially.

TABLE 14.1 // THE VOLUNTARY MOVIE RATING SYSTEM

Rating	Description
G	**General Audiences:** All ages admitted; contains nothing that would offend parents when viewed by their children.
PG	**Parental Guidance Suggested:** Parents urged to give "parental guidance" as it may contain some material not suitable for young children.
PG-13	**Parents Strongly Cautioned:** Parents should be cautious because some content may be inappropriate for children under the age of 13.
R	**Restricted:** The film contains some adult material. Parents/guardians are urged to learn more about it before taking children under the age of 17 with them.
NC-17	**No one 17 and under admitted:** Adult content. Children are not admitted.

Source: Motion Picture Association of America, "What Do the Ratings Mean?" accessed May 1, 2009, www.mpaa.org /FlmRat_Ratings.asp.

The First Amendment, Broadcasting, and the Internet

As the film industry developed, the lack of clarity regarding the First Amendment's protection of expression in movies prompted the industry to regulate itself. And as additional new media arose that our nation's founders could not have envisioned—namely, broadcasting and the Internet— legislators and industry players once again began debating the question of how free these media are under the First Amendment. Different types of protections and levels of regulation developed in broadcast and cyber- space. While film eventually received protections similar to print in the 1952 Supreme Court ruling, broadcast is subject to fewer protections. The Internet is so relatively new that people are still debating how First Amendment rights might apply to it.

Two Pivotal Court Cases

Drawing on the argument that limited broadcast signals constitute a scarce national resource, Congress passed the Communications Act of 1934. The act mandated that radio broadcasters operate in "the public interest, convenience, or necessity," suggesting that they were not free to air whatever they wanted. Since that time, station owners have challenged the "public interest" statute and argued that because the government is not allowed to dictate newspaper content, it similarly should not be permitted to control licenses or mandate broadcast programming. But the U.S. courts have outlined major differences between broadcast and print—as demonstrated by two cases.

The first case—*Red Lion Broadcasting Co. v. FCC* (1969)—began when WGCB, a small-town radio station in Red Lion, Pennsylvania, refused to give airtime to author Fred Cook. Cook wrote a book criticizing Barry Goldwater, the Republican Party's presidential candidate in 1964. On a syndicated show WGCB aired, a conservative radio preacher and Goldwater fan verbally attacked Cook on-air. Cook asked for response time from the stations that carried the attack. Most complied, but WGCB snubbed him. He appealed to the FCC, which ordered the station to give Cook free time. The station refused, claiming the First Amendment gave it control over its programming content. The Supreme Court sided with the FCC and ordered the station to give Cook airtime, arguing that the public interest—in this case, the airing of differing viewpoints—outweighs a broadcaster's rights.

The second case—*Miami Herald Publishing Co. v. Tornillo* (1974)—centered on the question of whether the newspaper in this case, the *Miami Herald*, should have been forced to give political candidate Pat Tornillo Jr. space to reply to an editorial opposing his candidacy. In contrast to the *Red Lion* decision, the Supreme Court sided with the paper. The Court argued that forcing a newspaper to give a candidate space violated the paper's First Amendment right to decide what to publish. Clearly, print media had more freedom of expression than did broadcasting.

Dirty Words, Indecent Speech, and Hefty Fines

Like the Supreme Court's rulings in the *Red Lion* and *Miami Herald* cases, regulators' actions regarding indecency in broadcasting reflected the idea that broadcasters had less freedom of expression than print media did. In theory, communication law says that the government cannot censor (prohibit before the fact) broadcast content. However, the government may punish broadcasters *after* the fact for **indecency**.

Concerns over indecent broadcast programming cropped up in 1937 when the FCC scolded NBC for airing a sketch featuring sultry comedian-actress Mae West. After

The sexual innuendo of an "Adam and Eve" radio sketch between sultry film star Mae West and dummy Charlie McCarthy (voiced by ventriloquist Edgar Bergen) enraged many listeners. The networks banned West from further radio appearances for what was considered "indecent" speech.

the sketch, which West peppered with sexual innuendos, the networks banned her from further radio appearances for "indecent" speech. Since then, the FCC has periodically fined or reprimanded stations for indecent programming, especially during times when children might be listening. For example, after an FCC investigation in the 1970s, several stations lost their licenses or were fined for broadcasting *topless radio*, which featured deejays and callers discussing intimate sexual subjects in the afternoon. (Topless radio would reemerge in the 1980s, this time with doctors and therapists—instead of deejays—offering intimate counsel to listeners.)

The current precedent for regulating broadcast indecency stems from a complaint to the FCC that came in 1973. In the middle of the afternoon, WBAI, a nonprofit Pacifica network station in New York, aired George Carlin's famous comedy sketch about the "seven dirty words" that can't be said on TV. A man riding in a car with his fifteen-year-old son heard the program and complained to the FCC, which sent WBAI a letter of reprimand. Although no fine was issued, the station appealed on principle—and won its case in court. The FCC promptly appealed to the Supreme Court. Though no court had legally defined indecency (which remains undefined today), the Supreme Court sided with the FCC in the 1978 *FCC v. Pacifica Foundation* case. The decision upheld the FCC's authority to require broadcasters to air adult programming only at times when children were not likely to be listening. The FCC banned indecent programs from most stations between 6:00 A.M. and 10:00 P.M.

The current precedent for indecency is based on a complaint about comedian George Carlin's sketch about the "seven dirty words" that could not be aired.

Political Broadcasts and Equal Opportunity

In addition to indecency rules, another law affecting broadcasting but not the print media is **Section 315** of the 1934 Communications Act. The section mandates that during elections, broadcast stations must provide equal opportunities and response time for qualified political candidates. In other words, if broadcasters give or sell time to one candidate, they must give or sell the same opportunity to others. Local broadcasters and networks have fought this law for years, claiming that because no similar rule applies to newspapers or magazines, the law violates their First Amendment right to

CONVERGING MEDIA
Case Study

Convergent Bullying

In his 2008 report "The Trolls among Us," Mattathias Schwartz describes a variety of cruel pranks and anonymous bullying online: hacking the MySpace account of a teen suicide victim and altering photos to make him look like a zombie, or attacking the Epilepsy Foundation's Web site and posting flashing seizure-inducing graphics on its discussion forums.[1] These sorts of acts have spawned a number of state laws meant to curb online harassment and bullying, but bullies know the new laws are virtually impossible to enforce. Local police usually do not have the technical know-how and resources needed to track down an anonymous troll, and federal agencies have larger concerns in terms of Internet crime, like identity theft, terrorism, and child pornography.

Internet-based convergence means that many people need not stay in front of a computer screen to access e-mail, Twitter, Facebook, and other social media; bullies, then, can follow their victims virtually anywhere. Though some of this harassment depends on anonymity, the most devastating form of cyberbullying is committed by people who know the victim. This was certainly the case in a series of widely reported teen suicides over the last ten years. One, thirteen-year-old Megan Meier, ended her life after receiving a MySpace message: "The world would be a better place without you." Megan thought the message was from a cute boy named Josh Evans. But Josh Evans turned out to be the invention of a forty-seven-year-old woman named Lori Drew who lived down the street from Megan. Megan had recently ended her friendship with Drew's daughter, a decision that prompted Drew to create the Josh Evans MySpace page and, as she put it to another neighbor, "mess with Megan." Though Drew's subsequent conviction of a misdemeanor violation of the Computer Fraud and Abuse Act would later be overturned, the case prompted Missouri to

update its harassment law to cover the Internet. It also inspired the proposed Megan Meier Cyberbullying Prevention Act, which would have made it a felony to transmit by electronic means any message "with the intent to coerce, intimidate, harass, or cause substantial emotional distress to a person." Though supported by such groups as Web Wise Kids, the bill also attracted the scorn of free-speech advocates who pointed out the proposed legislation was inconsistent with First Amendment protections. As a consequence, the bill never made it out of committee.

Online bullying demonstrates another way in which the virtual world and "real" world have converged, and that while online harassment may seem less real, it can have equally dire consequences. As such, the ubiquity of the Internet makes it subject to the same tough questions regarding freedom of speech as other media, and raises even more difficult questions of what is considered allowable free speech and what constitutes harassment or hate speech. Hateful forms of speech may indeed be the acid test of a vibrant democracy, a test with such paradoxical implications as tolerating intolerance, or defending the indefensible. Such contradictions are at the heart of living as an informed, media-literate citizen in a diverse and conflicted democracy.

control content. Many stations decided to avoid political programming entirely, ironically reversing the rule's original intention. The TV networks managed to get the law amended in 1959 to exempt newscasts, press conferences, and other events—such as political debates—that qualify as news. For instance, if a senator running for office appears in a news story, opposing candidates cannot invoke Section 315 and demand free time.

Supporters of the equal opportunity law in broadcasting argue that it enables lesser-known candidates representing views counter to those of the Democratic and Republican parties to add their perspectives to political dialogue. It also gives less wealthy candidates a more affordable channel than newspaper and magazine ads for getting their message out to the public.

Fair Coverage of Controversial Issues

Considered an important corollary to Section 315, the **Fairness Doctrine** was to controversial issues what Section 315 is to political speech. Initiated in 1949, this FCC rule required stations to air programs about controversial issues affecting their communities and to provide competing points of view during the programs. Broadcasters again protested that the print media did not have to obey these requirements. And once more, many stations simply avoided airing controversial issues. The Fairness Doctrine ended with little public debate in 1987 after a federal court ruled that it was merely a regulation, not an extension of Section 315 law.

Since 1987, however, support for reviving the Fairness Doctrine has surfaced periodically. Its advocates argue that broadcasting is fundamentally different from—and more pervasive than—print media. Thus, it should be more accountable to the public interest. The end of the Fairness Doctrine might have contributed to a more polarized political climate, fed in part by news networks unburdened by the requirement to provide different points of view. On the other hand, the lack of requirements could also allow the dissemination of other views that might not otherwise garner much attention.

Communication Policy and the Internet

Because the Internet is not regulated by the government, not subject to the Communications Act of 1934, and has done little self-regulating, many people see it as the one true venue for unlimited free speech under the First Amendment. Its current global expansion is comparable to the early days of broadcasting, when economic and technological growth outstripped law and regulation.

Early debates about what forms of expression should be allowed on the Internet typically revolved around issues such as civility and pornography. Those discussions have continued (see "Converging Media Case Study: Online Bullying" on page 437), but the debate has expanded to issues like government surveillance and how traditional means like wiretapping and search warrants can be expanded to include the turning over of Internet browsing histories and other data. As this medium continues to expand rapidly, we will need to consider some important questions: Will the Internet remain free of government attempts to contain it, change it, and monitor who has access to it? Can the Internet continue to serve as a democratic forum for regional, national, and global interest groups? Many global movements use this medium to fight political oppression. Human Rights Watch, for example, encourages free-expression advocates to use blogs "for disseminating information about, and ending, human rights abuses around the world."[9]

The First Amendment in a Democratic Society

Ultimately, questions about the First Amendment's implications for freedom of expression in mass media are really about democracy. And when it comes to our democracy, the news media—whether print, TV, radio, or the Internet—play a particularly important role. For most of our nation's history, citizens have counted on journalists to alert them to abuses in government and business. But today, news stories tend to address us more as consumers instead of citizens, focusing, for example, on how a business merger affects the immediate price of a product rather than the long-term social and economic impact on workers and communities. Moreover, as newspapers, TV stations, radio stations, and Internet corporations are merged into larger entertainment corporations, or media workers' jobs are threatened by outsourcing and consolidation, it has become more difficult for journalists to adequately cover and lead critical discussions about media ownership, media regulation, and business practices in general.

For these reasons, it has become more important than ever for citizens to share the watchdog role with journalists. Citizen action groups like Free Press, the Media Access Project, and the Center for Digital Democracy have worked to bring media ownership issues into the mainstream. They remind us that the First Amendment protects not only the news media's free-speech rights but also the rights of all of us to speak out. Mounting concerns over who can afford access to the media go to the heart of free expression. As we struggle

WikiLeaks editor Julian Assange launched the site in 2007. He claims that WikiLeaks has released more classified documents than the rest of the world press combined.

to determine the future of converging print, electronic, and digital media and to broaden the democratic spirit underlying media technology, we need to take part in spirited public debates about media ownership and control, about the differences between commercial speech and free expression. As citizens, we must pay attention to who is included and excluded from opportunities not only to buy products but also to voice their views and thereby shape our nation's cultural and political landscape. To accomplish this, we have to challenge government and business leaders—rather than assuming that journalists will do so.

In this regard, the Web site WikiLeaks represents the most extreme, controversial, and effective of the organizations devoted to "getting the unvarnished truth out to the public." Officially launched in 2007, WikiLeaks is known for generating headlines by publishing sensitive corporate communications and secret government documents provided by anonymous sources. For example, in November 2010, the organization supplied five newspapers with the first of 250,000 leaked diplomatic cables from 274 U.S. embassies around the world. Cables addressing the corruption of Tunisian President Ben Ali reportedly helped rally activists in the first of the successful "Arab Spring" revolutions.[10]

But the site's most celebrated and notorious work to date attracted worldwide attention with a "data spill" of classified U.S. military documents. The most sensational of this material was the release in April 2010 of video taken from one of two helicopters firing on a crowd of armed and unarmed people in Baghdad. Eighteen were killed in the attack, including two reporters from the Reuters news agency. Later in 2010, Julian Assange, the "editor in chief" of WikiLeaks, worked with journalists at the *New York Times*, the *Guardian*, and *Der Spiegel* to publish more classified material, though care was taken to redact names and not print information that might put lives at risk.[11]

WikiLeaks continues to release classified and sensitive documents acquired from anonymous sources. It also raises a number of troubling questions about freedom of speech in the age of convergent media. Are there limits to the public's right to know? Under what conditions do secrecy and confidentiality serve the public interest? Who benefited from the release of military footage of the helicopter attack in Baghdad? Who suffered? What ultimately was accomplished by this action?

Regardless of views on WikiLeaks, the health of our democracy demands an informed electorate, not one that is kept in the dark about who we really are, what we stand for, why we go to war, and how those wars are fought. We need not approve of the methods employed by WikiLeaks in order to recognize the worth of such watchdog groups devoted to keeping the government—and the press—honest.

CHAPTER ESSENTIALS

Now that you have finished reading this chapter, you can use the following tools:

REVIEW

Track the Origins of Free Expression and Free Press

- In the United States, freedom of speech and freedom of the press are protected by the First Amendment in the Bill of Rights. However, Americans have long debated what constitutes "free expression." Around the globe, four different interpretations emerged of what "free expression" means: the **authoritarian model** (which tolerates little criticism of government or public dissent), the **state model** (in which the government controls the press), the **social responsibility model** (in which the press is privately owned and functions as a **Fourth Estate**—an unofficial branch of government that watches for abuses of power by the legislative, judicial, and executive branches), and the **libertarian model** (which encourages vigorous criticism of government and supports the highest degree of individual and press freedoms) (pp. 417–420).

- Though the First Amendment prohibits censorship, which is defined as **prior restraint**—meaning that courts and governments cannot block any publication or speech *before* it actually occurs—two pivotal court cases have tested this idea: the Pentagon Papers case and the *Progressive* magazine case (pp. 420–422).

- Some forms of expression are not protected under the Constitution. These forms include sedition, copyright infringement (a **copyright** legally protects the rights of the authors and producers to their published or unpublished writing for a specified period of time, after which the work enters the **public domain**, allowing the public free access to the work), and **libel** or defamation of someone's character (which differs from **slander** or spoken defamation). To win a libel case, public officials must prove falsehood, damages, negligence, and **actual malice** (meaning that a reporter or an editor knew the statement was false and printed it anyway). Defenses against libel include the truth and the rule of **opinion and fair comment**—the notion that opinions, unlike statements of factual information, are protected from libel. Other forms of expression not protected by the Constitution are **obscenity**, which people have had difficulty defining over the years, and violation of privacy (the **right to privacy** addresses a person's right to be left alone without personal information becoming public property) (pp. 422–425, 428–429).

- The First Amendment has clashed with the Sixth Amendment, which guarantees accused individuals the right to speedy and public trials by impartial juries. **Gag orders** (speech restrictions) and laws governing use of cameras in the courtroom put restrictions on speech and other forms of expression for the sake of Sixth Amendment rights, whereas **shield laws** protect reporters from revealing confidential sources of information used in news stories (pp. 430–431).

Discuss the Relationship between the First Amendment and Film

- The advent of film presented new challenges for those seeking to determine whether expression in film should be protected. For the first half of the twentieth century, citizen groups and the Supreme Court failed to recognize movies as protected speech. The movie industry began regulating itself to safeguard its profits and avoid further government oversight (pp. 431–434).

Explain the Relationship between the First Amendment, Broadcasting, and the Internet

- Because it uses the public airwaves, broadcasting receives fewer protections than film and print. Though government cannot censor broadcast content, it may punish broadcasters after the fact for **indecency** or profanity. In addition, **Section 315** of the 1934 Communications Act mandates that during elections, broadcast stations must provide equal opportunities and response time for qualified political candidates. From 1949 to 1987, an important corollary to Section 315, the **Fairness Doctrine**, required stations to air programs about controversial issues affecting their communities and to provide competing points of view during the programs (pp. 435–436, 438).

- Since the Internet is not regulated by the government, not subject to the Communications Act of 1934, and has done little self-regulating, many consider it a true venue for free speech, though debates exist about what forms of expression should be allowed (pp. 438–439).

Understand the Role of the First Amendment in Our Democratic Society

- Questions about the First Amendment's influence over freedom of expression in mass media are centered on democracy (p. 439).

- As journalism becomes compromised by the business of media, sites like WikiLeaks have become de facto watchdog groups, raising questions about the public's right to know sensitive information (pp. 440–441).

STUDY QUESTIONS

1. What is the basic philosophical concept that underlies America's notion of free expression?
2. How did both the Motion Picture Production Code and the current movie rating system come into being?
3. How does the Supreme Court view print and broadcasting as different forms of expression?
4. Why is the future of watchdog journalism in jeopardy?

MEDIA LITERACY PRACTICE

Broadcasters are required to operate in "the public interest, convenience, or necessity." But these days, renewing a radio or TV station license is a relatively easy thing and can be done on a postcard every eight years. Work in groups of three or four to explore how well broadcasters serve your area. Ask each person to visit a radio or TV station during business hours to view their FCC file. (They are required by law to let you read it.)

DESCRIBE the content of the files of each station, noting what activities have been in the public interest over several years. Share your descriptions with the group.

ANALYZE the patterns in the public files. Do some stations contribute in a greater capacity than others?

INTERPRET what these patterns mean. Do the activities constitute operations in "the public interest, convenience, or necessity"? Are these things the station would likely be doing anyway, or do the federal requirements compel it to do more extraordinary things?

EVALUATE the stations' commitment to the public interest. Do they do enough in the public interest to merit their broadcast license?

ENGAGE with the community by writing to the stations to criticize or commend them on their commitment to public interest in your community. Make sure to send a copy to the FCC, since your letter will become part of the stations' public record.

⊚ ONLINE RESOURCES

Go to **bedfordstmartins.com/mediaessentials** for review quizzes, links, and more.

Visit the site's **VIDEOCENTRAL: MASS COMMUNICATION** section for videos like the one on page 430. There, you can find additional exclusive videos related to Chapter 14, including:

THE FIRST AMENDMENT AND STUDENT SPEECH
Legal and newspaper professionals explain how student newspapers are protected by the First Amendment.

FREEDOM OF INFORMATION
Ken Bunting, executive director of the National Freedom of Information Coalition, explains the importance of government transparency and accountability, particularly in an age of digital communication.

15

Media Economics and the Global Marketplace

In the 1880s, Benjamin Wonsal, a Polish cobbler, and his wife, Pearl Eichelbaum, brought their family to America. The New World promised a fresh start, and in the next century, four of their sons would give credence to the myth of America as the land of opportunity, a land that enabled the humblest of immigrants to achieve great power and wealth—though that story would not be punctuated with a standard happy ending.

In 1903, Ben and Pearl's three oldest sons (Hirsz, Aaron, and Szmul) pooled their resources to purchase a motion picture projector. With this device, they traveled through the hinterlands of Ohio and Pennsylvania exhibiting films like *The Great Train Robbery*. Nickel by nickel, they more than recovered their investment, and by 1907—the year the family name was changed to Warner—the brothers used their savings to open their first permanent movie theater. In 1918, the men now known as Harry, Albert, and Sam Warner—along with younger brother, Jack—relocated to Hollywood, where they opened a studio. In 1925, the visionary Sam convinced his siblings to gamble their profits on a new technology that was destined to forever change the movies. Thanks to this daring investment, Warner Brothers Pictures would release *The Jazz Singer*, the world's first talkie, in 1927. Starring Al Jolson, the game-changing film told the bittersweet story of Jewish assimilation into the

American melting pot. Tragically, Sam Warner (the brother most responsible for the studio's venture into sound) died just two days before the film's triumphant opening.

In forcing the conversion to sound, the Warner brothers unleashed a change that swept away many of the stars and studios that had dominated the silent era. On their ruins, a new movie oligopoly emerged made up of a handful of vertically integrated movie companies that would be called the "Big Five." Warner Brothers Pictures enjoyed membership in this elite group and became home to the gangster film and hard-boiled stars like James Cagney, Edward G. Robinson, Barbara Stanwyck, Bette Davis, and Humphrey Bogart. Bugs Bunny, Daffy Duck, Tweety Bird, and Porky Pig also enhanced the Warner's brand during this period in the hugely popular *Looney Tunes* and *Merrie Melodies* cartoon series. In 1942, the studio produced the greatest of Hollywood's patriotic wartime romances, *Casablanca*.

During the postwar period, Warner Brothers Pictures, like the rest of Hollywood, suffered from the competition of television and the inquisition of the House Un-American Activities Committee (HUAC), accusing film artists of communist propaganda. But the saddest moment in the family business, at least since Sam's death, came in 1956 when Jack double-crossed Harry and Albert to seize total control of the studio. Harry's collapse from a mild heart attack on learning of Jack's betrayal sent his health on a fatal tailspin that would culminate in his death in 1958.

Jack sold the studio in 1966 to Seven Arts Productions for $32 million, and the Warner brand took on a life of its own separate from its founding brothers. Marked by acquisition, takeover, and merger, the brand would survive several incarnations: Warner Bros.-Seven Arts (1966), Warner Communication (1972), Time Warner (1990), AOL Time Warner (2000), and again Time Warner (2003). A decade after the disastrous merger with AOL, a brand that quickly declined, Time Warner still ranks as the world's second largest entertainment conglomerate in terms of revenue (behind Disney).

TIME WARNER AND DISNEY ARE TWO EXAMPLES OF ENORMOUSLY SUCCESSFUL entertainment conglomerates that have survived years of leadership changes and power struggles. But not all of the mergers, takeovers, and acquisitions that have swept through the global media industries in the last twenty years have capitalized on the histories and reputations of the corporations involved. Take, for instance, the ill-timed purchase of MySpace by News Corp. in 2005. Paying $580 million for what was then the world's most popular social media site, Rupert

Murdoch would watch a newcomer named Mark Zuckerberg (and his site Facebook) reduce the value of MySpace to $35 million, the price Justin Timberlake and Specific Media, Inc., paid for the service in 2011. Despite such spectacular exceptions, many other cases of ownership convergence have provided even more economic benefit to the massive multinational corporations that dominate the current media landscape. As a consequence, we currently find ourselves enmeshed and implicated in an immense media economy characterized by consolidation of power and corporate ownership in just a few hands. This phenomenon, combined with the advent of the Internet, has made our modern media world markedly distinct from that of earlier generations—at least in economic terms. Not only has a handful of media giants—from Time Warner to Google—emerged, but the Internet has permanently transformed the media landscape. The Internet has dried up newspapers' classified-ad revenues; altered the way music, movies, and TV programs get distributed and exhibited; and forced almost all media businesses to rethink the content they will provide and how they will provide it.

In this chapter, we explore the developments and tensions shaping this brave new world of mass media by:

- examining the transition our nation has made from a manufacturing to an information economy, by considering how the media industries' structures have evolved, the impact of deregulation, the rise of media powerhouses through consolidation, trends that shape and reshape media industries, and theories about why U.S. citizens tend not to speak up about the dark side of mass media

- analyzing today's media economy, including how media organizations make money and formulate strategies, and how the Internet has changed the rules of the media game

- assessing the specialization and use of synergy currently characterizing media, by tracing the story of the Walt Disney Company as an example

- taking stock of the social challenges the new media economy has raised, such as subversion of antitrust laws, consumers' loss of control in the marketplace, and American culture's infiltration into other cultures

- evaluating the media marketplace's role in our democracy, by considering questions such as whether consolidation of media hurts or helps democracy and what impact recent media reform movements might have

In 1911 John D. Rockefeller Sr., considered the richest businessman in the world, saw his powerful monopoly, Standard Oil, busted into more than thirty separate companies.

The Transition to an Information Economy

In the first half of the twentieth century, the U.S. economy was built on mass production, the proliferation of manufacturing plants, and intense rivalry with businesses in other nations. By mid-century, this manufacturing-based economy began transitioning into an economy fueled by information (which new technologies made easier to generate and exchange anywhere) and by cooperation with other economies. Offices displaced factories as major work sites, centralized mass production declined in the United States and other developed nations, and American firms began outsourcing manufacturing work to developing countries where labor was cheap and environmental standards were lax.

Mass media industries seized the opportunity to expand globally. They began marketing music, movies, television programs, and computer software overseas. And the media mergers-and-acquisitions (M&A) drive that had begun in the United States in the 1960s expanded into global media consolidation by the 1980s.

This transition from a manufacturing-based to an information-based economy had several defining points: Early regulation designed to break up monopolies in

CHAPTER 15 // TIMELINE

1928 Disney Founded
Disney begins as a small animation studio in Hollywood.

1952 News Corp.
Rupert Murdoch inherits two Australian newspapers from his father, beginning what will grow into the News Corp. media empire.

1980s AT&T
AT&T, a telephone monopoly approved and regulated by the government for more than a hundred years, is broken up.

1985 GE Buys NBC
The merger sets off a wave of media consolidation.

1994 NAFTA and WTO
NAFTA in 1994 and the WTO in 1995 further encourage trade and the export of certain jobs.

1995 Disney Empire
Disney buys ABC.

manufacturing-related industries such as oil, railroads, and steel gave way to deregulation, which ultimately catalyzed the M&A drive that created media powerhouses. These information-based corporations in turn fueled new trends in the industry (including a decline of unionized labor and a growing wage gap). Soon a new society took shape—one in which the biggest media companies defined the values that dominated culture not only in the United States but also around the globe.

How Media Industries Are Structured

Most industries that make up the media economy have one of three common structures: monopoly, oligopoly, and limited competition.

Monopoly

A **monopoly** arises when a single firm dominates production and distribution in a particular industry—nationally or locally. For example, at the national level, AT&T ran a rare government-approved and -regulated monopoly—the telephone business—for more than a hundred years until the government broke it up in the mid-1980s. And Microsoft dominates the worldwide market for business computer operating systems.

On the local level, monopolies have proved more plentiful, arising in any city that has only one newspaper or one cable company. The federal government has encouraged

Microsoft remains one of the most powerful monopolies of the Digital Age. Here, CEO Steve Ballmer discusses the company's new media products.

1996 Time Warner The company buys Turner Broadcasting.

1996 Media Merger The Telecommunications Act of 1996 unleashes a huge wave of media mergers.

2001 AOL and Time Warner AOL, the largest Internet service provider at the time, merges with Time Warner, the largest media corporation.

2009 More Cable Deregulation A U.S. federal court strikes down the FCC's regulation limiting a cable company's holdings to not more than 30 percent of the U.S. cable market.

2011 Comcast Buys NBC Cable giant Comcast completes a deal to buy a majority share of NBC Universal.

owner diversity since the 1970s by prohibiting a newspaper from operating a broadcast or cable company in the same city. But since 2003, the Federal Communication Commission (FCC) has made several efforts to relax cross-ownership rules, arguing that the Internet and cable and satellite television provide sufficient informational diversity for citizens. Media activists have countered that the large traditional media are still the dominant news media in any market, and that when they merge, it results in fewer independent media voices.

Oligopoly

In an **oligopoly**, just a few firms dominate an industry. For example, in the late 1980s, the production and distribution of the world's music was controlled by only six corporations. By 2004, after a series of acquisitions, the "big six" had been reduced to the "big four"—Time Warner (U.S.), Sony (Japan), Universal (France), and EMI (Great Britain). In late 2011, Universal purchased EMI at auction; the deal, when finalized, will leave only three corporations controlling the vast majority of the world's music. The Internet is also changing the music game, enabling companies like Apple to gain new dominance with innovative business models such as the iTunes store. Time will reveal whether "the big three" maintain their status as an oligopoly.

Firms that make up an oligopoly face little economic competition from small independent firms. However, many oligopolies have purchased independent companies to nurture the fresh ideas and products the small companies have generated. Without the financial backing of an oligopoly, those ideas and products might not have made it to market.

Limited Competition

Limited competition characterizes a media market that has many producers and sellers but only a few products within a particular category.[1] For instance, hundreds of independently owned radio stations operate in the United States. However, most of these commercial stations feature just a few formats—such as country, classic rock, news/talk, or contemporary hits. Fans of other formats—including blues, alternative country, and classical music—may not be able to find a radio station that matches their interests. Of course, as with music, the Internet is changing radio, too, enabling companies like Pandora and Spotify to offer streaming audio for a huge array of formats.

Deregulation Trumps Regulation

Starting in the early twentieth century, Congress passed several acts intended to break up corporate trusts and monopolies, which often fixed prices to force competitors out of business. But later in the century, many business leaders began complaining that such regulation was restricting the flow of capital essential for funding business activities. U.S. President Jimmy Carter (1977–81) initiated deregulation, and President Ronald Reagan (1981–89) dramatically weakened most controls on business (e.g., environmental and worker safety rules). Many corporations in a wide range of industries flourished in this new procommerce climate. Deregulation also made it easier for companies to merge, diversify, and, in industries such as airlines, energy, communications, and financial services, to form oligopolies.[2]

In the broadcast industry, the Telecommunications Act of 1996 (under U.S. President Bill Clinton) lifted most restrictions on how many radio and TV stations one corporation could own. The act further permitted regional telephone companies to buy cable firms. In addition, cable operators regained the right to raise their rates with less oversight and to compete in the local telephone business. Why this shift to deregulation in the communications industry? With new cable channels, DBS, and the Internet, lawmakers no longer saw broadcasting as a scarce resource—once a major rationale for regulation as well as government funding of noncommercial and educational stations.

Not surprisingly, the 1996 act unleashed a wave of mergers in the industry, as television, radio, cable, telephone, and Internet companies fought to become the biggest corporations in their business sector and acquire new subsidiaries in other media sectors. The act also revealed legislators' growing openness to make special exemptions for communications companies. For example, in 1995, despite complaints from NBC, News Corp. had received a special dispensation from the FCC and Congress that allowed the firm to continue owning and operating the Fox network and a number of local TV stations.

Today, regulation of the communications industry is even looser. In late 2007, the FCC relaxed its rules further when it said that a company located in a Top 20 market (ranging in size from New York to Orlando, Florida) could own one TV station and one newspaper as long as there were at least eight TV stations in that market. Previously, a company could not own a newspaper and a broadcast outlet (a TV or radio station) in the same market. In 2009, a U.S. federal court struck down the FCC's regulation limiting a cable company's holdings to not more than 30 percent of the U.S. cable market, opening the possibility for a new round of unlimited cable mergers and acquisitions.

The Rise of Media Powerhouses

Until the 1980s, antitrust rules attempted to ensure diversity of ownership among competing businesses. Sometimes this goal was achieved in media industries.

In the mid-1980s, for instance, the Justice Department broke up AT&T's century-old monopoly, creating competition in the telephone industry. Other times this goal was not achieved. For example, monopolies persisted among local newspaper and cable companies. But overall, there has been much more consolidation than competition in the world of mass media.

One reason is that twentieth-century antitrust laws have been unevenly applied in media industries, forcing competition in some industries while allowing consolidation in others. For example, as the Justice Department broke up AT&T to create competition in the telephone industry, it also authorized several mass media mergers that concentrated power in the hands of a few behemoths. These included General Electric's purchase of RCA/NBC in the 1980s, Disney's acquisition of ABC for $19 billion in 1995, and Time Warner's buying of Turner Broadcasting for $7.5 billion in 1996. In 2001, AOL acquired Time Warner for $106 billion—the largest media merger in history at the time. In 2011, cable giant Comcast purchased a majority share of NBC Universal, once the deal was approved by regulatory agencies.

As traditional mass media corporations have grown bigger, in the twenty-first century we've also seen the rise of new media powerhouses. Companies like Apple, Google, Amazon, and Facebook aren't experts at creating media programming, but they've envisioned new ways for us to experience media content—buying content from their retail stores (e.g., the iTunes store and Amazon.com), consuming content on their innovative devices (e.g., the iPad, the Kindle Fire, a Google Android mobile phone), and linking us to other media content (via Google search, and our friends on Facebook). Imagine experiencing the mass media without using a product or service of one of these companies, and you begin to understand how this "digital turn," with these four companies leading the way, has transformed the mass communication environment in less than a decade (see "Converging Media Case Study: Shifting Economics" on page 455).

VideoCentral ⊚
**bedfordstmartins.com
/mediaessentials**

The Impact of Media Ownership
Media critics and professionals debate the pros and cons of media conglomerates.
Discussion: This video argues that it is the drive for bottom-line profits that leads to conglomerates. What solution(s) might you suggest to make the media system work better?

Analyzing the Media Economy

The immense reach and heft of the mass media economy raises some complicated questions—such as what role government should play in regulating media ownership. Should citizens step up demands for more accountability from media? Is American culture, expressed through our mass media, hurting other cultures? And is concentration of ownership

CONVERGING MEDIA
Case Study

Shifting Economics

The advent of the Internet has brought about a number of major economic changes, and as media continue to converge, we can expect the status quo to keep shifting. For example, when the Internet was first emerging as a mass medium in the early 1990s, one of the most popular ways of accessing it was through a subscription to America Online (AOL). AOL offered a simple, easy-to-use interface with its own e-mail, chat, and other content, as well as early Web browsing. As the World Wide Web became more popular, AOL stock soared as it made the then-novel experience of exploring the Web manageable, and its "walled garden" approach to access helped parents shield children from unsavory aspects of the Internet.

But as the Internet became less mysterious and more commonplace, that model of access became less relevant; while AOL's 2001 merger with Time Warner failed, Time Warner found greater success with another telecommunication spin-off: Time Warner Cable, which began to offer high-speed Internet access in the late 1990s. This model—getting Internet service from a cable or phone company—has become more dominant.

This development has, in turn, changed the way many people pay for media content. Before the converged Internet, the easiest way to gain constant access to a particular song, album, or movie was to buy it, on discs or cassettes. Some consumers still buy physical CDs or Blu-ray discs, of course, but those particularly conscious of clutter, budget, or their own shifting tastes may instead opt to stream their music online on services like Spotify, watch TV shows on Hulu, or, it must be said, download media illegally. All of this requires a high-speed Internet connection, meaning that money that might have gone to music labels or movie studios now heads toward telecommunication providers.

Authors and owners of media content are still trying to figure out how best to navigate this altered economic landscape, experimenting with different methods of generating revenue. Cable television, for example, so often packaged with high-speed Internet, could eventually become outmoded like AOL as more people subscribe to services like Netflix or Hulu Plus, where programming is less bound by particular channels or airtimes—and fees don't match those charged by cable companies. These services also pay studios to license their programming, which could be a path to traditional profitability for individual movies and TV shows. The main hubs of digital convergence—Apple, Google, Amazon, and Facebook—have become important conduits for mass media content, with their applications, online stores, and enormous user bases and may continue to grow. Consumers, of course, will continue to spend money on media and communication, but where that money ultimately goes, and who reaps the greatest rewards, may not stay constant.

in the media damaging our democracy? To explore possible answers to these questions, we examine how media industries are structured, how companies in these industries operate, and how the Internet is transforming the media economy.

How Media Companies Operate

In analyzing how media companies operate, economists pay attention to several things—including how these firms make money, and how they formulate strategies for establishing their prices, marketing their offerings, and meeting stakeholders' expectations and demands.

Making Money

Media companies bring in money from two sources: direct and indirect payments. **Direct payments** come from consumers who buy media products, such as books, movies, and Internet or cable TV services. **Indirect payments** derive from advertisers—companies that purchase ads in various media to attract specific consumers of those media. Over-the-air radio and TV broadcasting, daily newspapers, consumer magazines, and most Web sites rely on indirect payments for most of their revenue. But many media companies generate revenue through direct *and* indirect payments. These include newspapers, magazines, online services, and cable systems, which charge subscription fees in addition to selling commercial space and time to advertisers.

Increasingly, new media products must blur the line between the two forms of payment. Sales and rentals of physical media such as CDs and DVDs are declining (though legal downloads contribute to direct payments), while streaming services for music, TV, and movies are becoming more popular. This leads to consumers making direct payments for access to services like Netflix, Hulu, and Spotify, as well as to telecommunication companies who provide the Internet service needed to use those services, rather than direct payments to the companies who produce the content itself. Indirect payments are then made to the content producers by the various services and telecommunications companies.

Formulating Business Strategies

Media companies formulate strategies governing all their business processes. For instance, a local newspaper determines how high it can raise its monthly print or digital subscription price before enough disgruntled readers will drop their subscriptions and offset any profits made from the price increase. Or a book publisher tries to achieve **economies of scale** by increasing production levels to reduce the cost for each book printed.

Expectations of stakeholders—including customers, investors, and regulators—also strongly shape media companies' business strategies. For example, economists, media critics, and consumer organizations have asked the mass media to meet certain performance criteria. These criteria include meeting profit goals, introducing new technologies to the marketplace, making media products and services available to less affluent people, facilitating free expression and robust political discussion, watching for wrongdoing in government and business, monitoring crises, playing a positive role in education, and maintaining the quality of culture.[3]

Media companies are living up to some of these expectations better than others. To illustrate, news executives may trim budgets and downsize the staff to improve profit margins, but those actions may also undermine the newsroom's ability to adequately cover crucial topics and work as watchdogs of society.

How the Internet Is Changing the Game

Historically, media companies have operated in separate industries. That is, the newspaper business functioned separately from book publishing, which operated differently from radio, which in turn worked totally unlike the film industry.

The Internet has changed all that. This medium has not only provided a whole new portal through which people can consume older media forms, it has also pressured virtually all older media companies to establish an online presence. Today newspapers, magazines, book publishers, music companies, radio and TV stations, and film studios all have Web sites or mobile apps marketing digital versions and ancillaries of their products.

This development has presented new opportunities for some media organizations. For example, it enables noncommercial public broadcasters to bring in ad revenue. Public radio and TV stations, which are prohibited by FCC regulations from taking advertising, face no such prohibitions online. Many have begun raising money by posting advertisements on their Web sites.

However, the Internet has also posed new challenges for some older media companies, who must navigate territory with less established payment models. For instance, when Internet sites like YouTube display content from traditional broadcast and cable services, the companies selling those services lose direct-payment revenue every time someone consumes that content on the Internet rather than paying for services. But this availability may also create exposure for media companies' offerings. Traditional companies must then ask whether that new awareness translates into an increase in *paying* customers. Internet-based companies like Hulu are already offering different levels of access:

free, ad-supported but limited versions of their services alongside pay models with greater libraries of media offerings and more versatile formats.

Business Trends in Media Industries

Consolidation and digitization are not the only trends redefining the mass media business landscape. Additional trends shaping business overall have further affected the media economy. These include the growth of flexible markets and the decline of labor unions, as well as downsizing and a growing wage gap.

Flexible Markets and the Decline of Labor Unions

As many U.S. companies export manufacturing work and rely on other sources of labor, the power of American workers and membership in labor unions have decreased.

In today's economy, markets are flexible—that is, business and consumer needs and preferences change continually and quickly. Companies seeking to increase profitability alter their products, services, and production processes as needed to satisfy specialized, ever-shifting demands. Making niche products for specialized markets is expensive, and most new products fail in the marketplace. To offset their losses from product failures, companies need to score a few major successes—such as a blockbuster movie or a game-changing handheld device. Large companies with access to the most capital—such as media powerhouses—can more easily absorb losses than small businesses with limited capital. Thus the powerhouses stand the best chance of surviving in today's flexible markets.

To lower their costs and earn back their investments in product development, companies have begun relying heavily on cheap labor—sometimes exploiting poor workers in domestic and international sweatshops—and on quick, high-volume sales. Many U.S. companies now export manufacturing work, such as production of computers, CD players, TV sets, VCRs, and DVDs, to avoid the more expensive unionized labor at home. (Today, many companies outsource even technical and customer support services for their products.) As U.S. firms have gained access to alternative sources of labor, American workers' power has decreased. Since the early 1980s, membership in labor unions has declined dramatically.

Downsizing and the Wage Gap

With the advantage to large companies in this age of flexible markets, the disadvantaged are the many workers who have lost their jobs as companies have "downsized" to become "more productive, more competitive, [and] more flexible."[4] Many people today scramble for paid work, often working two or three part-time and low-wage jobs. In his 2006 book *The Disposable American*, Louis Uchitelle noted unintended side effects of downsizing, including companies' difficulty in developing innovative offerings after gutting their workforces. In the news media, reporting staffs have been downsized by more than 25 percent since the early 1990s. As a result, traditional news reporting has given way to other forms—such as online news sites and blogs.

The Age of Hegemony

As media corporations have grown larger, they also have been able to manage public debate and dissent about their increasing power. How? One explanation is their ability to exercise **hegemony** in our society. In a hegemony, society's least powerful members are persuaded to accept the values defined by its most powerful members.

In his 1947 article "The Engineering of Consent," Edward Bernays, a founder of modern public relations (see Chapter 12), expressed the core concept behind hegemony: Companies cannot get people to do what they want until the people consent to what those companies are trying to do—whether it is getting more people to smoke cigarettes, or persuading more of them to go to war. To win people's consent to his clients' goals, Bernays tried to convince Americans that his clients' interests were "natural" and "common sense."

Framing companies' goals in this way makes it unlikely that anyone will challenge or criticize those goals. After all, who is going to argue with common sense? Yet definitions of common sense change over time. For example, it was once common sense that the world was flat and that people who did not own property shouldn't be allowed to vote. When people buy uncritically into common sense, they inadvertently perpetuate the divisions that some common sense can create. And they shut out any viewpoints suggesting that these divisions are *not* natural.

The mass media—through the messages they convey in their products—play a powerful role in defining common sense and therefore setting up hegemony in society. Every time we read an article in a newspaper; read a book or magazine; or watch a movie, our favorite TV show, or a video clip on YouTube, we absorb messages suggesting what is important and how the world works. If we consume enough of these "stories," we might conclude that what we are seeing in these media products is "just the way things are." And if we believe this is "just the way things are," we probably won't challenge these trends or come up with other, better possibilities.

The reason the narratives "work" is that they identify with a culture's dominant values. In the United States, "Middle American" virtues dominate our culture, and include allegiances to family, honesty, hard work, religion, capitalism, health, democracy, moderation, loyalty, and so forth. These kinds of Middle American virtues are the ones

American Dream stories are distributed through our media. Early television shows in the 1950s like *The Adventures of Ozzie and Harriet* idealized the American nuclear family as central to the American Dream.

that our politicians most frequently align themselves with in the political ads that tell their stories.

These virtues lie at the heart of powerful American Dream stories that for centuries have told us that if we work hard and practice such values, we will triumph and be successful. Hollywood, too, distributes these shared narratives, celebrating characters and heroes who are loyal, honest, and hardworking. Through this process, the media (and the powerful companies that control them) provide the commonsense narratives that keep the economic status quo relatively unchallenged, leaving little room for alternatives. In the end, hegemony helps explain why we may sometimes support economic plans and structures that may not be in our best interest.

Specialization and Global Markets

The outsourcing and offshoring of many jobs and the breakdown of global economic borders were bolstered by trade agreements made among national governments in the mid-twentieth century. These included NAFTA (North American Free Trade Agreement) in 1994 and the creation of the WTO (World Trade Organization) in 1995. Such agreements enabled the emergence of transnational media corporations and stimulated business deals across national borders. Technology helped, too, making it possible for consumers around the world to easily swap music, TV shows, and movies on the Internet (legally and illegally). All of this has in turn accelerated the global spread of media products and cultural messages.

As globalization gathered momentum, companies began specializing to enter the new, narrow markets opening up to them in other countries. They also began seeking ways to step up their growth through synergies— opportunities to market different versions of a media product.

The Rise of Specialization and Synergy

As globalization picked up speed, several mass media—namely, the magazine, radio, and cable industries—sought to tap specialized markets in the United States and overseas, in part to counter television's mass appeal. For example, cable channels such as Nickelodeon and the Disney Channel serve the under-eighteen market, HISTORY draws older viewers, Lifetime and Bravo go after women, and BET targets young African Americans.

In addition to specialization, media companies sought to spur growth through **synergy**—the promotion and sale of different versions of a media product across

Disney's reach extends beyond animation and movies to Broadway shows and music. The TV movie *Lemonade Mouth*, for example, spawned a successful soundtrack featuring musical performances by the cast; promotional merchandise, concert tours, and sequels often follow.

a media conglomerate's various subsidiaries. An example of synergy is Time Warner's HBO cable special about "the making of" a Warner Brothers movie reviewed in *Time* magazine. Another example is Sony's buying up movie studios and record labels and playing their content on its electronic devices (which are often prominently displayed in their movies). But of all the media conglomerates, the Walt Disney Company perhaps best exemplifies the power of both specialization and synergy.

Disney: A Postmodern Media Conglomerate

After Walt Disney's first cartoon company, Laugh-O-Gram, went bankrupt in 1922, Disney moved to Hollywood and found his niche. He created Mickey Mouse (originally named Mortimer) for the first sound cartoons in the late 1920s and developed the first feature-length cartoon, *Snow White and the Seven Dwarfs*, completed in 1937.

For much of the twentieth century, the Disney Company set the standard for popular cartoons and children's culture. Nonetheless, the studio barely broke even because cartoon projects took time (four years for *Snow White*) and commanded the company's full array of resources. Moreover, the market for the cartoon film shorts that Disney specialized in was drying up, as fewer movie theaters were showing the shorts before their feature films.

Driving to Diversify

With the demise of the cartoon film short in movie theaters, Disney expanded into other specialized areas. Its first nature documentary short, *Seal Island*, came in 1949; its first live-action feature, *Treasure Island*, in 1950; and its first feature documentary, *The Living Desert*, in 1953. In the same year, Disney started Buena Vista, a distribution company. This was the first step in the studio's becoming a major player in the film industry.

Disney also counted among the first film studios to embrace television. In 1954, the company launched a long-running prime-time show, and TV became an even more popular venue than theaters for displaying Disney products. Then, in 1955, the firm added another entirely new dimension to its operations: It opened its Disneyland theme park in Southern California. (Walt Disney World in Orlando, Florida, would begin operation in 1971.) Eventually, Disney's theme parks would produce the bulk of the company's revenues.

Capturing Synergies

Walt Disney's death in 1966 triggered a period of decline for the studio. But in 1984 a new management team, led by Michael Eisner, initiated a turnaround. The

company's newly created Touchstone movie division reinvented the live-action/
animation hybrid for adults and children in *Who Framed Roger Rabbit?* (1988). A
string of hand-drawn animated hits followed, including *The Little Mermaid* (1989)
and *Beauty and the Beast* (1991). In a rocky partnership with Pixar Animation
Studios, Disney also distributed a series of computer-animated blockbusters, including *Toy Story* (1995) and *Finding Nemo* (2003).

Since then, Disney has come to epitomize the synergistic possibilities of
media consolidation. It can produce an animated feature for theatrical release
and DVD distribution. Because it owns ABC, it can place a series based on the
movie on ABC's Saturday-morning schedule. It can release a book version of
the movie through its publishing arm, Hyperion, and air "the-making-of"
versions on cable's Disney Channel or ABC Family. It can also publish stories
about the movie's characters in *Disney Adventures*, the company's popular
children's magazine. Indeed, characters have become attractions at Disney's
theme parks, which themselves have spawned lucrative Hollywood blockbusters like the *Pirates of the Caribbean* series. Some Disney films have had as
many as seventeen thousand licensed products—from clothing to toys to
dog food bowls. And in New York City, Disney even renovated several theaters
and launched versions of *Mary Poppins*, *The Lion King*, and *Spider-Man* as successful Broadway musicals.

Expanding Globally

Building on the international appeal of its cartoon features, Disney extended its
global reach by opening a successful theme park in Japan in 1983. Three years
later, the company started marketing cartoons to Chinese television—attracting
an estimated 300 million viewers per week. Disney also launched a magazine in
Chinese and opened several Disney stores and a theme park in Hong Kong. Disney
continued its international expansion in the 1990s with the opening of EuroDisney
(now called Disneyland Paris). In 1997, Orbit—a Saudi-owned satellite relay station
based in Rome—introduced Disney's twenty-four-hour cable channel to twenty-three
countries in the Middle East and North Africa.

Facing Challenges and Seizing Opportunities

From 2000 to 2003, Disney grew into the world's second-largest media
conglomerate. Yet the cartoon pioneer encountered major challenges as well as
new opportunities presented by the Digital Age. Challenges included a recession,
failed films and Internet ventures, declining theme-park attendance, and damaged
relationships with a number of partners and subsidiaries (including Pixar and
Miramax).

By 2005, Disney had fallen to No. 5 among movie studios in U.S. box-office sales—down from No. 1 in 2003. A divided and unhappy board of directors forced Eisner out in 2005 after he had served twenty-one years as CEO.[5] The following year, new CEO Robert Iger repaired the relationship between Disney and Pixar: He merged the companies and made Steve Jobs, founder of Pixar and Apple Computer, a Disney board member.

The Pixar deal showed that Disney was ready to seize the opportunities presented by the Digital Age. The company decided to focus on television, movies, and its new online initiatives. To that end, it sold its twenty-two radio stations and the ABC Radio Network to Citadel Broadcasting for $2.7 billion in 2007. Disney also made its movies and TV programs (and ABC's content) available for download at Apple's iTunes store, revamped its Web site as an entertainment portal, and in 2009 joined News Corp. and NBC Universal as a partner in the video-streaming site Hulu.com. In 2009 Disney made another big investment by purchasing Marvel Entertainment for $4 billion, bringing Spider-Man, Hulk, the X-Men, and other superheroes into the Disney pool of characters, providing additional financial assets even when other projects, like their costly underperforming movies *Mars Needs Moms* and *John Carter*, grossed less than anticipated. Disney mourned the death of Steve Jobs in 2011 but continued producing animated movies from Pixar and its in-house studios and had an enormous Marvel-branded hit with *The Avengers* in 2012. Disney also expanded its products globally, adding a fourth ship to its international cruise line and a new nationwide Disney channel in Russia, and starting construction of the Shanghai Disney Resort in China, scheduled for a 2015 opening.

The Growth of Global Audiences

As Disney's story shows, international expansion has afforded media conglomerates key advantages, including access to profitable secondary markets and opportunities to advance and leverage technological innovations. As media technologies have become cheaper and more portable (from the original Walkman to the iPad), American media have proliferated inside and outside U.S. boundaries.

Today, greatly facilitated by the Internet, media products easily flow into the eyes and ears of people around the world. And thanks to satellite transmission, North American and European TV is now available at the global level. Cable services such as CNN and MTV have taken their national acts to the international stage—delivering their content to more than two hundred countries.

This growth of global audiences has permitted companies that lose money on products at home to profit in overseas markets. Roughly 80 percent of American movies, for instance, do not earn back their costs in U.S. theaters; they depend on foreign circulation as well as home video formats to make up for early losses. The same is true for the television industry.

Social Issues in Media Economics

Mergermania has sparked criticism in some quarters. (See "Media Literacy Case Study: From Fifty to a Few: The Most Dominant Media Corporations" on pages 466–467.) Some opponents lament the limits of antitrust laws. Others decry consumers' loss of control in the marketplace when just a few companies determine what messages and media content are produced. Still others warn against the infiltration of American culture and media messages into every corner of the globe.

The Limits of Antitrust Laws

Despite the intent of antitrust laws to ensure diversity of corporate ownership, companies have easily avoided these laws since the 1980s. They have done so by diversifying their holdings and by forming local monopolies, especially in newspapers and cable. These efforts have resulted in fewer voices in the marketplace and less competition among industry players.

Expanding through Diversification

Diversification promotes oligopolies in which a few large companies control the majority of production and distribution of media content. Most media companies diversify among different media products (such as television stations and film studios), never fully dominating a particular media industry. Time Warner, for example, spreads its holdings among television programming, film, publishing, cable channels, and its Internet divisions. However, Time Warner competes directly with only a few other big companies like Disney, Viacom, and News Corp.

This kind of economic arrangement makes it difficult for companies outside the oligopoly to compete in the marketplace. For example, an independent film production company may be unable to attract enough investment to get its movies distributed nationwide.

MEDIA LITERACY
Case Study

From Fifty to a Few: The Most Dominant Media Corporations

When Ben Bagdikian wrote the first edition of *The Media Monopoly*, published in 1983, he warned of the chilling control wielded by the fifty elite corporations that owned most of the U.S. mass media. By the publication of the book's seventh edition in 2004, the number of corporations controlling most of America's daily newspapers, magazines, radio, television, books, and movies had dropped from fifty to five. Today, most of the leading corporations have a high profile in the United States, particularly through ownership of television networks: Time Warner (CW), Disney (ABC), News Corp. (Fox), CBS Corporation (CBS and CW), and Comcast/GE-owned NBC Universal (NBC).

The creep of consolidation over the past few decades requires us to think differently about how we experience the mass media on a daily basis. Potential conflicts of interest abound. For example, should we trust how NBC News covers Comcast or GE or how ABC News covers Disney? Should we be wary if *Time* magazine hypes a Warner Brothers film? More important, what actions can we take to ensure that the mass media function not just as successful businesses for stockholders but also as a necessary part of our democracy?

APPLYING THE CRITICAL PROCESS

DESCRIPTION To help you get a better understanding of how our media landscape is changing, look at Table 15.1, which lists the Top 10 media companies for 1980, 1996, and 2011.

ANALYSIS What patterns do you notice?

INTERPRETATION Based on what you have discovered, what do these patterns mean? How do they reflect larger trends in the media? That is, seven of the major companies in 1980 were mostly print businesses, but in 2009, none were. Why?

EVALUATION While the subsidiaries of these companies often change, the charts demonstrate the wide reach of large conglomerations. Are these large media corporations good or bad for the economy? How do they affect democracy?

ENGAGEMENT Think about how much of your daily media intake is owned by the top ten corporations and about the influence they have on your news and entertainment intake. Ask two or three others around you to do the same, and compare your responses.

TABLE 15.1 // TOP 10 U.S. MEDIA COMPANIES, 1980, 1996, 2011

1980

Rank	Company	Revenue in $ millions
1	American Broadcasting Cos.	$2,204.5
2	CBS Inc.	2,001.0
3	RCA Corp.	1,521.8
4	Time Inc.	1,348.5
5	S.I. Newhouse & Sons	1,250.0
6	Gannett Co.	1,195.0
7	Times Mirror Co.	1,128.4
8	Hearst Corp.	1,100.0
9	Knight-Ridder Newspapers	1,099.0
10	Tribune Co.	1,048.7

1996

Rank	Company	Revenue in $ millions
1	Time Warner	$11,851.1
2	Walt Disney Co.	6,555.9
3	Tele-Communications Inc.	5,954.0
4	NBC TV (General Electric Co.)	5,230.0
5	CBS Corp.	4,333.5
6	Gannett Co.	4,214.4
7	News Corp.	4,005.0
8	Advance Publications	3,385.0
9	Cox Enterprises	3,075.3
10	Knight-Ridder	2,851.9

2011

Rank	Company	Revenue in $ millions
1	Comcast Corp.	$44,544
2	DirecTV Group	20,676
3	Walt Disney Co.	18,596
4	Time Warner	18,208
5	Time Warner Cable	16,836
6	News Corp.	16,822
7	AT&T	12,712
8	DISH Network Corp.	12,544
9	Cox Enterprises	11,585
10	CBS Corp.	11,310

Source: Ad Age's 100 Leading Media Companies *report, December 7, 1981;* "100 Companies by Media Revenue," Advertising Age, *August 18, 1997;* "100 Leading Media Companies," Advertising Age, *October 3, 2011.*

Building Local Monopolies

Antitrust laws aim to curb *national* monopolies, so most media monopolies today operate locally. Nearly every cable company has been granted monopoly status in its local community. These firms alone decide which channels are made available and what rates are charged. Independent voices have little opportunity or means to raise the questions that regulatory groups—such as the Justice Department and the FCC—need to hear in order to shape the laws.

A Vast Silence

Despite the concerns expressed by some critics, there has been little public debate overall about the tightening oligopoly structure of international media. Experts have identified two forces behind this vast hegemonic silence: citizens' reluctance to criticize free markets because they equate them with democracy, and the often unclear distinction between how much choice and control consumers have in the marketplace.

Equating Free Markets with Democracy

Throughout the Cold War period in the 1950s and 1960s, many Americans refused to criticize capitalism, which they saw as synonymous with democracy. Any complaints about capitalism were viewed as an attack on the free marketplace. And attacks on free markets in turn sounded like criticism of free speech. That is in part because business owners saw their right to operate in a free marketplace as an extension of their right to buy commercial speech in the form of advertising. This line of thinking, which originated in corporate efforts to equate capitalism with democracy, still casts a shadow over American culture today, making it difficult for many people to openly question the advertising-supported economic structure of the mass media.

Debating Consumer Choice versus Consumer Control

In discussing free markets, economists distinguish between *consumer control* over marketplace goods and freedom of *consumer choice:* "The former requires that consumers participate in deciding what is to be offered; the latter is satisfied if [consumers are] free to select among the options chosen for them by producers."[6] Most Americans and the citizens of other economically developed nations clearly have *choice:* options among a range of media products. Yet the choices sometimes obscure the fact that consumers have limited *control:* power in deciding what kinds of media get created and circulated. Consumers thus have little ability to shape the messages conveyed through media products about what is important and how the world should work. Instead, they can only react to those messages.

Yet independent and alternative producers, artists, writers, and publishers have provided a ray of hope. When their work becomes even marginally popular, big media companies often capitalize on these innovations by acquiring it—which enables these works to get out to the public. Moreover, business leaders "at the top" depend on independent ideas "from below" to generate new product lines. Fortunately, a number of transnational corporations encourage the development of promising local artists.

Cultural Imperialism

The increasing dominance of American popular culture around the world has sparked heated debate in international circles. On the one hand, people in other countries seem to relish the themes of innovation and rebellion expressed in American media products, and the global spread of access to media (particularly the ease of digital documentation via mobile devices) have made it harder for political leaders to secretly repress dissident groups. On the other hand, American styles in fashion and food, as well as media fare, dominate the global market—a situation known as **cultural imperialism**. Today, numerous international observers contend that consumers in countries inundated by American-made movies, music, television, and images have even less control than American consumers. Even the Internet has a distinctively American orientation. The United States got a head start in deploying the Internet as a mass medium and has been the dominant force ever since. Although the Internet is worldwide and in many languages, the majority of the Web's content is still in English, the United States controls the top domains like .com and .org (without the requirement to have a nation-identifying domain name, such as .jp for Japan or .fr for France), and leading global sites like Google, Facebook, Amazon, YouTube, and *Wikipedia* are all American in design.

Defenders of American popular culture's dominance argue that a universal culture creates a *global village* and fosters communication and collaboration across national boundaries. Critics, however, point out that two-thirds of the world's population cannot afford most of the products advertised on American,

Ever since Hollywood gained an edge in film production and distribution, U.S. movies have dominated the box office in Europe, Asia, and the rest of the world. Worldwide grosses are in turn more important to Hollywood than ever.

Japanese, and European television. Yet they see, hear, and read about consumer abundance and middle-class values through TV and other media, including magazines and the Internet. Critics worry that the obvious disparities in economic well-being and the frustration that must surely come with not having the money to buy advertised products may lead to social unrest.

The Media Marketplace in a Democratic Society

Amy Goodman is cohost of *Democracy Now!*, a radio/TV newscast airing daily on more than 800 public and college radio stations, satellite television, and the Internet. *Democracy Now!* argues that it maintains editorial independence by accepting funding only from listeners, viewers, and foundations, and rejecting government funding, corporate underwriting, and advertisers.

Multinational giants are controlling more and more aspects of production and distribution of media products. This is particularly worrisome when it comes to news media: Media conglomerates that own news companies have the capacity to use those resources to promote their products and determine what news receives national coverage. When news coverage is determined by fewer decision makers, citizens cannot be certain they are receiving sufficient information with which to make decisions. That's bad news for any democracy.

Media powerhouses are also increasingly shaping the regulatory environment. Politicians in Washington, D.C. regularly accept millions of dollars from media conglomerates and their lobbying groups to finance their campaigns. Companies that provide such financial support stand a better chance of influencing regulatory decisions. Indeed, they have successfully pushed for more deregulation, which has enabled them to grow even more and come under fewer constraints. This is also bad news for our democracy, especially because the journalism subsidiaries of major media conglomerates are not completely independent of the powerful corporate and political forces on which they report. Who will tell us the news about big media and their political allies?

Despite the forces we have examined that are discouraging energetic debate about these realities, some grassroots organizations have arisen to challenge the power and reach of media behemoths. Such movements—like the annual National Conference for Media Reform—are usually united by geographic ties, common political backgrounds, or shared concerns about the state of the media. The Internet has also enabled media reform groups to form globally, uniting around such efforts as fostering independent media, contesting censorship, or monitoring the activities of multinational corporations.

This development is encouraging news: It suggests that we consumers—whether in America or elsewhere—might be willing to look more closely at the media marketplace's impact on our lives. And we may start demanding that media companies take more responsibility for fulfilling one of their key missions: making democratic life better for those of us consuming their products and absorbing their messages.

VideoCentral ⊚

bedfordstmartins.com /mediaessentials

The Power of Images: Amy Goodman on Emmett Till

Amy Goodman discusses how images have incredible story-telling power.

Discussion: Goodman's description of this event can help form a mental image of Emmett Till. Describe another historical image that can be considered powerful in the same way, and why it is important.

CHAPTER ESSENTIALS

Now that you have finished reading this chapter, you can use the following tools:

REVIEW

Discuss the Transition to an Information Economy

- Media industries have one of three common structures: **monopoly** (when a single firm dominates production and distribution in a particular industry), **oligopoly** (when a few firms dominate the industry), or **limited competition** (when there are many producers and sellers but only a few products within a particular category) (pp. 451–452).

- By the mid-twentieth century, the U.S. shifted from a manufacturing-based economy to one fueled by information and cooperation with other economies, causing mass media industries to expand globally. Although early regulation was designed to break up monopolies, deregulation of the industries won out, leading to a growth of mergers and acquisitions (pp. 452–453).

- Today's media powerhouses avoid monopoly charges by purchasing diverse types of media rather than controlling just one medium (pp. 453–454).

Explain the Media Economy

- Media companies make money from **direct payments**, which come from consumers who buy media products, and **indirect payments**, which come from advertisers and companies that purchase ads to attract specific customers. Companies also come up with specific business strategies to maximize profits. For example, many try to achieve **economies of scale**, the economic process of increasing production levels so as to reduce the overall cost per unit (pp. 456–457).

- Historically, media companies have operated in separate industries; however, the Internet is changing the way people consume media. It presents new opportunities for some media organizations while posing challenges for some older media companies (pp. 457–458).

- Other trends that have affected the media economy include flexible markets and the decline of unionized labor, and a growing wage gap (pp. 458–459).

- All these trends take place, in part, because mass media play a powerful role in establishing **hegemony** in society, where its least powerful members are persuaded to accept the values defined by its most powerful members (pp. 459–460).

Analyze Specialization and Global Markets

- As globalization increased, companies began specializing to enter the new, narrow markets in other countries. They also sought to spur growth through **synergy**—the promotion and sale of different versions of a media product across a media conglomerate's various subsidiaries (pp. 461–462).

- The Walt Disney Company is an example of a media conglomerate that has excelled at specialization and synergy. The company has also had success with its global expansion (pp. 462–463).

- Following Disney's model, many media conglomerates look to international expansion as a way to access markets and to provide opportunities to advance (pp. 464–465).

Trace the Social Issues in Media Economics

- Critics of mergers and media consolidation argue that antitrust laws are limited, that there are still fewer voices in the marketplace and less competition among industry players (p. 465).

- Others decry consumers' loss of control in the marketplace when just a few companies determine what messages and media content are produced (pp. 467–469).

- Still others warn against the infiltration of American culture and media messages into every corner of the globe—a situation known as **cultural imperialism** (pp. 469–470).

- Democracy suffers when news coverage is determined by fewer decision makers and when media powerhouses increasingly shape the regulatory environment. Grass-roots organizations and the Internet have enabled media reform groups to form globally, suggesting that consumers might be willing to look more closely at the media marketplace's impact on our lives (pp. 470–471).

STUDY QUESTIONS

1. How are the three basic structures of mass media organizations—monopoly, oligopoly, and limited competition—different from one another? How is the Internet changing everything?
2. Why has the federal government emphasized deregulation at a time when so many media companies are growing so large? How have media mergers changed the economics of mass media?
3. How do global and specialized markets factor into the new media economy? Using Disney as an example, what is the role of synergy in the current climate of media mergers?
4. What are the differences between freedom of consumer choice and consumer control? What is cultural imperialism, and what does it have to do with the United States?
5. What do critics and activists fear most about the concentration of media ownership? What are some promising signs regarding the relationship between media economics and democracy?

MEDIA LITERACY PRACTICE

One of the most difficult things to comprehend about the largest media corporations is their sheer size and synergies. To investigate this topic, explore examples of such synergies.

DESCRIBE the various subsidiaries and synergies of a media corporation—try Time Warner, Disney, or News Corp. You can begin by looking at the corporate Web site and *Columbia Journalism Review*'s ownership site, www.cjr.org/resources. Also, read corporate press releases and news stories about the media corporation's businesses.

ANALYZE the patterns in synergies. Which subsidiaries work with other subsidiaries? Are there any divisions that operate independently? Which kinds of products have the most extensive synergies (e.g., news? prime-time television? comic book characters?)

INTERPRET what these patterns mean. For example, do the synergies result in higher quality or more profitable media content? Do synergies result in overexposure of some media content?

EVALUATE the media corporation's business structure. Is synergy a good thing or a bad thing? Can journalism function well in a large media corporation?

ENGAGE with the community by writing a letter to a local newspaper or online publication (or a journalism outlet within the media corporation itself) that reveals the good and bad about synergies within corporate media.

⊙ ONLINE RESOURCES

Go to **bedfordstmartins.com/mediaessentials** for review quizzes, links, and more.

Visit the site's **VIDEOCENTRAL: MASS COMMUNICATION** section for videos like the ones on pages 454 and 471. There, you can find additional exclusive videos related to Chapter 15, including:

THE MONEY BEHIND THE MEDIA
Producers, advertisers, and advocates discuss how ownership systems and profits shape media production.

IT **GETS** BETTER PROJECT.

< BROWSE MORE VIDEOS

It Gets Better: Dan and Terry

Tweet ⟨0⟩   f SHARE

It Gets Better: Dan and Terry

👍 Like   👎 Share   ⤓ More info

▶ 🔊 5:32 / 8:32   CC ⚙ 🕐 YouTube ⤢

16

Social Scientific and Cultural Approaches to Media Research

In 2010, soon after widely publicized stories attributing fifteen-year-old Billy Lucas's suicide to antigay bullying, commentator and author Dan Savage launched the "It Gets Better Project" with a YouTube video created to inspire hope for young people enduring homophobic harassment at school and online. His idea snowballed into a worldwide movement generating over 30,000 user-created videos as well as submissions from celebrities, politicians, and media personalities. But even after the barrage of positive, inspiring messages, there are still stories like that of fourteen-year-old Jamey Rodemeyer, who had posted a video on Savage's YouTube channel, but took his own life the following year. Rodemeyer had been bullied at school since the fifth grade—and had endured online messages like "I wouldn't care if you died. No one would. So just do it :) It would make everyone WAY more happier!"[1]

In 2011, six people were killed and twelve wounded in a town near Tucson, Arizona. The attack took place in a supermarket parking lot, and the main target of the gunman was U.S. Representative Gabrielle Giffords, who was shot in the head. The deranged man responsible for the attack had posted a number of antigovernment messages on MySpace and YouTube. The attack prompted calls for stiffer gun control laws, as well as appeals to tone down the hyperbole and vitriol of political rhetoric associated with political activism during the heat of the Tea Party movement. Though Representative Giffords survived the shooting, she resigned her congressional seat in 2012 to focus on her medical recovery.

In 2012, the blogging site Tumblr announced a ban on blogs that "actively promote self-harm" including those facilitating or glorifying suicide, self-mutilation, anorexia, bulimia, or other eating disorders. Before launching the policy, Tumblr's staff considered continuing to allow users to publish such material, but with public service messages warning users of the content and providing information about helplines and other support services. Ultimately, the staff adopted the ban after deciding that "sometimes Tumblr gets used for things that are just wrong."[2]

These and other similar events have raised important questions: What power do the mass media have over individuals and society, and how do the media contribute to social problems like homophobia, bullying, suicide, self-mutilation, and eating disorders? And what should we do about it?

THE IDEA THAT MEDIA HAVE A SIGNIFICANT IMPACT on society has fueled the development of two types of research in the study of mass communication: social scientific and cultural studies.

Social scientific research attempts to understand, explain, and predict the impact of mass media on individuals and society. The main goal of this type of research is to define the problem with a testable hypothesis, collect data through one of various methodologies, and draw conclusions based on the data. Researchers who focus on **cultural studies** explore how people make meaning, understand reality, articulate values, and interpret their experiences through use of cultural symbols in media. Cultural studies scholars also examine how groups such as corporate and political elites use media to circulate their messages and serve their interests. Such research focuses on daily cultural experience, examining the subtle intersections among mass communication, history, politics, and economics.

In this chapter, we look at how these two forms of media research have evolved over time by:

- examining early media research methods, including propaganda analysis, public opinion research, social psychology studies, and marketing research

- assessing social scientific media research, including theories about how media influence people's behaviors and attitudes and the benefits and limitations of such research

- taking stock of cultural approaches to media research, including early and contemporary cultural studies theories and the strengths and limitations of such research

- considering the role of media research in our democracy, exploring questions such as how effectively such research addresses real-life problems

Early Media Research Methods

During most of the nineteenth century, philosophers such as Alexis de Tocqueville based their analysis of news and print media on moral and political arguments.[3] More scientific approaches to mass media research did not emerge until the late 1920s and 1930s. In 1920, Walter Lippmann's *Liberty and the News* called on journalists to operate more like scientific researchers in gathering and analyzing facts. Lippmann's next book, *Public Opinion* (1922), was the first to apply the principles of psychology to journalism. Considered by many academics to be "the founding book in American media studies,"[4] *Public Opinion* deepened Americans' understanding of the effect of media, emphasizing data collection and numerical measurement. According to media historian Daniel Czitrom, by the 1930s "an aggressively empirical spirit, stressing new and increasingly sophisticated research techniques, characterized the study of modern communication in America."[5] Czitrom traces four trends between 1930 and 1960 that contributed to the rise of modern media research: propaganda analysis, public opinion research, social psychology studies, and marketing research.

Propaganda Analysis

Propaganda analysis was a major early focus of mass media research. After World War I, some researchers began studying how governments used propaganda to advance the war effort. They found that during the war, governments routinely relied on propaganda divisions to spread "information" to the public. Though propaganda was considered important for mobilizing public support during the war, researchers after the war criticized it as "partisan appeal based on half-truths and devious manipulation of communication channels."[6] Harold

Propaganda analysis researchers studied the impact of war posters and other government information campaigns to determine how audiences could be persuaded through stirring media messages about patriotism and duty.

Lasswell's 1927 study *Propaganda Technique in the World War* defined propaganda as "the control of opinion by significant symbols, . . . by stories, rumors, reports, pictures and other forms of social communication."[7]

Public Opinion Research

After the two world wars, researchers went beyond the study of wartime propaganda and began examining how the mass media filter information and shape public attitudes. Social scientists explored these questions by conducting *public opinion research* through citizen surveys and polls.

Public opinion research on diverse populations has provided insights into how different groups view major national events, such as elections, and how those views affect their behavior. However, journalists became increasingly dependent on polls, particularly for political insight.

Today, some critics argue that this heavy reliance on measured public opinion adversely affects Americans' participation in the political process. For example, people who read poll projections and get the sense that few others are voting for their favored candidate may not bother casting a ballot. "Why should I vote," they tell themselves, "if my vote isn't going to make a difference?" Some critics of incessant polling also argue that polls mainly measure opinions on topics of interest to business, government, academics, and the mainstream news media. The public responds passively to polls, without getting anything of value in return. Professional pollsters object to **pseudo-polls**— typically call-in, online, or person-in-the-street polls that the news media use to address a "question of the day." Such polls, which do not use a random sample of the population and therefore are not representative of the population as a whole, nevertheless persist on news and entertainment Web sites, radio, and television news programs.

Social Psychology Studies

While opinion polls measure public attitudes, *social psychology studies* measure the behavior, attitudes, and cognition of individuals. The most influential early social psychology media studies efforts, the Payne Fund Studies, comprised thirteen research projects conducted by social psychologists between 1929 and 1932. Named after the private philanthropic organization that funded the research, the Payne Fund Studies were a response to a growing national concern about the effects of motion pictures on young people. The studies, which some politicians later used to attack the movie industry, linked frequent movie attendance to juvenile delinquency, promiscuity, and other problematic behaviors, arguing that movies took "emotional possession" of young filmgoers.[8]

The conclusions of this and other Payne Fund Studies contributed to the establishment of the film industry's production code, which tamed movie content from the 1930s through the 1950s. (See Chapter 14.) As forerunners of today's research into TV violence and aggression, the Payne Fund Studies became the model for media research, although social psychology is also used to study the mass media's relationship to body image, gender norms, political participation, and a wide range of other topics. (See Figure 16.1 for one example of a contemporary policy that has developed from media research. Also see "Media Literacy Case Study: What to Do about Television Violence?" on page 482.)

The following categories apply to programs designed solely for children:

 All Children
This program is designed to be appropriate for all children. Whether animated or live-action, the themes and elements in this program are specifically designed for a very young audience, including children from ages 2–6. This program is not expected to frighten young children.

Directed to Older Children — Fantasy Violence
For those programs where fantasy violence may be more intense or more combative than other programs in this category, such programs will be designated **TV-Y7-FV**.

 Directed to Older Children
This program is designed for children age 7 and above. It may be more appropriate for children who have acquired the developmental skills needed to distinguish between make-believe and reality. Themes and elements in this program may include mild fantasy violence or comedic violence, or may frighten children under the age of 7. Therefore, parents may wish to consider the suitability of this program for their very young children.

The following categories apply to programs designed for the entire audience:

 General Audience
Most parents would find this program suitable for all ages. Although this rating does not signify a program designed specifically for children, most parents may let younger children watch this program unattended. It contains little or no violence, no strong language and little or no sexual dialogue situations.

Parental Guidance Suggested
This program contains material that parents may find unsuitable for younger children. Many parents may want to watch it with their younger children. The theme itself may call for parental guidance and/or the program may contain one or more of the following: some suggestive dialogue (D), infrequent coarse language (L), some sexual situations (S), or moderate violence (V).

Parents Strongly Cautioned
This program contains some material that many parents would find unsuitable for children under 14 years of age. Parents are strongly urged to exercise greater care in monitoring this program and are cautioned against letting children under the age of 14 watch unattended. This program may contain one or more of the following: intensely suggestive dialogue (D), strong coarse language (L), intense sexual situations(S), or intense violence (V).

Mature Audiences Only
This program is specifically designed to be viewed by adults and therefore may be unsuitable for children under 17. This program may contain one or more of the following: crude indecent language (L), explicit sexual activity (S), or graphic violence (V).

**FIGURE 16.1 //
TV PARENTAL
GUIDELINES**

The TV industry continues to study its self-imposed rating categories, promising to fine-tune them to ensure that the government keeps its distance. These standards are one example of a policy that was shaped in part by media research.

Source: TV Parental Guidelines Monitoring Board, www.tvguidelines .org, 7/10/06.

MEDIA LITERACY
Case Study

What to Do about Television Violence?

The debate over violent television programming is almost as old as television, with the first congressional hearings on the matter occurring in 1952. More than a half-century later, the debate continues. In 2007, the FCC released a lengthy report, "Violent Television Programming and Its Impact on Children," and recommended action to address violent programming.

The commission agreed with research that suggests "exposure to violence in the media can increase aggressive behavior in children, at least in the short term." Yet as the report tried to make conclusive statements about violent programming, it raised only more questions about what to do. The FCC cited several troubling statistics:

- An average American household has the television set turned on eight hours, eleven minutes, daily.
- Children watch on average between two and four hours of television every day.
- Depending on their age, one- to two-thirds of children have televisions in their bedrooms.
- By the time most children begin the first grade, they will have spent the equivalent of three school years in front of the television set.
- By the time the average child is eighteen years old, he or she will have watched more than ten thousand hours of television.
- By age eighteen, an American child will have seen upwards of 15,000 simulated murders and about 200,000 acts of violence on television.[1]

But dealing with television violence has been persistently confounded by several problems. First is the problem of defining violent content, at least in a way that could be used in government policies.

The show *24* is often used as an example of violent programming on television.

Courts have struck down vague definitions that call for regulating excessive violence, noting that many classic stories from the Bible, Greek mythology, and fairy tales are filled with gruesome violence.

A second problem is determining which television programming to regulate. Most proposals include prime-time programming, but what about news, sports, commercials, and promotional announcements? And how should regulations treat cable and satellite television providers, who aren't subject to the same level of FCC oversight as broadcasters? Third is the issue of free speech. Courts have ruled that the First Amendment protects depictions of violence and violent speech. Although broadcasters have less First Amendment protection than other mass media and are subject to daytime restrictions on indecent content to protect children, it is not clear that similar rules could be applied to violent content.

Fourth, although a majority of Americans think there is too much violence on television, nearly all parties have fallen short in using existing tools to deal with it. The FCC charged that broadcast networks are inconsistent in how they voluntarily rate and label programs for violent content, and often "underlabel" programs with less restrictive ratings to increase advertiser incentives. Although the ratings have been around since 1997, many parents don't understand them. One in five parents has never heard of the ratings system, and only 8 percent can correctly identify the categories. The V-chip, much touted when it became a television set standard in 2000 to enable parents to block violent programming, is rarely used, and not all parents are aware of blocking features on newer digital sets. Moreover, changing viewing habits, with shows often available via DVR, streaming video, and iTunes, among others, makes programming more difficult to track or control.

Finally, for all of the research suggesting that TV violence causes violent behavior, there are still significant questions that such effects even exist. Although the FCC sided with effects researchers, the report also noted that controlled laboratory environments and experimental measures of aggression (e.g., hitting dolls, "killing" characters in video games) can't be generalized to the real world and that there is—at least as yet—no demonstrable correlation between media violence and crime statistics.

APPLYING THE CRITICAL PROCESS

DESCRIPTION Keep track of your TV viewing habits in one week. Devise a chart and create categories for the types of shows you watch (e.g., sitcoms, dramas, reality programs).

ANALYSIS Take note of the content in each program— what topics are covered, and whether or not there is violence. What shows seem to feature more violence than others? How much violence do you find overall?

INTERPRETATION What do your findings mean? Are you surprised by the appearance of violence in any seemingly nonviolent shows? Do broadcast network shows (e.g., ABC, CBS, NBC, Fox, CW) feature more, similar amounts of, or less violent programming than cable or satellite television shows?

EVALUATION How does exposure to violence in these shows affect you? Do you agree with the FCC statement that "exposure to violence in the media can increase aggressive behavior in children, at least in the short term"? Why or why not?

ENGAGEMENT Aside from TV shows, examine other forms of entertainment that you enjoy, such as your collection of movies or video games, for the presence of violent content. Are the rating systems for these products effective? File your comments or concerns online with the FCC (www.fcc.gov).

Marketing Research

Marketing research emerged in the 1920s, when advertisers and consumer-product companies began conducting surveys on consumer buying habits and other behaviors. For example, ratings systems arose that measured how many people were listening to commercial radio on a given night. By the 1930s, radio networks, advertisers, large stations, and advertising agencies all subscribed to ratings services. However, compared with print media, whose circulation departments kept track of customers' names and addresses, radio listeners were more difficult to trace. The problem prompted experts to develop increasingly sophisticated marketing research methods to determine consumer preferences and media use, such as direct-mail diaries, television meters, phone surveys, telemarketing, and eventually Internet tracking. In many instances, product companies paid consumers a small fee to take part in these studies.

Social Scientific Research

Concerns about public opinion measurements, propaganda, and the impact of media on society intensified just as journalism and mass communication departments gained popularity in colleges and universities. As these forces dovetailed, media researchers looked increasingly to behavioral science as the basis of their work. Between 1930 and 1960, "Who says what to whom with what effect?" became the key question "defining the scope and problems of American communications research."[9] To address this question, researchers asked more specific questions, such as this: If children watch a lot of TV cartoons (stimulus or cause), will this influence their behavior toward their peers (response or effect)? New social scientific models arose to measure and explain such connections—which researchers referred to as *media effects*.

Early Models of Media Effects

Between the 1930s and the 1970s, media researchers developed several paradigms about how media affect individuals' behavior. These models were known as hypodermic needle, minimal effects, and uses and gratifications.

Hypodermic Needle

The notion that powerful media adversely affect weak audiences has been labeled the **hypodermic needle** (or **magic bullet**) **model**. It suggests that the media "shoot" their effects directly into unsuspecting victims.

One of the earliest challenges to this model came from a study of Orson Welles's legendary October 30, 1938, radio broadcast of *War of the Worlds*. The broadcast presented H. G. Wells's Martian-invasion novel in the form of a news report—which frightened millions of listeners who didn't realize it was fictional. (See Chapter 6.) In 1940, radio researcher Hadley Cantril wrote a book-length study of the broadcast and its aftermath titled *The Invasion from Mars: A Study in the Psychology of Panic*. Cantril argued that, contrary to what the hypodermic needle model suggested, not all listeners thought the radio program was a real news report. In fact, the relatively few listeners who thought there was an invasion from Mars were those who tuned in late and missed the disclaimer at the beginning of the broadcast, and who were also predisposed (because of religious beliefs) to think that the end of the world was actually near. Although social scientists have since disproved the hypodermic needle model, many people still subscribe to it, particularly when considering the media's impact on children.

Early media researchers concerned about Adolf Hitler's use of national radio to indoctrinate the German people in the 1930s found his international broadcasts to be failures. Because so many media messages competed with Nazi propaganda in democratic countries, Hitler's radio programs had little impact there.

Minimal Effects

Cantril's research helped lay the groundwork for the **minimal effects** (or **limited effects**) **model** proposed by some media researchers. With the rise of empirical research techniques, social scientists began discovering and demonstrating that media alone do not cause people to change their attitudes and behaviors. After conducting controlled experiments and surveys, researchers argued that people generally engage in **selective exposure** and **selective retention** with regard to media. That is, people expose themselves to media messages most familiar to them, and retain messages that confirm values and attitudes they already hold. Minimal effects researchers have argued that in most cases mass media *reinforce* existing behaviors and attitudes rather than change them.

Indeed, Joseph Klapper, in his 1960 research study, *The Effects of Mass Communication*, found that mass media influenced only those individuals who did not already hold strong views on an issue. Media, Klapper added, had a greater impact on

The uses and gratifications model discusses media as being an "electronic hearth" that people gather around to share experiences. Here, we see people uniting in a sports bar to cheer on their favorite team.

poor and uneducated audiences. Solidifying the minimal effects argument, Klapper concluded that strong media effects occur largely at an individual level and do not appear to have large-scale, measurable, and direct effects on society as a whole.[10]

Uses and Gratifications

The **uses and gratifications** model arose to challenge the notion that people are passive recipients of media. This model holds that people instead actively engage in using media to satisfy various emotional or intellectual needs; for example, turning on the TV in the house not only to be entertained but also to use it as an "electronic hearth," making the space feel more warm and alive. Researchers supporting this model use in-depth interviews to supplement survey questionnaires. Through these interviews, they study the ways in which people used the media. Instead of asking, "What effects do media have on us?" these researchers ask, "Why do we use media?"

Although the uses and gratifications model addresses the *functions* of the mass media for individuals, it does not address important questions related to the impact of the media on society. Consequently, the uses and gratifications model has never become a dominant or enduring paradigm in media research. But the rise of Internet-related media technologies has brought a resurgence in uses and gratifications research to understand why people use new media.

Conducting Social Scientific Media Research

As researchers investigated various theories about how media affect people, they also developed different approaches to conducting their research. These approaches vary depending on whether the research originates in the private or public sector. *Private research,* sometimes called *proprietary research,* is generally conducted for a business, a corporation, or even a political campaign. It typically addresses some real-life problem or need. *Public research* usually takes place in academic and government settings. It tries to clarify, explain, or predict—in other words, to theorize about—the effects of mass media rather than to address a consumer problem.

Most media research today focuses on media's impact on human characteristics such as learning, attitudes, aggression, and voting habits. This research employs the **scientific method**, which consists of seven steps:

1. Identify the problem to be researched.
2. Review existing research and theories related to the problem.
3. Develop working hypotheses or predictions about what the study might find.
4. Determine an appropriate method or research design.

5. Collect information or relevant data.
6. Analyze results to see whether they verify the hypotheses.
7. Interpret the implications of the study.

The scientific method relies on *objectivity* (eliminating bias and judgments on the part of researchers), *reliability* (getting the same answers or outcomes from a study or measure during repeated testing), and *validity* (demonstrating that a study actually measures what it claims to measure).

A key step in using the scientific method is posing one or more **hypotheses**: tentative general statements that predict the influence of an *independent variable* on a *dependent variable*, or relationships between variables. For example, a researcher might hypothesize that frequent TV viewing among adolescents (independent variable) causes poor academic performance (dependent variable). Or, a researcher might hypothesize that playing first-person-shooter video games (independent variable) is associated with aggression in children (dependent variable).

Researchers using the scientific method may employ experiments or survey research in their investigations.

Experiments

Like all studies that use the scientific method, **experiments** in media research isolate some aspect of content; suggest a hypothesis; and manipulate variables to discover a particular medium's impact on people's attitudes, emotions, or behavior. To test whether a hypothesis is true, researchers expose an *experimental group*—the group under study—to selected media images or messages. To ensure valid results, researchers also use a *control group* that is not exposed to the selected media content and thus serves as a basis for comparison. Subjects are picked for each group through **random assignment**, meaning that each subject has an equal chance of being placed in either group.

For instance, suppose researchers wanted to test the effects of violent films on preadolescent boys. The study might take a group of ten-year-olds and randomly assign them to two groups. The experimental group watches a violent action movie that the control group does not see. Later, both groups are exposed to a staged fight between two other boys, and researchers watch how each group responds. If the control subjects try to break up the fight but the experimental subjects do not, researchers might conclude that the violent film caused the differences in the groups' responses. (See the "Bobo doll" experiment photos on page 489.)

When experiments carefully account for independent variables through random assignment, they generally work well to substantiate cause-effect hypotheses. Although experiments can sometimes take place in field settings, where people can be observed using media in their everyday environments, researchers have less control over variables. Conversely, a weakness of more carefully controlled experiments is that they are often conducted in the unnatural conditions of a laboratory environment, which can affect the behavior of the experimental subjects.

Survey Research

Through **survey research**, investigators collect and measure data taken from a group of respondents regarding their attitudes, knowledge, or behavior. Using random sampling techniques that give each potential subject an equal chance to be included in the survey, this research method draws on much larger populations than those used in experimental studies. Researchers can conduct surveys through direct mail, personal interviews, telephone calls, e-mail, and Web sites, thus accumulating large quantities of information from diverse cross sections of people. These data enable researchers to examine demographic factors in addition to responses to questions related to the survey topic.

Surveys offer other benefits as well. Because the randomized sample size is large, researchers can usually generalize their findings to the larger society as well as investigate populations over a long time period. In addition, they can use the extensive government and academic survey databases now widely available to conduct **longitudinal studies**, where they compare new studies with those conducted years earlier.

But like experiments, surveys also have several drawbacks. First, they cannot show cause-effect relationships. They can only show **correlations**—or associations—between two variables. For example, a random survey of ten-year-old boys that asks about their behavior might demonstrate that a correlation exists between acting aggressively and watching violent TV programs. But this correlation does not identify the cause and the effect. (Perhaps people who are already aggressive choose to watch violent TV programs.) Second, surveys are only as good as the wording of their questions and the answer choices they present. Thus, a poorly designed survey can produce misleading results.

Content Analysis

As social scientific media researchers developed theories about the mass media, it became increasingly important to more precisely describe the media content being studied. As a corrective, they developed a method known as **content analysis** to systematically describe various types of media content.

Content analysis involves defining terms and developing a coding scheme so that whatever is being studied—acts of violence in movies, representations of women in television commercials, the treatment of political candidates in news reports—can be accurately judged and counted. One annual content analysis study is conducted by the Gay and Lesbian Alliance Against Defamation (GLAAD) each year to count the quantity, quality, and diversity of gay, lesbian, bisexual, and transgender (GLBT) characters on television. In 2011, GLAAD's content analysis found that ABC Family led all networks with 55 percent of its programming hours featuring GLBT characters. TBS and A&E were at the bottom of their list, each with just 5 percent of its programming time featuring GLBT characters.

These photos of the "Bobo doll" experiments show that the children who observed adults punching and kicking the Bobo dolls were more likely to imitate the adult model's behavior when returned to a room with many toys.

Content analysis has its own limitations. For one thing, this technique does not measure the effects of various media messages on audiences or explain how those messages are presented. Moreover, problems of definition arise. For instance, how do researchers distinguish slapstick cartoon aggression from the violent murders or rapes shown during an evening police drama?

Contemporary Media Effects Theories

By the 1960s, several departments of mass communication began graduating PhD-level researchers (the first had been at the University of Iowa in 1948) schooled in experiment and survey research techniques as well as content analysis. These researchers began developing new theories about how media affect people. Five particularly influential contemporary theories emerged. These are known as social learning theory, agenda-setting, the cultivation effect, the spiral of silence, and the third-person effect theory.

Social Learning Theory

Some of the best-known studies suggesting a link between mass media and behavior are the "Bobo doll" experiments, conducted on children by psychologist

Albert Bandura and his colleagues at Stanford University in the 1960s. Although many researchers criticized the use of Bobo dolls as an experimental device (since the point of playing with Bobo dolls is to hit them), Bandura argued that the experiments demonstrated a link between violent media programs, such as those on television, and aggressive behavior. Bandura developed **social learning theory**, which he believed involved a four-step process: *attention* (the subject must attend to the media and witness the aggressive behavior), *retention* (the subject must retain the memory of what he or she saw for later retrieval), *motor reproduction* (the subject must be able to physically imitate the behavior), and *motivation* (there must be a social reward or reinforcement to encourage modeling of the behavior).

Supporters of social learning theory often cite real-life imitations of aggression depicted in media (such as the Columbine massacre) as evidence that the theory is correct. Critics argue that real-life violence actually stems from larger social problems (such as poverty or mental illness), and that the theory makes mass media scapegoats for those larger problems.

Agenda-Setting

A consequence of agenda-setting is that the stories that don't get attention from the mass media don't make it on to the public and political agendas. The Human Rights Watch organization works to publicize the high maternal mortality rate in rural India and provide aid for women there.

Researchers who hold the **agenda-setting theory** believe that when mass media focus their attention on particular events or issues, they determine—that is, set the agenda for—what people discuss and what they pay attention to. Media thus do not so much tell us *what* to think as what to think *about*.

The first investigations into the possibility of agenda-setting began in the late 1960s, when scholars Maxwell McCombs and Donald Shaw compared issues cited by undecided voters on election day with issues covered heavily by the media. Since then, researchers exploring this theory have demonstrated that the more stories the news media do on a particular subject, the more importance audiences attach to that subject. For instance, the extensive news coverage of Hurricane Katrina in fall 2005 sparked a corresponding increase in public concern about the disaster. Today, with national news coverage of the aftereffects of Katrina almost nonexistent, public interest in the impact of Katrina has ebbed—even though many of the areas affected by the hurricane still lie in ruins.

The Cultivation Effect

The **cultivation effect theory** holds that heavy viewing of TV leads individuals to perceive the world in ways consistent with television portrayals. The major research into this hypothesis grew from the TV violence profiles of George Gerbner and his colleagues, who attempted to make broad generalizations about the impact of televised violence. Beginning in the late 1960s, these social scientists categorized and counted different types of violent acts shown on network television. Using a methodology that combines annual content analyses of TV violence with surveys, the cultivation effect suggests that the more time individuals spend viewing television and absorbing its viewpoints, the more likely their views of social reality will be "cultivated" by the images and portrayals they see on television.[11] For example, Gerbner's studies concluded that, although fewer than 1 percent of Americans are victims of violent crime in any single year, people who watch a lot of television tend to overestimate this percentage.

Some critics have charged that cultivation research has provided limited evidence to support its findings. In addition, some have argued that the cultivation effects recorded by Gerbner's studies have been minimal. When compared side by side, these critics argue, perceptions of heavy television viewers and nonviewers regarding how dangerous the world is are virtually identical.

The Spiral of Silence

Developed by German communication theorist Elisabeth Noelle-Neumann in the 1970s and 1980s, the **spiral of silence theory** links mass media, social psychology, and public opinion formation. The theory proposes that those who believe that their views on controversial issues are in the minority will keep their views to themselves for fear of social isolation. The theory is based on social psychology studies, such as the classic conformity studies of Solomon Asch in 1951. In Asch's study on the effects of group pressure, he demonstrated that a test subject is more likely to give clearly wrong answers to questions about line lengths if everyone else in the room (all secret confederates of the experimenter) unanimously state an incorrect answer. Noelle-Neumann argued that this effect is exacerbated by mass media, particularly television, which can quickly and widely communicate a real or presumed majority public opinion.

Noelle-Neumann acknowledges that not everyone keeps quiet if they think they hold a minority view. In many cases, "hard-core nonconformists" exist and remain vocal even in the face of possible social isolation. These individuals can even change public opinion by continuing to voice their views.

Third-Person Effect

Identified in a 1983 study by W. Phillips Davison, the **third-person effect theory** suggests that people believe others are more affected by media messages than they are themselves. In other words, this theory posits the idea that "we" can escape the worst effects of media while still worrying about people who are younger, less educated, less informed, or otherwise less capable of guarding against media influence.

Under this theory, we might fear that other people will, for example, take tabloids seriously, imitate violent movies, or get addicted to the Internet, while

VideoCentral ◉
**bedfordstmartins.com
/mediaessentials**

Media Effects Research
Experts discuss how media
effects research informs media
development.
Discussion: Why do you
think the question of media's
effects on children has been
such a continually big
concern among researchers?

dismissing the idea that any of those things could happen to us. It has been argued that the third-person effect is instrumental in censorship, as it would allow censors to assume immunity to the negative effects of any supposedly dangerous media they must examine.

Evaluating Social Scientific Research

Media effects research has deepened our understanding of the mass media. This wealth of research exists partly because funding for studies on media's impact on young people remains popular among politicians and has drawn ready government support since the 1960s. But funding restricts the scope of some media effects research, particularly if the agendas of government agencies, businesses, or other entities do not align with researchers' interests. Moreover, because media effects research operates best in examining media's impact on individual behavior, few of these studies explore how media shape larger community and social life. Some research has begun to address these deficits, as well as to explore the impact of media technology on international communication.

Cultural Approaches to Media Research

In the 1960s, cultural approaches to research emerged to challenge social scientific media effects theories and to compensate for those theories' limitations. In contrast to social scientific media research, the *cultural studies* mode of media research involves interpreting written and visual "texts" or artifacts as symbols that contain cultural, historical, and political meanings. For example, researchers might argue that the wave of police and crime shows that flooded the TV landscape in the mid-1960s was a response to Americans' fears about urban unrest and income disparity. A cultural approach thus offers interpretations of the stories, messages, and meanings that circulate throughout society.

Like social scientific media research, cultural studies media research has evolved in the decades since it first appeared.

Early Developments in Cultural Studies Media Research

In Europe, media studies have always favored interpretive rather than scientific approaches. Researchers there have approached the media from the perspective of literary or cultural critics rather than experimental or survey researchers. These approaches were built on the writings of political philosophers such as Karl Marx and Antonio Gramsci, who investigated how mass media support existing hierarchies in society.

In the United States, early criticism of media effects research came from the Frankfurt School, a group of European researchers who emigrated from Germany to America to escape Nazi persecution in the 1930s. Under the leadership of Max Horkheimer, T. W. Adorno, and Leo Lowenthal, this group advocated augmenting experimental approaches with historical and cultural approaches to investigate mass media's long-range effects on audiences.

Since the time of the Frankfurt School, criticisms of the media effects tradition and its methods have continued, with calls for more interpretive studies of the rituals of mass communication. Academics who have embraced a cultural approach to media research try to understand how media and culture are tied to the actual patterns of communication in daily life. For example, in the 1970s, Stuart Hall and his colleagues studied the British print media and the police, who were dealing with an apparent rise in crime and mugging incidents. Arguing that the close relationship between the news and the police created a form of urban surveillance, the authors of *Policing the Crisis* demonstrated that the mugging phenomenon was exacerbated, and in part created, by the key institutions assigned the social tasks of controlling crime and reporting on it.[12]

Contemporary Cultural Studies Approaches

Cultural research investigates daily experiences, especially through the lenses of race, gender, class, and sexuality, and of imbalances of power and status in society. Such research emphasizes how some groups have been marginalized and ignored throughout history, particularly African Americans, Native Americans, Asians and Asian Americans, Arabic peoples, Latinos, Appalachians, gay men and lesbians, immigrants, and women. Cultural studies researchers also seek to recover these lost or silenced voices. The major approaches they use are textual analysis, audience studies, and political economy studies.

Textual Analysis

Textual analysis entails a close reading and interpretation of cultural messages, including those found in books, movies, and TV programs—such as portrayals of Arab and Arab American characters in popular films.[13] Whereas social scientific research approaches media messages with the

Media critic Jack Shaheen analyzes the cultural messages behind portrayals of Arabs and Arab Americans in film and TV, like the Bugs Bunny cartoon shown here.

CONVERGING MEDIA
Case Study

Studying Digital Natives

During Michael Wesch's graduate training in anthropology, he spent a total of eighteen months in New Guinea studying the impact of print, mapping, and census-taking on the natives of the remote Mountain Ok region. Today, he continues to study cultural changes wrought by the introduction of communication media. But, instead of studying print, he focuses on Web 2.0. And instead of studying isolated villages untouched by contemporary communication technologies, he studies globally connected virtual cultures that are the very products of the newest media. That is, Wesch studies digital natives—people who are most at home with converged media.

Wesch's methods would be labeled qualitative in conventional media research; he conducts ethnographies of the way people use digital media in their everyday lives. This method surrenders claims of objectivity in favor of attaining insights through participant observation. Instead of studying the digital media strictly in terms of information exchange, which is the tendency in quantitative research, Wesch's Digital Ethnography Working Group looks at the much more complicated process of producing, sharing, contesting, and negotiating meaning, as it relates to media and media users.

Wesch emerged as a leading public intellectual in the area of Web 2.0 when, after working for months on an academic paper that would explain the significance of new Web tools, he realized that he needed to exploit digital media in order to explain the digital media. On January 31, 2007, he posted the results of this epiphany, a frenetic 271-second YouTube video titled "The Machine is Us/ing Us." Wesch used screen shots of editing source code, bookmarking sites, creating blogs, and posting images to create a compelling and concise multimedia message, framed with a high-lighted composite quote from "We Are the Web" by

Kevin Kelly and followed by an appeal to move beyond thinking of Web 2.0 as mere information processing, noting that "the Web is no longer just linking information . . . the Web is linking people."

The simplicity and eloquence of Wesch's presentation attracted immediate attention in the blogosphere, and thanks to Digg, Delicious, and Technorati, "The Machine is Us/ing Us" quickly became the most-viewed video on the Web, even beating out all the Super Bowl ads that appeared the next weekend.[1] In its first six weeks, the video attracted 1.8 million views. Today, that number has grown to 11 million.

Wesch serves not only as a leading figure for researchers studying the convergent media, but also as a model of sorts for students who are considering careers in media research. Wesch demonstrates that research motivated by the quest for meaning provides avenues for gaining deep insights into how our identities and our values have been shaped by mediated experiences. Ultimately, his work on digital natives is designed to make us more self-conscious about the impact of converged media. This orientation on self-knowledge and how it relates to media literacy is apparent in the only question that appears on final exams in his anthropology classes: "Why are you here?"

principles of modern science in mind—replicability, objectivity, and data—textual analysis looks at rituals, narratives, and meaning.

Although textual analysis has a long and rich history in film and literary studies, it gained new significance for mass media in 1974 with the publication of Horace Newcomb's *TV: The Most Popular Art*, the first academic book to analyze television shows. Newcomb studied why certain TV programs and formats, such as the *Beverly Hillbillies*, *Bewitched*, and *Dragnet*, became popular. Trained as a literary scholar, Newcomb argued that content analysis and other social science approaches to popular media often ignored artistic traditions and social context.

Before Newcomb's work, textual analysis focused only on "important" or highly regarded works of art—debates, films, poems, and books. But by the end of the 1970s, a new generation of media studies scholars, who had grown up on television and rock and roll, began studying less elite forms of culture. By shifting the focus to daily popular culture, such studies shone a spotlight on the more ordinary ways that "normal" people (not just military, political, or religious leaders) experience and interpret their daily lives through messages in media.

Audience Studies

Audience studies differ from textual analysis in that the subject being researched is the audience for the text, not the text itself. For example, in her book *Reading the Romance: Women, Patriarchy and Popular Literature*, Janice Radway studied a group of midwestern women who enjoyed romance novels. Using her training in literary criticism and employing interviews and questionnaires, Radway investigated the meaning of romance novels to these women. She argued that reading romance novels functions as personal time for some women. The study also suggested that these particular romance-novel fans identified with the active, independent qualities of the romantic heroines they most admired.

As a cultural study, Radway's work did not claim to be scientific, and her findings cannot be generalized to all women. Rather, Radway investigated and interpreted the relationship between reading popular fiction and ordinary life for a specific group of women.[14] Such studies help to define culture as comprising both the *products* a society fashions (such as romance novels) and the *processes* that forge those products (see "Converging Media Case Study: Studying Digital Natives" on page 494).

Political Economy Studies

A focus on the production of popular culture and the forces behind it is the topic of **political economy studies**, which examine interconnections among economic interests, political power, and ways in which that power is used. Major concerns of such studies include the increasing consolidation of media ownership. With this consolidation, the production of media content is being controlled by fewer and fewer organizations, investing those for-profit companies with more and more power to dominate public discourse. The theory is that money—not democratic expression—is now the driving force behind public communication and popular culture.

Political economy studies work best when combined with textual analysis and audience studies to provide fuller context for understanding a media product: the cultural content of the media product, the economics and politics of its production, and audiences' responses to it.

Evaluating Cultural Studies Research

A major strength of cultural studies research is that researchers can more easily examine the ties between media messages and the broader social, economic, and political world since such research is not bound by precise control variables. For instance, social science research on politics has generally concentrated on election polls and voting patterns. But cultural research has broadened the discussion to examine class, gender, and cultural differences among voters and the various uses of power by individuals and institutions in positions of authority.

Yet just as social scientific media research has its limits, so does cultural studies media research. Sometimes cultural studies have focused exclusively on the meanings of media programs or "texts," ignoring their effect on audiences. Some cultural studies have tried to address this deficiency by incorporating audience studies. Both social scientists and cultural studies researchers today have begun to look more closely at the limitations of their work, and to borrow ideas from each other to better assess media's meaning and impact.

Media Research in a Democratic Society

One charge frequently leveled at academic studies is that they don't address the everyday problems of life and thus have little practical application. To be sure, media research has built a growing knowledge base and dramatically advanced what we know about mass media's effect on individuals and societies. But the larger public has had little access to the research process, even though cultural studies research tends to identify with marginalized groups. Any scholarship is self-defeating if its complexity removes it from the daily experience of the groups it examines. Researchers themselves have even found it difficult to speak to one another because of differences in the discipline-specific language they use to analyze and report their findings.

In addition, increasing specialization in the 1970s began isolating many researchers from life outside the university. Academics were criticized as being locked away in their "ivory towers," concerned with seemingly obscure matters the general public could not relate to. However, academics across many fields moved to mitigate this isolation, becoming increasingly active in political and cultural life in the 1980s and 1990s. For example, essayist and cultural critic Barbara Ehrenreich has written frequently about labor and economic issues in magazines such as *Time* and the *Nation* and has written several books on such issues.

Public intellectuals like Barbara Ehrenreich (*center*) cross the boundary between academics and the general public.

In recent years, public intellectuals have also encouraged discussion of the new challenges posed by media production in a digital world. Stanford University law professor Lawrence Lessig has been a leading advocate of efforts to rewrite the nation's copyright laws to enable noncommercial "amateur culture" to flourish on the Internet. He publishes his work in print and online. American University's Pat Aufderheide, longtime media critic for the alternative magazine *In These Times*, worked with independent filmmakers to develop the *Documentary Filmmakers' Statement of Best Practices in Fair Use*. The statement calls for documentary filmmakers to have reasonable access to copyrighted material for their work.

Like journalists, public intellectuals based on campuses help advance the conversations taking place in larger society. They actively circulate the most important new ideas of the day—including those related to mass media—and serve as models for how to participate in public life.

CHAPTER ESSENTIALS

Now that you have finished reading this chapter, you can use the following tools:

REVIEW

Explain Early Media Research Methods

- Scientific approaches to mass media research did not emerge until the late 1920s and 1930s (p. 479).

- Four trends that contributed to the rise of modern media research include **propaganda analysis** (the study of propaganda's effectiveness in influencing and mobilizing public opinion), public opinion research (which utilizes social scientific methods to conduct surveys and polls to examine how the mass media filter and shape public attitudes; **pseudo-polls**—typically call-in, online, or person-in-the-street polls—don't use random samples, and the results therefore don't represent the population as a whole), social psychology studies (which measure the behavior and thinking processes of individuals), and marketing research (which conducts surveys on consumer buying habits and other behaviors) (pp. 479, 481, 484).

Evaluate Social Scientific Research

- Between the 1930s and 1970s, media researchers developed several models about how media affect individuals' behavior. These models include the **hypodermic needle** or **magic bullet** (whose model suggests that powerful media adversely affect weak audiences), **minimal effects** or **limited effects** (whose model attempts to understand, explain, and predict the impact—or effects—of the mass media on individuals in society and argues that people generally engage in **selective exposure** and **selective retention**, exposing themselves to media messages most familiar to them), and **uses and gratifications** (which holds that people actively engage in using media to satisfy various emotional or intellectual needs) (pp. 484–486).

- At the same time, researchers developed different approaches to conducting their research. Most media research today focuses on media's impact and employs the **scientific method**, whose key step includes posing one or more **hypotheses** (general statements that predict the influence of an independent variable on a dependent variable). Researchers using the scientific method may conduct **experiments** (which isolate some aspect of content by using a control group picked through **random assignment**) or **survey research** (which is a method of collecting and measuring data taken from a group of respondents) (pp. 486–488).

- Researchers can use extensive government and academic survey databases now widely available to conduct **longitudinal studies**, where they compare new studies with those conducted years earlier. Surveys can show only **correlations**—or associations—between two variables, not demonstrable causes and effects. Another approach researchers can follow is **content analysis** (which describes media content and its elements by systematically categorizing and coding it) (pp. 488–489).

- By the 1960s, researchers began developing new theories about how media affect people, such as **social learning theory** (which suggests a link between mass media and subjects who learn and then model media behavior), **agenda-setting theory** (which states that when the mass media pay attention to particular events or issues, they determine the major topics of interest for individuals and society), the **cultivation effect theory** (which suggests that heavy television viewing leads individuals to perceive reality in ways that are consistent with the portrayals they see on television), the **spiral of silence theory** (which links the mass media, social psychology, and the suppression of public opinion), and the **third-person effect theory** (which suggests that people believe others are more affected by media messages than they are themselves) (pp. 489–492).

Discuss Cultural Studies Approaches to Media Research

- In the 1960s, **cultural studies** approaches to research emerged to challenge mainstream media effects theories. Early cultural studies research was built on the writings of political philosophers such as Karl Marx and Antonio Gramsci and the criticisms of media effects research from the Frankfurt School (pp. 492–493).

- Contemporary cultural studies approaches focus on **textual analysis** (a close reading and interpretation of cultural messages), **audience studies** (which differs from textual analysis in that the subject being researched is the audience for the text, not the text itself), and **political economy studies** (which examine interconnections among economic interests, political power, and ways in which that power is used) (pp. 493, 495–496).

Assess the Role of Media Research in Our Democratic Society

- Although media research has advanced what we know about mass media's effect on individuals and society, most people do not have access to the actual research process, which makes it hard to connect scholarship to the daily experience of the groups such research examines (p. 496).

- We rely on public intellectuals to help advance the conversations taking place in larger society and culture. These individuals encourage discussion of the new challenges posed by media (p. 497).

STUDY QUESTIONS

1. What are ways in which the mass media might be implicated in social problems like bullying, gun violence, and vitriolic political speech, and how might the social scientific and cultural studies research traditions respond differently to them?
2. What are pseudo-polls, and what about them makes them less reliable than social scientific polls and surveys?
3. What are the main ideas behind social learning theory, agenda-setting, the cultivation effect, the spiral of silence, and the third-person effect theory?
4. Why did cultural studies develop in opposition to social scientific media research?
5. What role do media researchers have in public debates about the mass media?

MEDIA LITERACY PRACTICE

In the beginning of this chapter, three stories suggested relationships between the media and (a) antigay bullying, (b) gun violence, and (c) "self-harm" behaviors. Investigate one of these topics through a content analysis. Work in groups of three.

DESCRIBE the nature of the problem and define coding categories for identifying content (e.g., accounts of homophobic or other bullying, stories associated with gunplay, or images glorifying unhealthy bodies) in certain types of media (e.g., the teen blogosphere, social media sites, action movies, or fashion advertisements). Then, have two others individually apply your coding scheme to the same media content. (If this is an effective coding scheme, their answers should agree at least 80 percent of the time. If not, rethink your definitions and coding scheme.)

ANALYZE the patterns in the data.

INTERPRET what these patterns mean. For example, do social media posts and blogs describing behaviors hurtful to oneself or others make those behaviors seem more acceptable? Do action movies suggest that surviving deadly gun battles makes one a hero? Do images of fashion models represent a limited range of body types?

EVALUATE the effectiveness of content analysis as a method. Do your original definitions affect the outcome of the analysis? How far does the content data go in proving any kind of media effects or impact?

ENGAGE with the community by presenting your conclusions to your class for feedback. If your research is strong enough, consult with your instructor and consider presenting your paper at an academic conference.

◉ ONLINE RESOURCES

Go to **bedfordstmartins.com/mediaessentials** for review quizzes, links, and more.

Visit the site's **VIDEOCENTRAL: MASS COMMUNICATION** section for videos like the one on page 491.

Notes

1 Mass Communication: A Critical Approach

1. See "Media Fasting: On 'Internet Addiction' and the Changing Face of News," *You Just Get Me*, April 29, 2010, http://blogs.psychsterdata.com/yjgm/2010/04/off-the-internet-for-24-hours-world-of-psychology.html.
2. James W. Carey, *Communication as Culture: Essays on Media and Society* (Boston: Unwin Hyman, 1989), 203.
3. For a historical discussion of culture, see Lawrence Levine, *Highbrow/Lowbrow: The Emergence of Cultural Hierarchy in America* (Cambridge, Mass.: Harvard University Press, 1988).
4. For overviews of this position, see Neil Postman, *Amusing Ourselves to Death: Public Discourse in the Age of Show Business* (New York: Penguin Books, 1985), 19; and Stuart Ewen, *Captains of Consciousness: Advertising and the Social Roots of the Consumer Culture* (New York: McGraw-Hill, 1976).
5. See Carey, *Communication as Culture*.
6. Tasha N. Dubriwny, "Constructing Breast Cancer in the News: Betty Ford and the Evolution of the Breast Cancer Patient," *Journal of Communication Inquiry*, 33(2), (2009): 104–125.
7. Charles K. Atkin, Sandi W. Smith, Courtnay McFeters, and Vanessa Ferguson, "A Comprehensive Analysis of Breast Cancer News Coverage in Leading Media Outlets Focusing on Environmental Risks and Prevention," *Health Communication* 13 (January/February 2008): 3–19.
8. Brooks Barnes, "Lab Watches Web Surfers to See Which Ads Work," *New York Times*, July 26, 2009, http://www.nytimes.com/2009/07/27/technology/27disney.html.
9. See Jon Katz, "Rock, Rap and Movies Bring You the News," *Rolling Stone*, March 5, 1992, 33.

CONVERGING MEDIA CASE STUDY: Disney and Steve Jobs, p. 10

1. See "Disney Buys Pixar for $7.4 bn," *Rediff India Abroad*, January 25, 2006, http://rediff.com/money/2006/jan/25disney.htm.
2. "Disney Now Largest Media Company,"*Huffington Post*, May 2, 2009, http://www.huffingtonpost.com/2009/04/01/disney-now-the-largest-me_n_181670.html.
3. Walt Disney Company, "Company Overview," accessed February 7, 2012, http://corporate.disney.go.com/corporate/overview.htm.

MEDIA LITERACY CASE STUDY: Bedouins, Camels, Transistors, and Coke, p. 22

1. Václav Havel, "A Time for Transcendence," *Utne Reader*, January/February 1995, 53.

2 Books and the Power of Print

1. Jack Zipes, quoted in Henry Kisor, "Way Too Many Books . . . ," *Chicago Sun-Times*, December 25, 2005, p. 9B.
2. See Elizabeth Eisenstein, *The Printing Press as an Agent of Change* (Cambridge: Cambridge University Press, 1980).
3. For a comprehensive historical overview of the publishing industry and the rise of publishing houses, see John A. Tebbel, *A History of Book Publishing in the United States*, 4 vols. (New York: R. R. Bowker, 1972–81).
4. Bibb Porter, "In Publishing, Bigger Is Better," *New York Times*, March 31, 1998, p. A27.
5. National Association of College Stores, "FAQ on College Textbooks," May 2008, http://nacs.org/common/research/faq_textbooks.pdf.
6. Claire Cain Miller and Julie Bosman, "E-books Outsell Print Books at Amazon," *New York Times*, May 19, 2011, www.nytimes.com/2011/05/20/technology/20amazon.html.

CONVERGING MEDIA CASE STUDY: Self-Publishing Gets Redefined, p. 49

1. Rikki Novetsky, "E-book Revolution," *Eye*, September 29, 2011, http://eye.columbiaspectator.com/?q=article/2011/09/29/e-book-revolution.
2. David Streitfeld, "Amazon Signs Up Authors, Writing Publishers Out of Deal," *New York Times*, October 16, 2011, http://www.nytimes.com/2011/10/17/technology/amazon-rewrites-the-rules-of-book-publishing.html.
3. Kevin Bloom, "Analysis: If Amazon Ruled Book Publishing, Too..." *Daily Maverick*, October 19, 2011, http://dailymaverick.co.za/article/2011-10-19-analysis-if-amazon-ruled-book-publishing-too.
4. Streitfeld, "Amazon Signs Up Authors."

3 Newspapers: The Rise and Decline of Modern Journalism

1. See Brooke Kroeger, *Nellie Bly: Daredevil, Reporter, Feminist* (New York: Times Books/Random House, 1994).
2. "Newspaper Ad Revs Fall 7% in Q1," *News & Tech*, June 3, 2011,http://www.newsandtech.com/news/article_85a668a2-8c6e-11e0-9f93-001cc4c002e0.html.
3. Michael Schudson, *Discovering the News: A Social History of American Newspapers* (New York: Basic Books, 1978), 23.
4. See David T. Z. Mindich, "Edwin M. Stanton, the Inverted Pyramid, and Information Control," *Journalism Monographs* 140 (August 1993).
5. Curtis D. MacDougall, *The Press and Its Problems* (Dubuque, IA: William C. Brown, 1964), 143, 189.

6. Walter Lippmann, *Liberty and the News* (New York: Harcourt, Brace and Howe, 1920), 92.

7. Dianiela Gevson, "Spanish-Language Dailies Expand a Bitter Battle," *New York Sun*, January 21, 2004, p. 2.

8. Project for Excellence in Journalism, *The State of the News Media 2007*, http://www.stateofthemedia .org/2007.

9. See Mark Fitzgerald, "ASNE Survey: Over Last Year, Dailies Shrank Their Newsrooms by the Biggest Margin in Three Decades," *Editor & Publisher*, April 13, 2008, www.editorandpublisher.com.

10. "The New Face of Washington's Press Corps," Pew Research Center Publications, February 11, 2009, http://pewresearch.org/pubs/1115/washington-press -corps-study.

11. Pew Research Center's Project for Excellence in Journalism, *The State of the News Media 2011*, http://www.stateofthemedia.org/2011/.

12. Seth Mnookin, "The Kingdom and the Paywall," *New York*, July 24, 2011, http://nymag.com/news/media/new-york -times-2011-8/.

13. John Carroll, "News War, Part 3," *Frontline*, PBS, February 27, 2007, http://www.pbs.org/wgbh/pages /frontline/newswar/etc/script3.html.

MEDIA LITERACY CASE STUDY: Covering Business News, p. 72

1. Alan Rusbridger, "How We Broke the Murdoch Scandal," *Newsweek*, July 17, 2011, http://www.thedailybeast.com /newsweek/2011/07/17/how-the-guardian-broke-the -news-of-the-world-hacking-scandal.html.

CONVERGING MEDIA CASE STUDY: News Aggegration, p. 86

1. "What Is Newser?" *Newser*, accessed December 2011, http://www.newser.com/what-is-newser.aspx.

2. Mark Cuban, "My Advice to Fox & MySpace on Selling Content—Yes You Can," *Blog Maverick*, August 8, 2009, http://blogmaverick.com/2009/08/08/my-advice-to-fox -myspace-on-selling-content-yes-you-can/.

3. Michael Wolff, "Mark Cuban Is a Big Fat Idiot—News Will Stay Free," *Huffington Post*, August 12, 2009, http://www .huffingtonpost.com/michael-wolff/mark-cuban-is-a-big -fat-i_b_257483.html.

4. See "The New News," James Cameron Memorial Lecture, September 22, 2010, http://image.guardian.co.uk/sysfiles /Media/documents/2010/09/23/DownieCameron.pdf; and

Jack Shaffer, "Len Downie Calls Arianna Huffington a Parasite," *Slate*, September 23, 2010, http://www.slate.com /articles/news_and_politics/press_box/2010/09 /len_downie_calls_arianna_huffington_a_parasite.html.

5. Arianna Huffington, "Leonard Downie's Downer," *Guardian*, September 23, 2009, http://www.guardian .co.uk/commentisfree/cifamerica/2010/sep/23 /huffington-post-washington-post.

4 Magazines in the Age of Specialization

1. See Theodore Peterson, *Magazines in the Twentieth Century* (Urbana: University of Illinois Press, 1964), 5.

2. Pew Research Center's Project for Excellence in Journalism, "Magazines: By the Numbers," *State of the News Media 2011*, http://stateofthemedia.org/2011 /magazines-essay/data-page-4/.

3. See "Readex Research Survey Finds Professionals Not Replacing Print with Digital," October 2011, http://www .marketwatch.com/story/readex-research-survey-finds -professionals-not-replacing-print-with-digital-2011-10-19.

4. See Gloria Steinem, "Sex, Lies and Advertising," *Ms.*, July–August 1990, 18–28.

MEDIA LITERACY CASE STUDY: The Evolution of Photojournalism, p. 104

1. Andrew Adam Newman, "3 Magazines Are Accused of Retouching Celebrity Photos to Excess," *New York Times*, May 28, 2007, http://www.nytimes.com/2007/05 /28/business/media/28fitness.html.

CONVERGING MEDIA CASE STUDY: Print, Web, and Synergy, p. 114

1. See "*Newsweek* and the *Daily Beast* Combine," *Daily Beast*, November 12, 2010, http://www.thedailybeast.com /articles/2010/11/12/newsweek-daily-beast-merge -announcement.html.

5 Sound Recording and Popular Music

1. Zacharly Lazar, "The 373-Hit Wonder," *New York Times*, January 6, 2011, http://www.nytimes.com/2011/01/09 /magazine/09GirlTalk-t.html.

2. Mark Coleman, *Playback: From the Victrola to MP3* (Cambridge, Mass.: Da Capo Press, 2003).

3. Mick Jagger, quoted in Jann S. Wenner, "Jagger Remembers," *Rolling Stone*, December 14, 1995, 66.

4. See Mac Rebennack (Dr. John) with Jack Rummel, *Under a Hoodoo Moon* (New York: St. Martin's Press, 1994), 58.

5. Ken Tucker, quoted in Ed Ward, Geoffrey Stokes, and Ken Tucker, *Rock of Ages: The Rolling Stone History of Rock & Roll* (New York: Rolling Stone Press, 1986), 521.
6. See "The Nashville Sound Begins," *Living in Stereo*, September 19, 2006, http://livinginstereo.com/?p=252.
7. See "What Is Countrypolitan Music?" http://www.countrypolitan.com/intro0101.php.
8. Ben Sisario, "Music Sales Fell in 2008, but Climbed on the Web," *New York Times*, January 1, 2009, http://www.nytimes.com/2009/01/01/art/music/01indu.html.
9. RIAA, *2008 Year-End Shipment Statistics*, http://76.74.24.142/1D212C0E-408B-F730-65A0-C0F5871C369D.pdf.
10. "It Isn't Pretty: RIAA 2010 Sales Music Data," April 29, 2011, http://www.hypebot.com/hypebot/2011/04/it-isnt-pretty-riaa-2010-music-sales-data-chart.html.
11. IFPI, *IFPI Digital Music Report 2008*, January 24, 2008, http://www.ifpi.org/content/section_resources/dmr2008.html.
12. Sisario, "Music Sales Fell in 2008."
13. "It Isn't Pretty."
14. Steven Winodgrasky, "Artist Royalties from iTunes: New Media, Same Old Battle," March 17, 2008, *The Royalty Report*, http://apo.org.au/node/17151.

CONVERGING MEDIA CASE STUDY: 360 Degrees of Music, p. 150
1. "For Radiohead Fans, Does 'Free' + 'Download' = 'Freeload'?" comScore, November 5, 2007, http://www.comscore.com/Press_Events/Press_Releases/2007/11/Radiohead_Downloads.
2. See Sara Karubian, "360 Degree Deals: An Industry Reaction to the Devaluation of Recorded Music," *Southern California Interdisciplinary Law Journal* 18, no. 395 (2009): 395–462, http://www-bcf.usc.edu/~idjlaw/PDF/18-2/18-2%20Karubian.pdf.
3. Karubian, "360 Degree Deals."

6 Popular Radio and the Origins of Broadcasting

1. Tom Lewis, *Empire of the Air: The Men Who Made Radio* (New York: HarperCollins, 1991), 181.
2. Michael Pupin, "Objections Entered to Court's Decision," *New York Times*, June 10, 1934, p. E5.
3. For a full discussion of early broadcast history and the formation of RCA, see Eric Barnouw, *Tube of Plenty* (New York: Oxford University Press, 1982); Susan Douglas, *Inventing American Broadcasting, 1899–1922* (Baltimore: Johns Hopkins University Press, 1987); and Christopher Sterling and John Kitross, *Stay Tuned: A Concise History of American Broadcasting* (Belmont, Calif.: Wadsworth, 1990).
4. Michele Hilmes, *Radio Voices: American Broadcasting, 1922–1952* (Minneapolis: University of Minnesota Press, 1997).
5. "Amos 'n' Andy Show," Museum of Broadcast Communications, http://www.museum.tv/archives/etv/A/htmlA/amosnandy/amosnandy.htm.
6. Radio Advertising Bureau, "Radio Marketing Guide," http://www.rab.com/public/marketingGuide/marketingGuide.pdf.
7. Peter DiCola, "False Premises, False Promises: A Quantitative History of Ownership Consolidation in the Radio Industry," Future of Music Coalition, December 2006, http://www.futureofmusic.org/research/radiostudy06.cfm.
8. "Statement of FCC Chairman William E. Kennard on Low Power FM Radio Initiative," March 27, 2000, http://www.fcc.gov/Speeches/Kennard/Statements/2000/stwek024.html.

CONVERGING MEDIA CASE STUDY: Streaming Music, p. 183
1. Jefferson Graham, "Pandora Sees a Huge Jump in Audience," *USA Today*, January 17, 2012, http://www.usatoday.com/tech/columnist/talkingtech/story/2012-01-17/pandora-radio/52623102/1.
2. Alexandre Roche, "Listen to Music with Your Friends," *Facebook Blog*, January 12, 2012, http://blog.facebook.com/blog.php?post=10150457932027131.

7 Movies and the Impact of Images

1. Douglas Gomery, *Shared Pleasures: A History of Movie Presentation in the United States* (Madison: University of Wisconsin Press, 1992), 18.
2. Douglas Gomery, *Movie History: A Survey* (Belmont, Calif.: Wadsworth, 1991), 167.
3. Based on MPAA reports over the past ten years.
4. Motion Picture Association of America, *Theatrical Market Statistics 2011*, http://www.mpaa.org/policy/industry.
5. Kinsey Lowe, "Cinema's Digital Takeover: The Decline and Fall of Film as We Have Known it," *Deadline Hollywood*, February 4, 2012, http://www.deadline.com.

MEDIA LITERACY CASE STUDY: Breaking through Hollywood's Race Barrier, p. 208
1. Douglas Gomery, *Shared Pleasures: A History of Movie Presentation in the United States* (Madison: University of Wisconsin Press, 1992), 155–170.

CONVERGING MEDIA CASE STUDY: Movie Theaters and Live Exhibition, p. 217

1. "Comedy: Amos 'n' Andy," Radio Hall of Fame, accessed February 10, 2012, http://www.radiohof.org/comedy/amosnandy.html.

2. "NCM Fathom Entertainment Events," National CineMedia, updated March 30, 2011, http://www.ncm.com/content/pdf/NCM_Fathom_Events_Chronology.pdf.

3. "Cinedigm's Live 3-D Broadcast of BCS Championship Game Sees Huge Turnout," Cinedigm Digital Cinema Corp., accessed October 6, 2012, http://investor.cinedigm.com/releasedetail.cfm?releaseid=358745.

4. Richard Verrier, "Movie Theaters Turn to Live Event Screenings to fill Seats," *Los Angeles Times*, April 20, 2010, http://articles.latimes.com/2010/apr/20/news/la-ct-theater20-20100420.

8 Television, Cable, and Specialization in Visual Culture

1. See Horace Newcomb, *TV: The Most Popular Art* (Garden City, N.Y.: Anchor Books, 1974), 31, 39.

2. See "Just the Facts: Consumer Choice Explodes, 1992–2012," National Cable & Telecommunications Association, http://www.ncta.com/statistic/statistic/Consumer-Choice-Explodes.aspx.

3. *United States v. Midwest Video Corp.*, 440 U.S. 689 (1979).

9 The Internet and New Technologies: The Media Converge

1. David Pogue, "The Year of the Cellphone," *New York Times*, December 13, 2007, http://www.nytimes.com/indexes/2007/12/13/technology/circuitsemail/index.html.

2. "John Seigenthaler Sr. Wikipedia Biography Controversy," *Wikipedia, The Free Encyclopedia*, accessed March 3, 2008, http://en.wikipedia.org/w/index.php?title=John_Seigenthaler_Sr._Wikipedia_biography_controversy&oldid=45268872.

3. Steven Musil, "Week in Review: Windows Woes," *New York Times*, February 29, 2008, http://www.nytimes.com/cnet/CNET_2100-1083_3-6232545.html.

4. See Federal Trade Commission, *Privacy Online: Fair Information Practices in the Electronic Marketplace*, May 2000, http://www.ftc.gov/reports/privacy2000.pdf.

CONVERGING MEDIA CASE STUDY: Fragmentation, Polarization, and Convergence, p. 283

1. Corbin Hiar, "How the Tea Party Utilized Digital Media to Gain Power," MediaShift, PBS.org, October 28, 2010, http://www.pbs.org/mediashift/2010/10/how-the-tea-party-utilized-digital-media-to-gain-power301.html.

10 Electronic Gaming and the Media Playground

1. Entertainment Software Association, "Essential Facts about the Computer and Video Game Industry," 2012, http://www.theesa.com/newsroom/release_detail.asp?releaseID=174.

2. Brett Staebell, "BoxeR in Brief," *Escapist*, April 6, 2010, http://www.escapistmagazine.com/articles/view/issues/issue_248/7378-BoxeR-in-Brief.

3. Erkki Huhtamo, "Slots of Fun, Slots of Trouble: An Archaeology of Arcade Gaming," in *Handbook of Computer Games*, ed. Joost Raessens and Jeffrey Goldstein (Cambridge, Mass.: MIT Press, 2005).

4. Ibid, 9–10.

5. Seth Porges, "11 Things You Didn't Know about Pinball History," *Popular Mechanics*, accessed April 5, 2012, http://www.popularmechanics.com/technology/gadgets/toys/4328211-new#slide-1.

6. "Magnavox Odyssey," PONG-Story, accessed April 5, 2012, http://pong-story.com/odyssey.html.

7. Fantasy Sports Trade Association, "Welcome to the Official Site of the FSTA," accessed April 5, 2012, http://www.ftsa.org.

8. Henry Jenkins, "Interactive Audiences?: The 'Collective Intelligence' of Media Fans," in *The New Media Book*, ed. Dan Harries (London: British Film Institute, 2002).

9. "South Korean Couple Starved Child while Raising 'Virtual Baby,'" *CNN World*, March 5, 2010, http://articles.cnn.com/2010-03-05/world/korea.baby.starved_1_online-addiction-virtual-world-online-game?_s=PM:WORLD.

10. Entertainment Software Association, "Essential Facts about the Computer and Video Game Industry."

11. "What Is GameSpot.com Fuse?" GameSpot.com, May 24, 2011, http://www.gamespot.com/forums/topic/28672086.

12. "Top 10 Most Expensive Video Game Budgets Ever," DigitalBattle.com, February 20, 2010, http://digitalbattle.com/2010/02/20/top-10-most-expensive-video-game-budgets-ever/.

13. "IGA Worldwide," YouTube.com, April 8, 2009, http://www.youtube.com/watch?v=dGKum-lo9V8.

14. "Top 10 Most Expensive Video Game Budgets Ever."

15. "John Madden Net Worth," CelebrityNetworth.com, accessed April 5, 2012, http://www.celebritynetworth.com/richest-athletes/nfl/john-madden-net-worth/.

16. Entertainment Software Rating Board, *Game Ratings & Descriptor Guide*, accessed April 5, 2012, http://www.esrb.org/ratings/ratings_guide.jsp.

17. Evan Narcisse, "Supreme Court: Video Games Qualify for First Amendment Protection," *Time Techland*, Time.com, June 27, 2011, http://techland.time.com/2011/06/27 /supreme-court-video-games-qualify-for-first-amendment -protection/.

MEDIA LITERACY CASE STUDY: Writing about Games, p. 312
1. "Bow, Nigger," always_black.com, September 22, 2004, http://www.alwaysblack.com/blackbox/bownigger.html.
2. Kieron Gillen, "The New Games Journalism," always_black.com, September 22, 2004, http://www .alwaysblack.com/?p=11.

11 Advertising and Commercial Culture

1. Stuart Elliott, "Advertising's Big Four: It's Their World Now," *New York Times*, March 31, 2002, sec. 3 (Money and Business), p. 1.
2. Randall Rothenberg, *Where the Suckers Moon: An Advertising Story* (New York: Alfred A. Knopf, 1994), 20.
3. See Bettina Fabos, "The Commercialized Web: Challenges for Libraries and Democracy," *Library Trends* 53, no. 4 (Spring 2005): 519–523.
4. See Michael Schudson, *Advertising: The Uneasy Persuasion* (New York: Basic Books, 1984), 36–43; and Andrew Robertson, *The Lessons of Failure* (London: MacDonald, 1974).
5. Katharine Q. Seelye, "About $2.6 Billion Spent on Political Ads in 2008," *The Caucus*, nytimes.com, December 2, 2008, http://thecaucus.blogs.nytimes.com/2008/12/02 /about-2.6-billion-spent-on-political-ads-in-2008.

12 Public Relations and Framing the Message

1. Christie D'Zurilla, "Ashton Kutcher's Paterno Tweet Sends Actor Running for PR Cover," *Ministry of Gossip, Los Angeles Times*, November 10, 2011, http://latimesblogs .latimes.com/gossip/2011/11/ashton-kutcher-paterno -tweet-aplusk-ashton-kutcher.html.
2. Matthew J. Culligan and Dolph Greene, *Getting Back to the Basics of Public Relations and Publicity* (New York: Crown Publishers, 1982), 100.
3. Marvin N. Olasky, "The Development of Corporate Public Relations, 1850–1930," *Journalism Monographs* 102 (April 1987): 15.
4. Michael Schudson, *Discovering the News: A Social History of American Newspapers* (New York: Basic Books, 1978), 136.
5. "Lobbying: Overview," OpenSecrets.org, accessed October 7, 2012, http://www.opensecrets.org/lobby /index.php.

6. Philip Shenon, "3 Partners Quit Firm Handling Saudis' P.R.," *New York Times*, December 6, 2002, http://www.nytimes .com/2002/12/06/international/middleeast/06SAUD .html?ex=1040199544&ei=1&en=c061b2d98376e7ba.

CONVERGING MEDIA CASE STUDY: YouTube and Wartime PR, p. 365
1. Cori E. Dauber, *YouTube War: Fighting in a World of Cameras in Every Cell Phone and Photoshop on Every Computer*, Strategic Studies Institute, U.S. Army War College, November 2009, http://www .strategicstudiesinstitute.army.mil/pdffiles/pub951.pdf.

MEDIA LITERACY CASE STUDY: Improving the Credibility Gap, p. 368
1. Nia Elizabeth Shepherd et al., "Who's Who: The Eco-Guide," *Time*, April 20, 2006, http://www.time.com/time /magazine/article/0,9171,1185518,00.html.

13 The Culture of Journalism: Values, Ethics, and Democracy

1. For another list and an alternative analysis of news criteria, see the Missouri Group, *News Reporting and Writing*, 10th ed. (New York: Bedford/St. Martin's, 2011), 5–6.
2. Herbert Gans, *Deciding What's News* (New York: Pantheon, 1979), 42–48.
3. Ibid.
4. *SPJ Code of Ethics*, Society of Professional Journalists, 1996, http://www.spj.org/ethicscode.asp.
5. Ibid.
6. For reference and guidance on media ethics, see Clifford Christians, Mark Fackler, and Kim Rotzoll, *Media Ethics: Cases and Moral Reasoning*, 4th ed. (White Plains, N.Y.: Longman, 1995); and Thomas H. Bivins, "A Worksheet for Ethics Instruction and Exercises in Reason," *Journalism Educator* (Summer 1993): 4–16.
7. Mike Royko, quoted in "News Media: A Searching of Conscience," *Newsweek*, May 4, 1981, 53.
8. Davis "Buzz" Merritt, *Public Journalism and Public Life: Why Telling the News Is Not Enough* (Hillsdale, N.J.: Lawrence Erlbaum, 1995), 113–114.
9. Katharine Q. Seelye, "Best-Informed Also View Fake News, Study Finds," *New York Times*, April 16, 2007.
10. David Broder, quoted in "Squaring with the Reader: A Seminar on Journalism," *Kettering Review* (Winter 1992): 48.
11. Christopher Lasch, "Journalism, Publicity and the Lost Art of Argument," *Gannett Center Journal* 4(2) (Spring 1990): 1.

MEDIA LITERACY CASE STUDY: Bias in the News, p. 388
1. Harris Poll #52, "News Reporting Perceived as Biased . . . ," Harris Interactive, June 30, 2006, http://www.harrisinteractive.com/harris_poll.
2. *Random House Webster's Unabridged Dictionary*, 2nd ed., s.vv. "conservative," "liberal."
3. See Herbert Gans, *Deciding What's News* (New York: Pantheon, 1979).
4. See Bernard Goldberg, *Bias: A CBS Insider Exposes How the Media Distort the News* (New York: Perennial, 2003).
5. See Eric Alterman, *What Liberal Media? The Truth about Bias and the News* (New York: Basic Books, 2003).

14 Legal Controls and Freedom of Expression

1. Jenna Worthan, "Public Outcry over Antipiracy Bills Began as Grass-Roots Grumbling," *New York Times*, January 19, 2012, http://www.nytimes.com/2012/01/20/technology/public-outcry-over-antipiracy-bills-began-as-grass-roots-grumbling.html?_r=2&pagewanted=1&ref=technology.
2. Laurence Tribe, "The 'Stop Online Piracy Act' (SOPA) Violates the First Amendment." http://www.serendipity.li/cda/tribe-legis-memo-on-SOPA-12-6-11-1.pdf.
3. "European Parliament Resolution on the EU-US Summit of 28 November 2011," European Parliament, http://www.europarl.europa.eu/sides/getDoc.do?type=MOTION&reference-P7-RC-2011-0577&language=EN.
4. See Douglas M. Fraleigh and Joseph S. Tuman, *Freedom of Speech in the Marketplace of Ideas* (New York: St. Martin's Press, 1998), 77.
5. Fred Siebert, Theodore Peterson, and Wilbur Schramm, *Four Theories of the Press* (Urbana: University of Illinois Press, 1956).
6. Hugo Black, quoted in New York Times Co. v. United States, 403 U.S. 713 (1971), http://www.law.cornell.edu/supct/html/historics/USSC_CR_0403_0713_ZC.html.
7. Robert Warren, quoted in United States v. Progressive, Inc., 467 F. Supp. 990 (W.D. Wis. 1979), http://www.bc.edu/bc_org/avp/cas/comm/free_speech/progressive.html.
8. See Edward W. Knappman, ed., *Great American Trials: From Salem Witchcraft to Rodney King* (Detroit, Mich.: Visible Ink Press, 1994), 517–519.
9. Human Rights Watch, "Become a Blogger for Human Rights," accessed June 17, 2008, http://hrw.org/blogs.htm.
10. "'First Wikileaks Revolution': Tunisia Descends into Anarchy as President Flees after Cables Reveal Country's Corruption," *Daily Mail*, January 15, 2011, http://www.dailymail.co.uk/news/article-1347336/First-Wikileaks-Revolution-Tunisia-descends-anarchy-president-flees.html.

11. Bill Keller, "Dealing with Assange and the WikiLeaks Secrets," *New York Times Magazine*, January 26, 2011, http://www.nytimes.com/2011/01/30/magazine/30Wikileaks-t.html?pagewanted=1&_r=3&ref=magazine#.

CONVERGING MEDIA CASE STUDY: Convergent Bullying, p. 437
1. Mattathias Schwartz, "The Trolls among Us," *New York Times Magazine*, August 3, 2008, http://www.nytimes.com/2008/08/03/magazine/03trolls-t.html.

15 Media Economics and the Global Marketplace

1. Douglas Gomery, "The Centrality of Media Economics," in *Defining Media Studies*, ed. Mark R. Levy and Michael Gurevitch (New York: Oxford University Press, 1994), 202.
2. David Harvey, *The Condition of Postmodernity: An Enquiry into the Origins of Cultural Change* (Oxford: Basil Blackwell, 1989), 171.
3. Gomery, "The Centrality of Media Economics," 203–204.
4. Thomas Geoghegan, "How Pink Slips Hurt More Than Workers," *New York Times*, March 29, 2006, p. B8.
5. See James Stewart, *Disney War* (New York: Simon & Schuster, 2005).
6. Edward Herman, "Democratic Media," *Z Papers* (January–March 1992): 23.

16 Social Scientific and Cultural Approaches to Media Research

1. Sarah Anne Hughes, "Jamey Rodemeyer, Bullied Teen Who Made 'It Gets Better' Video, Commits Suicide," blogPOST, washingtonpost.com, September 21, 2011, http://www.washingtonpost.com/blogs/blogpost/post/jamey-rodemeyer-bullied-teen-who-made-it-gets-better-video-commits-suicide/2011/09/21/gIQAVVzxkK_blog.html.
2. Aylin Zafar, "Tumblr Bans Pro-Eating Disorder and Other Self-Harm Blogs," *Time NewsFeed*, Time.com, February 24, 2012, http://newsfeed.time.com/2012/02/24/tumblr-bans-pro-eating-disorder-and-other-self-harm-blogs/.
3. Steve Fore, "Lost in Translation: The Social Uses of Mass Communications Research," *Afterimage* 20 (April 1993): 10.
4. James Carey, *Communication as Culture: Essays on Media and Society* (Boston: Unwin Hyman, 1989), 75.
5. Daniel Czitrom, *Media and the American Mind: From Morse to McLuhan* (Chapel Hill: University of North Carolina Press, 1982), 122–125.
6. Ibid., 123.

7. Harold Lasswell, *Propaganda Technique in the World War* (New York: Alfred A. Knopf, 1927), 9.

8. See W. W. Charters, *Motion Pictures and Youth: A Summary* (New York: Macmillan, 1934); and Garth Jowett, *Film: The Democratic Art* (Boston: Little, Brown, 1976), 220–229.

9. Czitrom, *Media and the American Mind*, 132; see also Harold Lasswell, "The Structure and Function of Communication in Society," in *The Communication of Ideas*, ed. Lyman Bryson (New York: Harper and Brothers, 1948), 37–51.

10. See Joseph Klapper, *The Effects of Mass Communication* (New York: Free Press, 1960).

11. See Nancy Signorielli and Michael Morgan, *Cultivation Analysis: New Directions in Media Effects Research* (Newbury Park, Calif.: Sage, 1990).

12. See Stuart Hall et al., *Policing the Crisis: Mugging, the State, and Law and Order* (London: Macmillan, 1978).

13. See Jack G. Sheehan, *Reel Bad Arabs: How Hollywood Vilifies a People* (Northampton, Mass.: Interlink Publishing Group, 2001).

14. See Janice Radway, *Reading the Romance: Women, Patriarchy and Popular Literature* (Chapel Hill: University of North Carolina Press, 1984).

MEDIA LITERACY CASE STUDY: What to Do about Television Violence? p. 482

1. Federal Communications Commission, "Violent Television Programming and Its Impact on Children," April 25, 2007, http://hraunfoss.fcc.gov/edocs_public /attachmatch/FCC-07-050A1.pdf.

Glossary

A&R (artist & repertoire) agents talent scouts of the music business who discover, develop, and sometimes manage performers.

access channels in cable television, a tier of nonbroadcast channels dedicated to local education, government, and the public.

account executives in advertising, client liaisons responsible for bringing in new business and managing the accounts of established clients.

account reviews in advertising, the process of evaluating or reinvigorating an ad campaign, which results in either renewing the contract with the original ad agency or hiring a new agency.

acquisitions editors in the book industry, editors who seek out and sign authors to contracts.

actual malice in libel law, a reckless disregard for the truth, such as when a reporter or an editor knows that a statement is false and prints or airs it anyway.

ad impressions how often online ads are seen.

adult contemporary (AC) one of the oldest and most popular radio music formats, typically featuring a mix of news, talk, oldies, and soft rock.

affiliate stations radio or TV stations that, though independently owned, sign a contract to be part of a network and receive money to carry the network's programs; in exchange, the network reserves time slots, which it sells to national advertisers.

agenda-setting theory a media-research argument that says that when the mass media pay attention to particular events or issues, they determine—that is, set the agenda for—the major topics of discussion for individuals and society.

album-oriented rock (AOR) the radio music format that features album cuts from mainstream rock bands.

alternative rock nonmainstream rock music, which includes many types of experimental music.

AM (amplitude modulation) a type of radio and sound transmission that stresses the volume or height of radio waves.

analog recording a recording that is made by capturing the fluctuations of the original sound waves and storing those signals on record grooves or magnetic tape—analogous to the actual sound.

analysis the second step in the critical process, it involves discovering significant patterns that emerge from the description stage.

anthology drama a popular form of early TV programming that brought live dramatic theater to television; influenced by stage plays, anthologies offered new teleplays, casts, directors, writers, and sets from week to week.

arcade an establishment gathering multiple coin-operated games together in a single location.

ARPAnet the original Internet, designed by the U.S. Defense Department's Advanced Research Projects Agency (ARPA).

association principle in advertising, a persuasive technique that associates a product with some cultural value or image that has a positive connotation but may have little connection to the actual product.

astroturf lobbying phony grassroots public affairs campaigns engineered by public relations firms; coined by U.S. Senator Lloyd Bentsen of Texas (named after AstroTurf, the artificial grass athletic field surface).

Atari a video game development company that released Pong, the first big hit arcade game, and established the home video game market through a deal with Sears.

audience studies cultural studies research that focuses on how people use and interpret cultural content; also known as *reader-response research*.

audiotape lightweight magnetized strands of ribbon that make possible sound editing and multiple-track mixing; instrumentals or vocals can be recorded at one studio and later mixed onto a master recording in another studio.

authoritarian model a model for journalism and speech that tolerates little criticism of government or public dissent; it holds that the general public needs guidance from an elite and educated ruling class.

avatar an identity created by an Internet user in order to participate in a form of online entertainment, such as *World of Warcraft* or *Second Life*.

bandwagon effect an advertising strategy that incorporates exaggerated claims that everyone is using a particular product, so you should too.

barter in TV, giving a program to a local station in exchange for a split in the advertising revenue.

basic cable in cable programming, a tier of channels composed of local broadcast signals, nonbroadcast access channels (for local government, education, and general public use), a few regional PBS stations, and a variety of popular channels downlinked from communication satellites.

Big Six the six major Hollywood studios that currently rule the commercial film business: Warner Brothers, Paramount, Twentieth Century Fox, Universal, Columbia Pictures, and Disney.

block booking an early tactic of movie studios to control exhibition involving pressuring theater operators to accept marginal films with no stars in order to get access to films with the most popular stars.

block printing a printing technique developed by early Chinese printers, who hand-carved characters and illustrations into a block of wood, applied ink to the block, and then printed copies on multiple sheets of paper.

blogs sites that contain articles in chronological journal-like form, often with reader comments and links to other articles on the Web (from the term Web log).

blues originally a kind of black folk music, this music emerged as a distinct category in the early 1900s; it was influenced by African American spirituals, ballads, and work songs in the rural South, and by urban guitar and vocal solos from the 1930s and 1940s.

book challenge a formal complaint to have a book removed from a public or school library's collection.

boutique agencies in advertising, small regional ad agencies that offer personalized services.

broadband data transmission over a fiber-optic cable — a signaling method that handles a wide range of frequencies.

broadcasting the transmission of radio waves or TV signals to a broad public audience.

browsers information-search services, such as Firefox and Microsoft's Internet Explorer, that offer detailed organizational maps to the Internet.

cathode-ray tube a key component of early television and computer screens that allowed the display of images.

CATV (community antenna television) early cable systems that originated where mountains or tall buildings blocked TV signals; because of early technical and regulatory limits, CATV contained only twelve channels.

celluloid a transparent and pliable film that can hold a coating of chemicals sensitive to light.

chapter shows in television production, situation comedies or dramatic programs whose narrative structure includes self-contained stories that feature a problem, a series of conflicts, and a resolution from week to week (for contrast, see **serial programs** and **episodic series**).

cinema verité French term for *truth film*, a documentary style that records fragments of everyday life unobtrusively; it often features a rough, grainy look and shaky, handheld camera work.

citizen journalism a grassroots movement wherein activist amateurs and concerned citizens, not professional journalists, use Internet tools like blogs to disseminate news and information.

click through how often users land briefly on a Web site before clicking through to the next site.

codex an early type of book in which paperlike sheets were cut and sewed together along the edge, then bound with thin pieces of wood and covered with leather.

collective intelligence video game tips and cheats shared by players of the games, usually online.

commercial speech any print or broadcast expression for which a fee is charged to the organization or individual buying time or space in the mass media.

common carrier a communication or transportation business, such as a phone company or a taxi service, that is required by law to offer service on a first-come, first-served basis to whoever can pay the rate; such companies do not get involved in content.

compact discs (CDs) playback-only storage discs for music that incorporate pure and very precise digital techniques, thus eliminating noise during recording and playback.

conflict of interest considered unethical, a compromising situation in which a journalist stands to benefit personally from the news report he or she produces.

conflict-oriented journalism found in metropolitan areas, newspapers that define news primarily as events, issues, or experiences that deviate from social norms; journalists see their role as observers who monitor their city's institutions and problems.

consensus narrative cultural products that become popular and command wide attention, providing shared cultural experiences.

consensus-oriented journalism found in small communities, newspapers that promote social and economic harmony by providing community calendars and meeting notices and carrying articles on local schools, social events, town government, property crimes, and zoning issues.

console a device used specifically to play video games.

contemporary hit radio (CHR) originally called Top 40 radio, this radio format encompasses everything from hip-hop to children's songs; it remains the most popular format in radio for people ages eighteen to twenty-four.

content analysis in social science research, a method for systematically studying and coding media texts and programs.

cookies information profiles about a user that are usually automatically accepted by the Web browser and stored on the user's own computer hard drive.

copy editors the people in magazine, newspaper, and book publishing who attend to specific problems in writing such as style, content, and length.

copyright the legal right of authors and producers to own and control the use of their published or unpublished writing, music, and lyrics; TV programs and movies; or graphic art designs.

Corporation for Public Broadcasting (CPB) a private, nonprofit corporation created by Congress in 1967 to funnel federal funds to nonprofit radio and public television.

correlation an observed association between two variables.

country claiming the largest number of radio stations in the United States, this radio format includes such subdivisions as old-time, progressive, country-rock, western swing, and country-gospel.

cover music songs recorded or performed by musicians who did not originally write or perform the music; in the 1950s, cover music was an attempt by white producers and artists to capitalize on popular songs by blacks.

critical process the process whereby a media-literate person or student studying mass communication employs the techniques of description, analysis, interpretation, evaluation, and engagement.

cultivation effect theory in media research, the idea that heavy television viewing leads individuals to perceive reality in ways that are consistent with the portrayals they see on television.

cultural imperialism the phenomenon of American culture (e.g., media, fashion, and food) dominating the global market and shaping the cultures and identities of other nations.

cultural studies in media research, the approaches that try to understand how the media and culture are tied to the actual patterns of communication used in daily life; these studies focus on how people make meanings, apprehend reality, and order experience through the use of stories and symbols.

deadheading the practice in the early twentieth century of giving reporters free rail passes as bribes for favorable stories.

deficit financing in television, the process whereby a TV production company leases its programs to a network for a license fee that is actually less than the cost of production; the company hopes to recoup this loss later in rerun syndication.

demographic editions national magazines whose advertising is tailored to subscribers and readers according to occupation, class, and zip-code address.

demographics in market research, the gathering and analysis of audience members' age, gender, income, ethnicity, and education characteristics to better target messages to particular audiences.

description the first step in the critical process, it involves paying close attention, taking notes, and researching the cultural product to be studied.

design managers publishing industry personnel who work on the look of a book, making decisions about type style, paper, cover design, and layout.

desktop publishing a computer technology that enables an aspiring publisher/editor to inexpensively write, design, lay out, and even print a small newsletter or magazine.

developmental editors in book publishing, the editors who provide authors with feedback, make suggestions for improvements, and obtain advice from knowledgeable members of the academic community.

development budget the money spent designing, coding, scoring, and testing a video game.

digital communication images, texts, and sounds that use pulses of electric current or flashes of laser lights and are converted (or encoded) into electronic signals represented as varied combinations of binary numbers, usually ones and zeros; these signals are then reassembled (decoded) as a precise reproduction of a TV picture, a magazine article, or a telephone voice.

digital divide the socioeconomic disparity between those who do and those who do not have access to digital technology and media, such as the Internet.

digital recording music recorded and played back by laser beam rather than by needle or magnetic tape.

digital video the production format that is replacing celluloid film and revolutionizing filmmaking because the cameras are more portable and production costs are much less expensive.

digital video recorder (DVR) a device that enables users to find and record specific television shows (and movies) and store them in a computer memory to be played back at a later time or recorded onto a DVD.

digitization the translation of information in analog form into binary code.

dime novels sometimes identified as pulp fiction, these cheaply produced and low-priced novels were popular in the United States beginning in the 1860s.

direct broadcast satellites (DBS) satellite-based services that for a monthly fee downlink hundreds of satellite channels and services; they began distributing video programming directly to households in 1994.

directories review and cataloguing services that group Web sites under particular categories (e.g., Arts & Humanities, News & Media, Entertainment).

direct payment in media economics, the payment of money, primarily by consumers, for a book, a music CD, a movie, an online computer service, or a cable TV subscription.

documentary a movie or TV news genre that documents reality by recording actual characters and settings.

e-book a digital book read on a computer or electronic reading device.

e-commerce electronic commerce, or commercial activity, on the Web.

economies of scale the economic process of increasing production levels so as to reduce the overall cost per unit.

electromagnetic waves invisible electronic impulses similar to visible light; electricity, magnetism, light, broadcast signals, and heat are part of such waves, which radiate in space at the speed of light, about 186,000 miles per second.

electronic publisher a communication business, such as a broadcaster or a cable TV company, that is entitled to choose what channels or content to carry.

e-mail electronic mail messages sent by the Internet; developed by computer engineer Ray Tomlinson in 1971.

engagement the fifth step in the critical process, it involves actively working to create a media world that best serves democracy.

Entertainment Software Rating Board the video game industry's self-regulating system, designed to inform parents of sexual and violent content that might not be suitable for younger players.

episodic series a narrative form well suited to television because main characters appear every week, sets and locales remain the same, and technical crews stay with the program; episodic series feature new adventures each week, but a handful of characters emerge with whom viewers can regularly identify (see also **chapter shows** and **serial programs**).

ethnocentrism an underlying value held by many U.S. journalists and citizens, it involves judging other countries and cultures according to how they live up to or imitate American practices and ideals.

evaluation the fourth step in the critical process, it involves arriving at a judgment about whether a cultural product is good, bad, or mediocre; this requires subordinating one's personal taste to the critical assessment resulting from the first three stages (description, analysis, and interpretation).

evergreens in TV syndication, popular, lucrative, and enduring network reruns, such as the *Andy Griffith Show* or *I Love Lucy*.

evergreen subscriptions magazine subscriptions that automatically renew on subscribers' credit cards.

experiments in regard to the mass media, research that isolates some aspect of content, suggests a hypothesis, and manipulates variables to discover a particular text's or medium's impact on attitudes, emotions, or behavior.

Fairness Doctrine repealed in 1987, this FCC rule required broadcast stations to both air and engage in controversial-issue programs that affected their communities and, when offering such programming, to provide competing points of view.

famous-person testimonial an advertising strategy that associates a product with the endorsement of a well-known person.

feature syndicates commercial outlets or brokers, such as United Features and King Features, that contract with newspapers to provide work from well-known political writers, editorial cartoonists, comic-strip artists, and self-help columnists.

Federal Communications Act of 1934 the far-reaching act that established the FCC and the federal regulatory structure for U.S. broadcasting.

Federal Communications Commission (FCC) an independent U.S. government agency charged with regulating interstate and international communications by radio, television, wire, satellite, and cable.

Federal Radio Commission (FRC) established in 1927 to oversee radio licenses and negotiate channel problems.

feedback responses from receivers to the senders of messages.

fiber-optic cable thin glass bundles of fiber capable of transmitting thousands of messages converted to shooting pulses of light along cable wires; these bundles of fiber can carry broadcast channels, telephone signals, and all sorts of digital codes.

fin-syn (Financial Interest and Syndication Rules) FCC rules that prohibited the major networks from running their own syndication companies or from charging production companies additional fees after shows had completed their prime-time runs; most fin-syn rules were rescinded in the mid-1990s.

first-run syndication in television, the process whereby new programs are specifically produced for sale in syndication markets rather than for network television.

flipper bumper an addition to the pinball machine that transformed the game from one of chance into a challenging game of skill, touch, and timing.

FM (frequency modulation) a type of radio and sound transmission that offers static-free reception and greater fidelity and clarity than AM radio by accentuating the pitch or distance between radio waves.

focus group a common research method in psychographic analysis in which a moderator leads a small-group discussion about a product or an issue, usually with six to twelve people.

folk music music performed by untrained musicians and passed down through oral traditions; it encompasses a wide range of music, from Appalachian fiddle tunes to the accordion-led zydeco of Louisiana.

format radio the concept of radio stations developing and playing specific styles (or formats) geared to listeners' age, race, or gender; in format radio, management, rather than deejays, controls programming choices.

Fourth Estate the notion that the press operates as an unofficial branch of government, monitoring the legislative, judicial, and executive branches for abuses of power.

fringe time in broadcast television, the time slot either immediately before the evening's prime-time schedule (called *early fringe*) or immediately following the local evening news or the network's late-night talk shows (called *late fringe*).

gag orders legal restrictions prohibiting the press from releasing preliminary information that might prejudice jury selection.

gangster rap a style of rap music that depicts the hardships of urban life and sometimes glorifies the violent style of street gangs.

gatekeepers editors, producers, and other media managers who function as message filters, making decisions about what types of messages actually get produced for particular audiences.

general-interest magazine a type of magazine that addresses a wide variety of topics and is aimed at a broad national audience.

genre a narrative category in which conventions regarding similar characters, scenes, structures, and themes recur in combination.

grunge rock music that takes the spirit of punk and infuses it with more attention to melody.

HD radio a digital technology that enables AM and FM radio broadcasters to multicast two to three additional compressed digital signals within their traditional analog frequency.

hegemony the acceptance of the dominant values in a culture by those who are subordinate to those who hold economic and political power.

hidden-fear appeal an advertising strategy that plays on a sense of insecurity, trying to persuade consumers that only a specific product can offer relief.

high culture a symbolic expression that has come to mean "good taste"; often supported by wealthy patrons and corporate donors, it is associated with fine art (such as ballet, the symphony, painting, and classical literature), which is available primarily in theaters or museums.

high-definition the digital standard for U.S. television sets that has more than twice the resolution of the system that served as the standard from the 1940s through the 1990s.

hip-hop music that combines spoken street dialect with cuts (or samples) from older records and bears the influences of social politics, male boasting, and comic lyrics carried forward from blues, R&B, soul, and rock and roll.

Hollywood Ten the nine screenwriters and one film director subpoenaed by the House Un-American Activities Committee (HUAC) who were sent to prison in the late 1940s for refusing to discuss their memberships or to identify communist sympathizers.

HTML (HyperText Markup Language) the written code that creates Web pages and links; a language all computers can read.

human-interest stories news accounts that focus on the trials and tribulations of the human condition, often featuring ordinary individuals facing extraordinary challenges.

hypodermic-needle model an early model in mass communication research that attempted to explain media effects by arguing that the media shoot their powerful effects directly into unsuspecting or weak audiences; sometimes called the *magic bullet theory*.

hypotheses in social science research, tentative general statements that predict a relationship between a dependent variable and an independent variable.

illuminated manuscripts books from the Middle Ages that featured decorative, colorful designs and illustrations on each page.

indecency the government may punish broadcasters for indecency or profanity after the fact; over the years a handful of radio stations have had their licenses suspended or denied over indecent programming.

indie rock independent-minded rock music, usually distributed by smaller labels.

indies independent music and film production houses that work outside industry oligopolies; they often produce less mainstream music and film.

indirect payment in media economics, the financial support of media products by advertisers, who pay for the quantity or quality of audience members that a particular medium attracts.

individualism an underlying value held by most U.S. journalists and citizens, it favors individual rights and responsibilities over group needs or institutional mandates.

infotainment a type of television program that packages human-interest and celebrity stories in TV news style.

instant book in the book industry, a marketing strategy that involves publishing a topical book quickly after a major event occurs.

instant messaging (IM) a Web feature that enables users to chat with buddies in real time via pop-up windows assigned to each conversation.

intellectual properties the material in video games—stories, characters, personalities, music, etc.—that requires licensing agreements.

Internet the vast central network of high-speed digital lines designed to link and carry computer information worldwide.

Internet radio online radio stations that either "stream" simulcast versions of on-air radio broadcasts over the Web or are created exclusively for the Internet.

Internet service provider (ISP) a company that provides Internet access to homes and businesses for a fee.

interpretation the third step in the critical process, it asks and answers the "What does that mean?" and "So what?" questions about one's findings.

interpretive journalism a type of journalism that involves analyzing and explaining key issues or events and placing them in a broader historical or social context.

inverted-pyramid style a style of journalism in which news reports begin with the most dramatic or newsworthy information—answering *who*, *what*, *where*, and *when* (and less frequently *why* or *how*) questions at the top of the story—and then tail off with less significant details.

irritation advertising an advertising strategy that tries to create product-name recognition by being annoying or obnoxious.

jazz an improvisational and mostly instrumental musical form that absorbs and integrates a diverse body of musical styles, including African rhythms, blues, big band, and gospel.

joint operating agreement (JOA) in the newspaper industry, an economic arrangement, sanctioned by the government, that permits competing newspapers to operate separate editorial divisions while merging business and production operations.

kinescope before the days of videotape, a 1950s technique for preserving television broadcasts by using a film camera to record a live TV show off a studio monitor.

kinetograph an early movie camera developed by Thomas Edison's assistant in the 1890s.

kinetoscope an early film projection system that served as a kind of peep show in which viewers looked through a hole and saw images moving on a tiny plate.

leased channels in cable television, channels that allow citizens to buy time for producing programs or presenting their own viewpoints.

libel in media law, the defamation of character in written or broadcast expression.

libertarian model a model for journalism and speech that encourages vigorous government criticism and supports the highest degree of freedom for individual speech and news operations.

limited competition in media economics, a market with many producers and sellers but only a few differentiable products within a particular category; sometimes called *monopolistic competition*.

linotype a technology introduced in the nineteenth century that enabled printers to set type mechanically using a typewriter-style keyboard.

literary journalism the adaptation of fiction techniques, such as detailed setting descriptions or extensive dialogue, to nonfiction material and in-depth reporting.

lobbying in government public relations, the process of attempting to influence the voting of lawmakers to support a client's or an organization's best interests.

longitudinal studies a term used for research studies that are conducted over long periods of time and often rely on large government and academic survey databases.

low culture a symbolic expression allegedly aligned with the questionable tastes of the "masses," who enjoy the commercial "junk" circulated by the mass media, such as soap operas, rock music, talk radio, comic books, and monster truck pulls.

low-power FM (LPFM) a class of noncommercial radio stations approved by the FCC in 2000 to give voice to local groups lacking access to the public airwaves; the 10-watt and 100-watt stations broadcast to a small, community-based area.

magalogs a combination of a glossy magazine and retail catalog that is often used to market goods or services to customers or employees.

magazine a nondaily periodical that comprises a collection of articles, stories, and ads.

manuscript culture a period during the Middle Ages when priests and monks advanced the art of bookmaking.

market research in advertising and public relations agencies, the department that uses social science techniques to assess the behaviors and attitudes of consumers toward particular products before any ads are created.

mass communication the process of designing and delivering cultural messages and stories to diverse audiences through media channels as old as the book and as new as the Internet.

mass customization the process whereby product companies and content providers customize a Web page, print ad, or other media form for an individual consumer.

massively multiplayer online role-playing game (MMORPG) an online fantasy game set in a virtual world in which users develop avatars of their own design and interact with other players.

mass market paperbacks low-priced paperback books sold mostly on racks in drugstores, supermarkets, and airports, as well as in bookstores.

mass media the cultural industries—the channels of communication—that produce songs, novels, news, movies, online services, and other cultural products and distribute them to a large number of people.

mass media channel newspapers, books, magazines, radio, television, and the Internet.

media buyers in advertising, the individuals who choose and purchase the types of media that are best suited to carry a client's ads and reach the targeted audience.

media convergence the process whereby old and new media are available via the integration of personal computers and high-speed digital distribution.

media effects (social scientific) research the mainstream tradition in mass communication research, it attempts to understand, explain, and predict the impact—or effects—of the mass media on individuals and society.

media literacy an understanding of the mass communication process through the development of critical-thinking tools—description, analysis, interpretation, evaluation, engagement—that enable a person to become more engaged as a citizen and more discerning as a consumer of mass media products.

mega-agencies in advertising, large firms or holding companies that are formed by merging several individual agencies and that maintain worldwide regional offices; they provide both advertising and public relations services and operate in-house radio and TV production studios.

megaplexes movie theater facilities with fourteen or more screens.

messages the texts, images, and sounds transmitted from senders to receivers.

microprocessors miniature circuits that process and store electronic signals, integrating thousands of electronic components into thin strands of silicon along which binary codes travel.

minimal-effects model a mass communication research model based on tightly controlled experiments and survey findings; it argues that the mass media have limited effects on audiences, reinforcing existing behaviors and attitudes rather than changing them. Also called the *limited effects* model.

modern era period from the Industrial Revolution to the twentieth century that was characterized by working efficiently, celebrating individuals, believing in a rational order, and rejecting tradition and embracing progress.

monopoly in media economics, an organizational structure that occurs when a single firm dominates production and distribution in a particular industry, either nationally or locally.

Morse code a system of sending electrical impulses from a transmitter through a cable to a reception point; developed in the 1840s by the American inventor Samuel Morse.

movie palaces ornate, lavish single-screen movie theaters that emerged in the 1910s in the United States.

MP3 short for MPEG-1 Layer 3, an advanced type of audio compression that reduces file size, enabling audio to be easily distributed over the Internet.

muckraking a style of early-twentieth-century investigative journalism that referred to reporters' willingness to crawl around in society's muck to uncover a story.

multiple-system operators (MSOs) large corporations that own numerous cable television systems.

multiplexes contemporary movie theaters that exhibit many movies at the same time on multiple screens.

must-carry rules rules established by the FCC requiring all cable operators to assign channels to and carry all local TV broadcasts on their systems, thereby ensuring that local network affiliates, independent stations (those not carrying network programs), and public television channels would benefit from cable's clearer reception.

narrative films movies that tell a story, with dramatic action and conflict emerging mainly from individual characters.

narrowcasting any specialized electronic programming or media channel aimed at a target audience.

National Public Radio (NPR) noncommercial radio established in 1967 by the U.S. Congress to provide an alternative to commercial radio.

network a broadcast process that links, through special phone lines or satellite transmissions, groups of radio or TV stations that share programming produced at a central location.

network era the period in television history, roughly from the mid-1950s to the late 1970s, that refers to the dominance of the Big Three networks—ABC, CBS, and NBC—over programming and prime-time viewing habits; the era began eroding with a decline in viewing and with the development of VCRs, cable, and new TV networks.

news the process of gathering information and making narrative reports—edited by individuals in a news organization—that create selected frames of reference and help the public make sense of prominent people, important events, and unusual happenings in everyday life.

news and talk radio the fastest-growing radio format in the 1990s.

newshole the space left over in a newspaper for news content after all the ads are placed.

newspaper chain a large company that owns several papers throughout the country.

newsreels weekly ten-minute magazine-style compilations of filmed news events from around the world organized in a sequence of short reports; prominent in movie theaters between the 1920s and the 1950s.

newsworthiness the often unstated criteria that journalists use to determine which events and issues should become news reports, including timeliness, proximity, conflict, prominence, human interest, consequence, usefulness, novelty, and deviance.

nickelodeons the first small makeshift movie theaters, which were often converted cigar stores, pawnshops, or restaurants redecorated to mimic vaudeville theaters.

objective journalism a modern style of journalism that distinguishes factual reports from opinion columns; reporters strive to remain neutral toward the issue or event they cover, searching out competing points of view among the sources for a story.

obscenity expression that is not protected as speech if these three legal tests are all met: (1) the average person, applying contemporary community standards, would find that the material as a whole appeals to prurient interest; (2) the material depicts or describes sexual conduct in a patently offensive way; (3) the material, as a whole, lacks serious literary, artistic, political, or scientific value.

off-network syndication in television, the process whereby older programs that no longer run during prime time are made available for reruns to local stations, cable operators, online services, and foreign markets.

offset lithography a technology that enabled books to be printed from photographic plates rather than metal casts, reducing the cost of color and illustrations and eventually permitting computers to perform typesetting.

oligopoly in media economics, an organizational structure in which a few firms control most of an industry's production and distribution resources.

online fantasy sports games where players assemble teams of real-life athletes and use actual sports results to determine scores.

open-source software noncommercial software shared freely and developed collectively on the Internet.

opinion and fair comment a defense against libel which states that libel applies only to intentional misstatements of factual information rather than opinion, and which therefore protects said opinion.

opt-in policies regulations that require a Web site to obtain explicit permission before collecting a consumer's browsing-history data.

Pacifica Foundation a radio broadcasting foundation established in Berkeley, California, by journalist and World War II pacifist Lewis Hill; he established KPFA, the first nonprofit community radio station, in 1949.

pack journalism a situation in which reporters stake out a house or follow a story in such large groups that the entire profession comes under attack for invading people's privacy or exploiting their personal tragedies.

paperback books books made with less expensive paper covers, introduced in the United States in the mid-1800s.

papyrus one of the first substances to hold written language and symbols; obtained from plant reeds found along the Nile River.

Paramount decision the 1948 Supreme Court decision that ended vertical integration in the film industry by forcing the studios to divest themselves of their theaters.

parchment treated animal skin that replaced papyrus as an early pre-paper substance on which to document written language.

partisan press an early dominant style of American journalism distinguished by opinion newspapers, which generally argued one political point of view or pushed the plan of the particular party that subsidized the paper.

pass-along readership the total number of people who come into contact with a single copy of a magazine.

payola the unethical (and often illegal) practice of record promoters paying deejays or radio programmers to favor particular songs over others.

pay-per-view (PPV) a cable-television service that allows customers to select a particular movie for a fee, or to pay $25 to $40 for a special one-time event.

paywall an arrangement restricting Web site access to paid subscribers.

penny arcade an early version of the modern video arcade, with multiple coin-operated mechanical games gathered together in a single location.

penny papers (also *penny press*) refers to newspapers that, because of technological innovations in printing, were able to drop their price to one cent beginning in the 1830s, thereby making papers affordable to working and emerging middle classes and enabling newspapers to become a genuine mass medium.

phishing an Internet scam that begins with phony e-mail messages that pretend to be from an official site and request that customers send their credit card numbers, passwords, and other personal information to update the account.

photojournalism the use of photos to document events and people's lives.

pinball machine a mechanical game where players score points by manipulating the path of a metal ball on a playfield in a glass-covered case, and an early ancestor of today's electronic games.

plain-folks pitch an advertising strategy that associates a product with simplicity and the common person.

podcasting enables listeners to download audio program files from the Internet for playback on computers or digital music players.

political advertising the use of ad techniques to promote a candidate's image and persuade the public to adopt a particular viewpoint.

political economy studies an area of academic study that specifically examines interconnections among economic interests, political power, and how that power is used.

pop music popular music that appeals either to a wide cross section of the public or to sizable subdivisions within the larger public based on age, region, or ethnic background; the word *pop* has also been used as a label to distinguish popular music from classical music.

populism a political idea that attempts to appeal to ordinary people by setting up a conflict between "the people" and "the elite."

portal an entry point to the Internet, such as a search engine.

postmodern period a contemporary historical era spanning the 1960s to the present; its social values include opposing hierarchy, diversifying and recycling culture, questioning scientific reasoning, and embracing paradox.

premium channels in cable programming, a tier of channels that subscribers can order at an additional monthly fee over their basic cable service; these may include movie channels and interactive services.

press agents the earliest type of public relations practitioner, who sought to advance a client's image through media exposure.

press releases in public relations, announcements—written in the style of a news report—that give new information about an individual, a company, or an organization and pitch a story idea to the news media.

prime time in television programming, the hours between 7 and 11 p.m. (or 7 and 10 p.m. in the Midwest), when networks have traditionally drawn their largest audiences and charged their highest advertising rates.

printing press a fifteenth-century invention whose movable metallic type technology spawned modern mass communication by creating the first method for mass production; it reduced the size and cost of books, made them the first mass medium affordable to less affluent people, and provided the impetus for the Industrial Revolution, assembly-line production, modern capitalism, and the rise of consumer culture.

prior restraint the legal definition of censorship in the United States, which prohibits courts and governments from blocking any publication or speech before it actually occurs.

product placement the advertising practice of strategically placing products in movies, TV shows, comic books, and video games so the products appear as part of a story's set environment.

professional books technical books that target various occupational groups and are not intended for the general consumer market.

Progressive Era the period of political and social reform lasting roughly from the 1890s to the 1920s that inspired many Americans—and mass media—to break with tradition and embrace change.

propaganda in advertising and public relations, a communication strategy that tries to manipulate public opinion to gain support for a special issue, program, or policy, such as a nation's war effort.

propaganda analysis the study of propaganda's effectiveness in influencing and mobilizing public opinion.

pseudo-events in public relations, any circumstance or event created solely for the purpose of obtaining coverage in the media.

pseudo-polls typically call-in, online, or person-in-the-street polls that don't use random samples and whose results thus don't represent the population as a whole.

psychographics in market research, the study of audience or consumer attitudes, beliefs, interests, and motivations.

Public Broadcasting Act of 1967 the act by the U.S. Congress that established the Corporation for Public Broadcasting, which oversees the Public Broadcasting Service (PBS) and National Public Radio (NPR).

Public Broadcasting Service (PBS) the noncommercial television network established in 1967 as an alternative to commercial television.

public domain the end of the copyright period for a cultural or scientific work, at which point the public may begin to access it for free.

publicity in public relations, the positive and negative messages that spread controlled and uncontrolled information about a person, a corporation, an issue, or a policy in various media.

public journalism a type of journalism, driven by citizen forums, that goes beyond telling the news to embrace a broader mission of improving the quality of public life; also called *civic journalism*.

public relations the total communication strategy conducted by a person, a government, or an organization attempting to reach and persuade its audiences to adopt a point of view.

public service announcements (PSAs) reports or announcements, carried free by radio and TV stations, that promote government programs, educational projects, voluntary agencies, or social reform.

pulp fiction a term used to describe many late-nineteenth-century popular paperbacks and dime novels, which were constructed of cheap machine-made pulp material.

punk rock rock music that challenges the orthodoxy and commercialism of the recording business; it is characterized by loud, unpolished qualities, a jackhammer beat, primal vocal screams, crude aggression, and defiant or comic lyrics.

QR codes square bar codes, often seen on advertisements, that can be scanned by smartphone cameras, linking to videos and Web pages.

Radio Act of 1912 the first radio legislation passed by Congress, it addressed the problem of amateur radio operators increasingly cramming the airwaves.

Radio Act of 1927 the second radio legislation passed by Congress; in an attempt to restore order to the airwaves, it stated that licensees did not own their channels but could license them as long as they operated in order to serve the "public interest, convenience, or necessity."

Radio Corporation of America (RCA) a company developed during World War I that was designed, with government approval, to pool radio patents; the formation of RCA gave the United States almost total control over the emerging mass medium of broadcasting.

radio waves a portion of the electromagnetic wave spectrum that was harnessed so that signals could be sent from a transmission point and obtained at a reception point.

random assignment a social science research method for assigning research subjects; it ensures that every subject has an equal chance of being placed in either the experimental group or the control group.

rating in TV audience measurement, a statistical estimate expressed as a percentage of households tuned to a program in the local or national market being sampled.

receivers the target of messages crafted by a sender.

reference books dictionaries, encyclopedias, atlases, and other reference manuals related to particular professions or trades.

regional editions national magazines whose content is tailored to the interests of different geographic areas.

responsible capitalism an underlying value held by many U.S. journalists and citizens, it assumes that businesspeople compete with one another not primarily to maximize profits but to increase prosperity for all.

rhythm and blues (R&B) music that merged urban blues with big-band sounds.

right to privacy addresses a person's right to be left alone, without his or her name, image, or daily activities becoming public property.

rockabilly music that mixed bluegrass and country influences with those of black folk music and early amplified blues.

rock and roll music that mixed the vocal and instrumental traditions of popular music; it merged the black influences of urban blues, gospel, and R&B with the white influences of country, folk, and pop vocals.

rotation in format radio programming, the practice of playing the most popular or best-selling songs many times throughout the day.

satellite radio pay radio services that deliver various radio formats nationally via satellite.

saturation advertising the strategy of inundating a variety of print and visual media with ads aimed at target audiences.

scientific method a widely used research method that studies phenomena in systematic stages; it includes identifying the research problem, reviewing existing research, developing working hypotheses, determining appropriate research design, collecting information, analyzing results to see if the hypotheses have been verified, and interpreting the implications of the study.

search engines computer programs that allow users to enter key words or queries to find related sites on the Internet.

Section 315 part of the 1934 Communications Act; it mandates that during elections, broadcast stations must provide equal opportunities and response time for qualified political candidates.

selective exposure the phenomenon whereby audiences seek messages and meanings that correspond to their preexisting beliefs and values.

selective retention the phenomenon whereby audiences remember or retain messages and meanings that correspond to their preexisting beliefs and values.

senders the authors, producers, agencies, and organizations that transmit messages to receivers.

serial programs radio or TV programs, such as soap operas, that feature continuing story lines from day to day or week to week (see **chapter shows**).

share in TV audience measurement, a statistical estimate of the percentage of homes tuned to a certain program, compared with those simply using their sets at the time of a sample.

shield laws laws protecting the confidentiality of key interview subjects and reporters' rights not to reveal the sources of controversial information used in news stories.

situation comedy (sitcom) a type of comedy series that features a recurring cast and set as well as several narrative scenes; each episode establishes a situation, complicates it, develops increasing confusion among its characters, and then resolves the complications.

sketch comedy short television comedy skits that are usually segments of TV variety shows; sometimes known as *vaudeo*, the marriage of vaudeville and video.

slander in law, spoken language that defames a person's character.

small-town pastoralism an underlying value held by many U.S. journalists and citizens, it favors the small over the large and the rural over the urban.

snob-appeal approach an advertising strategy that attempts to convince consumers that using a product will enable them to maintain or elevate their social station.

social learning theory a theory within media-effects research that suggests a link between the mass media and behavior.

social networking sites Internet Web sites that allow users to create personal profiles, upload photos, create lists of favorite things, and post messages to connect with old friends and to meet new ones.

social responsibility model a model for journalism and speech, influenced by the libertarian model, that encourages the free flow of information to citizens so they can make wise decisions regarding political and social issues.

social scientific research the mainstream tradition in mass communication research, it attempts to understand, explain, and predict the impact—or effects—of the mass media on individuals and society.

soul music that mixes gospel, blues, and urban and southern black styles with slower, more emotional, and melancholic lyrics.

sound bite in TV journalism, the equivalent of a quote in print; the part of a news report in which an expert, a celebrity, a victim, or a "person on the street" is interviewed about some aspect of an event or issue.

space brokers in the days before modern advertising, individuals who purchased space in newspapers and sold it to various merchants.

spam a computer term referring to unsolicited e-mail.

Spanish-language radio one of radio's fastest-growing formats, concentrated mostly in large Hispanic markets such as Miami, New York, Chicago, Las Vegas, California, Arizona, New Mexico, and Texas.

spiral of silence a theory that links the mass media, social psychology, and the formation of public opinion; it proposes that people who find their views on controversial issues in the minority tend to keep these views silent.

split-run editions editions of national magazines that tailor ads to different geographic areas.

spyware software with hidden codes that enable commercial firms to "spy" on users and gain access to their computers.

state model a model for journalism and speech that places control in the hands of an enlightened government, which speaks for ordinary citizens and workers in order to serve the common goals of the state.

stereo the recording of two separate channels or tracks of sound.

storyboard in advertising, a blueprint or roughly drawn comic-strip version of a proposed advertisement.

studio system an early film production system that constituted a sort of assembly-line process for movie-making; major film studios controlled not only actors but also directors, editors, writers, and other employees, all of whom worked under exclusive contracts.

subliminal advertising a 1950s term that refers to hidden or disguised print and visual messages that allegedly register on the subconscious, creating false needs and seducing people into buying products.

subsidiary rights in the book industry, selling the rights to a book for use in other media forms, such as a mass market paperback, a CD-ROM, or the basis for a movie screenplay.

supermarket tabloids newspapers that feature bizarre human-interest stories, gruesome murder tales, violent accident accounts, unexplained phenomena stories, and malicious celebrity gossip.

superstations local independent TV stations, such as WTBS in Atlanta or WGN in Chicago, that have uplinked their signals onto a communication satellite to make themselves available nationwide.

survey research in social science research, a method of collecting and measuring data taken from a group of respondents.

syndication leasing TV stations the exclusive right to air older TV series.

synergy in media economics, the promotion and sale of a product (and all its versions) throughout the various subsidiaries of a media conglomerate.

talkies the name given to the first motion pictures with sound following the silent film era.

Telecommunications Act of 1996 the sweeping update of telecommunications law that led to a wave of media consolidation.

telegraph invented in the 1840s, it sent electrical impulses through a cable from a transmitter to a reception point, transmitting Morse code.

textbooks books made for the el-hi (elementary and high school) and college markets.

textual analysis in media research, a method for closely and critically examining and interpreting the meanings of culture, including architecture, fashion, books, movies, and TV programs.

third-person effect theory a theory suggesting that people believe others are more affected by media messages than they are themselves.

Top 40 format the first radio format, in which stations played the forty most popular hits in a given week as measured by record sales.

trade books the most visible book industry segment, featuring hardbound and paperback books aimed at general readers and sold at bookstores and other retail outlets.

trade publications specialty magazines aimed at a narrowly defined audience.

transistor invented by Bell Laboratories in 1947, this tiny technology, which receives and amplifies radio signals, made portable radios possible.

TV newsmagazine a TV news program format, pioneered by CBS's *60 Minutes* in the late 1960s, that features multiple segments in an hour-long episode, usually ranging from a celebrity or political feature story to a hard-hitting investigative report.

underground press radical newspapers, run on shoestring budgets, that question mainstream political policies and conventional values; the term usually refers to a journalism movement of the 1960s.

university press the segment of the book industry that publishes scholarly books in specialized areas.

urban one of radio's more popular formats, primarily targeting African American listeners in urban areas with dance, R&B, and hip-hop music.

uses and gratifications model a mass communication research model, usually employing in-depth interviews and survey questionnaires, that argues that people use the media to satisfy various emotional desires or intellectual needs.

Values and Lifestyles (VALS) a market-research strategy that divides consumers into types and measures psychological factors, including how consumers think and feel about products and how they achieve (or do not achieve) the lifestyles to which they aspire.

vellum a handmade paper made from treated animal skin, used in the Gutenberg Bibles.

vertical integration in media economics, the phenomenon of controlling a mass media industry at its three essential levels: production, distribution, and exhibition; the term is most frequently used in reference to the film industry.

videocassette recorders (VCRs) recorders that use a half-inch video format known as VHS (video home system), which enables viewers to record and play back programs from television or to watch movies rented from video stores.

video news release (VNR) in public relations, the visual counterpart to a press release; it pitches a story idea to the TV news media by mimicking the style of a broadcast news report.

video-on-demand (VOD) cable television technology that enables viewers to instantly order programming, such as movies, to be digitally delivered to their sets.

viral marketing short videos or other content which marketers hope will quickly gain widespread attention as users share it with friends online, or by word of mouth.

vitascope a large-screen movie projection system developed by Thomas Edison.

webzines magazines that publish on the Internet.

Wi-Fi a standard for short-distance wireless networking, enabling users of notebook computers and other devices to connect to the Internet in cafés, hotels, airports, and parks.

Wikis Internet Web sites that are capable of being edited by any user; the most famous of these sites is *Wikipedia*.

WiMax a communication technology that provides data over long distances in multiple ways, from traditional cell phone connections to services that link mobile phones to traditional mass media.

Wireless Ship Act the 1910 mandate that all major U.S. seagoing ships carrying more than fifty passengers and traveling more than two hundred miles off the coast be equipped with wireless equipment with a one-hundred-mile range.

wireless telegraphy the forerunner of radio, a form of voiceless point-to-point communication; it preceded the voice and sound transmissions of one-to-many mass communication that became known as broadcasting.

wireless telephony early experiments in wireless voice and music transmissions, which later developed into modern radio.

wire services commercial organizations, such as the Associated Press, that share news stories and information by relaying them around the country and the world, originally via telegraph and now via satellite transmission.

yellow journalism a newspaper style or era that peaked in the 1890s; it emphasized high-interest stories, sensational crime news, large headlines, and serious reports that exposed corruption, particularly in business and government.

Credits

Text Credits

13, Table 1.1: Data from "Hours Per Person Per Year Using Consumer Media." Veronis Suhler Stevenson Communications Industry Forecast. **36,** Table 2.1: Figures through 1945 from John Tebbel, *A History of Book Publishing in the United States,* 4 vols. (New York: Bowker, 1972-81); figures after 1945 from various editions of *The Bowker Annual Library and Book Trade Almanac* (Information Today, Inc.) and Bowker press releases. **42,** Figure 2.1: Milliot, Jim. "Penguin, Hachette Gained in Tough 2008." *Publishers Weekly,* May 4, 2009. Copyright 2009 Reproduced with permission of PWXYZ, LLC in the format Republish in a textbook/"other" book via Copyright Clearance Center. **45,** Figure 2.2: "Where the New Textbook Dollar Goes." © 2011 by the National Association of College Stores. **48,** Figure 2.3: "E-Bookstore Purchases by iPad Owners." From Jim Milliot, "Amazon Ups Its Edge," *Publishers Weekly,* January 24, 2011. **51,** Table 2.2: "How a Paperback's Revenue is Divided." From Arianne Cohen, "A Publishing Company: Random House." *New York Magazine,* June 3, 2007. Copyright © 2007. Reprinted by permission. **80,** Figure 3.1: "Selected Alternative Newspapers in the United States." Reprinted by permission of Alternative Newsmedia. **87,** Figure 3.2: "Digital Devices and the News." From *State of the News Media 2012,* "Mobile Devices and News Consumption." Copyright © 2012. Reprinted by permission of the Pew Research Center's Project for Excellence in Journalism. **107,** Table 4.1: "The Top 10 Magazines" from MPA the Association of Magazine Media, 2012, www.magazine.org. **120,** Table 4.2: "Major Magazine Chains." From Advance.net, Hearst.com, meredith.com, TimeInc.com, accessed January 2012. **133,** Figure 5.1: "Annual vinyl, tape, CD, mobile, and digital sales." From Recording Industry Association of America, 2010 year-end statistics. Reprinted with permission from the Recording Industry Association of America. **177,** Figure 6.1: "Radio Today." Fall 2010. www.arbitron.com. **178–179,** Media Literacy Case Study, Chapter 6: Foster, David Wallace. Excerpted from "Host: The Origins of Talk Radio," the *Atlantic Monthly,* April 2005, 66–68. Reprinted by permission of the Hill Nadell Literary Agency on behalf the David Foster Wallace Literary Trust. **214,** Figure 7.1: "Market Share of U.S. Film Studios and Distributors, 2011." From Box Office Mojo, Studio Market Share, http://boxofficemojo.com/studio/. **232,** Figure 8.1: "A Basic Cable Television System." Reprinted by permission of Clear Creek Communications. **252,** Figure 8.2: From Brian Steinberg, "'American Idol,' NFL Duke It Out for Priciest TV Spot." AdAge Mediaworks, October 24, 2011. **255,** Figure 8.3: "Top 10 U.S. Video Programming Distributors, 2011." National Cable & Telecommunications Association, August 2012. www.ncta .com. Copyright © 2012 SNL Kagan, a division of SNL Financial LC. All Rights Reserved. **267,** Figure 9.1: "Distributed Networks." Reprinted with the permission of Simon & Schuster, Inc., from *Where Wizards Stay Up Late* by Katie Hafner and Matthew Lyon. Copyright © 1996 by Katie Hafner and Matthew Lyon. **329,** Figure 11.1: "Revenue for the World's Four Largest Agencies." Reprinted with permission from the June 16, 2009 issue of Advertising Age/American Demographics. Copyright © 2009 Crain Communications, Inc. **340,** Table 11.1: "The Top 10 Global Brands." From "BrandZ Top 100 Most Powerful Brands 2011." Millward Brown Optimor. http://www .millwardbrown.com/brandz/2011/report/. **363,** Figure 12.1: "The Top Six Holding Firms with Public Relations Subsidiaries." From "Agency Family Trees 2012," *Advertising Age,* April 25, 2012. http://adage.com /datacenter/agencyfamilytrees12. **375,** Table 12.1: Public Relations Society of America (PRSA) Member Statement of Professional Values. Reprinted with permission from the Public Relations Society of America (www.prsa.org /ethics). **426–427,** Media Literacy Case Study Box, Chapter 14: Excerpted from John L. Seigenthaler, Sr. "A False *Wikipedia* Biography." *USA Today,* November 30, 2005. Reprinted by permission of the author. **434,** Table 14.1: "The Voluntary Movie Rating System." From the Motion Picture Association of America, "What Do the Ratings Mean?" © 2011 Motion Picture Association of America, Inc. All rights reserved. **466–467,** Media Literacy Case Study Box, Chapter 15: From *Ad Age's 100 Leading Media Companies* report, December 7, 1981; "100 Companies by Media Revenue," *Advertising Age,* August 18, 1997; "100 Leading Media Companies," *Advertising Age,* October 3, 2011. Reprinted with permission of *Advertising Age.* Copyright © 1981, 1996, 2011. **481,** Figure 16.1: "TV Parental Guidelines." Reprinted by permission of the TV Parental Guidelines Monitoring Board.

Photo Credits

Key: AP-WW = Associated Press; CO = Corbis Pictures; CO-BA = CO/Bettmann Archive; CO-SY = CO/Sygma; GI = Getty Images; PF = Photofest

xv, SIME/eStock Photo; **xvi,** Red Huber/Orlando Sentinel/ MCT via GI; **xvii,** the Granger Collection; **xviii,** Santi Visalli/GI; **xix,** (t.) Jay West/WireImage/GI; (b.) ZUMA Press/Newscom; **xx,** Copyright © 20th Century Fox. All rights reserved/ courtesy Everett Collection; **xxi,** Photo by Richard

Index